MW01055780

Inside TCP/IP

Third Edition

A Comprehensive Introduction to Protocols and Concepts

Karanjit S. Siyan, Ph.D.

New Riders Publishing, Indianapolis, Indiana

Inside TCP/IP, Third Edition

By Karanjit S. Siyan, Ph.D.

Published by:
New Riders Publishing
201 West 103rd Street
Indianapolis, IN 46290 USA

Printed in the United States of America 1 2 3 4 5 6 7 8 9 0

Library of Congress Cataloging-in-Publication Data

CIP data available upon request

ISBN: 1-56205-714-6

Warning and Disclaimer

This book is designed to provide a comprehensive introduction to TCP/IP protocols and concepts as well as information about how to integrate the protocol suite into existing network environments. Every effort has been made to make this book as complete and as accurate as possible, but no warranty or fitness is implied.

The information is provided on an "as is" basis. The author(s) and New Riders Publishing shall have neither liability nor responsibility to any person or entity with respect to any loss or damages arising from the information contained in this book or from the use of the discs or programs that may accompany it.

Publisher *David Dwyer*
Marketing Manager *Mary Foote*
Executive Editors *Julie Fairweather, Laurie Petrycki*
Managing Editor *Sarah Kearns*

Acquisitions Editor
Julie Fairweather

Development Editor
Stacia Mellinger

Project Editor
Daryl Kessler

Copy Editors
Jennifer Clark
Noelle Gasco
Matt Litten
Barbara Potter

Technical Editor
Rick Fairweather

Software Product Developer
Steve Flatt

Software Acquisitions and Development
Dustin Sullivan

Assistant Marketing Manager
Gretchen Schlesinger

Team Coordinator
Amy Lewis

Manufacturing Coordinator
Brook Farling

Book Designer
Glenn Larsen

Cover Designer
Sandra Schroeder

Cover Production
Casey Price

Director of Production
Larry Klein

Production Team Supervisor
Laurie Casey

Graphics Image Specialists
Laura Robbins
Marvin Van Tiem

Production Analysts
Dan Harris
Erich J. Richter

Production Team
Lori Cliburn
Kim Cofer
Kristy Nash
Laure Robinson

Indexer
Kevin Fulcher

About the Author

Karanjit S. Siyan is president of Kinetics Corporation. He has authored international seminars on Solaris and SunOS, TCP/IP networks, PC network integration, Windows NT, Novell networks, and Expert Systems using Fuzzy Logic. He teaches advanced technology seminars in the United States, Canada, Europe, and the Far East. Dr. Siyan has published articles in *Dr. Dobbs Journal, The C Users Journal, Databased Advisor,* and research journals, and is actively involved in Internet research. Karanjit has worked with computer networks for Unix, NetWare, Windows NT, and OS/2, and with computer languages such as C/C++, Pascal, LISP, Algol, Ada, MSL, Jovial, Java, and so on, for many years. He has written compilers for a number of these languages. Karanjit holds a Ph.D. in Computer Science, a Master's degree in Electrical Engineering and Computer Science, and a Bachelor's degree in Electronics and Electrical Communication Engineering. He is a member of IEEE and ACM, and his career achievements are recorded in Marquis' *Who's Who in the World, Who is Who in America, Who's Who in Finance and Industry,* and *Who's Who in Science and Engineering.*

Before working as an independent consultant, Karanjit worked as a senior member of technical staff at ROLM Corporation, and as a software developer and technical manager on numerous projects. As part of his consulting work, Karanjit has written a number of custom compiler and operating system development tools. His interests include UNIX-based, NetWare-based, Windows NT-based, and OS/2 networks. He is actively involved in the application of many computer science disciplines such as networks, operating systems, programming languages, databases, expert systems, and computer security. Dr. Siyan holds certification credentials for a number of commercial operating system products, and has written numerous books.

Trademark Acknowledgments

Acknowledgments

One of the more pleasurable tasks of being an author is to thank the people responsible for the success of a book. I wish to thank my family: Ahal Singh, Tejinder, Harjeet, Jagjit, Kookie, Dolly, and Dei. Special thanks to Mother, Saint Germain, El Morya Khan, Kuan-Yin, Bhagwan Krishna, and Babaji. Without their spiritual support, this book would not have been possible.

I want to thank Bob Sanregret and Anders Amundson, who initially got me interested in writing teaching materials about computers. I also wish to thank the many people at Learning Tree for their help and support on various projects. In particular I would like to thank Professor John Moriarty, Rick Adamson, Dr. David Collins, Eric Garen, Marti Sanregret, Nancy Harrison, Richard Beaumont, David O'Neil, Robin Johnston, and Tom Spurling.

I wish to thank Stacia Mellinger, this book's development editor, for her experience and professionalism, Julie Fairweather for her encouragement and cheerful attitude, and Daryl Kessler, Jennifer Clark, Noelle Gasco, Matt Litten, and Barbara Potter for their help in developing this book.

I also wish to thank Drew and Blythe Heywood for their friendship, support, and encouragement throughout the many years it has been my pleasure to know them.

Contents at a Glance

Table Contents

Introduction

This book, *Inside TCP/IP, Third Edition (A Comprehensive Introduction to Protocols and Concepts)*, introduces the fundamentals of the TCP/IP protocol suite. The TCP/IP protocol suite is a collection of communication protocols that enable computing devices to be linked together in a network. Traditionally, TCP/IP was used for Wide Area Networks such as the Internet. More recently, TCP/IP has been widely used in the building of corporate intranets. The approach taken in this book gives you a solid understanding of the theories, techniques, and practices of deploying TCP/IP-based networks.

Inside TCP/IP, Third Edition, is designed for advanced users and system administrators who plan to work with the TCP/IP protocol suite. If you are new to TCP/IP networks, you will be able to use the information in this book to understand the working of TCP/IP networks, regardless of the type of operating systems and TCP/IP implementations. The in-depth discussion of TCP/IP in this book applies to all TCP/IP implementations. There are many books that focus on the configuration issues of a particular TCP/IP implementation such as Unix or Windows NT. However, although these books go into great detail about the commands, mouse clicks, and key strokes necessary to configure or implement TCP/IP, they typically do not provide an in-depth explanation of the theory and principles behind the workings of TCP/IP. While this book is not operating-system specific, it does give, where it is useful, configuration and implementation issue details. But most of the discussion in this book is cross-platform and can apply to any TCP/IP implementation.

One of the unique features of this book is a detailed discussion and analysis of TCP/IP protocols captured in a real life network. The behavior of the protocols is explained in terms of the actual packet sequences that implement the TCP/IP protocols and their field values in the headers. These packet sequences, also called protocol traces, are discussed for many of the basic TCP/IP protocols.

Every chapter in this book ends with a list of questions for review that help you better understand the chapter material. While some of the questions are conceptual and have a one- or two-line answer, other questions require deep thinking and understanding of the application of the information covered in the chapter. As you ponder these questions, you will come to understand some of the deeper issues concerning TCP/IP.

The material in this book and the review questions at the end of each chapter can also be used as an introductory course in TCP/IP for technical colleges and institutes. The chapters follow a logical sequence and can be covered in the order in which they are introduced in this book.

How This Book Is Organized

The following sections offer a brief outline on the chapters in this book.

Part I: TCP/IP Layering Model and Physical Infrastructure

Chapter 1, "Introduction to TCP/IP," introduces the TCP/IP protocol suite and gives you an overview of the more common TCP/IP protocols, such as IP, TCP, UDP, Telnet, FTP, DNS, and HTTP. This chapter gives you a brief introduction to these protocols and how they fit together in the TCP/IP protocol suite.

Chapter 2, "TCP/IP Protocol Layering Concepts," discusses the TCP/IP protocol hierarchy. The concept of protocol layering as a means to simplify the writing of TCP/IP software (TCP/IP implementation) and understand the TCP/IP protocol suite is described. Specifically, ISO's OSI model and the DoD model are discussed in relationship to the TCP/IP protocol suite.

Chapter 3, "Network Support for TCP/IP," discusses LAN/WAN technologies that are used to support TCP/IP. Basic LAN technologies such as Ethernet, Token Ring, Fast Ethernet, and IEEE LANs, are discussed. The role of interconnection devices such as repeaters, bridges, routers, and gateways is also explained. This chapter also discusses the encapsulation of TCP/IP packets in the data link layer frames of the hardware technologies.

Part II: TCP/IP Internetworking Infrastructure

Chapter 4, "IP Addressing," presents the structure, format, and representation of IPv4 and IPv6 addresses. The different IPv4 address classes and their meanings and usage are discussed. Also described are the roles of multicast, broadcast, limited broadcast, and directed broadcast addresses.

Chapter 5, "Address Resolution Protocols," discusses the protocols used for binding IP addresses with hardware addresses. The packet format and operation of ARP and RARP are explained in great detail. ARP and RARP protocol decodes on a real life network are discussed in great detail.

Chapter 6, "The Internet Protocol," explains the IPv4 protocol that provides a virtual view of the network where all nodes are treated as IP nodes. The nature of the IP connectionless service and its features are presented. The protocol format and operation of IP is discussed along with an in-depth explanation of IP options. IP protocol decodes for a real-life network are provided.

Chapter 7, "IP Routing Concepts," explains how IP can be used to build arbitrarily complex networks using routers. This chapter describes the role and behavior of an IP router and explains the differences between Static and Dynamic routing. Other important concepts covered include Direct versus Indirect delivery, structure of routing table, default routes, IP routing logic, and processing of incoming IP datagrams.

Chapter 8, "The ICMP Protocol," discusses the ICMP protocol and its format and operation. ICMP is part of the implementation of IP modules. The ICMP protocol is very helpful in troubleshooting and diagnosing the problems in IP networks. Examples of ICMP protocol traces and decodes are presented.

Chapter 9, "IP Subnetting and Supernetting," explains how to overcome the inefficient address allocation resulting from the straightforward usage of the standard IP address classes A, B, and C. The use of subnetting and supernetting results in a more efficient address allocation. This chapter describes the use of Variable Length Subnet Masking (VLSM) and Classless Internet Domain Routing (CIDR) in the context of several practical examples. The Internet Group Management Protocol (IGMP), which is used in IP multcast networks, is also discussed.

Chapter 10, "IP Routing Protocols," defines autonomous systems and the use of autonomous system routing protocols called Interior Gateway Protocols (IGPs). The Vector Distance and Link State routing protocols are explained. RIP and OSPF are discussed as examples of the Vector Distance and Link State routing protocols.

Chapter 11, "Transfer Protocols," explains the features, operation, and packet format of TCP and UDP. The transfer protocols are host-to-host protocols that enable important mechanisms to interface with user applications. The TCP protocol provides a reliable data stream and the techniques used to increase its reliability and efficiency are discussed in detail. Protocol decodes for both TCP and UDP are discussed.

Part III: TCP/IP Application Services

Chapter 12, "Automatic Configuration," discusses the BOOTP and DHCP protocol features, formats, and operations used to provide TCP/IP parameters from a central location such as BOOTP or DHCP server. The operation of DHCP in terms of a finite state machine is described. The protocol decodes for BOOTP/DHCP are also presented in this chapter.

Chapter 13, "Application Services," discusses some common application services on TCP/IP networks. These services include Domain Name System (DNS), Mail protocols (SMTP, POP3, and IMAP4), Remote Access protocols (Telnet and Berkeley r*), file transfer protocols (FTP and TFTP), file access protocols (NFS and Web NFS), and Web Access Protocols (HTTP/HTML and Gopher).

Chapter 14, "TCP/IP Network Management," presentss the network management model used in TCP/IP networks. Specifically, the Simple Network Management Protocol (SNMP), which is widely used in the industry, is discussed.

Part IV: Future Directions

Chapter 15, "IP Next Generation and ATM," discusses two exciting technologies that can do much to shape the future of the new generation of intranets and internets: IP Next Generation, also called IPv6, and ATM. The features and protocol format of IPv6 headers are explained. The basics of ATM and how TCP/IP packets are sent on ATM networks are also discussed.

Appendix

The appendix, "Standard Protocols," contains listings of the standard protocols and RFCs and their current statuses.

Conventions Used in This Book

Throughout this book, certain conventions are used. Please take a moment to examine these conventions:

- Information you type is displayed in **boldface**. This applies to individual letters or numbers as well as to text strings. This convention, however, does not apply to special keys, such as Enter, Esc, or Ctrl.
- New terms appear in *italic*.
- Text that is displayed on-screen, such as prompts or messages, appears in a `monospace` font.

Special Text Used in This Book

Throughout this book, you will see examples of special text. These passages have been given special treatment so that you can instantly recognize their significance and can locate them easily.

Note A note includes "extra" information that you should find useful, but which complements the discussion at hand rather than being a direct part of it. A note might describe situations that can arise when you use an application under certain circumstances, and then explain what steps to take when you find yourself in such a situation.

Tip A tip provides quick instructions for getting the most from your system as you follow steps outlined in the general discussion. A tip might show you how to speed up a procedure or how to implement one of many timesaving and system-enhancing techniques. A tip might also tell you how to avoid a potential problem with your system.

Warning A warning tells you when a procedure might be dangerous—that is, when you run the risk of losing data, locking your system, or perhaps damaging your hardware. A warning might explain how to avoid such risks or might describe the steps you should take to remedy a loss.

New Riders Publishing

The staff of New Riders Publishing is committed to bringing you the very best in computer reference material. Each New Riders book is the result of months of work by authors and staff who research and refine the information contained within its covers.

As part of this commitment to you, New Riders invites your input. Please let us know if you enjoy this book, if you have trouble with the information and examples presented, or if you have a suggestion for the next edition.

Please note, however that New Riders staff cannot serve as a technical resource for TCP/IP or TCP/IP protocol-related questions or for questions about software- or hardware-related problems. Please refer to the documentation that accompanies your software or to the applications' Help systems.

If you have a question or comment about any New Riders book, there are several ways to contact New Riders Publishing. We will respond to as many readers as we can. Your name, address, or phone number will never become part of a mailing list or be used for any purpose other than to help us continue to bring you the best books possible.

You can write us at the following address:

New Riders Publishing
Attn: Publisher
201 W. 103rd Street
Indianapolis, IN 46290

If you prefer, you can fax New Riders Publishing at:

317-817-7448

You can also send electronic mail to New Riders/Sams/Que at the following Internet address:

networking@mcp.com

New Riders Publishing is an imprint of Macmillan Computer Publishing. To obtain a catalog or information, or to purchase any Macmillan Computer Publishing book, call 800-428-5331 or visit our Web site at http://www.mcp.com.

Thank you for selecting *Inside TCP/IP, Third Edition*!

PART I

TCP/IP Layering Model and Physical Infrastructure

CHAPTER 1

Introduction to TCP/IP

Computer networks have come to play an increasingly important role in the lives of people. The motivation for the widespread use of computer networks is the need for people with common and shared interests to communicate with each other. People who are a part of a business organization need to communicate and share information with each other. Because information can more easily be represented and manipulated in electronic form, the employees of the business organization have access to terminals attached to mainframes/minicomputers, personal computers, or computer workstations. To meet the need to share and communicate information, the computers need to be connected. When computers are connected to each other, a data communication network—the computer network—is created.

Within a business organization at a single location, the computer network is usually a local area network (LAN). When the business organization needs to communicate with other businesses or individuals at a different location, a wide area network (WAN) is created to connect the different sites together (see fig. 1.1).

Figure 1.1 Local area and wide area computer networks.

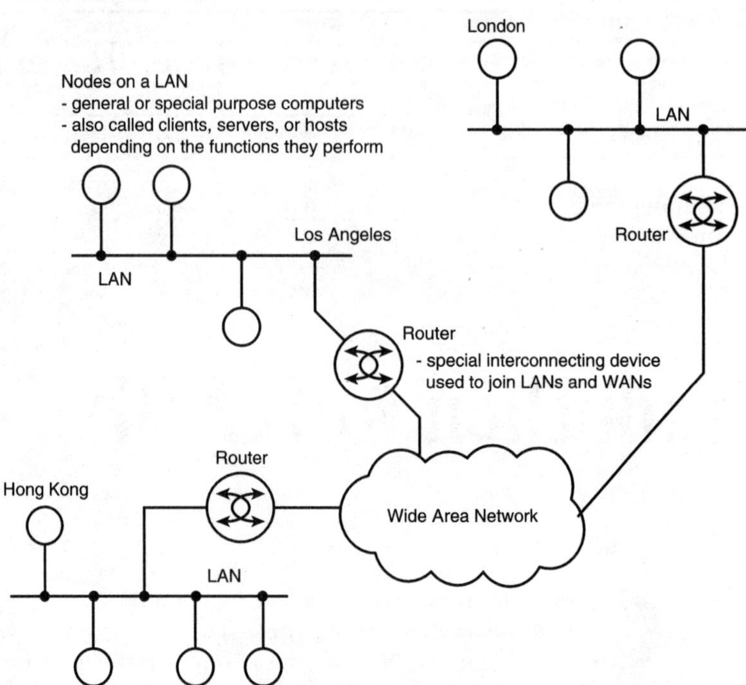

The example that has been given is of a business organization. However, today's networks have grown to encompass people from different backgrounds and organizations, as can be seen in the phenomenal growth of the Internet, the world-wide network that links private individuals, business organizations, nonprofit organizations, governments, international organizations, and educational institutions. Also, it is not necessary that the users of computer network be people; the users can be devices performing a certain controlling function. For example, in the case of an aircraft, ship, or automobile, several computers may be monitoring different aspects of the control systems that need to communicate control information.

This book focuses its attention on computer networks that have been built with a networking technology lumped under the name TCP/IP, which stands for Transmission Control Protocol/Internet Protocol. Networks that use this technology are called TCP/IP networks.

This technology plays a major part in the world-wide Internet and many business networks. Perhaps one reason for the appeal of TCP/IP networks is that they are based on an open specification that is not controlled by any vendor.

This chapter examines the origins of TCP/IP networks and the commercial uses of this protocol. It also gives a brief overview of the more common application services that use the TCP/IP protocol. This chapter is very conceptual in nature and offers you a more general, introductory look at the technology. Upcoming chapters deal more specifically with how TCP/IP literally works.

Overview of TCP/IP Networks

Before examining the details of TCP/IP networks in later chapters, an overview of TCP/IP would be helpful in giving you a more general perspective of TCP/IP networks. To assist you in understanding TCP/IP networks, the following sections will give you a clear definition as well as the history that led to the commercial uses of TCP/IP.

What Is TCP/IP?

When people use the acronym TCP/IP, it can refer to a number of different concepts and ideas. The most popular use of the term TCP/IP is *a communications protocol for data transport*. The TCP stands for Transmission Control Protocol and IP stands for Internet Protocol.

What is a communications protocol? A communications protocol is a set of rules and regulations by which computers networked together can communicate. Just as people require the use of a commonly understood language to communicate, so do computers. If people are talking to each other in a room, chances are very high that they are speaking in a common language. In a room full of diplomats from different countries, such as in the United Nations, you can expect different languages to be spoken. But in this case, you can also expect to find translators who can help the people understand each other. Computer networks mimic the communications methods used by human beings. This situation is not exactly a coincidence because computer networks are designed by human beings. A very common and popular language used in computer networks is the TCP/IP protocol. If other protocol languages are to be used in the computer network, you need translator computer devices, which can translate to a common language.

The term TCP/IP is not limited just to the Transmission Control Protocol (TCP) and the Internet Protocol (IP). The term can also refer to a group of protocols—such as the User Datagram Protocol (UDP), File Transfer Protocol (FTP), Terminal Emulation Protocol (Telnet), Hypertext Transfer Protocol (HTTP), and so on—that are associated with TCP/IP.

Figure 1.2 shows a sample TCP/IP network that uses TCP/IP. In this figure, TCP/IP refers to the communications protocol and the applications—such as FTP, Telnet, HTTP—that use TCP/IP.

Figure 1.2 Example TCP/IP internet.

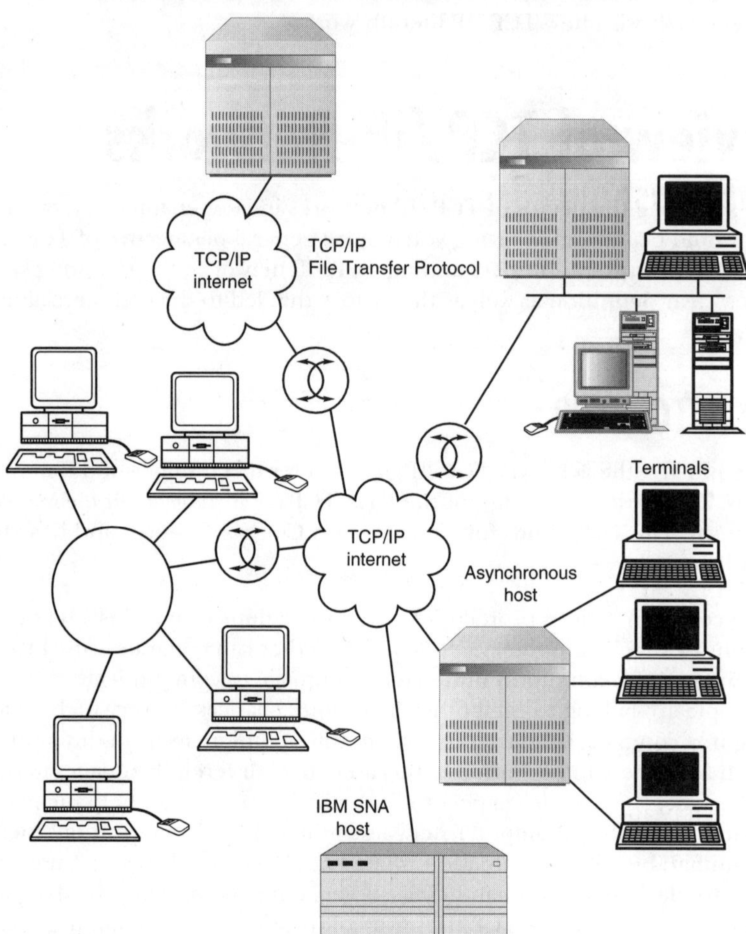

Networks that use TCP/IP are called TCP/IP *internets.* Figure 2.1 is an example of a TCP/IP internet. A distinction must be made between a TCP/IP *internet* and the *Internet.* A TCP/IP internet is any network that uses TCP/IP protocols that may or may not be connected to other networks. *The* Internet is currently the largest network in the world with thousands of computers. It spans several continents and is predominantly based on TCP/IP.

When businesses use Internet services—particularly the World Wide Web service implemented by the HTTP protocol—on their own private network, the TCP/IP internet is called an *intranet*. Application services used on intranets are either the same as those used on the Internet or are modified versions of the Internet application programs.

The discussion of the TCP/IP technology in this book covers internets, intranets, and the global Internet.

TCP/IP: Past and Present

In the late 1960s, DARPA (Defense Advanced Research Projects Agency) of the United States noticed that there was a rapid proliferation of computers in military communications. Computers, because they could be easily programmed, provided flexibility in achieving network functions that was not available with other types of communications equipment. The computers that were used in military communications were manufactured by different vendors and were designed to interoperate with computers from that vendor only. Vendors used proprietary protocols in their communications equipment. The military had a multivendor network but no common protocol to support the heterogeneous equipment from different vendors.

Role of DARPA

To solve these problems, the U.S. Department of Defense (DoD) mandated that the Defense Advanced Research Projects Agency (DARPA) define a common set of protocols. The reasons for having a common set of protocols include the following:

- **Procurement simplification.** By mandating a common set of protocols, it is possible for the military to have a Request for Proposal, which specifies that communications products use the common protocol.
- **Fostering of competition among vendors.** Vendors can compete with each other based on the merits of their implementation of a standard protocol. If a common set of protocols is not required, vendors can implement their proprietary protocols against which other vendors cannot compete.
- **Interoperability.** By having vendors use a common set of protocols, interoperability between equipment from different vendors becomes a reality. If this equipment does not interoperate, the problem is probably due to a difference in implementation. The vendors can then refer to the standard specification of the protocol to isolate the problem.
- **Vendor productivity and efficiency.** Vendors can focus their attention on a single protocol rather than spread their efforts trying to implement several protocols. This condition makes the vendors' efforts more productive.

The Early DARPA Experiments

In 1969, an interesting experiment was conducted by DARPA to use a computer network to connect the following four sites:

1. University of California, Los Angeles (UCLA)
2. University of California, Santa Barbara (UCSB)
3. University of Utah
4. SRI International

Figure 1.3 shows the sites that were involved. This experiment was the beginning of the famous ARPAnet (Advanced Research Projects Agency Network). The experiment was a success. Additional sites were added to the network.

Figure 1.3 The four-node ARPAnet experiment.

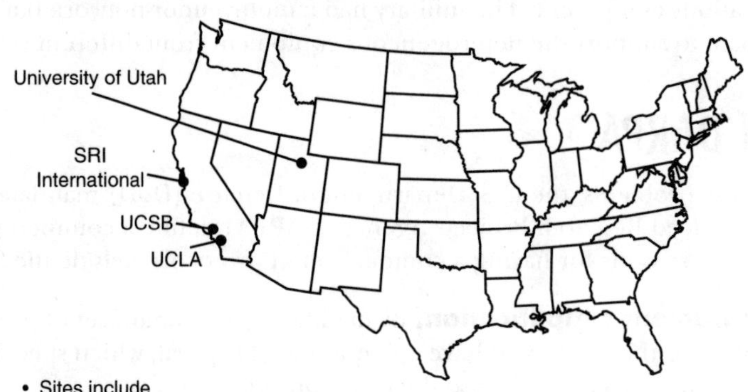

- Sites include
  - University of California, Los Angeles (UCLA)
  - University of California, Santa Barbara (UCSB)
  - University of Utah
  - SRI International

ARPAnet = Advanced Research Projects Agency Network

In 1972, an ARPAnet demonstration was done with 50 packet-switched nodes (PSNs) and 20 hosts. Like the preceding 4-node experiment, this one was also a success, and it set the stage for large-scale deployment of PSNs and hosts on the ARPAnet.

The term *node* in computer networks is a generic name for any device that connects to a network. This device can be a packet-switching device, as mentioned in relationship to the four-node ARPAnet experiment; or it can be any computer, including a personal computer, workstation, minicomputer, or mainframe.

Another term that is frequently used is *host,* which historically refers to a large computer that can support a number of terminals connected to it. Today, the term *host* is used to refer to any computer that provides services to users. This kind of computer can be a personal computer, workstation, minicomputer, or mainframe.

Another term that is frequently used is *server*. This term is used for any personal computer, workstation, minicomputer, or mainframe that is running server software. Server software provides services to other user software components called *clients*.

The ARPAnet Evolution

The ARPAnet continued to grow and went through a series of transformations. Prior to 1984, the ARPAnet consisted of specialized military networks connected with the ARPAnet (see fig. 1.4). After 1984, the specialized military networks formed their own network that was not connected to any other network. The US Military Defense Data Network (DDN) was created with links to the ARPAnet (see fig. 1.5).

Figure 1.4 **Pre-1984 ARPAnet.**

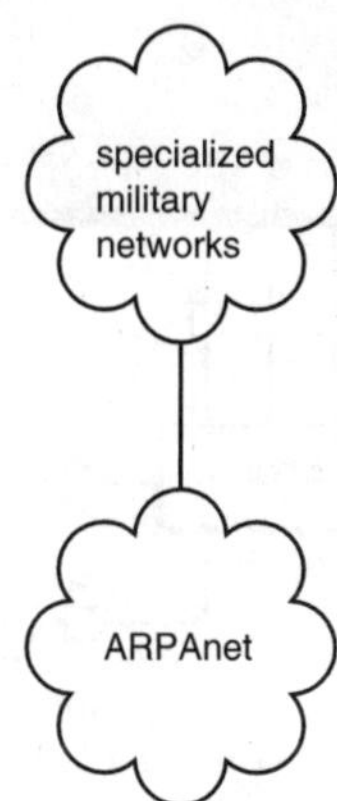

Figure 1.5 **ARPAnet in 1984.**

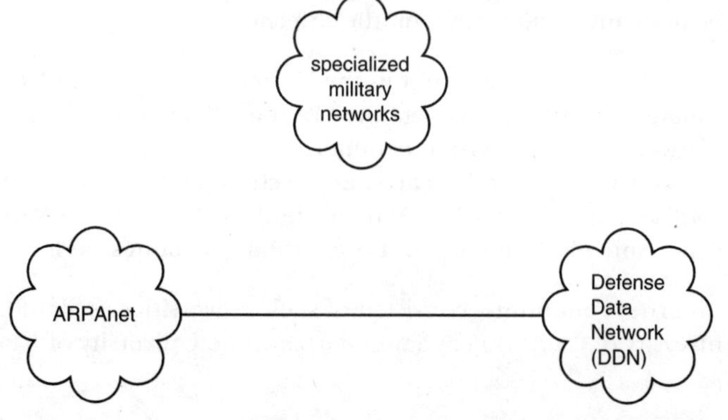

By 1986, the ARPAnet had expanded to encompass all major universities, the military network called MILNET, Research Laboratories such as Cadre and Tartan at Carnegie-Mellon University (CMU), and satellite links to several international sites (see fig.1.6).

Figure 1.6 ARPAnet in 1986.

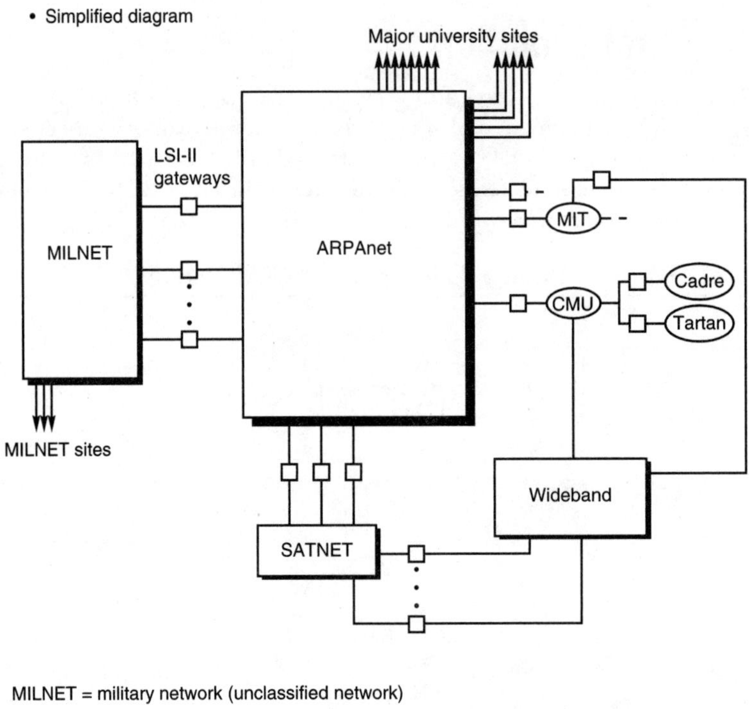

Gradually the ARPAnet itself was replaced by the Internet. The Internet is experiencing a rapid commercialization and is no longer the exclusive domain of universities and research organizations. There is currently more network traffic from commercial organizations than any other source on the Internet.

The original backbone of the Internet in the United States was NSFNET (National Science Foundation Network). Management of the NSFNET was contracted to ANS (Advanced Network Services). When commercialization of the Internet began, an ANSNET backbone was formed for carrying the commercial traffic. The ANSNET backbone was also managed by ANS. Actually, both NFSNET and ANSNET traffic was carried over the same physical links, but two virtual backbones were run over it.

The earlier Internet community consisted of such universities as Stanford, UCLA, MIT, the University of California at Santa Barbara, the University of Utah, the

University of Hawaii, and the University of California at Berkeley. This community also consisted of research organizations such as the SRI International, Rand Corporation, the Institute of Advanced Computation, and Bolt, Beranek and Newman (BBN).

Currently the Internet community has expanded to include commercial organizations and individual users. The Internet community includes all major universities, research organizations, corporations, schools, individual users, and Internet providers.

Internet providers are commercial organizations that sell access to the Internet. Table 1.1 shows a list of some of the Internet providers. This list is by no means complete or exhaustive and is shown as an example of what is available in the United States. It is difficult to keep such lists updated because Internet providers go out of business and new ones spring up; however, you can find complete books on listings of the regional Internet providers in various countries.

TABLE 1.1
Example List of Internet Providers

Internet Access Provider	Contact
AlterNet	UUNET Technologies, Inc. 800-488-6383 703-204-8000 alternet-info@uunet.uu.net
USANET (Internet Express)	719-520-1700 ID "new," password "newuser" Local access area codes: 303, 719 info@usa.net
DELPHI	800-365-4636 walthowe@delphi.com
Dial-in-cerf	Provided by CERFNET 800-876-2373 or 619-455-3900 Local access area codes: 213, 310, 415, 510, 619, 714, 818 help@cerf.net
NEARnet	617-873-8730 Local access codes: 508, 603, 617 nearnet-join@nic.near.net

continues

Table 1.1, Continued
Example List of Internet Providers

Internet Access Provider	Contact
NETCOM	408-554-UNIX info@netcom.com
NorthWestNet	206-562-3000 nic@nwnet.net
NYSERnet	315-453-2912 info@nysernet.org
PSInet	703-620-6651 all-info@psi.com
Well	The Whole Earth 'Lectronic Link 415-332-6106 ID "newuser" info@well.sf.ca.us
World	Software Tool & Die 617-739-9753 ID "new" 617-739-0202 office@world.std.com

Transition from Proprietary Networks to Open TCP/IP Networks

Earlier commercial computers were based around proprietary vendor products. Two classic examples are IBM's SNA (System Network Architecture) network and Digital's DECnet (see fig 1.7).

IBM's SNA network has traditionally been hierarchical. The IBM host communicates with communications controllers that off-load the communications processing from the IBM host. The communications controller in turn communicates with an IBM cluster controller that acts like a terminal server to IBM 3278/3279 page-mode display terminals.

Figure 1.7 Example proprietary networks.

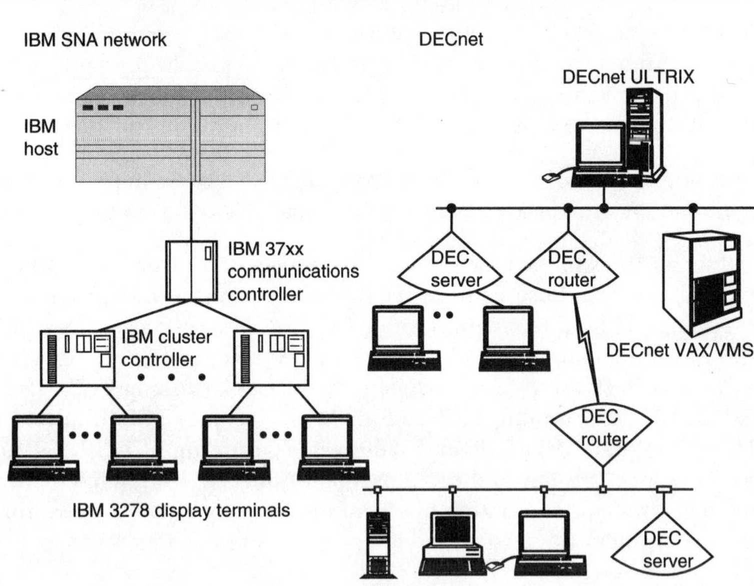

Digital's DECnet Phase IV is built around the DECnet suite of protocols, and DECnet Phase V uses both DECnet and OSI (Open Systems Interconnect) protocols. DECnet has a more peer-to-peer orientation at both the physical network and protocol levels when compared with IBM's SNA network.

IBM's SNA networks have evolved to become more peer-to-peer at the API- and upper-protocol level, as can be seen with the introduction of APPC (Advanced Peer-to-Peer Communications) and APPN (Advanced Peer-to-Peer Networks).

Both of these proprietary solutions, IBM's SNA and Digital's DECnet, have become more open with the availability of standard TCP/IP support (and also OSI support). IBM, VAX, or Alpha-based hosts can be accessed by using TCP/IP protocols and services.

Both IBM and DEC have intensified their efforts in the TCP/IP marketplace. For example, IBM now off-loads TCP/IP processing from the IBM mainframes to the IBM Interconnect Controller or to a RISC System 6000 running TCP/IP. The IBM Interconnect Controller acts as a front-end processor and gets the host out of processing TCP/IP communications. The IBM Interconnect Controller is an Intel processor micro-channel platform running TCP/IP on OS/2. This off-load technology is primarily aimed at MVS, which are VM mainframes that are currently at peak capacity.

A Multivendor Network

Vendors have begun providing more open solutions based around TCP/IP because users have demanded freedom from proprietary solutions. Proprietary solutions lock users to a particular vendor's platform. Although this situation may be advantageous to vendors, it can lead to more expensive networking solutions for the user.

Using a common protocol such as TCP/IP promotes a more competitive market where users can pick the best TCP/IP protocol stack from a wide range of choices.

Figure 1.8 shows an example of a multivendor network based around TCP/IP. This figure shows a variety of hosts running TCP/IP. This figure shows an HP-9000 class machine running HP-UX that comes with TCP/IP software. It also shows SUN workstations running SunOS or Solaris, VAX/VMS running TCP/IP for VMS or Wollongong's TCP/IP for VMS, Novell NetWare 3.x/4.x running TCP/IP, Unix TCP/IP, IBM VM host running TCP/IP for VM or Fibronics TCP/IP, IBM PC with NCSA TCP/IP software, MacTCP, and Windows NT running TCP/IP. Because of restrictions of space, this figure shows a partial list only. TCP/IP implementations are available on every major computing platform ranging from mainframes, minicomputers to microcomputers.

The HP-UX, SunOS/Solaris, and UnixWare are examples of TCP/IP implementations on a Unix platform. TCP/IP is implemented as a standard part of BSD Unix and Unix System V.

Figure 1.8 Example multivendor TCP/IP implementations.

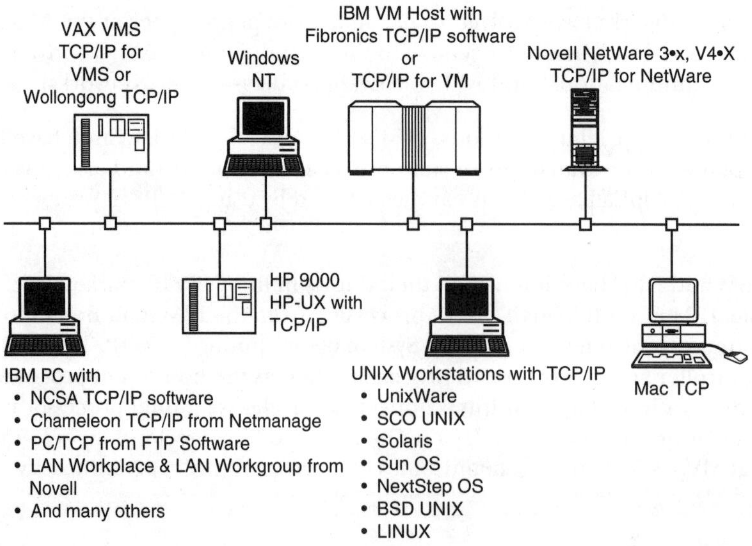

Originally, TCP/IP was implemented in the kernel of the BSD 4.2 Unix operating system. BSD 4.2 Unix was a very seminal version of Unix and is one of the reasons for TCP/IP's widespread popularity. Most universities and many research organizations use BSD Unix. Today, many host machines on the Internet run a direct descendant of BSD Unix. In addition, many commercial versions of Unix, such as SUN's SunOS and Digital's Ultrix, were derived from BSD 4.2 Unix. Unix System V TCP/IP implementation has also been heavily influenced by BSD Unix.

Shift in TCP/IP Vendor Revenues

If this book is your first introduction to TCP/IP, you should feel good about the fact that you are interested in it. Many job opportunities in the area of computer networks require knowledge of TCP/IP. Figures 1.9 and 1.10 show the shift in TCP/IP vendor revenues and the number of TCP/IP vendors. Both of these graphs indicate a rising interest in TCP/IP. Figure 1.9 shows that the market size, in terms of revenues, has increased for U.S.-based companies. It also shows that most of the growth has been in the commercial sector.

Figure 1.9 **TCP/IP vendor revenues.**

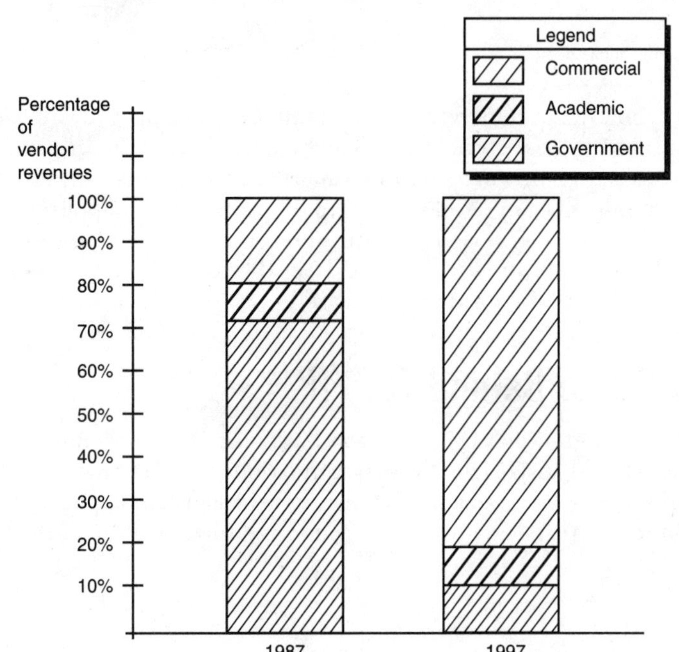

Source: Infonetics, *Network World*, Newton-Evans Research Co.

Figure 1.10 Number of TCP/IP vendors.

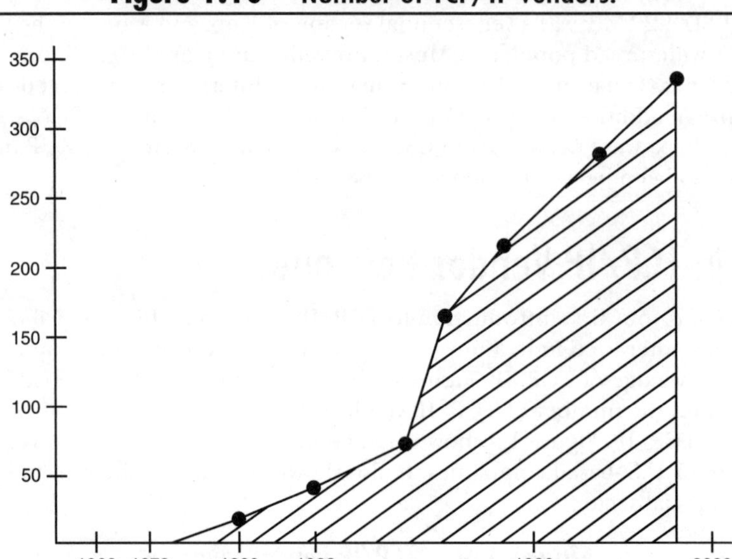

Source: Infonetics

Figure 1.10 shows a rapid increase in the number of vendors providing TCP/IP-based products around 1985. Several reasons can be attributed to this growth. One of the major reasons is that the microcomputer market grew dramatically around this time, and several vendors began developing TCP/IP protocols and applications for microcomputers. Another reason is that vendors grew tired of waiting for OSI protocols to mature while there was already a mature TCP/IP protocol suite and services that had a proven track record for a number of years.

Driving Force Behind TCP/IP

TCP/IP delivers today what OSI protocols have promised for a number of years. The areas where TCP/IP was originally weak compared to OSI protocols was in the area of application services. OSI had a far richer variety of standard application services than TCP/IP. In recent years, as a result of strenuous efforts by those in the Internet community, TCP/IP proponents have narrowed the gap between OSI application offerings and TCP/IP applications. Some of the more promising OSI applications, such as X.500, are now implemented on TCP/IP-based networks.

The three factors driving growth in TCP/IP today are as follows:

- **Promise of interoperability.** Having a common protocol allows the interoperability of products from different vendors. For true interoperability, vendors should use not only TCP/IP but TCP/IP application services, too.
- **Interest in the commercialization of the Internet.** The Internet today is predominantly based on TCP/IP protocols and application services. As the general public's interest in using the Internet and the ensuing Information Superhighway continues to increase, you can expect a corresponding increase in interest in TCP/IP protocols and services.
- **Growth in network management tools.** The most widely implemented network management protocol today is SNMP (Simple Network Management Protocol). This protocol makes use of TCP/IP protocols. Many network vendors of products such as hubs, bridges, and routers provide SNMP agents. These SNMP agents use the TCP/IP stack. The graph in figure 1.10, therefore, also includes hardware vendors.

TCP/IP Time-Line Evolution

Figure 1.11 shows the TCP/IP time-line evolution. This figure shows notable events that occurred with respect to TCP/IP growth. The time-line begins with the four-node ARPAnet experiment in 1969 and the ARPAnet demonstration in 1972. In the 1978–1980 time frame, there was a great deal of interaction between the TCP/IP researchers and implementers and the researchers at Xerox's Palo Alto research facility, who were working on XNS (Xerox Network System). As a result of this interaction, XNS's RIP (Routing Information Protocol) was adopted for use in BSD Unix. Because BSD Unix was popular, RIP became widely used on TCP/IP networks. The influence of BSD Unix was felt around 1980, when this operating system was deployed at many sites.

Figure 1.11 TCP/IP time-line evolution.

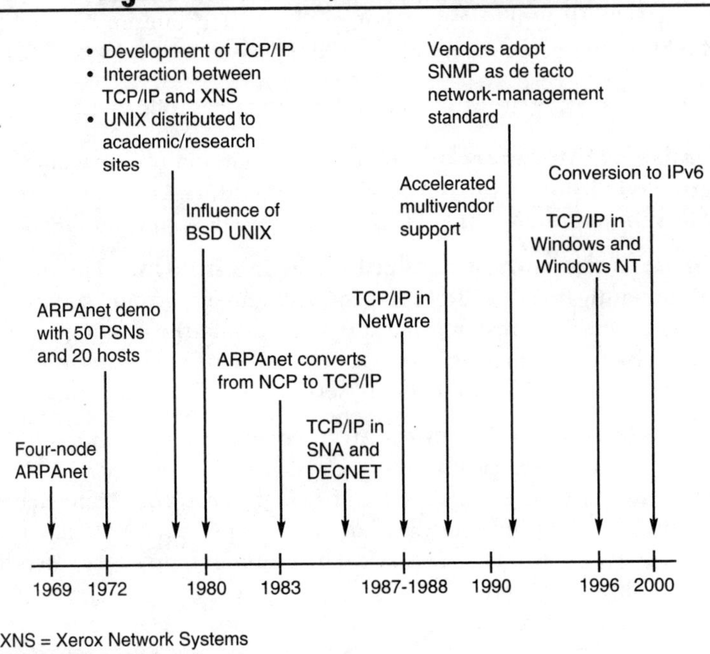

In 1983, the ARPAnet—which was up to this time using NCP—began converting to TCP/IP.

In the late 1980s, there was accelerated multivendor support for TCP/IP. In the early 1990s, SNMP became a de facto standard for management of TCP/IP networks. SNMP is not restricted to using TCP/IP protocols. For example, SNMP can also run on Novell's IPX protocol (Internetwork Packet Exchange protocol) and OSI's CLNP (Connectionless Network Protocol).

TCP/IP Applications Overview

Several TCP/IP applications, such as File Transfer Protocol (FTP) and Telnet (Terminal Emulation), were mentioned earlier in this chapter. This section will provide an overview of these applications. Later chapters in this book will discuss additional details of these application services.

Figure 1.12 shows some of the more popular TCP/IP applications. This figure shows a TCP/IP internet with users that are accessing TCP/IP applications on hosts that are remote from the users.

Figure 1.12 TCP/IP applications overview. (Courtesy Learning Tree)

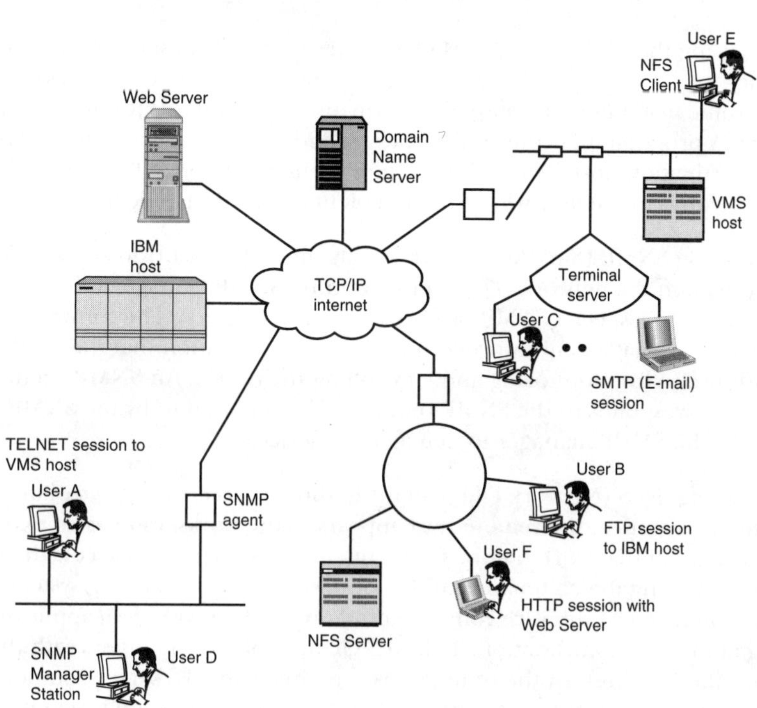

User A in this figure is at a workstation and using a Telnet session to log on remotely to a VMS host. The Telnet application enables a user to access another host remotely. For this action to take place, two components of software must be running. You need a Telnet *client* application running at the user's workstation. The Telnet client application takes the user's keystrokes and sends them (character at a time or a line at a time) to the remote host. At the remote host, you need a Telnet *server* component. This Telnet server component takes the user's typed-in characters and submits them to the operating system as if they were typed in by a locally attached terminal. The Telnet server is responsible for taking the host's response and sending it to the Telnet client running at the user's workstation.

User B is using an FTP session to perform file transfers between his workstation and an IBM host. The FTP application enables a user to access another host's file system interactively. After an FTP session is established, the user can type special FTP commands that enable the user to browse directories and files on the remote system. The user can issue commands for *uploading* or *downloading* files between the workstation and the FTP host. For an FTP session to work, you need two software components. You need an FTP *client* application running at the user's workstation. The FTP client application enables you to send interactive commands to the FTP host. At the remote host, you need an FTP *server* component. This FTP server component processes the user's FTP commands and interacts with the file system of the host that it runs on.

User C is using the SMTP (Simple Mail Transfer Protocol) to send electronic mail to other users on the network. The mail software running at the user's workstation takes the electronic mail message composed by the user and deposits it into an outgoing mail area. A program that runs in the background takes the electronic mail and sends it to the destination host. The mail is then deposited in the mailbox on the host. This mailbox belongs to the user who is the recipient of the electronic mail.

User D is using SNMP (Simple Network Management Protocol) to access information about devices on the network. The user is running SNMP manager software that sends requests in a special SNMP message format to a device. The software queries the device for management information, which is information that the SNMP manager finds useful for monitoring and controlling the device. An SNMP agent running on the device responds to the SNMP requests. The replies sent by the SNMP agent are used by the SNMP manager to manage the device.

User E is using NFS (Network File System) to directly access file services on a remote host. The file system at the remote host appears to the workstation as an extension of the file system on that workstation. This setup enables the user to access the remote file system by using the commands of the local workstation operating system. For NFS to work, you need two software components. You need an NFS *client* application running at the user's workstation. The NFS client application *connects* with the file system on the NFS host. At the remote host, you need an NFS server component. This NFS server component interacts with the file system of the host on which it runs and enables its file system to be treated as a local file system at the user's workstation.

User F is using a web browser to access a set of hyperlinked text and a graphics document on a remote web server. Using the web browser and the underlying application service protocol (HTTP), the user can browse web documents on the web server. The web browser implements the HTTP client and renders graphically the web documents delivered by the web server that implements the HTTP server. The web documents are encoded by using a special syntax called the Hypertext Markup Language (HTML).

The Domain Name System (DNS) server that is shown in figure 1.12 is used for TCP/IP applications to refer to host names by their symbolic names rather than by their network address. When a TCP/IP application such as Telnet wants to log on to the VMS host, it can use a symbolic name for the VMS host. The DNS server will resolve this symbolic name to the network address that will be used by the Telnet application to contact the VMS host.

Table 1.2 summarizes the TCP/IP applications discussed in this section.

TABLE 1.2
TCP/IP Applications Summary

Application Service	Description
Telnet	Enables a user to log in remotely across a TCP/IP network to any host supporting this protocol. The remote login gives a user the appearance of being directly connected to the remote machine. The keystrokes that the user enters at the computer or terminal are delivered to the remote machine, and the remote computer's response is delivered back to the user's computer or terminal. The delivery of the keystrokes and the computer's response is accomplished by the Telnet protocol. The Telnet protocol, in turn, uses the TCP/IP protocol as its communications protocol.
FTP	Enables users to transfer files among computers on a TCP/IP network. The files that are transferred can be of arbitrary sizes. The user logs into the remote FTP server and enters into an interactive session with the FTP server. The user's computer runs a special program called the FTP client. Using the FTP client, the user can issue interactive commands to view files at the remote server and transfer files to and fro from the FTP server.
SMTP	Enables users to send electronic mail to other users on the TCP/IP network. The electronic mail is composed in the form of a memo. The user enters the electronic mail address of the recipient, subject information, and so on in the header of the electronic mail. SMTP uses TCP/IP as the underlying protocol to relay the message to a mail server. The mail servers act as a network of mail relay agents that work together to deliver the message to the destination.
SNMP	Enables remote management of such devices as bridges, routers, and gateways on the network. Devices that are to be monitored by using SNMP must run a special agent called the SNMP agent, which has knowledge of the device parameters and how to access them. An SNMP manager station sends SNMP requests to read or modify the values of the device parameters; therefore, the SNMP manager station can control and manage the device. SNMP uses UDP and IP as the communications protocol.

continues

Table 1.2, Continued
TCP/IP Applications Summary

Application Service	Description
DNS	Acts as an electronic directory and clearing house for names of network resources. DNS treats computer names as symbolic addresses. DNS defines a hierarchical naming scheme that enables computers to be accessed symbolically. For example, a chess-playing computer at IBM may have the following symbolic or DNS name: trueblue.chess.ibm.com. DNS names are also important for electronic mail because the electronic mail addresses use host DNS names as part of the electronic mail address. Thus a user called bob may have the following electronic mail address: bob@trueblue.chess.ibm.com. The name after the @ sign is a DNS name of the mail system that holds the user's electronic mailbox. DNS uses UDP and IP as the communications protocol.
HTTP	Enables hypertext-linked documents to be delivered to a web browser. The hypertext documents and embedded graphics, audio, and video files are rendered for display on the user's screen by the web browser. HTTP uses TCP/IP as the communications protocol.

Again, this section merely offers you a taste of the different TCP/IP applications and what they have to offer. More detailed coverage is found in upcoming chapters.

The Internet

The former ARPAnet has gradually been replaced by the Internet. The Internet is not a single network; rather, it is a conglomeration of several networks. The Internet uses mainly TCP/IP-based protocols and applications. But not all networks on the Internet use TCP/IP. Two examples of this exception include the BITNET and the CREN networks, which use IBM's SNA protocols. In order for these networks to interact with other networks that use TCP/IP, protocol translations by *gateways* need to be done.

Even though the Internet continues to undergo commercialization, it provides an incomparable test network for developing new protocols and application services. For example, a great deal of experimentation and research on OSI application services is conducted on the Internet even though the OSI application services were originally designed to work with a different set of protocols.

The following section describes examples of networks that comprise the Internet.

Example Networks on the Internet

Table 1.3 contains some of the networks that make up the Internet. The list is by no means exhaustive, and some of the networks are of historical interest. This list is meant to give you an idea of the range of participation on the Internet by international communities.

Table 1.3
Examples of Networks on the Internet

Network	Description
NSFNET	National Science Foundation Network. It is the backbone network in the United States, but it has been largely replaced by newer backbones from ANSNET and MCI.
CSNET	Computer Science Network. It is an affordable Internet service that uses X.25 for small schools and organizations.
Cypress Net	Provides low cost and low volume Internet access centered around Purdue University.
MILNET	U.S. Department of Defense (DoD) Network. It was originally part of ARPAnet.
BITNET	Because It's Time Network. It uses IBM mainframes and low-cost 9600 bps links.
CREN	Consortium for Research and Education Network. It is the successor to CSNET and BITNET.
EARN	European Academic Research Network. It uses BITNET technology and is the network for Europe, the Middle East, and Africa.
JANET	Joint Academic Network. It is the network for universities and research institutions in the United Kingdom.
CDNet	The Canadian Development Network provides network services to the Canadian research, education, and advanced development community.
NRCnet	Canadian National Research Council Network. It is modeled after NSFNET.

continues

Table 1.3, Continued
Examples of Networks on the Internet

Network	Description
ACSnet	Australian Computer Science Network. It is used by universities, research institutions, and industry.
Kogaku-bu	Established in 1987, it uses TCP/IP over a Toshiba 100 Mbps fiber backbone network that connects Ethernet LANs.

The NFSNET is a general-purpose internet providing access to scientific computing resources, data, and information. NFSNET was initially organized and partly funded by NSF. NFSNET is a three-level inter-network consisting of the following elements:

- **The backbone.** A transcontinental network that connects separately administered networks to NSF supercomputer centers
- **Mid-level networks.** Regional, discipline-based, and supercomputer consortium networks
- **Campus-wide networks.** Connected to mid-level networks

Management and operation of NFSNET are the responsibility of Merit, Inc. and, later on, ANSNET. End-user support of NFSNET is provided by a Network Information Center (NIC) at Bolt Beranek and Newman, Inc. (BBN). The NFSNET has an interesting architecture. It uses packet-switched nodes called NSS (nodal switching subsystems). Each NSS consists of nine IBM RT/PCs running AIX connected to token-ring networks for redundancy. Within each NSS, a routing control processor (NCP) mediates access between more than one NSS. Backbone routing software within each NSS uses IS-IS (a routing protocol called Intermediate System to Intermediate System). Mid-level networks are connected by using the Exterior Gateway Protocol (EGP).

Established in January 1981, CSNET consisted of the computer science departments of schools and universities. Membership is now more general and includes industrial, academic, government, and nonprofit institutions that are engaged in computer-related research or advanced development in science and engineering. The network is confined mostly to the United States and Canada, but it has links to Australia, Finland, France, Germany, Israel, Japan, Korea, New Zealand, Sweden, Switzerland, the People's Republic of China, and the United Kingdom. The CSNET CIC (Computer and Information Center) was administered by Bolt Beranek and Newman, Inc. (BBN).

BITNET is a cooperative network that serves more than 2,300 hosts (IBM) at several hundred sites in 32 countries. The underlying protocol is NJE, with some sites running NJE on top of TCP/IP. In Europe, there are plans to migrate to ISO protocols. Major constituents of BITNET are in the United States, Mexico, Japan,

Singapore, Taiwan, and Korea. Asian parts are known as Asianet; Canadian parts, as NetNorth; and European parts, as EARN.

In October 1988, the boards of CSNET and BITNET voted to merge the two into a single network called the CREN. The merger was completed in 1989.

EARN was formed in 1983. The charter statutes of EARN state that it is a network for Europe, the Middle East, and Africa. Recent voting has ratified Morocco, Tunisia, Egypt, and India as members. Administratively, EARN is registered in France, and its board of directors consists of members from each member country. EARN uses the technology used in BITNET and is part of BITNET. Many EARN hosts are IBM VM and DEC VAX VMS machines. Gateways exist to other networks, such as JANET in the United Kingdom and HEANET in Ireland.

JANET was established to provide consolidated links among universities and research institutions in the United Kingdom. JANET is funded by the Computer Board for Universities and Research Councils (CB) and is limited to the following members:

- Universities
- Laboratories or institutes funded by research councils
- Individual members of polytechnics or other institutes of higher education that hold research council grants
- Polytechnics that can join the network but are charged

Services in JANET include mail, file transfer, remote login, and remote job entry. LANs connected to JANET tend to be X.25 campus switches, Cambridge Rings (CR82 standard), Ethernet, and IEEE 802.3. Wide area links are X.25 at the network layer. JANET packet-switching exchanges (JPSE) are based on GEC 4000 processors. JANET uses a domain name system similar to the Internet DNS, but the order of the domain name parts is opposite, with the root on the left. For example, to send mail from JANET to the Internet, the gateway is at `uk.ac.ucl.cs.nss` at the University of London Computer Center (ULCC).

CDNet is administered by the CDNet Headquarters at the University of British Columbia (UBC) and is independent of the Canadian Department of Defense. Most machines are DEC VAX or Sun file servers (about 60 percent Unix and 40 percent VMS). Most wide area links are X.25 at 2,400 bps (with a range varying from 1,200 bps to 9,600 bps) provided through DATAPAC. There are leased-line connections to the NFSNET backbone. Gateways exist to CSNET and BITNET.

NRCnet is modeled after NFSNET to provide faster services than currently offered by NetNorth and CDNet. NRCnet uses the three-level model of backbone, mid-level, and campus LANs.

ACSnet is based on the Sydney Unix Network (SUN) software developed at the University of Sydney. The network was started in 1979. It provides mail- and file-transfer traffic among researchers, academia, and industry. Wide area links include leased lines, dial-up lines, and X.25

Kogaku-bu, established in 1987, uses TCP/IP over a Toshiba 100 Mbps fiber backbone network that connects Ethernet LANs. Protocols are not FDDI because the technology predates FDDI. The data link protocol on the ring is called TOTOLAN/RING. Applications include Telnet and FTP. Mainframe remote login access that uses Japanese character sets has been managed by putting Telnet in the transparent mode and by using the character conversion capabilities of the IBM TSS TIOP2 program on the mainframe.

The IAB and the Internet Society

Figure 1.13 shows the interrelationship between the various bodies that have an impact on the Internet.

Figure 1.13 Structure of the IAB.

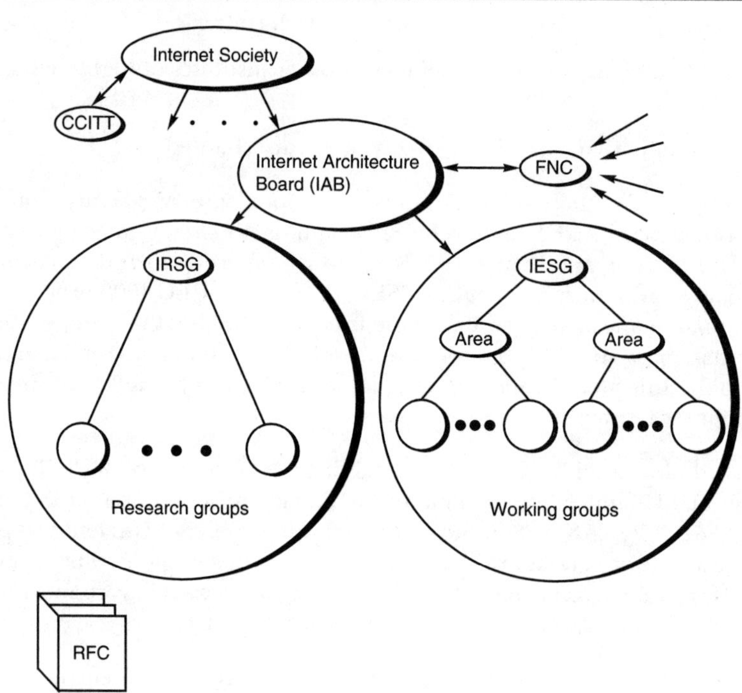

CCITT = Comité Consultatif Internationale Télégraphique et Téléphonique
IESG = Internet Engineering Steering Group
IRSG = Internet Research Steering Group
FNC = Federal Networking Council

The Internet Architecture Board (IAB) provides a focus, direction, and coordination of TCP/IP-related protocols. This body guides the evolution of the Internet. It is comprised of the Internet Research Task Force (IRTF) and the Internet Engineering Task Force (IETF). The Federal Networking Council (FNC) is the U.S. government regulatory body that serves as an advisory body. As the Internet gets even more commercialized, the influence of the FNC has been reduced.

The Internet Engineering Task Force is managed by the Internet Engineering Steering Group (IESG). The task force is divided into *areas*, with the areas divided into *working groups*. The IETF focuses on short- to medium-term engineering problems.

The Internet Research Task Force is managed by the Internet Research Steering Group (IRSG). The task force focuses on long-term research problems.

The IETF has the following broad eight technical areas; the actual areas may change over time, depending on the needs of the Internet:

- Applications
- Host protocols
- Internet protocols
- Routing
- Network management
- OSI interoperability
- Operations
- Security

The IETF has many working groups. Some of these are authentication, domain names, dynamic host configuration, host requirements, interconnectivity, Internet MIB, joint management, Telnet, user documents, and so on. The term *IETF* is also used to refer to the entire body of engineering effort carried out under IESG; IETF includes the IESG, its chairman, and its working groups.

In 1992, the Internet Society was formed to promote the use of the Internet for collaboration on research topics on the Internet. The society provides a forum for industry, educators, government, and users. It is involved with the recommendation of procedures and technical standards for the global Internet and private internets.

Membership to the Internet Society is open to everyone for an annual membership fee. You can contact the Internet Society through the following methods:

Postal Address:
Internet Society
Suite 100
1895 Preston White Drive
Reston, VA 22091-5434
U.S.A

Internet e-mail:
isoc@isoc.org

Telephone:
703-648-9888

Fax:
703-620-0913

RFCs, STDs, and IENs

The primary method for communicating new ideas on protocols, research, and standards is through Request for Comments (RFCs). When a researcher comes up with a new protocol, research, or a tutorial on a topic, the researcher can submit his findings as an RFC document. Thus, RFCs consist of Internet standards, proposals for new or revised protocols, implementation strategies, tutorials, collective wisdom, and so on.

Protocols that are to become standards in the Internet go through a series of states that describe their maturity levels. These levels are the proposed standard, draft standard, and standard. Each level involves an increased amount of scrutiny and testing. When a protocol completes this process, it is assigned an STD number.

As technology advances, some protocols are superseded by better ones, or they may be unused. These protocols are documented with the *historic* designation. The results of early protocol research and development work are documented in some RFCs. These protocols are designated as *experimental.*

Protocols that are developed by other standards organizations or by particular vendors and individuals may be of interest or may be recommended for use on the Internet. The specifications of such protocols may be published as RFCs for the convenience and ease of distribution to the Internet community. These protocols are labeled *informational.*

Sometimes, protocols may achieve widespread implementation without the approval or involvement of the IESG. This situation may occur because of the evolution of protocols in the marketplace or because of political reasons. Some of these vendor protocols may even become very important to the Internet community because business organizations may have deployed them within their intranets. The position of the IAB is that it strongly recommends that the standards process be used in the evolution of the protocol to maximize interoperability and to prevent incompatible protocol requirements from arising.

Not all the protocols are required to be implemented in all systems because there is such a variety of possible systems where a protocol implementation may not make sense. For example, some Internet devices—such as gateways, routers, terminal servers, workstations, and multiuser hosts—have a different set of requirements.

Not all RFCs are Internet protocol standards, even though all Internet protocol standards have an RFC number. The list of official Internet protocol standards is published regularly. This list is also an RFC. When a new RFC is published on the same topic, it contains a statement about which RFC it replaces. Thus RFC 2200 is published as

> 2200 S J. Postel, "INTERNET OFFICIAL PROTOCOL STANDARDS,"(Obsoletes RFC 2000) (STD 1)

Notice that this RFC listing states that RFC 2200 is an Internet official protocol standard and that it makes obsolete RFC 2000 on the same topic. If you examine the RFC index, you will notice that there is a letter *S* next to the number. This letter means that the number is an Internet standard. Other codes that are used are *PS* for a proposed standard; *DS* for a draft standard; *I* for informational purposes; and *E* for documenting results of experiments (see table 1.4 for a detailed discussion). RFC 2200 is also described as being STD 1. The Internet standards are numbered starting with STD 1, STD 2, and so on. These standards are described by RFCs whose numbers are described in the STD 1 document.

TABLE 1.4
Status Definitions of Protocols as per RFC 2000

Status	Definition
Standard protocol	The IESG has established an official standard protocol for the Internet. These protocols are assigned STD numbers that are separated into two groups: an IP protocol and higher, which include protocols that apply to the whole Internet; and network-specific protocols, which include specifications about how to do IP on particular types of networks.
Draft standard protocol	The IESG is actively considering this protocol as a possible standard protocol. Substantial and widespread testing and comments are desired. Comments and test

continues

Table 1.4, Continued
Status Definitions of Protocols as per RFC 2000

Status	Definition
	results should be submitted to the IESG. Changes can still be made in a draft standard protocol before it becomes a standard protocol.
Proposed standard protocol	These are protocol proposals that may be considered by the IESG for standardization in the future. Implementation and testing by several groups are desirable. Revision of the protocol specification is likely.
Experimental protocol	A system should not implement an experimental protocol unless it is participating in the experiment and has coordinated its use with the developer of the protocol. Typically, experimental protocols are those that are developed as part of an ongoing research project that is not related to an operational service offering. An experimental protocol may go up the ranks to become a standard protocol, but its designation as *experimental* suggests that the protocol is not intended for operational use.
Informational protocol	Protocols developed by other standards organizations and vendors, or protocols that are outside the purview of the IESG may be published as RFCs for the convenience of the Internet community. These kinds of protocols are informational protocols.
Historic protocol	These are protocols that are unlikely to become standards in the Internet community because they have been superseded by later developments or because of lack of interest.

As part of the standardization process, sufficient time is allowed for the Internet community to consider and react to the standardization proposals. There is usually a minimum delay of six months before a proposed standard can be advanced to a draft standard, and four months before a draft standard can be promoted to a standard. Thus the minimum time for a proposed standard to be adopted is ten months.

To ensure that a standard can be implemented, it is general practice that no proposed standard can be promoted to a draft standard without at least two independent implementations and the recommendation of the IESG. Therefore, before the proposed standard can be promoted, the Internet community can examine the implementation of the proposed standard. Promotion from draft standard to standard generally requires the approval of the IESG. The promotion also requires the operational experience and demonstrated interoperability of two or more implementations.

If there is uncertainty as to the proper decision concerning a proposed standard, a special review committee may be appointed. The review committee consists of experts from the IETF, IRTF, and the IAB, and the committee recommends the appropriate action to be taken concerning the proposed standard.

The advancement of a protocol to proposed standard is an important step because it puts the protocol on the standards track. In other words, the protocol is a candidate for eventual standardization. As the protocol advances to a draft standard status, it is a signal to the Internet community that, unless major objections are raised or flaws are discovered, the protocol is likely to be advanced to a standard.

Figure 1.14 shows a matrix that describes the different states in the evolution of a proposed protocol. At any given time, a protocol occupies a cell in the matrix. Protocols that are more likely to be in cells are shown with a larger number of *X*s in the cells. Therefore, a new protocol is most likely to start in the proposed standard/elective cell or the experimental/limited use cell. For a complete list of the standard protocols, see Appendix A.

Figure 1.14 State of proposed protocol.

STATE \ STATUS	Req	Rec	Ele	Lim	Not
Std	X	XXX	XXX		
Draft	X	X	XXX		
Prop		X	XXX		
Info					
Expr				XXX	
Hist					XXX

Earlier documents and standards on the ARPAnet were written as Internet engineering notes (IENs). These notes have been replaced by RFCs. Some of the RFCs are actually poems. Some examples are RFC 968 and RFC 1121. Some interesting poems by Vincent Cerf, the father of the Internet and a codeveloper of the TCP/IP protocol can be found in the following sidebars.

'Twas the Night Before Startup by Vint Cerf, 1985 (RFC 968)

'Twas the night before startup and all through the net,
not a packet was moving; no bit nor octet.
The engineers rattled their cards in despair,
hoping a bad chip would blow with a flare.
The salesmen were nestled all snug in their beds,
while visions of data nets danced in their heads.
And I with my datascope tracings and dumps
prepared for some pretty bad bruises and lumps.
When out in the hall there arose such a clatter,
I sprang from my desk to see what was the matter.
There stood at the threshold with PC in tow,
an ARPAnet hacker, all ready to go.
I could see from the creases that covered his brow,
he'd conquer the crisis confronting him now.
More rapid than eagles, he checked each alarm
and scrutinized each for its potential harm.
On LAPB, on OSI, X.25!
TCP, SNA, V.35!
His eyes were afire with the strength of his gaze;
no bug could hide long; not for hours or days.
A wink of his eye and a twitch of his head,
soon gave me to know I had little to dread.
He spoke not a word, but went straight to his work,
fixing a net that had gone plumb berserk;
And laying a finger on one suspect line,
he entered a patch and the net came up fine!
The packets flowed neatly and protocols matched;
the hosts interfaced and shift-registers latched.
He tested the system from Gateway to PAD;
not one bit was dropped; no checksum was bad.
At last he was finished and wearily sighed
and turned to explain why the system had died.
I twisted my fingers and counted to ten;
an off-by-one index had done it again...

Rosencrantz and Ethernet by Vint Cerf, 1989 (RFC 1121)

All the world's a net! And all the data in it merely packets
come to store-and-forward in the queues a while and then are
heard no more. 'Tis a network waiting to be switched!
To switch or not to switch? That is the question. Whether
'tis wiser in the net to suffer the store and forward of
stochastic networks or to raise up circuits against a sea
of packets and, by dedication, serve them.
To net, to switch. To switch, perchance to slip!
Aye, there's the rub. For in that choice of switch,
what loops may lurk, when we have shuffled through
this Banyan net? Puzzles the will, initiates symposia,
stirs endless debate and gives rise to uncontrolled
flights of poetry beyond recompense!

Anyone can submit a document for publication as an RFC. Submissions must be made via electronic mail to the RFC editor. While RFCs are not refereed publications, they are subject to technical review from the task forces, individual technical experts, or the RFC editor. You should read RFC 1543 on "Instructions to RFC Authors" before submitting an RFC. You can get the information you need at the following address:

1543 I J. Postel, "Instructions to RFC Authors," 10/28/1993.
(Pages=16) (Format=.txt) (Obsoletes RFC1111)

New RFCs must be submitted it to the editor-in-chief whose e-mail address is

RFC-Editor@ISI.EDU

Obtaining RFCs

You can obtain a Request for Comments from several sources. If you do not have access to the Internet, you can contact the following to obtain a request:

SRI International, Room EJ291
333 Ravenswood Avenue
Menlo Park, CA 94025
415-859-3695
NIC@SRI-NIC.ARP

Table 1.5 shows some of the RFC sites that are available. The primary repositories will have the RFC available when it is first announced, as will many secondary repositories. Some secondary repositories may take a few days to make available the most recent RFCs.

Table 1.5
RFC Sites

Host Name	Primary/Secondary
DS.INTERNIC.NET	Primary
NIS.NSF.NET	Primary
NISC.JVNC.NET	Primary
VENERA.ISI.EDU	Primary
WUARCHIVE.WUSTL.EDU	Primary
SRC.DOC.IC.AC.UK	Primary
FTP.CONCERT.NET	Primary
FTP.SESQUI.NET	Primary
SUNIC.SUNET.SE	Secondary
CHALMERS.SE	Secondary
WALHALLA.INFORMATIK.UNI-DORTMUND.DE	Secondary
MCSUN.EU.NET	Secondary
FUNET.FI	Secondary
UGLE.UNIT.NO	Secondary
FTP.DENET.DK	Secondary
MUNNARI.OZ.AU	Secondary
NIC.CERF.NET	Secondary
FTP.UU.NET	Secondary

If you have web access to the Internet, you can obtain copies of RFCs from `http://ds.internic.net`.

Summary

TCP/IP-based networks play an increasingly important role in computer networks. TCP/IP networks are based on an open protocol specification that is not controlled by any vendor. This chapter fully and completely defined TCP/IP. It examined the origins of TCP/IP networks and the commercial uses of this protocol. The chapter briefly explained some common uses of TCP/IP protocols. This chapter also discussed the relationship between the Internet and the older ARPAnet, and the professional bodies that influence research and development of the Internet protocols. You should also have an understanding of how a protocol proposal evolves to a standard protocol on the Internet.

Test Yourself

1. What is a communications protocol?
2. Give an example of how human communications is similar to computer communications.
3. What does the term *TCP/IP* typically mean?
4. Give a brief explanation of the distinctions, if any, between internets, intranets, and the Internet.
5. List some of the reasons why the U.S. Department of Defense (DoD) mandated a common set of protocols.
6. Name some vendor or openly available system that offers TCP/IP solutions to build a multivendor network.
7. What are some of the forces driving the growth of TCP/IP?
8. Give a brief description of the following services: Telnet, FTP, SMTP, SNMP, DNS, and HTTP.
9. What is the purpose of the IAB and the Internet Society?
10. What are RFCs, STDs, and IENs?
11. Are all RFCs standards? Give examples of RFCs that are not standards.
12. Read RFC 1160 and describe the charter of the IAB.
13. How can you obtain a copy of an RFC?
14. RFCs have a state associated with them. Describe these different states.

CHAPTER 2

TCP/IP Protocol Layering Concepts

The TCP/IP applications utilized by users of TCP/IP intranets and the Internet depend upon the smooth interaction of a number of protocol components. These protocol components are called protocol layers. The term *protocol layers* suggests that there is an interaction between the protocol components, and this is indeed so. Each protocol layer interacts with the one next to it using an idealized interface.

Building systems, such as protocols, in layers, has a number of advantages. Each layer can be designed so that it can perform a well-defined function. The layer can be treated as a "black box." This means the implementation details can be treated independently of the function performed by the layer. From a functional point of view, for example, you give the protocol layer some data, and the layer performs the specified function with the data. Examples of this include representing the data in a particular way, delivering the data reliably across the network, or ensuring that the data is delivered using the most optimal route in the network, and so on.

By isolating the function of the layer from its implementation, you can make changes to the implementation of a protocol layer with minimum impact on other protocol layers. You see an example of this in modern networks where the networking hardware, which implements a specific protocol layer function, keeps on improving; that is, it gets faster and more reliable. As a network designer and planner, you can improve the network performance by replacing older network hardware with faster, better, and often cheaper network hardware. Moreover, you can do this without changing the protocol software and applications that run on the network hardware.

To realize the importance of protocol layering, consider the alternative situation of not using protocol layering. In this case the network applications are dependent on the communications protocol and the network hardware. If you made changes to any of these components—the applications, communications protocols, and network hardware—you would have to make major changes to the other components. Why? Because if some form of layering is not used to isolate these functions, the implementation of the components are intertwined in complex ways. Making changes to any one component result in complex, and hidden changes to other components, subsequently doing major changes in other components to accommodate these new changes. Not only that, but you also become dependent on the vendor of that networking system. In the long run, this is bad for the vendor and the customer. The vendor loses its competitive edge as it obtains a lock on its customer base, and the customer is locked into the vendor's networking platform.

The computer industry is still very young. Even so, it is interesting to see how history tends to repeat itself within this industry. Over a decade ago, many Information Technology (IT) professionals had the view that a single vendor solution would solve all their problems. It would be a one-stop place for buying their hardware or software and a one-stop place for obtaining technical help and maintenance for networks. As companies went through "down sizing" and "re-engineering" to became more competitive and cost conscious, they realized that while the single vendor solution avoided the Information Technology professionals from having to learn about competing solutions in the market place, the single vendor solution was either very costly or technologically stagnant as the company was unable to take advantage of improvements in technology as they were left waiting for the vendor to catch up with the latest technological innovations. One literally had to "bet" one's network on a particular vendor solution with the hope that the vendor would remain competitive in the market place. With the uncertainty of the market place and the ever changing shifts in the fortunes of companies in the stock market, it is not a good idea to bet your company on the future well-being of any vendor.

Today, there is even more of a temptation to fall into the trap of a single vendor solution as technology changes at faster and faster rates and Information Technology professionals have to work harder to keep up with these changes. IT professionals have to constantly learn about new technologies and become more adept at discerning truth from fiction in the marketing campaigns of the vendors. If IT professionals do not take a pro-active stance in evaluating and keeping up with technology and the management of the company loses it confidence in its IT staff, this doesn't bode well for the company. In many cases the management has been known to make a decision on behalf of its IT staff; for example, deciding on networking solutions when it is not properly equipped to do so. If things don't work out right, the IT staff will have to shoulder the blame.

By using open standards that are based on protocol layering and freedom of choice to select open application specifications, one can eliminate the need to buy into a single vendor solution. One can mix and match equipment from different vendors based on the business needs of the organization. This idea of having open specifications and protocol layering is the very theme of both this chapter and the protocol layer models.

The two models of primary importance in describing protocol layers are the DoD model and the OSI model. The DoD model was developed specifically for TCP/IP, whereas the OSI model was developed later and takes into account other protocols besides TCP/IP. The models are important for both the implementer of the protocols and the IT professionals who deploy these protocols for gaining an understanding of the TCP/IP protocol elements. At the very least, you must have a working familiarity with TCP/IP layering concepts because these models provide insight into the different protocol elements needed for interoperability of TCP/IP applications. In addition, the models define a vocabulary that is widely used in discussing TCP/IP protocols.

Principles of Protocol Layering

A TCP/IP network such as that shown in figure 2.1 can be organized into the following major network elements:

- Physical connections
- Protocols
- Applications

Figure 2.1 Elements of a TCP/IP network.

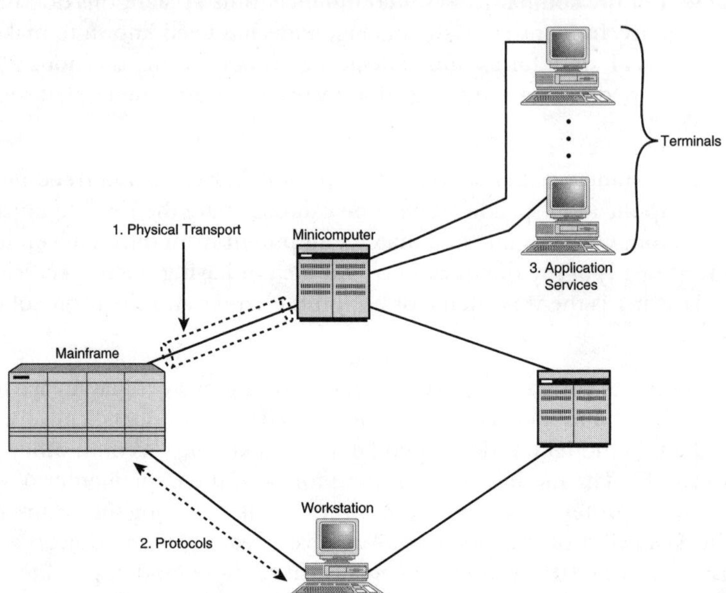

The physical connections provide the medium over which the bits comprising the messages can be transmitted. The physical connections could be coaxial cable, twisted-pair wiring (shielded or unshielded), fiber optic, telephone lines, leased lines, microwave links, infrared links, radio links, or satellite links. There are indeed many choices for the physical connections of a network. Typically, you must make your choice based on factors such as bandwidth of medium, ease of installation, maintenance, media cost, and end equipment cost.

The physical connections represent the lowest level of logical functionality needed by the network. To operate the network, you need to have a standard set of rules and regulations that all devices must obey to be able to communicate and interoperate with each other. The rules and regulations by which devices on the network communicate are called *protocols.* A variety of such rules and regulations (protocols) exist, and these rules provide different types of functions for a network.

Network applications use the underlying network protocols to communicate with network applications running on other network devices. The network protocols, in turn, use the physical network connections to transmit the data.

When you consider that network operation consists of physical connections, protocols, and applications, you can see that these network elements form a hierarchy. In this hiearchy, the applications are at the very top and the physical connections exist at the bottom. The protocols provide a "bridge" between the applications and the physical connections.

To understand the hierarchy between the network elements and the functions that they perform, you need a "yardstick" or model for defining these functions. One commonly accepted model is the OSI reference model, while another model is the DoD model, which was designed for describing TCP/IP protocols in particular.

The OSI Model

The OSI Reference Model was developed in 1978 by the *International Organization of Standards* (ISO) to specify a standard that could be used for the development of open systems and as a yardstick to compare different communication systems. Network systems designed according to OSI framework and specifications speak the same language; that is, they use similar or compatible methods of communication. This type of network system allows systems from different vendors to interoperate.

In the early days of computer networks (prior to the OSI model), the proprietary computer network architecture reigned supreme. In those days, an organization that was interested in installing a computer network examined the choices available, including IBM, DEC, HP, Honeywell, and Sperry and Burroughs (now Unisys). Each of those companies had their own proprietary architecture; therefore, the capability to interconnect networks from different vendors was almost nonexistent.

Once committed to buying equipment from a specific vendor, the organization was virtually "locked in." Updates or modifications to the system were provided by the vendor, and because the vendor had a closed proprietary architecture, no one could compete with that vendor in supplying equivalent services. Prices were determined based on what the customer could bear without complaining too much!

Today's users probably realize that in many areas of the computer industry, this picture has not changed much. Proprietary architectures are still around. For now, the OSI model can, at the very least, provide you with a clearer picture of how the different components of a network relate to each other.

Layers of the OSI Model

The OSI model has seven layers, as shown in figure 2.2.

Figure 2.2 The OSI Reference Model.

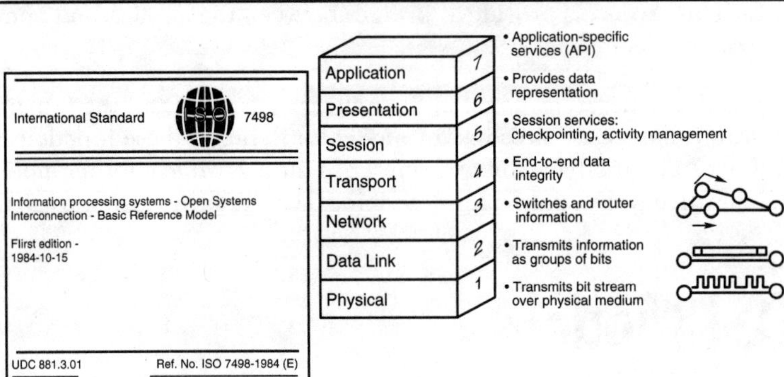

API = application programming interface

The layers, working from the bottom up, are as follows:

- Physical
- Data Link
- Network
- Transport
- Session
- Presentation
- Application

Five principles were applied when arriving at the layers and are included in the following:

1. A layer should be created only when a different level of abstraction is needed.
2. Each layer should provide a well-defined function.
3. The function of each layer should be chosen so that it defines internationally standardized protocols.
4. The layer boundaries should be chosen to minimize the information flow across layer interfaces.
5. Distinct functions should be defined in separate layers, but the number of layers should be small enough that the architecture does not become unwieldy.

The application of these five principles creates an idealized model where each layer performs only one of the major functions and depends on the services of the immediately lower layer. Conversely, each layer also provides services to the layer immediately above it. The Network layer, for example, uses the services of the layer immediately below it (the Data Link layer), and it provides services to the layer immediately above it(the Transport Layer).

The Physical and Application layers exist at the extremity of the OSI Reference model. The *Physical layer* does not use the services of any other layer but must provide the physical network connectivity to the layer above it, the Data Link layer. The *Application layer* uses the services of the Presentation layer, and provides services to any custom end-user applications that make use of the Application layer.

The functions of each of the layers are summarized in more detail in the following sections.

Physical Layer

The *Physical layer* transmits bits over a communication channel. The bits may represent database records or file transfers, however, the physical layer is oblivious to what those bits represent. The bits can be encoded as digital 1s and 0s or in analog form (see fig. 2.3). The Physical layer deals with the mechanical, electrical, and procedural interfaces over the physical medium. Popular forms of physical media are twisted-pair wiring, coaxial cable, fiber optics, and wireless communications.

Figure 2.3 Physical layer options shown along with the type of signal.

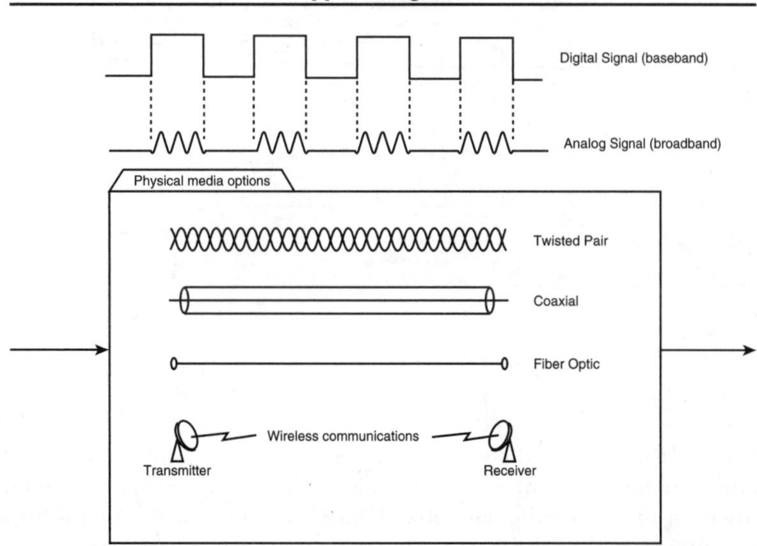

The Physical layer has no knowledge of the structure of the data that it is required to transmit or receive. The Physical layer is responsible for transmitting data bits over the physical media using an appropriate signaling technique that is agreed upon by the devices that communicate over that physical media. In addition, the Physical layer can also receive signals over the media and convert it to data bits that are delivered to the Data Link layer.

Data Link Layer

The *Data Link layer* builds on the transmission capability of the Physical layer and provides services to the Network layer. The bits that are transmitted or received are grouped in logical units called a *frame*. In the context of LANs, a frame could be a Token Ring or Ethernet frame, an FDDI frame, or another LAN type frame. For WAN links, this could be a SLIP, PPP, X.25, or an ATM cell frame or another WAN type frame.

The bits in a frame have special meanings. The beginning and ending of a frame may be marked by special bit patterns. Additionally, the bits in a frame are divided into an address field, control field, data field, and error control field. Figure 2.4 shows a typical Data Link frame. You see more specific examples of the Data Link frame in the discussion of Ethernet and Token Ring LANs discussed later in this chapter.

Figure 2.4 A typical Data Link layer frame.

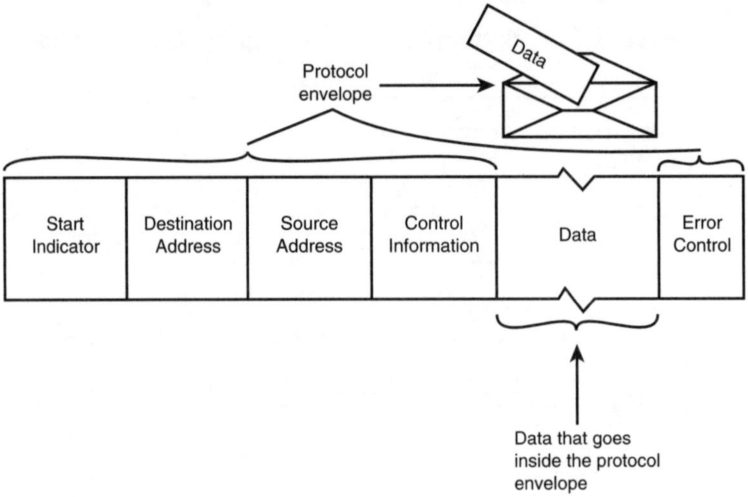

The *address field(s)* contains the sender and receiving node address. The *control field* is used to indicate the different types of data link frames, which include data frames and frames used for managing the data link channel. The *data field* contains the actual data being transmitted by the frame. The *error control field* usually detects errors in the data link frame.

The Data Link layer is the first layer which attempts to handle transmission errors. The error control field is usually a hardware-generated *checksum* that is used to detect errors in the data link frame. For the most part, modern networks use a Cyclic Redundancy Checksum (CRC). For LANs, this is typically a 32-bit CRC checksum. Additionally, for WAN links that are inherently slower than LAN links, a 16-bit CRC checksum is used to avoid the overhead of transmitting additional checksum bits.

The details of the CRC calculation are beyond the scope of this book, so it is sufficient to say that the CRC checksums can detect any of the following errors:

- All single-bit errors, two isolated single-bit errors
- All odd number of bit errors
- All burst errors of 16 bits or less for 16-bit CRC, and 32 bits or less for 32-bit CRC.

A burst error is an error condition where a series of contiguous bits in the received frame are in error (see fig. 2.5). The probability of burst error that is larger than the CRC size being undetected is 1 ÷ (2××S), where S is the CRC size.

Figure 2.5 CRC error detection properties.

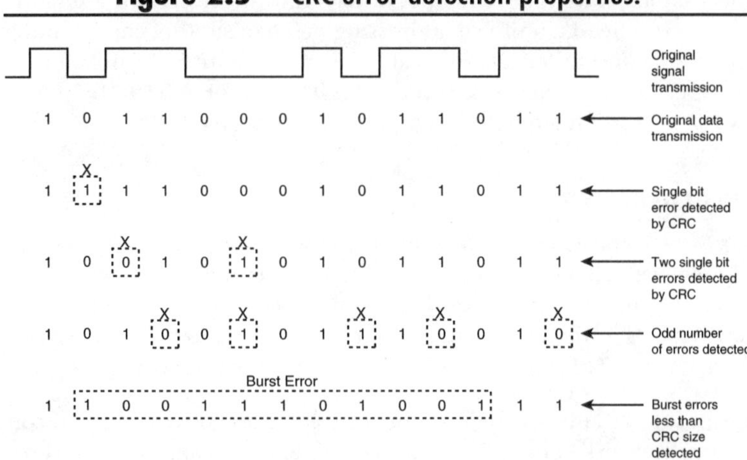

In TCP/IP networks, the Data Link layer implementations include any of the follow technologies: Token Ring, Ethernet, FDDI, Frame Relay, X.25, SLIP, PPP, ATM.

Network Layer

The *Network layer* builds on the node-to-node connection provided by the Data Link layer. The node-to-node data link services are extended across a network by this layer. An additional service provided by the Network layer is how to route *packets* (units of information at the network layer) between nodes connected through an arbitrarily complex network (see fig. 2.6).

Figure 2.6 Network layer function.

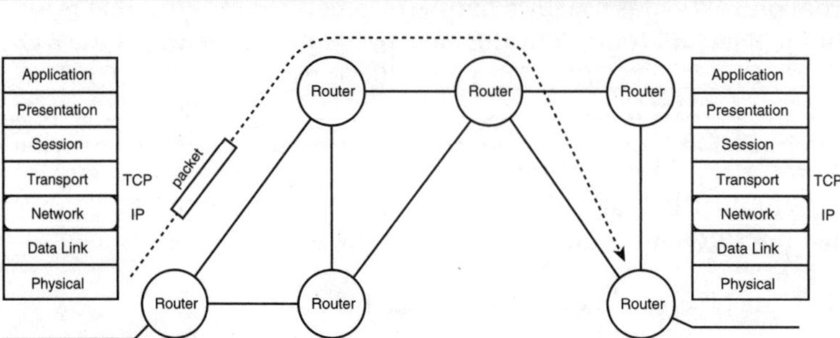

- Router is a device that acts like a switch and determines the next destination to forward the packet
- Router examines the Network layer header, which contains a uniform network addressing mechanism

Besides routing, the Network layer helps eliminate congestion as well as regulate the flow of data. The Network layer also makes it possible for two networks to be interconnected by implementing a uniform addressing mechanism. Token Ring or Ethernet LANs, for instance, have different types of data link addresses. To interconnect these two networks, you need a uniform addressing mechanism that can be understood by both Token Ring and Ethernet. You will learn more about Ethernet and Token Ring addresses in Chapter 3, "Network Support for TCP/IP." For TCP/IP based networks the Network layer is implemented using the *Internet Protocol (IP)*.

Transport Layer

The *Transport layer* provides enhancements to the services of the Network layer. This layer helps ensure reliable data delivery and end-to-end data integrity. To ensure reliable delivery, the transport layer builds on the error control mechanisms provided by the lower layers. If the lower layers don't do an adequate job, the transport layer has to work harder. This layer is the last chance for error recovery.

The Transport layer also may be responsible for creating several logical connections over the same network connection, a process called *multiplexing*. Multiplexing (or time sharing) occurs when a number of transport connections share the same network connection. Figure 2.7 illustrates the properties of the Transport layer.

Figure 2.7 Transport layer functions.

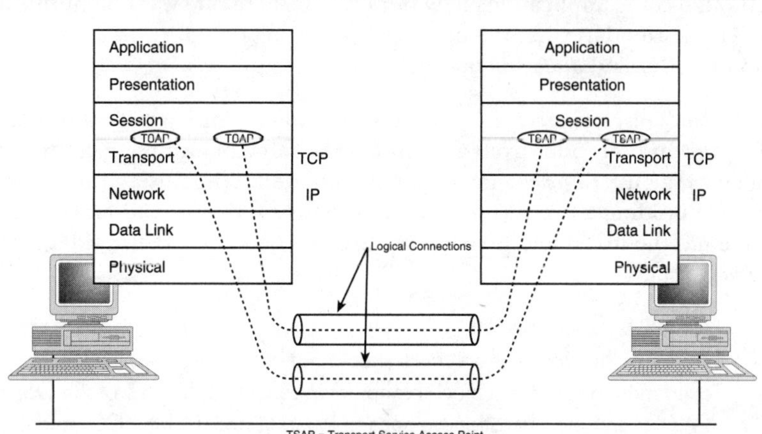

The Transport layer is the middle layer of the OSI model. The three lower layers constitute the *subnet* (portion of the network model), and the three upper layers are usually implemented by networking software on the node. The Transport layer is also usually implemented on the node. Its job is to convert an unreliable subnet into a more reliable network.

In TCP/IP networks, the Transport layer is implemented by the Transmission Control Protocol (TCP) and User Datagram Protocol (UDP).

The Transport layer implements multiplexing in which several software elements (OSI terminology uses the term *protocol entity*) share the same network layer address. To uniquely identify the software elements within the Transport layer, a more general form of addressing is necessary. These addresses, called *transport addresses,* usually are a combination of the Network layer address and a *Transport Service Access Point (TSAP)* number. In TCP/IP networks the term *port numbers* is used to identify transport addresses.

Session Layer

The *Session layer* makes use of the Transport layer to provide enhanced session services. Examples of a session include a user being logged in to a host across a network or a session being established for the purpose of transferring files.

The Session layer may provide some of the following enhancements:

- Dialog control
- Token management
- Activity management

A session, in general, allows two-way communications (*full duplex*) across a connection, although some applications may require alternate one-way communications (*half duplex*). The session layer has the option of providing one-or two-way communications, an option called *dialog control.*

For some protocols, it is essential that only one side attempt a critical operation at a time. To prevent both sides from attempting the same operation, a control mechanism, such as the use of *tokens,* must be implemented. When using the token method, only the side holding a token is permitted to perform the operation. Determining which side has the token and how it is transferred between the two sides is known as *token management.*

Note The use of the word "token" here should not be confused with Token Ring operation. Token management is a much higher level concept at layer 5 of the OSI model. IBM's Token Ring operation belongs to layers 2 and 1 of the OSI model.

Figure 2.8 illustrates some of the functions of the Session layer.

Figure 2.8 Session layer functions with token management enabled.

Session
Dialog Unit
Major Synchronization Point
Minor Synchronization Point
Application
Presentation
SSAP SSAP
Session Token
TCP Transport
IP Network
Data Link
Physical
If token is used in communication session, the session entity that has the token controls session-related operations.
Application
Presentation
SSAP SSAP
Session
Transport TCP
Network IP
Data Link
Physical

If you are performing a one hour file transfer between two machines, and network crashes occur approximately every 30 minutes, you may never be able to complete the file transfer. After each transfer aborts, you have to start all over again. To avoid this problem, you can treat the entire file transfer as a single activity with checkpoints inserted into the data stream. That way, if a crash occurs the session layer can synchronize to a previous checkpoint. These checkpoints are called synchronization points (see fig. 2.8). There are two types of synchronization points and are given as follows:

- Major
- Minor

A major synchronized point inserted by any communicating side must be acknowledged by the other communicating side, whereas a minor synchronization point is not acknowledged. That portion of the session that is between two major synchronization points is called a *dialog unit.* The operation of managing an entire activity is called *activity management.* An activity can consist of one or more dialog units.

TCP/IP networks do not have a general session layer protocol. This is because some of the characteristics of the Session layer are provided by the TCP protocol. If TCP/IP applications require special session services they provide their own. An example of such a TCP/IP application services is the Network File System (NFS) which implements its own Session layer service, the Remote Procedure Call (RPC) protocol. Figure 2.9 shows the Session layer functions for TCP/IP networks. Many TCP/IP applications do not use any Session layer services and the Session layer is *null* for these applications.

Figure 2.9 Session layer protocols demonstrated for TCP/IP networks.

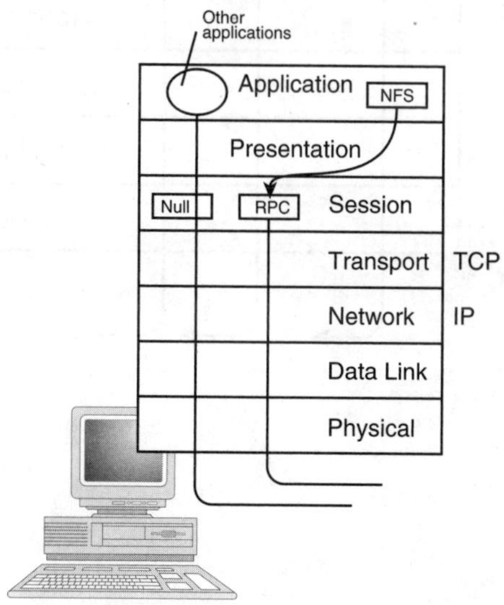

Presentation Layer

The *Presentation layer* manages the way data is represented. Many ways of representing data exist, such as ASCII and EBCDIC for text files, and 1s or 2s for numbers. If the two sides involved in communication use different data representations, they will not be able to understand each other. The Presentation layer represents data with a common syntax and semantics. If all the nodes used and understood this common language, misunderstanding in data representation could be eliminated.

An example of this common language is *Abstract Syntax Representation, Rev 1* (ASN.1), an OSI recommendation. In fact, ASN.1 is used by the Simple Network Management Protocol (SNMP) to encode its high level data. The Network File System (NFS) protocol also uses its own session layer service, the External Data Representation (XDR) protocol. Figure 2.10 shows the Presentation layer functions for TCP/IP networks. Many TCP/IP applications do not use any Presentation layer services and the Presentation layer is *null* for these applications.

Figure 2.10 Presentation layer functions for TCP/IP networks.

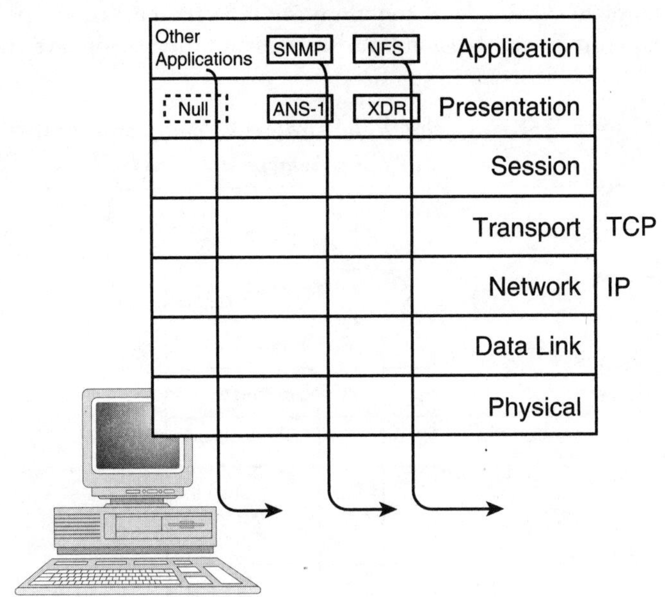

Application Layer

The *Application layer* contains the protocols and functions needed by user applications to perform communication tasks. Examples of common functions include the following:

- Protocols for providing remote file services, such as open, close, read, write, and shared access to files
- File transfer services and remote database access
- Message handling services for electronic mail applications
- Global directory services to locate resources on a network
- A uniform way of handling a variety of system monitors and devices
- Remote job execution

Many of these services are called Application Programming Interfaces (APIs). APIs are programming libraries that an application writer can use to write network applications.

Some examples of TCP/IP application services (see fig. 2.11) are File Transfer Protocol (FTP), Trivial File Transfer Protocol (TFTP), Network File System (NFS), TELNET, Simple Mail Transfer Protocol (SMTP), Simple Network Management Protocol (SNMP), HyperText Transfer Protocol (HTTP).

Figure 2.11 Application layer functions in TCP/IP networks.

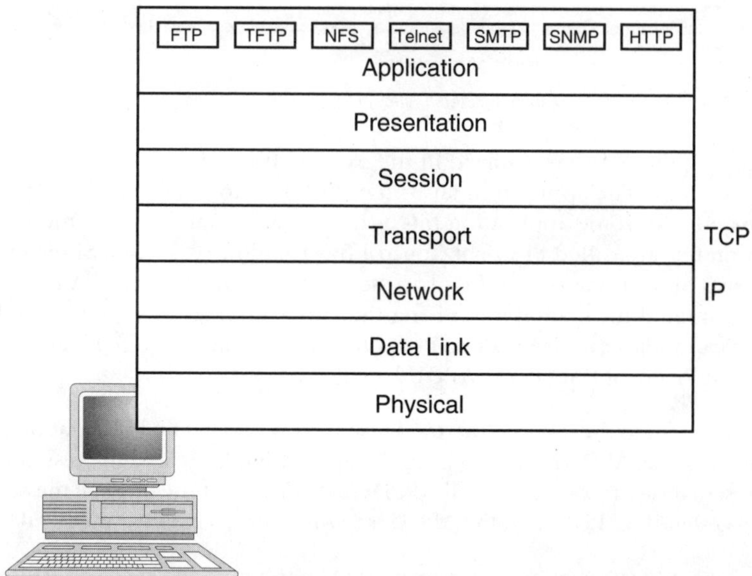

Data Traversal in the OSI Model

Figure 2.12 shows an example of how data traverses the network. For the sake of simplicity only the communication between two computers, A and B, are shown. The sending process on computer A, wants to send data to a receiving process in computer B.

Figure 2.12 Data traversal in the OSI model.

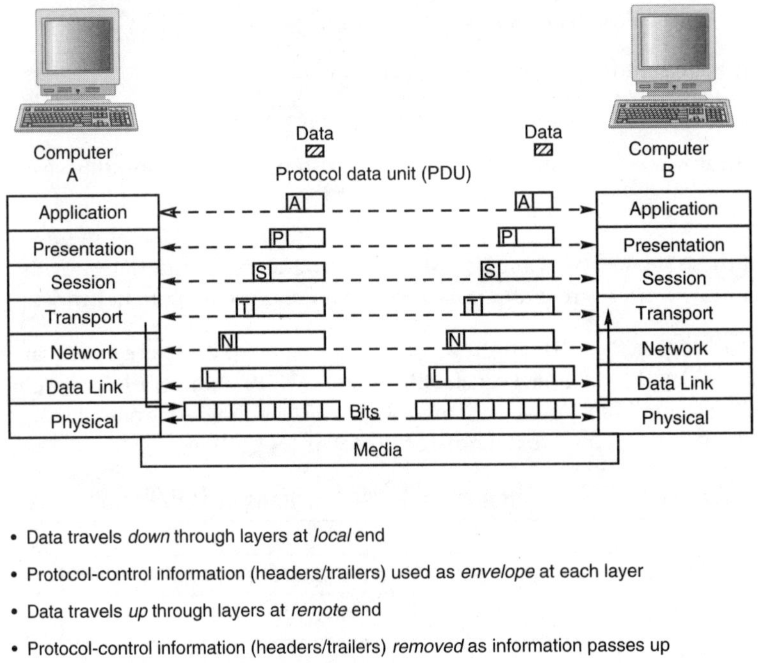
Computer A
Computer B
Data
Data
Protocol data unit (PDU)
Application
Presentation
Session
Transport
Network
Data Link
Physical
A
P
S
T
N
L
Bits
Media
Application
Presentation
Session
Transport
Network
Data Link
Physical
• Data travels *down* through layers at *local* end
• Protocol-control information (headers/trailers) used as *envelope* at each layer
• Data travels *up* through layers at *remote* end
• Protocol-control information (headers/trailers) *removed* as information passes up

The two computer systems involved in the exchange are called *End Systems* (ES) in OSI terminology. The application layer in each ES performs its processing on the message and adds some application bits as header information to the message. These application bits are called Protocol Control Information (PCI) in OSI terminology and consists of information on the processing done on the message. Additionally, the PCI may contain information identifying the application entities (source and destination application layer address). The PCI, plus the original message is called the Application Protocol Data Unit (APDU).

The APDU is sent to the layer below, the Presentation Layer. The Presentation Layer adds its PCI to the data (APDU) received from the application layer, and the resulting message is the Presentation Protocol Data Unit (PPDU). At this point the original message is encapsulated in the APDU, and the APDU is in turn encapsulated as the PPDU.

As each layer adds its own header information to the message received from its upper layer, it's like taking the data and placing it inside an envelope. The envelope with its contents—forms the PDU (or packet) for that layer.

This process continues all the way down to the Physical layer. At the Data Link layer, usually a *trailer field* is added to the data. This trailer field is a checksum field, usually the CRC checksum, and covers the Data Link layer frame. The checksum is generated by the Data Link layer hardware mechanism (network boards). It is added at the end because the hardware mechanism computes the checksum as the data is pumped out serially over the line.

At the Physical layer the "header" information may take the form of an indication informing the receiver of a packet arrival. On Ethernet networks, this is a 56-bit preamble that is used by the receiver to synchronize itself.

At the remote end (computer B), the physical layer receives the bits and strips off any physical layer synchronization bits and send the resulting data to the Data Link layer. The remote Data Link layer groups the bits received into a frame and checks to see if the CRC is valid. After the Data Link layer processes the received frame, it strips off the Data Link PCI (Data Link header and CRC) and sends the resulting NPDU (Network PDU) to the Network layer for processing.

At each remote end-system layer, the PDU is processed based on the PCI (header) information for that layer. The PCI is removed and the data portion of the PDU sent to the upper layer. This process continues until the remote Application layer completes its processing and the original data is recovered.

If you examine layers at the local end-system and the remote end-system, it appears as if the layers in the OSI model communicate with the corresponding *peer layer*. For this reason the OSI model describes peer-to-peer protocols between the layers. The transport layer at the two end-systems, for example, appear to be communicating with each other. In order to accomplish this communication it has to make use of the infrastructure provided by the layers (Network, Data Link, Physical layers)below it.

The active elements in each OSI layer are called *protocol entitites*. Protocol entities implement the services in each OSI layer and communicate with peer protocol entities in a peer layer on another system. A protocol entity could be a piece of software (software entity) or hardware (micro-chip, electronic circuits, and so on). Typically, the Physical layer and Data Link layer protocol entities are implemented in hardware, and the Network layer and above protocol entities are implemented in software. In devices such as routers, a hybrid of software and hardware called *firmware* may be used to implement the protocol entities.

The OSI model provides a conceptual view of communication that is easy to comprehend. In actual practice, the layers are not as well defined as shown in the OSI model. An implementation, for example, may not have a distinct separation between the Presentation and Application layer. Many of the functions of the Presentation layer, such as universal data encoding and decoding, may be performed in the Application Layer by calling appropriate data encoding and decoding programming language functions.

The DoD Model

The OSI model was created in 1979, although protocol layering concepts existed long before they were formalized by the OSI model. An example of an earlier successful protocol that used protocol layering concepts was the TCP/IP protocol suite. Because of TCP/IP's historic ties with the Department of Defense (DoD), the TCP/IP protocol layering is called the DoD model.

Figure 2.13 describes the DoD model, which consists of four layers.

Figure 2.13 The DoD model.

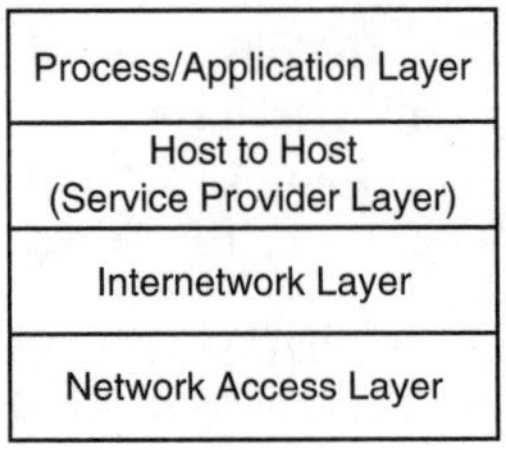

Process/Application Layer
Host to Host (Service Provider Layer)
Internetwork Layer
Network Access Layer

The layers (from bottom-to-top) are as follows:

- Network Access layer
- Internetwork layer
- Host-to-Host layer
- Process/Application layer

Network Access Layer

The bottom most layer is the Network Access layer. The Network Access layer represents the physical connection components such as the cables, transceivers, network boards, link protocols, LAN access protocols (such as CSMA/CD for Ethernet and token access for Token Ring), token bus, and FDDI. The Network Access layer is used by the Internetwork layer.

Internetwork Layer

The Internetwork layer is responsible for providing a logical address for the physical network interface. The DoD model's implementation of the Internetwork layer is the Internet Protocol (IP). The IP protocol layer provides a mapping between the logical address and the physical address provided by the Network Access layer, by using Address Resolution Protocol (ARP) and Reverse Address Resolution Protocol

(RARP). Problems, diagnostic information, and unusual conditions associated with the IP protocol are reported by a separate protocol called the Internet Control Message Protocol (ICMP) that also operates at the Internetwork layer.

The Internetwork layer is also concerned with routing of packets between hosts and networks. The Internetwork layer is used by the DoD upper layers. The upper layer that directly uses the Internetwork layer is the Host-to-Host layer.

Host-To-Host Layer

The Host-to-Host protocol, as the name implies, implements connections between two hosts across a network. The DoD model implements two host-to-host protocols: the Transmission Control Protocol (TCP) and the User Datagram Protocol (UDP). The TCP protocol is responsible for reliable, simultaneous, full-duplex connections. The term reliable means TCP takes care of transmission errors by resending the portion of data that was in error. The Process/Application layers that use TCP, however, do not have to be concerned with reliability of data transmission because this is handled by TCP.

TCP also provides for simultaneous connections. Several TCP connections can be established at a host and data can be sent simultaneously, independent of data on other connections. TCP provides full-duplex connections, which means that data can be sent and received on a single connection.

The UDP protocol is not as robust as TCP and can be used by applications that do not require the reliability of TCP at the Host-to-Host layer.

Process/Application Layer

The Process/Application layer provides applications that use the Host-to-Host layer protocols (TCP and UDP). Examples of these applications are File Transfer Protocol (FTP), Terminal Emulation (TELNET), Electronic Mail (SMTP), and Simple Network Management Protocol (SNMP). The Process/Application layer represents the user's interface to the TCP/IP protocol stack.

Data-Flow Across TCP/IP Networks Using the DoD Model

Figure 2.14 shows communication between two hosts using the DoD model. The data transmitted by a host is encapsulated by the header protocol of the Process/Application Services layer. The Application/Process layer data is in turn encapsulated by the Host-to-Host (TCP or UDP) layer. The Host-to-Host layer protocol is in turn encapsulated by the Internetwork layer (IP). Finally, the Internetwork layer protocol is encapsulated by the Network Access layer protocol.

Figure 2.14 DoD Protocol layering and communications.

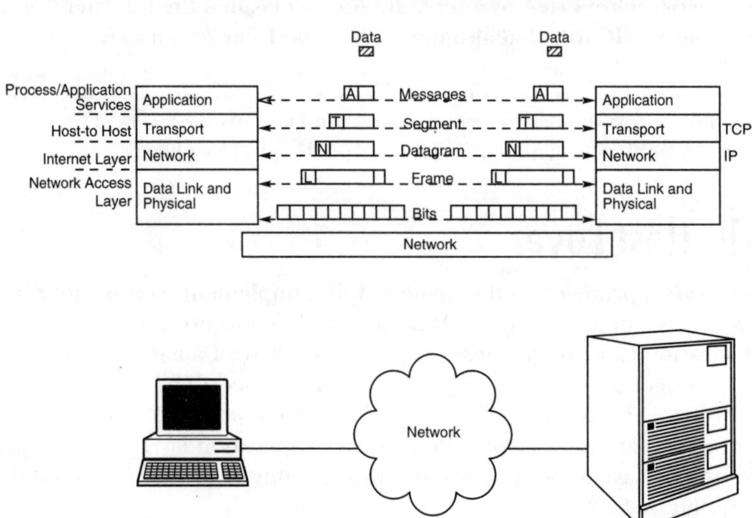

When the encapsulated data is received by the remote host (the second, receiving host), it decapsulates the headers at each of the DoD model layers and sends the resulting data to the layer above it until the original data is recovered.

Comparing the DoD Model and the OSI Model

If you compare the functionality of the DoD model with the OSI model, you can see that they are similar. Figure 2.15 shows these similarities.

Figure 2.15 OSI model compared to DoD model.

	OSI Reference Model	DoD Model	
7	Application Layer	Process/Application Layer	4
6	Presentation Layer		
5	Session Layer		
4	Transport Layer	Host-to-Host Layer (Service Provider Layer)	3
3	Network Layer	Internetwork Layer	2
2	Data Link Layer	Network Access Layer	1
1	Physical Layer		

The Network Access layer of the DoD model corresponds to two layers of the OSI model: the Physical layer and the Data Link layer.

The Internetwork layer of the DoD model corresponds to the Network layer of the OSI model.

The Host-to-Host layer of the DoD model corresponds to the Transport layer of the OSI model.

The Process/Application layer of the DoD model corresponds to three layers of the OSI model: Session layer, Presentation layer, and Application layer.

Table 2.1 summarizes these connections.

TABLE 2.1
DoD and OSI Comparison Summary

DoD Layer	OSI Layer Number	OSI Layer
Network Access	1	Physical
	2	Data link
Internetwork	3	Network
Host-to-Host	4	Transport
Process/Application	5	Session
	6	Presentation
	7	Application

An important difference between the OSI and DoD models is the difference in terminology used to describe data at each layer. In the OSI model, the term Protocol Data Unit (PDU) was used to describe data at a layer. In the DoD model, the term *message* is used to describe data at the Process/Application layer. The term *segment* is used to describe data at the Host-to-Host layer. The term *datagram* is used to describe data at the Internetwork layer, and the term *frame* is used to describe data at the Network Access layer.

TCP/IP Implementation Hierarchy

The TCP/IP protocol suite has evolved to include a rich set of application services that can utilize a variety of physical networking technologies, such as WANs, LANs, radio, satellite links, and Integrated Services Digital Network (ISDN) lines. The TCP/IP protocol modules and their relationship with each other is called the *TCP/IP implementation hierarchy.*

Figure 2.16 shows a partial list of TCP/IP application services and a large variety of Network Access protocols that support TCP/IP. The application services are shown in relationship to the OSI model. An implementation may support only a few of the application services or other protocols, such as ARP, RARP, proxy ARP, and routing protocols. The TCP/IP host in figure 2.16, for example, supports only the TCP/IP application services FTP, TELNET, and SMTP.

Figure 2.16 TCP/IP implementation hierarchy. (Courtesy Learning Tree)

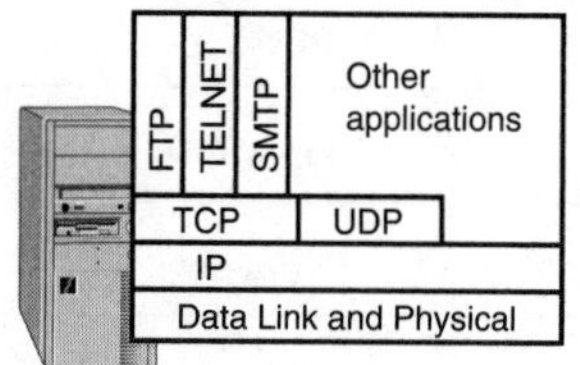

TCP/IP protocols are implemented as a layered hierarchy

TCP, UDP, and IP provide infrastructure for application services

A TCP/IP host may implement only some of the application services

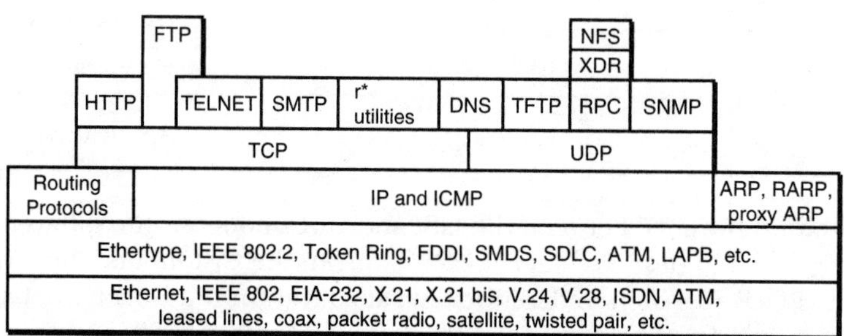

The application services in figure 2.16 are called "TCP/IP application services" because of their historical association with the TCP/IP protocol. There is nothing to prevent the application services described by the Process/Application layer from being built around a different transport or Network layer protocol. SNMP, for example, is historically associated with TCP/IP but can also run on an IPX protocol stack (RFC 1420), AppleTalk protocol stack (RFC 1419), and the OSI protocol stack (RFC 1418). Similarly, services that are traditionally non-TCP/IP based, such as Server Message Block (SMB) and NetBIOS, which normally runs on a NetBEUI network protocol (RFC 1001 and 1002), and X.500, which uses the OSI protocols, can also run on TCP/IP. The ISO Development Environment (ISODE) provides X.500 services over TCP/IP.

An important concept in TCP/IP is protocol multiplexing and demultiplexing, which enables many upper-layer protocols to use a common lower-layer protocol. This concept is discussed next.

Protocol Multiplexing and Demultiplexing

Figure 2.17 shows TCP/IP communications between two hosts. Each host is running TCP/IP application services such as FTP, TELNET, Trivial File Transfer Protocol (TFTP), and SMTP.

Figure 2.17 **Protocol multiplexing and demultiplexing. (Courtesy Learning Tree)**

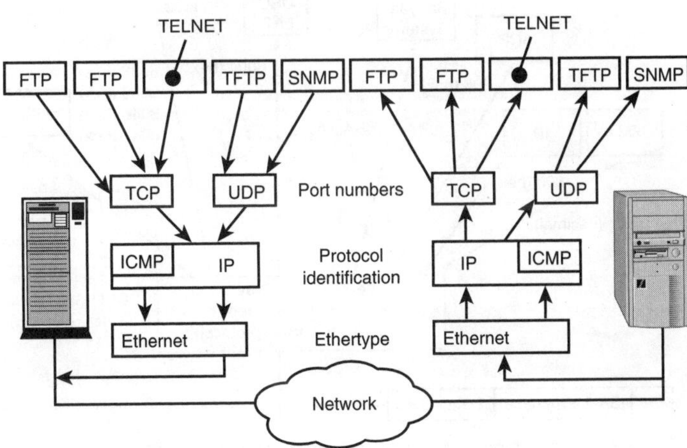

Several sessions exist between the hosts that use FTP. You might ask the question: How does networking software on each host distinguish between multiple applications or protocols at a given layer?

The Ethernet in figure 2.17, for example, shows a mixed protocol environment that supports IP and ICMP protocols and potentially other protocols, such as IPX and

AppleTalk's IDP. How does Ethernet determine that a packet arriving from a network interface is destined for IP or ICMP? To make this distinction, Ethernet uses a 2-byte Ethertype field that is part of the Ethernet frame (see fig. 2.18). Table 2.2 shows some of the values of Ethertype fields used for Network layer protocols. Using table 2.2, you can see that IPX has been assigned an Ethertype of 8137 and 8138.

Figure 2.18 A 2-byte Ethertype field used for protocol multiplexing/demultiplexing.

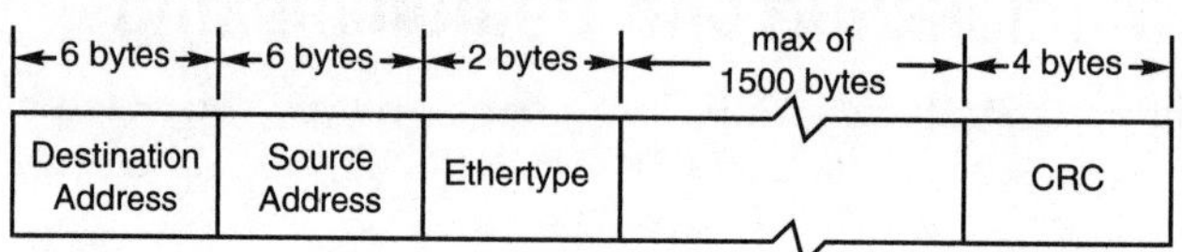

The Ethertype field at the Data Link layer makes it possible to multiplex several network protocols at the sender and demultiplex them at the receiver (see fig. 2.19).

Figure 2.19 Multiplexing/demultiplexing using the Ethertype field.

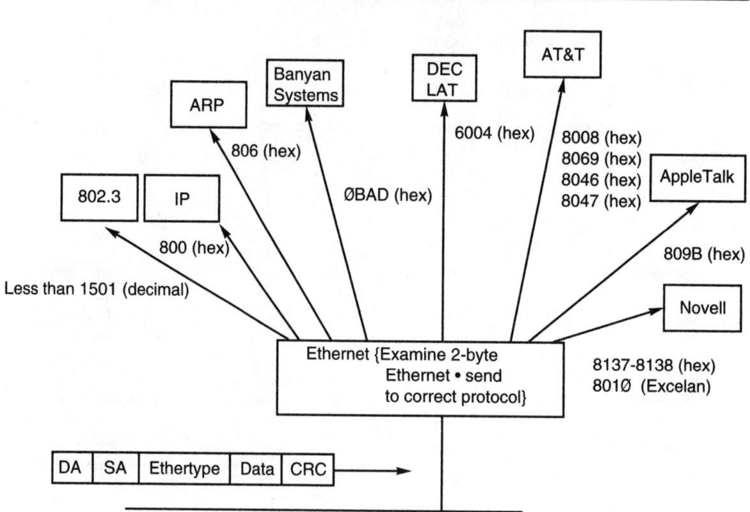

Table 2.2
Ethertype Values Used for Data Link Layer Multiplexing/Demultiplexing.

Ethertype Value (decimal)	Ethertype Value (hexadecimal)	Ethertype Field Assignment
0–1500	0–05DC	IEEE 802.3 length field
1536	0600	XEROX NS IDP
2048	0800	DoD IP
2049	0801	X.75 Internet
2050	0802	NBS Internet
2051	0803	ECMA Internet
2052	0804	Chaosnet
2053	0805	X.25 Level 3
2054	0806	ARP (Address Resolution Protocol)
2055	0807	XNS Compatibility
2076	081C	Symbolics Private
2184–2186	0888–088A	Xyplex
2304	0900	Ungermann-Bass Net Debugger
2560	0A00	Xerox IEEE 802.3 PUP
2561	0A01	PUP Address Translation
2989	0BAD	Banyan Systems
4096	1000	Berkeley Trailer Negotiation
4097–4101	1001–100F	Berkeley Trailer encapsulation/IP
5632	1600	Valid Systems
16962	4242	PCS Basic Block Protocol

continues

Table 2.2, Continued
Ethertype Values Used for Data Link Layer Multiplexing/Demultiplexing

Ethertype Value (decimal)	Ethertype Value (hexadecimal)	Ethertype Field Assignment
21000	5208	BBN Simnet
24576	6000	DEC Unassigned (Experimental)
24577	6001	DEC MOP Dump/Load
24578	6002	DEC MOP Remote Console
24579	6003	DEC DECNET Phase IV Route
24580	6004	DEC LAT
24581	6005	DEC Diagnostic Protocol
24582	6006	DEC Customer Protocol
24583	6007	DEC LAVC, SCA
24584–24585	6008–6009	DEC Unassigned
24586–24590	6010–6014	3COM Corporation
28672	7000	Ungermann-Bass download
28674	7002	Ungermann-Bass dia/loop
28704–28713	7020–7029	LRT
28720	7030	Proteon
28724	7034	Cabletron
32771	8003	Cronus VLN
32772	8004	Cronus Direct
32773	8005	HP Probe
32774	8006	Nestar
32776	8008	AT&T
32784	8010	Excelan (Novell)

Ethertype Value (decimal)	Ethertype Value (hexadecimal)	Ethertype Field Assignment
32787	8013	SGI diagnostics
32788	8014	SGI network games
32789	8015	SGI reserved
32790	8016	SGI bounce server
32793	8019	Apollo Computers
32815	802E	Tymshare
32816	802F	Tigan, Inc.
32821	8035	Reverse ARP
32822	8036	Aeonic Systems
32824	8038	DEC LANBridge
32825–32828	8039–803C	DEC Unassigned
32829	803D	DEC Ethernet Encryption
32831	803F	DEC LAN Traffic Monitor
32832–32834	8040–8042	DEC Unassigned
32836	8044	Planning Research Corp.
32838–32389	8046–8047	AT&T
32841	8049	ExperData
32859	805B	Stanford V Kernel exp.
32860	805C	Stanford V Kernel prod.
32864	805D	Evans & Sutherland
32866	8062	Counterpoint Computers
32869–32870	8065–8066	University of Massachussetts at Amherst

continues

Table 2.2, Continued
Ethertype Values Used for Data Link Layer Multiplexing/Demultiplexing

Ethertype Value (decimal)	Ethertype Value (hexadecimal)	Ethertype Field Assignment
32871	8067	Veeco Integrated Auto
32872	8068	General Dynamics
32873	8069	AT&T
32874	806A	Autophon
32876	806C	ComDesign
32877	806D	Computgraphic Corp.
32878–32887	806E–8077	Landmark Graphics Corp.
32890	807A	Matra
32891	807B	Dansk Data Elektronik
32892	807C	Merit Internodal
32893–32895	807D–807F	Vitalink Communications
32896	8080	Vitalink TransLAN III
32897–32899	8081–8083	Counterpoint Computers
32923	809B	AppleTalk
32924–32926	809C–809E	Datability
32927	809F	Spider Systems Limited
32931	80A3	Nixdorf Computers
32932–32947	80A4–80B3	Siemens Gammasonics, Inc.
32960–32963	80C0–80C3	DCA Data Exchange Cluster
32966	80C6	Pacer Software
32967	80C7	Applitek Corporation
32968–32972	80C8–80CC	Intergraph Corporation

Ethertype Value (decimal)	Ethertype Value (hexadecimal)	Ethertype Field Assignment
32973–32975	80CD–80CE	Harris Corporation
32975–32978	80CF–80D2	Taylor Instruments
32979–32980	8CD3–80D4	Rosemount Corporation
32981	80D5	IBM SNA Service on Ethernet
32989	80DD	Varian Associates
32990–32991	80DE–80DF	Integrated Solution TRFS
32992–32995	80E0–80E3	Allen-Bradley
32996–33008	80E4–80F0	Datability
33010	80F2	Retix
33011	80F3	AppleTalk AARP (Kinetics)
33012–33013	80F4–80F5	Kinetics
33015	80F7	Apollo Computer
33023	80FF–8103	Wellfleet Communications
33031–33033	8107–8109	Symbolics Private
33072	8130	Waterloo Microsystems
33073	8131	VG Laboratory Systems
33079–33080	8137–8138	Novell, Inc.
33081	8139–813D	KTI
33100	814C	SNMP Research
36864	9000	Loopback
36865	9001	3COM(Bridge) XNS System Management
36866	9002	3COM(Bridge) TCP Sys

continues

TABLE 2.2, CONTINUED
Ethertype Values Used for Data Link Layer Multiplexing/Demultiplexing

Ethertype Value (decimal)	Ethertype Value (hexadecimal)	Ethertype Field Assignment
36867	9003	3COM(Bridge) loopdetect
65280	FF00	BBN VITAL–LanBridge cache

When the IP layer receives a packet from Ethernet it has to distinguish between packets that need to be processed by the TCP or UDP protocol module. It does this by examining an 8-bit Protocol Id field of the IP packet. Table 2.3 shows some common values for the Protocol Id field. Most TCP/IP implementations store the values in a special file called the *protocols* file in their system configuration area.

TABLE 2.3
Protocol Id Values Used for Network Layer Multiplexing/Demultiplexing

Protocol Id	Next Layer Protocol in IP Packet
0	Reserved
1	Internet Control Message Protocol (ICMP)
2	Internet Group Management Protocol (IGMP)
4	IP in IP encapsulation
5	Stream IP
6	Transmission Control Protocol (TCP)
8	Exterior Gateway Protocol (EGP)
9	Any private interior gateway protocol (example: CISCO's IGP)
11	Network Voice Protocol (NVP-II)
12	Parc Universal Protocol (PUP)
16	Chaos protocol
17	User Datagram Protocol (UDP)

Protocol Id	Next Layer Protocol in IP Packet
21	Packet Radio Measurement (PRM)
22	XEROX NS IDP (XNS-IDP)
29	ISO Transport Protocol Class 4 (ISO-TP4)
30	Bulk Transfer Protocol (NETBLT)
36	Express Transport Protocol (XTP)
37	Datagram Delivery Protocol (DDP)
75	Packet Video Protocol (PVP)
80	ISO Internet Protocol (ISO-IP)
83	VINES

When the TCP or UDP protocol modules receive a packet from the IP layer, they have to distinguish between packets that need to be processed by an application service such as FTP, TELNET, SMTP, and SNMP and those that don't. The TCP and UDP protocol modules do this by examining the 16-bit port number field of their respective packets. Tables 2.4 and 2.5 show a few common values for port numbers for TCP and UDP. Because TCP and UDP protocol modules are distinct from each other, their port number address spaces are distinct.

Also notice that some TCP/IP applications are listed in tables 2.4 and 2.5 with the same port number. As you might think, this is because these application services are available over both TCP and UDP. Most TCP/IP implementations store the values in the table /etc/services file on Unix hosts.

Table 2.4
Port Number Values Used for TCP Multiplexing/Demultiplexing

TCP Port Number	Application Layer Service
0	Reserved
1	TCP Port Service Multiplexor
2	Management Utility
3	Compression Process

continues

TABLE 2.4, CONTINUED
Port Number Values Used for TCP Multiplexing/Demultiplexing

TCP Port Number	Application Layer Service
5	Remote Job Entry
7	Echo
9	Discard
11	Active Users (systat)
13	Daytime
17	Quote of the Day (QUOTD)
20	FTP data port
21	FTP control port
23	Telnet
25	SMTP
35	Any private printer server
37	Time
39	Resource Location Protocol
42	Host name server (nameserver)
43	Who Is (nicname)
49	Login Host Protocol (login)
52	XNS Time Protocol
53	Domain Name Server (domain)
54	XNS clearing house
66	Oracle SQL*NET (sql*net)
67	Bootstrap Protocol Server (bootps)
68	Bootstrap Protocol Client (bootpc)

TCP Port Number	Application Layer Service
70	Gopher protocol
79	Finger protocol
80	World Wide Web HTTP
88	Kerberos
94	Trivoli Object Dispatcher (objcall)
95	SUPDUP
102	ISO-TSAP
107	Remote Telnet Service (rtelnet)
108	SNA Gateway Access Server (snagas)
110	Post Office Protocol—Version 3 (POP3)
111	Sun Remote Procedure Call (sunrpc)
119	Network News Transfer Protocol (NNTP)
123	Network Time Protocol (NTP)
134	INGRES-NET Service
137	NETBIOS Naming Service (netbios-ns)
138	NETBIOS Datagram Service (netbios-dgm)
139	NETBIOS Session Service (netbios-ssn)
142	Britton-Lee IDM
191	Prospero
194	Internet Relay Chat Protocol (irc)
201	AppleTalk Routing Maintenance (at-rtmp)
202	AppleTalk Name Binding (at-nbp)
213	IPX

continues

Table 2.4, Continued
Port Number Values Used for TCP Multiplexing/Demultiplexing

TCP Port Number	Application Layer Service
215	Insigniax (Soft PC)
217	dBASE UNIX
372	UNIX Listserv
519	unixtime
525	Time Server (timed)
533	For emergency broadcasts (netwall)
556	RFS server (remoterfs)
565	Who Am I (whoami)
749	Kerberos Administration (kerberos-adm)
767	Phone (phonebook)
1025	Network Blackjack (blackjack)
1352	Lotus Notes (lotusnote)
7000–7009	Used by Andrew File System (AFS)
17007	ISODE Directory User Agent (isode-dua)

Table 2.5
Port Number Values Used for UDP Multiplexing/Demultiplexing

UDP Port Number	Application Layer Service
0	Reserved
2	Management Utility
3	Compression Process
5	Remote Job Entry
7	Echo

UDP Port Number	Application Layer Service
9	Discard
11	Active Users (systat)
13	Daytime
17	Quote of the Day (QUOTD)
35	Any private printer server
37	Time
39	Resource Location Protocol
42	Host name server (nameserver)
43	Who Is (nicname)
49	Login Host Protocol (login)
52	XNS Time Protocol
53	Domain Name System server (domain)
54	XNS clearing house
66	Oracle SQL*NET (sql*net)
67	Bootstrap Protocol Server (bootps)
68	Bootstrap Protocol Client (bootpc)
69	Trivial Transfer Protocol (tftp)
70	Gopher protocol
79	Finger protocol
80	World Wide Web HTTP
88	Kerberos
94	Trivoli Object Dispatcher (objcall)
95	SUPDUP

continues

Table 2.5, Continued
Port Number Values used for UDP Multiplexing/Demultiplexing

UDP Port Number	Application Layer Service
102	ISO-TSAP
107	Remote Telnet Service (rtelnet)
108	SNA Gateway Access Server (snagas)
110	Post Office Protocol—Version 3 (POP3)
111	Sun Remote Procedure Call (sunrpc)
119	Network News Transfer Protocol (NNTP)
123	Network Time Protocol (NTP)
134	INGRES-NET Service
137	NETBIOS Naming Service (netbios-ns)
138	NETBIOS Datagram Service (netbios-dgm)
139	NETBIOS Session Service (netbios-ssn)
142	Britton-Lee IDM
161	SNMP
162	SNMP Traps
191	Prospero
194	Internet Relay Chat Protocol (irc)
201	AppleTalk Routing Maintenance (at-rtmp)
202	AppleTalk Name Binding (at-nbp)
213	IPX (Used for IP Tunneling)
215	Insignia (Soft PC)
217	dBASE UNIX
372	UNIX Listserv

UDP Port Number	Application Layer Service
513	Maintains database on who is logged in to machines on a local net and the load average of the machine (who)
519	unixtime
525	Time Server (timed)
533	For emergency broadcasts (netwall)
556	RFS server (remoterfs)
565	Who Am I (whoami)
749	Kerberos Administration (kerberos-adm)
767	Phone (phonebook)
1025	Network Blackjack (blackjack)
1352	Lotus Notes (lotusnote)
7000–7009	Used by Andrew File System (AFS)
17007	ISODE Directory User Agent (isode-dua)

TCP/IP Implementation and the Host Operating System

The performance of a TCP/IP implementation, its configuration, and its ease of maintenance depend on the operating system platform on which it runs. To show the interaction between the TCP/IP protocol and the application, vendors try to show the operating system as part of the OSI model. Unfortunately, the operating system does not fit neatly into the OSI model because the OSI model is designed for communication functions. The operating system has its own multiple-layer model. One such model is shown in figure 2.20.

Compare this figure with figure 2.2 and you can see that the operating system and the OSI models are distinct. An operating system is a program that is a resource manager. On the other hand, the network communication system (modeled by the OSI model) is just one resource the operating system has to manage.

Figure 2.20 Operating system layering.

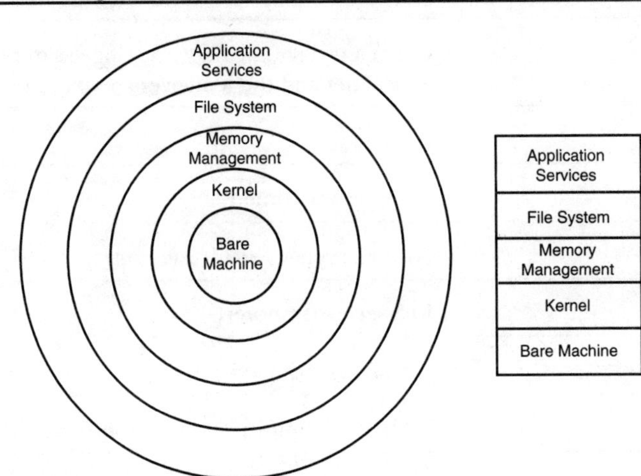

Although the operating system is theoretically not necessary for running TCP/IP—the TCP/IP protocol could be embedded in ROM in an embedded application—most commercial implementations of TCP/IP interact with the operating system.

TCP/IP's interaction with the operating system can be classified in any of the following ways:

- As part of the operating system kernel
- As a device driver
- As an application process

In operating systems such as Unix and NetWare, TCP/IP is implemented as part of the operating system kernel. This type of TCP/IP implementation tends to be fast because there is little overhead in accessing the OS kernel for communication functions.

Operating systems that have device driver implementations of TCP/IP include Microsoft Windows NT/Windows 95, VMS, OS/2, Microsoft Windows, and MS-DOS. In Microsoft Windows that runs on top of MS-DOS, the VxD virtual device driver implements the TCP/IP stack as a 32-bit driver that uses extended memory and avoids the use of base memory of the Intel processor.

Operating systems that have application process implementations of TCP/IP are IBM's mainframe operating systems MVS and VM, MS Windows, and MS-DOS. Some MS-Windows and MS-DOS TCP/IP implementations use terminate-and-stay-resident (TSR) programs and Dynamic Link Libraries (DLLs).

Summary

TCP/IP applications are built in a hierarchical fashion using a series of protocol components that are layered on top of each other. These protocol components are called protocol layers. There are two models that are used to describe the relationship between the protocol layers: the OSI model and the DoD model. The OSI model is more dominant within the industry in describing the protocol layering and for this reason a greater number of pages were devoted to discussing this model. Both models provide an invaluable assistance in helping you understand how the different protocol elements interact with each other. The protocol layer models are important in another way—they help define the vocabulary used in discussing TCP/IP protocols.

Test Yourself

1. Name the models used to describe TCP/IP protocols.
2. What are the three major elements of a computer network?
3. Name the layers of the OSI and the DoD models.
4. What were the five principles used to determine the layers of the OSI model?
5. Which OSI layer typically deals with CRC error detection?
6. The IP protocol corresponds to which OSI layer?
7. The TCP protocol corresponds to which OSI layer?
8. Which OSI layer is responsible for end-to-end data delivery and error integrity?
9. Which OSI layer deals with uniform data representation?
10. What are the differences between the OSI model and the DoD model?
11. Give examples of two implementations of the Presentation layer protocol used by TCP/IP applications. Name the TCP/IP applications that use these Presentation layer protocols.
12. Give a short description of protocol multiplexing/demultiplexing in TCP/IP networks.
13. In Ethernet networks what information in the Ethernet frame is used for protocol multiplexing/demultiplexing?
14. Use table 2.2 to determine the Ethertype value used for the IP protocol.
15. In TCP/IP networks, which field in an IP packet is used to perform protocol multiplexing/demultiplexing?

16. Explain why protocol multiplexing/demultiplexing is needed in networks.
17. Use table 2.3 to determine the Protocol ID values used for the TCP and UDP protocols.
18. What field in a TCP or UDP packet is used to determine the TCP/IP application service that uses the TCP or UDP protocol?
19. Use tables 2.4 and 2.5 to determine the port number and the transport layer protocol used by TELNET, SMTP, SNMP, HTTP, TFTP and DNS.
20. Name the three methods used to implement TCP/IP protocols in most operating systems. Give examples of operating systems that use these methods.

CHAPTER 3

Network Support for TCP/IP

One of the reasons for the popularity of TCP/IP networks is that TCP/IP can run on a variety of networks and computing devices. The TCP/IP protocol suite can run on computers such as main frames, mini computers, workstations, personal computers, hand-held computers and organizers, and even cellular phones!

The actual network hardware and software is usually transparent to the user of the network. In fact, most users are not even aware that they are using the TCP/IP protocol let alone the type of network hardware. However, this book is written for you, the network professional, who wants to learn about TCP/IP, the "glue" that ties together the different network components. The networking hardware and how TCP/IP runs on top of it is therefore of concern to you and is discussed in this chapter.

Overview of Networking Hardware that Run TCP/IP

By networking hardware, what is meant is layers two and one of the OSI model. Recall from the discussion in Chapter 2, "TCP/IP Protocol Layering Concepts," that layer two of the OSI model is the Data Link layer and layer one of the OSI model is the Physical layer. The Data Link layer transmits and receives data units called frames and interacts with the Physical layer that is responsible for sending and receiving the frame over a physical media. Network interface cards are the pieces of network hardware that go inside a computer and connect the computer to the physical network. Network interface cards typically implement the functionality of the Data Link and Physical layers of the OSI model.

Before describing the variety of networking hardware available for running TCP/IP applications and protocols, you might ask a very fundamental question: Why do I need so many different types of network hardware to run TCP/IP?

The motivation for having so many different types of hardware is that it is difficult for a single type of hardware to satisfy all the requirements of a real-life network. Most organizations use a Local Area Network (LAN) at a given location, because LANs provide high speeds at relatively low implementation costs. However, LANs are restricted to limited distances and cannot span the distances needed by widely separated sites that need to be connected by a network.

For spanning long distances, Wide Area Networks (WANs) that connect remote sites are used. Most WANs use a fundamentally different technology fromLANs. As their name implies, they are designed for connecting networks over long distances. While WANs can span longer distances than LANs, they typically have limited speeds and are slower than LANs. So we see that a single LAN or WAN may not meet the needs of an organization. What is needed in this case is a LAN/WAN combination (see fig. 3.1).

Such a network consists of one or more LAN and WAN networks. The LANs and WANs differ from each other in the distances they can span, the speeds they provide, and the fundamentally different network hardware technologies they use. Networks that use such different network hardware technologies need to be tied together by special "glue" devices. These devices are called *bridges, routers,* or *gateways.* (This chapter will discuss the roles of bridges and routers to connect different network hardware technologies. You will learn more about routers, gateways, and Internet routing protocols in later sections of this book.)

One of the goals of connecting different types of networks is to provide users access to resources on the network regardless of the location of the user. This access should be provided in a manner that is transparent to the user. In other words, the complexity of the network and its underlying technologies, protocols, hardware devices, and cabling should be hidden from the user. While the network details are hidden from the user, they cannot be hidden from the network designer/implementer. From a network designer/implementer perspective, the network components and resources must interoperate and be easy to manage and maintain. The network designer or implementer needs to be knowledgeable about the network hardware and protocol components to determine which kinds of devices can be connected to each other and how they interoperate.

Figure 3.1 LAN/WAN combination network.

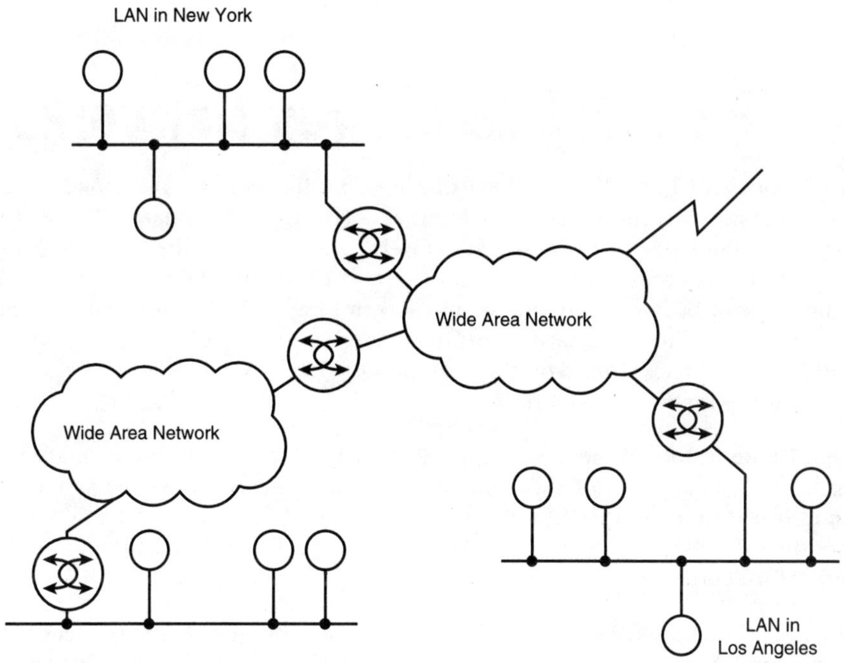

Figure 3.1 shows a network that consists of LANs and WANs. In each of these categories (LANs, WANs), there are several different types of hardware that are available. The network designer or implementer must make this choice based on the business needs of the organization. The following are some of the more common types of LAN technologies:

- IEEE LANs
- Ethernet
- Token Ring
- Switched networks
- FDDI

The following are some of the more common types of technologies:

- X.25
- Frame Relay
- SMDS
- MAN
- SLIP/PPP/CSLIP
- ATM

TCP/IP on IEEE Local Area Networks

As you work with TCP/IP network hardware, you will encounter references to the Institute of Electrical and Electronic Engineers (IEEE) 802 standards. These are ubiquitous standards for LANs and are closely connected with the first two OSI layers: the Data Link layer and the Physical layer. The IEEE standard defines Ethernet LANs by the name of IEEE 802.3 standard, and Token Ring LANs by the name of IEEE 802.5 standard. These standards constitute a large number of LAN networks that run TCP/IP. A brief background on the evolution of IEEE LAN standards will be helpful here, and this section offers just that.

The IEEE undertook Project 802 in February of 1980 to identify and formalize LAN standards for data rates not exceeding 20 megabits per second (Mbps). Standardization efforts resulted in the IEEE 802 LAN standards. The number 802 was chosen to mark the calendar date when IEEE undertook the LAN standardization efforts (80 for 1980, 2 for February).

Figure 3.2 shows the IEEE LAN standards in relationship to the OSI model discussed in Chapter 2. You can see that the primary emphasis of the IEEE committee was to standardize the hardware technologies used at the Physical and Data Link layers. This is not surprising considering that networking hardware such as network interface cards and LAN wiring can be modeled completely by the two lower OSI layers.

The IEEE standards divide the OSI data link layer into two sublayers:

- Media Access Control (MAC)
- Logical Link Control (LLC)

Figure 3.2 Relationship of the IEEE 802 Standard to the OSI model. (Courtesy IEEE Standard 802-1990)

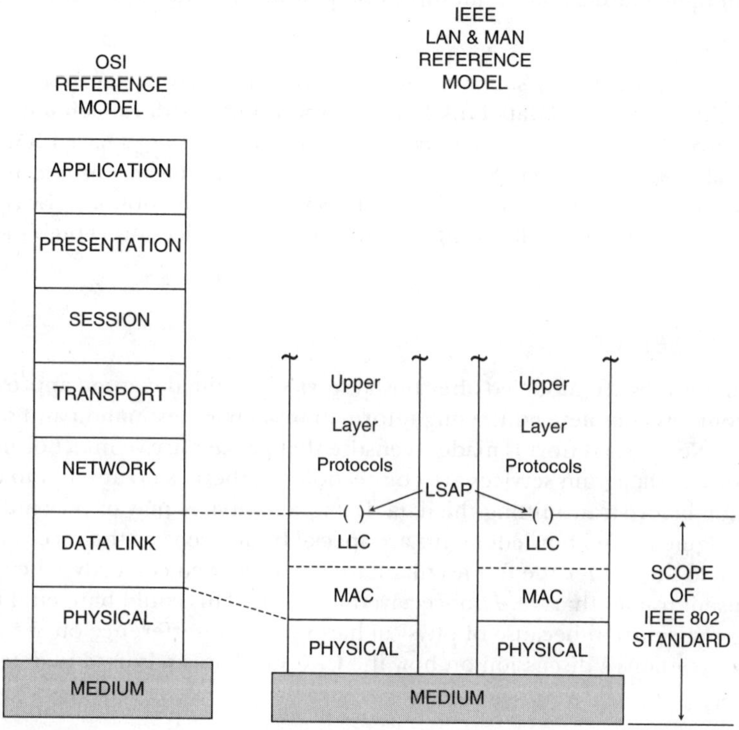

Media Access Control (MAC)

The MAC layer deals with media access techniques utilized to control access to a shared physical medium. Token Ring and Ethernet have different implementations of the MAC layer because they use different methods to share the physical media. This also means that if your TCP/IP network needs to link Ethernet and Token Ring networks, you must use one of the "glue" devices such as a bridge or router between the Ethernet and Token Ring networks.

Logical Link Control (LLC)

All IEEE LANs have the same LLC layer as defined by standard 802.2. The advantage of a common sublayer such as the LLC is that upper-layer mechanisms can be the same regardless of what kind of networking hardware you use.

Figure 3.2 shows the interface between Upper Layer Protocols and the LLC layer defined by *Link Service Access Points* (*LSAPs*). LSAPs are logical data link addresses. A single MAC address, such as an Ethernet address, can have multiple LSAP addresses. These multiple addresses allow multiple end-point connections between two nodes on a LAN.

The LLC layer is the upper sublayer within the Data Link layer. Recall from the previous chapter that the Data Link layer is responsible for transmission of data between two adjacent nodes on a network. These adjacent nodes have LSAP addresses that are called the *Destination Service Access Point (DSAP)* and *Source Service Access Point (SSAP)* within the LLC layer. The LLC layer also provides the options of virtual circuit (connections-oriented) or datagram (connectionless) services or a combination of these two.

Datagram Services

Datagram services are modeled after postal services. In the datagram approach, every packet contains complete addressing information such as destination and source addresses. No special effort is made to ensure that packets arrive intact or in the correct order. Datagram services are connectionless; there is no attempt to create a connection before transmitting the data. Datagram services may or may not use acknowledgments. Acknowledgments are special frames sent by the receiver that announce to the sender the frames that have been received correctly. They are used to retransmit frames that were not received correctly. This could happen if there are errors in transmission because of physical hardware or interference on the line. Chapter 2 contains a discussion on how the CRC mechanism is used to detect errors in frames.

Unacknowledged datagram services means that datagrams are sent but no attempt is made at the Data Link layer to retransmit frames that were incorrectly received. For applications that require a guarantee that packets were received correctly, this guarantee is delivered by the Transport layer of the OSI model (refer to Chapter 2). In TCP/IP networks, the Transport layer is implemented by TCP.

Unacknowledged datagram service for IEEE LANs is called Type 1 service. The Internet Protocol, which implements layer 3 of the OSI model, also does not use acknowledgments; that is, it is a connectionless service. This makes it easier to map the IP datagram into the frames used by LANs. Typically, a single IP datagram fits inside a LAN frame (see fig. 3.3). Where the size of the IP datagram is too large to fit inside a single LAN frame, the IP datagram is fragmented into sizes suitable to fit inside a LAN frame, and each IP datagram fragment is sent inside a LAN frame (see fig. 3.4). You will learn in later chapters that there are mechanisms in the header of the IP datagram to keep track of the individual IP data fragments.

Figure 3.3 An IP datagram is transported inside a LAN frame.

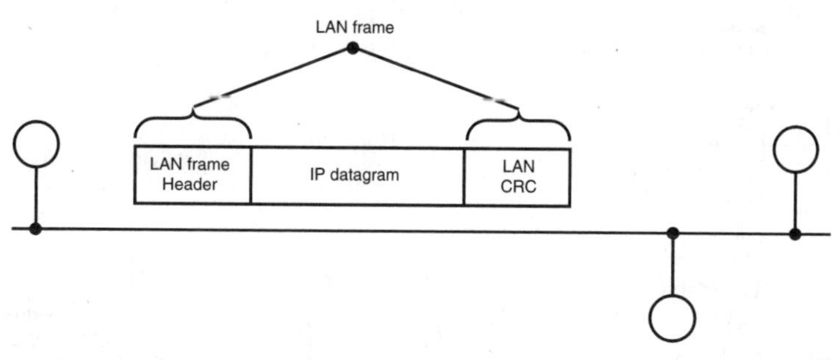

Figure 3.4 IP datagram fragments are transported inside LAN frames.

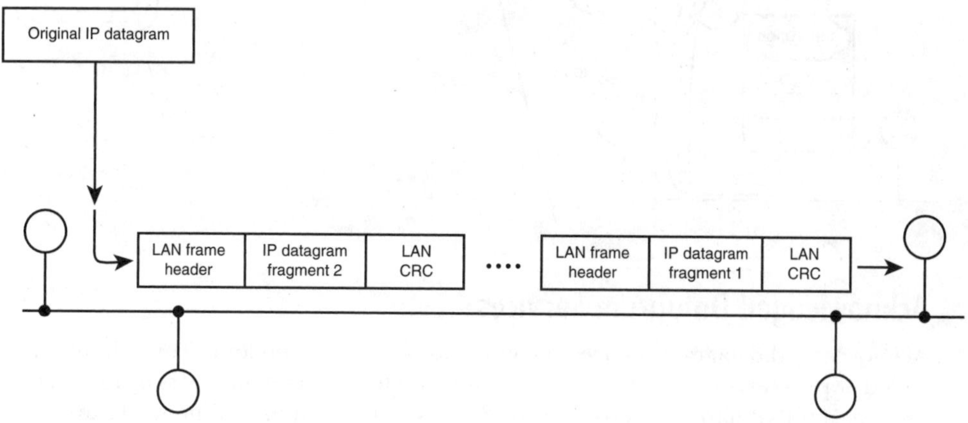

Virtual Circuit

In a *virtual-circuit* approach a special effort is made to ensure that packets arrive error-free in the order they were sent. Virtual circuits are modeled after the telephone system and require that a connection be established between two nodes before data can be exchanged between them. When data transfer is complete, this virtual circuit needs to be closed or terminated. Virtual-circuit services are called Type 2 services. In TCP/IP networks, virtual circuits are seldom used at the level of a MAC layer in LANs. This is because the TCP protocol is used to build an end-to-end virtual circuit (see fig. 3.5). The difference between an end-to-end virtual circuit provided by a TCP and the Type 2 service of LANs is that the LAN virtual circuits are between two nodes on the same LAN or two compatible LANs connected by a bridge. LAN virtual circuits cannot provide end-to-end virtual circuits across WAN links of the type shown in figure 3.5.

Figure 3.5 TCP virtual circuits versus LAN virtual circuits.

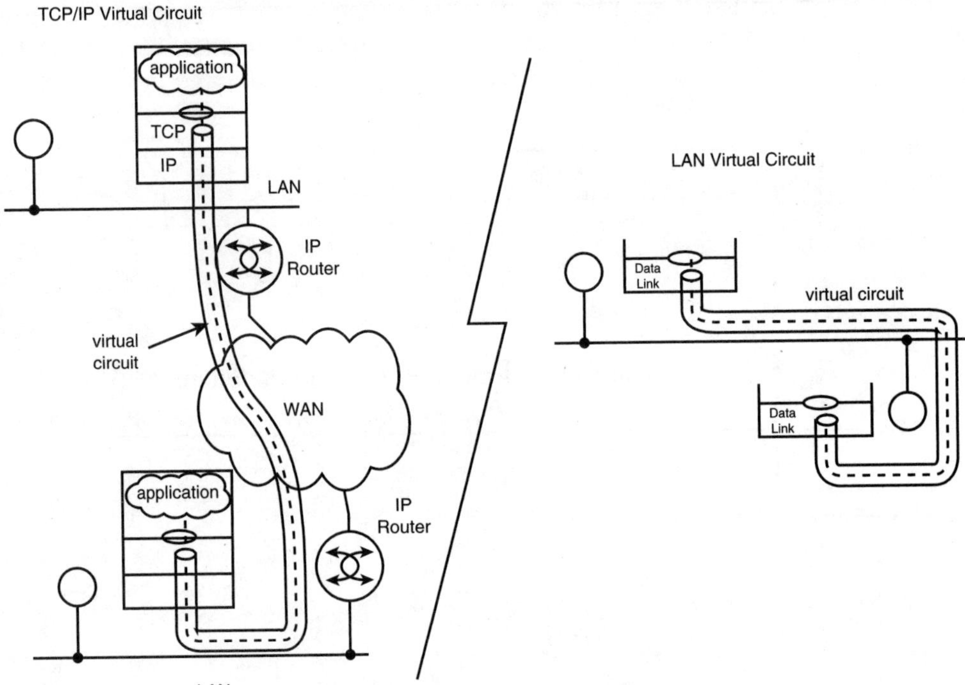

Acknowledged Datagram Services

Acknowledged datagram services, a combination of datagram and virtual circuits, are called Type 3 services, in which an effort is made to correct data errors by retransmitting packets that have data errors. Type 3 services are used in IBM networks for transmitting SNA data over LANs.

In summary, the types of services provided by LLC are as follows:

- **Type 1.** Unacknowledged, datagram service. Supports point-to-point, multipoint, and broadcast transmission.
- **Type 2.** Virtual-circuit service. Provides sequenced, flow-controlled, error-free services between LSAPs.
- **Type 3.** Acknowledged, datagram service. Provides datagram point-to-point service with acknowledgments.

Figure 3.6 shows how the IEEE committee has identified the choices at the different layers.

Figure 3.6 Services defined by various IEEE 802 standards.

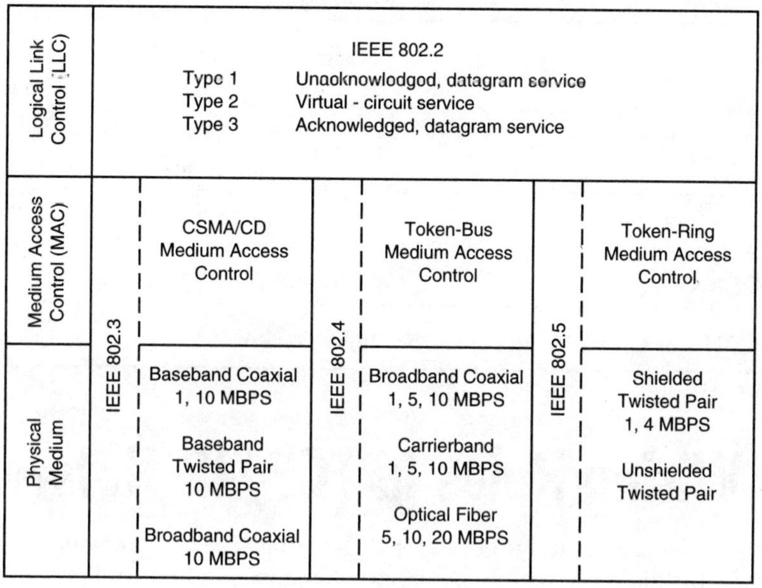

	IEEE 802.3	IEEE 802.4	IEEE 802.5
Logical Link Control (LLC)	IEEE 802.2 Type 1 Unacknowledged, datagram service Type 2 Virtual - circuit service Type 3 Acknowledged, datagram service		
Medium Access Control (MAC)	CSMA/CD Medium Access Control	Token-Bus Medium Access Control	Token-Ring Medium Access Control
Physical Medium	Baseband Coaxial 1, 10 MBPS Baseband Twisted Pair 10 MBPS Broadband Coaxial 10 MBPS	Broadband Coaxial 1, 5, 10 MBPS Carrierband 1, 5, 10 MBPS Optical Fiber 5, 10, 20 MBPS	Shielded Twisted Pair 1, 4 MBPS Unshielded Twisted Pair

Each of the choices represents a standard protocol or specification. Their IEEE numbers and meaning are described in table 3.1.

TABLE 3.1
IEEE Standards

IEEE Standard	Meaning
IEEE 802.1	LAN bridging
IEEE 802.2	Logical Link Control (LLC)
IEEE 802.3	Standardization of Ethernet Technology
IEEE 802.4	Token Bus standard
IEEE 802.5	Token Ring standard
IEEE 802.6	Metropolitan Area Network (MAN)

continues

Table 3.1, Continued
IEEE Standards

IEEE Standard	Meaning
IEEE 802.7	Broadband technical advisory
IEEE 802.8	Fiber optic technical advisory
IEEE 802.9	Integrated Voice/Data (IVD)
IEEE 802.10	LAN security
IEEE 802.11	Wireless LANs
IEEE 802.12	100 VG-AnyLAN

LAN Wiring Rules in TCP/IP Networks

Each LAN standard has its own rules for LAN wiring. These rules define the connecting media, the hardware requirements, and the way the various components are arranged. Two primary concerns exist with regard to media:

- Arrangement of cables
- Media type (usually some type of cable)

Arrangement

The geometrical arrangement of the wiring scheme is called the *topology*. The topologies that are common in LANs are the following:

- Star
- Bus
- Ring

These are shown in figure 3.7.

Figure 3.7 LAN topologies.

CE

Star Topology

CE = Central Element

- Media not shared
- CE performs centralized switching/connection function

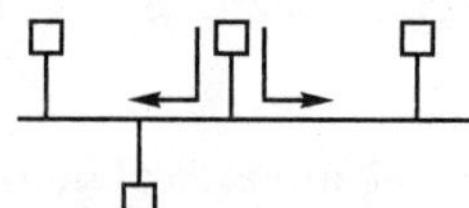

Bus Topology

- Shared media
- Access to shared media done by distributed control
- Bidirectional broadcast

Ring

Ring Topology

- Shared media
- Access to shared media done by distributed control
- Unidirectional broadcast

The Star Topology

In the *star* topology, communication between any two nodes must go through a central device or switching element. The devices that connect to the central switch tend to be simple, with all of the complexity residing in the central switch. The central switching element should be reliable and provide signal isolation between ports so that failures at any one port are not propagated to other ports.

Classic examples of star topology are mainframe and minicomputer architectures in which the host is the central switch. If the host breaks down, communication between the nodes in the network is broken also. This points out the vulnerability of the star wiring topology: it is vulnerable to a single point of failure.

If, on the other hand, the central switching element both is reliable and provides signal isolation between the ports, the star topology is one of the best topologies. This explains why it is used in Token Ring, FDDI, and 10BASE-T LANs. Another advantage is that it is easy to connect or remove stations from a central location. In many LANs, these central elements (hubs) come with advanced network management features like *Simple Network Management Protocol (SNMP)*.

The Bus Topology

The *bus* topology consists of a linear cable to which stations are attached. Signals sent by a station on the bus propagate in both directions. Every transmission is available to every station on the network more or less simultaneously. A classic example of a bus topology is *Ethernet.*

The Ring Topology

The *ring* topology consists of a cable in the form of a loop with stations attached to it. Signals are sent in only one direction, and the ring can be implemented by point-to-point *simplex* (one direction flow) links. Stations see only the transmissions that happen to pass by them in the ring. An example of a network that uses the ring topology is a Token Ring LAN.

An important distinction should be noted between physical and logical network topologies. The *physical* topology of a network describes the way in which the actual cables are laid out. The *logical* topology describes the way that the network behaves. You can see and touch the physical topology of the network. The person who installs the cable and hardware sees the physical topology. You cannot see the logical topology; it is the network from the perspective of how data is sent through the network.

Token Ring is described as a ring topology because data is passed from station to station until it returns to the starting point. Data behaves as though it travels around a ring. Token Ring networks always are wired with an individual cable that extends from a central wiring hub to each workstation. Because the wiring system looks like a star, Token Ring has a star logical topology. Similarly, Ethernet always has a logical bus topology even when it is wired in a star using the new and popular 10BASE-T system.

Media Choices

This section briefly reviews common LAN media choices in TCP/IP networks, such as coaxial, twisted pair, and fiber optic, as seen in figure 3.8.

Coaxial Cable

Coaxial (coax) cable consists of an inner conductor (usually made of a copper alloy) that is used for sending a signal. The return signal flows through the shield that is separated from the central conductor by a *dielectric* (electrically insulating material). The shield provides good bandwidth capabilities and electrical noise immunity. This cable type is the "granddaddy" of LAN media because some of the earliest LANs were built using it. Coax cables are typically found in bus LAN topologies.

Figure 3.8 Twisted pair, coaxial, and fiber optic cables.

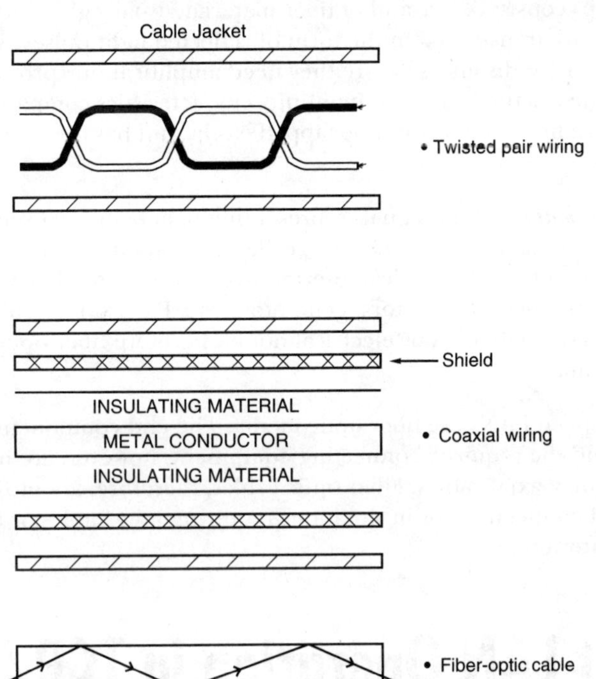

Twisted Pair Wiring

Twisted pair (TP) wiring consists of a pair of wires wrapped around each other. These wires are twisted to minimize radiation and electrical interference. Twisted pair wiring can have a shield around it to improve its data transmission quality. Both *shielded twisted pair (STP)* and *unshielded twisted pair (UTP)* wiring are available for LANs. One wire is used for sending the signal, and the other wire acts as a signal return. Twisted pair wiring is cheap and easy to install. Many buildings are already pre-wired with data-grade twisted pair wiring.

Shielded cables surround the center conductors with a jacket of fine, braided wires. The shield helps prevent outside electrical interference from affecting the conductors and also reduces the risk of broadcasting signals interfering with nearby electronic devices. Although shielded cables once were required for nearly all local area network installations, today, use of unshielded twisted pair wire is more popular. Unshielded twisted pair wire for LANs is similar to that used for telephone communications. Networks can often use telephone wire that is already installed.

Fiber Optic Cable

Fiber optic cables consist of a strand of fiber material, usually glass, inside a protective jacket. Signals are transmitted in the form of reflected light pulses. Signals can propagate over long distances before they need amplification (provided by repeaters). Fiber optic has the best noise immunity characteristics compared to other wiring, is secure because it cannot be tapped easily, and has the best bandwidth characteristics.

What is *noise immunity*? If the signals representing data being transmitted in the media are unaffected by electrical interference, called *noise*, then the media has good noise immunity. The sources of electrical interference or noise could be wireless devices, fluorescent lights, electrical motors/generators, etc. Fiber optic cables use light signals, which are unaffected by electrical noise; therefore fiber optic cables have good noise immunity.

Today's high-speed LANs use fiber optic media. The end-component costs for fiber optic cables and the required connecting equipment, however, are higher than twisted pair and coaxial cables. Fiber optic cables, therefore, are most commonly used for high-speed connections or in situations requiring long cables or better immunity to electrical interference.

Ethernet LAN Operation in TCP/IP Networks

Robert Metcalfe, along with David Boggs and others who worked for Xerox Corporation, developed a LAN based on carrier sensing mechanisms. This LAN spanned a distance of one kilometer, supported 100 personal stations, and achieved data rates of 2.94 Mbps. This system was called Ethernet in honor of that elusive substance called ether through which electromagnetic radiation was once thought to propagate.

Ethernet was proposed as a standard by Digital Equipment Corporation, Intel, and Xerox. The first Ethernet standard was published in September 1981 and was called the DIX 1.0. DIX stands for Digital (DEC), Intel, and Xerox. DIX 1.0 was followed by DIX 2.0 published in November 1982. The DIX 2.0 standard is also called Ethernet II.

Meanwhile, Project 802 from the IEEE had undertaken LAN standardization efforts. Not surprisingly, Digital, Intel, and Xerox proposed the adoption of Ethernet as a standard. IBM proposed the Token Ring as a standard, based on prototypes built at IBM's Zurich lab. The Ethernet proposal became known as the IEEE 802.3 and the Token Ring proposal became the IEEE 802.5.

True to the nature of committee design, the IEEE 802.3 standard is not quite the same as the Ethernet standard; there are important differences. Although 802.3 and Ethernet are incompatible standards, the term *Ethernet* is used in TCP/IP LANs to designate 802.3-compliant networks. This book bows to common usage and uses the term Ethernet for both standards, making distinctions as required when a specific standard is discussed.

Ethernet is also known by other names. In 1982, the European Computer Manufacturers Association (ECMA) adopted it as the ECMA 80/82/82 standard. The U.S. Federal Government adopted "Ethernet" in the FIPS PUBS 107 publication, in 1984. In 1989, the International Organization of Standards and International Electrotechnical Commission adopted it as the ISO/IEC 8802-3 standard.

The following sections discuss Ethernet as it relates to LAN operation in TCP/IP networks in greater detail.

Ethernet Operation

Before an Ethernet station transmits, it listens for activity on the transmission channel (see fig. 3.9). Ethernet frequently is described as a "listen before talking" protocol. *Activity* is any transmission caused by other Ethernet stations. The presence of a transmission is called a *carrier*. The station electronics can sense the presence of a carrier.

Figure 3.9 Carrier-sense mechanism in Ethernet.

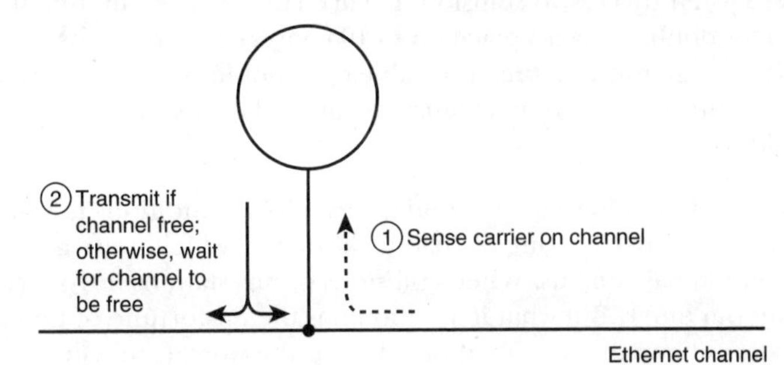

If a station detects a busy channel, the station refrains from transmission. After the last bit of the passing frame, the Ethernet data link layer continues to wait for a minimum of 9.6 microseconds to provide proper interframe spacing. At the end of this time, if a data frame is waiting for transmission, and the channel is free, transmission is initiated. If the station has no data to transmit, it resumes the *carrier sense* (listening for a carrier) operation. The interframe gap provides recovery time for other Ethernet stations.

If a station tried to transmit when the channel is busy, a garbled transmission would result. Garbled transmissions are called *collisions.*

If the channel is free (no carrier detected), the station is free to transmit. Because multiple stations attached to the Ethernet channel use the carrier-sense mechanism, it is called a *Carrier Sense with Multiple Access (CSMA).*

What if two stations decide to transmit at the same time and there was no activity on the channel? A collision would occur. Collisions occur during the normal operation of Ethernet LANs because stations transmit based only on one fact: the presence of a carrier on the channel. They do not know if packets are queued for transmission on other stations. Furthermore, the CSMA operation is complicated by the fact of *propagation delay* in LANs. In Ethernet, for example, signals propagate at 0.77 times the speed of light for standard (thick) cables and 0.65 times the speed of light on thin Ethernet cables. A delay occurs before a transmission is heard by all stations, and a station may transmit because it has yet to hear another station's transmission.

Collisions are a fact of life in Ethernet LANs. Ethernet stations minimize the effects of collision by detecting the collisions as they occur. Hence the name CSMA/CD to describe the Ethernet media access mechanism (CD stands for *Collision Detect*). The stations involved in the collision abort their transmissions. The first station to detect the collision sends out a special jamming pulse to alert all stations that a collision has taken place. After a collision occurs, all stations set up a random interval timer. Transmission takes place only after this interval timer expires. Introducing a delay before transmission can reduce the probability of collisions.

What happens when successive collisions occur? The average random time out value is doubled. This doubling takes place up to 10 consecutive collisions. Beyond that, doubling the average random time out value does not improve the performance of the network significantly. This mechanism is called the *truncated binary exponential back-off algorithm.*

How long does a station have to wait under heavy load conditions to transmit a frame? A station may experience a string of "bad luck" during which every time it transmits some other station has the bus. When collisions occur, stations introduce a delay using the random timer. But what if a station has the misfortune of timing out after the other stations have already timed out? Under the worst-case scenario, a station may have to wait indefinitely. This is not acceptable for real time applications. Hence Ethernet is not suited for real-time applications. Because Ethernet technology is simple, cheap, and easy to implement, many real-time networks used in factory automation use Ethernet with a modified CSMA/CD mechanism to guarantee network availability. This modified Ethernet is of course no longer the standard Ethernet discussed in this book.

The next section examines different Ethernet options.

Ethernet Cable Options

Coaxial cable serves as the medium for two variations of Ethernet: the Standard Ethernet and the Thin Ethernet. Ethernet can also can run on UTP wiring. These options are shown in figure 3.10.

Figure 3.10 IEEE options for 802.3 Ethernet.

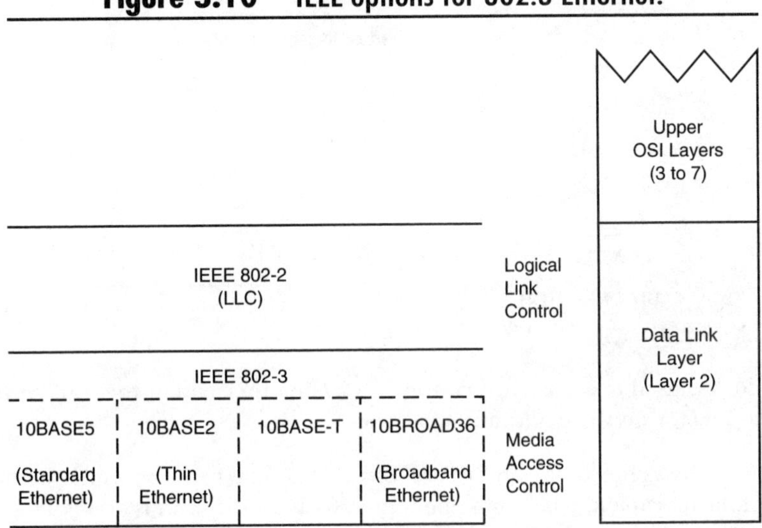

Standard Ethernet Wiring Rules

Another name for Standard Ethernet is Thick Wire Ethernet because the coaxial cable it uses is much thicker than that used for Thin Wire Ethernet. The cable type used for Thick Wire Ethernet is RG-8. The IEEE version of standard Ethernet is called 10BASE5. The 10 stands for 10 Mbps operation; the BASE stands for baseband operation; and the 5 stands for 500 meters per segment.

Figure 3.11 shows some standard Ethernet components. The network board shown in this figure has an AUI connector socket and a coaxial connection. The coaxial connection is used to connect to Thin Wire Ethernet. This particular card can be used with both Thick/Thin Wire Ethernet.

Stations on Thick Ethernet communicate to the external network through external transceivers attached to the shared media. The shared media is called the *trunk segment cable* or just the *segment.* Because of signal attenuation, a segment cannot be longer than 500 meters.

The external transceiver and the Network board are connected by a transceiver cable. The DIX connector plug mates with the DIX connector socket on the Network board.

Figure 3.11 Thick Ethernet network cable and hardware.

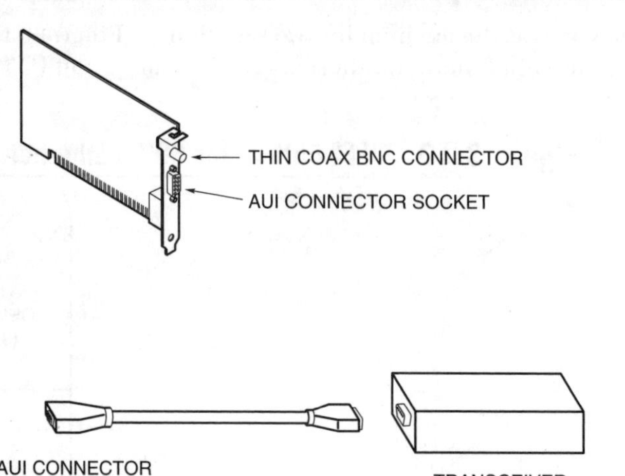

A slide lock is used to secure this connection. The other end of the transceiver fits into a connector on the external transceiver.

Figure 3.12 shows the Thick Ethernet cable used to make up the trunk segments. Thick Ethernet cable is a 0.4-inch diameter, 50-ohm cable and is available in various precut lengths with an N-series connector plug attached to each end. You also can purchase Thick Ethernet cable in spools or bulk quantities. These come without the N-series connectors attached at the ends.

Figure 3.12 also shows the N-series *barrel connector* that can be used to join two lengths of Ethernet cable. A trunk segment must be terminated with an N-series *terminator.* The N-series terminator is a 50-ohm resistor that blocks electrical interference on the segment. Additionally, it cancels out any signal reflections caused by signals reaching the end of the cable. The N-series terminator is attached to the male N-series terminator on the end of the segment. N-series terminators come with a grounding wire. One end of the cable must be grounded; the other end must remain ungrounded to avoid *ground-loop* currents.

Figure 3.13 shows an example of a Thick Ethernet network. Two trunk segments are joined together by a device called a repeater in Thick Ethernet networks. A *repeater* is an active device that allows an Ethernet LAN to expand beyond a single segment by linking two segments together. The repeater amplifies and regenerates the signal so the signal can be transmitted over longer distances. A multiport repeater such as a DEMPR (Digital Equipment's multiport repeater) can link a number of Ethernet segments together.

Figure 3.12 Thick Ethernet coaxial cable connectors.

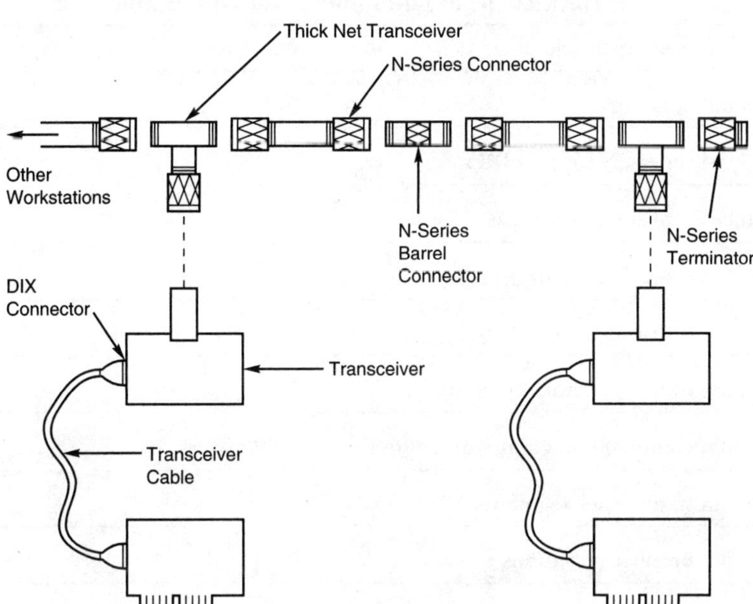

Figure 3.13 Example of a Thick Ethernet network.

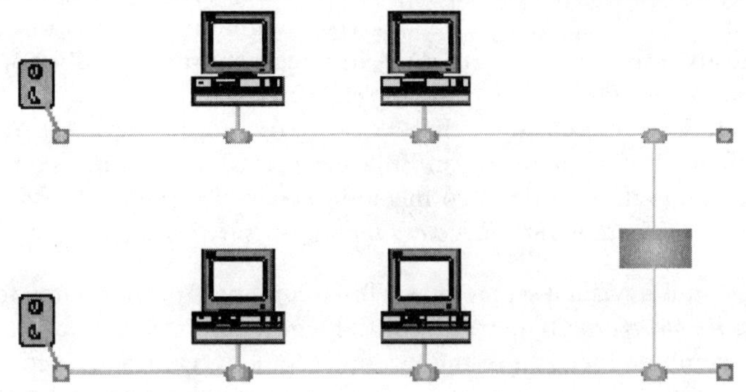

Table 3.2 describes the rules you must follow with Thick Ethernet wiring.

TABLE 3.2
Thick Ethernet Parameters and Wiring Rules

Thick Ethernet Parameters	Value
Maximum data rate	10 Mbps
Maximum repeaters without IRLs	2
Maximum repeaters with IRLs	4
Maximum coaxial segment length	500 meters
Maximum transceiver cable length	50 meters
Maximum number of link segments	2
Maximum combined link segment length	1000 meters
Maximum stations per segment	100
Maximum number of stations	1024
Distance between stations	Multiples of 2.5 meters

To travel from one station to another station on an Ethernet LAN that consists of coaxial trunk segments only (see fig. 3.14), a signal cannot travel through more than two *full repeaters.* A full repeater joins two coaxial segments together directly. A coaxial segment is distinct from a link segment. A link segment made of fiber optic or twisted pair cable can be used to join two coaxial segments over a longer distance. The purpose of a link segment is to extend the range of an Ethernet LAN. You can have a maximum of two link segments on an Ethernet LAN. Link segments do not have stations attached to them and are connected to coaxial segments by repeaters. Another name for them is *Inter-Repeater Link-segments (IRLs).*

A *half-repeater* joins a coaxial segment to a link segment. Another name for a half-repeater is a *remote repeater.* The trunk coaxial segment length cannot exceed 500 meters. The combined lengths of the two link segments cannot exceed 1000 meters. Using these wiring parameters, you can deduce the maximum length of an Ethernet LAN.

Figure 3.15 illustrates the longest possible Ethernet. T1 through T6 represent transceivers.

Figure 3.14 Longest Thick Ethernet network formed by using full repeaters only.

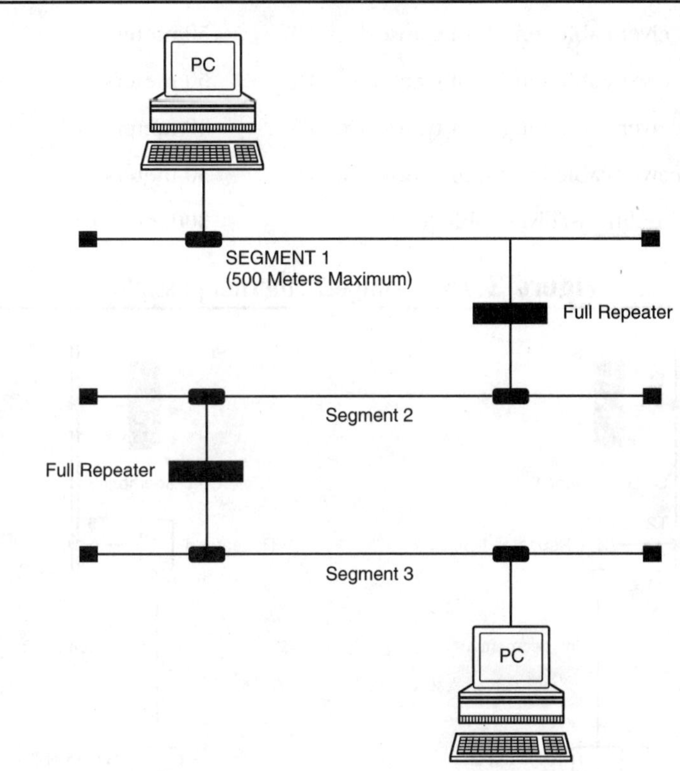

Using this diagram, you can calculate the length of this network:

Coax Segment 1 length = 500 meters

Coax Segment 2 length = 500 meters

Coax Segment 3 length = 500 meters

Combined Link Segment 1 and 2 length = 1000 meters

Total Ethernet Length = 2500 meters

Some people take advantage of the considerable length of transceiver cables to extend the range of the LAN even farther by adding the transceiver cable lengths to transceivers T1, T2, T3, T4, T5, and T6 in figure 3.15. Because the maximum transceiver cable length is 50 meters, this gives a combined transceiver length of 300 meters. The following calculations show how to arrive at this number:

Transceiver cable length of transceiver T1	50 meters
Transceiver cable length of transceiver T2	50 meters
Transceiver cable length of transceiver T3	50 meters
Transceiver cable length of transceiver T4	50 meters
Transceiver cable length of transceiver T5	50 meters
Transceiver cable length of transceiver T6	50 meters
Combined transceiver cable length	300 meters

Figure 3.15 Longest Ethernet possible.

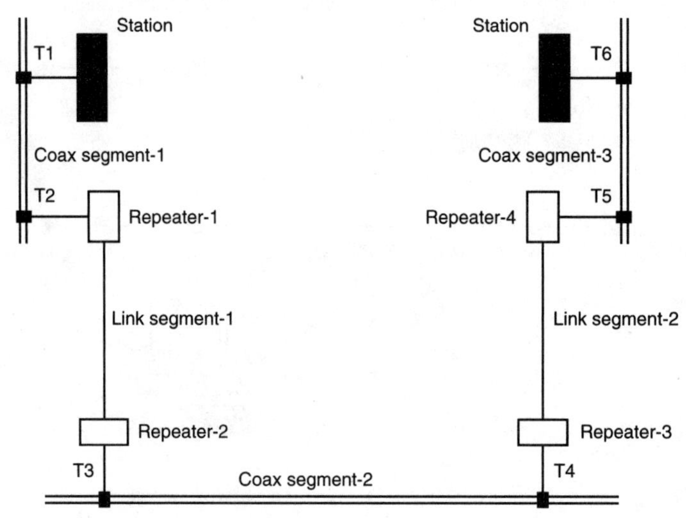

By using maximum transceiver lengths, the maximum Ethernet length is 2500 meters plus 300 meters, which is 2800 meters.

The maximum number of stations that you can attach to a Thick Ethernet segment is 100, and the total number of stations cannot exceed 1024. The repeater attachment to a segment counts as one station. The minimum distance between any two stations is 2.5 meters. It is recommended that you separate stations at distances of multiples of 2.5 meters to minimize interference caused by standing waves on an Ethernet segment. *Standing waves* are formed by the presence of electrical signals on the segment.

Thin Wire Ethernet Wiring Design Rules

Other names for Thin Wire Ethernet are *Thinnet* and also *Cheapernet* (because it is cheaper than Standard Ethernet). The coaxial cable it uses is much thinner than that used for Thick Wire Ethernet. The IEEE version of Thin Wire Ethernet is called *10BASE2.* The 10 stands for 10 Mbps operation; the BASE stands for baseband operation; and the 2 stands for approximately 200 meters (actually, 185 meters) per segment.

Figure 3.16 shows some of the Thin Wire Ethernet components. The network board or Network board, in this figure, has a coaxial connection.

Figure 3.16 Thin Ethernet components.

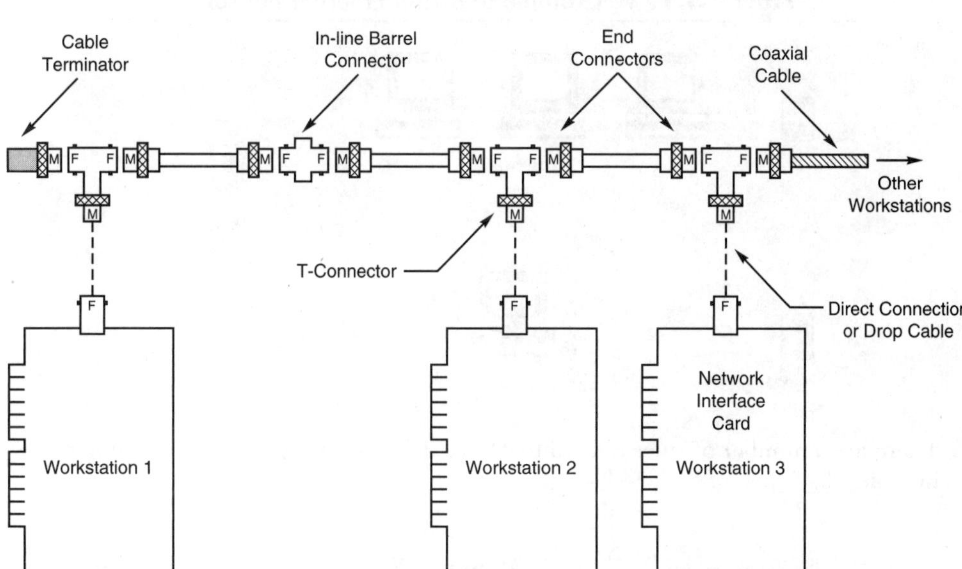

The transceiver functions for a Thin Wire Ethernet are performed by the on-board network electronics. No external transceiver connections are made to the network. BNC T-connectors are used to connect the Network board with the cable. The two opposing jacks of the T-connector are used to join two lengths of Thin Wire Ethernet cable. The remaining plug is attached to the BNC connector jack on the Network board.

Due to signal attenuation, a thin wire segment cannot be longer than 185 meters. Thin Ethernet cable has a 0.2-inch diameter and RG-58 A/U 50-ohm cable, and is available in various precut lengths with a standard BNC plug attached to each end. Thin Ethernet cable also can be purchased in spools or bulk quantities that come without the BNC connectors attached at the ends. Using special crimping tools you can construct cables of arbitrary lengths.

You also can use the BNC barrel connector to join two lengths of Ethernet cable. A trunk segment must be terminated with a BNC terminator. The *BNC terminator* is a 50-ohm resistor that blocks electrical interference on the segment. Additionally, it cancels out any signal reflections caused by signals bouncing off the end of the cable. The BNC terminator is attached to one of the two jacks on a T-connector to which no cable is attached. There is a grounded BNC terminator that has a grounding wire. One end of the cable must be grounded; the other end must remain ungrounded to avoid ground loop current.

Figure 3.17 shows an example of a Thin Ethernet network. In this network, there are two trunk segments that are joined together by a repeater. The repeater in figure 3.17 has two ports to attach a maximum of two segments.

Figure 3.17 Example of a Thin Ethernet network.

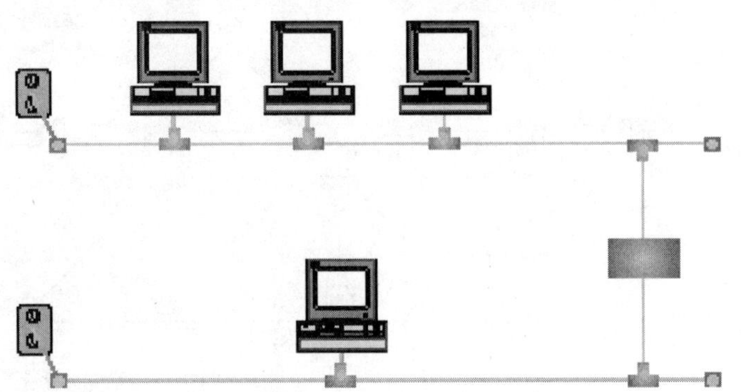

There are a number of rules related to Thin Ethernet wiring. These are summarized in table 3.3.

TABLE 3.3
Thin Ethernet Parameters and Wiring Rules

Thin Ethernet Parameters	Value
Maximum data rate	10 Mbps
Maximum repeaters without IRLs	2
Maximum repeaters with IRLs	4
Maximum coaxial segment length	185 meters
Maximum number of link segments	2

Thin Ethernet Parameters	Value
Maximum stations per segment	30
Maximum number of stations	1024
Minimum distance between stations	0.5 meters

The repeater rules for Thin Ethernet are the same as for Thick Ethernet.

The trunk coaxial segment length for Thin Ethernet cannot exceed 185 meters. The maximum number of stations that can be attached to a Thin Ethernet segment is 30, and the total number of stations cannot exceed 1024. The repeater attachment to a segment counts as one station. The minimum distance between any two stations is 0.5 meters.

10BASE-T Wiring Design Rules

An increase in interest for 10BASE-T began in 1990 due to the lower cost components and ease of configuring networks based in UTP wiring. 10BASE-T is a technology that is used to implement Ethernet. 10BASE-T is an implementation option for the IEEE 802.3 standard. The 10 stands for 10 Mbps operation; the BASE stands for baseband operation; and the T stands for twisted pair wiring.

In figure 3.18, the Network board has a telephone-type RJ-45 port, which is officially called a *Media Dependent Interface (MDI)* port. The Network board shown in the figure also has a DIX connector. The DIX connector is used to connect by means of a transceiver to Thick Wire Ethernet. This particular card can be used with both 10BASE-T and Thick Ethernet. Many network boards require a switch setting to enable either the 10BASE-T or DIX port, whereas others have an auto-sense mechanism. The transceiver functions for a 10BASE-T are performed by the onboard network board electronics.

The 10BASE-T uses a physical star topology with the 10BASE-T concentrator (also called *hub*) serving as the central switching element. The 10BASE-T plug and connector are shown in figure 3.19. Each concentrator accepts cables to several workstations. UTP wiring is used to connect a 10BASE-T concentrator to the workstation. This wiring normally consists of 0.4 to 0.6 mm diameter (26 to 22 AWG) unshielded wire in a multipair cable. The performance specifications are generally met by 100 meters of 0.5 mm telephone twisted pair.

Figure 3.18 Connectors on a 10BASE-T network adapter card.

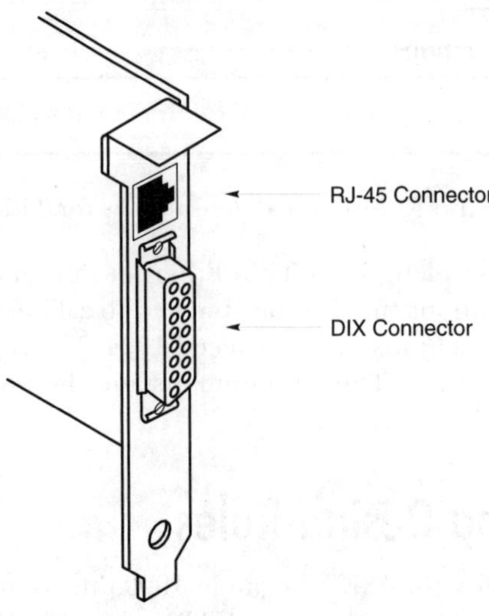

Figure 3.19 10BASE-T plug and connector. (Source: IEEE Standard 802.3i-1990).

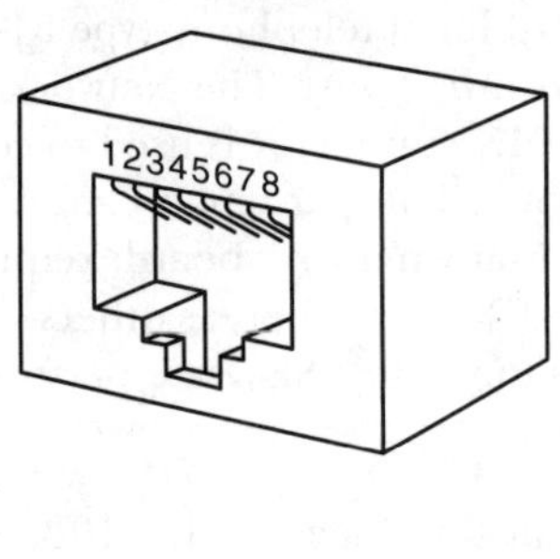

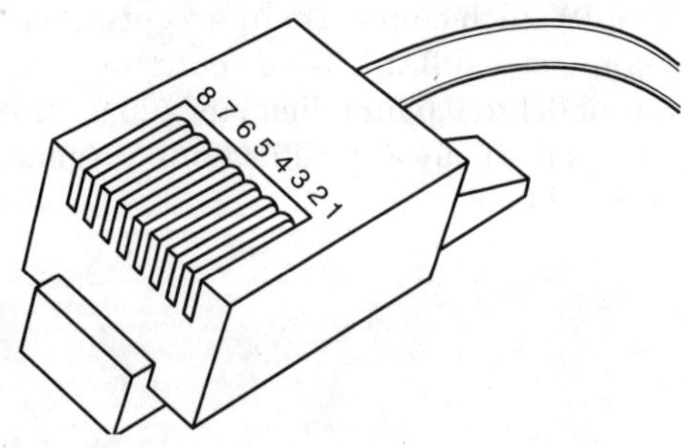

There are two twisted pairs (four wires) between each network board and the concentrator, as shown in figure 3.20. Each two-wire path forms a simplex link segment. One simplex segment is used for transmitting and the other for receiving.

Figure 3.20 Simplex segments used in 10BASE-T. (Source: IEEE Standard 802.3l-1990).

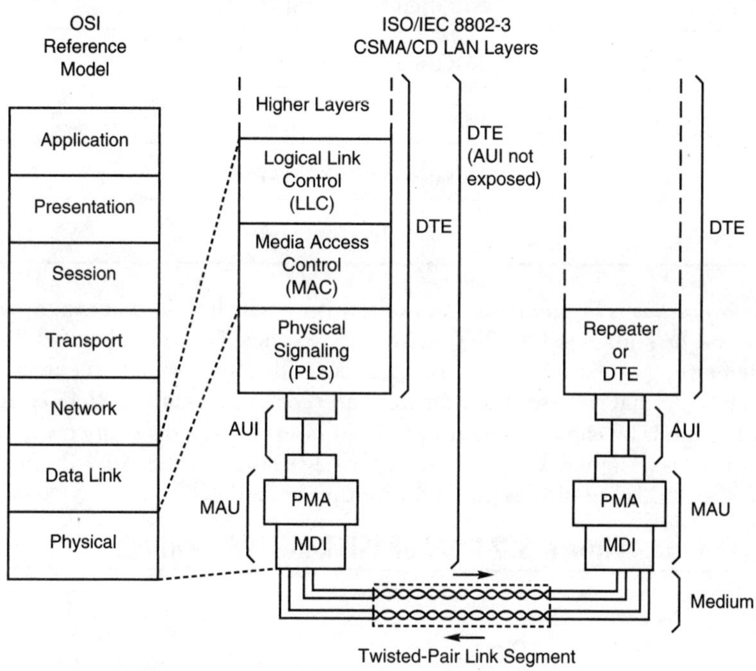

Table 3.4 shows the pin assignments for a 4-pair twisted pair wiring. Only two pairs, one for transmission (TD) and another for receiving (RD), are used.

TABLE 3.4
Pin Assignments for the MDI Connector

Contact	MDI signal
1	TD+
2	TD_

continues

Table 3.4, Continued
Pin Assignments for the MDI Connector

Contact	MDI signal
3	RD+
4	Not used by 10BASE-T
5	Not used by 10BASE-T
6	RD_
7	Not used by 10BASE-T
8	Not used by 10BASE-T

A *crossover function* is implemented in every twisted pair link so that the transmitter at one end will be connected to the receiver at the other. Figure 3.21 shows the two ways of implementing crossover functions. One way to do this is to use an external crossover UTP cable that reverses the transmit and receive pairs at the RJ-45 connector at one end of the UTP cable. A second way is an internal crossover function, in which the crossover is designed as part of the internal circuitry in the 10BASE-T device. An MDI port with this function is marked with the symbol "X."

Figure 3.21 10BASE-T crossover wiring.

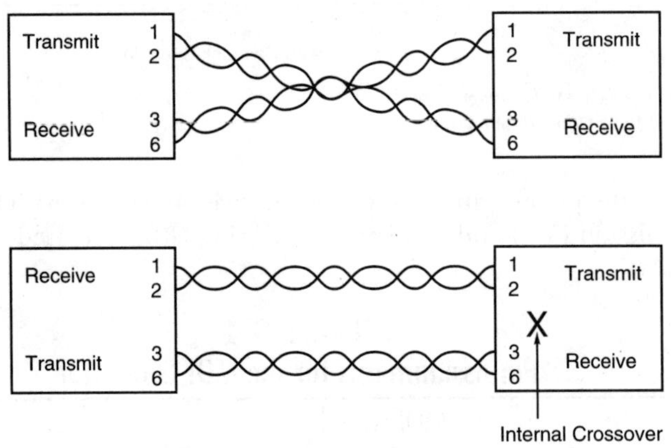

Figure 3.22 shows a single concentrator 10BASE-T network.

Figure 3.22 A single concentrator 10BASE-T network.

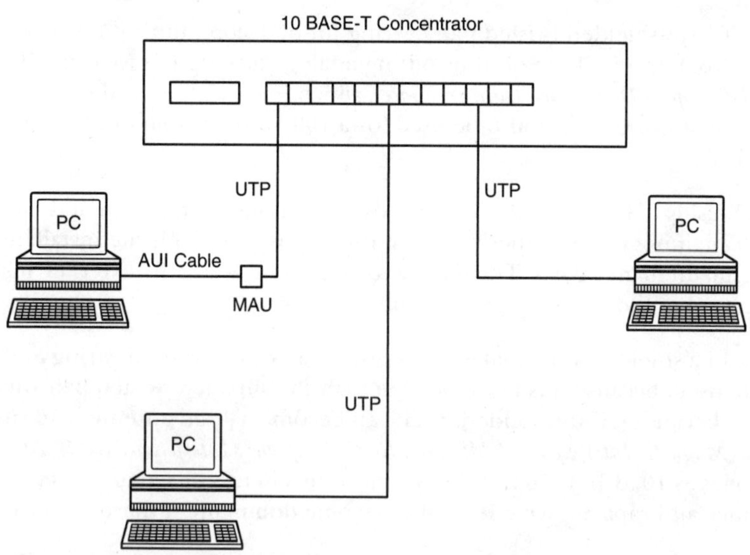

The concentrator has 12 RJ-45 ports. If the station's Network board has a 10BASE-T (RJ-45) connector, the connections can be made directly through UTP cable. For stations with 10BASE5 network boards, a 10BASE-T MAU (10BASE-T transceiver) is needed to connect the AUI cable to the station.

The 10BASE-T concentrator serves the role of a repeater. It performs the following functions:

- Data packet retiming (IEEE 802.3 standard)
- Per-port Link Integrity Test ("Good Link Test")
- Per-port autopartitioning, which disconnects the port in the event of 30 consecutive collisions, an excessively long single collision, or jabber input

The proper operation of the CSMA/CD 10BASE-T network requires network size to be limited to control round-trip propagation delays (the time it takes a signal to reach extremity of network and come back). The configuration rules for more than one concentrator are as follows:

- Maximum of four concentrators in the data path between any two stations
- UTP segments should be no longer than 100 meters

UTP Wiring Considerations

Use of UTP (unshielded twisted pair) wiring for data communications has come a long way from its initial use of transmitting analog voice signals to its use in 10BASE-T and *CDDI (Copper Distributed Data Interface),* which is a variation of the FDDI LAN that runs at 100 Mbps. UTP can also be used for a 100 Mbps version of Ethernet called 100BASE-T.

Although using UTP for LAN wiring needs can simplify installation and reduce wiring costs, it can, if not done properly, do just the opposite: complicate installations and increase maintenance costs. The factors to consider for an effective UTP installation are discussed in the upcoming paragraphs.

The lack of a shield in UTP makes it cheaper than other types of wiring and also easier to install because it is more flexible than the shielded twisted pair wiring. However, because it is unshielded, UTP can become a good antenna and susceptible to *Electro-Magnetic Interference (EMI)* and *Radio-Frequency Interference (RFI)*. At such frequencies as 10 to 100 Mbps, UTP wiring results in loss of signal due to attenuation. Inductance and capacitance effects also become dominant at these high frequencies.

The *inductance* is caused by the electromagnetic field that surrounds the UTP wire when the high-frequency signals pass through it. It can be likened to the transformer effect that induces a voltage on the secondary of the transformer due to electromagnetic coupling. The *capacitance* effect is caused because the conductors that make up the twisted pair wire are separated by an insulating material. These effects reduce the quality of the signal and limit the distance that can be used between devices connected by UTP.

The twists that are used in twisted pair wiring help reduce inductance by creating a magnetic field that essentially cancels out inductance. For this reason, an important parameter in measuring the quality of a cable is the twists per inch of the wire. This can reduce the amount of *cross-talk,* which is the inductive coupling to other pairs of wires or noise sources. Cross-talk can lead to signal distortion (often called *jitter*) and, in the case of Ethernet networks, can be mistaken for collisions, which could degrade the network performance.

In Token Ring networks, cross-talk can generate hard errors that can cause the Token Ring networks to go through reconfigurations. Reconfigurations are time-consuming and result in slow networks.

Flat silver satin wire, which works just fine in low-speed data networks such as 19.2 Kbps, has zero twists per inch. This type of cabling is common in telephone networks; however, if voice telephone cable is used in data networks that operate in the Mbps range, it can result in disaster. Besides causing the network to fail, it can create a great deal of EMI noise that can cause other devices to fail also.

The signal that is used in both Ethernet and Token Ring networks is a baseband signal. *Baseband signals* are digital signals that have sharp edges. The capacitance effect in a wire causes the signal to lose some of its sharpness so that it becomes rounded. The resistance effect causes the signal to lose its strength (attenuation). The inductance and capacitance effect can make the signal vulnerable to external noise sources to the point that the signal can be completely distorted. Figure 3.23 illustrates these effects.

Figure 3.23 Signal distortion and noise in cables.

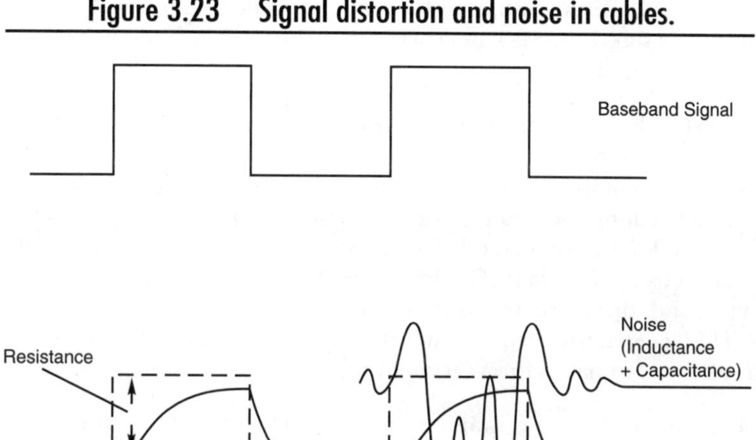

Another factor to consider is that signals with sharp edges or rapidly changing signals result in high-frequency harmonics. Mathematically speaking, the *ds/dt*—the rate at which the signal changes—is high for the edges of the baseband signal. If the signal is periodic, it can be expressed as the sum of sine wave harmonics of the fundamental frequency of the signal, in which the sine wave may have different phase (starting point) differences. This means that a 20 Mbps signal is really not just a 20 Mbps signal, but a sine wave with 20 MHz fundamental frequency and harmonic components of 40 MHz, 60 MHz, 80 MHz, 100 MHz, 120 MHz, and so on. The higher harmonics are smaller in magnitude. What this means in practical terms is that the cable must be able to carry the higher harmonic components of the data signal. If it does not do this well, the signal can become distorted.

Some of these factors can be mitigated by using high-quality twisted pair wiring. The characteristics of cables can be defined in terms of attenuation, which is measured in decibels per 100 feet. Decibels is a logarithmic scale (to the base 10) for comparing power levels. It is defined as log (P2/P1)

where

P2 = Power at output

P1 = Power applied at input

LAN designers specify maximum distance lengths for cable segments based on attenuation characteristics of the cable medium for the frequency of data transmission. For this reason, 10BASE-T networks have a limit of 100 meters between station and wiring concentrator.

The type of sheath used to enclose the twisted pair wire affects its plenum rating. *Plenum rating* determines whether or not the cable must be encased in a conduit for fire resistance as required by some building codes. PVC (polyvinyl chloride) is the most common coating used and is not fire resistant. Another type of cable coating called *TFEP* (teflon fluorinated ethylene propylene) is rated as fire resistant. It also has a lower dielectric constant. The lower the dielectric constant, the lower the capacitance, and, therefore, the lower the signal distortion. Because of these characteristics, TFEP-coated wire can transmit the signal over longer distances with less signal distortion compared to PVC-coated wires.

In telephone networks, it is common to use a punch-down block called the 66 Block. Whereas this type of punch-down block works fine for telephone networks, it is not designed to carry data. For data networks that need to carry data in the Mbps range, you must use punch-down blocks specifically designed for data. These include punch-down blocks known as the 110s, 3m 7000D, and Krone. Data grade punch-down blocks include gold-plated or silver-plated contact points, labeling, and so forth. Data-grade patch panels also are available. Some of their features are cross-connect circuits etched on the wafer board itself. These patch panels can carry high-frequency signals in a manner similar to printed circuit boards.

Mixed Media Ethernet Networks

You can combine the different media (coaxial, twisted pair, and fiber) into one Ethernet LAN. If you combine mixed media networks, use a fiber optic, twisted pair, or coaxial cable to implement the link segment. Figures 3.24 and 3.25 show examples of mixed media networks.

Figure 3.24 An 802.3 network using fiber optic cable.

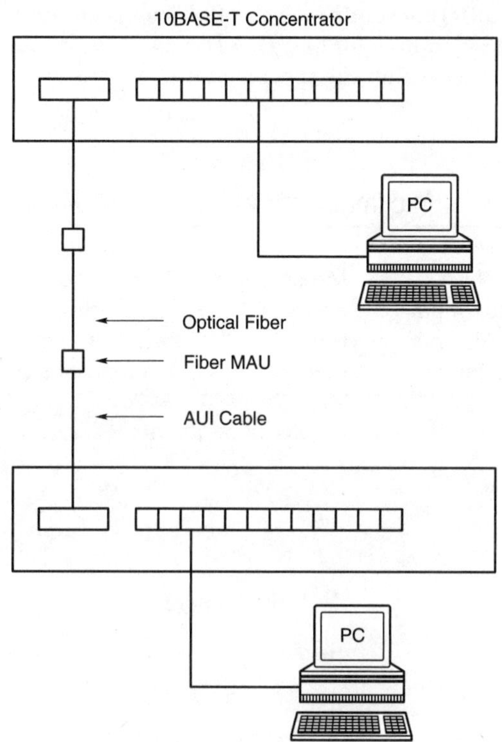

Figure 3.25 An 802.3 network with a coaxial backbone.

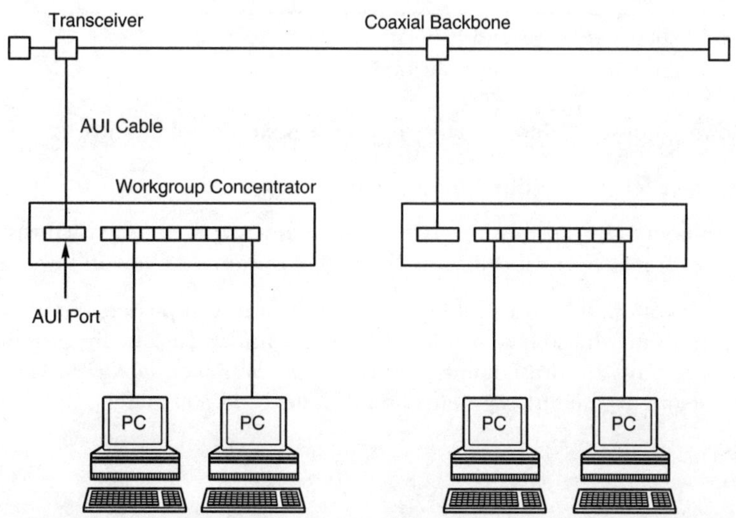

Table 3.5 summarizes the maximum delays of the various media segments. This table is important for the LAN manager because Ethernet segments can be built by combining cables from different vendors, each of which may differ from the specifications by small amounts. Test equipment like *Time Domain Reflectometers (TDRs)* can be used to see that the delays are within the specifications.

TABLE 3.5
Maximum Delays for Ethernet Media

Media Segment Type	Maximum MAUs per Segment	Maximum Segment Length (meters)	Minimum Propagation Velocity (fraction of speed of light)	Maximum Delay per Segment (nanoseconds)
		Coaxial Segment		
10BASE5	100	500	0.77c	2165
10BASE2	30	185	0.65c	950
		Link Segment		
FOIRL	2	1000	0.66c	5000
10BASE-T	2	100	0.59c	1000
		AUI (Transceiver Cable)		
AUI	DTE/1 MAU	50	0.65c	257

c = 300,000,000 meters/second (velocity of light in vacuum)
FOIRL = Fiber Optic Inter Repeater Link

The following network topology rules apply for mixed media networks:

1. Repeater sets are required for all segment interconnections.
2. The maximum transmission path between any two stations may consist of up to five segments, four repeater sets (including optional AUIs), and two MAUs.
3. If a network path consists of five segments and four repeaters sets, up to three segments may be coaxial trunks and the remainder must be link segments. If five segments are present and *Fiber Optic Inter-Repeater Link (FOIRL)* is used as the link segment, the link segment should not exceed 500 meters.

4. If a network path consists of four segments and three repeater sets, the maximum allowable length of the FOIRL segments is 1000 meters each.

Rule 2 is illustrated in figure 3.26. Notice that this rule does not tell us how many segments are coaxial trunks with multiple station attachments and how many are link segments with no station attachments. Rule 3 clarifies this problem.

Figure 3.26 Maximum Ethernet transmission path with three coaxial segments. (Source: IEEE Std 802.3l-1990)

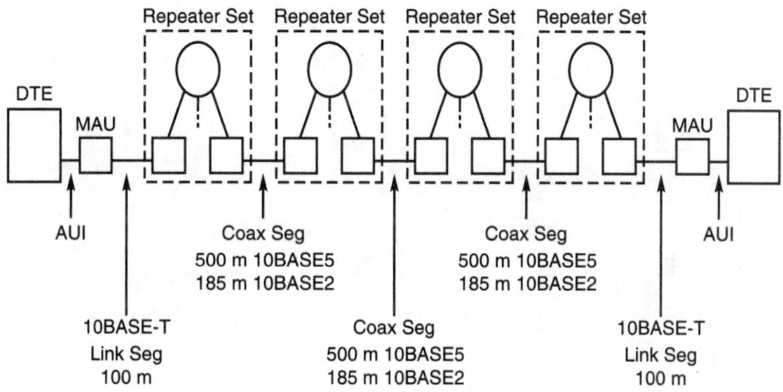

Rule 3 is illustrated in figure 3.27. This figure shows a multimedia Ethernet network. The media used in this network is a combination of coaxial, fiber, and twisted pair. Notice in figure 3.27 that there are five repeater sets. This may at first glance seem to contradict the rule of a maximum of four repeater sets, but between any two stations, there are no more than four repeaters in the transmission path. There is a total of ten segments: seven twisted pair, two fiber optic, and one coaxial. However, there are no more than five segments between any two stations. Also, there is a maximum of one coaxial segment, which is within the maximum three coaxial segment rule. When the coaxial segment is included in the transmission path, the remaining four segments are link segments: three twisted pair and one fiber optic link segment. Because there is a maximum of five segments and four repeaters in the transmission path, the maximum FOIRL length is 500 meters. This follows from Rule 3. The maximum span of this network is 1300 meters, not including AUI drops.

Rule 4 is illustrated in figure 3.28. There are three repeater sets and six segments: four twisted pair and two fiber optic. There are no coaxial segments in this figure. Between any two stations, there is a maximum of four segments and three repeaters. The four segments consist of two fiber optic and two twisted pair cables. Each of the FOIRL links has a maximum length of 1000 meters. The maximum span of this network is 2200 meters, not including AUI drops.

Figure 3.27 Maximum transmission path using 802.3 coaxial segments, 10BASE-T link segments, and fiber optic link segments. (Source: IEEE Standard 802.3i-1990)

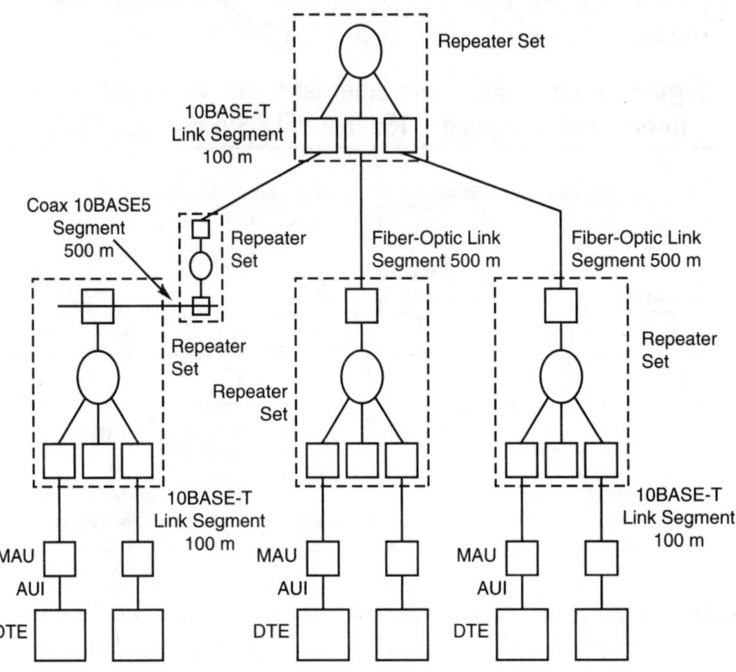

If you are extending an existing network and plan to use a different cable type, you can do so by using the methods discussed in the following sections.

Combining Thin/Thick Cable in a Segment

You can combine thin and thick Ethernet cable in a single segment by using as much thin cable as possible. Thin cable is cheaper and easier to install than thick cable. Figure 3.29 illustrates a network layout using segments made up of a combination of thin and thick cable.

Combined thin/thick cables are between 185 meters and 500 meters long. The minimum length is 185 meters because coaxial segments shorter than 185 meters can be built with thin cable exclusively. The maximum of 500 meters is the limit for a segment made out of thick coaxial exclusively.

Figure 3.28 Maximum transmission path with three repeater sets and four link segments. (Source: IEEE Standard 802.3i-1990)

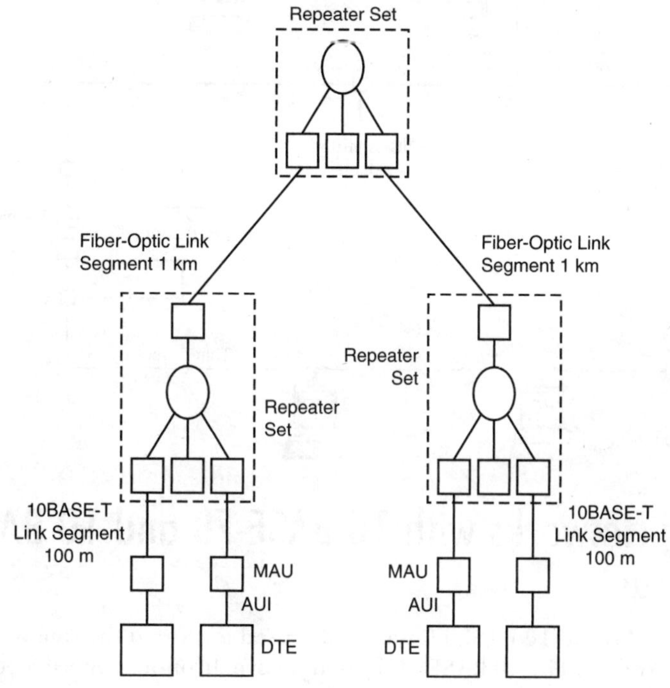

To compute the number of meters of thin cable you can use (thinLen) in one combination trunk segment, use the following equation:

thinLen = (500 – trunkLen)/3.28 meters

(trunkLen = Length of trunk segment you want to build)

If you want to build a trunk segment of 400 meters, for example, the maximum length of thin coaxial cable you can use is

thinLen = (500 – 400) ÷ 3.28 = 30.48 meters

You can use 30.48 meters of thin coaxial with 400 – 30.48 = 369.52 meters of thick cable. Thin and thick coaxial cable must be connected by means of an N-series to a BNC jack.

Figure 3.29 Combining Thick and Thin coaxial Ethernet.

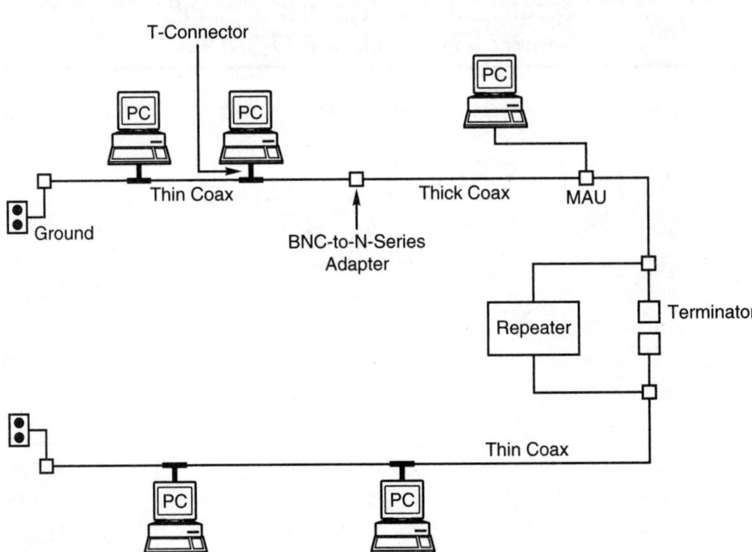

Linking Networks with 10 BASE-FB and 10 BASE-FL Standards

The 10 BASE-FB and 10 BASE-FL standard is used to extend the range of existing Ethernet networks. The 10 BASE-FL is used for synchronous Ethernet connections and the 10 BASE-FL is used for asynchronous connections between a station and the Ethernet segment. The 10 BASE-FB was ratified by the IEEE 802 committees in September 1993. Prior to the 10 BASE-FL and 10 BASE-FB standards the Fiber Optic Inter-Repeater Link (FOIRL) was used to link Ethernet segments at distances up to 1 kilometer. The 10 BASE-FB and 10 BASE-FL extends the range between Ethernet segments to two kilometers. The two kilometers is an IEEE specification limit. Actual products may be able to go beyond the two-kilometer limit, to distances of up to four kilometers.

Understanding Framing for TCP/IP Networks

Both Ethernet-II and IEEE 802.3 have a minimum frame size of 64 bytes and a maximum frame size of 1518 bytes. There are differences between the frame structures of IEEE 802.3 and Ethernet-II. It is possible to configure some nodes on a single

LAN segment to use either the IEEE 802.3 frame or Ethernet-II frame. If this is done, a node configured with Ethernet-II frames will not be able to communicate with a node configured with IEEE 802.3 frames. The following sections elaborate on this issue while discussing the differences in frame structures between Ethernet-II and IEEE 802.3.

The Ethernet-II Frame

The Ethernet-II frame (see fig. 3.30) begins with a preamble of eight octets (one octet = eight bits) consisting of an alternating pattern 1010 that ends in 101011. At 10 Mbps, this preamble is of 6.4 microsecond duration and is sufficient time for the receiving station to synchronize and get ready to receive the frame.

Figure 3.30 Comparison of 802.3 and Ethernet II frame structures.

7 octets	1 octet	6 octets	6 octets	2 octets	46 to 1500 octets	4 octets	
Preamble	Start Frame Delimiter	Destination Address	Source Address	Length ≤1500	LLC Data	Frame Check Sequence	IEE802.3

8 octets	6 octets	6 octets	2 octets	46 to 1500 octets	4 octets	
Preamble	Destination Address	Source Address	Type > 1500	Upper Layer Data	Frame Check Sequence	Ethernet II

The Destination Address (DA) and the Source Address (SA) fields follow this preamble. Each address field is six octets long. The first three octets represent a manufacturer's code and the remaining three octets are assigned by the manufacturer. This assignation is made so that an Ethernet card will have a unique six-octet address. This address is usually burned into a ROM chip on the Ethernet card. The least significant bit (LSB) of the first octet is the Physical/Multicast bit. It is 0 for an Ethernet address. A value of 1 for this LSB indicates a multicast address. For instance, a hex value of FFFFFFFFFFFF, all 1s, for the DA field represents a broadcast. The manufacturer's code was formerly assigned by Xerox; it is now assigned by IEEE.

The Type field, also referred to as Ethertype, is a two-octet field used to indicate the type of data in the data field. Thus, if the Ethernet frame is used to carry TCP/IP data, the Ethertype value will be 800 hex. The Ethertype field is used by network drivers or the network layer to demultiplex data packets to the appropriate protocol stack. It allows multiple protocol stacks to run on a single Ethernet card.

The Data Unit field is a variable length field that can range from 46 to 1500 octets. The remaining fixed length fields add up to 18 bytes.

The Frame Check Sequence (FCS) field is generated by the Ethernet hardware at the end of the data field and is a 32-bit *Cyclic Redundancy Checksum (CRC)* over the address, type, and data fields. It is used to detect errors in transmission. Bad frames are retransmitted.

Understanding IEEE 802.3 Frames

The IEEE frame (also shown in figure 3.30) begins with a preamble of seven octets (one octet = eight bits) consisting of an alternating pattern 1010. At 10 Mbps, this preamble is 5.6 microseconds in duration, and this is sufficient time for the receiving station to synchronize and get ready to receive the frame.

The Start Frame Delimiter (SFD) follows after the preamble and is defined by the pattern 10101011. Note the following:

IEEE 802.3 preamble + SFD = Ethernet preamble

The IEEE 802.3 preamble and the SFD field combined are identical to the eight-octet Ethernet preamble.

The DA and the SA fields follow the SFD. Each address field can be six octets or two octets long. The six-octet addressing is the most common. The first three octets represent a manufacturer's code and the remaining octets are assigned by the manufacturer. This assignation is made so that any two Ethernet and IEEE cards will have a unique six-octet address. This address is usually burned into a ROM chip on the IEEE 802.3 card. The LSB of the first octet represents the Individual/Group field and is similar to the Physical/Multicast field in Ethernet. The next bit is the *Universe/ Local* (U/L) field and indicates if the addressing is global or local.

The Length field follows the address fields and is two octets long. It indicates the data size of the LLC layer. A minimum of 46 octets of LLC is required to make up the minimum size of 64 octets. The maximum value of this field is 1500 to make a maximum frame size of 1518 octets.

The Data Unit field is a variable length field containing 46 to 1500 octets of LLC data.

The FCS field is generated by the IEEE 802.3 hardware at the end of the Data field and is a 32-bit Cyclic Redundancy Checksum (CRC) over the Address, Type, and Data fields. It is used to detect errors in transmission. Bad frames are retransmitted.

Differences Between Ethernet-II and IEEE 802.3

There are differences between Ethernet-II and IEEE 802.3. You can see that Ethernet-II uses a two-byte Type field to indicate the type of data. The Type field values were at one time assigned by Xerox; they are now assigned by IEEE. Instead of the Type field,

IEEE 802.3 has a two-byte Length field. The Length field for Ethernet Packets is supplied by a higher layer. In some cases, the Network board can determine the length of the frame based on signal duration and passes this information to upper layers. For IEEE 802.3 frames, the type information is supplied by the IEEE 802.2 (Logical Control Layer) frame that is part of the Data Unit field.

Ethernet has no provision to pad the data to make a minimum Ethernet frame of 64 bytes. IEEE 802.3 frames have a Length field to encode the pad information. In Ethernet, the padding has to be performed by upper layers.

The SNAP Header

The LLC frame type format is illustrated in figure 3.31. Normally, all communication is performed using 802.2 Type 1. Recall from the discussion in section "TCP/IP on IEEE Local Area Networks" earlier in this chapter that Type 1 communication is connectionless and type 2 communication is connection-oriented. Consenting systems on the same IEEE 802 network may use 802.2 Type 2 communication after verifying that it is supported by both nodes. This is accomplished using the 802.2 Exchange Identification (XID) mechanism, which consists of special LLC frames that are sent to determine the communication settings of another IEEE 802.2 node. Type 1 communication is the recommended method and must be supported by all implementations.

Figure 3.31 LLC frame in IEEE 802.3.

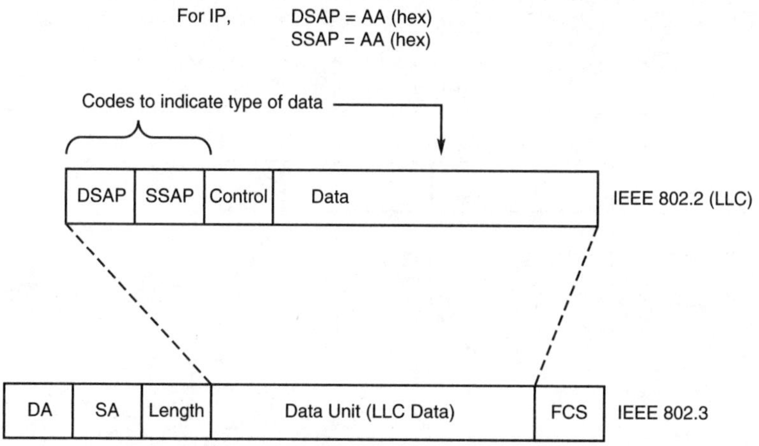

A hex code of AA for SSAP and DSAP in the LLC frame is reserved to transmit upper layer packets that were generated by non-IEEE LANs. This special code of AA hex indicates that the *Sub Net Access Protocol (SNAP)* mechanism is in use. The SNAP protocol describes a header that is placed just inside the LLC header, as illustrated in figure 3.32.

Figure 3.32 SNAP Header with IP encapsulation. (Courtesy Learning Tree)

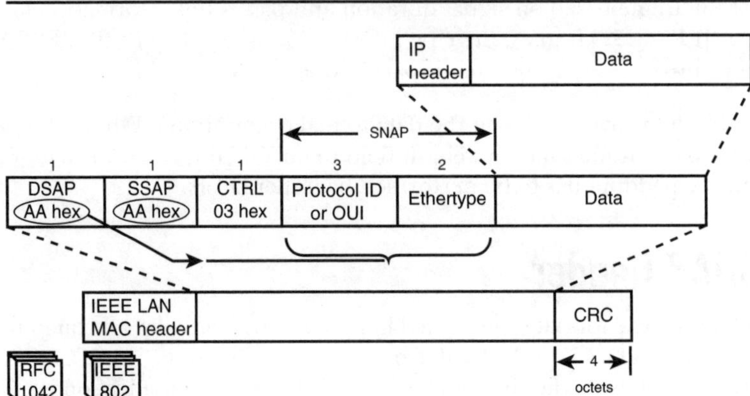

The SNAP header is five octets long and consists of a three-octet *Organizational Unit Identifier (OUI)* and a two-octet Ethertype field value. The OUI represents the organization authority responsible for the encoding of the octets that follow the OUI. For TCP/IP networks, an OUI value of zero is used; this means that a two-byte Ethertype field follows. By encoding the Ethertype field in the SNAP header, it is possible to connect non-IEEE 802 LANs such as Ethernet to IEEE 802 LANs without losing the Ethertype field information that is used in Ethernet LANs (see fig. 3.33). The requirement for non-IEEE LANs is that they must use LLC frames (IEEE 802.2 framing) with SNAP headers.

Figure 3.33 You can connect Ethernet LANs to non-Ethernet LANs.

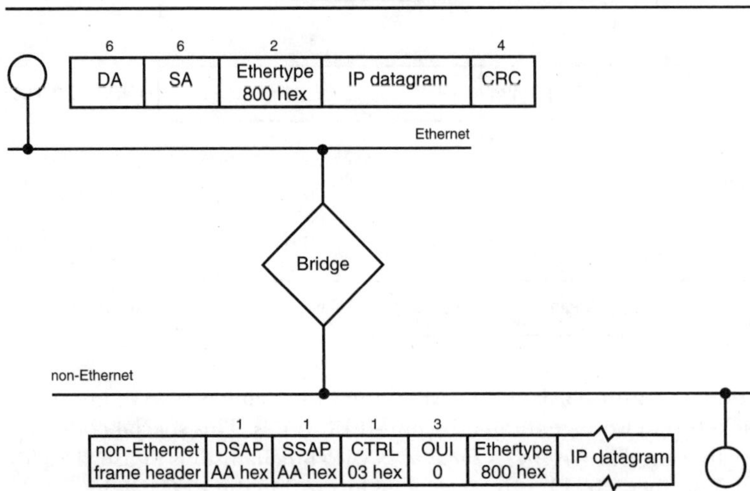

A complete description of SNAP can be found in RFC 1042.

Fast Ethernet for TCP/IP

As network-based applications become more commonplace and complex, they place greater demands on network bandwidth. Examples of applications that need greater network bandwidth are computer-aided design, computer-aided training, document management, image processing, real-time video, and multimedia. While Ethernet with its maximum data rate of 10 Mbps has been used for these applications, a faster network is needed for these applications. Examples of a faster network are Fast Ethernet and the 100 BASE-VG specification (both discussed later in the section) that operates at 100 Mbps.

Before discussing the high-speed Ethernet standards, a brief background of the position of these standards in relationship to the installed base of existing Ethernet networks will be helpful.

The IEEE 802.3 specification defined a *Physical Media Dependent (PMD)* communication protocol that consisted of LLC/MAC layer and the PMD layer (see fig. 3.34). The *LLC (Logical Link Control)* and the *MAC (Media Access Control)* layers correspond to layer 2, the Data Link layer, of the OSI model. The PMD layer corresponds to layer 1, the Physical layer, of the OSI model.

Figure 3.34 IEEE 802.3 specification components.

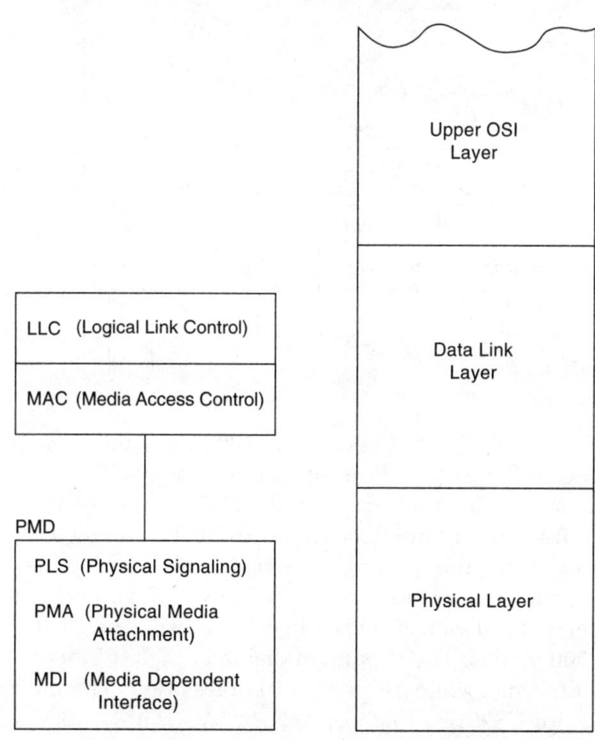

The distinguishing characteristic of IEEE 802.3 is the MAC layer. The MAC layer is responsible for the format of the Ethernet frame and the CSMA/CD arbitration mechanism that is used to gain access to a shared media. Keeping the MAC layer independent of the Physical layer enables the IEEE 802.3 specification to specify a number of different media types (see fig. 3.35). It also enables the MAC layer to be defined in a speed-independent fashion. With the exception of the *interpacket gap* time, which is the minimum time that must elapse between packets that are sent, all MAC time parameters are expressed in bit-time intervals. This means that it is possible to use Ethernet at data rates faster than the original 10 Mbps operation speed for Ethernet.

Figure 3.35 **IEEE 802.3 physical media support.**

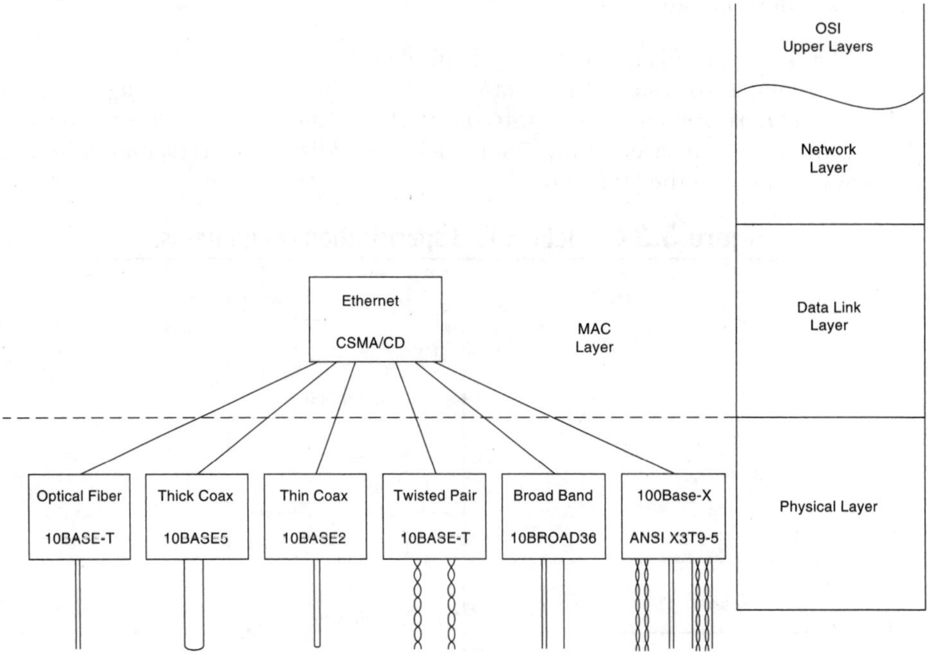

Fast Ethernet as it is currently defined operates at 100 Mbps, and represents a tenfold scaling of the Ethernet 10 Mbps MAC layer operation. The scaling is possible because of the independence of the Physical layer from the MAC layer. The Physical layer for IEEE 802.3 is responsible for sending/receiving the data bit stream to the attached medium, encoding/decoding the bit stream, carrier sense, collision detection, and electrical and mechanical interface to the attached medium. Fast Ethernet's maximum network diameter is 250 meters. This is in contrast with the 10 Mbps Ethernet, whose diameter is 2500 meters. The maximum diameter of Fast Ethernet is one tenth that of the 10 Mbps Ethernet, while its speed is 10 times faster. There is a trade-off of speed versus distance for CSMA/CD networks. For CSMA/CD to work, a station must transmit long enough to detect a collision with a station transmitting from the farthest end of the network. At 10 Mbps and a maximum diameter of 2500 meters, the packet must be transmitted for at least 57.6 microseconds to meet these requirements. The minimum number of bits to be transmitted is therefore computed as shown: Minimum transmitted bits = 10 Mbps × 57.6 microseconds = 576 bits.

The 576 bits includes the Ethernet/IEEE 802.3 preamble, which is 64 bits long; therefore, the minimum Ethernet/IEEE 802.3 frame size is 576 – 64 = 512 bits (64 bytes). In Fast Ethernet, the MAC layer is the same as for Ethernet. This means that the Ethernet frame format and size is the same for these versions of Ethernet. The minimum Ethernet frame size for Fast Ethernet is also 64 bytes. A collision must be detected while transmitting the preamble and the minimum frame size (576 bits). Since Fast Ethernet transmits data 10 times more quickly than Ethernet, 576 bits will be transmitted in 5.76 microseconds, instead of the 57.6 microseconds for Ethernet. The network diameter must therefore be 10 times smaller to detect a collision with a station transmitting from the farthest end of the network. That is, Fast Ethernet's diameter is 2500 ÷ 10 = 250 meters.

In general, if the data transfer rate is *R* Mbps for a CSMA/CD network, the network diameter (*D*) for maintaining compatibility with the Ethernet frame format and size is

$$D = 25000 \div R \text{ meters}$$

For a 10 Mbps CSMA/CD Ethernet, the diameter is 25000 ÷ 10 = 2500 meters.

For a 100 Mbps CSMA/CD Fast Ethernet, the diameter is 25000 ÷ 100 = 250 meters.

For a 500 Mbps CSMA/CD (hypothetical) Ethernet, the diameter would be 25000 ÷ 500 = 50 meters.

An AT&T study done in the late 1980s showed that the majority (greater than 90 percent) of the networks have desktops that are within 100 meters of the local wiring closet. This is within the 250 meter maximum diameter of Fast Ethernet.

Fast Ethernet supports a variety of different types of physical media. One such physical layer specification is the 100 BASE-TX proposal from Grand Junction Networks, Inc., an early player in the Fast Ethernet specification. The 100 BASE-TX proposal uses two pairs for Category 5 *UTP (Unshielded Twisted Pair)*, IBM Type 1 (two pairs of shielded twisted pair data grade), and optical fiber support. The 100 BASE-TX uses the ANSI Twisted Pair X3T9.5 *Physical Media Dependent (PMD)* layer. The ANSI TP-X3T9.5 PMD was endorsed in 1992 as technology for reliably and economically transmitting a 100-Mbps signal over twisted pair wiring for *CDDI (Copper Distributed Data Interface)*. CDDI is the twisted pair version of *FDDI (Fiber Distributed Data Interface)*. Figure 3.36 shows the relationship between Fast Ethernet MAC and the ANSI X3T9.5 PMD layer. The 100 BASE-TX combines the Ethernet MAC layer with the ANSI X3T9.5 PMD standard. The ANSI X3T9.5 supports Category 5 UTP, IBM Type 1, and optical fiber cabling.

Figure 3.36 Relationship between Fast Ethernet, 100 BASE-X, and ANSI X3T9.5 PMD.

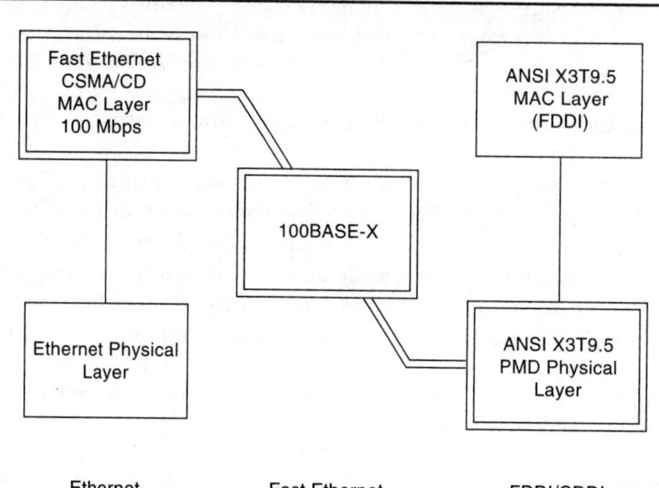

The TP-PMD uses stream cipher scrambling for security, and MLT-3 bit encoding. 100 BASE-TX can also use the FDDI Fiber PMD that uses the 62.5/25 micron fiber multimode cable. The Fiber PMD is unscrambled and uses 4B/5B encoding and *NRZI (Non Return to Zero Inverted)* signaling. The 4B/5B uses four out of five bits for data symbols. This results in 16 data symbols and 16 control symbol bit patterns. The bit patterns for the data symbols are such that long strings of 0s and 1s are avoided. This enables the use of NRZI signaling, which cannot encode clocking information if a long string of 0s and 1s is used. To use FDDI's Fiber PMD, the 100 BASE-TX specifies the use of a special convergence sublayer (see fig. 3.37). The *convergence sublayer* translates continuous signaling of the Fiber PMD to the start-stop, half duplex signaling expected by the Ethernet MAC.

The 100 BASE-TX supports unshielded twisted pair wiring consisting of two pairs of Category 5 UTP. The 10 BASE-T specification is designed to use two pairs of Category 3 UTP (voice grade UTP). For those sites that need to use Fast Ethernet and only have Category 3 UTP, but do not want to upgrade their cabling to Category 5 UTP, an alternate proposal called the "4T+" has been specified by the Fast Ethernet Alliance. The 4T+ uses four pairs of Category 3 UTP. The workstation-to-repeater hub distance is 100 meters for 4T+ signaling, but hub-to-hub distance is 10 meters. This type of network is called 100BASE-T4.

The 4T+ is a new encoding method that uses an eight binary/six ternary (8B/6T) code set. It is similar to the MLT-3 signaling used with Category 5 UTP, but has a limited bandwidth of 30 MHz. Figure 3.38 shows how the four pairs of Category 3 UTP are used. Pair 1 is used for collision indication and pairs 2, 3, and 4 are used for carrying data.

Figure 3.37 Convergence sublayer for Fiber PMD in 100BASE-TX.

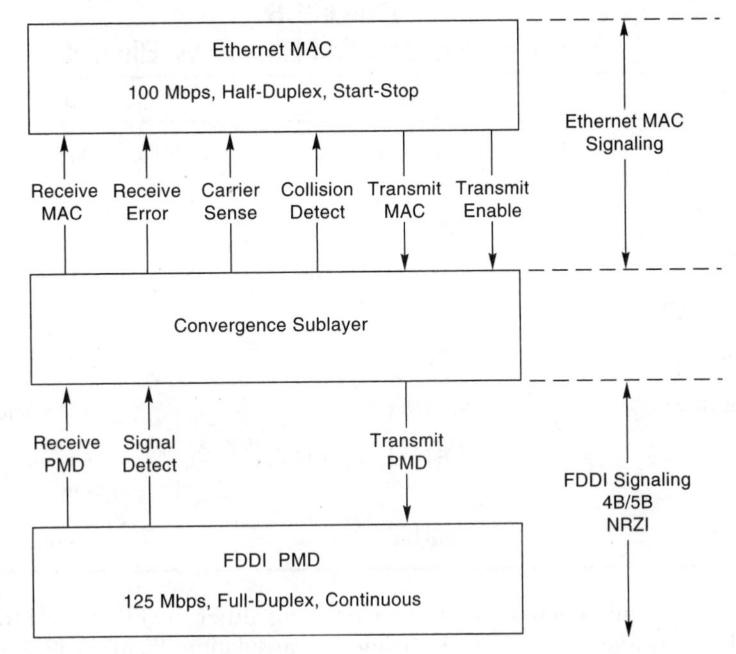

Figure 3.38 4T+ Twisted Pair Usage.

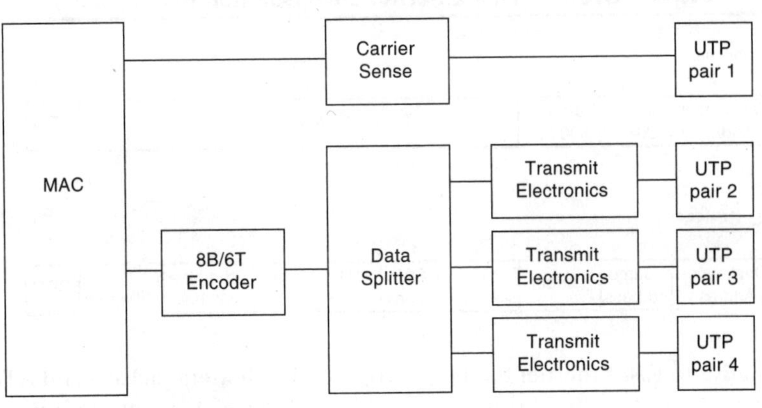

Another variation of the Fast Ethernet is the use of fiber optic cable for transmission. This type of standard is called 100BASE-TF.

The parameter values used by Fast Ethernet are shown in table 3.6.

TABLE 3.6
Parameter values for Fast Ethernet vs. Ethernet

Parameter	Ethernet	Fast Ethernet
slotTime	512 bit-times	512 bit-times
interFrameGap	9.60 microseconds	960 nanoseconds
attemptLimit	16	16
backoffLimit	10	10
jamSize	32 bits	32 bits
maxFrameSize	1518 octets	1518 octets
minFrameSize	64 octets (512 bits)	64 octets (512 bits)
addressSize	48 bits	48 bits

TCP/IP packets can be sent on Fast Ethernet using either the Ethernet II frame encapsulation or the LLC with SNAP header encapsulation. Figure 3.39 shows both methods.

Figure 3.39 Fast Ethernet encapsulation of TCP/IP.

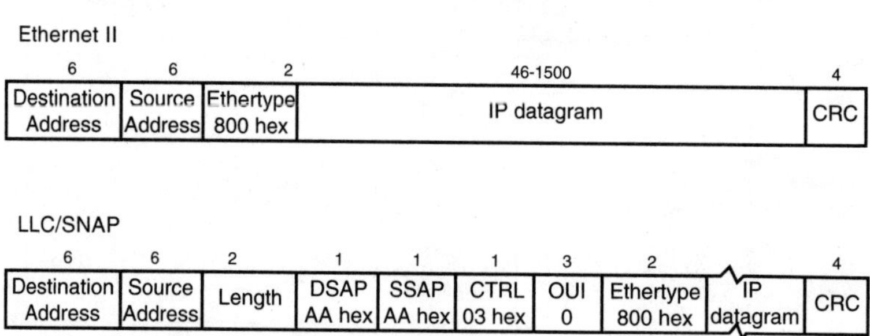

An alternative to Fast Ethernet has been proposed by Hewlett-Packard and AT&T. This scheme uses a Demand Priority Access Method in which a network hub device controls access to the network based on a priority scheme. Because this scheme uses a different access method than CSMA/CD, it cannot be classified as an "Ethernet" scheme even though it retains the frame format structure of Ethernet. This scheme is the subject of study by the IEEE 802.12 committee.

The HP and AT&T proposal (IEEE 802.12) uses four pairs of Category 3 UTP. This Demand Based Priority Access method is called 100BASE-VG because it uses a the voice grade Category 3 UTP. It can also be configured to use Shielded Twisted Pair (STP), Category 5 UTP, and fiber optic cables.

Figure 3.40 summarizes the wiring approaches used by the Fast Ethernet and the IEEE 802.12.

Figure 3.40 UTP type used for Fast Ethernet and IEEE 802.12.

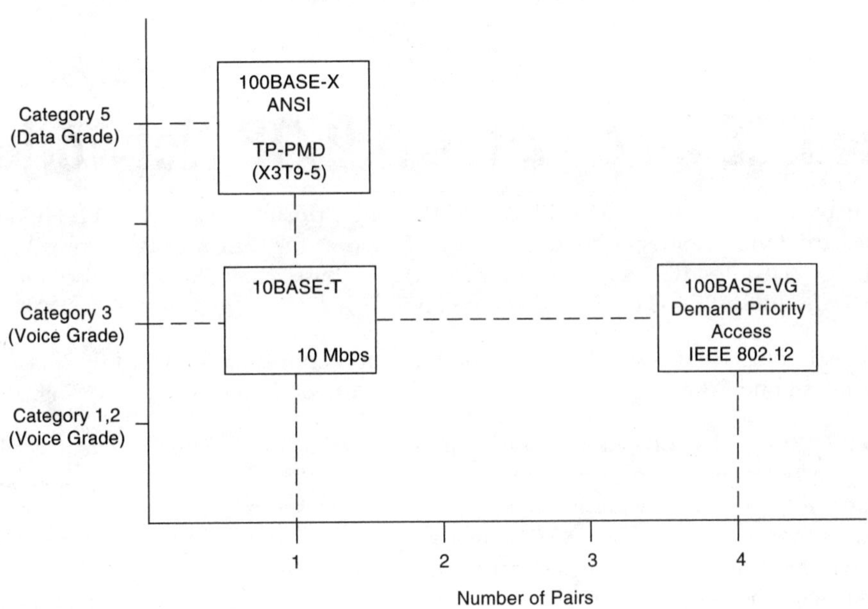

The Politics of Numbering: IEEE 802.13, IEEE 802.14, IEEE 802.30, or IEEE 802.3?

This may be a strange section in a book of this nature but it is necessary to understood why the Fast Ethernet proposal has been at different times called the IEEE 802.14 and the IEEE 802.30.

The Fast Ethernet was initially considered as part of the IEEE 802.3 specification. The chairman of the IEEE 802.3 committee felt that the use of TP-PMD (Twisted

Pair - Physical Media Dependency) warranted sufficient changes to the MAC layer that a new working group was needed. The next number after IEEE 802.12 would have been IEEE 802.13. It was felt that the number "13" in the IEEE 802.13 designation would place the Fast Ethernet proposal at a disadvantage because 13 is considered to be "unlucky" in western culture. Consequently the number designation of IEEE 802.14 was used for Fast Ethernet. This number designation was later changed to IEEE 802.30. The chair of the IEEE 802 committee said that allowing the Fast Ethernet to remain in the IEEE 802.3 committee would give the Fast Ethernet proponents an unfair advantage over the IEEE 802.12 proposal. At the next meeting of the IEEE 802 working group in 1993, the chair resigned to head the IEEE 802.12 group. The new chairman brought the IEEE 802.30 group back under the aegis of the IEEE 802.3 group where it had originally begun.

The IEEE 802.12 for TCP/IP Networks

The primary sponsor of the IEEE 802.12 Demand Priority access method is Hewlett-Packard. Other vendors who have expressed support for IEEE 802.12 include AT&T Microelectronics, IBM, Proteon, and Ungermann-Bass. This standard is also referred to as the 100BASE-VG or the 100VG-AnyLAN.

The advantage of this standard is that it performs better than the Fast Ethernet Standard under heavy loads. It also prermits the use of Category 3 UTP wiring.

In the IEEE 802.12 proposal, networks are designed around a central repeater called the *root* repeater. The root repeater polls its ports in the *port order* to determine if a station or another repeater hub attached at the port is waiting to transmit. Figure 3.41 shows an example of a IEEE 802.12 network. The root repeater polls its port number 1, then port number 2, then port number 3. At port number 3, another repeater is attached. This is called a Level 2 repeater, to distinguish it from the Level 1 repeater, which is the root repeater. Polling port number 3 of the root repeater results in the Level 2 repeater polling its ports in the port order. If the Level 2 repeater has eight ports, the polling action will continue as 3-1, 3-2, 3-3, 3-4, 3-5, 3-6, 3-7, 3-8. After the Level 2 repeater connected to port 3 finishes its polling, the polling action will be transferred back to the root repeater, which will continue polling its port 4, port 5, and so on. In figure 3.41, there is another Level 2 repeater attached to port 8 of the root repeater. After polling port 7 of the root repeater, the polling action will continue to the Level 2 repeater attached to port 8 of the root repeater. This will result in the following ports being polled in the order specified: 8-1, 8-2, 8-3, 8-4, 8-5, 8-6, 8-7, 8-8. After this the polling action will revert to the root repeater, which will repeat the pooling starting from its port 1.

Figure 3.41 IEEE 802.12 Polling Scheme.

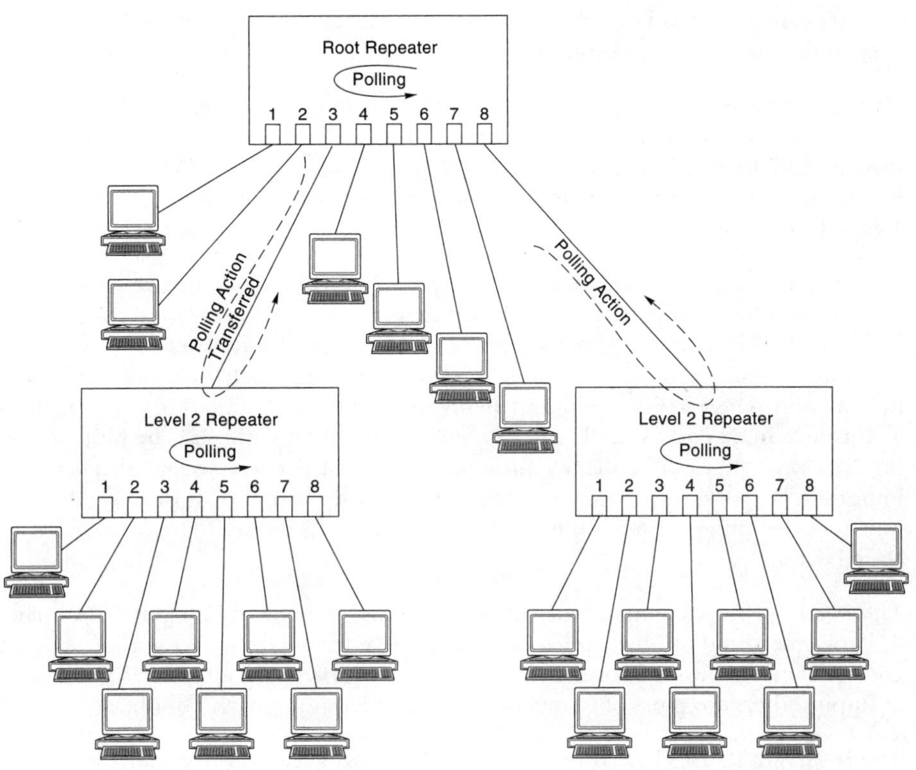

In the diagram in figure 3.41 only two levels of repeaters are shown. IEEE 802.12 permits the cascading of up to three levels of repeater hubs. The distance between a workstation and a repeater hub can be a maximum of 100 meters. An IEEE 802.12 based network can span a maximum distance of 4000 feet.

Because of the polling action of IEEE 802.12, the time an application has to wait for gaining access to the network can be predicted with precision. This is of great importance in real-time applications. To further support applications that may need immediate access to the network, a priority scheme is introduced. In this priority scheme, requests for transmission can be classified as high priority requests or normal priority requests. High priority requests are serviced before normal priority requests. Multiple levels of priority are proposed to support real time traffic.

With any priority based scheme, it is possible for low priority stations to be denied access for long periods of time. To ensure fairness, normal priority requests that are waiting for more than 250 milliseconds are given a boost in priority so that they can be satisfied. Additionally, no station is permitted to transmit twice in a row if another station has a request pending at the same level. At the root repeater, a high priority request cannot preempt a lower priority request that is in progress. However, at lower level repeaters such as Level 2 and Level 3 repeaters, a high priority request can preempt a lower priority request even if the lower priority request is in progress.

The 802.12 standard can use either an Ethernet frame or a Token Ring frame format. In its current form the 802.12 proposal requires all hubs in a priority domain to support either the Ethernet or Token Ring format, but not both. An extension to the 802.12 standard is being considered so that a hub can support both Ethernet and Token Ring frame types.

The encoding method used by 802.12 is a *quartet* signaling encoding scheme. This method uses four sequential code streams that are sent on four twisted pairs of a Category 3 UTP. The encoding that is used is the *NRZ (Non Return to Zero)* with 5B/6B encoding scheme. The NRZ encoding minimizes the signal changes needed to send information. The 5B/6B encoding scheme, uses five out of six bits for data symbols. This results in 32 data symbols and 32 control symbol bit patterns. The bit patterns in the data symbols are such that a continuous strings of 1s or 0s is avoided. This is important because, with NRZ encoding, a continuous strings of 1s or 0s would result in loss of clocking information needed by the receiving station to recover the encoded data.

The 802.12 proposal contains an option for using two pairs of Category 5, two pairs of STP, or one strand of fiber optic cable. With these wiring options, the four sequential code streams that would normally be sent over four pairs of Category 3 UTP are multiplexed on two pairs of Category 5 or STP, or a single strand of fiber.

The IEEE 802.12 uses LLC framing. TCP/IP packets are encapsulated in an LLC, plus a SNAP header as shown in figure 3.42. As required by SNAP, the DSAP and SSAP values for SNAP encapsulation are set to AA hex, and the OUI value is set to zero.

Figure 3.42 TCP/IP framing for IEEE 802.12.

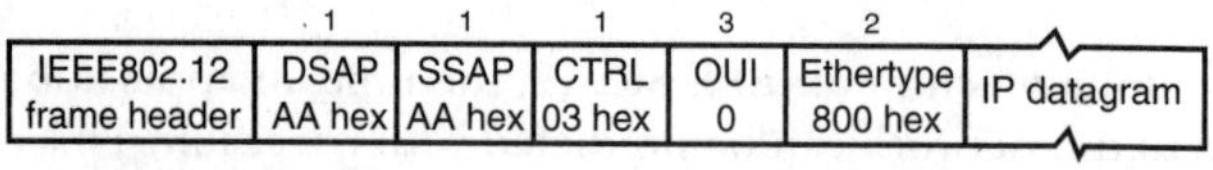

	1	1	1	3	2	
IEEE802.12 frame header	DSAP AA hex	SSAP AA hex	CTRL 03 hex	OUI 0	Ethertype 800 hex	IP datagram

Ethernet Switches

An interesting variation of Ethernet implementation is the Ethernet switching hubs. Ordinarily, Ethernet uses a media that is shared by all the attached devices that participate in the CSMA/CD arbitration mechanism. The maximum bandwidth on Ethernet is 10 Mbps. This bandwidth has to be shared by the devices that attach to the Ethernet LAN (see fig. 3.43). If this data bandwidth were to be divided equally among N attached devices, each device will have to be allocated a bandwidth of $10/N$ Mbps.

For $N = 1024$, which is the maximum devices on a single Ethernet LAN, the average bandwidth per attached device is 10 Kbps. In actual practice not all the N devices will be actively transmitting on the network. Even assuming 10 devices ($N = 10$) actively participating on the Ethernet LAN, the average bandwidth is 1 Mbps.

Figure 3.43 Ethernet bandwidth for shared media.

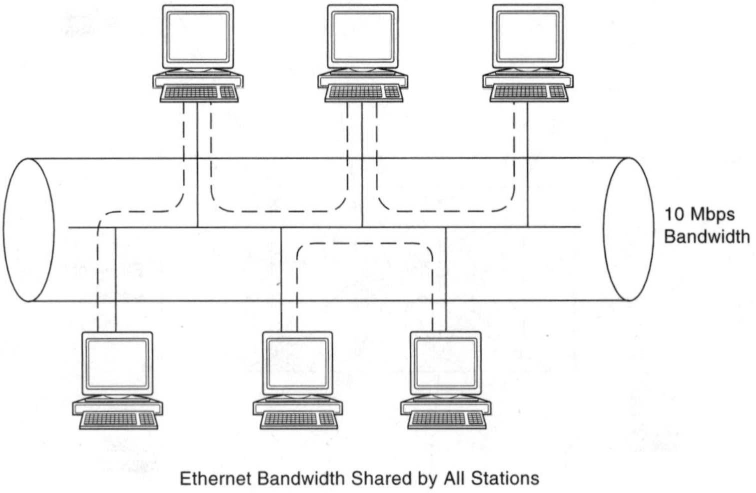

10 Mbps Bandwidth

Ethernet Bandwidth Shared by All Stations

To increase the bandwidth available for applications, some vendors make a special hub called the *Ethernet switch* (see fig. 3.44), where each port of the Ethernet switch is attached to a LAN that operates at 10 Mbps. Each port of the Ethernet switch stores the addresses of the devices attached to that port. It must, therefore, have sufficient memory associated with each port to store the addresses of all the nodes that can be attached to that node.

The Ethernet switch uses the addresses stored at each port to send a packet received on one port to the appropriate destination port. This action is called *switching*. The criterion that is used to perform the switching function is the destination address of the Ethernet frame. Each Ethernet segment attached to a port of the Ethernet switch forms a separate CSMA/CD collision domain. Collisions generated on one Ethernet segment are not transmitted to other Ethernet segments. In this regard, the Ethernet switch can be seen as a bridge. The aggregate capacity of a network that uses an Ethernet switch is multiplied by the number of ports on the Ethernet switch. If there are M ports in the Ethernet Switch, the formula for aggregate capacity is $10 \times M$ Mbps.

Thus for a 12-port Ethernet switch, the Ethernet switch must be able to switch data rates up to 120 Mbps.

Figure 3.44 Ethernet switch.

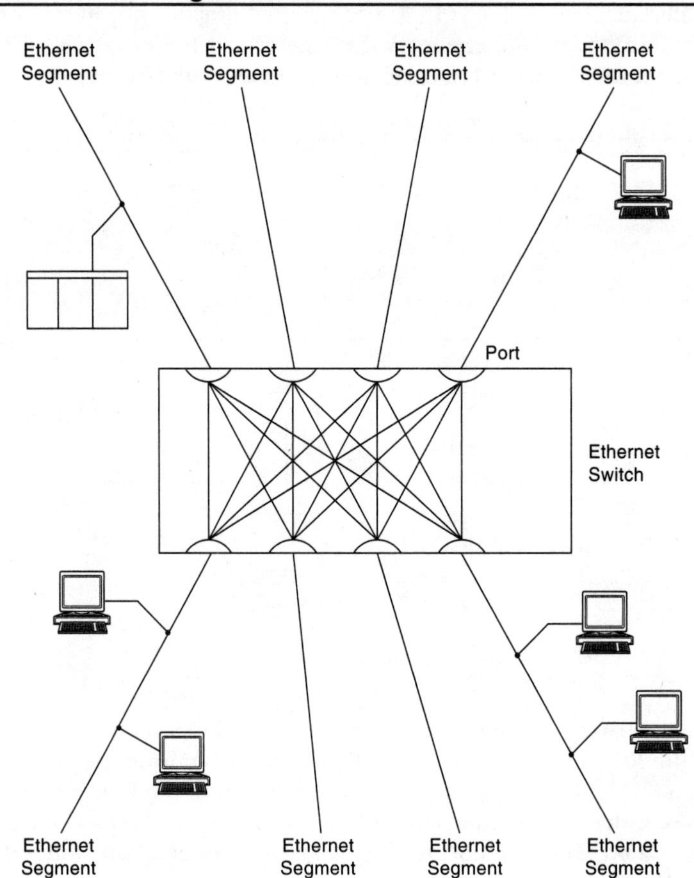

Some vendors offer a variety of switching options with their Ethernet switches. A few of the common ones are the following:

- Store and forward switching
- Fast forward switching
- Fragment free switching

In *store and forward switching* the entire packet is received at the port before a decision is made to switch the packet to its appropriate port. Receiving the entire packet allows the Ethernet switch to check the Ethernet packet for CRC errors. Packets with invalid CRCs are rejected. This mode, while the most reliable, has the highest latency of the switching modes because the entire packet has to be stored before being switched.

In *fast forward switching* a decision is made to switch the packet after receiving only the address header. This reduces the *latency* or the wait time for a packet, but can result in a packet with a bad CRC being sent to another port, since the CRC is not checked. This mode, while the fastest, is the least reliable of the switching modes. It is called the "Cut Through" mode by many vendors. Errors in the packet can still be detected by upper-layer protocol software running on Ethernet stations.

Fragment free switching represents a compromise between the store and forward switching and fast forward switching. In fragment free switching, the Ethernet switch examines the packet long enough to determine that it is at least 64 bytes long, which is the minimum packet size for Ethernet and the size of the Ethernet collision window. Packets that are smaller than 64 bytes are called *fragments* and can result from collisions on an Ethernet segment or a malfunctioning card at an Ethernet station. Another distinguishing characteristic of Ethernet switches is whether they allow only a single station or an entire segment to attach to the Ethernet switch port. By attaching Ethernet segments to a port on the Ethernet switch, you can relieve congestion at high-traffic locations on the network by providing a higher aggregate bandwidth than is possible with non-switched Ethernet hubs.

Because network traffic can be concentrated at the server, faster ports such as the 100 Mbps port are used for the server devices. An alternative solution is to install 20 Mbps Full Duplex Ethernet cards at the server. Ethernet operates in a half-duplex mode at 10 Mps. By attaching two ports to a single Ethernet card, each port having a separate link to the Ethernet switch, you can double the bandwidth of traffic between the server and the switch.

Some Ethernet switch products offer a *secure address mode* in which the station addresses associated with each port can be entered into a table. This prevents non-authorized users from using the Ethernet switch. In Ethernet switches where only a single station can attach to a port on the Ethernet switch, the port can be disabled if an unauthorized station is detected.

In many networks a major network bottleneck is the network traffic that is handled by the server. Consider an Ethernet switch that provides a 10 Mbps private channel for each station attached to its port, and where the server is attached to one of the Ethernet switch's ports. If M stations were to access the server simultaneously, the server would have to handle $10 \times M$ Mbps of data (see fig. 3.45). If there were ten stations that needed to access the server at 10 Mbps, the server would have to handle $10 \times 10 = 100$ Mbps of data. An ordinary Ethernet switch would not be able to provide a solution to this problem. What is needed here is an Ethernet switch that has dedicated ports that can handle 100 Mbps of data. Up to 12 simultaneous conversations can exist between the 10 Mbps private Ethernet channels and a 100 Mbps port. This yields an aggregate bandwidth of the following:

$$12 \times 10 + 1 \times 100 = 120 + 100 = 220 \text{ Mbps}$$

Figure 3.45 Traffic problem at server port for Ethernet switch.

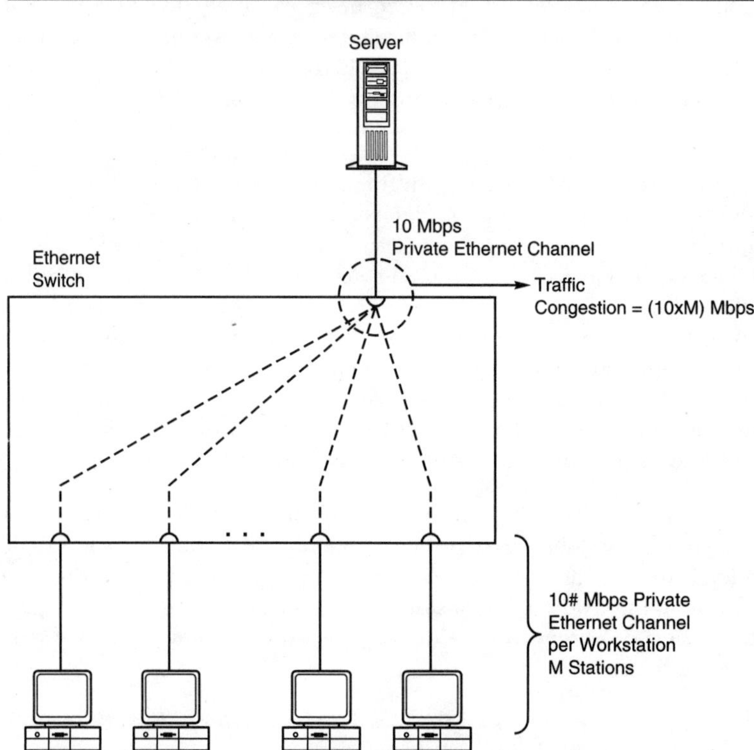

TCP/IP on Token Ring Networks

From table 3.1, you can see that there are two Token passing standards. The Token Ring LAN you encounter most often is the IEEE 802.5. This LAN is often referred to as the IBM Token Ring because IBM was the prime mover behind the IEEE 802.5 standard. The IEEE 802.5 is the Token Ring standard discussed in this section. The IEEE 802.4 also uses a token passing method, but this is implemented on a bus rather than on a ring.

Note This Token Bus method simulates Token Ring operation on a bus LAN and is seldom used in commercial networks. Token Bus networks were designed for the *Manufacturing Automation Protocol (MAP)*, which is now primarily a historical network. ARCnet, also a Token Bus network, has seen a decline in its use. For these reasons, Token Bus networks are not discussed in this chapter.

Operation of Token Ring LANs

Token Ring-based networks have been around for many years. Ring LANs are a concatenation of point-to-point links, and as such are not really broadcast LANs like Ethernet. They may be considered to be sequential broadcast LANs with the point-to-point links forming a circle. The technology of ring LANs is digital, unlike that of Ethernet LANs, where the carrier sense mechanism may be analog. An attractive feature of ring-based LANs is their deterministic response time, even under heavy load conditions. *Deterministic time* means that for a given Token Ring, you can predict the longest maximum delay a node on the ring will experience before it can send data. In contrast to this, Ethernet works are non-deterministic because you cannot predict the worst case maximum delay for obtaining access to the network.

Figure 3.46 illustrates Token Ring operation. The Token Ring LAN can be seen as a concatenation of point-to-point links. Each station acts like a repeater providing the necessary amplification and correcting for signal jitter. The links can be made up of any medium such as coaxial, twisted pair, and fiber optic. For the IBM Token Ring, twisted pair is the medium of choice. Fiber optic links can be used to extend Token Ring operation over longer distances.

Figure 3.46 Token Ring operation.

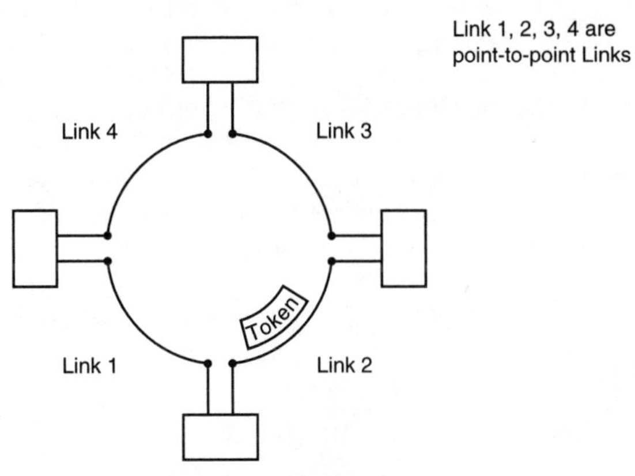

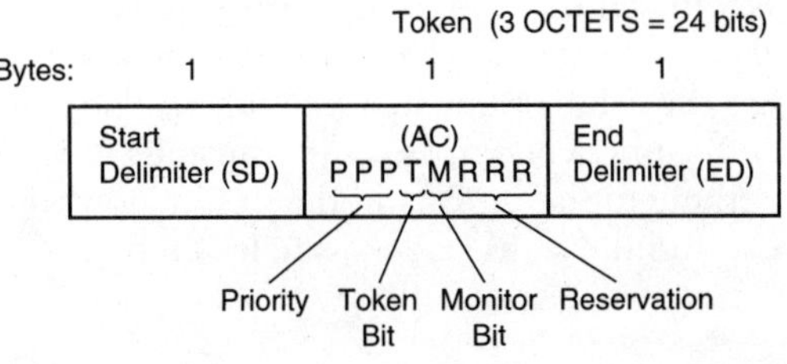

The *token* is a special frame used by stations to access the Token Ring network. Stations that want to send data wait for a token to go by. A bit in the Token frame indicates whether the token is in use. After a station acquires a token, it changes the token from a free to a busy token and sends its data. For proper operation of the ring, the token must circulate continuously even if there is no activity on the ring. There are 24 bits (three octets) in the token, and the ring must have enough latency or delay to hold 24 bits. If the bit rate on the ring is 4 Mbps, the ring must have a latency of 24 ÷ 4 Mbps = 6 microseconds. Six microseconds may seem like a very short delay, but consider a twisted pair medium where the propagation velocity is 0.59 times the speed of light. To compute the size of the ring that will have a latency of six microseconds, use the following formula:

Size of Ring = Latency × Propagation speed of media

= 0.0000006 × 0.59 × 3 × 100,000,000 meters

= 1062 meters

= 1.062 km

Thus the minimum size of the ring would be 1 km! This size is enormous, considering that you might want to install a few stations in a single room. For this reason, a special station designated as the Active Monitor adds a 24-bit delay buffer to the ring. This buffer also compensates for any accumulated phase jitter on the ring. The Active Monitor is important for maintaining normal operation of the ring.

Under normal operation of the ring, stations may be powered down. What happens to the bits that need to go across an inactive station? Token Ring networks are wired as star networks with a hub or wiring center. Each station's connection is controlled by a relay in the hub. In figure 3.47 the relays are held open by power from the station. When a station is powered down, the relay closes, bypassing the inactive station.

As illustrated in figure 3.48, a token ring station operates in one of four modes:

- Transmit mode
- Listen mode
- Bypass mode
- Receive mode

Figure 3.48 shows four stations operating in these modes. Station A is in the transmit mode. To enter this mode, it seizes a free token. The token has a token bit called the *T bit*. This T bit has the value of one in a free token. The transmitting station changes this T bit to a 0, indicating a busy token and transmits the data frame. Station A is sending this data frame to station D, and the destination address field will hold station D's address, and the source address field will hold A's address.

Figure 3.47 Token Ring relay bypass mechanism.

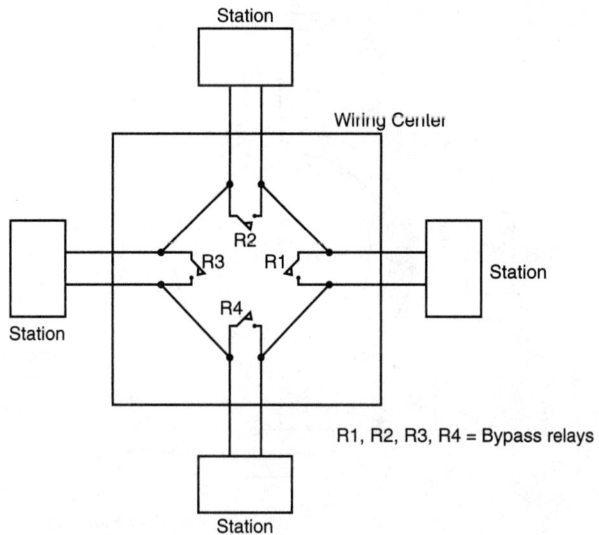

Station B is operating in the listen mode. It checks the destination address field of the frame to see if it holds its address (B's address). Because the frame is addressed to station D, it enters the listen mode. In the listen mode, a station copies the incoming bits to the output link.

Station C has been powered down and is therefore in the bypass mode. The bits flow through the bypass relay.

Station D examines the destination address field. It discovers that it is indeed the addressed station and, therefore, enters the receive mode. In the receive mode, the data frame is copied into the station's memory and also sent along the ring.

A number of flags called Frame Status flags are modified to indicate proper reception of the data frame. Station A receives the data frame that it sent and examines the Frame Status flags. The Frame Status flags serve the purpose of a hardware-based acknowledgment. The sending station can determine these flags and determine if the frame was received correctly. The Frame Status flags are the following:

- Address-recognized (A) flag
- Frame-copied (C) flag
- Error (E) flag

The E flag is computed and set by every station. The A and C flags are set by the destination station only. Table 3.7 defines these flags.

Figure 3.48 Token Ring station modes.

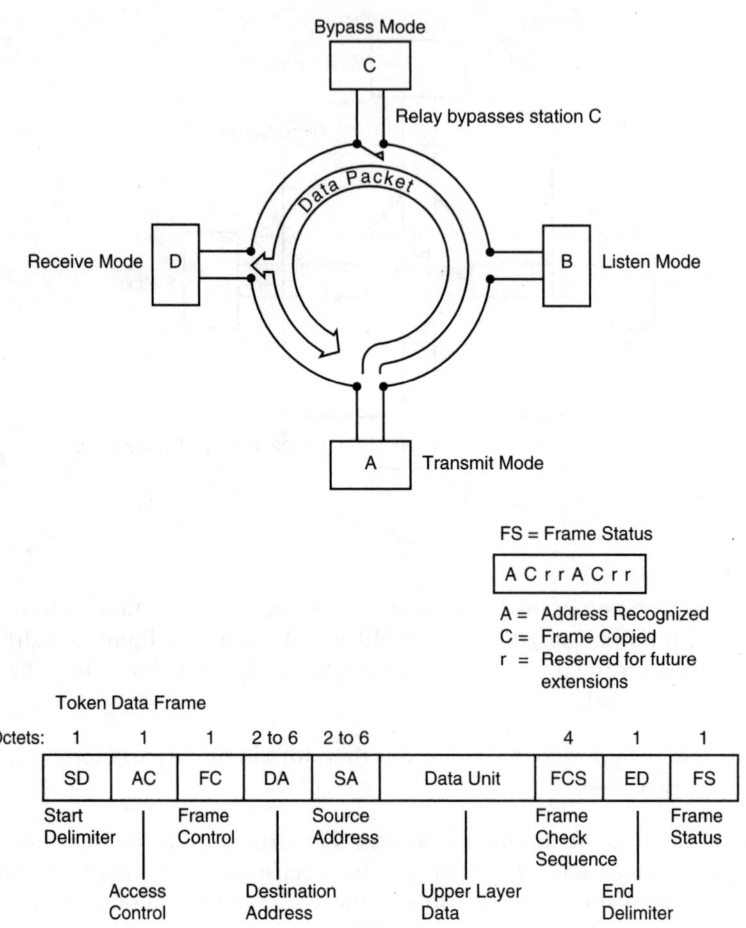

TABLE 3.7
Frame Status Flags

Frame Flags	Value	Meaning
A	1	Address recognized
A	0	Address not recognized
C	1	Frame copied successfully
C	0	Frame not copied

Frame Flags	Value	Meaning
E	1	Bad Frame (CRC error)
E	0	Good Frame

The legal combinations (that is, combinations that are possible) of these flags are as follows:

- AC = 00 implies that the address was not recognized and, therefore, the copy operation did not take place.
- AC = 10 implies that the station exists, but the frame was not copied. If E = 1, a bad frame was received. If the E flag is 0, then the frame was not copied for unknown reasons.
- AC = 11 implies that the station exists and the frame was copied to the station. If E = 1 and AC = 11, this indicates that the error was produced after the frame was copied.

The only illegal combination is AC = 01, which indicates that the station was not recognized, but a user still copied the frame. In other words, some station illegally copied the data frame. This is clearly an improper condition.

As the bits that were sent by station A come back to it, they are removed from the ring.

What if station A was powered down before the frame that it sent came back? Because it is the responsibility of the sending station to remove the frame that it sent, this frame would circulate endlessly. There are many similar scenarios that could disrupt the normal ring operation. What if the token was destroyed by noise on the ring? Would stations wait for the token indefinitely? The Token Ring operation contains self-healing mechanisms to correct for these and many other possibilities. These situations are detected and handled by special control frames called MAC frames and are one of the reasons why the IEEE 802.5 operation is more complex than that of IEEE 802.3. The following discussion describes just a few of these self-healing mechanisms.

Although all stations seem equal, some stations are more equal than others. One such station is called the *Active Monitor.* There is a *monitor bit (M-bit)* in the token that is set to 0 by the transmitting station. The Active Monitor examines this M-bit and changes it to a 1, if it is a 0. If the Active Monitor bit sees an M-bit value of 1, it concludes that this data frame has been circulating around once too often. This could be because of a crash of the transmitting station, which failed to remove the data frame from the ring.

If the token is lost because it got mangled by noise on the ring, the Active Monitor times out and generates a new token. The Active Monitor keeps track of this *Token Rotation Time (TRT)* and times out if it exceeds a threshold value. For small token ring networks, the typical value of TRT is eight microseconds. Under heavy load conditions this value may rise.

The Active Monitor is not a station with special networking hardware. Any station on the Token Ring can become an Active Monitor. All other stations act as Standby Monitors. The choice of which station becomes an Active Monitor is realized through a ring-initialization procedure. You may ask, what if the Active Monitor fails? In this case, one of the Standby Monitors becomes the Active Monitor.

When no data frames are circulating around the ring, the Active Monitor issues an Active Monitor Present (AMP) MAC frame. This frame is sent at regular intervals of usually seven seconds. Other stations in the role of Standby Monitors send Standby Monitor Present (SMP) MAC frames. Standby monitors detect the AMP frame and conclude that the Active Monitor is doing its job. If the Active monitor skips a beat—if it does not send out the AMP frame when it should—one of the Standby Monitors takes over the role of the Active Monitor. The Standby Monitor that detects the failure of the Active Monitor sends its claim on the Token Ring in the form of *Claim Token (CL_TK)* MAC frames. The Standby Monitor stops sending these frames if one of the following conditions occurs:

- **Another CL_TK frame is received and the sender's address is greater than this station's address.** If two or more stations send out CL_TK, the station with the higher address becomes the Active Monitor.
- **A Beacon (BCN) MAC frame is received.** This frame is sent as a result of a major ring failure such as a ring break. The BCN frame is used to locate and isolate the fault. In this case, the ring needs to be healed before deciding the winner of this contest.
- **A Purge (PRG) MAC frame is received.** This frame is sent out at the end of the Claim Token procedure by the station that has become the new Active Monitor. This means that the race has already been won by another station, and so there is no point in continuing.

In any of the preceding cases, the Standby Monitor backs off. If a station receives the CL_TK frame it generated, it becomes the Active Monitor (new king of the hill!) and issues an RG MAC frame to inform other stations that there is a new Active Monitor. At this point, the new Active Monitor adds the 24-bit latency buffer to the ring and commences monitoring the network.

Before joining a ring, a new station sends out the *Duplicate Address Test (DAT)* MAC frame as part of the ring initialization procedure. The DAT frame is sent with its own address in the DA field. If another station responds with the AC bits set to 11, then another station has the same address. The new station returns an appropriate status code. Network monitoring software can detect this code and process it with an appropriate error message.

Another feature of the IEEE 802.5 is the priority access mechanism. The token has two fields:

- The Priority field
- The Reservation field

Each field consists of three bits. A total of eight priorities values can be defined (0 to 7). The Reservation field is set to 0 by the transmitting station. If a station wants priority access, it can place its priority value in the Reservation field. After the transmitting station receives the frame it sent, it copies the Reservation field value in the Priority field of the new token that it generates. The token now has the requested Priority value. Only stations with higher or equal priority can access this token.

Token Ring Options

The IEEE 802.5 specifies Token Ring implementation options (see fig. 3.49) at data rates of 1 Mbps, 4 Mbps, and 16 Mbps. The 1 Mbps uses UTP wiring. Initially the 4 Mbps and 16 Mbps used STP wiring. A demand within the industry is to have the 4 Mbps and 16 Mbps run on UTP wiring. Several products are available to support UTP wiring for 4 and 16 Mbps Token Rings. For a long time, a 16 Mbps UTP version was not available from IBM. IBM has teamed with Synoptics Communications to propose a 16 Mbps UTP standard to the IEEE 802.5 committee.

Figure 3.49 IEEE 802.5 options for Token Ring.

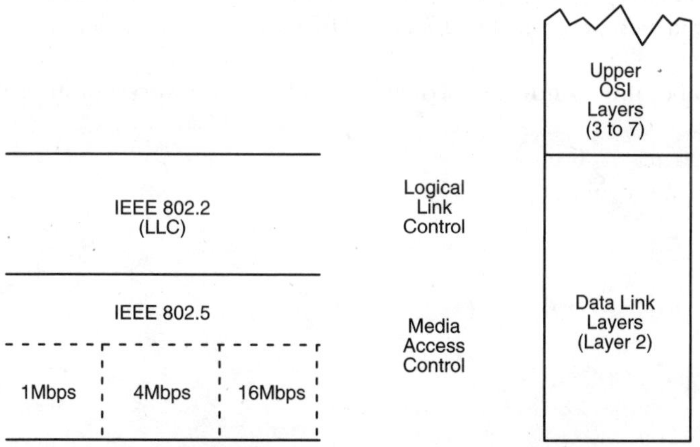

The 16 Mbps stations do not wait for the return of the data frame to place the token on the network, which is called the *early token release mechanism.* This mechanism allows up to two data frames to be transmitted on a Token Ring LAN at a time.

Token Ring LAN Components

The Token Ring network board has a 9-pin socket when Shielded Twisted Pair wiring is used. You might also have the option of using Type 3 Unshielded Twisted Pair cabling with RJ-45 connectors.

The *Multistation Access Unit,* also called *MAU*—not to be confused with the *Media Attached Unit (MAU)* in IEEE 802.3—is a wiring center that allows up to eight stations to be connected to it. The two end ports, called *Ring In (RI)* and *Ring Out (RO),* are not used to connect Token Ring stations. These are used to connect multiple MAUs together. Four port wiring centers (also called hubs) also are available. MAUs also are available that contain a number of network management features. These are called smart or intelligent MAUs.

The MAU Setup Aid device is used to test each port by checking the operation of the bypass relay mechanism for each port.

The IBM Token Ring network adapter cable is made of eight feet of IBM Type 1 cable. Type 6 cable also can be used, although these are recommended as patch cables between wiring centers. One end of this cable connects to the Token Ring adapter and the other end is a dual-gender connector that plugs into one of the station ports in the IBM 8228 MAU.

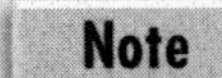

While the IBM Type 3 cable is the same as the Category 3 UTP cabling discussed in this book, Type 1, Type 2, Type 6, and Type 9 are IBM cable type designations, and must not be confused with the UTP category type classifications.

The method of interconnecting Token Ring MAUs and workstations is illustrated in figure 3.50.

Figure 3.50 Token Ring network cabling components.

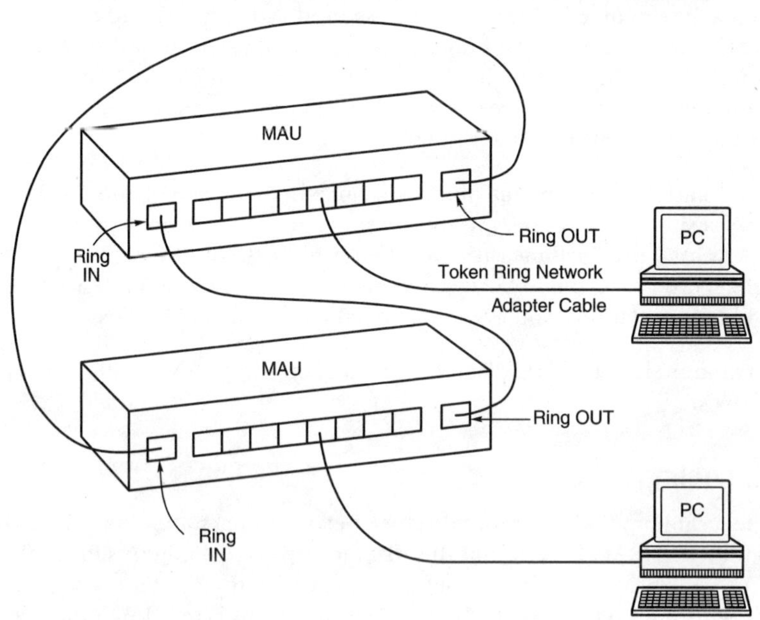

IEEE 802.5 Design Rules

Table 3.8 summarizes the rules for Token Ring wiring.

TABLE 3.8
Token Ring Wiring Rules

Token Ring Parameters	Type 1, 2	Type 3
Maximum devices per ring	260	96
Tested data rates	16 Mbps	4 Mbps
Station to single MAU LAN	300 meters	100 meters
Station to multiple MAU LAN	100 meters	45 meters
Maximum MAUs per LAN	12	2
MAU to MAU distance	200 meters	120 meters

The following sections discuss these rules in detail.

Type 1, 2 Cabling

Although a maximum of 260 stations can be used with Types 1 and 2 cables, a more reasonable number is 100. The limit on the maximum stations is due to accumulated clock jitter. Interestingly enough, if you use the MAU, which has a maximum of eight ports, you only use 12 MAVs (see table 2.7 in Chapter 2); you have a maximum of 8 × 12 = 96 stations on the Token Ring.

For Type 1 and 2 cables, the maximum distance between workstation to MAU is 300 meters for a single MAU LAN, but this distance drops to 100 meters for multiple MAU LANs. As a practical measure, it is better to work with the tighter constraint of 100 meters, even for a single MAU LAN, because LANs have a tendency to grow and, as you add more stations, you eventually need a multiple MAU LAN.

The maximum MAU to MAU distance for a Token Ring LAN is 200 meters for Type 1 and 2 cables.

Type 3 Cabling

For Type 3 cabling, the maximum distance between workstation to MAU is 100 meters for a single MAU LAN, but this distance drops to 45 meters for multiple MAU LANs. As a practical measure, it is better to work with the tighter constraint of 45 meters even for a single MAU LAN. The reason for this is that LANs have a tendency to grow, and as we add more stations, we would eventually need a multiple MAU LAN.

The maximum MAU to MAU distance for a Token Ring LAN is 120 meters for Type 3 cabling.

Guidelines for Token Ring Cabling

There are general guidelines for Token Ring cabling. These rules are as follows:

1. Stations located within eight feet of the MAU can be connected by using eight-foot adapter cables.
2. Stations farther than eight feet from the MAU can be connected by using extension cords (or you can build longer adapter cables).
3. To form a ring by using multiple MAUs, connect a patch cable from the RO of the first MAU to the RI of the second MAU. Continue doing this for all the MAUs until you reach the last MAU. Connect the RO of the last MAU to the RI of the first MAU.
4. You cannot connect stations to the RI and the RO ports. The RI and RO ports are only used for interconnecting multiple MAUs.
5. Patch cables (IBM Type 6) should not be spliced.

6. Patch cables (IBM Type 6) should not be used in any duct, plenum, or other space used for air handling. IBM Type 9, which is a plenum-rated cable, can be used instead.

Token Ring Troubleshooting Considerations on TCP/IP Networks

For the Token Ring to work correctly, the physical token loop must be maintained. Any problem that would disrupt the flow of data on the physical wire will cause the token ring to malfunction. Also, because the data flows through each workstation (each station acts as a repeater), a malfunctioning workstation can cause the entire ring to fail. For these reasons, troubleshooting token ring networks can be challenging.

Most modern Token Ring networks, especially those from IBM, contain built-in hardware diagnostics that can rapidly detect cable faults and isolate problem nodes on the network. Additionally, network management software is available from vendors for troubleshooting Token Ring networks.

The Size of the Token Ring

Token Ring networks using STP cabling such as the IBM Type 1 and Type 2 cables have a limit as to the maximum number of stations that can be placed in a single physical ring. This limit is 260 stations for the IBM Token Ring using STP cables. Adding workstations above this limit causes clock jitter problems that make the ring fail. To have a useful ring, the minimum number of physical stations is 2. The actual number of stations on a ring is a number between the limits of 2 and 260.

An important consideration when determining the number of stations is to keep a physical ring large enough to provide useful work but small enough to make troubleshooting easier. In a smaller ring, it is much easier to physically isolate the offending station or isolate the problem in the ring.

One way to keep a ring to a reasonable size to facilitate troubleshooting is to use Token Ring bridges, as illustrated in figure 3.51. *Bridges* are devices that allow physical rings to be separate in terms of MAC Layer operation. For instance, in figure 3.51, two rings are joined by a bridge. Each ring has its own token, which is used to implement the MAC mechanism. The token is restricted to the physical ring on which it operates. Using this approach, it is possible to construct complex ring networks, in which each ring operates independently of the others but can still communicate to other stations in other rings through the bridges. The bridges participate in the MAC mechanism of the rings they are connected to.

Figure 3.51 Separate token mechanism of rings connect with a bridge.

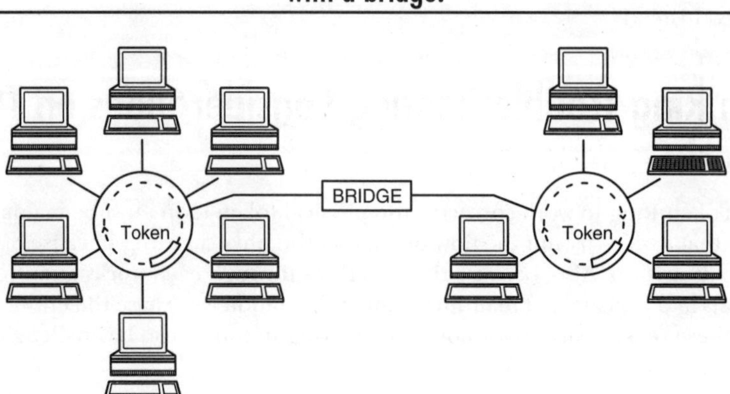

Built-In Diagnostics for Token Ring Networks

The IEEE 802.5 specification for the Token Ring specifies built-in diagnostics that are used by workstations to isolate problems with the Token Ring. Many of these diagnostics refer to the concept of a fault domain or failure domain.

The *fault domain* is a section of the ring (fig. 3.52) that consists of the following three components:

- ◆ The station transmitting the BCN Frame
- ◆ The beaconing station's Nearest Active Upstream Neighbor (NAUN)
- ◆ The cable between the beaconing station and its NAUN

Because the data flow in a ring is unidirectional, every station has a neighbor that is upstream with respect to its position in the ring. This *upstream neighbor* is the station from which the data frame is received and is called the NAUN. The use of the word *Active* implies that the NAUN may not be the nearest physical upstream neighbor because the physically closest neighbor may not be participating in the ring. The NAUN for each station is set in the Neighbor Notification process activated by the Active Monitor.

When a station discovers a *hard error,* caused by hardware malfunction, it sends a beacon MAC frame that contains its NIC address, the NAUN, and the *beacon type,* which indicates additional information about the nature of the fault. The contents of the beacon frame essentially define the fault domain. The beacon type is helpful in diagnosing the cause of the error. An example of a beacon type is a cable fault. The beacon frame is broadcast to all stations. All other stations enter the Beacon Repeat mode in which they copy and repeat the frame around the ring. The beacon frame is generated repeatedly by the station that detects the hard error. After the NAUN copies the beacon frame eight times, it removes itself from the ring and conducts a series of self-tests such as the DAT and the Lobe Media Test. In the Lobe Media test, the NIC transmits a Lobe Test MAC frame to the MAU port to test if it receives the frame correctly. If it receives the frame incorrectly, the *lobe* (cable between the NIC and the MAU port) is suspect.

Figure 3.52 Token Ring fault domain.

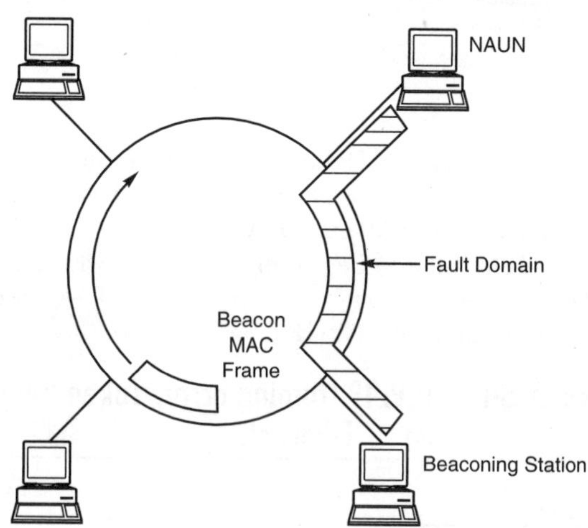

If the NAUN station fails, it removes itself from the ring. Because the NAUN, which was the cause of the problem, is off the ring, the beaconing station will receive the BCN frames it sends. At this point, the station stops beaconing and retransmits the token frame onto the ring. The ring has now auto-recovered.

If the NAUN station passes its self-test, it reinserts itself in the ring. After a certain time, the beaconing station assumes that the NAUN has passed the self-test. The problem could then be with the beaconing station. Therefore, the beaconing station goes through the same series of self-tests. If the beaconing station fails its tests, it will remove itself from the ring. The Active Monitor will then initiate a Ring Recovery by issuing a Ring Purge control frame followed by a Claim Token control frame. If the beaconing station passes its test, it will reinsert itself in the ring. If the beaconing condition persists, the problem requires manual troubleshooting. The problem is most likely caused by the cabling media (including the MAU) between the beaconing station and its NAUN.

TCP/IP Framing in IEEE 802.5 Networks

The IEEE 802.5 standard uses the Logical Link Control (LLC) framing to encapsulate upper layer protocol data. For sending TCP/IP data the SNAP header extension is used (see fig. 3.53).

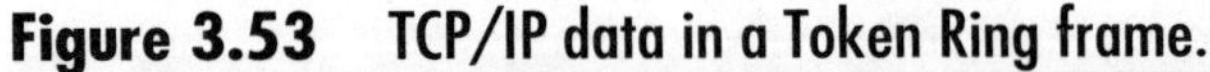

Figure 3.53 TCP/IP data in a Token Ring frame.

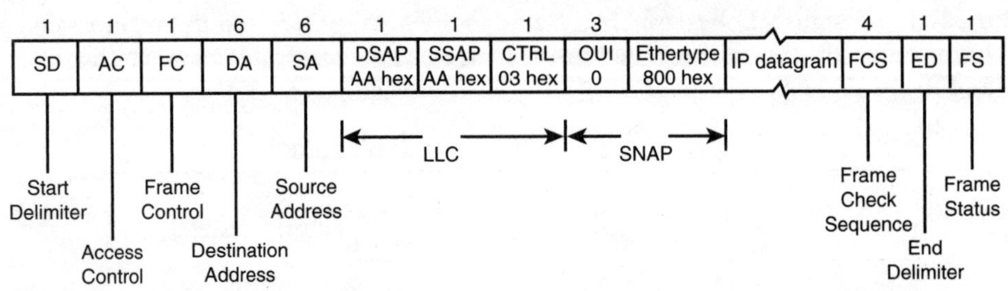

The Ethertype field value in the SNAP header is set to a value of 800 hexadecimal. This is the standard value assigned for encapsulating TCP/IP data in Ethernet frames. Using the SNAP header whose LSAP and DSAP values are set to AA hexadecimal enables the Ethertype field value to be preserved in cases where Ethernet and Token Ring networks are connected. This can be seen in figure 3.54, which shows the Token Ring and Ethernet frame carrying TCP/IP data.

Figure 3.54 TCP/IP framing across Token Ring and Ethernet.

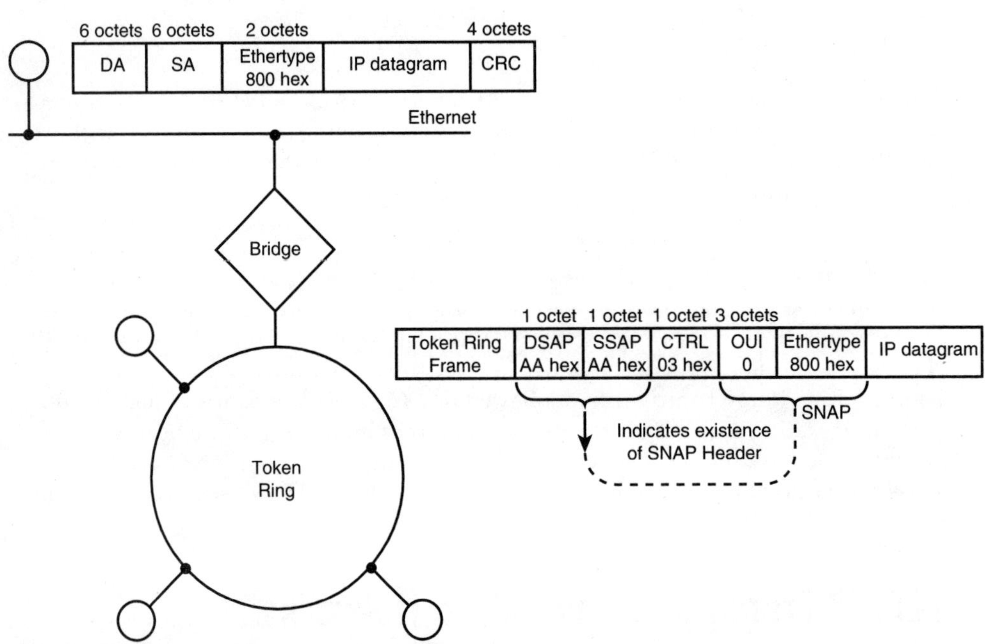

TCP/IP on FDDI Networks

Fiber Distributed Data Interface (FDDI) is regarded as a high speed LAN (100 Mbps). Because it can span a distance of 100 kilometers, FDDI has some of the properties of a WAN, as far as its ability to interconnect LANs. FDDI spans layers 2 and 1 of the OSI model and can be used to provide IEEE 802.2 or LLC services to upper layers (see fig. 3.55). FDDI can be used to run client/server applications that rely on IEEE 802.2 services, including NetWare, which provides IEEE 802.2 encapsulation. The FDDI physical station address follows the IEEE 48-bit (6 octet) addressing convention.

Figure 3.55 FDDI spans layers 1 and 2 of the OSI model.

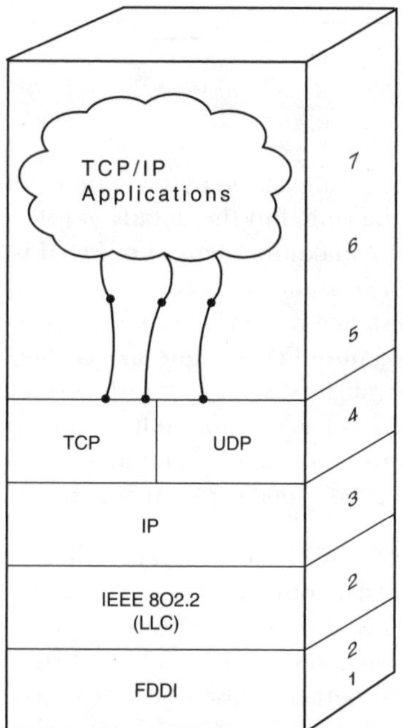

FDDI Operation

A full FDDI configuration consists of two fiber rings. The primary ring is used for data transfer, and the secondary ring serves as a backup ring, in case the primary ring fails. If the primary ring fails, an auto-sense mechanism causes a ring wrap so that traffic is diverted to the secondary ring (see fig. 3.56). Only stations that have a dual-attachment (are connected to primary and secondary rings) tolerate this type of failure.

Figure 3.56 FDDI ring with dual and single attachments.

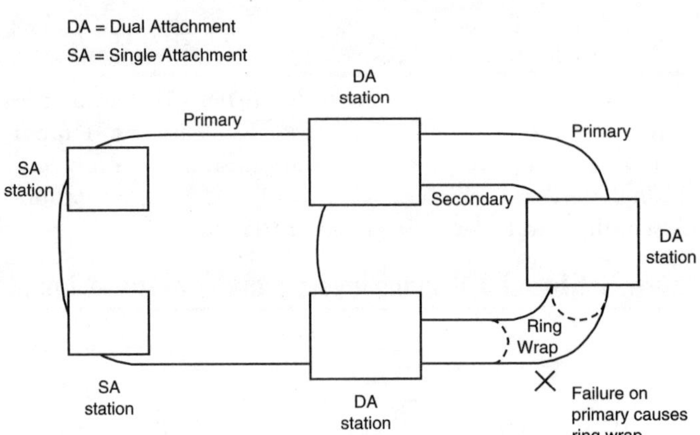

FDDI is based on the Token Ring access method that runs at 100 Mbps. A token is used to control access to the ring, but the details of token management are different from IEEE 802.5 LANs. The maximum length of FDDI is 200 kilometers (100 kilometers for dual rings), and the distance between two nodes on a FDDI LAN cannot exceed two kilometers. Distance parameters are based on a maximum latency (delay) of 1.617 milliseconds. Maximum FDDI frame size is 4500 bytes. This size makes it suited for high-speed file transfers, such as transfers of graphic, image, and other data files. Because the frame size is larger, more data can be packed into the frame and fewer packets are needed to send the file. The total number of connections to an FDDI ring cannot exceed 2000 (1000 for dual-attached stations).

The FDDI network expects that PC workstations will not be attached directly to it, but attached by means of an FDDI concentrator or router (see fig. 3.57). If nodes are connected directly to the FDDI ring, their powering on and off causes frequent ring reconfigurations that may become costly in a large FDDI network. PC workstations connected directly to FDDI networks also may not keep up with the high data rates in FDDI.

The FDDI concentrators, also called *Multi Access Station Units (MAUs),* serve as a fan-out box so that multiple stations can be connected. Several FDDI concentrators can be cascaded to increase the fan-out. Although the FDDI concentrator has a dual attachment, the stations attached to the concentrator have a single attachment to save on FDDI NIC costs. FDDI concentrators should be powered on all the time to reduce ring reconfigurations.

FDDI token management enables several FDDI frames to be resident on the ring at a time, which better utilizes the data bandwidth on the ring.

Figure 3.57 FDDI network with router.

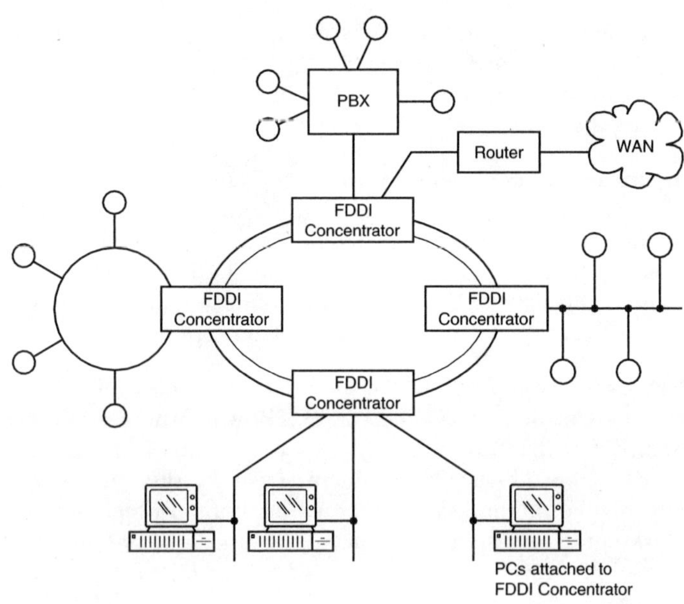

The FDDI ring operates in two modes:

- Synchronous
- Asynchronous

In *synchronous mode*, stations are guaranteed a percentage of total bandwidth available on the ring. This bandwidth allocation is calculated in terms of percentage of Target Token Rotation Time (TTRT). The *TTRT* is the expected token rotation time for the expected traffic on the network and is negotiated during ring initialization. A station with synchronous bandwidth allocation can transmit data for a period of time not to exceed the percentage of TTRT allocated to it. Any remaining time that is left after all stations finish synchronous transmission is allocated to the remaining nodes. Thus, if the actual *Token Rotation Time (TRT)* is less than TTRT, the leftover time (TTRT – TRT) is used for asynchronous transfer.

In *asynchronous mode*, transfer can take place in two modes:

- Restricted
- Nonrestricted

A station can perform an extended transfer in restricted asynchronous mode. The *Station Management (SMT)* negotiates a maximum restricted time. Stations running in restricted asynchronous mode should not take up the entire ring for a period of time greater than TTRT.

In nonrestricted mode, leftover time is divided between any nodes that wants to send data. This mode of operation is the default. The division of time can be based on priority schemes in which stations have a threshold TRT. Stations with lower threshold TRT are cut off earlier.

FDDI uses multimode fiber. Extensions to FDDI that use single-mode fiber are also in use. Although multimode can use a mix of light frequencies, a single-mode fiber uses laser and a smaller-core diameter fiber. Single-mode fiber has less signal attenuation and can be used over longer distances. With these FDDI extensions, two stations can be up to 60 kilometers apart. FDDI-II permits circuit switching in the synchronous mode with up to 16 synchronous channels of 6.144 Mbps each.

Many vendors are interested in running the FDDI protocols over a copper medium. Some vendors use Unshielded Twisted Pair (UTP) wire, whereas other vendors favor Shielded Twisted Pair (STP) wire. Using copper-based FDDI wiring is cheaper than using the fiber-based products. One problem of using twisted pair wiring is compliance with FCC regulations and signal attenuation, both of which limit the distance between a workstation and the FDDI concentrator to about 100 meters. Products that use copper-based FDDI, called *CDDI (Copper Distributed Data Interface)*, are available today.

TCP/IP Framing on FDDI Networks

Even though FDDI LANs were developed by ANSI and not IEEE, FDDI uses LLC to encapsulate upper layer protocols. This enables the use of a SNAP header in conjunction with LLC framing to allow framing of TCP/IP packets. The framing of TCP/IP packets in FDDI LANs is illustrated in figure 3.58. The DSAP and SSAP fields of the LLC header are set to AA hexadecimal, and the Ethertype field in the SNAP header contains the value of 800 hexadecimal for IP packets.

Figure 3.58 Framing of TCP/IP packets in FDDI LANs.

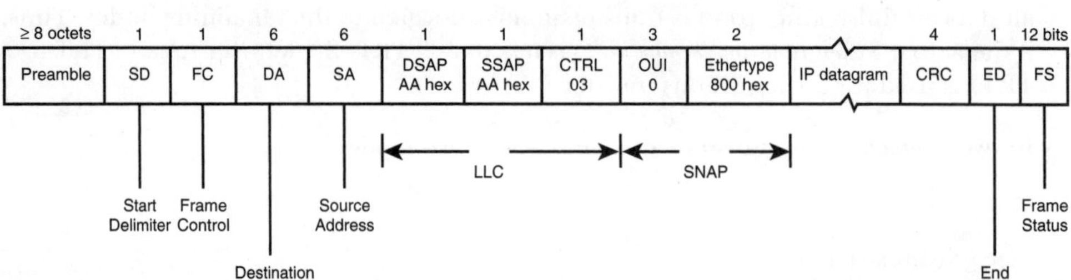

Extending Local Area Networks Using Wide Area Networks

When several LANs need to be connected over long distances, WAN links or WAN networks must be used. LANs and WANs are usually connected by special devices called bridges or routers. The remainder of this chapter gives a brief introduction to bridges and routers and discusses the different WAN technologies.

The Roles of Repeaters, Bridges, and Routers

Repeaters, bridges, and routers (each of which is defined in greater detail in upcoming sections) are devices that extend the range of a LAN. Although you can use repeaters to go beyond a single cable segment, there are limitations on the number of repeaters you can use and the distance you can extend the LAN with repeaters. If you use bridges and routers, you can go beyond the LAN distance. For example in an Ethernet LAN, there is a maximum distance of 2500 meters. You can use bridges or routers to extend this distance. Each Ethernet LAN still has the 2500-meter and four repeater rule, but once a packet crosses a bridge it is on another logical LAN and subject to the restrictions of that LAN only.

You can also use an interconnecting device such as a repeater, bridge, or router to go beyond the limit of the maximum number of nodes that can be placed on a physical LAN segment or network. For example, in 10BASE5 Ethernet, you can have a maximum of 100 station attachments per Ethernet cable segment. If you want to place more than 100 stations on an Ethernet LAN, you can use a repeater to connect another segment and place the additional nodes on this new segment. Similarly, if you want to go beyond the 1024 station attachment limit for an Ethernet LAN, you can use a bridge or a router to connect to another Ethernet LAN and place the additional nodes on the new Ethernet LAN.

Bridges and routers do more than extend the range of a LAN. You can use them to connect dissimilar LANs and to alleviate traffic bottleneck problems.

Although bridges and routers are described as devices, they consist of a computer that runs algorithms to perform bridging or routing functions. If high performance is desired, these devices are implemented as special dedicated computers that can perform bridging and routing functions efficiently. For bridges, the algorithms are usually encoded in EPROM (firmware) for rapid execution. Routers, as you learn shortly, are more complicated than bridges and may require periodic updates by the vendor to correct problems and enhance functionality. It is easier to implement the routing algorithms in software so that they can be changed more easily. Many router vendors store the software in flash RAM.

Many vendors allow you to incrementally expand the capabilities of their bridges and routers. Hardware modules that consist of one or more network boards can be used to connect to different types of networks. These hardware modules fit into a slot in the bridge or router and connect to a high-speed backplane bus that is used for data transfer between the modules.

Defining a Repeater

A *repeater* operates at the Physical layer of the OSI model (see fig. 3.59). It takes a signal from one LAN, reconditions and re-times it, and sends it to another LAN. The reconditioning usually amplifies and boosts the power level of the signal. The repeater has no knowledge of the meaning of the individual bits in the packet. A repeater cannot be addressed individually; no address field exists in the packet for a repeater.

Figure 3.59 Repeater definition and the OSI Model.

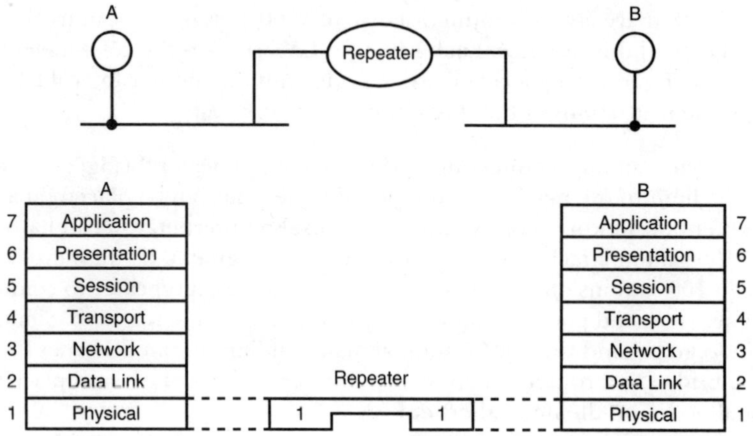

The repeater's job is simple: detect the signal, amplify and retime it, and send it through all the ports except the one on which the signal was seen. In the case of Ethernet, the signals that are transmitted include data packets and even collisions. The segments of the LAN that are connected participate in the media access mechanism such as CSMA/CD or Token Access. For Token Ring LANs, each station performs the repeater function so that usually no separate repeater device is needed. Some fiber optic media extensions to the Token Ring may use special repeater devices to boost the signal over long distances.

Defining a Bridge

Bridges connect two separate networks to form a logical network. An example of a bridge between an IEEE 802.3 and IEEE 802.5 LAN is shown in figure 3.60. This bridge has two network cards: a Token Ring card and an Ethernet network card. The Token Ring card is used to connect the bridge to the Token Ring LAN and the Ethernet card is used to connect to the Ethernet LAN.

Figure 3.60 Bridge between IEEE 802.3 and IEEE 802.5 LAN.

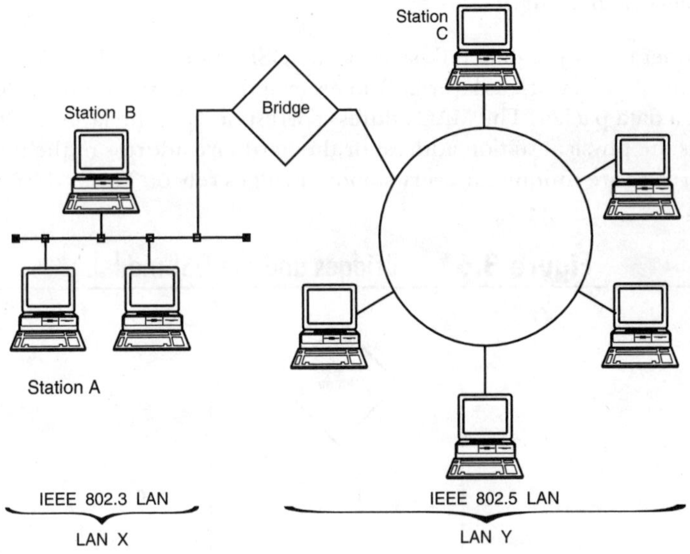

One way of looking at this concept is that a bridge has a "split personality." It behaves as a Token Ring station and also as an Ethernet station, and herein lies the key to understanding its function. In figure 3.61, a packet sent from station A to station B does not cross the bridge in its normal mode of operation. The bridge detects that stations A and B are on the same LAN and a bridging function is not required.

If, however, station A sends a packet to station C, the bridge realizes that station C is on another LAN (Token Ring) and places the packet on the Token Ring LAN. It cannot place the Ethernet packet directly to the Token Ring LAN because the Ethernet frame cannot be understood by the Token Ring LAN. The bridge must remove the Ethernet header and replace it with a Token Ring header containing station C's address. The bridge also must wait for a free token before placing the packet on the Token Ring LAN. As it waits, other packets may be sent to it for transmission to the Token Ring LAN. These packets must be queued for processing. A bridge, therefore, must have storage capacity to store frames and acts as a store-and-forward device.

In figure 3.60, most of the stations on LAN X communicate among themselves. Occasionally, stations in LAN X may need to communicate with stations in LAN Y. Another way of saying this is that most of the traffic is intra-LAN (within a LAN), and a small fraction is inter-LAN (between multiple LANs). A good rule of thumb is the *80/20 rule.* About 80 percent or more of traffic should be intra-LAN traffic and 20 percent or less should be inter-LAN traffic.

If the 80/20 rule is violated frequently, the stations generating excessive inter-LAN traffic should be detected and relocated to another LAN so that they do not cause excessive inter-LAN traffic. Stations generating excessive traffic can be detected by using protocol analyzers. *Protocol analyzers* are devices that can monitor, store, and analyze packets on a ring.

A bridge operates at the data link layer of the OSI model (see fig. 3.61). A bridge performs most of its work at layer 2. Bridges examine the *Media Access Control (MAC)* header of a data packet. The MAC address corresponds to the layer 2 address and represents the physical station address or the hardware address of the network board. MAC addresses are unique for every station. Bridges rely on MAC addresses for their operation.

Figure 3.61 Bridges and the OSI model.

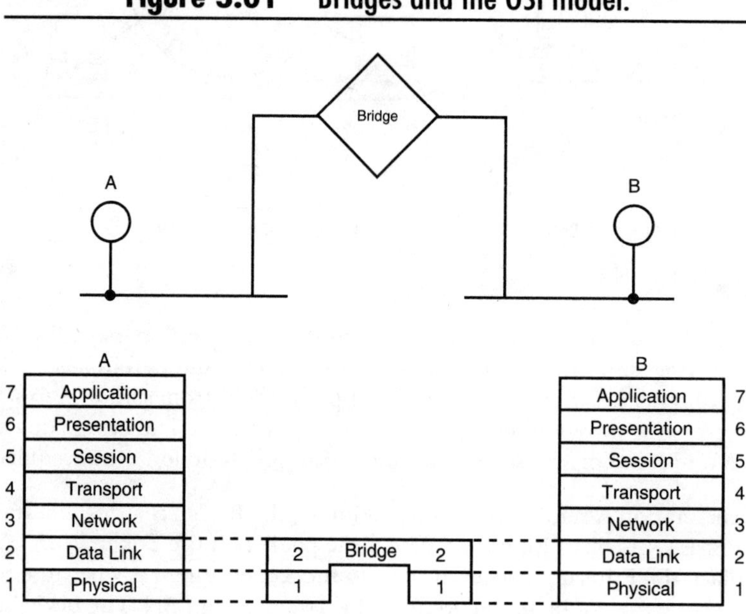

Unlike a repeater, a bridge actually sees the data packet. Bridge ports have unique MAC addresses. A bridge has an understanding of the data packet up to the data link layer and can decode it up to this level. Bridges isolate the media access mechanisms of the LANs to which they are connected. Thus, collisions in a CSMA/CD LAN do not propagate across a bridge. In the case of Token Ring LANs joined by a bridge, the token does not cross a bridge. Because bridges are selective about which data packets can be transferred, they help solve traffic bottleneck problems.

Bridges are effective for a small number of LANs, but as the number of LANs grows, the number of possible paths between the sender and receiving station become very large. Not all the possible paths are optimal. Some paths involve roundabout ways of getting to the destination, and this can create unnecessary traffic. If a bridge is to be effective for large LANs, it must have knowledge about the optimal path. But a bridge only operates at the Data Link layer, and the routing information is part of layer 3 (Network layer) operation. By definition, therefore, bridges cannot make decisions about routes through the network because information on routes is encoded in the network address, and the network address is accessible only by the Network layer.

Although a bridge can seem limited, it is a simple and an inexpensive way to interconnect two LANs. To perform intelligent routing decisions, you need a router.

Defining Routers and Gateways

A *router* operates at the network layer of the OSI model (see fig. 3.62). A router performs most of its work at layer 3. Bridges are limited to examining the MAC address of a data packet, but routers can examine the network address. For a router to work, the protocol being routed must have a Network layer address, also called the *network address.* For TCP/IP networks, the network address is called *the IP address.*

Figure 3.62 Routers and the OSI model.

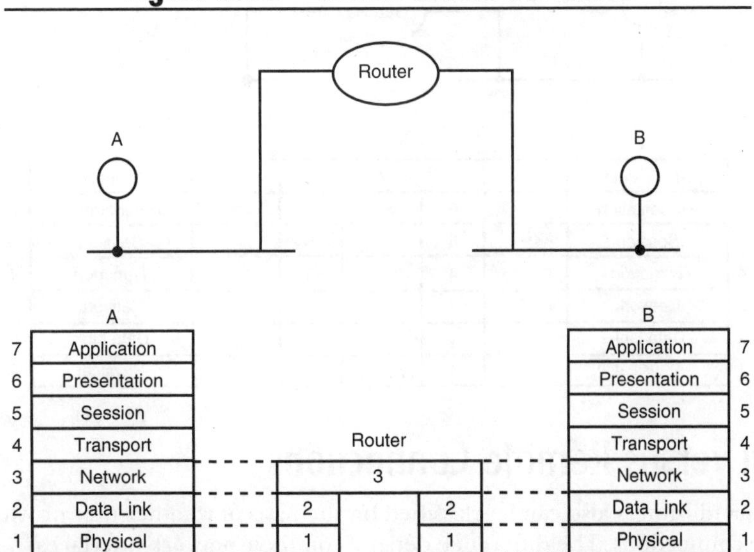

Because the network address usually has routing information encoded in it, routers can make use of this capability to make intelligent decisions. Thus, a *route* in a network consists of network addresses and paths. Routers are aware of how to forward a datagram get to a destination and also are aware of which path is the most optimal.

Because routers operate at a higher layer of the OSI model compared to bridges, they can do more things with a packet than a bridge can, and they also are more complex. Their complexity makes routers costlier to develop and they might cost more. Routers do more processing of the packets than a bridge; therefore, they tend to be slower than bridges.

Routers are the devices of choice to use to interconnect large LANs in TCP/IP networks. You also can use routers to connect LANs over long distances. In earlier literature on the Internet, routers were called *gateways.* To some extent the legacy of this older terminology still exists in the naming of routing protocols and TCP/IP configuration parameters for hosts. In modern networks, a gateway is a device that operates at higher levels than routers.

In figure 3.63, a gateway device is shown operating at layer 7. In general, a *gateway* is a device that can operate at any layer of the OSI model and provides translation between two incompatible protocols. A gateway operating at layer 7 is an Application layer gateway.

Figure 3.63 Gateways and the OSI model.

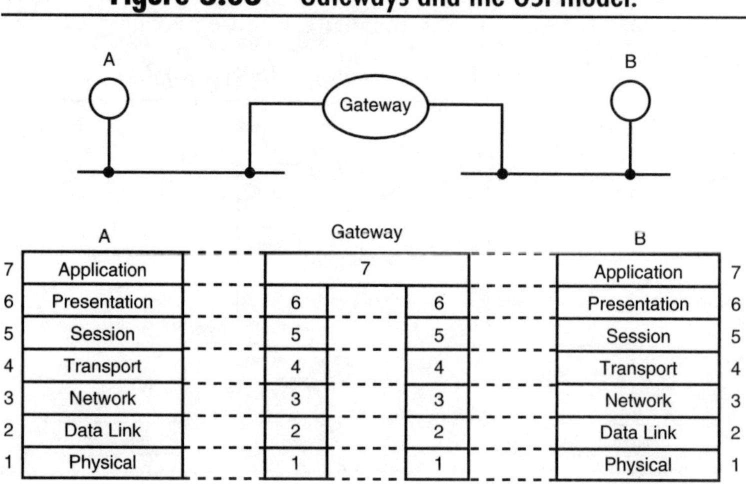

Local versus Remote Connections

Bridges and routers also can be classified on the basis of whether they provide local or remote connections. The difference depends on their network interfaces or ports.

Local bridges and routers have ports that connect them to local transmission media over relatively short distances. An example of this setup is the transceiver cable used in Ethernet LANs. You can choose from a variety of choices such as coaxial, twisted pair, and fiber optic media to connect local devices to a network. The actual media choice often is dictated by the LAN that is being connected.

Remote bridges and routers require ports that can connect them to long-haul transmission media. You have fewer interface choices for long transmission media. Some popular choices include RS-232 ports and V.35 ports. Many remote devices have two or more remote connections and at least one local connection. In figure 3.64, router A has two local ports and one remote port. Router B has one remote port and one local port. The remote ports are connected by a point-to-point link. You can run a number of connection protocols on these point-to-point links. Some of the choices include X.25, Frame Relay, T1, SONET, and SMDS.

Figure 3.64 Remote routers.

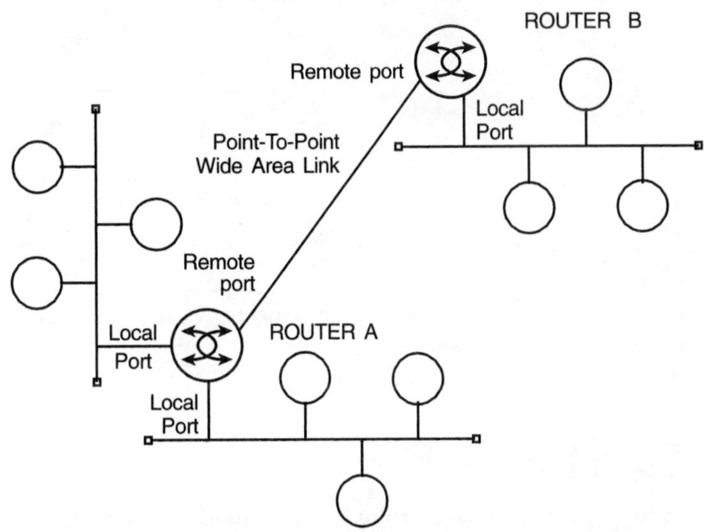

Besides point-to-point links, you also can use *cloud* technologies to connect LANs. *Point-to-point* links are telephone circuits, or T1 circuits, that you can lease from telephone companies or other vendors. Because these lines are dedicated for the communications from the sender point to a destination point, they are named point-to-point. *Cloud* technologies, such as the type shown in figure 3.65, are based on switching systems. The router, acting as *the Customer Premise Equipment (CPE)* is used to connect to the cloud. The details of the cloud are not known to the LAN. It may use an X.25/X.75 protocol, Frame Relay, SMDS switches, ATM, or a proprietary technology. The cloud or wide area network (WAN) is managed by the organization that provides the long-haul service.

Figure 3.65 Routers connected by means of WAN cloud technologies.

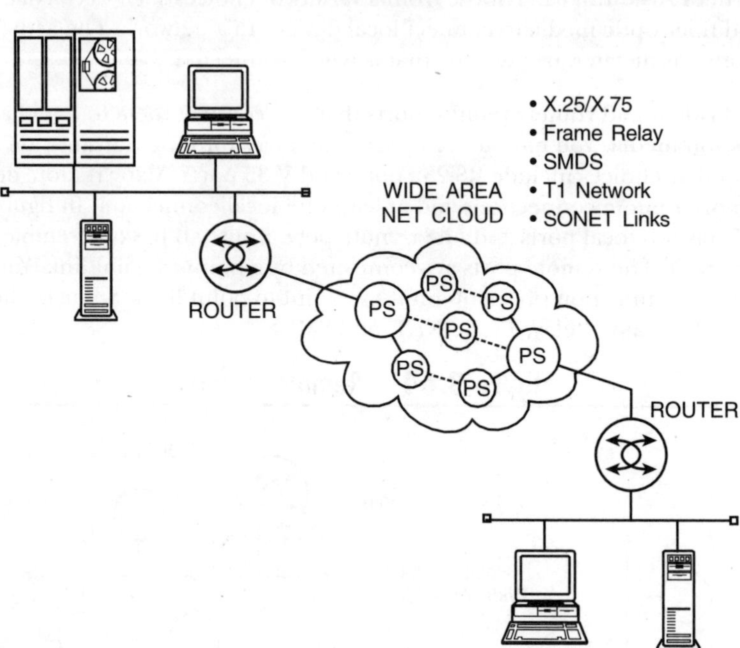

A difference between local and remote bridges and routers is the cost of the connection. Because local connections are managed entirely by the organization that owns the LAN, no additional cost is incurred. For remote connections, you must pay for the services provided by the long-haul vendor.

Bridge Operation

While routers are a general purpose solution for extending the range of TCP/IP networks, bridges can be used to extend the range of small TCP/IP networks. Because bridges operate at layer 2 (Data Link layer) of the OSI model, they are not aware of the IP protocol that corresponds to layer 3 (Network layer) of the OSI model. LANs that are linked together with bridges appear as a single logical network to an IP router.

The two predominant methods of bridging are as follows:

- Transparent bridge (TB)
- Source-Routing (SR) bridge

In transparent bridging (also called spanning tree bridging), the decision to relay packets is made by the bridge and is transparent to workstations.

Figure 3.66 shows a transparent bridge network. Each bridge maintains a table that keeps track of station addresses. Transparent bridges examine the source address of every packet they see and record this source address in the bridge table along with the number of the port on which the packet was seen. Transparent bridges also maintain a timeout field for each table entry so that old entries can be periodically purged.

Figure 3.66 Transparent bridge network.

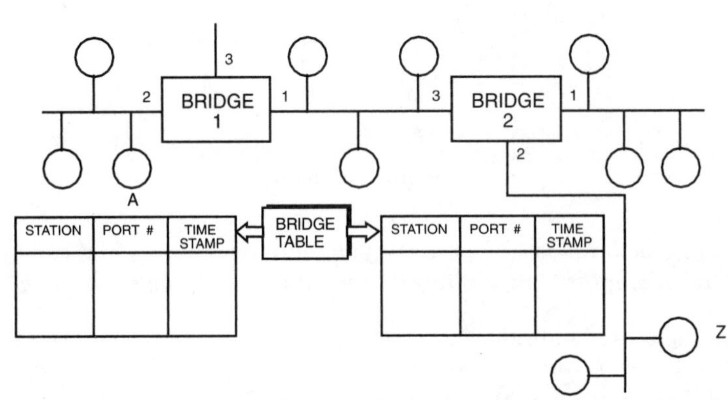

Consider what happens if station A transmits a packet to station Z. Bridge 1 sees the packet and consults its table to see whether or not it has an entry for station Z. If it does not, it forwards the packet through all of its out ports, excluding the port on which the packet was observed. Bridge 1 also checks the source address field of the packet and records in its table that station A can be reached at its port 2. When Bridge 2 sees the packet, it repeats the algorithm just described. If there is no entry for station Z, it forwards the packet through all its outgoing ports (flooding). It also records the fact that station A can be reached through its port 3. When station Z acknowledges the message from station A, it sends a packet with source address Z and destination address A. After Bridge 2 consults its table, it notes that station A can be reached through port 3, and forwards the packet only through port 3. It also records that station Z can be reached through its port 2.

To prevent endless circulation of packets, transparent bridge networks cannot have loops. The transmission path forms a spanning tree that covers all the stations on the network. If there are bridges that could form a loop, as shown in figure 3.67, these bridges must remain inactive. The inactive bridges act like redundant bridges. Redundant bridges are activated after the spanning tree topology changes. Topology changes are transmitted by *Bridge Protocol Data Units (BPDUs)*. This special protocol is used to maintain the overall spanning tree topology. The process of arriving at the spanning tree is called the *spanning tree algorithm.* One bridge in the spanning tree becomes the *root* and all other bridges transmit frames in the direction of the root by using a least-cost metric.

Figure 3.67 Avoiding loops on transparent bridge networks.

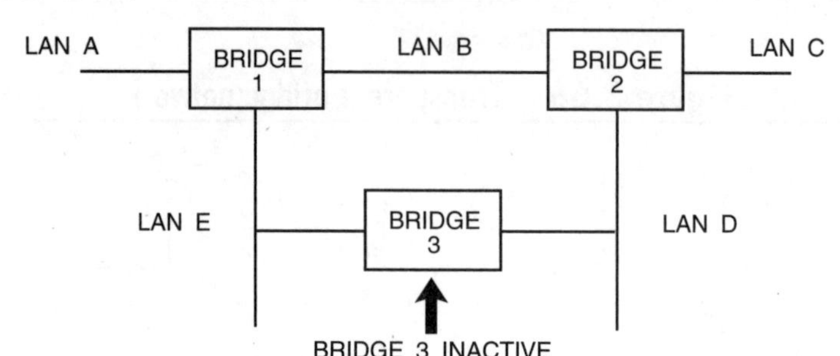

The spanning tree bridge is the preferred method for Ethernet and IEEE 802.3 networks and is supported by vendors that manufacture bridges for these LANs.

Source routing is used in bridges used to connect Token Ring networks. In Source Routing, the source (sender) must determine the best path to get to a destination. After this path is discovered, the source station maintains this path in its routing table and includes this path in the *Routing Information (RI)* field for every packet that is sent. The RI field is shown in figure 3.68 along with its relationship to the Token Ring packet. The RI field is present whenever the I/G bit of the source address is set to 1. This I/G bit also is referred to as the *Routing Information Indicator (RII)* bit. The Token Ring frame structure is discussed in Chapter 2. The *Routing Designator (RD)* fields contain the path the packet must follow to arrive at the destination. RD fields consist of a ring number and a bridge number pair. SR bridges simply follow the directions in the routing information field. A total of 14 RD fields are possible, which limits the largest transmission path to 13 bridges or hops. IBM's implementation currently limits total RD fields to eight, which corresponds to seven bridges or hops.

Figure 3.69 shows the path from station A to Z using source routing. The details of the routing field also are shown.

The key to the operation of source routing is discovering the initial route. This is done by sending a *discovery frame* that is broadcast by the source node when it wants to discover the best path to a destination. The discovery frame circulates on the network and arrives at the destination with a record of the path taken. The discovery frames are returned to the sender, who then selects the best possible path.

Figure 3.68 Routing information field.

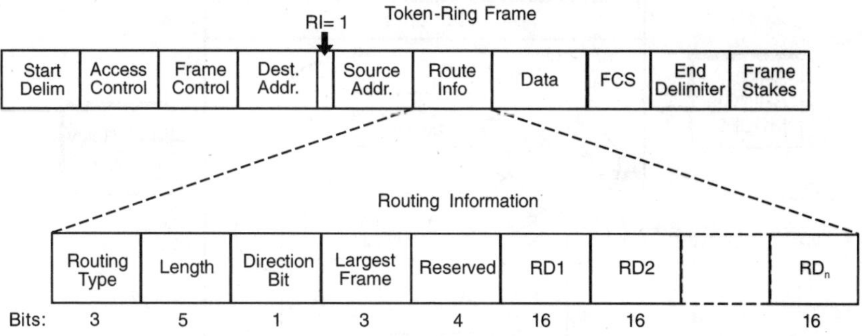

Figure 3.69 Transmission using source routing.

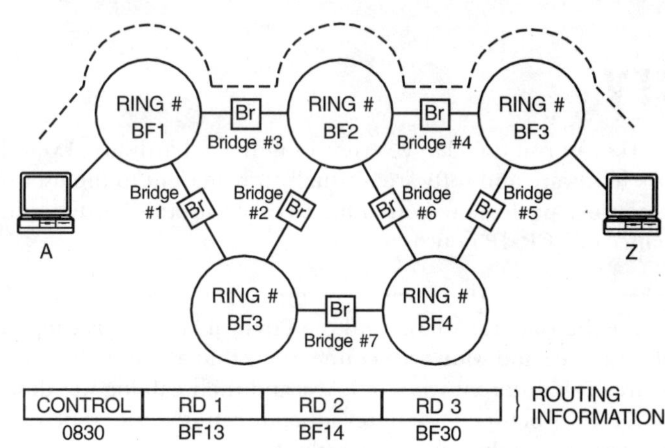

IEEE 802.5 networks prefer the source routing method. How do you connect IEEE 802.3 networks that use Transparent Bridges with IEEE 802.5 networks that use source routing? One method is to have a bridge, such as the IBM 8209 bridge, that provides translation of routing information between the two separate bridge mechanisms. Another method is to use a bridge that is a combination of source routing and transparent bridges. These bridges are called *Source Routing Transparent (SRT)* bridges. In SRT, transparent bridging is used when there is no RI field; otherwise, source routing is used. The model for SRT bridges is shown in figure 3.70. The MAC layer entity consists of SR and TB algorithms. These algorithms are invoked depending on the setting of the RII bit.

Figure 3.70 Source Routing Transparent (SRT) bridges.

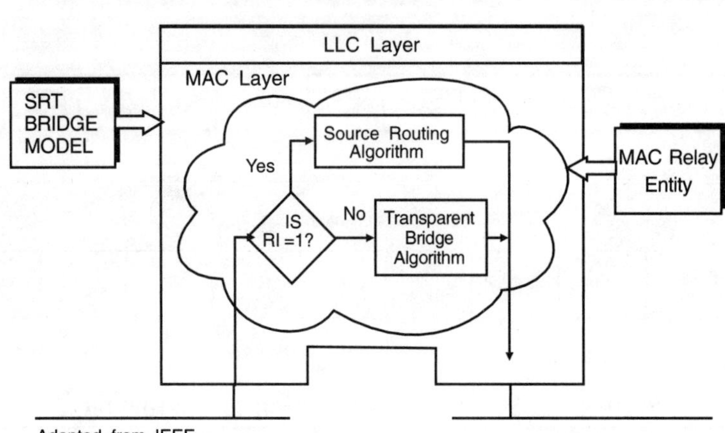

Summary

TCP/IP networks can run on a large variety of network hardware. Even though the actual network hardware and software is usually transparent to the user of the network, the network professional often has to deal with this hardware in the building and maintenance of TCP/IP networks.

Network hardware for TCP/IP networks corresponds to layers 2 and 1 of the OSI model. These are the Data Link layer and the Physical layer. This chapter described the variety of local area and wide area connections that are available for running TCP/IP software. The different types of LANs and their cabling was described in detail. The differences between the different connecting devices such as repeaters, bridges, and gateways and their uses are outlined.

Test Yourself

1. Why are there so many different types of network hardware to run TCP/IP? Are there any advantages?
2. Name two devices that can be used to connect networks that use different network hardware.
3. The IEEE LAN standards describe which two layers of the OSI model?
4. What is the relationship of the LLC layer to the MAC layer? Draw a diagram describing this relationship, and the relationship of these layers to the OSI model.

5. Write the names of the link SAP addresses for the LLC layer.
6. Describe briefly the different types of services available at the LLC layer.
7. LANs typically use which type of LLC service: Type 1, Type 2, or Type 3? State the reason or reasons why LANs use this service.
8. Write the names of the IEEE standards deal with CSMA/CD and Token Passing mechanisms.
9. List the different types of Ethernet/802.3 LANs and give a brief description of each of these types.
10. Draw an Ethernet frame showing how it can carry TCP/IP data. Label each field.
11. What is the SNAP header extension mechanism? Why is it used? Which LANs use the SNAP header extension for carrying TCP/IP data?
12. Draw a Token Ring frame showing how it can carry TCP/IP data. Label each field.
13. Draw a FDDI frame showing how it can carry TCP/IP data. Label each field.
14. What is the function of an Active Monitor in the IEEE 802.5 network? Why is a similar mechanism not needed for Ethernet networks?
15. How can you extend the range of a LAN?
16. Give a description of the different types of devices used to extend the range of a LAN.
17. With the help of a diagram explain the operation of a spanning tree bridge.
18. With the help of a diagram explain the operation of a source routing bridge.
19. What are the advantages of using switched Ethernet networks over regular Ethernet networks? What kinds of TCP/IP applications are best suited for switched Ethernet?
20. Is there any similarity between switched Ethernet and spanning tree Ethernet bridges? What are the differences between them?
21. What are some of the fundamental differences between a bridge and a router?

PART II

TCP/IP Internetworking Infrastructure

CHAPTER 4

IP Addressing

One of the primary tasks in building a TCP/IP network is the assignment of Internet addresses to the nodes on the network. Internet addresses in TCP/IP networks are called *IP addresses.* While assigning IP addresses is on the surface a simple task, you need to consider a number of factors. One factor to consider is that each IP network address needs to be unique. IP addresses possess a certain structure. You cannot just connect a node to an IP network and assign it a unique IP address; You must, additionally, ensure that the IP address is consistent with the IP addresses of other nodes on that network segment. If you are implementing TCP/IP on a network, one of the tasks that you must perform is to select and configure IP addresses correctly.

This chapter explores IP addressing in great detail. It fully defines the concept, covers special IP addresses, and discusses both assigning and configuring IP addresses. Although the chapter deals mainly with IP version 4 addresses, it does take a brief look at IP version 6.

Note There are two versions of IP: IP version 4 and IP version 6. IP version 4, which is still the dominant Internet Protocol on the Internet, uses 32-bit addresses. IP version 6 is the next generation protocol that is designed to replace IP version 4. IP version 6 uses 128-bit addresses.

What Is a Network Address?

For nodes to be connected in an Internet consisting of more than one network (see fig. 4.1), a consistent logical addressing scheme must be used throughout the network. *Logical addresses* are unique identifiers that can be number value assignments or names. *Network addresses* are the Service Access Point (SAP) identifiers at the Network layer of the OSI model (see fig. 4.2). The Network SAP (NSAP) addresses must be unique for all protocol entities communicating at the Network layer of the OSI model.

Figure 4.1 Multiple network Internets should use a consistent logical addressing scheme.

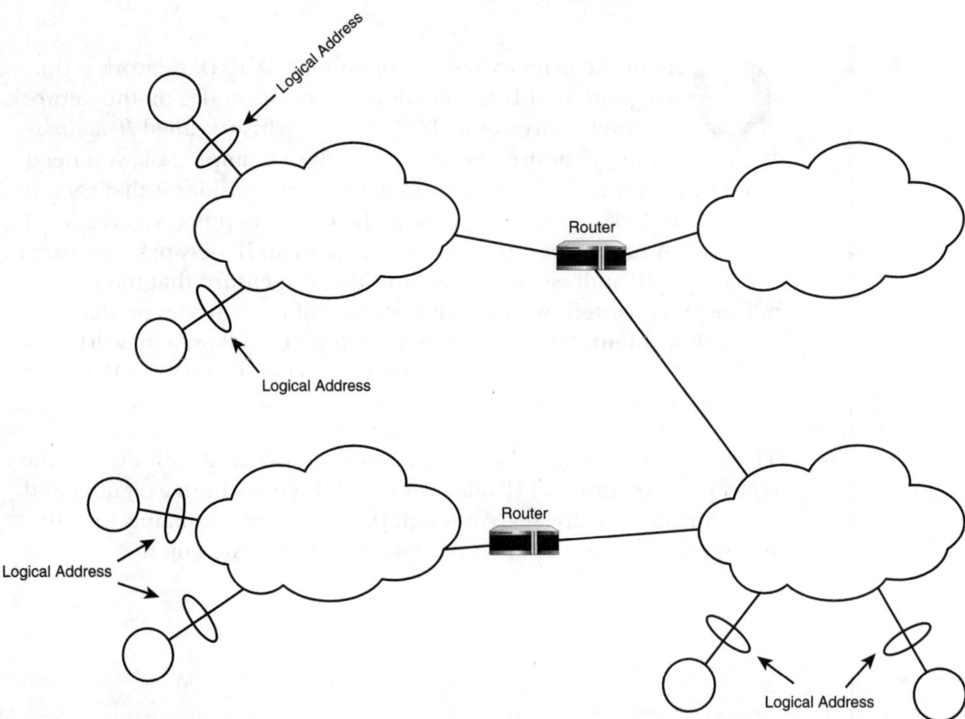

Figure 4.2 Network SAPs must be unique.

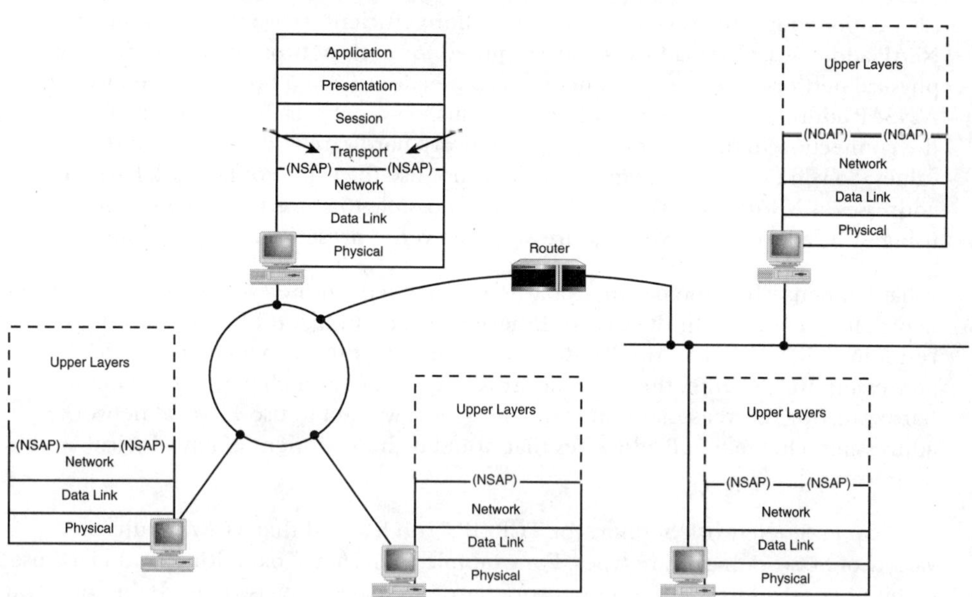

Address Values for NSAPs

At the level of the Network layer in the OSI model, it is more common to use a number value than a name value for NSAP addresses. This is because it is more efficient for protocols at lower layers of the OSI model to work with number values than symbolic names. Names are typically used in applications that are closer to human users. This is because human users find that names are more pronounceable and easier to deal with than numbers. Protocol software such as the Internet software, however, works more efficiently with number representations of addresses.

The Internet Protocol (IP) works at the Network layer of the OSI model. The Network layer of the OSI model is concerned with routing issues. The IP address should be structured to ensure routing efficiency. Routing computations are more efficient with binary numbers than symbolic names. This is another reason why number values are more suitable for network addresses than symbolic names.

Generally speaking, upper layers of the OSI model tend to use addresses that are closer to names. Names as addresses are typically used by the Application layer of the OSI model.

NSAP Independence from Network Hardware

As mentioned in the previous section, it is more efficient to use number values for NSAP addresses. NSAP addresses are required for each network connection to the physical network. If there are *N* network connections from a host, you need to assign *N* NSAP addresses. The network hardware, such as a network board, is used to make the connection to the network, and the network hardware addresses are number values. So you might ask the question: Why not use the values of network hardware addresses as NSAP addresses? In theory, it is possible to come up with a scheme for using MAC addresses as NSAP addresses; however, it presents a few problems.

What happens when the network boards are changed (in the event of a faulty network board, for example)? In the case of Ethernet, Token Ring, and FDDI, this would result in a change in the MAC address and, consequently, a change in the NSAP address. In this scheme, the NSAP address is dependent on changes in the network hardware. For this reason, the Internet designers wanted to use a logical network addressing scheme for IP addresses that would be independent of any physical layer addresses.

In Chapter 3, "Network Support for TCP/IP," you learned that TCP/IP runs on a variety of network hardware types. For example, Ethernet, Token Ring, and FDDI use 48-bit physical addresses. Other network hardware types may use 8-bit, 16-bit, or 32-bit addresses. By using logical addresses rather than physical addresses, the Internet Protocol does not have to be concerned with the hardware peculiarities of the underlying network. The different hardware addresses should be mapped to a logical network address (see fig. 4.3). For IP addresses, special address resolution protocols are used to perform this mapping. Address resolution protocols are discussed in Chapter 5, "Address Resolution Protocols."

Figure 4.3 Hardware addresses should be mapped to a logical address.

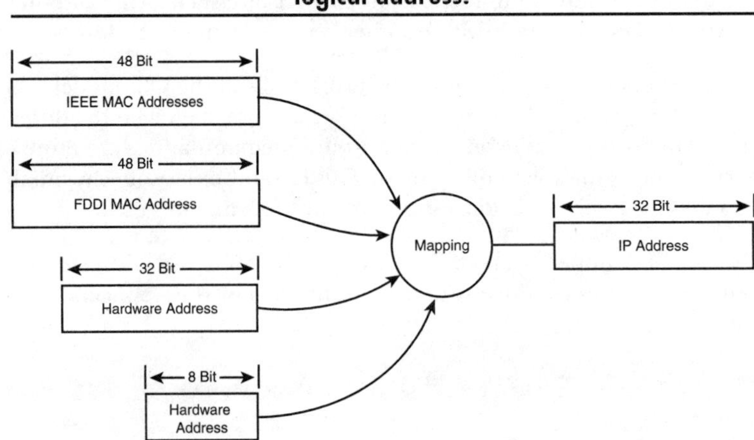

Because the IP addresses are not dependent on hardware addresses, you can replace the underlying hardware with newer hardware without having to change the logical address. In other words, you can upgrade your network with more efficient and faster technologies without having to change logical addresses.

The IP Address

The Internet was designed as a logical network of computers, connecting devices and software. This logical view of the network is independent of the underlying hardware technology (see fig. 4.4). Although this concept may seem simple, it is one of the most powerful and flexible aspects of the Internet. Independence of the network from underlying hardware has allowed the Internet network to expand and grow to become the world's largest network, containing every kind of computing device imaginable. New kinds of computing devices can be connected to the network without changing the logical view of the network.

Figure 4.4 A logical network is independent of the underlying hardware.

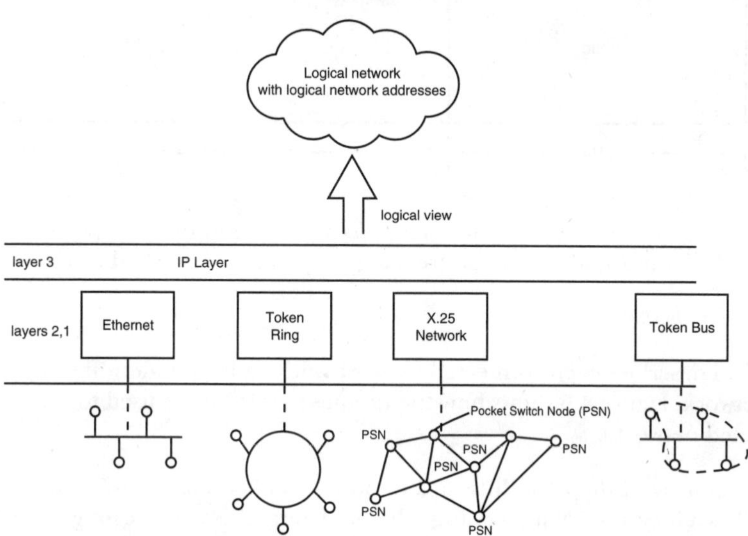

Structuring the IP Address

The logical view of the Internet creates a virtual network. Each network connection to the virtual network is identified by a unique identity, which is the NSAP or IP address. The network designers can select the size of the IP address based on how big they expect the virtual network to become. The designers of the Internet selected a 32-bit number for the IP address. With a 32-bit size for the NSAP address, the maximum number of connections that you can have on the network at the same time are 2^{32}, which is equal to 4,294,967,296 or about 4 billion connections. As you will learn later, however, you cannot have that many connections because some bit representations of the IP address have special reserved meanings and cannot be assigned to individual network connections.

The virtual network consists of networks tied together with connecting devices such as routers and gateways (see Chapter 3 for an understanding of the role of routers and gateways). To route IP datagrams, routers must be able to distinguish between the different logical networks. The designers decided to structure the IP address to enable it to make this distinction between the different logical networks. A certain number of bits in the IP address are used to identify the individual network in the virtual network, and the remaining bits are used to identify the host within the network. Figure 4.5 illustrates the division of the IP address.

Figure 4.5 Use the IP address to identify the network and host.

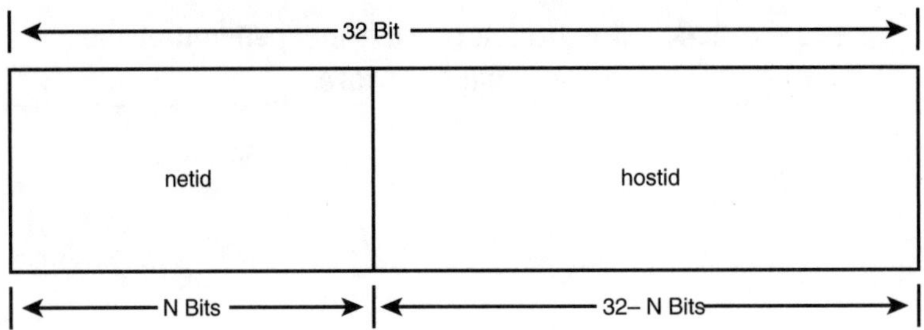

The network portion is called the *network ID* or *netid,* and the host portion is called the *host ID* or the *hostid.* The IP address logically can be described by the following:

{*netid, hostid*}

The netid describes each connected network and the hostid identifies the host within that network. Figure 4.6 shows how the unique netids can be used to identify the connected networks.

The structuring of the IP address to a network number and a host number within that network is a hierarchical addressing scheme. Hierarchical addressing is designed to make routing more efficient. Many hierarchical schemes are tied to a geographical region, but the IP address hierarchical addressing is a logical hierarchical addressing rather than a geographical hierarchical addressing.

The routers' primary concern is getting an IP datagram to the correct network. To do this, they have to store information about the *netids* and not the *hostids.* There are less netids than hostids, which makes the amount of information that the routers have to know more manageable. If no distinction was made between network number and host number—that is, a flat addressing scheme was used instead of a hierarchical addressing scheme—the routers would have to potentially store all 4 billion IP addresses!

Figure 4.6 **Example network showing netid's values for identifying networks.**

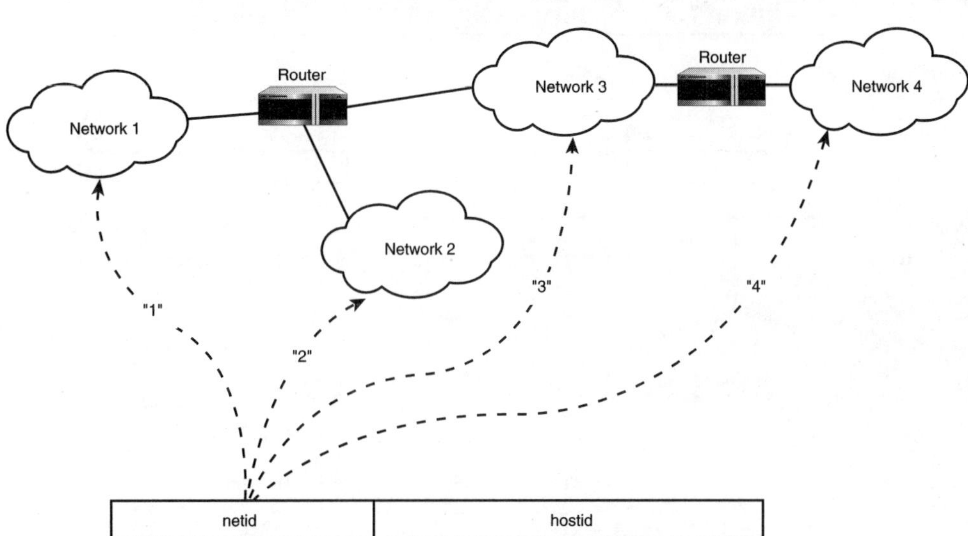

IP Address Classes

All hosts connected to the same network have the same netid (see fig. 4.7) and, of course, a different hostid. In figure 4.7, the netid and hostid values are shown as hexadecimal numbers; hexadecimal numbers are a shorthand way of representing binary numbers in groups of four bits. (If you are not familiar with hexadecimal numbers, consult table 4.2). The netid identifies the network uniquely. Interconnected networks must have unique netids for routing to work correctly.

Networks that have the same netid have a common prefix that represents the IP addresses of hosts inside the network. What is the size of this common prefix? Given a 32-bit number for the IP address, the Internet designers decided to use either the first, first two, or first three bytes as the netid:

- **First byte (Class A).** If the first byte is used for the netid, the remaining three bytes are used for the hostid. This type of address format for an IP address is called a class A address.

- **First two bytes (Class B).** If the first two bytes are used for the netid, the remaining two bytes are used for the hostid. This type of address format for an IP address is called a class B address.
- **First three bytes (Class C).** If the first three bytes are used for the netid, the remaining byte is used for the hostid. This type of address format for an IP address is called a class C address.

Figure 4.7 Sharing a common netid on a network.

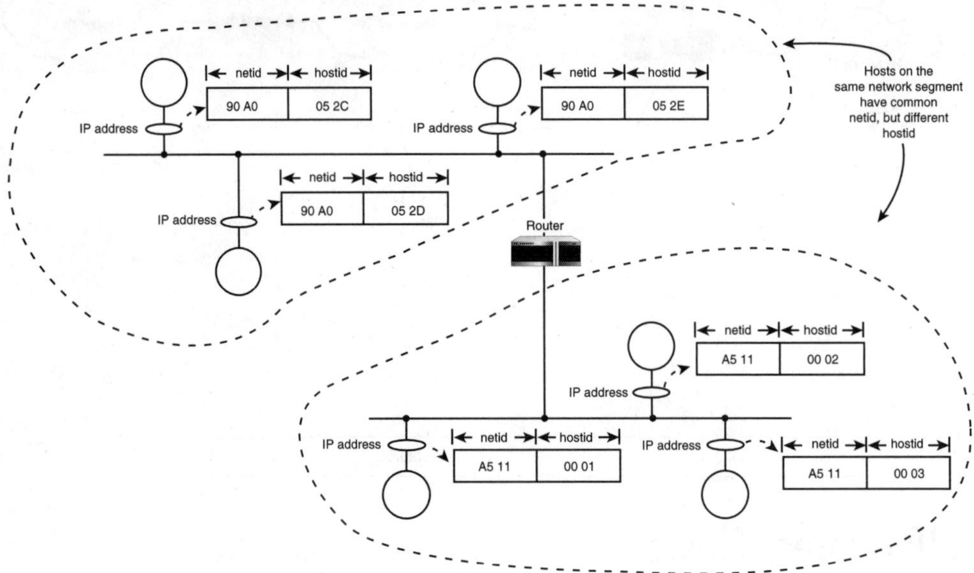

The Internet designers chose to partition the IP address into netid and hostid pairs on a byte boundary, resulting in three address classes that could be assigned for network connections. Using a byte boundary was a simplification in the design; they could have partitioned the IP address on any bit boundary with *N* bits assigned for the netid and 32 – *N* bits assigned for the hostid.

How do you make the distinction between the different IP address formats? The most significant bits are used to determine the IP address format—that is, the number of bits that are used for the netid and the hostid.

Besides the three address classes A, B, and C, two other address classes, D and E, are currently defined (see fig. 4.8). Of these classes, A, B, and C addresses are assignable. Class D is reserved for *multicasting*, which is used by special protocols to transmit messages to a select group of nodes. Class E is reserved for future use.

Figure 4.8 Defined IP address classes.

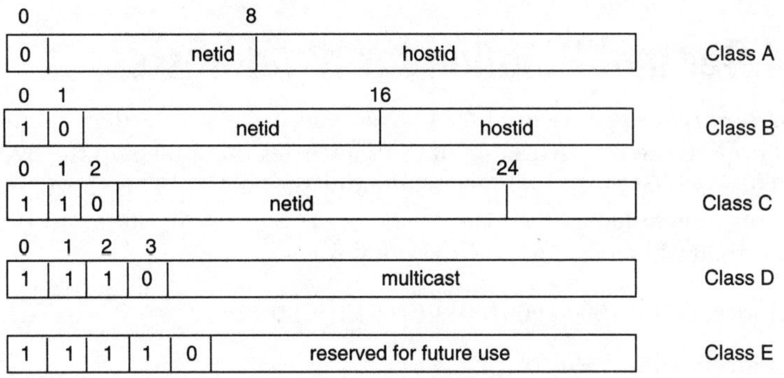

Bit positions	Fields	Class
0, 8	0 | netid | hostid	Class A
0 1, 16	1 | 0 | netid | hostid	Class B
0 1 2, 24	1 | 1 | 0 | netid |	Class C
0 1 2 3	1 | 1 | 1 | 0 | multicast	Class D
	1 | 1 | 1 | 1 | 0 | reserved for future use	Class E

Reasons for Using Specific Address Classes

The different types of IP address classes are defined to meet the needs of networks of different sizes. On request, the network registration authority assigns a network number (the netid field) to an organization. Once an organization has been allocated a network number, it is its responsibility to assign the host numbers (the values for the hostid field).

The number of hosts that can be assigned for a given network number depends on the number of bits in the hostid field. The number of bits in the hostid field depends on the address class to which the network number belongs. A class A network number has the largest number of bits in the hostid field and, therefore, the largest number of hosts. Similarly, a class C address has the smallest number of bits in the hostid field and, therefore, the smallest number of hosts. Table 4.1 shows the number of networks and nodes that are possible with each address class.

TABLE 4.1
Number of Networks and Nodes Possible with Each Address Class

Address Class	Number of Networks	Number of Nodes
A	127	16,777,214
B	16,383	65,534
C	2,097,151	254

Class A networks are suited for very large networks, but because their netid field (refer to fig. 4.8) is only seven bits, there can be only 127 such networks. The original ARPANET is an example of a class A network. Class B networks are medium-size networks that are suited for medium to large organizations. Class C networks are suited for small organizations, in which each network can have no more than 254 nodes.

Dotted Decimal Notation for IP Addresses

The 32-bit number is represented for convenience sake as four decimal numbers corresponding to the decimal value of the four bytes that make up the 32-bit IP address. The decimal numbers are separated by periods (.). This shorthand notation for IP addresses is called *dotted decimal notation.* The following shows an IP address in its binary form and as a dotted decimal notation.

IP Address = 10010000 00010011 01001010 11001001

IP Address = 144.19.74.201

Note

How is the binary number 10010000 equal to the decimal number 144? Binary numbers use the base 2 just as decimal numbers use the base 10. The decimal number 144 is actually the following arithmetic expression:

$$1 \times 10^2 + 4 \times 10 + 4 \times 1 = 144$$

Similarly, the binary number 10010000 is equivalent to the following expression:

$$1 \times 2^7 + 0 \times 2^6 + 0 \times 2^5 + 1 \times 2^4 + 0 \times 2^3 + 0 \times 2 + 0 \times 1$$

$$= 2^7 + 2^4$$

$$= 144$$

Each 1 or 0 bit in a binary pattern is multiplied by 2 to the power of the number of bits to the right of this bit. The first term in the preceding expression, 1×2^7, is for the leftmost bit 1 in 10010000. The leftmost bit is called the most significant bit (msb), and the rightmost bit is called the leaset significant bit (lsb). There are 7 bits to the right of the msb. For this reason, the value represented by this bit is 1×2^7.

Chapter 9, "IP Subnetting and Supernetting," discusses binary numbers in greater detail in the section titled "Conversion Between Decimal and Binary Numbers."

Figure 4.9 shows the relationship between the binary representation of the IP address and the dotted decimal notation. From this figure, you can see that the first group of 8 bits (10010000, which has a decimal value of 144) becomes the first decimal number of the dotted decimal IP address. Similarly, the second, third, and fourth group of 8 bits are each represented by their decimal values in the dotted decimal notation.

Some TCP/IP implementations use a hexadecimal dotted notation. Hexadecimal numbers use the base 16, and are a shorthand way of expressing binary numbers. Table 4.2 shows the symbols used for the hexadecimal numbers and their corresponding decimal values as well as the binary representation.

Figure 4.9 Dotted decimal notation.

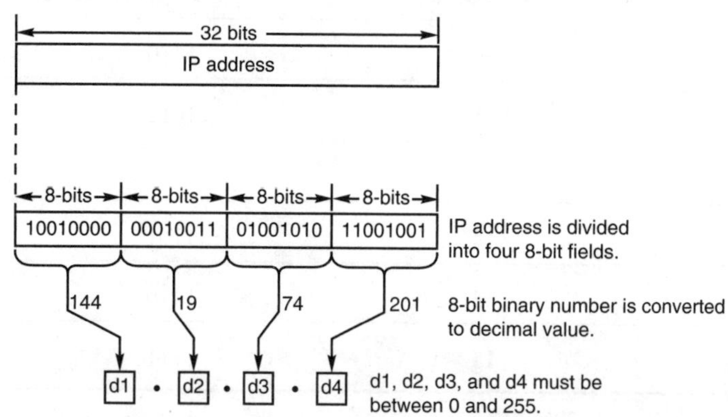

TABLE 4.2
Hexadecimal Values

Hexadecimal Code	Decimal Value	Binary Representation
0	0	0000
1	1	0001
2	2	0010
3	3	0011
4	4	0100
5	5	0101
6	6	0110
7	7	0111
8	8	1000
9	9	1001

continues

Table 4.2, Continued
Hexadecimal Values

Hexadecimal Code	Decimal Value	Binary Representation
A	10	1010
B	11	1011
C	12	1100
D	13	1101
E	14	1110
F	15	1111

The IP address of 144.19.74.201 would therefore be expressed as follows in the hexadecimal dotted notation:

0x90.0x13.0x4A.0xC9

The "0x" prefix is used to indicate the digits that follow are hexadecimal.

Leading zeros for dotted decimal notation should be omitted. Many TCP/IP implementations will ignore leading zeros; however, some TCP/IP implementations interpret leading zeros to indicate that the number that follows is octal. Thus, you should not write the IP address of 129.12.33.61 as 129.012.033.061. In TCP/IP implementations that ignore leading zeros, the two dotted decimal formats are equivalent. However, if the TCP/IP implementation uses a leading zero to indicate octal numbers, the IP address of 129.012.033.061 is *not* 129.12.33.61; instead, it is equivalent to 129.9.24.43!

Calculating an Address Class

Given an IP address in the dotted decimal notation form, it is important to know to which address class it belongs. The IP address class determines the number of bits assigned to the hostid field. The size of the hostid field limits the number of hosts that can be on the network. Another reason for knowing the address class is because it can be used to determine how to divide a network into smaller networks called *subnets.*

One method of determining the IP address class is to convert the IP address into its binary form and to examine the first few most significant bits (bits on the left of the binary pattern for the IP address). The most significant bits of an IP address determine the IP address class. From figure 4.8, you can see that if the most significant bit of the IP address is a 0, the IP address is a class A address. If the first two most significant bits of the IP address are 10, the IP address is a class B address; and if the first three most significant bits of the IP address are 110, the IP address is a class C address. These rules are summarized in table 4.3.

TABLE 4.3
Determining IP Address Class from the Most Significant Bits of the IP Address

Most Significant Bits	IP Address Class
1	Class A
10	Class B
110	Class C
1110	Class D

Consider an IP address of 137.65.4.1. If you convert this IP address to its binary representation, you will obtain the following 32-bit pattern:

1001001 01000001 00000100 00000001

The most significant two bits of this bit pattern are 10. Therefore, the IP address 137.65.4.1 is a class B address.

Consider, another example where the IP address is 199.245.180.10. If you convert this IP address to its binary representation, you will obtain the following 32-bit pattern:

1100111 11110101 10110100 00001010

The most significant three bits of this bit pattern are 110. Therefore, the IP address 199.245.180.10 is a class C address.

While the technique outlined previously works, it is a laborious way of determining the IP address class because it involves converting the IP address to a bit pattern. Fortunately, there is a simpler way. Consider the class B address shown in figure 4.10. For a class B address, the two most significant bits are 10. The minimum value of the first 8 bits is reached when the remaining 6 bits are 0; the maximum value is reached when the remaining 6 bits are 1.

Therefore, the minimum value of the first 8 bits of a class B address is 10000000 and the maximum value is 10111111. These minimum and maximum values correspond to decimal values of 128 and 191. This means that if the first decimal number of an IP address in the dotted decimal notation is a number between 128 and 191 (inclusive), the IP address is a class B address. In the previous example of the IP address 137.65.4.1, the number 137 is between 128 and 191; therefore, 137.65.4.1 is a class B address.

Figure 4.10 Determining IP address class.

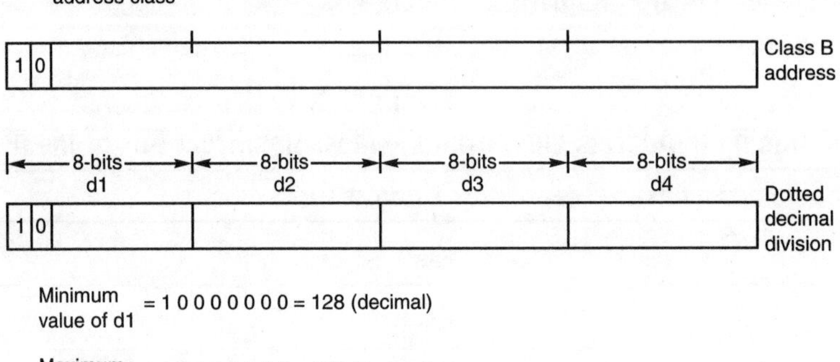
• First decimal number in dotted decimal IP address tells the address class
1 0
Class B address
8-bits d1
8-bits d2
8-bits d3
8-bits d4
Dotted decimal division
Minimum value of d1 = 1 0 0 0 0 0 0 0 = 128 (decimal)
Maximum value of d1 = 1 0 1 1 1 1 1 1 = 191 (decimal)
• Conclusion: For a class B address, the first decimal number must be between 128 and 191

Using the same reasoning, the minimum and maximum for the first decimal numbers of both a class A and class C address in their dotted decimal notation forms can be worked out as demonstrated in the following example:

> Minimum value of first decimal for class A = 00000000 = 0
>
> Maximum value of first decimal for class A = 01111111 = 127
>
> Minimum value of first decimal for class C = 11000000 = 192
>
> Maximum value of first decimal for class C = 11011111 = 223

Table 4.4 shows the range of values for the first decimal number of an IP address in the dotted decimal notation. This table can be used to determine the IP address class simply by examining the first decimal number of an IP address.

TABLE 4.4
Determining IP Address Class from the First Decimal Number of an IP Address Expressed in Dotted Decimal Notation

IP Address Class	Minimum	Maximum
A	0	126
B	128	191
C	192	223

IP Address Class	Minimum	Maximum
D	224	239
E	240	247

Consider the following questions:

1. What is the IP address class for 40.12.33.1?
2. What is the IP address class for 191.122.65.234?
3. What is the IP address class for 204.17.206.10?

By examining table 4.4, the first decimal number of 40 in the IP address 40.12.33.1 indicates that it is a class A address. The first decimal number of 191 in the IP address 191.122.65.234 indicates that it is a class B address; and the first decimal number of 204 in the IP address 204.17.206.10 indicates that it is a class C address.

Special IP Addresses

There are certain special cases for IP addresses. RFC 1700 describes a special notation that can be used to express special IP addresses:

IP-address ::= { <Network-number>, <Host-number> }

The preceding defines an IP address as consisting of a network number and a host number. The <Network-number> corresponds to the netid and the <Host-number> corresponds to the hostid used earlier in this chapter.

A notation "–1" means that the field contains all 1 bits, while a value of "0" means that the field contains all 0 bits.

The following special IP addresses have been defined:

- {<Network-number>, 0}
- {<Network-number>, –1}
- { –1, –1}
- {0, 0}
- {0, <Host-number>}
- {127, <any>}

Addresses of all 0s and all 1s in the <Host-number> field cannot be assigned as individual IP addresses. This means that if there are N bits in the host number field, you can have only $2N$ IP address assignments.

These special addresses are discussed in the following sections. In addition to the previously listed special addresses, special addresses are used for broadcasting within subnets. The treatment of subnets is addressed in Chapter 9; it is not discussed in this introductory chapter on IP addresses.

Addressing "This" Network

A hostid value of all 0s is never assigned to an individual TCP/IP host. An IP address with a hostid value of 0 indicates the network itself (that is, "this" network). This special address is described using the following type:

{<Network-number>, 0}

Consider the IP address of 137.53.0.0. This is a class B network. Recall that in a class B network, the <Network-number> is 16 bits (2 bytes or the first two decimal numbers in the dotted decimal address) and the <Host-number> is the remaining 16 bits of the IP address. Therefore, the special address 137.53.0.0 refers to the class B network 137.53. Figure 4.11 shows several connected networks that use the special address notation for "this" network.

The two class B addresses 137.53.0.0 and 141.85.0.0 have a "0.0" for the hostid field. These addresses indicate all the nodes in that network. The {<Network-number>, 0} cannot be used as a source or destination IP address.

Figure 4.11 Using the {<Network-number>, 0} special address.

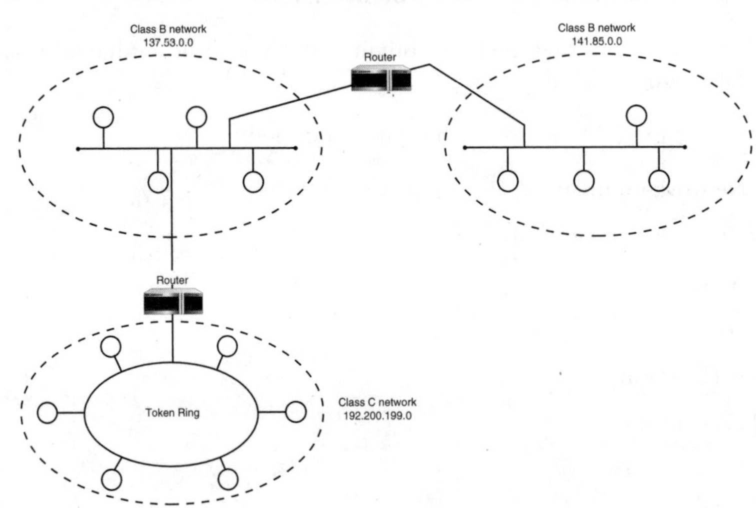

Directed Broadcast

A *directed broadcast* is one sent to all nodes in a specified network. If the hostid value contains all 1s in the bit pattern, it indicates a *directed broadcast address.* A directed broadcast address can occur in the destination IP address of an IP datagram, but never as a source IP address. This special address is described using the following type:

{<Network-number>, –1}

A directed broadcast address will be seen by all nodes on that network (see fig. 4.12). Therefore, for the network number 137.53, the broadcast address will be 137.153.255.255. The network number 137.53 is a class B address and has 16 bits (2 bytes or the first two decimal numbers in the dotted decimal address) in the hostid field. If 1s are used for the 16 bits of the hostid, they correspond to a decimal value of 255.255.

Figure 4.12 An IP broadcast with hardware broadcast support.

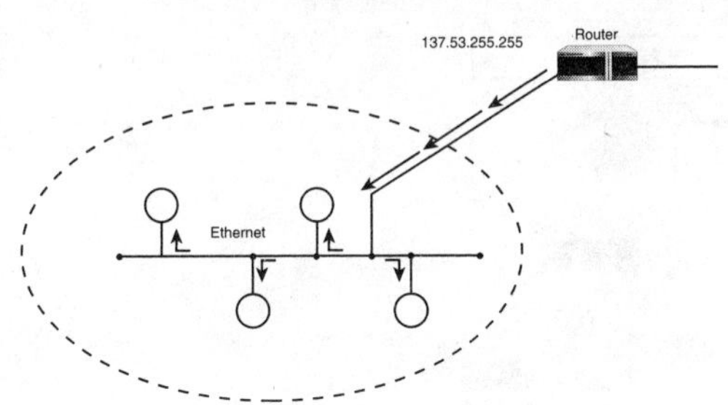

In the example in figure 4.12, the underlying network hardware is Ethernet, which supports broadcasts efficiently at the network hardware level. On other networks, such as point to point networks (see fig. 4.13), hardware level broadcast might not be supported efficiently. In this case, the broadcast is typically done by the IP protocol software by replicating the IP datagram across all possible links.

A directed broadcast is sent to a specific network that is identified in the <Network-number> field. Routers on the network configured to forward directed broadcasts send the IP datagram to the final router that connects the destination network <Network-number>. The destination network router will be obliged to send the IP datagram to all nodes on the network. If the destination network provides a hardware level broadcast, it is used to broadcast the IP datagram. Figure 4.14 shows an example of a directed broadcast where the Ethernet broadcast mechanism is used to broadcast the IP datagram on the destination network. In Ethernet, a destination address of all 1s indicates that the Ethernet frame is to be broadcast.

Figure 4.13 An IP broadcast without hardware broadcast support.

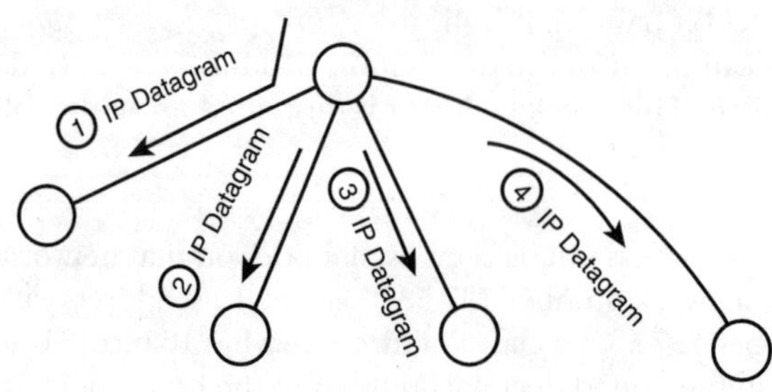

Figure 4.14 A directed broadcast example.

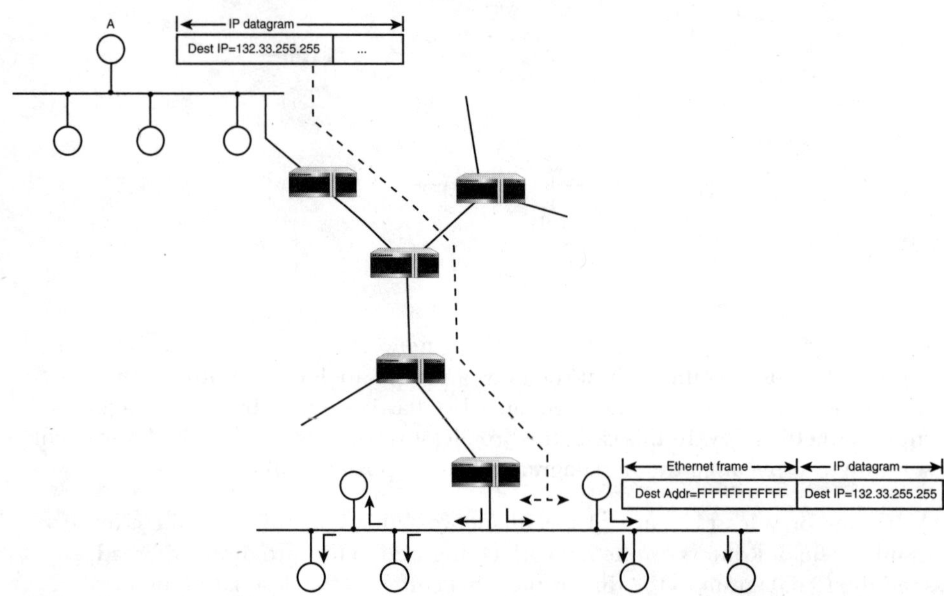

Routers can be configured not to forward directed broadcasts in situations where broadcast to other networks is not permitted.

Limited Broadcasts

A *limited broadcast* is one that is sent to all nodes on the same network as the source node sending the broadcast. The limited broadcast is represented by the value of 255.255.255.255. This special address is described using the following type:

{–1, –1}

The limited broadcast can be used in local area networks, where a broadcast never crosses a router boundary (see fig. 4.15).

Figure 4.15 Use of limited broadcast in LANs.

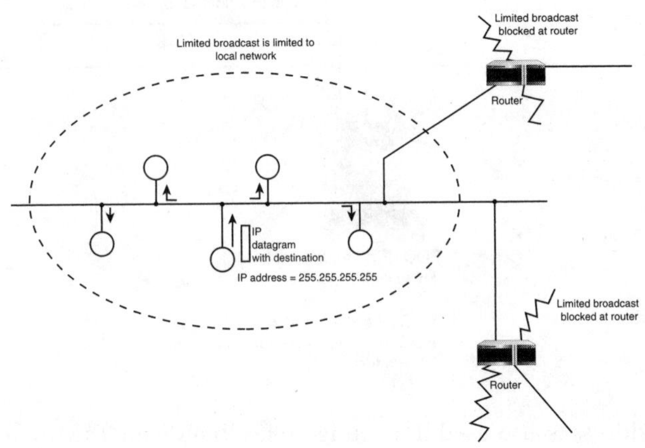

In a directed broadcast, the sender must supply the value of the <Network-number>. If broadcasting over the local network, you can use the limited broadcast that does not require knowledge of the <Network-number>.

A limited broadcast address can never appear as a source IP address; it can appear only as a destination IP address.

All Zeros IP Address

An all zeros IP address is a special address of the following type:

{0, 0}

The <Network-number> field is 0, which means "this" network. The <Host-number> field is also 0, which means "this" node on the network. This address typically occurs when an IP node is trying to determine its IP address. An example of this is the BOOTP protocol, which can be used by nodes on a network to assign an IP address from a central BOOTP server.

When the IP node sends an initial request to the BOOTP server, the IP node does not know its IP address (see fig. 4.16). It uses a value of 0.0.0.0 in the source IP address field to indicate that it could be "this" node (<Host-number> is 0) on "this" network (Network-number> is 0). Once the IP node learns its IP address from the BOOTP reply, it does not use the 0.0.0.0 address.

Figure 4.16 Use of an 0.0.0.0 IP address.

BOOTP Server
BOOTP Request
Source IP Address=0.0.0.0 ....
1. BOOTP client does not know its IP address.
2. BOOTP client sends a BOOTP request to determine its IP address.

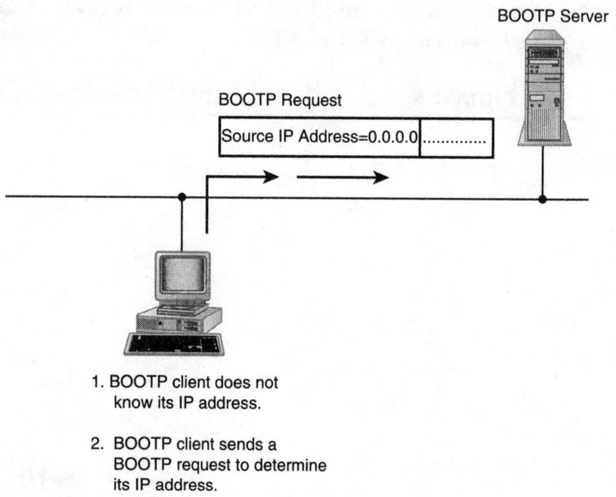

The 0.0.0.0 address is also used in routing tables to indicate the network entry for the default router's (often called the *default gateway*) IP address.

The IP address of 0.0.0.0 can be used only as a source IP address, and never as a destination IP address.

IP Address on "This" Network

A <Network-number> value of 0 with the <Host-number> value of non-zero means the specific host number in "this" network.

{0, <Host-number>}

If a node on a network receives a packet whose destination IP address has the <Network-number> set to 0, but the <Host-number> matches the receiver's <Host-number> field, the receiver will accept the packet. The receiver interprets the <Network-number> value of 0 to mean "this" network. Figure 4.17 shows an example of a receiver receiving a packet whose destination IP address is 0.0.0.23.

Figure 4.17 Receiving an IP datagram for "this" network.

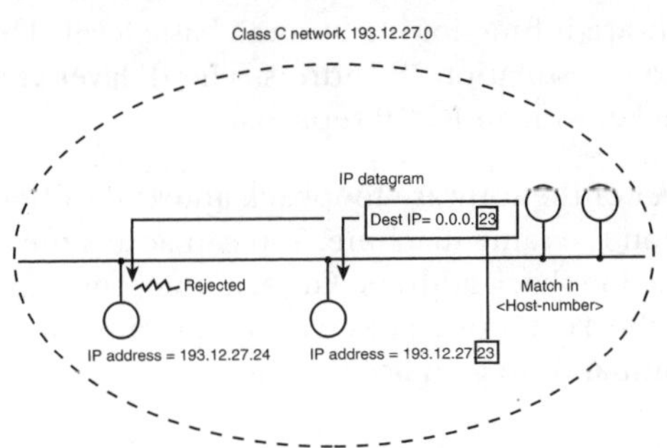

Software Loop-Back

If you examine table 4.4, you will see that the number 127, which should have been in the class A range of values, is missing. This number is reserved for the *loopback address.* The loopback address is the special address described by:

{127, <any>}

Any packet sent by a TCP/IP application to an IP address of 127.*X.X.X*, where *X* is a number from 0 to 255, results in the packet coming back to the application without reaching the network media. The packet is copied from transmit to receive buffer on the same computer (see fig. 4.18). This is why the IP address 127.*X.X.X* is called a loopback address.

Figure 4.18 In software loopback, the packet never reaches the network media.

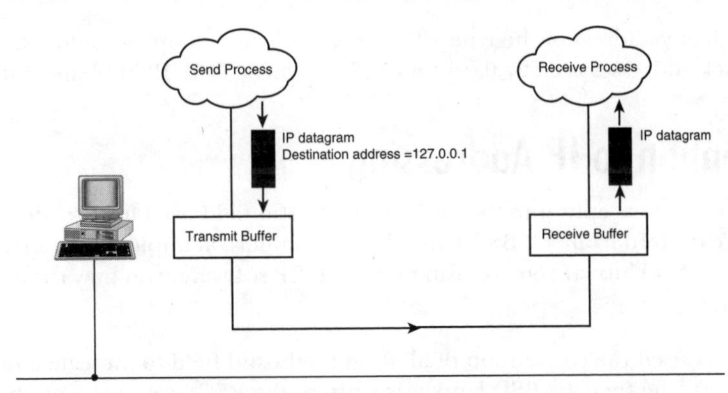

The software loopback address can be used to quickly verify that the TCP/IP software is properly configured. For example, you can use this with the "ping" tool to ensure that the IP layer software is functioning at some basic level. The "ping" tool sends an ICMP echo packet to a destination IP address. The IP layer at that address responds to an ICMP echo packet with an ICMP reply packet.

Another useful aspect of the software loopback address is when a TCP/IP client and service are running on the same machine. You can access the service on the same machine by using the loopback address. For example, you can use the Telnet or FTP client to connect to the Telnet or FTP server on the same machine by using the following typical commands to gain access:

telnet 127.0.0.1

ftp 127.0.0.1

You can use the preceding commands to check access to the Telnet and FTP server, as shown in figure 4.19.

Figure 4.19 Using a loopback address to access local services.

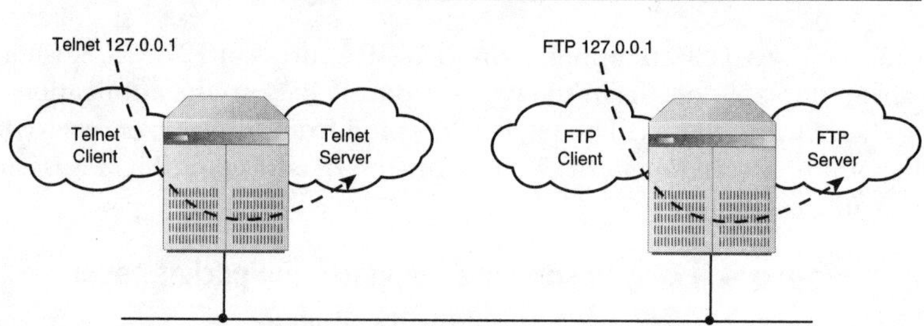

Alhough any address of the type 127.*X.X.X* indicates a loopback address, common loopback addresses are 127.0.0.1 and 127.1 in most TCP/IP implementations.

Exception to IP Addressing

An important exception to the all 1s in the hostid field used for broadcast is TCP/IP software derived from 4.2 BSD Unix. Many commercial implementations were derived from 4.2 BSD Unix. If you are using old TCP/IP software, you may run into this exception.

BSD Unix used the convention of all 0s in the hostid field to indicate a broadcast address. At the time 4.2 BSD Unix was written, the RFCs were unclear about the convention used for broadcast addresses. This was clarified in later RFCs, which stated that all 1s in the hostid field should be used for broadcast addresses. 4.3 BSD Unix was modified to conform to the RFCs. Software derived from 4.2 BSD Unix, unless modified, may still use the all 0s broadcast convention. If hosts that use all 0s broadcast are placed on the same physical network as hosts that use all 1s broadcast, the broadcast mechanism will not work as expected. Symptoms of this will be that the TCP/IP applications on that network will not work correctly.

Unicasting, Broadcasting, and Multicasting

When an IP datagram is sent to an individual IP address, it is called a *unicast IP datagram.* The process of sending the datagram is called *unicasting.* Unicasting is used when two IP nodes are communicating with each other.

When an IP datagram is sent to all nodes on a specific network, it is called *broadcasting.* In earlier sections, you saw examples of both directed and limited broadcasts.

There is a third mode of sending an IP datagram called *multicasting.* In multicasting, a class D address is used as the destination address. The IP datagram is delivered to a group of systems identified by a class D address. The systems that have the same multicast address are said to belong to a *multicast group.* Members of the multicast group, while being assigned a class D address, must also be assigned an IP address (from the class A, B, or C address group). The multicast group can receive an IP datagram in two ways:

- IP datagrams sent directly to their individual IP address (class A, B, C).
- IP datagrams sent to their multicast address (class D).

Class D addresses are those whose first decimal number in the dotted decimal notation is in the range of 224 to 239 inclusive (refer to table 4.4).

The Internet Assigned Number RFC defines permanently assigned multicast addresses listed in table 4.5.

TABLE 4.5
Standard Multicast Address Assignments

Multicast Address	Description
224.0.0.0	Base Address (Reserved)
224.0.0.1	All Systems on this Subnet
224.0.0.2	All Routers on this Subnet
224.0.0.3	Unassigned

continues

Table 4.5, Continued
Standard Multicast Address Assignments

Multicast Address	Description
224.0.0.4	DVMRP Routers
224.0.0.5	OSPFIGP All Routers
224.0.0.6	OSPFIGP Designated Routers
224.0.0.7	ST Routers
224.0.0.8	ST Hosts
224.0.0.9	RIP2 Routers
224.0.0.10	IGRP
224.0.0.11	Mobile-Agents
224.0.0.12–224.0.0.255	Unassigned
224.0.1.0	VMTP Managers Group
224.0.1.1	NTP Network Time Protocol
224.0.1.2	SGI-Dogfight
224.0.1.3	Rwhod
224.0.1.4	VNP
224.0.1.5	Artificial Horizons-Aviator
224.0.1.6	NSS-Name Service Server
224.0.1.7	AUDIONEWS-Audio News Multicast
224.0.1.8	SUN NIS+ Information Service
224.0.1.9	MTP Multicast Transport Protocol
224.0.1.10	IETF-1-LOW-AUDIO
224.0.1.11	IETF-1-AUDIO
224.0.1.12	IETF-1-VIDEO

Multicast Address	Description
224.0.1.13	IETF-2-LOW-AUDIO
224.0.1.14	IETF-2-AUDIO
224.0.1.15	IETF-2-VIDEO
224.0.1.16	MUSIC-SERVICE
224.0.1.17	SEANET-TELEMETRY
224.0.1.18	SEANET-IMAGE
224.0.1.19	MLOADD
224.0.1.20	Any private experiment
224.0.1.21	DVMRP on MOSPF
224.0.1.22	SVRLOC
224.0.1.23	XINGTV
224.0.1.24	microsoft-ds
224.0.1.25	nbc-pro
224.0.1.26	nbc-pfn
224.0.1.27–224.0.1.255	Unassigned
224.0.2.1	"rwho" Group (BSD) (unofficial)
224.0.2.2	SUN RPC PMAPPROC_CALLIT
224.0.3.000–224.0.3.255	RFE Generic Service
224.0.4.000–224.0.4.255	RFE Individual Conferences
224.0.5.000–224.0.5.127	CDPD Groups
224.0.5.128–224.0.5.255	Unassigned
224.0.6.000–224.0.6.127	Cornell ISIS Project

continues

Table 4.5, Continued
Standard Multicast Address Assignments

Multicast Address	Description
224.0.6.128–224.0.6.255	Unassigned
224.1.0.0–224.1.255.255	ST Multicast Groups
224.2.0.0–224.2.255.255	Multimedia Conference Calls
224.252.0.0–224.255.255.255	DIS transient groups
232.0.0.0–232.255.255.255	VMTP transient groups

For multicasting to work, a host must have the capability to join a multicast group or remove itself from the multicast group. This capability is usually implemented by a command line and is operating-system specific. The IP layer software must be able to recognize multicast addresses of incoming and outgoing IP datagrams. Older IP implementations may not recognize multicast addresses.

Any hosts on an IP Internet can join a multicast group. The hosts need not be on a single LAN and may be separated by routers. Consequently, routers need to understand how to forward multicast datagrams across the network. To do this efficiently, routers must know whether there are hosts on a locally attached network that are part of a multicast group. How do routers know this information? Routers exchange information amongst themselves and discover if there are group members on remote networks to which the IP multicast datagrams need to be forwarded.

Hosts that join or leave a multicast group use the Internet Group Management Protocol (IGMP) to report their group memberships to neighboring routers. The neighboring routers receive this report and update their internal tables about the hosts that are members of a multicast group. Routers can periodically poll hosts with queries about their current membership. These polls are sent, using the special multicast address 224.0.0.1 (refer to table 4.5), to all systems on this subnet.

When a multicast is sent to a LAN, that LAN's multicasting hardware capabilities are used. Recall from Chapter 3 that both Ethernet and IEEE 802 LANs have a multicasting bit that can be set in the most significant bit of the MAC address. The 23 low-order bits of the IP multicast address are placed in the low-order 23 bits of the Ethernet or IEEE 802 net multicast address.

The physical layer multicast address that is used is the following bit pattern:

10000000 00000000 011110010 xxxxxxxx xxxxxxxx xxxxxx

The “x” positions can be any bit values. The first “x” is set to 0, and so the physical layer multicast now becomes:

10000000 00000000 011110010 **0**xxxxxxx xxxxxxxx xxxxxxxx

The IP multicast is a class D address whose most significant bits are 1110 (refer to table 4.3). The bit representation for any multicast address is as follows:

1110xxxx xxxxxxxx xxxxxxxx xxxxxxxx

The “x” positions can be any bit values. Only the low-order bits of the IP multicast address are used to form the physical multicast address. These low-order bits are marked with “y” in the following multicast address format:

1110xxxx xyyyyyyy yyyyyyyy yyyyyyyy

The “x” bits in the previous class D multicast address are ignored in forming the physical multicast address, which now becomes the following:

10000000 00000000 011110010 0yyyyyyy yyyyyyyy yyyyyyyy

The translations described in the previous steps are done so that it is simple to translate an IP multicast address to a physical multicast address on a LAN.

Another point to note in the preceding discussion is that because only the lower 23 bits of the IP multicast address are used in the physical multicast address, many IP multicast addresses would map to the same physical IP multicast address. Consider the following IP multicast address:

1110xxxx xyyyyyyy yyyyyyyy yyyyyyyy

Regardless of the values of the “x” bits, the IP multicast address maps to the following single physical IP multicast address:

10000000 00000000 011110010 0yyyyyyy yyyyyyyy yyyyyyyy

Because several IP multicast addresses map to the same physical multicast address, the host may pick up IP multicast datagrams that it does not want. For this reason, the “x” bits in the IP multicast typically are set to zero. With the “x” bits set to zero, the IP multicast addresses have the following format:

1110**0000 0**yyyyyy yyyyyyyy yyyyyyyy

In dotted decimal notation, these are IP addresses in the following range:

224.0.0.0 to 224.127.255.255

Assigning IP Addresses

If your network is going to be connected to other networks such as the Internet, you must apply to a central authority to obtain a unique netid (network number) that is not in use by anyone else. Once you have obtained a network number, you are responsible for making the host number assignments for the given network numbers. The central Internet Address Network Authority (IANA) sets the policy and has ultimate authority over the numbers assigned. The IANA is part of the Internet Registry, which in turn is controlled by the IAB. In actual practice, the network numbers are obtained from the InterNIC.

To connect to the MILNET, use the following contact information:

DDN Network Information Center
14200 Park Meadow Drive, Suite 200
Chantilly, VA 22021, USA
E-mail: hostmaster@nic.ddn.mil

To connect to the Internet, use the following contact information:

Network Solutions
InterNIC Registration Services
505 Huntmar Park Drive
Herndon, VA 22070 USA
E-mail: hostmaster@internic.net
WWW: www.internic.net

Two other NIC centers have been formed in Europe and Asia to meet the needs of these regions. These are the RIPE (Réseaux IP Européens) Network Coordination Center and the Asia Pacific Network Information Center (APNIC). Contact information for each follows:

RIPE Network Coordination Center
Kruislaan 409
NL-1098 SJ Amsterdam
The Netherlands
Phone: +31 20 592 5065
Fax: +31 20 592 5090
E-mail: ncc@ripe.net
WWW: www.ripe.net

Asia Pacific Network Information Center
c/o The United Nations University
53-70 Jingumae 5-Chome
Shibuya-ku
Tokyo, 150 Japan
Phone: +81 3 5467 7014
Fax: +81 3 5467 7015
E-mail: hostmaster@apnic.net
WWW: www.apnic.net

Private Network Addresses

To reduce the need for new IP addresses, RFC 1597 on Address Allocation for Private Internets was issued in March 1994. The authors of this RFC suggest a scheme for IP address assignments for private networks. *Private networks* are those not connected to other networks or those that have hosts and services that have limited interaction with the connected Internet. Hosts on a network can be classified into the following categories:

- Hosts that do not require access to hosts in other enterprises or the Internet at large.
- Hosts that need access to a limited set of outside services such as e-mail, FTP, netnews, remote login, and so on, which can be handled by an Application layer gateway (refer to Chapter 2, "TCP/IP Protocol Layering Concepts," for a definition of Application layer gateways).
- Hosts that need Network layer access outside the enterprise, which is provided via IP connectivity and includes router devices or hosts that are visible to the outside world.

Hosts in the first category can use IP addresses that are unique within the private network, but may not be unique across the Internet. Because no packet exchange occurs with these hosts outside the private network, the duplicate IP address problem will never be seen.

Hosts in the second category that are insulated from the external Internet by an Application level gateway do not need to have unique IP addresses across the Internet. This is because the Application level gateway hides the IP addresses of these hosts from the external network.

Hosts in the third category require IP addresses that are globally unique across the Internet.

By maintaining proper documentation on the network, you can easily identify hosts in category 1 and 2. These hosts do not need Network layer connectivity outside the organization's network.

RFC 1597 gives the following examples of hosts in categories 1 and 2:

- A large airport that has many arrival/departure displays individually addressable via TCP/IP. It is very unlikely that these displays need to be directly accessible from other networks.
- Large organizations, such as banks and retail chains, are switching to TCP/IP for their internal communication. Local workstations like cash registers, money machines, and equipment at clerical positions rarely need to have such connectivity.

For security reasons, many enterprises use Application layer gateways (such as firewalls) to connect their internal network to the Internet. The internal network usually does not have direct access to the Internet, and only one or more firewall hosts are visible from the Internet. In this case, the internal network can use non-unique IP numbers. Vendors also provide *Network Address Translation (NAT)* devices that can map between non-unique private IP addresses and a set of unique IP addresses.

If two enterprises communicate over their own private link, usually only a very limited set of hosts are reachable from the remote enterprise over this link. Only those hosts need globally unique IP numbers.

Interfaces of routers on an internal network usually do not need to be directly accessible from outside the enterprise.

Based on the request of the authors of RFC 1597, the IANA has reserved the following three blocks of the IP address space for private networks to be assigned for hosts in categories 1 and 2:

10.0.0.0 to 10.255.255.255	1 class A network
172.16.0.0 to 172.31.255.255	16 class B networks
192.168.0.0 to 192.168.255.255	256 class C networks

An enterprise that decides to use IP addresses out of the previously listed address space can do so without any coordination with IANA or an Internet registry. This address space can thus be used by many enterprises and reduces the need for assigning new network numbers. Addresses within this private address space are unique within the enterprise, but not unique across the network.

If an enterprise needs globally unique address space for applications and devices that are connected at the IP layer, it will have to obtain such addresses from an Internet registry. The IANA will not assign IP addresses from the private IP address space.

Because private addresses have no global meaning, routing information about private networks should not be propagated outside the enterprise. Routers in networks not using private address space, such as those of Internet Service Providers (ISPs), should have their filters set to reject routing information about private networks. Filtering out private address information should not be reported as a routing protocol error.

To use private address space, an enterprise needs to determine which hosts do not need to have Network layer connectivity. If the configuration of the hosts change and Network layer connectivity is needed to external networks, globally unique addresses must be assigned; that is, the IP address of these hosts must be changed from the private address space to the public address space. If an organization does not keep proper track of changing requirements for hosts, the organization can accidentally create a situation of duplicate IP address problems. Perhaps for this and other reasons, RFC 1627 was issued in July 1994.

The authors of RFC 1627, titled "Network 10 Considered Harmful (Some Practices Shouldn't be Codified)," argue that the recommendations in RFC 1597 reduce network reliability and security and are costly in terms of potential problems. For example, if two organizations that are using private address spaces need to connect directly, at least one of them will have to change its IP address assignments. RFC 1627 states that "RFC 1597 gives the illusion of remedying a problem, by creating formal structure to a long-standing informal practice. In fact, the structure distracts us from the need to solve these very real problems and does not even provide substantive aid in the near-term." Additionally, RFC 1627 states that the IANA has overstepped its mandate in recommending RFC 1597 without the benefit of the usual public review and approval by the IETF or IAB.

So what should you, the network designer, do in the midst of this controversy about using private addresses? If you plan on using the recommendations of RFC 1597, do so with great care. Ensure that you have proper documentation and understanding of which services are visible or non-visible to the outside world. Read RFC 1627 and understand the objections it raises.

Class C Address Allocation

The class C addresses from 192.0.0 through 223.255.245 have been divided into 8 blocks of addresses. Regional authorities are responsible for allocation of these blocks. Table 4.6 shows this address allocation.

TABLE 4.6
Class C Address Allocation

Address Range	Region
192.0.0–193.255.255	Multiregional. Includes addresses established before the region-based address allocation scheme was introduced.
194.0.0–195.255.255	Europe.
196.0.0–197.255.255	Used when there is need to assign IP addresses that are not based on region.
198.0.0–199.255.255	North America.
200.0.0–201.255.255	Central and South America.
202.0.0–203.255.255	Pacific Rim.
204.0.0–205.255.255	Used when there is need to assign IP addresses that are not based on region.

Address Range	Region
206.0.0–207.255.255	Used when there is need to assign IP addresses that are not based on region.
208.0.0–223.255.255	Available for assignment.

The IP address allocation information in table 4.6 can be useful if you have a protocol trace of packets coming into your network and you want to determine the region of the world from which the packets originated.

Configuring IP Addresses

Hosts on a TCP/IP network need to be configured using proper IP addresses. The actual configuration procedure depends on the operating system. The configuration procedure can be classified into the following categories:

- Command line based
- Menu interface
- Graphical User Interface based
- Obtained dynamically when host boots from a central server

Table 4.7 shows examples of operating systems that fit into these categories.

TABLE 4.7
Configuring IP Address and Other Parameters for Hosts

Method	Operating System/Protocol
Command line	Unix, VMS, Router devices, and MS-DOS.
Menu interface	Router devices, Unix, NetWare servers, and MS-DOS.
Graphical User Interface	Unix and Microsoft Windows products.
Dynamically assigned	DHCP and BOOTP protocols. Available on almost all major operating system platforms.

Many systems offer a command that can be executed to modify the IP address. In these systems, the command line is often placed in the startup script for the operating system. The menu interface is built using extended line drawing character sets. You are prompted to enter the IP address and other IP parameters. The Graphical User Interface is for systems—such as X-Windows and Microsoft's Windows operating systems—that offer a pixel-based graphical view. The dynamically assigned IP address is used in conjunction with BOOTP or DHCP protocol. When starting up, a device requests its IP address and other parameters from a central server that can deliver this information using either the BOOTP or the DHCP protocol.

The IP address information for the host is recorded in a number of places. When the IP address information is entered, it is cached in memory and is available for use by the TCP/IP software. Alternatively, this information can be recorded on a system file in the operating system. IP addresses of other systems can be discovered by consulting a special file, usually called the "hosts" file, or by using the DNS protocol. The DNS service is typically used to determine a host's IP address given its symbolic DNS name (refer to Chapter 1, "Introduction to TCP/IP"). In some systems, proprietary protocols can be used to discover an IP address on a network. An example of this is the WINS service used in Microsoft's operating systems.

You must consult your operating system manuals for actual details on configuring IP addresses. The following sidebar provides examples of configuring IP addresses for most Unix implementations, and for the Windows NT operating system.

Imagine that you are configuring a network interface to IP address 144.19.74.102, subnet mask 255.255.0.0, and directed broadcast address 144.19.255.255. (Subnet masks are discussed in Chapter 9.)

For a Unix Configuration

1. Log on as root user.
2. Run the following command:

   ifconfig eth0 144.19.74.102 netmask 255.255.0.0 broadcast 144.19.255.255

Replace eth0 with the Unix logical name of the network interface.

For Windows NT

1. Log on as Administrator user.
2. Select the following:
   - Start
   - Settings
   - Control Panel

continues

- ◆ Network
  - ◆ Select the TCP/IP protocol
  - ◆ Select Properties

3. You will see a dialog box in which you can enter the IP address and subnet mask.

Windows NT, by default, uses the appropriate directed broadcast address of 144.19.255.255 based on the subnet mask that you specify.

IP Version 6 Addresses

As noted earlier in this chapter, the 32-bit address space for IP addresses is running out as the Internet continues to grow in size. Notwithstanding RFC 1597, every IP network connection on the Internet requires a unique IP address. Some devices have more than one network connection, which results in the rapid consumption of assignable IP addresses.

It is estimated that the 32-bit IP addresses (also called IP version 4 addressing) can provide over 2,100,000 networks and a total of over 3720 million hosts. However, the IP address space allocation scheme is not very efficient because new network numbers are generally required to connect networks through Network layer relay devices such as routers.

In Chapter 9, you learn about subnetting and supernetting schemes that help you utilize the IP address space more efficiently. Even with subnetting, however, the IP address allocation scheme is not very efficient. For example, if you have a class B network assignment, you can have up to 65,534 hosts. However, a medium size organization may have only 15,000 hosts on the network, which leaves the remaining 50,534 addresses unused and unavailable to the Internet community.

IP addresses are quickly becoming a scarce resource. To overcome this problem, the IETF has studied methods for overcoming the address space problem and making improvements to the protocol so that it can run more efficiently over newer networking technologies. After studying a variety of proposals for solving limitations of the current IP protocol (called IP version 4 [IPv4], after the version number field value of 4 in the IP header), the IETF has decided on the "IP Next Generation" protocol, known as IPng or IP version 6 (IPv6). One of the design goals of IPv6 was to support at least one billion networks. To support this design criteria, IPv6 uses 128-bit addresses. This is four times the bit size of IPv4 addresses. IPv6 uses the concept of network numbers and host numbers, but extends this concept to several levels. The hierarchical addressing in IPv6 can support more efficient routing. The IPv6 address can contain an IPv4 address by using 32-bit IPv4 addresses in the lower bits of the IPv6 address and adding a fixed prefix of 96 bits. The 96-bit prefix consists of 80 zero bits followed by 16 zero or 16 one bits.

Unregistered IPv4 addresses can be used in IPv6 by adding a unique registered modifier so that the overall IPv6 address is unique.

IPv6 is designed to interoperate with IPv4 systems. This allows a period of coexistence for the two IP systems. The goal is to have current IPv4 systems eventually replaced by IPv6 systems. Routers with both IPv6 and IPv4 support could be used to relay information between networks running the IPv4 protocol and the newer IPv6 protocol.

IPv6 includes support for mobile portable systems. This permits portable computer and other device users to connect from anywhere within the network without having to perform manual configuration. Mobile systems automatically will be connected when joining the network at a new attachment point. In addition to automatic configuration for mobile systems, regular workstations are self-configuring. IPv6 supports encryption at the Internet layer and provides better support for real-time traffic. Real-time data traffic requires some guarantee of the maximum delay in transmitting datagrams across the network.

Because IPv6 addresses are 128 bits long, using dotted decimal notation is not a convenient notation for writing IPv6 addresses. If the dotted decimal notation was used for writing IPv6 addresses, you would have to write a string of 16 decimal numbers separated by dots!

Consider the following bit-pattern representation of an IPv6 address:

01011000 00000000 00000000 11000101

11100011 11000011 11110001 10101010

01001000 11100011 11011001 00100111

11010100 10010101 10101010 11111110

Notice that because there are 128 bits in the IPv6 address, it is not very convenient to write it as a bit pattern. If you use the dotted decimal notation, this IPv6 address would be written as follows:

88.0.0.192.227.195.241.170.72.227.217.39.212.149.170.254

As you can see from the preceding dotted decimal value, it is not a compact notation. The designers chose to use a *colon hexadecimal notation* to write the bit patterns. The hexadecimal values are written as 16 bits separated by the colon (:) character. The preceding IPv6 address is written as follows:

5800:00C3:E3C3:F1AA:48E3:D923:D495:AAFE

Using the colon hexadecimal notation requires fewer digits and separation characters. The colon hexadecimal notation specifies two shorthand techniques you can use to reduce the number of characters that you have to write.

The first technique is that you can skip leading zeros. Consider the following IPv6 address:

48A6:0000:0000:0000:0000:0DA3:003F:0001

By skipping the leading zeros, you can write this as the following simplified address:

48A6:0:0:0:0:DA3:3F:1

Note that 0000 is replaced by 0, 0DA3 is replaced by DA3, and 0001 is replaced by 1. In each case, leading zeros are skipped to reduce the number of characters that you have to write.

The second technique uses *zero compression,* in which a single string of repeated zeros is replaced by a double colon (::). In the preceding IPv6 address, there is a string of four 0s (0:0:0:0). These zeros can be replaced by "::." The preceding IPv6 address can therefore be written as follows:

48A6::DA3:3F:1

To expand the zero compressed IPv6 address, align whatever is to the left of the colon with the left 16-bit words of the IPv6 address. Next, align whatever is to the right of the double colon with the right 16-bit words of the IPv6 address. Fill the remaining 16-bit words of the IPv6 address with zeros. As an example, consider the following zero compressed IPv6 address:

5400:FD45::FFFF:3AFE

In the expanded form, this IPv6 address becomes the following:

5400:FD45:0:0:0:0:FFFF:3AFE

You can use the double colon only once in the notation to produce an unambiguous interpretation. The following IPv6 notation is illegal because the number of zeros that were compressed is ambiguous.

5400::45A1::23A6

The third technique is to use the double colon either as a prefix or suffix. Consider the following IPv6 representation of the IPv4 address 170.1.1.1:

0:0:0:0:0:0:AA01:101

This can be represented as the following:

::AA01:101

Summary

Assigning Internet addresses to the nodes on the network is a very common task you will perform when building a TCP/IP network. Two types of IP addresses exist: those for IP version 4 and those for IP version 6. This chapter discusses the format of both types of IP addresses. Because IP version 4 is the major networking protocol deployed on the Internet, the term IP address refers to an IPv4 address.

IP addresses must be unique on a network. In special cases, it is possible to introduce non-unique addresses, called private addresses, as outlined in RFC 1597.

IP addresses possess a certain structure; they are divided into a network number (netid) and a host number (hostid) portion. This chapter examines the strengths and weaknesses of this scheme. Not all IP addresses can be assigned as a unique identification for network connections. Only class A, B, and C addresses are assignable to individual network connections. Class D is used for IP multicasting. In addition, there are several special addresses used for broadcasting, loopback addresses, and special circumstances.

Test Yourself

1. If a host has five network connections over which IP transmission takes place, how many IP addresses does it need?
2. What is the OSI term for an IP address?
3. Discuss the advantages/disadvantages of using the MAC hardware address as the value of the NSAP address.
4. What is the advantage of using a logical address value for IP addresses?
5. How many address classes exist in IP? Name the address classes that can be used for individual IP addresses.
6. What are IP address classes D and E used for?
7. Draw the bit representation format for the different address classes. Show the values of the most significant bits and explain their importance.
8. What is the advantage/disadvantage in dividing the IP address into a netid and a hostid?
9. Prove that an IP dotted decimal notation whose first number is between 1 to 126 is a class A address.
10. Prove that an IP dotted decimal notation whose first number is between 128 to 191 is a class B address.

11. Prove that an IP dotted decimal notation whose first number is between 192 to 223 is a class C address.
12. Prove that an IP dotted decimal notation whose first number is between 223 to 239 is a class D address.
13. Explain the difference between a directed broadcast address and a limited broadcast address. Give example(s) of each address type.
14. What is a software loopback address? Describe its format. How many representations of the loopback address exist?
15. What does the IP address of 0.0.0.0 signify? Give examples of its usage.
16. What is the IP address of 255.255.255.255 used for?
17. On a class B network of 135.23.0.0, what does the address 0.0.45.23 mean?
18. Given a class C network address of 193.234.55.0, how many hosts are possible for that network? Give the reasoning behind your answer.
19. Given a class B network address of 167.45.0.0, how many hosts are possible for that network? Give the reasoning behind your answer.
20. Given a class A network address of 9.0.0.0, how many hosts are possible for that network? Give the reasoning behind your answer.
21. What are the differences between a unicast, broadcast, and multicast IP address?
22. What is the IP address 224.0.0.1 used for?
23. Given an IP multicast address of 224.0.0.1, write the physical multicast address value for an IEEE 802.5 network.
24. What is a private address? Write the possible range of values for private IP addresses. Which RFC describes its usage? Are any problems associated with its usage?
25. Under what circumstances would an organization want to use private addresses?
26. What types of hosts can be assigned a private IP address?
27. Can you assign a private IP address to a host or router that is visible to the outside world? Justify your answer.
28. Which authorities assign IP addresses in Europe and Asia?
29. Determine whether the following IP addresses are special addresses, unicast IP addresses, multicast IP addresses, or invalid addresses. Also, specify to which class, if any, these IP addresses belong.

    33.0.0.45 212.44.45.56
    128.0.35.0

212.0.0.0

100.78.189.1

100.0.0.0

0.0.0.0

190.34.0.0

127.33.45.255

255.255.255.255

10.255.255.255

137.256.34.0

127.1

33.55.260.35

127.0.0.1

0.0.22.45 on network 156.23.0.0

0.67.43.90 on network 7.0.0.0

0.0.0.252 on network 99.25.66.0

30. What is the theoretical limit to the number of IP multicast addresses?
31. If only the lower 23 bits of an IP multicast address are mapped to a physical multicast address, how many IP multicast addresses will potentially map to the same physical multicast address? Does this pose a potential problem? If so, what restrictions can be placed on the IP multicast address to solve this problem?
32. Given the scheme described in this chapter for mapping an IP multicast address to a physical multicast address, how many physical multicast addresses are possible?
33. Describe the methods used to enter IP address information at a host.
34. Write the colon hexadecimal notation for the following IPv6 addresses:

    01011000 10101011 01111001 10111101

    10100011 11011011 11110011 11110010

    11001000 10000011 10011001 10101111

    01010100 10111101 11101110 10000001

35. Convert the following IPv4 addresses to IPv6 addresses. Show both the compressed and expanded colon hexadecimal notation.

    127.0.0.1

    199.245.180.10

    255.255.255.255

    167.99.44.33

CHAPTER 5

Address Resolution Protocols

The IP address scheme is a logical addressing scheme designed to create the appearance of a virtual network. All interfaces on the network are modeled by a single 32-bit identifier called the IP address. However, the actual transmission of the IP datagrams on a physical network requires that the IP datagrams be encapsulated in Data Link layer (OSI layer 2) frames. The Data Link layer frames, such as Ethernet or Token Ring, need hardware addresses as part of their framing. This chapter discusses the techniques used in TCP/IP networks to create the association between hardware addresses and IP addresses. The protocols required to create the association between hardware addresses and IP addresses are called Address Resolution Protocols.

Need for Address Resolution

The DNS is used to provide an association between symbolic names for the host and the IP address. Knowing the symbolic name, a host can discover the corresponding IP address. In order to transmit a message to a host on a network with a broadcast capability, such as in Ethernet and Token Ring, the sender must know the hardware address of the destination host. The hardware address, also called the Media Access Control (MAC) address, is needed in the MAC header of the packet used to send a message. The host software knows the IP address of the destination by using DNS or a table lookup. The problem of determining the hardware address of the destination host is illustrated in figure 5.1.

Figure 5.1 Need for Address resolution. (Courtesy Learning Tree)

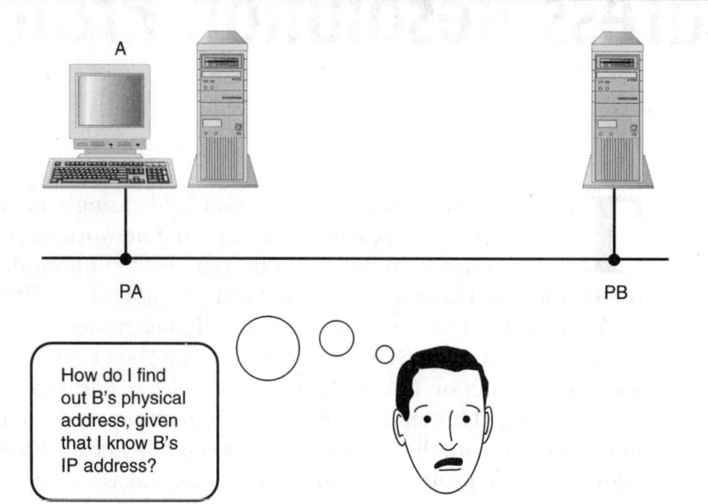

One method of solving the problem was to use a table of IP address and MAC address associations similar to the hosts file table discussed earlier. The problem with this approach is that if a network board is replaced on a host, the MAC address changes, and this table has to be updated. If a technician changes the network board, it is unlikely that he will inform the network administrator of this change immediately.

This approach of manually configuring a TCP/IP system to define the correspondence between IP addresses and MAC addresses was done in earlier systems. In modern systems, a more flexible scheme is needed to dynamically determine the MAC address knowing a host's IP address. This dynamic mechanism is implemented as a separate protocol called the Address Resolution Protocol.

Address Resolution Protocol (ARP)

Figure 5.2 shows a simplified view of how ARP works. In this figure, Host A wishes to determine the hardware address of destination B as a prelude to sending a message.

Figure 5.2 ARP Operation. (Courtesy Learning Tree)

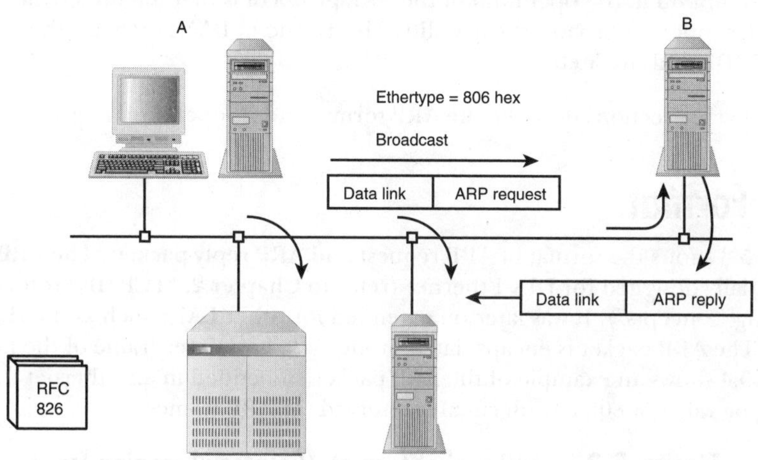

Host A sends a MAC broadcast frame called the ARP request frame on the network. The *ARP request frame* contains the sender Host A's IP and MAC addresses and the destination B's IP address. The ARP request frame contains a place-holder field for destination B's hardware address. All nodes on the physical network receive the broadcast ARP request frame. All other nodes who receive the broadcast frame compare their IP addresses to the IP addresses in the ARP request. Only the host that has the same IP address as the one requested in the ARP request frame responds.

If Host B exists on the network, it responds with its hardware address encoded in an ARP reply frame. The Host A initializes its ARP cache table (kept in RAM) with the answer contained in the ARP reply. The ARP cache entries are timed out after a certain period which can be configured in some TCP/IP implementations. Typically, the ARP cache time-out is 15 minutes. After an ARP cache entry has timed-out for a specific host, the ARP request frame is sent again to discover the host's hardware address. The ARP cache is consulted by a host before the host sends an ARP request. If the answer is found in the ARP cache, the host can avoid generating an ARP request.

The ARP request is sent with a hardware broadcast address because the hardware address of the target node is not known. The ARP reply that is sent by the target node *is not* a broadcast frame. Why? Because the target node knows the sender hardware address by examining the ARP packet or the sender hardware address in encapsulating Data Link frame. The ARP reply is, therefore, sent directly to the node that sent the ARP request.

The assumption in the operation of the ARP protocol is that the underlying physical network supports a broadcast capability. This is true in LANs such as Ethernet, Token Ring, FDDI, and ARCnet.

The following sections describe the ARP format and its operation in greater detail.

ARP Format

Figure 5.3 shows the format of ARP request and ARP reply packets. The ARP protocol was initially designed for DIX Ethernet (refer to Chapter 2, "TCP/IP Protocol Layering Concepts"). It was later on extended for other LANs such as the IEEE 802 LANs. The ARP packet is encapsulated in the Data Link layer frame of the network. Figure 5.4 shows an example of the ARP packet embedded in an Ethernet frame. An Ethertype value of 806 hexadecimal is reserved for ARP frames.

Figure 5.3 ARP packet format. (Courtesy Learning Tree)

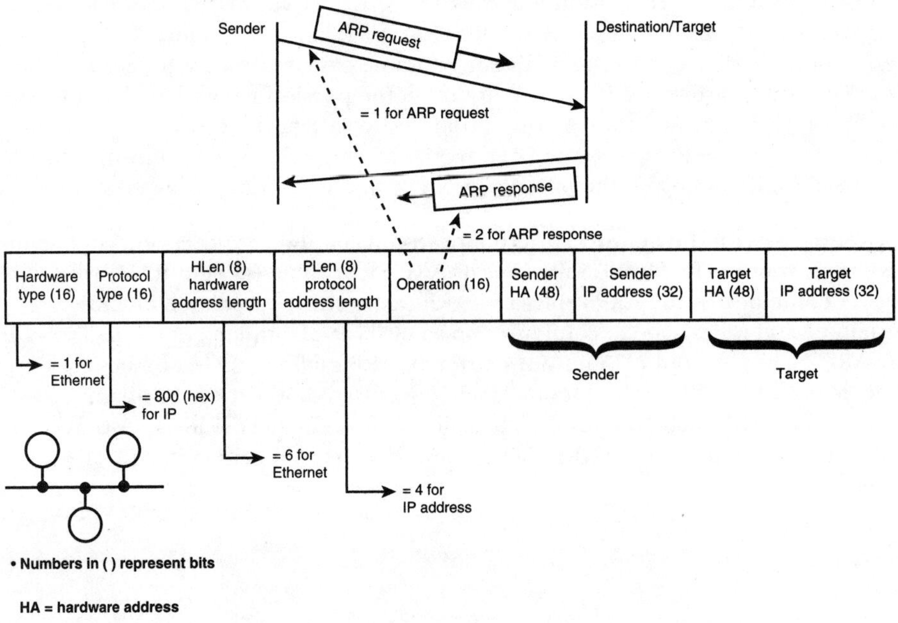

Figure 5.4 ARP packet encapsulated in an Ethernet frame.

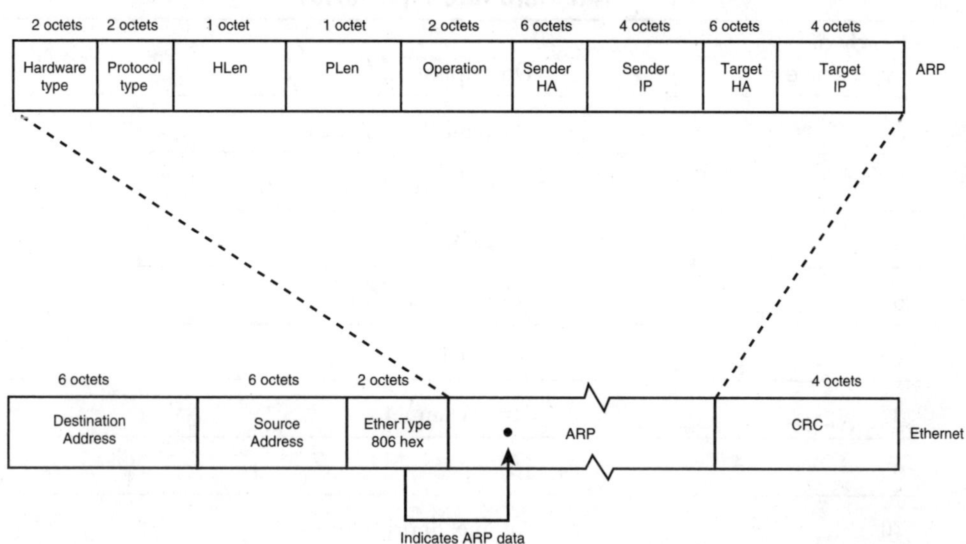

This section defines the ARP format by discussing, in detail, each of the ARP packet fields. (In figure 5.3 the numbers in parentheses are the size of the ARP field in bits.)

Looking at figure 5.3, the Hardware type field is the first field in the ARP packet. It is 2 octets (octet = 8 bits) long and indicates the type of hardware network. (The term octet is the same as the term byte for practical purposes. The term octet is more correct because on some older machine architectures a byte did not always have 8 bits.)

The value in the Hardware type field controls the setting of the HLen field (to be discussed presently). A value of 1 in the Hardware type field indicates an Ethernet network. Table 5.1 lists the codes assigned for the Hardware type values in the ARP packet for different networks.

TABLE 5.1
ARP Hardware Type Values

Hardware Type Value	Description of Network
1	Ethernet (10 Mbps)
2	Experimental Ethernet (3 Mbps)

continues

Table 5.1, Continued
ARP Hardware Type Values

Hardware Type Value	Description of Network
3	Amateur Radio AX.25
4	Proteon ProNET Token Ring
5	Chaos Net
6	IEEE 802 Networks
7	ARCNET
8	Hyperchannel
9	Lanstar
10	Autonet Short Address
11	LocalTalk
12	LocalNet
13	Ultra link
14	SMDS
15	Frame Relay
16	Asynchronous Transmission Mode (ATM)
17	HDLC
18	Fibre Channel
19	Asynchronous Transmission Mode (ATM)
20	Serial Line
21	Asynchronous Transmission Mode (ATM)

The Protocol type is the upper layer protocol address that was supplied for which the corresponding hardware address is desired. This field is 2 octets long. In the case of TCP/IP networks, the protocol address is the IP address for which the hardware address is needed. The Protocol type value is the same as the Ethertype value for the protocol. See table 2.2 in Chapter 2 for a list of common Ethertype values for a number of protocols. For the IP protocol, a value of 800 hexadecimal is used for the Protocol type field.

The HLen field is the length of the hardware address in octets. This field is 1 octet long. The HLen value is controlled by the value Hardware type field. If the Hardware type is 1, it indicates an Ethernet network whose hardware address is 8 octets. Therefore, the HLen field value is set to 8 for Ethernet networks. The HLen field determines the size of the Sender HA and the Destination HA fields. (HA is a common abbreviation for hardware addresses in TCP/IP protocols.) For Ethernet networks these fields are 8 octets long.

The PLen field is the length of the protocol address in octets. This field is 1 octet long. The PLen value is controlled by the value Protocol type field. If the Protocol type is 800 hexadecimal, it indicates the IP protocol whose IP address is 4 octets. Therefore, the PLen field value is set to 4 for IP networks. The PLen field determines the size of the Sender IP and the Destination IP fields. For IP networks these fields are 4 octets long.

The Operation field is two octets long and indicates whether the packet contains an ARP request or an ARP reply. Table 5.2 indicates the possible values that can exist in the Operation field. Some of the values in table 5.2 are for experimental protocols or proposed address resolution protocols, and you may never see them on existing networks.

TABLE 5.2
Operation Values for ARP Packet

Operation Field Value	Type of Operation
1	ARP-Request
2	ARP-Reply
3	RARP-Request
4	RARP-Reply
5	DRARP-Request
6	DRARP-Reply
7	DRARP-Error

continues

Table 5.2, Continued
Operation Values for ARP Packet

Operation Field Value	Type of Operation
8	InARP-Request
9	InARP-Reply
10	ARP-NAK

The Sender HA field contains the hardware address of the node sending the ARP request. The sender knows its hardware address by reading it from the network board, and it fills this field with the hardware address of the network board.

The Sender IP address contains the IP address of the node sending the ARP request. The sender knows its IP address by reading it from a configuration file or its memory cache, which contains network configuration information.

The Target HA field is the hardware address of the target. This value is not known by the sender in an ARP request. It is the value that the ARP request sender is trying to determine. This field is normally set to all zeros or all ones. STD 37 (also RFC826) on Address Resolution Protocol states that the Target HA is not set to anything in particular because it is this value that it is trying to determine. The Target HA could be set to the broadcast address for the hardware (all ones in the case of the Ethernet) if that makes it convenient for some aspect of the implementation.

The Target IP field in the ARP request contains the IP address of the node whose hardware address is to be determined. This value is supplied by the ARP request sender.

The ARP reply packet uses the same format as the ARP request packet, but the Operation field value is set to a value of 2 to indicate an ARP reply (see table 5.2).

Using the same format for ARP requests and replies enables an implementation to reuse the ARP request packet buffer for the ARP reply. The ARP reply has the same length as an ARP request, and several of the fields are the same.

When an IP node sends an ARP reply, it places its hardware address in the Sender HA field. Note that the value of the Sender HA field in the ARP reply packet is the reason for sending the ARP request—that is, it contains the target node's hardware address. The fields in the ARP packet reply are filled as follows:

- **Sender HA.** This contains the target node's hardware address (reason for original ARP operation).
- **Sender IP.** This contains the target node's IP address.

- **Target HA.** This contains the ARP request sender's hardware address. The target node knows this by examining the Sender HA field in the ARP request.
- **Target IP.** This contains the ARP request sender's IP address. The target node knows this by examining the Sender IP field in the ARP request.

In the Data Link frames that are used to send the ARP request and ARP replies, the address fields are filled as follows (see fig. 5.5):

- **ARP request packet**
  - *Data Link Source HA.* Value read from the network board of the ARP request sender.
  - *Data Link Destination HA.* Broadcast. Usually all 1s.
- **ARP reply packet**
  - *Data Link Source HA.* Value read from the network board of the target node generating the ARP reply.
  - *Data Link Destination HA.* Value read from the Sender HA field in the ARP request.

Figure 5.5 Data Link addresses for ARP request and ARP reply.

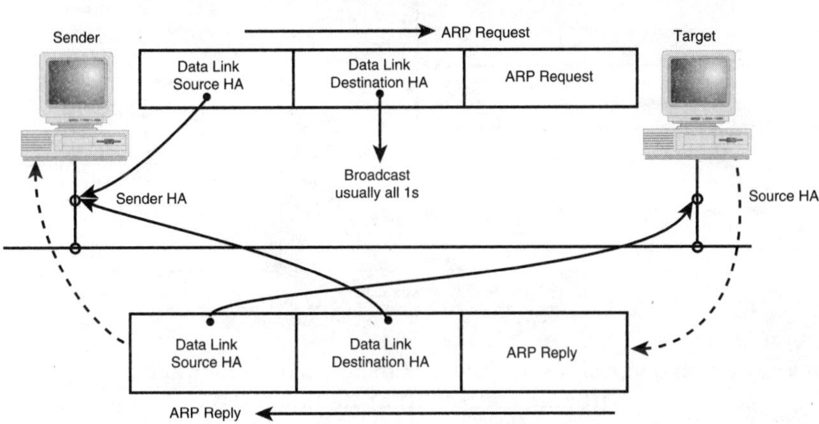

Note that the ARP request and ARP reply packets are variable in size because the hardware address and protocol address fields depend on the type of hardware and protocol of the network.

ARP Operation

As an IP packet is sent through the network layers of nodes in a TCP/IP internet, the routing component of the network layer determines the IP address of the next router (see fig. 5.6). The routing component of the network layer determines if the IP datagram is to be sent to a host on the local network or a host on a different network segment. The actual routing algorithm executed by a sender host is discussed in detail in Chapter 7, "IP Routing Concepts."

Figure 5.6 Routing component of network layer in sending host.

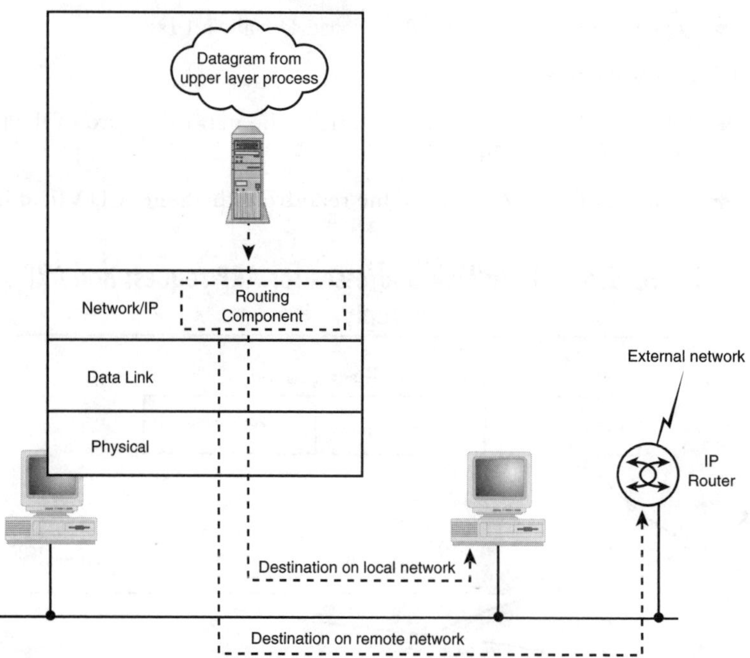

If the sender host determines that the destination is on the local network, it needs to find the destination's hardware address. If the destination is on a remote network (a different network than the local network), then the sender needs to find the hardware address of the router port to which the IP datagram is to be forwarded.

For broadcast networks ARP is used to find the hardware address of the target node, which is either the node on the local network or the router port on the local network.

ARP is implemented as part of the IP module in networks that need address resolution, such as broadcast LANs (Ethernet, Token Ring, and so on). The ARP protocol is directly encapsulated by the Data Link layer protocol; it is not encapsulated by the IP protocol (see fig. 5.7). This means that the ARP protocol cannot be routed—that is, it cannot cross a router boundary—because the IP encapsulation is required for a packet for it to be forwarded by an IP router.

Before sending the ARP request, the ARP module tries to find the target address in its local cache, also called the ARP cache table. The *ARP cache table* (see fig. 5.8) keeps pairs of entries of IP addresses and the corresponding hardware address.

Figure 5.7 Limit of ARP on local network segment.

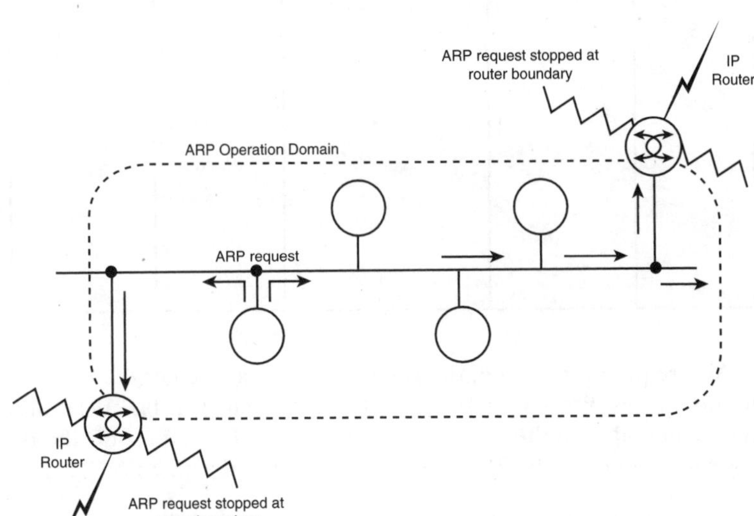

If the target IP address is found in the ARP cache table, it looks up the corresponding hardware address and returns it to the ARP module. The ARP module returns the hardware address to the network driver that made the request to discover the target node's hardware address. The network driver then transmits a Data Link layer frame containing the IP datagram with the target node's hardware address placed in the destination hardware address field. In the scenario just discussed, an ARP request is never generated because the target node's hardware address was discovered in the local cache.

What happens if the ARP cache does not contain the target node's hardware address? In this case, the ARP module generates a Data Link layer frame containing the ARP request to discover the target node's hardware address. The ARP request is broadcast at the Data Link layer to all nodes on the local network segment. As mentioned earlier, the ARP requests/replies are confined to the local network segment and do not cross router boundaries.

Figure 5.8 ARP cache table.

Protocol Type (IP)	Protocol Address (IP address)	Hardware Address	Interface Number	Time Stamp

When an ARP request is received, the Data Link layer at the target node gives the packet to the Address Resolution module. The ARP request is broadcast at the Data Link level, so all nodes on the local network receive it. However, only the node whose IP address corresponds to the Target IP address respond with an ARP reply.

The steps performed by the ARP module at the receiving node is listed as follows (they are also shown as a flow chart in figure 5.9):

1. Do I recognize hardware type in the Hardware Type field of the ARP request packet?
2. If the answer is yes in step 1, optionally check the hardware length HLen in the ARP request packet.
3. Do I know how to process the protocol in the Protocol Type field in ARP request packet?
4. If the answer is yes in step 3, optionally check the protocol length PLen in ARP request packet.
5. Set Merge_flag to *false* to control ARP processing in subsequent steps.
6. If the pair <protocol type, sender protocol address> is already in my translation table, update the sender hardware address field of the entry with the new information in the packet and set Merge_flag to *true*.

7. Am I the target protocol address?

   (This means is my IP address the same as that in the Target IP address field?)

8. If the answer is yes in step 7, then continue by determining if Merge_flag is false. If Merge_flag is *false*, add the triplet <protocol type, sender protocol address, sender hardware address> to the translation table.

9. Is the Operation field value a request?

10. If the answer is yes to step 9, then continue by swapping hardware and protocol fields, putting the local hardware and protocol addresses in the sender fields. Set the Operation field to ARP reply. Send the packet to the (new) target hardware address on the same hardware on which the request was received.

In the algorithm just described, the <protocol type, sender protocol address, sender hardware address> triplet is merged into the ARP cache table before the Operation field is examined in step 6. This step only occurs if a node has an entry for the sender's IP address in the ARP cache table. Figure 5.10 shows how an ARP cache table is modified by a single ARP request. Note that only the ARP cache table for nodes that have an entry for the sender IP address is modified.

Updating or adding ARP cache entries is done because the upper layers of the target node are likely to respond to the ARP request sender, and when the target generates a Data Link layer frame, it consults its ARP cache table and discovers that it already knows the hardware address of the sender. Thus an ARP request to discover the sender's hardware address is not required.

Note also that if the target node already has an entry in its ARP cache table for the <protocol type, sender protocol address> pair, then the new hardware address replaces the old address. This could occur in any of the following situations:

1. New network hardware was added in the ARP request sender to replace the existing one. In this case the hardware address of the node would be different.

2. The IP addresses were reassigned. The ARP request sender is another node that was assigned the IP address that is in the ARP cache table of the target. The hardware address of the ARP sender is different because it is a different node.

3. There is a duplicate address problem. Another node claims to have the same IP address as the one in the target node's ARP cache table.

While the first two situations are normal, the last situation of duplicate IP addresses is an error condition and is examined in detail in the later "Duplicate IP Addresses" sections in this chapter.

Figure 5.9 ARP Packet Reception flow diagram.

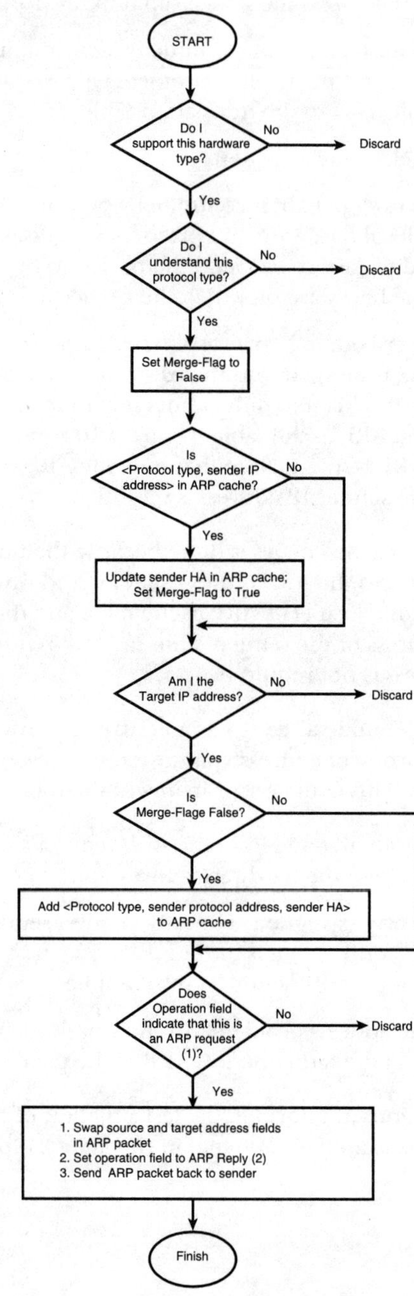

Figure 5.10 ARP request causing changes in ARP cache table as per RFC 826.

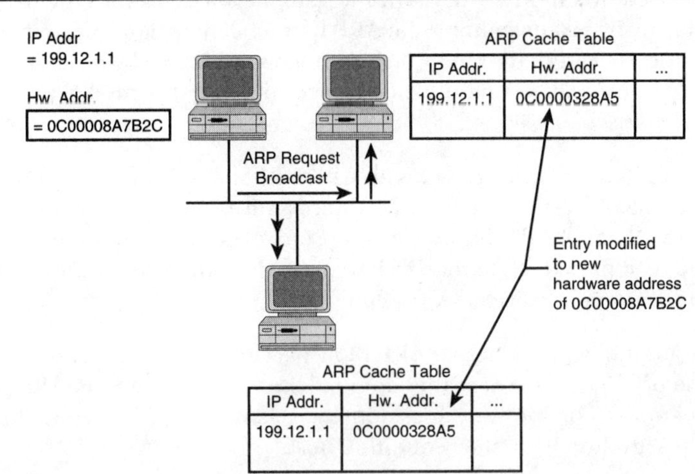

Comments on the ARP Protocol Design

In theory, the length fields HLen and PLen in the ARP packet format are redundant because the length of the hardware address and the protocol address can be determined by the value of the Hardware Type and Protocol Type fields. For instance, if the Hardware Type field has a value of 1, it indicates an Ethernet frame (see table 5.1).This implies an HLen value of 6 octets because Ethernet addresses are 6 octets long. Similarly, if the Protocol Type field indicates an IP protocol, the PLen value is 4 octets because IP addresses are 4 octets long.

The redundant HLen and PLen fields are included for optional consistency checking and for the use of network monitoring tools.

The Operation field is used to determine if this is a request or a reply to a previous request. Using a two-octet field is excessive considering the number of the operation codes that have been assigned thus far (see table 5.2). In retrospect, a one-octet field would have been sufficient.

The Sender HA and Sender IP address fields are needed because these fields are potentially recorded in the ARP cache tables of the receiving nodes. In the ARP request the Target HA has no meaning because its value is not known. Note that the answer is actually returned in the Sender HA field in the ARP reply. The Target HA is included for completeness and network monitoring.

The Target IP field is necessary in the ARP request so that a machine can determine whether or not it is the target node and therefore needs to send a reply. The Target IP field is not necessarily needed in the ARP reply if one assumes a reply is only provoked by a request. It could be used for network monitoring and to simplify the ARP request/reply processing algorithm.

Network Monitoring with ARP

ARP can be used by a monitoring device to gain knowledge about the higher level protocol activity by just examining the ARP frame headers. For example, the network monitoring device can determine which protocols are in use by examining the Protocol Type field value. A monitoring device could be designed along the lines suggested in this section.

When the monitoring device receives an ARP packet, it can enter the protocol type, sender protocol address, and sender hardware address in a table. Additionally, it can determine the length of the hardware and protocol address from the HLen and PLen fields of the ARP packet. Note that ARP requests are broadcast at the Data Link level, and a monitor would receive all ARP requests.

If the Operation field indicates an ARP reply packet, and the target protocol address matches the protocol address of the monitor, the monitor sends an ARP reply like any other target node. The monitor does not receive any other ARP replies because an ARP reply is sent directly to the requesting host.

Timeouts in ARP Cache Table

ARP cache tables are often implemented with a timeout mechanism. Entries in the ARP cache table may have time stamp values associated with them. This section discusses some of the timeout issues associated with ARP tables.

If a node is moved, it is usually shut down before moving. Shutting down a node clears its ARP cache table so old entries do not cause confusion. Other nodes on the network generally are not aware that a particular node has moved or been shut down.

If the node has been moved to a location on the same network segment, the ARP cache information about the moved node is still valid because the IP address and hardware address of the moved node has not changed (see fig. 5.11).

If the node is shut down, other nodes are not able to reach this node. They use their ARP cache information to access the node but are unable to make the connection. An implementation could use the failure to initiate a connection to a node to delete the information about the node in the ARP cache table (see fig. 5.12). It could also try accessing the node by sending a few more ARP requests before giving up.

If the node has been moved to a location on a different network segment (see fig. 5.13), it is behind a router boundary. Because IP addresses contain information about the network segment they are attached to (refer to Chapter 4, "IP Addressing"), the IP address of the moved node must change even though its hardware address remains the same. Recall that ARP transmissions do not go beyond a router boundary. For all practical purposes the new node can be assumed to be shut down or unavailable. This situation is discussed in the previous paragraph and in figure 5.12.

Figure 5.11 ARP cache information about a node moved to the same network segment does not change.

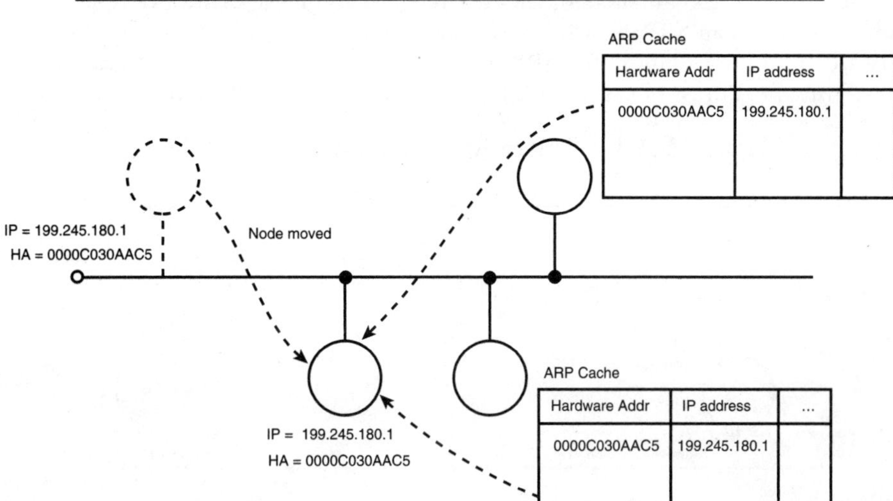

Figure 5.12 Update of ARP cache upon not being able to reach a node.

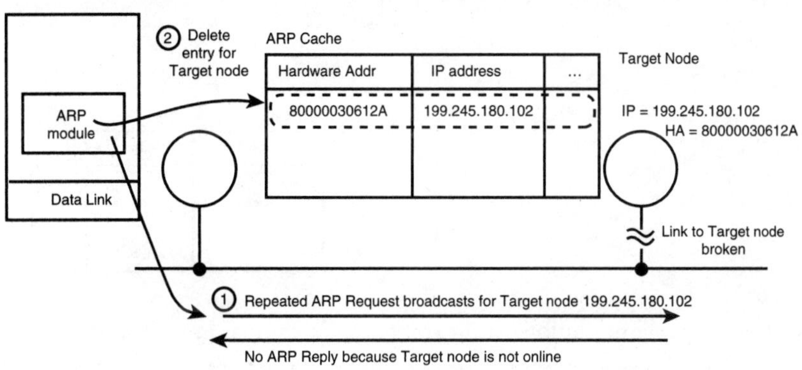

An ARP implementation typically updates the time stamps when the address resolution entry is used for transmitting packets to a node. The time stamps are also updated when ARP requests are received from a node whose entry exists in the ARP cache table. If no packets are received from a node for a suitable length of time (the ARP timeout value), the address resolution entry is discarded.

An ARP implementation may also have an independent process (also called a *daemon* process) check the ARP cache table periodically and time out old entries. In TCP/IP a default time out of 15 minutes is used for the ARP cache time out, and in some implementations this value could be configured by a system administrator. As a refinement, it is also possible for the ARP daemon to first send an ARP request to the node directly. If an ARP reply is not seen after a few retransmissions, the ARP entry is discarded. In this situation, the ARP request is sent directly and *not broadcast* because the hardware address of the node is known from the ARP cache table.

Figure 5.13 ARP cache table for a node moved to a different network segment.

IP address of moved node must change to match network prefix "200.1.20" at its new location
Hardware Address remains same
IP = 200.1.20.1
HA = 0000C030AAC5
Network = 200.1.10.0
Moved
IP =199.245.180.1
HA = 0000C030AAC5
IP Router
Network = 199.245.180.0
ARP Cache entry is invalid it still points to the old location
ARP Cache
Hardware Addr | IP address | ...
0000C030AAC5 | 199.245.180.1

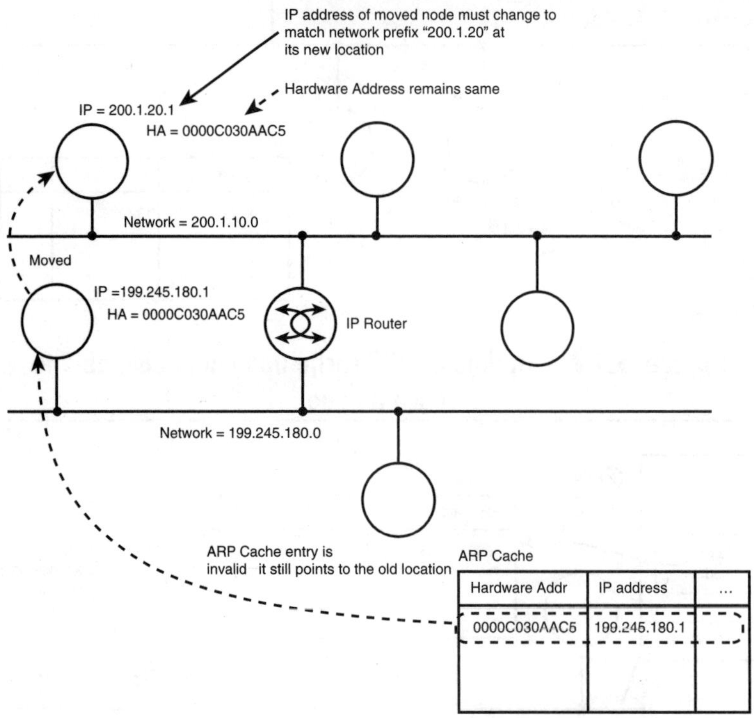

Many TCP/IP implementations allow you to make manual entries in the ARP cache table. Normally, there is no need to make manual entries in the ARP table, as the dynamic ARP operation determines the IP address and hardware associations. ARP entries made manually are not timed out and can be used to fix problems with incorrect entries in the ARP table because of duplicate IP address problems or malfunctioning software.

The tool used to view or make changes in the ARP table depends on the operating system. It can be a command-line tool or a graphical tool.

ARP in Bridged Networks

When a TCP/IP connection fails, the TCP protocol that is responsible for reliable delivery attempts to recover from the failure by retransmitting packets. If the failure was caused by a physical link failure and other paths to the destination are available, the IP datagrams get routed around the failed link. If TCP is unable to recover from the failure, recovery continues at the lower layers. At the lower layers, the ARP module attempts to recover from the connection by broadcasting an ARP request.

If the target node is on the local network segment, this is a viable technique for recovering from failure. However, a complication arises when the several nodes start sending ARP request broadcasts. This can happen when a central host is no longer available because of host or link failure (see fig. 5.14).

Figure 5.14 ARP broadcast traffic after failure.

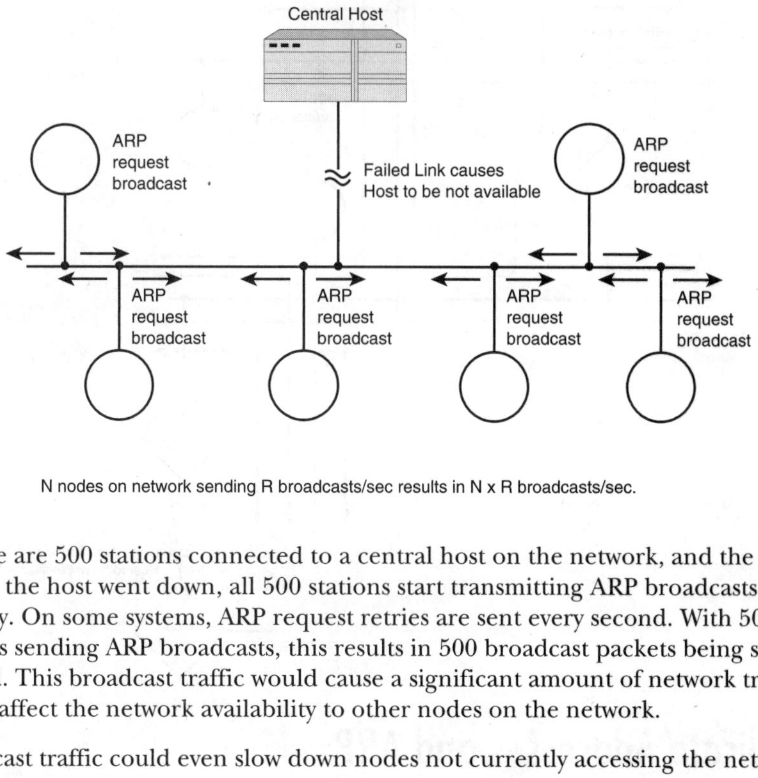

If there are 500 stations connected to a central host on the network, and the connection to the host went down, all 500 stations start transmitting ARP broadcasts simultaneously. On some systems, ARP request retries are sent every second. With 500 stations sending ARP broadcasts, this results in 500 broadcast packets being sent every second. This broadcast traffic would cause a significant amount of network traffic that would affect the network availability to other nodes on the network.

Broadcast traffic could even slow down nodes not currently accessing the network. This is because the network board and the associated software driver must examine every broadcast packet. In the case of ARP requests, the ARP module is also executed for every broadcast request. Processing even 50 ARP requests per second can take a fair amount of processing power and have a significant slowing down effect on a node. As a result all nodes on the network appear to slow down.

The repeated ARP broadcasts create further complications in a bridged network (see fig. 5.15). Network segments separated by bridges are considered to be part of the same MAC domain. ARP requests/replies must be transmitted across these bridges. Propagation of broadcast traffic across bridges can have a multiplying effect, and the network traffic could increase even more. Creating a large or complex network topology using bridges, therefore, is not desirable under these conditions.

Figure 5.15 ARP traffic on bridged networks.

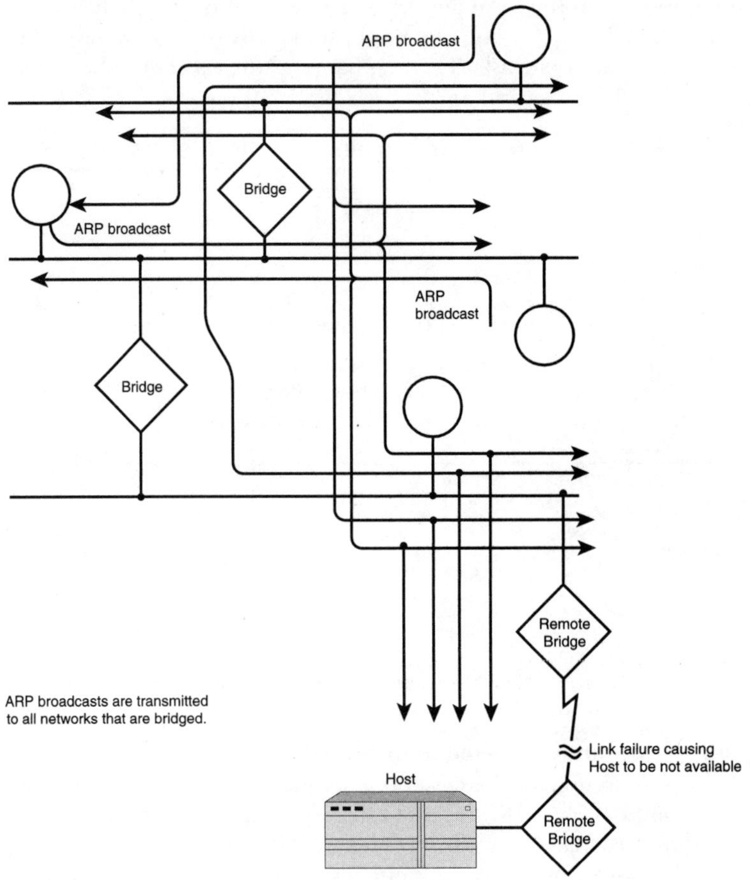

Duplicate Addresses and ARP

IP addresses on a network must be unique. How do you ensure this uniqueness? By proper documentation and assignment of IP addresses. Because of the human element involved in assigning IP addresses, it is possible to inadvertently assign nodes on a network with the same IP address. When this happens, chaos and confusion ensues. Networked applications work intermittently or sometimes mysteriously stop working altogether.

To help you understand the effect of duplicate IP addresses, the following sections discuss two scenarios:

- Duplicate IP addresses at TCP/IP clients
- Duplicate IP addresses at TCP/IP servers

Duplicate IP Addresses at TCP/IP Clients

Consider the situation in figure 5.16 that shows two TCP/IP clients called "workstation 1" and "workstation 2" accessing a central TCP/IP server at IP address 144.19.74.102. The server's hardware address is 080020021545.

Figure 5.16 **Duplicate IP addresses at TCP/IP clients - Step 1. (Courtesy Learning Tree)**

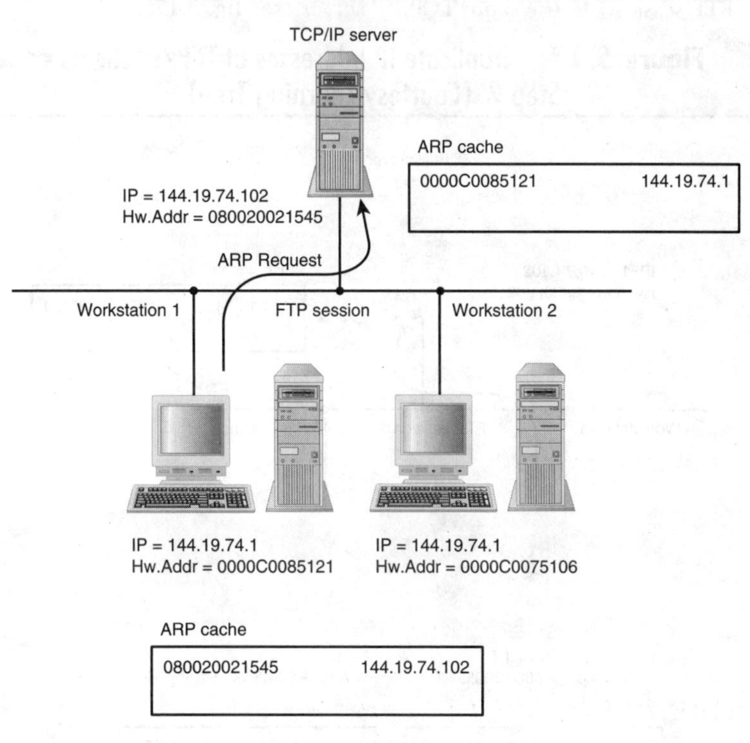

Workstations 1 and 2 are using the same IP address of 144.19.74.1. Their hardware addresses are 0000C0085121 and 0000C0075106, respectively.

Workstation 1 starts an FTP session with the TCP/IP server. Before the FTP session starts, workstation 1 issues an ARP broadcast request to discover the hardware address of the TCP/IP server. On receiving the ARP request, the TCP/IP server adds an entry for the ARP request sender (workstation 1) in its ARP cache table, and sends an ARP reply to the sender. On receiving the ARP reply, workstation 1 adds an entry for the TCP/IP server in its local ARP cache table. At this point the ARP cache table for the TCP/IP server is as follows:

IP Address	Hardware Address
144.19.74.1	0000C0085121

The ARP cache table for workstation 1 is as follows:

IP Address	Hardware Address
144.19.74.102	080020021545

In the second phase, workstation 2 attempts to establish a TCP/IP session (perhaps another FTP session) to the same TCP/IP server (see fig. 5.17).

Figure 5.17 Duplicate IP addresses at TCP/IP clients - Step 2. (Courtesy Learning Tree)

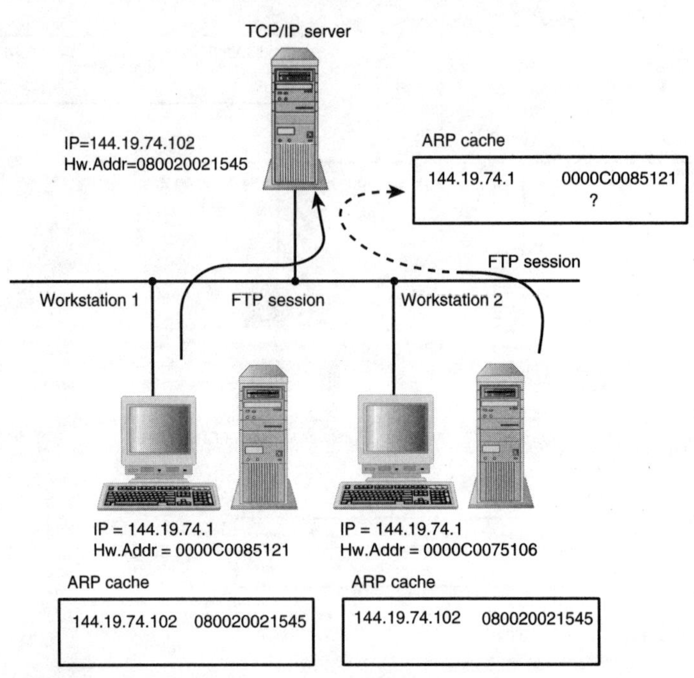

Before making the connection, workstation 2 must discover the TCP/IP server's hardware address. It attempts to do just that by sending an ARP request. On receiving the ARP request, the TCP/IP server wants to add an entry for the ARP request sender (workstation 2) in its ARP cache table, and send an ARP reply to the sender. The TCP/IP server finds that there is already an entry for 144.19.74.1 in its ARP cache table. As per RFC 826 on the Address Resolution Protocol, the TCP/IP server must replace the existing entry with the new one.

Most TCP/IP implementations perform this replacement silently without issuing any warning of a potential duplicate IP address problem. Some TCP/IP implementations issue a warning of a potential duplicate IP address problem. The TCP/IP server replies to the ARP request from workstation 2. On receiving the ARP reply, workstation 2 adds an entry for the TCP/IP server in its local ARP cache table. At this point, the ARP cache table for the TCP/IP server is as follows:

IP Address	Hardware Address
144.19.74.1	0000C0075106

The ARP cache table for workstation 2 is as follows:

IP Address	Hardware Address
144.19.74.102	080020021545

When the TCP/IP server wants to send data to workstation 1, it looks up the hardware address of workstation 1 at IP address 144.19.74.1 in its local ARP cache table and sends the data to this hardware address. Unfortunately, this is workstation 2's hardware address, and the data is sent to workstation 2. Workstation 1, on not receiving expected data, tries to resend its last transmission, and the TCP/IP server continues sending the response to workstation 2. Workstation 1, therefore, "hangs" waiting for a response. It eventually times out, or the workstation may have to be rebooted to recover from the error. In any case, an application that was working fine some time ago may suddenly stop working, much to the consternation of the user and system administrator alike!

Workstation 2, on receiving unexpected data destined for workstation 1, probably rejects it, optionally generates an error message, and continues with its session with the TCP/IP server. Alternatively, workstation 2 can become confused with unexpected data and also hangs.

If the user at workstation 1 reboots the hung computer and tries to reconnect to the TCP/IP server, the ARP cache entry for workstation 2 in the TCP/IP is replaced with that for workstation 1. This causes workstation 2 to hang, and the situation could repeat until the users give up in frustration.

If the users at workstations 1 and 2 are not in communication with each other about the problems they are experiencing, each experiences its side of the story—that is, their workstation "hangs" unexpectedly in the middle of accessing the TCP/IP server. If the users do not access the TCP/IP server at the same time, they never experience this problem and the duplicate IP address problem goes undetected. If the users experience the problem occasionally, they may dismiss the problem to a "fluke" on the network and never report it. Again, the problem goes undetected.

Duplicate IP Addresses at TCP/IP Servers

Consider the situation in figure 5.18 that shows two TCP/IP servers called "server 1" and "server 2". They are both set to the duplicate IP address of 144.19.74.102. The server's hardware addresses are 080020021545 and AA0004126750, respectively.

Figure 5.18 Duplicate IP addresses at TCP/IP servers. (Courtesy Learning Tree)

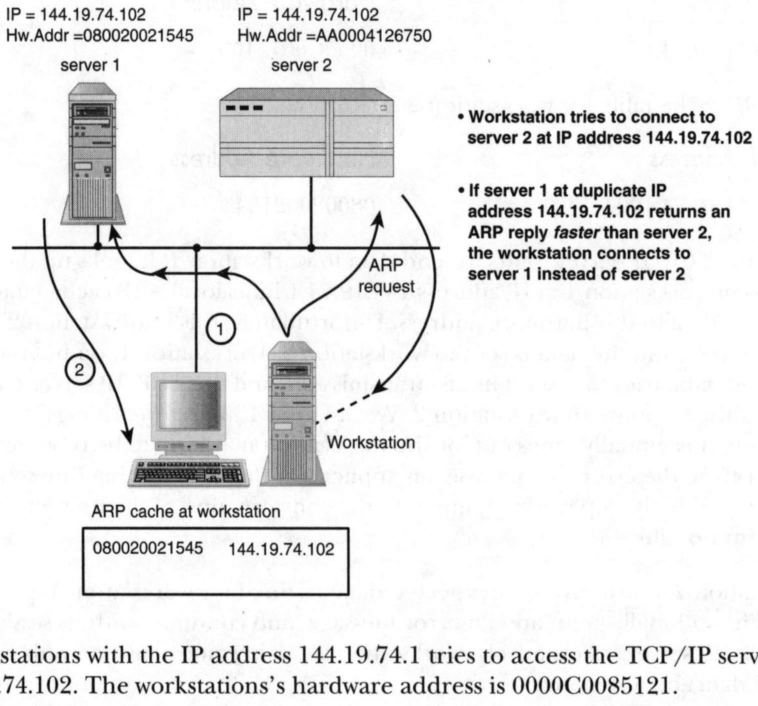

A workstations with the IP address 144.19.74.1 tries to access the TCP/IP server at 144.19.74.102. The workstations's hardware address is 0000C0085121.

The workstation tries to connect with server 2. Before making the TCP/IP connection, the workstation issues an ARP broadcast request to discover the hardware address of the TCP/IP server. There are two TCP/IP servers at the same target IP address of 144.19.74.102. On receiving the ARP request, both servers 1 and 2 add an entry for the ARP request sender (workstation) in their local ARP cache table and send an ARP reply to the sender. There are two responses sent on the network. The workstation accepts the first ARP reply and silently ignores the second response. If the server's ARP reply reaches the workstation first, the workstation adds an entry for server 2 in its local ARP cache table. At this point the ARP cache tables for the servers and the workstation are as follows:

Server 1 IP Address	Hardware Address
144.19.74.1	0000C0085121

Server 2 IP Address	Hardware Address
144.19.74.1	0000C0085121

Workstation IP Address	Hardware Address
144.19.74.102	080020021545

The workstation then continues interacting with server 2 instead of server 1, as it had originally intended. If server 2 does not have the expected service, the connection fails, and the user experiences an error message about the service not being supported at the server. This is puzzling to the user, especially if the user has successfully accessed services at server 1 on prior occasions.

If the server 2 has the service that the workstation expects, the user attempts to logon to that service. If the service is Telnet or FTP, a user logon and password are required. If the user is not alert, he may not notice that the FTP server or Telnet server name/version number reported on the screen is different than the one he expects. If the user does not have a logon account with the same name and password as server 1, logon is denied. If the logon account and password are the same on both servers, the user logs on to the wrong server. The user may not find the files or data he is expecting because he has logged on to the wrong server.

If the server is a multihomed host (server with multiple network connections) that acts as a router, there may be the possibility of even more confusion as packets destined to outside networks may not follow the expected route or may not get delivered because the wrong server has accepted the packets for delivery.

The ARP Duplicate Address Test

Many TCP/IP implementations broadcast an ARP request when starting up. The ARP request is sent with the Target IP field in the ARP request set to that of the node that is starting up (see fig. 5.19).

Figure 5.19 Initial ARP request on booting.

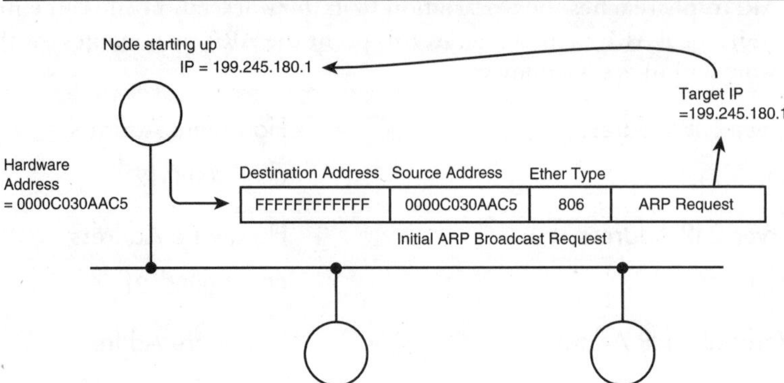

The purpose of this initial ARP request is to discover if there are any nodes that have a duplicate IP address. If an ARP reply is received, another node (the one generating the ARP reply) has the same IP address as that of the node that is booting up. The node that is starting up should report the duplicate IP address in a suitable manner. It is even possible for the node responding to the ARP request to do an extra check on the Sender IP field in the ARP request packet to see if it is the same as its own IP address. If the Sender IP and Target IP address fields match, the responding node can generate a suitable alert about a duplicate IP address problem.

The initial ARP frame can only discover duplicate IP address problems on the same network segment. Because ARP packets do not cross router boundaries, they cannot detect duplicate IP address problems for network segments connected by routers.

Another function of the initial ARP broadcast is for nodes that have an entry for the node that is starting up to update their ARP cache table. If the node that is starting up has a different hardware address (because the network hardware was changed), all nodes receiving the ARP broadcast discard the old hardware address and update their ARP cache tables with the new hardware address.

Protocol Trace for ARP

A *protocol analyzer* is a device that can be used for capturing network traffic; the captured traffic is called a *protocol trace.* The network driver for the protocol analyzer device places the network connection in a "promiscuous" mode of operation. In the promiscuous mode, the network board accepts all packets on that network segment, and even packets meant for other nodes. The protocol analyzer captures the network traffic in internal buffers and decodes it for analysis. Use of the protocol analyzer on networks is a security hazard, especially if sensitive data, such as user names and passwords, are sent in the "clear" (without any encryption).

The protocol analyzer can also be very useful in understanding and troubleshooting network protocols. The approach taken in this book is to present you with protocol traces for a real life network, and to show you its inner workings by analyzing the packet trace.

Figure 5.20 shows a typical ARP packet request/response sequence that was captured using a protocol analyzer. This protocol trace is further analyzed in figures 5.21, 5.22, and 5.23 discussed in the sections that follow.

Figure 5.20 ARP packet exchange summary.

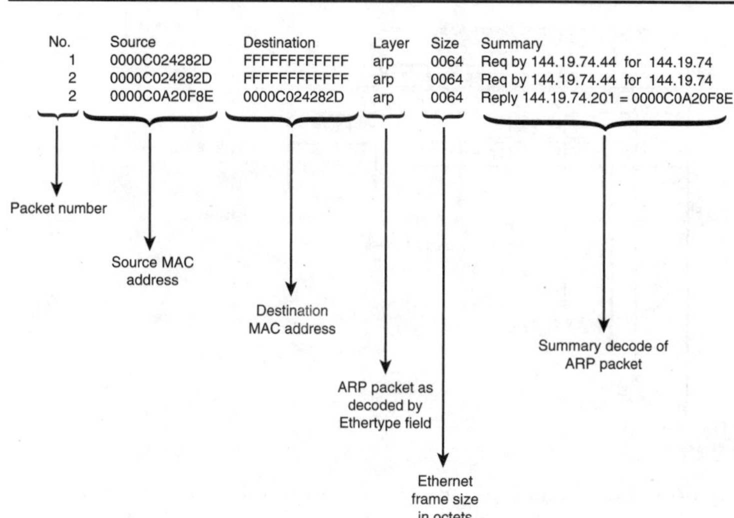

The ARP packet trace summary in figure 5.20 shows three ARP packets. Packet 1 is an initial ARP broadcast request sent on booting up by a station with IP address 144.19.74.44. Packet 2 is the ARP request for a specified target IP address, and packet 3 is the corresponding ARP reply.

Initial ARP Broadcast

When the station at IP address 144.19.74.44 started, it sent an ARP request to its own IP address. The purpose of broadcasting its own target IP address in the ARP is twofold:

1. Detect any duplicate IP addresses on the network segment.
2. Update ARP cache table of other nodes that may have information about 144.19.74.44.

Figure 5.21 shows a detailed description of the initial broadcast packet.

Figure 5.21 Initial ARP broadcast.

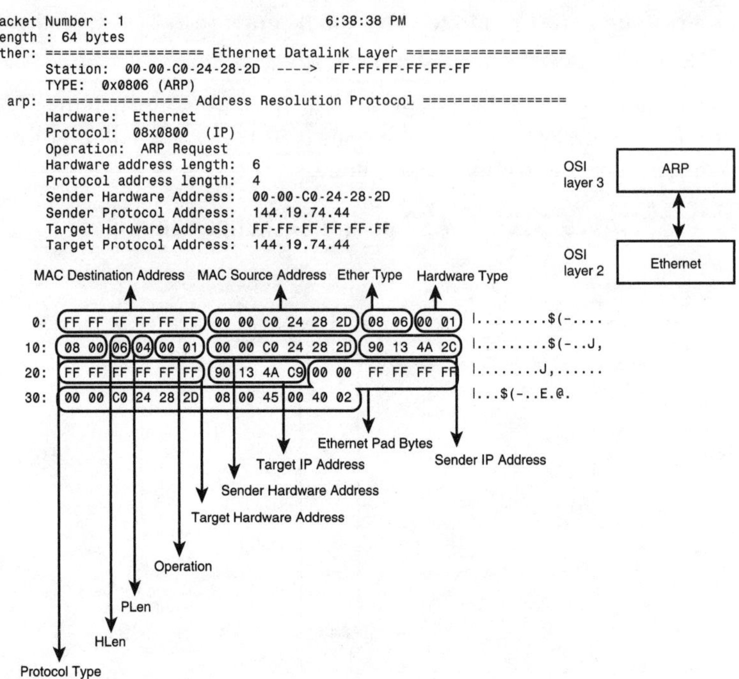

On examination of the Data Link layer that was used in transmitting the ARP request, you can see that this is an Ethernet frame with the following field values in hexadecimal:

Destination Address:	FFFFFFFFFFFF
Source Address:	0000C024282D
Ether Type:	0806

The Ethernet destination address of FFFFFFFFFFFF corresponds to all ones and is a broadcast address. The station sending the broadcast has the Ethernet address of 0000C024282D. The EtherType field is 806 hex, which is the EtherType value reserved for an ARP packet. This means that the ARP packet is encapsulated in an Ethernet frame.

The Operation field in the ARP packet has a value of 1, which indicates this is an ARP request. The Sender HA address and Sender IP field values are 0000C024282D and 144.19.74.44, respectively. The Target HA and Target IP address fields have a value of FFFFFFFFFFFF and 144.19.74.44, respectively. The Target HA address is not known, and an implementation usually places all zeros or all ones in this field. This particular TCP/IP implementation uses all ones.

The Target IP address of 144.19.74.44 is the same as that of the sender. This fact identifies this ARP request packet as an initial broadcast ARP packet that is sent on starting the TCP/IP protocol stack. Its purposes are to check for duplicate IP addresses on the network segment and update existing information in ARP cache about the station that is starting up.

Padding of Ethernet Frames

In the hexadecimal representation of the ARP packet in figure 5.21, several octets are marked with the label Ethernet Pad. Ethernet has a requirement of a minimum packet size of 64 octets (refer to Chapter 2). If the packet size to be sent falls below this minimum size, Ethernet pads the data to be sent so that the Ethernet frame size is 64 bytes. Many Ethernet drivers use whatever data is lying around in the transmit buffer to make the minimum packet size. You can see this in the packet decodes in figures 5.21, 5.22, and 5.23.

If you count the number of octets on the hexadecimal dump, there are actually only 60 octets, even though the packet length of 64 octets is reported at the very top of the packet decode in these figures. What happened to the remaining 4 bytes? The remaining 4 bytes are the CRC checksum used by Ethernet. Though the CRC checksum is part of the Ethernet frame, most protocol analyzers do not report this value.

ARP Request Packet

Figure 5.22 shows a detailed description of an ARP request packet sent to find the hardware address of a target station.

Figure 5.22 ARP request packet.

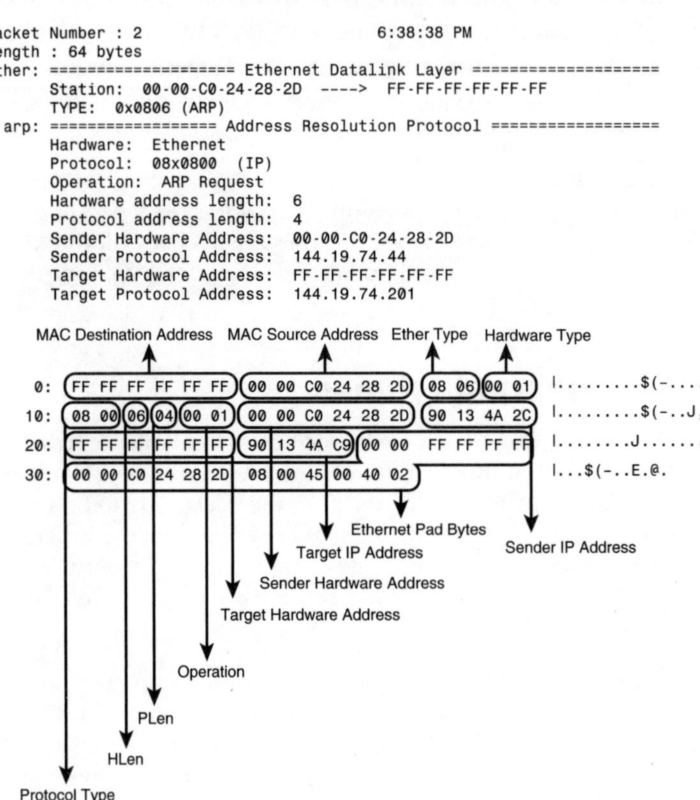

```
Packet Number : 2                                  6:38:38 PM
Length : 64 bytes
ether: ==================== Ethernet Datalink Layer =====================
       Station:  00-00-C0-24-28-2D  ---->  FF-FF-FF-FF-FF-FF
       TYPE:  0x0806 (ARP)
  arp: ================== Address Resolution Protocol ==================
       Hardware:  Ethernet
       Protocol:  08x0800  (IP)
       Operation:  ARP Request
       Hardware address length:  6
       Protocol address length:  4
       Sender Hardware Address:  00-00-C0-24-28-2D
       Sender Protocol Address:  144.19.74.44
       Target Hardware Address:  FF-FF-FF-FF-FF-FF
       Target Protocol Address:  144.19.74.201
```


Ethernet is the Data Link layer that was used in transmitting the ARP request. The packet decode shows an Ethernet frame with the following field values in hexadecimal:

Destination Address:	FFFFFFFFFFFF
Source Address:	0000C024282D
Ether Type:	0806

The Ethernet header fields are the same as that shown in figure 5.21. This is because the frame was sent by the same station, 144.19.74.44. Again note that the EtherType field is 806 hex, which is the EtherType value reserved for an ARP packet. This means that an ARP packet is encapsulated in an Ethernet frame.

The Operation field in the ARP packet has a value of 1, which indicates this is an ARP request. The Sender HA address and Sender IP field values are 0000C024282D and 144.19.74.44, respectively. The Target HA and Target IP address fields have a value of FFFFFFFFFFFF and 144.19.74.201, respectively. The Target HA address is not known and an implementation usually places all zeros or all ones in this field. This particular TCP/IP implementation uses all ones.

The Target IP address of 144.19.74.201 is that of the target node whose hardware address is being sought.

ARP Reply Packet

Figure 5.23 shows a detailed description of the ARP reply packet that was sent by the target node at 144.19.74.201 in response to the ARP reply packet of figure 5.22.

Figure 5.23 ARP reply packet.

```
Packet Number : 3                              6:38:38 PM
Length : 64 bytes
ether: ==================== Ethernet Datalink Layer ====================
       Station:  00-00-C0-A2-0F-8E  ---->  00-00-C0-24-28-2D
       TYPE:  0x0806 (ARP)
  arp: ================== Address Resolution Protocol ==================
       Hardware:  Ethernet
       Protocol:  08x0800  (IP)
       Operation:  ARP Reply
       Hardware address length:  6
       Protocol address length:  4
       Sender Hardware Address:  00-00-C0-A2-0F-8E
       Sender Protocol Address:  144.19.74.201
       Target Hardware Address:  00-00-C0-24-28-2D
       Target Protocol Address:  144.19.74.44
```

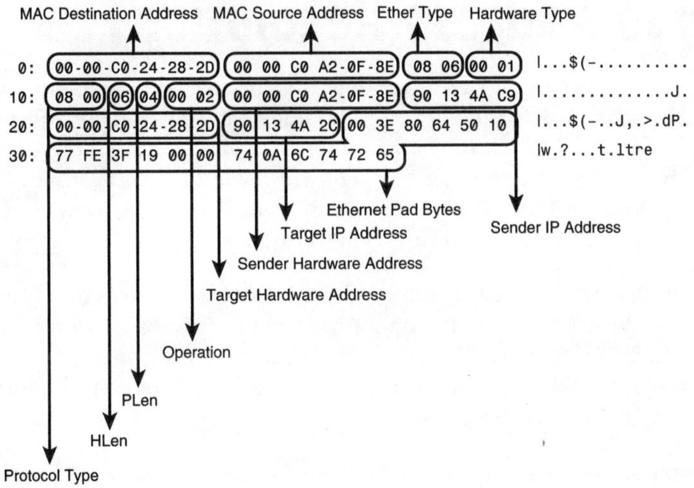

```
 0: 00-00-C0-24-28-2D 00 00 C0 A2-0F-8E 08 06 00 01   l...$(-..........
10: 08 00 06 04 00 02 00 00 C0 A2-0F-8E 90 13 4A C9   l.............J.
20: 00-00-C0-24-28 2D 90 13 4A 2C 00 3E 80 64 50 10   l...$(-..J,.>.dP.
30: 77 FE 3F 19 00 00 74 0A 6C 74 72 65               lw.?...t.ltre
```

Ethernet is the Data Link layer that was used in transmitting the ARP request. The packet decode shows an Ethernet frame with the following field values in hexadecimal:

Destination Address:	0000C024282D
Source Address:	0000C0A20F8E
Ether Type:	806

The Ethernet fields indicate that this Ethernet frame is sent to node with MAC address of 0000C024282D, the ARP request sender. Note that the ARP reply is not broadcast but sent directly to the ARP request sender. The EtherType field is 806 hex, which confirms that this is an ARP packet encapsulated in an Ethernet frame.

The Operation field in the ARP packet has a value of 2, which indicates this is an ARP reply. The Sender HA address and Sender IP field values are 0000C0A20F8E and 144.19.74.201, respectively. The Sender HA value of 0000C0A20F8E is the answer that was sought by the ARP request. It is the hardware address of the target 144.19.74.201. The Target HA and Target IP address fields have a value of 0000C024282D and 144.19.74.44, respectively. The Target HA is the hardware address of the ARP request sender, and the Target IP is its IP address.

Reverse Address Resolution

In the earlier examples of ARP usage, it was assumed that a node knew its IP address. How does a node know its IP address? The node can obtain its IP address from its local store, usually a file whose name and location is dependent on the TCP/IP implementation and the operating system. However, there is a class of computers that do not have local storage. These computers have all system information kept on a remote server. These computers are called "diskless stations."

Modern diskless stations may actually have a local disk, but this disk is used for speeding up the operation of the operating system and not for storing TCP/IP-related parameters that are kept at a remote server. For example, the local disk may only be used for holding a local swap area needed to implement the operating system's virtual memory mechanism.

Diskless stations also have a copy of the operating system image kept on remote servers. On startup the diskless station downloads a copy of the operating system image from the remote server to its memory. Before the diskless station can download its operating system image using TCP/IP file transfer protrocols, it needs an IP address. This IP address cannot be a random value; it must be unique and have the same prefix as the IP addresses of other nodes on that network segment. For example, if other stations on the network have IP addresses like 199.245.180.1, 199.245.180.5, and 199.245.180.7, then the common prefix is "199.245.180." The diskless station must also have the same common prefix. A common prefix is needed because information on how to route to a network segment is embedded as prefix value in the IP address.

The diskless station typically obtains its IP address by sending a request to servers on that network segment. Since it does not know the address information of the remote server, this request is sent as a Data Link layer broadcast. One mechanism to obtain IP addresses from remote servers is the *Reverse Address Resolution Protocol* (RARP). The protocol is called Reverse ARP because the information that it seeks is opposite to that sought by the ARP protocol. Figure 5.24 shows the type of information being sought by the RARP client and contrasts this with the type of information being sought by an ARP client. The RARP client, A, knows its hardware address (*Ha*), but not its IP address (*Ia*). In the case of ARP, the ARP client knows its hardware address and IP address, but does not know B's hardware address (*Hb*).

Figure 5.24 RARP and ARP operations contrasted.

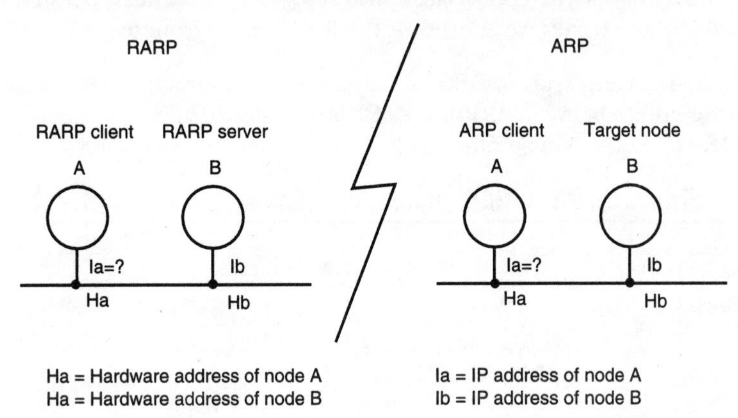

Diskless stations are used to reduce hardware costs, simplify node configuration and upgrades by keeping critical information in a central location, and reduce the possibility of viruses being introduced because the users cannot easily introduce programs through diskless workstations.

The next few section discuss RARP in greater detail.

RARP Operation

In RARP operation, the node that wants to discover its IP address (the RARP client), broadcasts a request called the RARP request. The *RARP request* is broadcast at the Data Link layer because the RARP client does not know the address (hardware or IP address) of the remote server. The remote server that processes the RARP request is called the RARP server. All nodes on the network segment receive the RARP request broadcast, but only the nodes acting as RARP servers respond.

If there is more than one RARP server, all RARP servers attempt to process the RARP request. The RARP client typically accepts, the first response it receives and silently ignores the rest.

The RARP server keeps a table of the IP address for nodes on the network segment. This table is indexed by a unique identifier that is specific to each machine. This unique identifier is sent in the RARP request. For diskless stations this unique identifier must be some hardware-specific parameter that it can easily read. The identifier cannot be a value stored in local storage because diskless stations do not have a local disk available for this purpose. The RARP designers (see STD 38, RFC 903) decided to use the hardware addresses as unique identifiers because they are unique for a network segment and can be easily read by the network drivers.

When an RARP server receives an RARP request, it consults its table of IP address and hardware address bindings (see fig. 5.25). If it finds an entry in the RARP table that matches the hardware address found in the RARP request, it returns the corresponding IP address in an RARP reply. The RARP reply is not broadcast because the RARP server looks up the hardware address of the RARP client from the RARP request.

The RARP request and reply packets use the same packet format as ARP packets (see fig. 5.3). The difference between ARP and RARP is the values that are placed in the fields. When RARP packets are in an Ethernet frame, an EtherType value of 8035 hex is used.

Figure 5.25 RARP operation. (Courtesy Learning Tree)

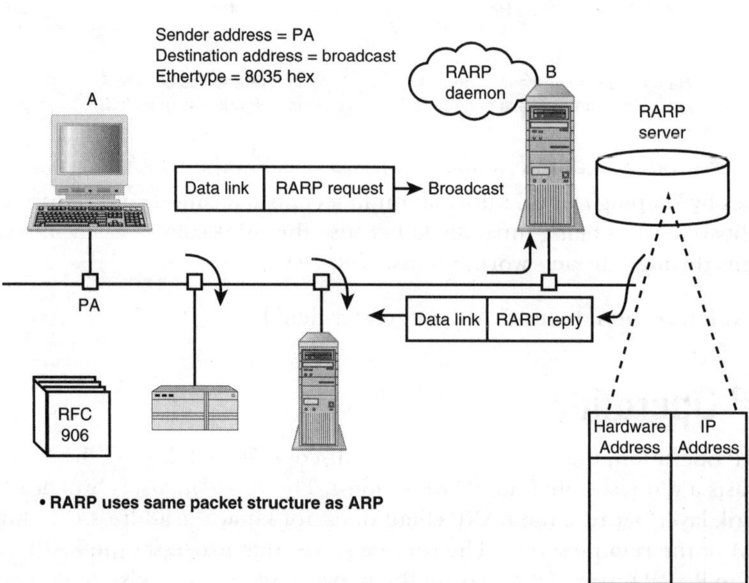

The RARP request fields are filled in as follows (all references to field names are that for the ARP packet structure in figure 5.3):

- **RARP Request**
  - Data Link Destination Hardware Address = *Broadcast*
  - Data Link Source Hardware Address = RARP client HA
  - DataLink EtherType = 8035 hex
  - Operation = 3 (RARP Request)
  - Sender HA = RARP client HA
  - Sender IP = Undefined. Usually 0.0.0.0 used.
  - Target HA = RARP client HA
  - Target IP = Undefined.
- **RARP Reply**
  - Data Link Destination Hardware Address = RARP client HA
  - Data Link Source Hardware Address = RARP server HA
  - DataLink EtherType = 8035 hex
  - Operation = 4 (RARP Reply)
  - Sender HA = RARP server HA
  - Sender IP = RARP server IP address
  - Target HA = RARP client HA
  - Target IP = RARP client IP address (this is the answer)

The Target HA address field in the RARP request is set to that of the RARP client. This is done as a convenience for the RARP server that does not then have to modify this field because it contains the RARP client hardware address in the RARP reply.

The network driver can examine the Ethertype field and know that this an RARP packet (EtherType = 8035 hex) and send the request to the RARP module. The Operation code fields used for RARP are 3 for an RARP request and 4 for an RARP reply. These fields could also be used to distinguish an ARP packet from an RARP packet. However, this approach is not very efficient, as the ARP module would have to examine the Operation field first, and if this indicated a RARP packet, the ARP module would then send it to the RARP module. By using the EtherType field protocol, demultiplexing (refer to Chapter 2) can be done efficiently at a lower layer.

In many implementations RARP is not automatically provided by the ARP or IP module. It must be run as a separate process, such as a daemon process, on the computer that is to act as an RARP-server.

RARP Storms

If the RARP server is unavailable because of a hardware link failure or because the RARP server is down, RARP clients are unable to boot up. RARP clients continually send out RARP broadcast requests. If there are many RARP clients simultaneously sending out RARP request broadcasts, this creates a heavy network traffic load (an RARP storm).

The situation of not receiving an RARP reply is more serious than not receiving an ARP reply. If there is no ARP reply, it means that a particular host and its services are not available. The ARP client can still try to access other nodes on the network. However, if there is no RARP reply, the RARP client cannot boot up. Many RARP clients continue to send RARP broadcast requests indefinitely in the hope that the RARP server may eventually become available. The situation of repeated RARP broadcast requests, therefore, is more serious than that of ARP requests because it can result in greater network traffic.

Primary and Backup RARP Servers

To make the availability of RARP services more reliable, multiple RARP servers can be used. With multiple RARP servers, all servers would attempt to answer to the RARP broadcast request simultaneously. Only one of the RARP replies is used by the RARP client. All other RARP replies are discarded and use up network bandwidth. One scheme to prevent multiple RARP replies is to designate one of the RARP servers as a primary and all others as secondary RARP servers.

On receiving an RARP request, the primary RARP server responds to the request. The secondaries do not respond but note the arrival time of the RARP request. If the primary does not respond within a time out interval, the secondary RARP server assumes that the primary RARP server is down and responds to the RARP request.

If there are multiple secondary RARP servers, all secondary servers attempt to respond at the same time. A refinement of this scheme is to have secondary RARP servers wait for a random time interval before responding. If the primary server is functioning normally, there are no additional delays in sending the RARP reply. If the primary server is down, there may be a small random delay before one of the secondary RARP servers responds.

RARP Packet Trace

This section analyzes the packet trace produced by an RARP client making an RARP request to initialize itself. The RARP client attempts to boot up and do a Telnet session to a host at IP address 199.245.180.10. An RARP server has been configured at

IP address 199.245.180.33. This situation is described in figure 5.26 where an RARP client sends a broadcast request to get its IP address. When the RARP server replies with the IP address of the RARP client, the RARP client then attempts to perform a Telnet session to the host at IP address 199.245.180.10. Before it can perform the Telnet session, the Telnet client must obtain the hardware address of the host. It does this by issuing an ARP request. The host returns its hardware address in the ARP reply. The Telnet client then proceeds with its Telnet session.

Figure 5.26 RARP operation example.

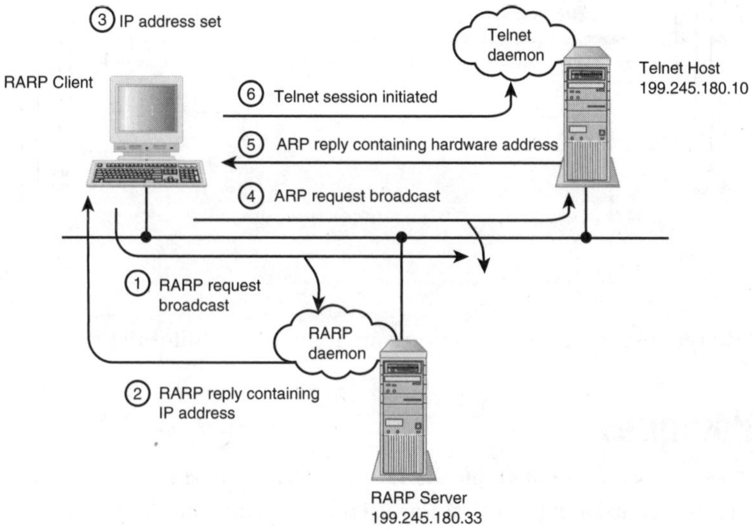

Figure 5.27 shows the packet trace produced on a real life network for the example in figure 5.26.

Notice that RARP packets 2–4 are repeated. This is because the RARP server is slow to respond to the RARP client. This illustrates one of the dangers of RARP broadcast storms when the RARP server does not respond quickly. The RARP request in packet 4 is responded to in the RARP reply in packet 5. On receiving this RARP request, the RARP client sets its IP address to the value 199.245.180.3 returned in the RARP reply. The RARP client then attempts to get the hardware address of the host using an ARP broadcast request. The ARP requests are sent in packets 6 and 7. Packet 7 is a repeat of the ARP request in packet 6 because the Telnet host does not respond quickly enough to the first ARP request. The Telnet host responds to the ARP request in packet 8 with its hardware address. The RARP client then opens a Telnet session in packets 9–11.

Figure 5.27 Protocol trace of RARP/ARP and Telnet packets.

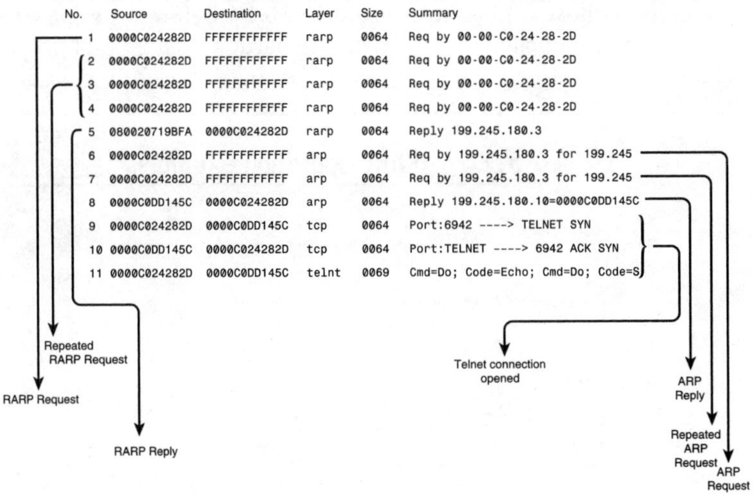

No.	Source	Destination	Layer	Size	Summary
1	0000C024282D	FFFFFFFFFFFF	rarp	0064	Req by 00-00-C0-24-28-2D
2	0000C024282D	FFFFFFFFFFFF	rarp	0064	Req by 00-00-C0-24-28-2D
3	0000C024282D	FFFFFFFFFFFF	rarp	0064	Req by 00-00-C0-24-28-2D
4	0000C024282D	FFFFFFFFFFFF	rarp	0064	Req by 00-00-C0-24-28-2D
5	080020719BFA	0000C024282D	rarp	0064	Reply 199.245.180.3
6	0000C024282D	FFFFFFFFFFFF	arp	0064	Req by 199.245.180.3 for 199.245
7	0000C024282D	FFFFFFFFFFFF	arp	0064	Req by 199.245.180.3 for 199.245
8	0000C0DD145C	0000C024282D	arp	0064	Reply 199.245.180.10=0000C0DD145C
9	0000C024282D	0000C0DD145C	tcp	0064	Port:6942 ----> TELNET SYN
10	0000C0DD145C	0000C024282D	tcp	0064	Port:TELNET ----> 6942 ACK SYN
11	0000C024282D	0000C0DD145C	telnt	0069	Cmd=Do; Code=Echo; Cmd=Do; Code=S

The RARP request and reply packets are analyzed in the following two sections.

RARP Request

Figure 5.28 shows the detailed decode of the RARP request broadcast packet. Ethernet is the Data Link layer that was used in transmitting the RARP request. The packet decode shows an Ethernet frame with the following field values in hexadecimal:

Destination Address:	FFFFFFFFFFFF
Source Address:	0000C024282D
Ether Type:	8035

Figure 5.28 RARP request packet.

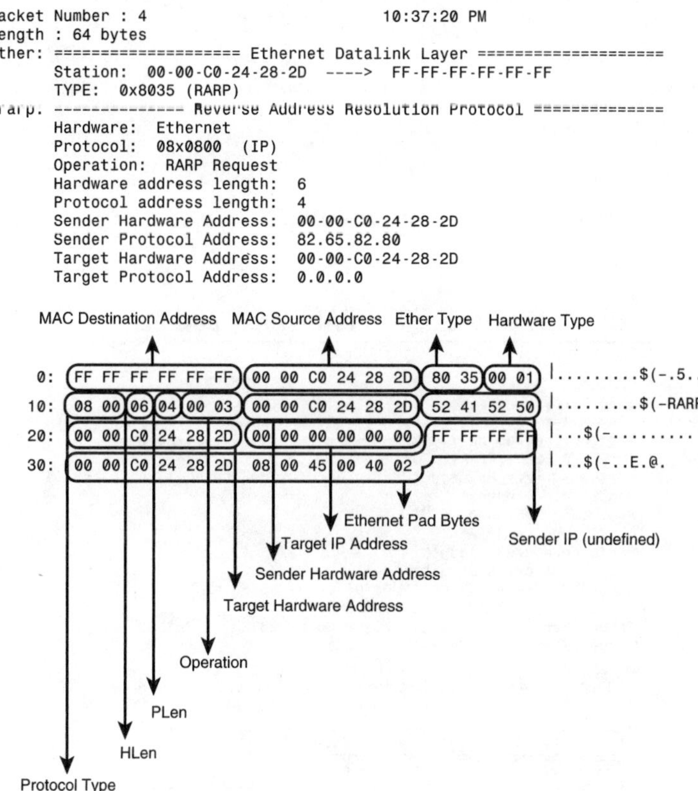

The EtherType field is 8035 hex, which is the EtherType value reserved for an RARP packet. This means that an RARP packet is encapsulated in an Ethernet frame.

The Operation field in the RARP packet has a value of 3, which indicates this is an RARP request. The Sender HA address and Sender IP field values are 0000C024282D and 82.65.82.80, respectively. The Sender IP address field is actually undefined. This field represents the IP address being sought in the RARP request. An implementation can use whichever value it wants here. Many implementations use a value of 0.0.0.0. Curiously enough this real life implementation uses a value of 82.65.82.80. The actual value used does not have any real significance.

The Target HA and Target IP address fields have a value of 0000C024282D and 0.0.0.0, respectively. In this TCP/IP implementation, the Target IP address is undefined, and its value is set to 0.0.0.0.

RARP Reply

Figure 5.29 shows a detailed description of the RARP reply packet that was sent by the RARP server at 144.19.74.33 in response to the RARP reply packet of figure 5.28. Ethernet is the Data Link layer that was used in transmitting the ARP request. The packet decode shows an Ethernet frame with the following field values in hexadecimal:

Destination Address:	0000C024282D
Source Address:	080020719BFA
Ether Type:	8035

Figure 5.29 RARP reply packet.

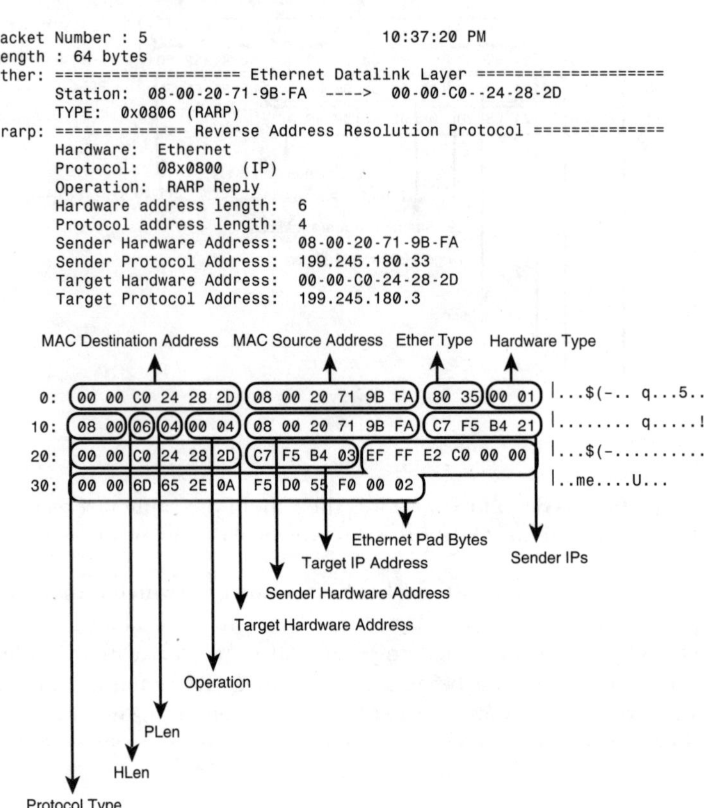

```
Packet Number : 5                              10:37:20 PM
Length : 64 bytes
ether: ==================== Ethernet Datalink Layer ====================
      Station:  08-00-20-71-9B-FA  ---->  00-00-C0--24-28-2D
      TYPE:  0x0806 (RARP)
 rarp: ============== Reverse Address Resolution Protocol ==============
      Hardware:  Ethernet
      Protocol:  08x0800  (IP)
      Operation:  RARP Reply
      Hardware address length:  6
      Protocol address length:  4
      Sender Hardware Address:  08-00-20-71-9B-FA
      Sender Protocol Address:  199.245.180.33
      Target Hardware Address:  00-00-C0-24-28-2D
      Target Protocol Address:  199.245.180.3
```


The Ethernet fields indicate that this Ethernet frame is sent to the RARP client at MAC address of 0000C024282D. Note that the RARP reply is not broadcast but sent directly to the RARP client. The EtherType field is 8035 hex, which confirms that this is an RARP packet encapsulated in an Ethernet frame.

The Operation field in the RARP packet has a value of 4, which indicates this is a RARP reply. The Sender HA address and Sender IP field values are 080020719BFA and 199.245.180.33, respectively. These are the parameters for the RARP server. The Target HA and Target IP address fields have a value of 0000C024282D and 199.245.180.3, respectively. The Target HA is the hardware address of the RARP client. The Target IP of 199.245.180.33 is the answer that was sought by the RARP request. It is the IP address to be assigned to the RARP client.

Displaying the ARP Cache

Normally, the network administrator does not add entries to the ARP cache table of a host because the ARP protocol is used by the IP module to add and delete entries in the ARP cache table. Many TCP/IP implementations, however, do provide a tool for displaying, adding, deleting, or modifying ARP cache table entries. The actual tool is operating system-specific.

As an example, both Unix and Windows NT provide a command-line tool called `arp` for manual maintenance of an ARP cache table. This `arp` tool is used for making temporary fixes so that IP addresses are bound to the correct hardware addresses. For the actual syntax of this command you must consult your operating system documentation.

Other Address Resolution Protocols

There are other address resolution protocols designed for specific uses. RFC 1293 describes the Inverse ARP (IARP) protocol that is used in frame relay connections to discover the IP address of the machine at the other end of the connection. Proxy ARP can be used in networks that use old TCP/IP software that does not understand subnetting. Proxy ARP is described in RFC 1027. RFC 1577 describes the ARP mechanism over ATM networks. RFC 1390 describes transmission of IP and ARP over FDDI Networks, and RFC 1374 describes ARP on HIPPI networks.

Summary

In broadcast networks, such as most LANs, a method is needed to dynamically discover hardware addresses and IP addresses. These methods are called address resolution protocols. ARP is designed to discover the target node's hardware address, given its IP address. ARP protocol is typically used at the start of a network connection to an application service residing on a LAN.

The RARP protocol is used by stations to discover their IP addresses. The IP addresses are stored in a central location, such as an RARP server. RARP is popularly used by diskless workstations. The RARP protocol is used to assign an IP address to a diskless workstation. Then, a file transfer protocol, such as the Trivial File Transfer Protocol (TFTP), is used to download the operating system image. The TFTP protocol is small enough to be implemented in the ROM of diskless workstations.

Test Yourself

1. What types of networks need an address resolution protocol?
2. What is the size of the ARP request/reply header?
3. Draw a picture showing the relationship between ARP, IP, and Ethernet at the protocol layering level and the implementation level.
4. Why are ARP requests sent as broadcast frames?
5. Under what condition would an ARP request be sent as a directed frame instead of a broadcast frame?
6. As you examine the packet structure for ARP and RARP sent in Ethernet frames, you may note that the Sender HA and Target HA fields may seem redundant because this information is also kept in the Ethernet header. Why is it necessary to keep this redundant information?
7. Why would broadcast traffic, such as that produced by repeated ARP requests, slow down nodes not currently accessing the network?
8. The ARP protocol corresponds to which layer of the OSI model? Give justifications for your answer.
9. What problems, if any, would be encountered if a host was statically configured with information about MAC addresses and the corresponding IP addresses?
10. Why is the initial ARP request sent as a broadcast?
11. Why is the ARP reply not sent as a broadcast?
12. Some ARP implementations send an initial ARP request broadcast containing the local IP address in the Target IP address field. What is the purpose of this broadcast frame?
13. Draw the structure of an ARP packet and explain the usage of the different fields. Also draw the structure of a RARP packet and explain how it differs from an RARP packet.
14. ARP and RARP are demultiplexed at the Data Link level. How is this done?

15. A host on a LAN boots up and tries to connect to a server on the same network. Assuming this is not a diskless node, will an ARP request be generated by the host? If the host is a diskless station and RARP is being used to discover the host's IP address, what kind of packets will be generated to make the connection? Will the diskless station generate any ARP requests?

16. Under what conditions will a host not need to send an ARP request?

17. How is an ARP duplicate IP address test done?

18. When an ARP request/reply is transmitted on an Ethernet, is any padding of the Ethernet frame required? If so, how many bytes need to be padded? Why is padding needed on Ethernet networks?

19. What is the impact of ARP/RARP broadcast storms on bridged networks?

20. There are two workstations each set to an IP address of 198.24.54.1. They are attempting to create a Telnet session with a central host at the IP address of 198.24.54.33. The MAC addresses of the two workstations are 0000C003A216B and 0800000DFCA90. Explain what would happen in this situation. Use drawings of the contents of the ARP cache table to explain what may happen in this scenario.

21. What would happen in the duplicate IP address for TCP/IP clients scenario discussed in this chapter if a TCP/IP implementation chose to ignore the RFC 826 recommendation about replacing the ARP cache entry with a new hardware address for an existing ARP cache entry? Would it alleviate the duplicate IP address problem? What other problems would this introduce?

22. Under what conditions would an RARP broadcast storm take place?

23. What is the role of the primary and secondary RARP servers? Describe how a secondary server can answer a RARP request.

24. Consider the following hexadecimal dump of a packet. What kind of a packet is this?

```
 0: 00 00 C0 24 28 2D 00 00 C0 DD 14 5C 08 00 45 00 ¦...$(-.....\..E.
10: 00 29 E9 86 40 00 80 06 19 4F C7 F5 B4 0A C7 F5 ¦.)..@....O......
20: B4 03 00 17 1B 1E 04 E2 87 09 01 31 E0 1C 50 18 ¦...........1..P.
30: 3F E5 BD 7E 00 00 32 FF 03 FF F0 00             ¦?..~..2.....
```

25. Consider the following hexadecimal dump of a packet. What kind of a packet is this? Decode the packet fully and explain its purpose.

```
 0: FF FF FF FF FF FF 00 00 C0 24 28 2D 08 06 00 01 ¦.........$(-....
10: 08 00 06 04 00 01 00 00 C0 24 28 2D 90 13 4A 2C ¦.........$(-..J,
20: FF FF FF FF FF FF 90 13 4A 2C 00 00 FF FF FF FF ¦........J,......
30: 00 00 C0 24 28 2D 08 00 45 00 40 02             ¦...$(-..E.@.
```

26. Consider the following hexadecimal dump of a packet. What kind of a packet is this? Decode the packet fully and explain its purpose.

```
 0: FF FF FF FF FF FF 00 00 C0 24 28 2D 08 06 00 01 ¦.........$(-....
10: 08 00 06 04 00 01 00 00 C0 24 28 2D 90 13 4A 2C ¦.........$(-..J,
20: FF FF FF FF FF FF 90 13 4A C9 00 00 FF FF FF FF ¦........J.......
30: 00 00 C0 24 28 2D 08 00 45 00 40 02             ¦...$(-..E.@.
```

27. Consider the following hexadecimal dump of a packet. What kind of a packet is this? Decode the packet fully and explain its purpose.

```
 0: 00 00 C0 24 28 2D 00 00 C0 A2 0F 8E 08 06 00 01 ¦...$(-..........
10: 08 00 06 04 00 02 00 00 C0 A2 0F 8E 90 13 4A C9 ¦..............J.
20: 00 00 C0 24 28 2D 90 13 4A 2C 00 3E 80 64 50 10 ¦...$(-..J,.>.dP.
30: 77 FE 3F 19 00 00 74 0A 6C 74 72 65             ¦w.?...t.ltre
```

28. Consider the following hexadecimal dump of a packet. What kind of a packet is this? Decode the packet fully and explain its purpose.

```
 0: FF FF FF FF FF FF 00 00 C0 24 28 2D 80 35 00 01 ¦.........$(-.5..
10: 08 00 06 04 00 03 00 00 C0 24 28 2D 52 41 52 50 ¦.........$(-RARP
20: 00 00 C0 24 28 2D 00 00 00 00 00 00 FF FF FF FF ¦...$(-..........
30: 00 00 C0 24 28 2D 08 00 45 00 40 02             ¦...$(-..E.@.
```

29. Consider the following hexadecimal dump of a packet. What kind of a packet is this? Decode the packet fully and explain its purpose.

```
 0: 00 00 C0 24 28 2D 08 00 20 71 9B FA 80 35 00 01 ¦...$(-.. q...5..
10: 08 00 06 04 00 04 08 00 20 71 9B FA C7 F5 B4 21 ¦........ q.....!
20: 00 00 C0 24 28 2D C7 F5 B4 03 EF FF E2 C0 00 00 ¦...$(-..........
30: 00 00 6D 65 2E 0A F5 D0 55 F0 00 02             ¦..me....U...
```

30. There are 50 nodes on a network that are each sending two broadcasts per second on a network because of the failure of the main RARP server. Assuming an Ethernet network, what percentage of the network bandwidth does the RARP traffic consume?

31. Derive a general formula for the percentage of network bandwidth consumed by ARP/RARP broadcast packets. Assume the following parameters for the network:

    Maximum network data rate = D bps

    Number of nodes sending ARP/RARP broadcast = N

    Rate of sending ARP/RARP transmissions = R packets/sec

32. Use this formula to verify your answer in question 30.

CHAPTER 6

The Internet Protocol

The Internet Protocol (IP) provides the first level of abstraction that provides a virtual view of the network where all nodes are treated as IP nodes. IP provides an abstract view of the network, a logical view wherein the network is viewed as an idealized network possessing properties that are described in this chapter.

Because of the abstraction layer that IP provides, protocols above the IP layers—such as the TCP and UDP protocols—can treat the network as an IP-only network. In reality, the network may not be an IP-only network; it may support other protocols besides TCP/IP. The IP node's network connections are identified by the 32-bit value known as the IP address. IP provides connectionless services to upper-layer services. The connectionless service is implemented using datagrams that contain the source and destination IP addresses and other parameters needed for IP operation. This chapter provides a strong conceptual understanding of how IP works in real life networks.

IP Abstraction

The IP layer relies on the underlying network hardware for its transmission. This means that IP datagram is encapsulated by the frames of the underlying network, such as Ethernet, Token Ring, or X.25.

The upper-layer protocols, such as TCP and UDP, need not be aware of the network hardware encapsulation and the underlying hardware. Upper-layer protocols may expect a certain quality of service, such as throughput and delay factors. These are called *Quality of Service* (QoS) parameters. The upper layers pass the QoS parameters along with the data to the IP layer. The IP layer may attempt to map the QoS parameters to services provided by the underlying network hardware. The underlying network hardware may or may not be able to supply this service.

Figure 6.1 shows that the IP host has three network connections. These connections are for Ethernet, Token Ring, and X.25 networks. In this example, IP runs on each of the three network connections. These network connections are identified by a unique 32-bit identifier called the IP address. The IP layer presents to the upper layers an abstraction for each of the three networks. This abstraction is independent of the physical attributes of the networks, such as address size, maximum transmission unit (MTU) size, network bandwidth, maximum data transmission rate, and so on. The MTU size is the maximum size of the data field for the underlying physical network. Since the data field contains IP datagrams for TCP/IP networks, the MTU size is also the maximum size of the IP datagram that can be carried on a physical network.

In the example network in figure 6.1, the MTU size of the Ethernet network is 1500 bytes. The MTU size is 4440 for the IEEE 802.5, 4 Mbps Token Ring network; it is 17940 for the IEEE 802.5, 16 Mbps network. For the X.25 network, the MTU size is negotiated as an option and can range from 64 bytes to 4 KB. IP networks are required to process datagrams of at least 576 bytes in size. Because the smallest IP datagram that all routers must process is 576 bytes, the lower values are not used as MTU sizes in an X.25 network carrying TCP/IP data.

Regardless of the MTU size and speed differences of the networks, the IP layer translates these networks into a common logical IP network that is independent of physical differences.

Figure 6.1 IP abstraction. (Courtesy Learning Tree)

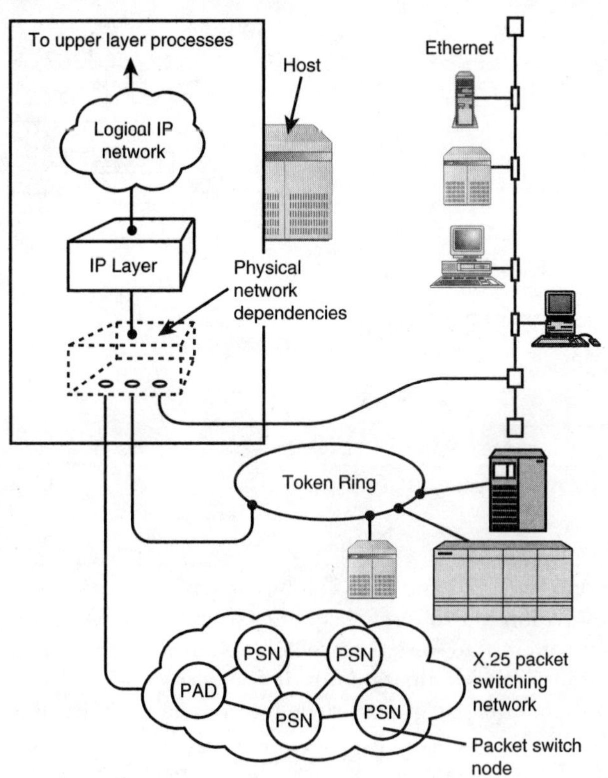

- **IP Layer**
  - Provides powerful logical abstraction
  - Hides Physical Layer dependency
- **Upper layer processes see a logical IP network**

PAD = packet assembler/disassembler

The abstract IP network is connectionless. Each datagram is independently routed. It is possible, therefore, for successive datagrams to be transmitted along different paths (see fig. 6.2).

Figure 6.2 Independent routing of IP datagrams.

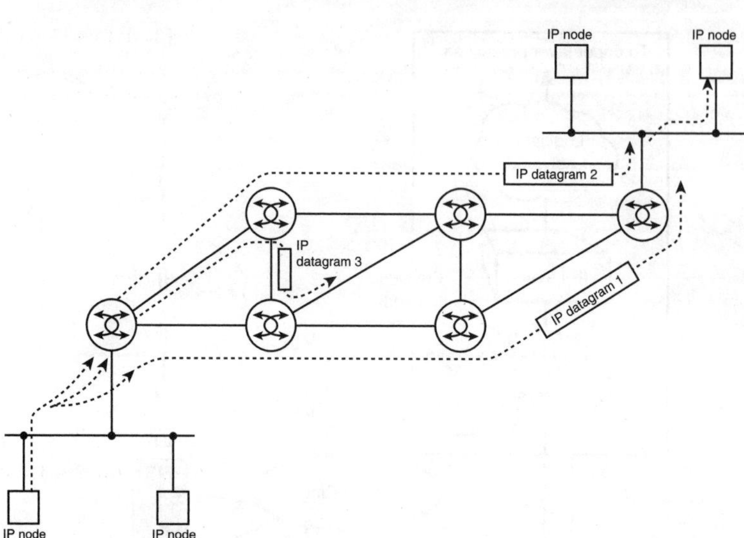

Because of the difference in time delays along the paths, it is possible for datagrams to arrive at the destination in a different sequence from that in which they were sent. The IP layer makes no attempt to solve the problem of ensuring that datagrams are delivered to applications in the destination host in the correct order. Nor does it make any attempt to ensure that the datagrams are delivered reliably to the destination. Delivering datagrams in the proper order is called *sequencing*. The sequencing problem and the problem of reliable data delivery is solved by an upper-layer protocol such as TCP.

Because IP does not attempt to solve the sequencing and reliable data delivery problem, it is easy to map IP onto a variety of network hardware. Upper-layer protocols can add additional levels of reliability as needed by applications.

It is important to realize that the IP network in itself, without the assistance of any higher-level protocols, is inherently unreliable. The IP network uses a best-effort delivery method; that is, it tries to do the best job it can delivering the IP datagram, but it cannot guarantee delivery of the datagram. This is why IP is almost always used in conjunction with upper-layer protocols, which provides added functionality.

The IP service is connectionless, and each datagram is routed independently of others. Each datagram includes the sender and destination IP address. The destination address is used by intervening IP routers to forward the IP datagram to the correct destination.

IP abstraction enables datagrams to be transmitted regardless of the MTU size of the network. IP nodes can fragment a large datagram when needed. The following sections explain this concept in greater detail.

IP Datagram Size

IP was designed to accommodate a variety of network hardware types. As pointed out earlier, different networks have different restrictions on the maximum data size that can be transmitted by the Data Link layer frame. Table 6.1 lists the MTU size of the different hardware types.

TABLE 6.1
MTU Sizes

Network Type	MTU (octets)
Ethernet	1500
IEEE 802.3	1492
Token Ring	4440 to 17940 (actual size depends on the Token Holding Time)
FDDI	4352
IEEE 802.4	8166
SMDS	9180
X.25	1007 (ARPANET via DDN Standard X.25) 576 (for Public Data Networks, but can be increased by negotiation)

Token Ring MTU sizes shown in table 6.1 depend on the Token Holding Time (THT), which is approximately 8.58 ms (milliseconds). For a 4 Mbps transmission rate, the maximum Token Ring frame size is computed as follows:

Maximum Token Ring frame size (@ 4Mbps) = 8.58 ms × 4 Mbps

= 8.58 × 4 × 1024 × 1024

= 36000 bits

= 36000 ÷ 8 octets = 4500 octets

In the previous calculations 1 Mbps is actually 1 Kbps × 1 Kbps = 1024 × 1024 bps.

Largest Token Ring frame header is computed as follows:

MAC Header	= 15 octets
Routing Information field	= 30 octets
LLC header	= 4 octets
SNAP header	= 5 octets
MAC trailer	= 6 octets
Total frame header	= 60 octets
MTU size for Token Ring @ 4 Mbps	= Maximum Frame size – Token Ring frame header size
	= 4500 – 60 = 4440 octets

For Token Ring at 16 Mbps, the maximum Token Ring frame size is computed as follows:

Maximum Token Ring frame size @ 16 Mbps	= 8.58 ms × 16 Mbps
	= 8.58 × 16 × 1024 × 1024
	= 144000 bits
	= 144000 ÷ 8 octets = 18000 octets
MTU size for Token Ring @ 4 Mbps	= Maximum Frame size – Token Ring frame header size
	= 18000 – 60 = 17940 octets

The FDDI MTU size in table 6.1 is computed as follows:

Maximum FDDI frame size using the 4B/5B encoding	= 4500 octets

Largest FDDI frame header is computed as follows:

MAC Header	= 16 octets
LLC header	= 4 octets
SNAP header	= 5 octets
MAC trailer	= 7 octets (approximately)
Total frame header	= 32 octets

To accommodate future expansion, it is recommended that 148 octets be allocated for the FDDI frame header.

MTU size for FDDI
@ 100 Mbps = Maximum Frame size – Adjusted FDDI frame header size

= 4500 – 148 = 4352 octets

The IP datagram can be up to 65536 bytes long. Most networks do not have an MTU size that is as big as 65536 bytes. The IP layer at the sender usually limits the size of the datagram to not exceed that of the MTU size of the local network. If an IP datagram must traverse intervening networks, the IP datagram cannot exceed the MTU size of the networks if the IP datagram is to be delivered in one whole piece. IP networks do not have any efficient mechanism to determine beforehand the MTU sizes of the intervening networks. If they did, the sender could send an IP datagram that does not exceed the MTU size of the intervening networks. Instead, IP networks depend on the fragmentation mechanism to deliver arbitrarily sized datagrams to any network.

IP Fragmentation

If an IP datagram exceeds the MTU size of the network it must traverse, it cannot be sent in one whole piece. The IP datagram must be broken into smaller fragments that do not exceed the MTU size of the network. This process is called *fragmentation*. Each fragment of the original datagram is sent as an IP datagram. The IP header carries sufficient information to identify the fragment. This information is used by the destination host in assembling the fragments.

Figure 6.3 illustrates the process of sending an IP datagram across networks. In this example, network B's MTU size is smaller than the datagram size. Router R1 detects this fact and fragments the IP datagram into smaller IP datagrams that do not exceed the MTU size of network B. The fragmented datagrams are routed independently and arrive at host C. Though the MTU size of network C can accommodate the original datagram, the router R2 at the boundary between networks B and C makes no attempt at reassembling the fragments to form the original datagram. Reassembly of the IP datagram fragments is performed by the destination IP module and never by intervening routers.

Figure 6.3 IP datagram fragmentation. (Courtesy Learning Tree)

What happens in figure 6.3 when host C needs to reply to host A? Host C will adjust the datagram size to not exceed the MTU size of network C. The datagram from host C can be delivered to host A without any fragmentation. However, the intervening routers will not attempt to combine multiple datagrams into a larger datagram to increase the efficiency of transmission.

In IP networks, only fragmented datagrams are assembled at the destination. Whole datagrams are never combined into a larger datagram to increase efficiency of transmission.

IP Datagram Format

The IP datagram format contains an IP header and the IP data from upper-layer protocols (see fig. 6.4). The IP header is designed to accommodate the features of the IP layer.

From what you have learned about the IP layer in the previous sections, the IP header must contain at least the following information:

- **IP address of source and destination.** This is needed because IP is a connectionless protocol, and complete source and destination address information must be included with every datagram.
- **Quality of service.** This field is needed to specify the type of service expected from the underlying network.

- **Fragmentation information.** Because the IP datagram can get fragmented on a network boundary, there should be fields that help identify the fragment within the original datagram.
- **Datagram size.** IP datagrams can be of variable size. For this reason, there should be a field identifying the total length of the IP datagram.
- **IP header size.** IP datagrams can include optional fields that specify the IP options used for security, source routing, and so on. This causes the IP header size to be of variable length. For this reason the actual IP header size must be indicated in the IP header.

Figure 6.4 IP datagram format.

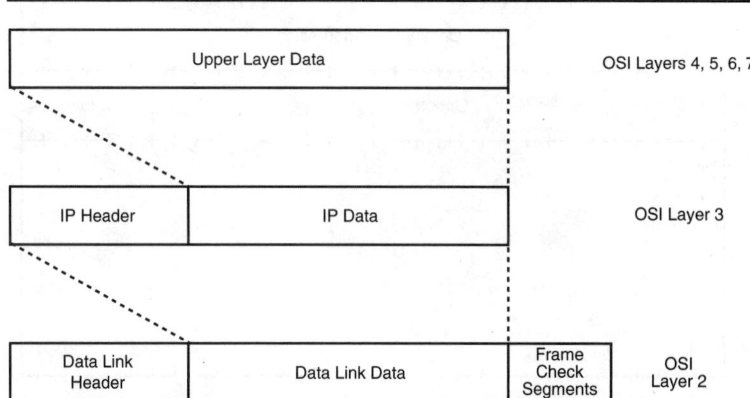

The following section discusses the details of the actual IP header format.

IP Header Format

The IP header has a minimum length of 20 octets. If IP options are specified in the IP datagram, the header length may be longer. Figure 6.5 shows the fields and structure of the IP header.

The IP header format is discussed in detail in RFC 791 and RFC 1122. RFC 1349 describes the use of the Type of Service (TOS) field in the IP header in detail.

Figure 6.5 IP header.

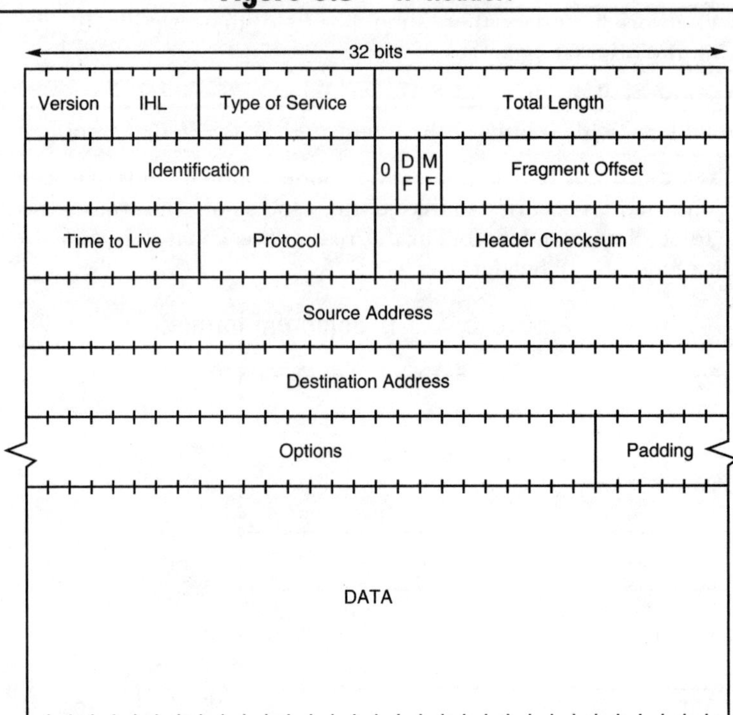

The Version Field

In figure 6.5, the *Version* field is four bits long and indicates the format of the IP header. This enables future IP packet structures to be defined. The current version number is 4, and this IP is called IPv4. The next generation of IP has a version number value of 6 and allows for 128-bit IP addresses. For this reason it is called IPv6. Table 6.2 shows the other possible values of the version number field.

Note Version number values of 7, 8, and 9 were assigned to experimental and proposed IP protocols to solve the limitation of the 32-bit IP address problem. These protocols have been superseded by Ipv6.

Table 6.2
IP Version Number Values

IP Version	Meaning
0	Reserved
1–3	Unassigned
4	IPv4
5	Stream IP Datagram Mode (Experimental IP)
6	IPv6. Also called IPng.
7	TP/IX: The Next Internet
8	The "P" Internet Protocol
9	TUBA
10–14	Unassigned
15	Reserved

The Version field is used by the sender, receiver, and any intervening routers to determine the format of the IP header. IP software is required to check the Version field to ensure that the IP header format is the one it expects. For example, if the IP software can only process version 4 datagrams, it will reject datagrams that have a different value than 4 in the Version field.

The following is an explanation of some of the entries that you see in table 6.2:

- The Stream IP protocol is an experimental protocol used to provide end-to-end guaranteed service across an internet. Stream IP is described in RFC 1819.
- The TP/IX, "P" Internet protocol, and TUBA were all at one time contenders for the replacement of IPv4. They are no longer serious contenders and are relegated to historical status, because IPv6 is the approach that has been adopted as a replacement for IPv4.
- The "P" Internet protocol is a new protocol with advanced features and variable-length addresses. It was later merged with Simple Internet Protocol (SIP). SIP uses 64-bit addressing and was merged with IP Address Encapsulation (IPAE), which describes how the transition between IPv4 and longer addressing would be achieved. SIP is described in RFC 1710.

- The TP/IX protocol (see table 6.2) is an older protocol that became the basis of the Common Architecture for the Internet (CATNIP) that integrates IPv4 with Internet Packet Exchange (IPX) and the OSI Connectionless Network Protocol (CLNP). The CATNIP protocol is primarily of historical interest. CATNIP is described in RFC 1707.
- TUBA stands for TCP and UDP with Bigger Addresses. TUBA is based on CLNP. TUBA is described in RFC 1347, RFC 1526, and RFC 1561.

The Internet Header Length Field

The *Internet Header Length* (IHL) field is the length of the header in 32-bit words. This field is 4 bits long and is required because the IP header contains a variable-length options field. All other fields have a fixed length. The options field is padded, if necessary, to be a multiple of 32-bit words. Typically, most IP headers do not have any options listed. Excluding the options field, the IP header length is 20 octets. The typical IHL value is, therefore, five 32-bit words. The maximal internet header is 60 octets and specifies the use of IP options. In this case the IHL value will be fifteen 32-bit words.

The Type of Service Field

The *Type of Service* (ToS) field informs the networks of the QoS desired, such as precedence, delay, throughput, and reliability. The meaning of this 8-bit field is shown in figure 6.6.

Figure 6.6 Type of Service field for IP packets.

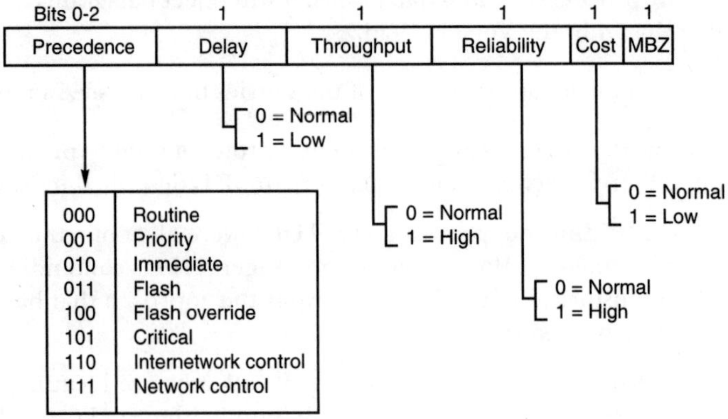

The first three bits deal with the Precedence value associated with the IP datagram. The *Precedence* field reflects the military origin of IP networks (the Department of Defense, which is discussed presently). The following are the meanings of some of the precedence values:

- **Flash.** ASAP (As Soon As Possible). Maximum priority on all circuits.
- **Immediate.** Within four hours.
- **Priority.** Same day.
- **Routine.** Within one day.

The Precedence values are 3 bits long. Table 6.3 lists the possible values and meanings of the precedence field:

Table 6.3
Precedence Values

Precedence	Meaning
000	Routine
001	Priority
010	Immediate
011	Flash
100	Flash-override
101	Critical
110	Internetwork control
111	Network control

The Precedence field was intended for Department of Defense applications of the Internet protocols. The use of non-zero values in this field is outside the scope of the IP standard specification. Vendors should consult the Defense Information Systems Agency (DISA) for guidance on the IP Precedence field and its implications for other protocol layers. Vendors should note that the use of precedence most likely will require that its value be passed between protocol layers in much the same way as the TOS field is passed. The IP layer must provide a means for the transport layer to set the TOS field of every datagram that is sent; the default is all 0 bits. The IP layer should pass received TOS values up to the transport layer.

The 4 bits that follow the Precedence field are a code for types of service. These codes are interpreted as shown in table 6.4.

Table 6.4
Types of Service Codes

TOS code	Meaning
1000	Minimum delay
0100	Maximum throughput
0010	Maximum reliability
0001	Minimum monetary cost
0000	Normal service

The last bit of the TOS field must be zero. This 1-bit field is called the must be zero (MBZ) field and is reserved for future use. IP protocols participating in Internet experiments may make use of this field. Routers and recipients of datagrams ignore the value of this field. This field is copied on fragmentation, which results in all the IP datagram fragments having the same type of service.

Most IP implementations and routing protocols—RIP, HELLO, and so on—ignore the Type of Service field. Although the TOS field has been little used in the past, it is expected to play an increasing role with routing protocols such as OSPF that could make use of the TOS field. The TOS field is expected to be used to control two aspects of router operations: routing and queuing algorithms. The TOS field also may be mapped into link-layer sharing of serial lines by different classes of TCP traffic.

The TOS field can be used as a hint to the routing algorithms to select the most appropriate path. If a router knows of more than one possible route to a destination, it can use the TOS field to select the route that more closely matches the TOS field value. For example, a router may know of two paths to a destination: one with a high-delay and high-throughput connection such as a satellite link, and one with a low-delay and low-throughput connection such as a leased line. If the application traffic carries interactive user keystrokes, the requirement is one of low delay but not very high throughput. Consequently, the router should select the leased line connection for routing this type of traffic. If the application traffic requires a high volume of file data transfer, throughput is important and the high delay is not so critical. In this case, the satellite link with high throughput is the best route.

Note RFC 1349 describes the use of the TOS field in detail.

The Total Length Field

The Total Length field contains the length of the IP header and data in bytes. This field is 16 bits long, which limits the datagram to a maximum size of 65535 octets. This number is the maximum value that can be represented by 16 bits and consists of 16 ones:

1111111111111111

The preceding number is equal to $2^{16} - 1$, a decimal value of 65535.

Datagrams that are as long as 65535 octets are impractical for most hosts and networks. Most networks have an MTU size that is far less than 65535 octets. It also is not efficient to design the communication buffers where IP datagrams can be as large as 65535 octets. Typical datagram size for most networks and hosts seldom exceeds 16 KB.

All IP nodes must be prepared to receive datagrams of at least 576 bytes whether they arrive whole or in fragments. The minimum size of 576 bytes is based on 512 bytes of data plus 64 bytes of protocol overhead.

Datagrams that are larger than the MTU size of the underlying network must be fragmented.

The Identification Field

The Identification field is set uniquely for each datagram, and is the datagram number. Each sending side numbers the datagram starting with some initial value (see fig. 6.7). Most IP implementations use a global memory counter that is incremented with each IP datagram that is sent. If you capture network traffic from hosts that have been up for some time, such as server computers, you will see Identification field values that start from a seemingly arbitrary initial value. This is because the hosts have been sending IP datagrams in previous network sessions, and the Identification field is incremented for each IP datagram that is sent.

Figure 6.7 Identification field values.

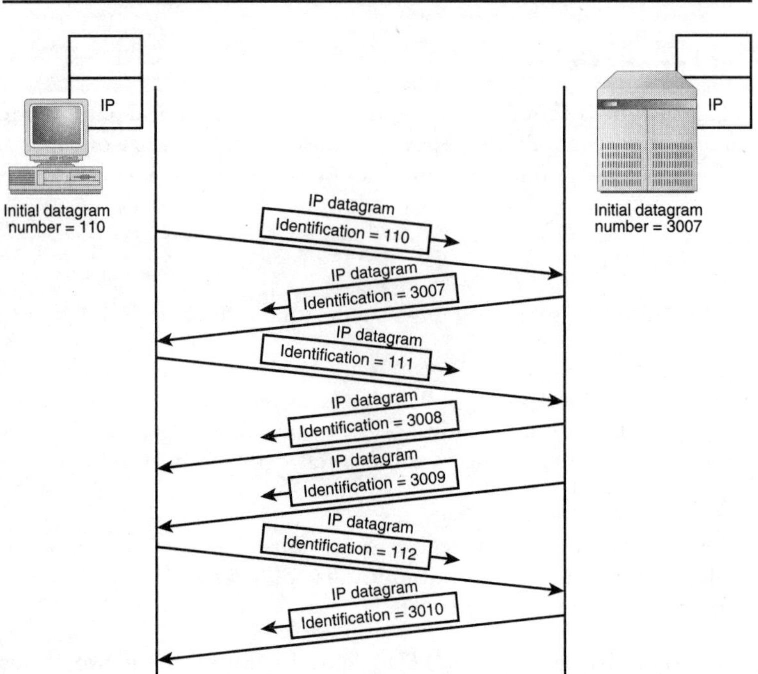

The identification field is 16 bits long. This allows for datagrams to be numbered from 0 to 65535.

The Identification field is used primarily to identify IP datagram fragments as belonging to a particular original IP datagram. The Identification field is used in conjunction with the fragment flags Don't Fragment (DF), More Fragments (MF), and Fragment Offset fields to reassemble the datagram.

Fragmentation Flags and Fragment Offset Fields

If the DF flag is set to 1, it means that the datagram should not be fragmented. This may be done if the sender knows that the receiver may not have sufficient capability to reassemble the fragments into the original datagram. An example of this is a bootstrap program running in the ROM of a computer that downloads data from a server machine. If the entire data is designed to fit inside a datagram, the sender can set the DF flag to 1. Another reason for setting the DF flag is in the situation where the sender wants to eliminate the delays caused by reassembly of IP datagram fragments at the receiver. If the DF flag is set to 0, it indicates that a router or host may fragment the IP datagram.

If the MF flag is set to 1, it indicates to the receiver that there are more fragments to come. An MF set to 0 indicates that it is the last fragment. For complete IP datagrams, the MF flag will always be set to 0 to indicate that there are no more fragments to this datagram.

In the ideal situation, the MTU size of all the networks that an IP datagram needs to traverse should have an MTU size that is larger than the largest IP datagram to be transmitted by a sender. In this case, there is no need to perform any fragmentation Even if the smallest MTU size along a path is known, you should realize that successive datagrams may follow a different path and, therefore, encounter a different smallest MTU size. (This is because each IP datagram is routed independently of other datagrams.)

How is an IP datagram fragmented? Consider the situation in figure 6.8 where a host on network A is sending IP datagrams to a host on network C. There is an intervening network B that the IP datagrams must traverse. The MTU sizes of networks A, B, and C are 1,500, 525, and 4,470 octets, respectively. Router Ra joins networks A and B, and router Rc joins networks B and C. Typically host A will send IP datagrams that fit inside the MTU size of network A. In this example, assume that an IP datagram with an Identification value of 5 and a size of 1500 octets is sent by host A. When the router Ra encounters this IP datagram, it will fragment the IP datagram before it can forward the datagram to network B because the MTU size of network B is smaller than the datagram size. The fragment size is selected so that it will fit inside the MTU size of network B (525 bytes). The *offset*, the start of the data field relative to the original unfragmented data, is placed in the Fragment Offset field of each IP datagram fragment.

Figure 6.8 Fragmentation example.

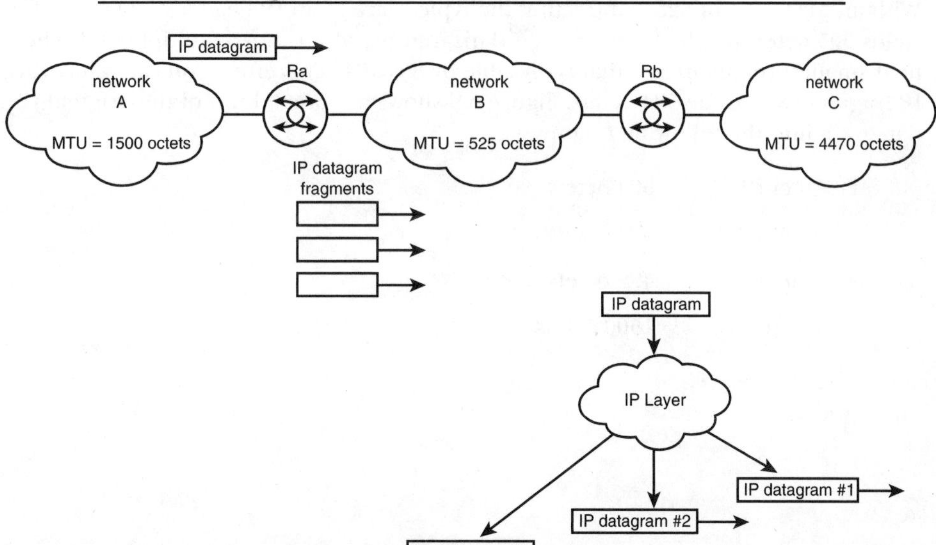

The Fragment Offset field indicates the position of the fragment's data relative to the start of the original datagram. (The specifics of the value of this field are discussed shortly.) The Fragment Offset field is 13 bits long. If you study the IP header format in figure 6.5, you will notice that only 13 bits are used because some of the other bits are used for the DF and MF flags.

Because the IP datagram can be up to 65535 octets long, this field is not sufficiently long to describe offset values greater than 8192 octets. For this reason, the Fragment Offset field is extended by appending three 0 bits:

fragment_offset_value000

The resulting fragment offset value is always a multiple of 8 bytes. Therefore, the fragment offset always describes fragments in units of 8-byte groups. The fragment offset value must be multiplied by 8 to get the actual offset of the fragment. This means that all fragments except the very last must be a multiple of 8. In addition the fragments must fit inside the MTU size of the network. In the example of the 1500-octet IP datagram, you may decide to divide this into sizes of 525 bytes as shown below:

Fragment 1 size = 525 octets

Fragment 2 size = 525 octets

Fragment 3 size = 450 octets

IP datagram size = 1500 octets

However, 525 bytes is not a multiple of 8. You also must take into account the size of the IP header (a minimum of 20 octets), which must also fit within the MTU size. With an MTU size of 525, subtracting the typical size of an IP header of 20 octets yields 505 octets for the fragment size. This number also is not a multiple of 8. The next smallest fragment size that is divisible by 8 is 504. Therefore, you can select the IP fragment size to be 504 octets. Figure 6.9 shows the breakdown of the original IP datagram into the following fragments:

Fragment 1 = 504 octets

Fragment 2 = 504 octets

Fragment 3 = 492 octets

IP datagram = 1500 octets

Figure 6.9 Fragmentation of the original IP datagram.

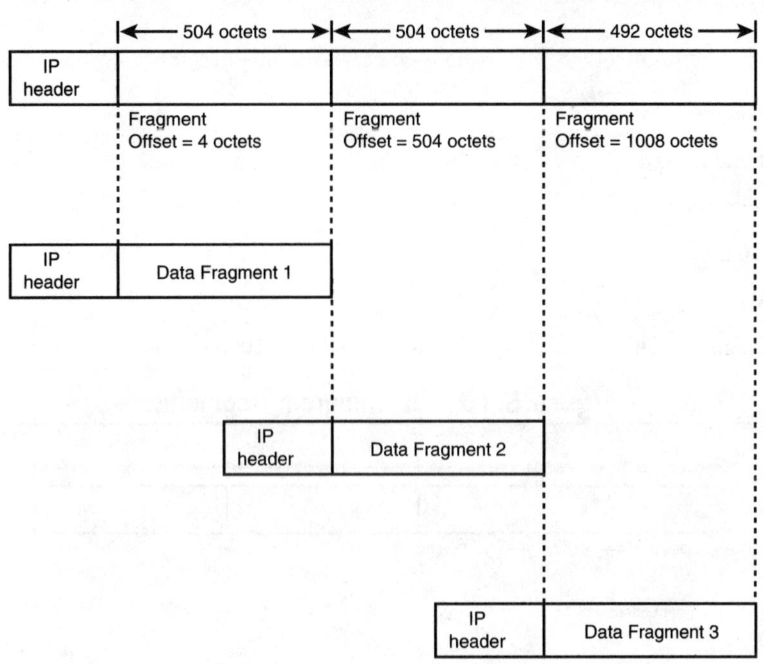

Each fragment must have its own IP header. The Identification field value in the fragmented IP datagrams have the value belonging to the original fragmented IP datagram. This identifies the IP fragment as belonging to a specific original IP datagram. The flag settings and fragment offset values of the fragmented IP datagrams (see fig. 6.10) are as follows:

Fragment 1:

Total Length = 504 octets

Identification = 5

DF flag = 0

MF = 1

Fragment Offset = 0

Fragment 2:

Total Length = 504 octets

Identification = 5

DF flag	= 0
MF	= 1
Fragment Offset	= 63 8-octet words (504 octets)

Fragment 3:

Total Length	= 492 octets
Identification	= 5
DF flag	= 0
MF	= 0
Fragment Offset	= 126 8-octet words (1008 octets)

Figure 6.10 IP datagram fragments.

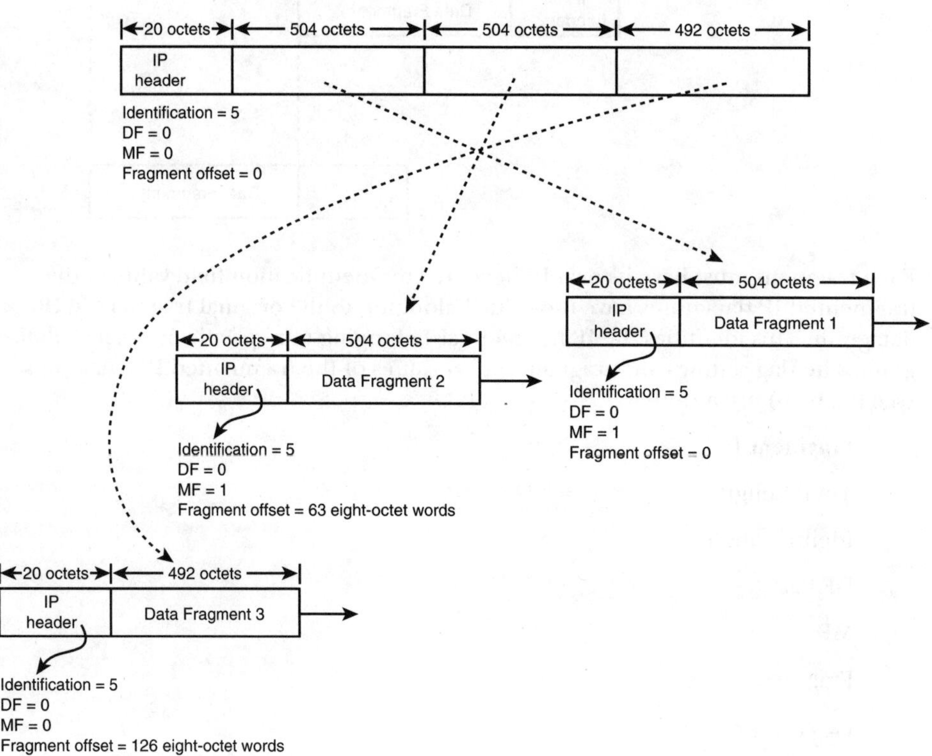

For the receiver to reassemble the IP datagram, it must obtain all fragments starting with the IP datagram fragment with a fragment offset value of 0, and going onto the highest fragment offset value. The receiver uses the size of each fragment (Total

Length field of the IP datagram header), the fragment offset value, and the MF flag to determine if it has received all the fragments. How does a receiver know that the last fragment has been received? The last fragment has an MF flag value set to 0. The first fragment is identified by an MF flag set to 1 and a fragment offset set to 0. All other intermediate fragments will have an MF flag set to 1 and a non-zero fragment offset value.

Once an IP datagram has been fragmented, the individual pieces travel to the destination along potentially separate paths. The IP fragments are reassembled at the receiver and never at an intervening router. This fact leads to the following issues:

- IP fragments travel from their point of fragmentation to the destination.
- Despite intervening networks having a larger MTU size than the fragment size, the fragments will be carried in small size packets, which results in poor protocol efficiency.
- Excessive fragmentation leads to excessive network traffic.

If a fragment is lost, the original datagram cannot be reassembled. Despite successful transmission of the remaining fragments, the original datagram must be discarded. In this case, upper-layer protocols such as TCP ensure that the original datagram is present, but this datagram will be fragmented again at the point where the IP datagram exceeds the MTU size.

The receiving IP node starts a reassembly timer upon receiving the first IP fragment. If this timer expires before all the other fragments arrive, the IP node discards the remaining fragments even though they were received correctly. As the number of fragments increases, so does the possibility of losing an IP datagram. This is because a loss of a single fragment results in the loss of the entire datagram. When the reassembly timer expires, an Internet Control Message Protocol (ICMP) message is sent to the sender announcing that the reassembly timer has expired. A monitoring device such as a protocol analyzer can be used to alert you to this problem.

The decision to reassemble the IP datagram at the receiver, while creating the problems described previously, has the advantage of keeping the router implementation simple. The IP routers do not have to be concerned about storing and reassembling the IP fragments. If there are several networks with a small MTU size, reassembling the IP fragments at intervening routers would be somewhat wasteful because the reassembled IP datagram would have to be fragmented before traversing a network with a small MTU size.

The TTL field

The *Time To Live* (TTL) is measured in seconds and represents the maximum time an IP datagram can live on the network. It should be decremented at each router by the amount of time taken to process the packet. When the TTL field becomes 0, the TTL timer expires. The intent is that TTL expiration causes a datagram to be discarded by a router, but not by the destination host. Hosts acting as routers by forwarding datagrams must follow the previously discussed behavior for TLL routing. The TTL field has two functions:

- Limits the lifetime of TCP segments
- Terminates Internet routing loops

When the TTL timer expires, an ICMP message announcing this fact is sent to the source.

Although TTL is measured in seconds, it is difficult for routers to estimate the exact transit time for IP datagrams on a network segment. Routers could note the time an IP datagram spends inside the router by noting the time when a datagram arrives and the time when it leaves the router. Because of the extra processing required to do so, many routers do not attempt to estimate the time an IP datagram spends inside a router and simply decrease the TTL value by 1. Because of this, the TTL field has some attributes of a hop count. Some earlier implementers mistakenly set the TTL value to 16 because 16 is infinity for RIP (Routing Information Protocol). TTL is independent of RIP metrics, however.

Other considerations for TTL fields are the following:

- A host must not send a datagram with a TTL value of 0, and a host must not discard a datagram just because it was received with a TTL less than 2.
- An upper-layer protocol may want to set the TTL to implement an expanding scope search for some Internet resource. This is used by some diagnostic tools and is expected to be useful for locating the "nearest" server of a given class using IP multicasting, for example. A particular transport protocol also may want to specify its own TTL boundary on maximum datagram lifetime.
- A fixed value must be at least big enough for the Internet *diameter*, the longest possible path. A reasonable value is about twice the diameter, which enables continued Internet growth.
- The IP layer must provide a means for the transport layer to set the TTL field of every datagram that is sent. When a fixed TTL value is used, that value must be configurable. Unfortunately, most implementations do not enable the initial TTL value to be set. A default value of 32 or 64 is very common.

The Protocol Field

The Protocol field is used to indicate the upper-layer protocol that is to receive the IP data. The Protocol field is used for multiplexing/demultiplexing of data to upper-layer protocols (refer to Chapter 2). For example, TCP has a Protocol field value of 6, UDP has a value of 17, and ICMP has a value of 1. When IP sees a Protocol field value of 6, it knows that the IP header encapsulates TCP data that must be delivered to the TCP module. If IP sees a Protocol field value of 17, it knows that this must be delivered to the UDP module. Similarly, when IP sees a Protocol field value of 1, it knows that this must be delivered to the ICMP module.

Table 6.5 shows the Protocol field values for IP.

TABLE 6.5
Protocol IDs

Protocol ID	Abbreviation	Meaning
0		(Reserved)
1	ICMP	Internet Control Message
2	IGMP	Internet Group Management
3	GGP	Gateway-to-Gateway
4	IP	IP in IP (encapsulation)
5	ST	Stream
6	TCP	Transmission Control
7	UCL	UCL
8	EGP	Exterior Gateway Protocol
9	IGP	any private interior gateway
10	BBN-RCC-MON	BBN RCC Monitoring
11	NVP-II	Network Voice Protocol
12	PUP	PUP
13	ARGUS	ARGUS
14	EMCON	EMCON
15	XNET	Cross Net Debugger
16	CHAOS	Chaos

continues

Table 6.5, Continued
Protocol IDs

Protocol ID	Abbreviation	Meaning
17	UDP	User Datagram
18	MUX	Multiplexing
19	DCN-MEAS	DCN Measurement Subsystems
20	HMP	Host Monitoring
21	PRM	Packet Radio Measurement
22	XNS-IDP	XEROX NS IDP
23	TRUNK-1	Trunk-1
24	TRUNK-2	Trunk-2
25	LEAF-1	Leaf-1
26	LEAF-2	Leaf-2
27	RDP	Reliable Data Protocol
28	IRTP	Internet Reliable Transaction
29	ISO-TP4	ISO Transport Protocol Class 4
30	NETBLT	Bulk Data Transfer Protocol
31	MFE-NSP	MFE Network Services Protocol
32	MERIT-INP	MERIT Internodal Protocol
33	SEP	Sequential Exchange Protocol
34	3PC	Third Party Connect Protocol
35	IDPR	Inter-Domain Policy Routing Protocol
36	XTP	XTP
37	DDP	Datagram Delivery Protocol
38	IDPR-CMTP	IDPR Control Message Transport Protocol

Protocol ID	Abbreviation	Meaning
39	TP++	TP++ Transport Protocol
40	IL	IL Transport Protocol
41	SIP	Simple Internet Protocol
42	SDRP	Source Demand Routing Protocol
43	SIP-SR	SIP Source Route
44	SIP-FRAG	SIP Fragment
45	IDRP	Inter-Domain Routing Protocol
46	RSVP	Reservation Protocol
47	GRE	General Routing Encapsulation
48	MHRP	Mobile Host Routing Protocol
49	BNA	BNA
50	SIPP-ESP	SIPP Encap Security Payload
51	SIPP-AH	SIPP Authentication Header
52	I-NLSP	Integrated Net Layer Security TUBA
53	SWIPE	IP with Encryption
54	NHRP	NBMA Next Hop Resolution Protocol
55–60		(Unassigned)
61		(Any host internal protocol)
62	CFTP	CFTP
63		(Any local network)
64	SAT-EXPAK	SATNET and Backroom EXPAK
65	KRYPTOLAN	Kryptolan
66	RVD	MIT Remote Virtual Disk Protocol

continues

TABLE 6.5, CONTINUED
Protocol IDs

Protocol ID	Abbreviation	Meaning
67	IPPC	Internet Pluribus Packet Core
68		(Any distributed file system)
69	SAT-MON	SATNET Monitoring
70	VISA	VISA Protocol
71	IPCV	Internet Packet Core Utility
72	CPNX	Computer Protocol Network Executive
73	CPHB	Computer Protocol Heart Beat
74	WSN	Wang Span Network
75	PVP	Packet Video Protocol
76	BR-SAT-MON	Backroom SATNET Monitoring
77	SUN-ND	SUN ND PROTOCOL-Temporary
78	WB-MON	WIDEBAND Monitoring
79	WB-EXPAK	WIDEBAND EXPAK
80	ISO-IP	ISO Internet Protocol
81	VMTP	VMTP
82	SECURE-VMTP	SECURE-VMTP
83	VINES	VINES
84	TTP	TTP
85	NSFNET-IGP	NSFNET-IGP
86	DGP	Dissimilar Gateway Protocol
87	TCF	TCF
88	IGRP	IGRP

Protocol ID	Abbreviation	Meaning
89	OSPFIGP	OSPFIGP
90	Sprite-RPC	Sprite RPC Protocol
91	LARP	Locus Address Resolution Protocol
92	MTP	Multicast Transport Protocol
93	AX.25	AX.25 Frames
94	IPIP	IP-within-IP Encapsulation Protocol
95	MICP	Mobile Internetworking Control Pro.
96	SCC-SP	Semaphore Communications Sec. Pro.
97	ETHERIP	Ethernet-within-IP Encapsulation
98	ENCAP	Encapsulation Header
99		(Any private encryption scheme)
100	GMTP	GMTP
101–254		(Unassigned)
255		(Reserved)

Header Checksum Field

The Header Checksum is used for the IP header only. The 1's complement of each 16-bit value making up the header is added (excluding the Header Checksum field). Then the 1's complement of the sum is taken. This field is recomputed at each router since the TTL field is decremented at the router, and this results in the modification of the IP header.

It is quite simple to compute checksum, and experimental evidence indicates that it is adequate in detecting errors in transmitting the datagram.

Source and Destination IP Addresses

The Source Address and Destination Address are the 32-bit IP addresses of the source and destination nodes. These are sent in every IP datagram because the IP network is a connectionless network, and each IP datagram must include the sender and destination IP addresses.

The routers use the destination IP address value to perform the routing for each IP datagram.

IP Options

IP implements facilities for indicating the security of a datagram, source routing information, and timestamp information. Because these facilities are infrequently used, they are implemented as optional fields called *IP options.*

The IP options are as follows:

- Security
- Record Route
- Strict Source Routing
- Loose Source Routing
- Internet Timestamp

The IP options must be handled by all IP nodes, and may optionally appear in IP datagrams near the end of the IP header. Their transmission in any particular datagram is optional, but their implementation is not. For example, in environments that need a high level of security, the Security option may be required in all IP datagrams.

The option field is variable in length, and values must be multiples of 32-bit words. Zero pad values may be added to make the options field size multiples of 32-bit words. There are two formats for IP option values (see fig. 6.11):

- **Option format 1.** A single octet of option-type.
- **Option format 2.** An option-type octet, an option-length octet, and the actual option-data octets. The option-length octet contains the overall size of this option including the octet-type, option-length, and option-data fields.

Figure 6.11 Option formats.

option-type

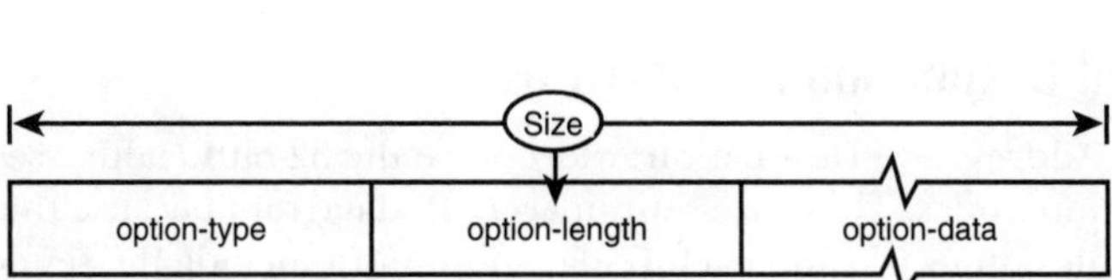

The option-type octet is the first octet that occurs in an option specification. In option format 1 the option-type octet is the only octet, and in option format 2 it is followed by two other fields. The option-type consists of the following three fields (see fig. 6.12):

- Copied flag (1 bit)
- Option-class (2 bits)
- Option-number (5 bits)

Figure 6.12 Option octet.

0	1	2	3	4	5	6	7
copied	option-class		option-number				

The Copied flag controls how routers process the options field during fragmentation. When set to 1, the Copied flag indicates that the options should be copied into all IP datagram fragments. When set to 0, the Copied flag indicates that the options should be copied into the first IP fragment and not into all IP datagram fragments.

The Option-class field is 2 bits long and can have a value from 0 to 3. The meanings of these values are listed in table 6.6.

TABLE 6.6
Option-Class Field Values in Option-Type Octet

Code	Meaning
0	Network control
1	Reserved for future use
2	Debugging and measurement
3	Reserved for future use

The class field is used to determine the general category of the option. The categories are for network control and debugging. The Option-number field is 5 bits long and enables the specification of up to 32 options for a given option category. Table 6.7 lists the different options that have been defined.

Table 6.7
IP Options

Option-class	Option-number	Length	Meaning
0	0	-	End of Option list. This option occupies only 1 octet and has no length octet. It is used if options do not end at an end of header.
0	1	-	No Operation. This option occupies only 1 octet; it has no length octet. It is used to align octets in a list of options.
0	2	11	Basic Security. This is used to carry Security, Compartmentation, User Group (TCC), and Handling Restriction Codes compatible with DoD requirements.
0	3	variable	Loose Source Routing. Used to route the IP datagram based on information supplied by the source.
0	5	variable	Extended Security. Used for specifying additional security.
0	7	variable	Record Route. Used to trace the route an IP datagram takes.
0	8	4	Stream ID. Used to carry the 16-bit SATNET stream identifier through networks that do not support the stream concept. It is now obsolete.
0	9	variable	Strict Source Routing. Used to route the IP datagram based on information supplied by the source.
2	4	variable	Internet Timestamp. Used to record timestamps along the route. This is currently the only option defined for the debugging and measurement category of option-class.

The following sections explain the different IP option types in greater detail.

End of Option List and the No Operation Options

The End of Option List and the No Operation options are the only single octet options. The End of Option list (refer to table 6.7) is a 1-octet option consisting of all zeros (see fig. 6.13):

Figure 6.13 The End of Option list.

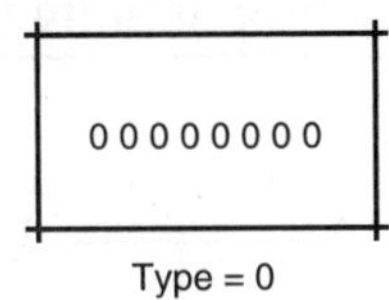

This option indicates the end of the option list, which may not coincide with the end of the internet header according to the IHL field. This option is used at the end of all options, and not at the end of each option. This option need only be used if the end of the options would not otherwise fall on a 32-bit boundary.

The No Option list (refer to table 6.7) is a 1-octet option consisting of the following bit pattern (see fig. 6.14):

Figure 6.14 The No Option list.

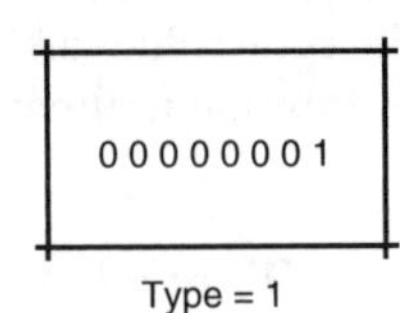

The No Operation option may be used between options to align the beginning of a subsequent option on a 32-bit boundary.

The Security Option

The Security option provides a way for hosts to send security, compartmentation, handling restrictions, and closed user group parameters. There are two types of Security options:

- **Basic Security.** Used to indicate sucurity level designations Confidential, Unclassified, Secret, and so on.
- **Extended Security.** Used to specify additional security per the needs of a military organization.

Basic Security Option

Figure 6.15 shows the Basic Security option format. It is characterized by an octet-type code of 130. The codes define protection authorities that have various rules concerning the treatment of the IP datagram. These protection authorities include the U.S. National Security Agency (NSA), Central Intelligence Agency (CIA), and Department of Energy (DOE).

Figure 6.15 Basic Security Option format.

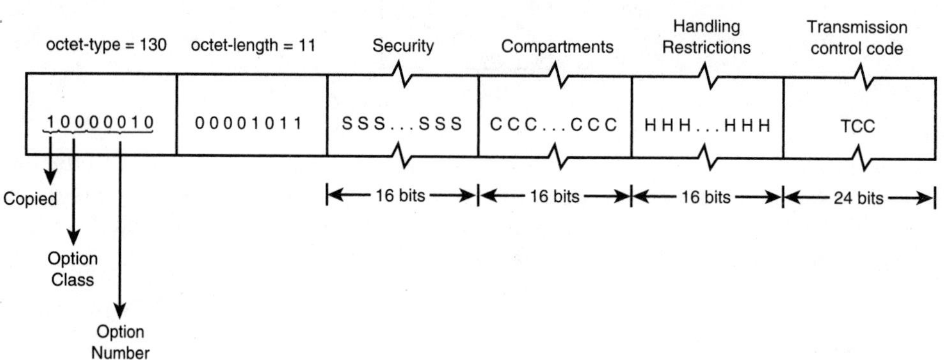

The Security field is 16 bits long and specifies one of 16 levels of security, 8 of which are reserved for future use. The security code values are described in table 6.8. Some of the code values have meanings that are internal to the various protection authorities.

TABLE 6.8
Security Code Values for IP Options

Code	Meaning
00000000 00000000	Unclassified
11110001 00110101	Confidential
01111000 10011010	EFTO
10111100 01001101	MMMM
01011110 00100110	PROG
10101111 00010011	Restricted
11010111 10001000	Secret

Code	Meaning
01101011 11000101	Top Secret
00110101 11100010	Reserved for future use
10011010 11110001	Reserved for future use
01001101 01111000	Reserved for future use
00100100 10111101	Reserved for future use
00010011 01011110	Reserved for future use
10001001 10101111	Reserved for future use
11000100 11010110	Reserved for future use
11100010 01101011	Reserved for future use

The Compartments field is 16 bits long and an all zero value is used when the information transmitted is not compartmented. Other values for the compartments field may be obtained from the Defense Intelligence Agency.

The Handling Restrictions is 16 bits long. The values represent control and release markings and are alphanumeric digraphs that are defined in the Defense Intelligence Agency Manual (DIAM) 65-19, "Standard Security Markings."

The Transmission Control Code (TCC) field is 24 bits long and is used to segregate traffic and define controlled communities of interest among subscribers. The TCC values are trigraphs and are available from the Defense Communication Agency (DCA).

Extended Security Option

The Extended Security option is used for specifying additional security requirements (see fig. 6.16). It is characterized by an octet-type code of 133.

Commercial routers may not support IP security options.

Record Route Option

The Record Route option is used by the sender to record the IP addresses of the routers that forward the IP datagram to the destination. The list of routers actually visited is recorded.

Figure 6.16 Extended Security option.

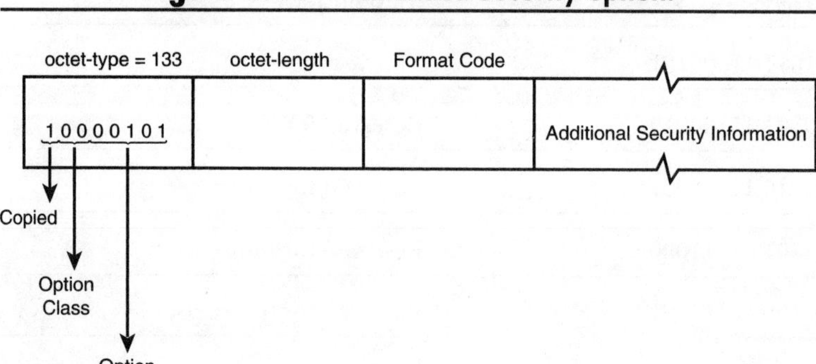

The Record Route option begins with the Option-type code of value 131 (see fig. 6.17). The second octet is the option length (the length of the entire option). The Record Data field contains slots for a list of IP address values. The third octet is the pointer into the Route Data field and indicates the start of the next slot to be processed. The pointer is relative to this option, and the smallest value for the pointer is 4. If the pointer value is greater than the Octet-length, there are no empty slots in the Record Data field; that is, the Record Data field is full. If the Record Data list is full, a router forwards the datagram without inserting itself in the list.

Figure 6.17 Record Route option.

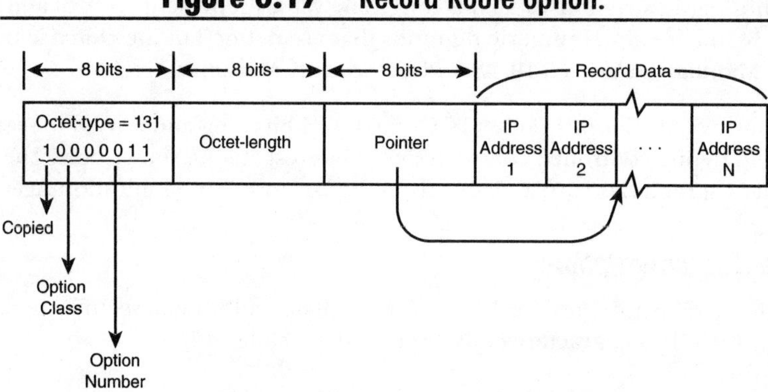

If the pointer is not greater than the Octet-length, the Record Data list is not full and there are empty slots available. The router inserts its IP address at the position specified by the pointer field and increments the pointer field value by 4, the size of the IP address. The recorded address is the IP address of the network interface of the router through which this datagram is being forwarded.

Both sender and receiver have to agree that record route information will be used and processed. The sender adds the Record Route option and sufficient slots for the

IP addresses to the IP datagram. The receiver agrees to process the list of IP addresses recorded in the Record Data field. If the receiver has not agreed to process the record route data, this information is ignored by the receiver.

Strict and Loose Source Routing

In source routing, the sender supplies the path to reach the destination. The path consists of a list of IP addresses of the routers that must be visited. Normally, the path to reach the destination is decided by the routers based on the optimal path determined by routing protocols. In source routing, the sender dictates the path that a datagram must follow in arriving at the destination. The source routing facility is useful in testing a particular path even when you know that the routers would not normally select that path. This also gives you the flexibility of routing datagrams through networks that are known to work reliably. The disadvantage of source routing is the presumption that you know the topology of the network and the list of routers that are used for forwarding a datagram. In a complex network, the topology and the actual path an IP datagram must follow may not be easy to determine.

There are two types of source routing:

- Strict source routing
- Loose source routing

In the Strict Source Routing option (see fig. 6.18), the sender includes a sequence of IP addresses that must be followed exactly in forwarding the datagram. The path between two successive IP addresses in the source route list can only be a single physical network segment. A single physical network segment can consist only of layers 1 (repeater) and 2 (bridge) devices, but not layer 3 (router) devices. If routers cannot follow the strict sequence of IP addresses, the datagram is rejected.

Figure 6.18 Strict source routing.

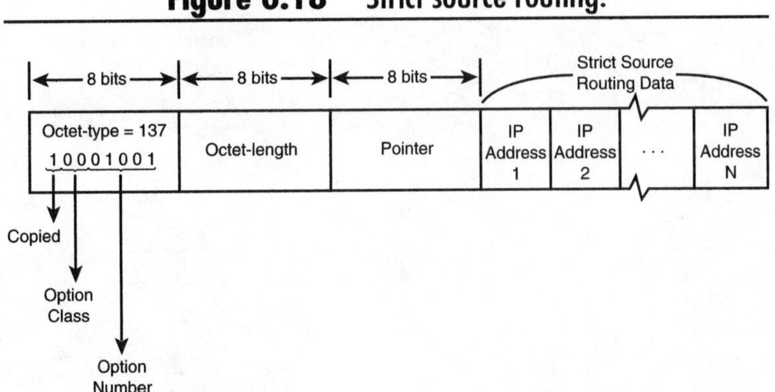

In the Loose Source Routing option (see fig. 6.19), the sender also includes a sequence of IP addresses that must be followed in forwarding the datagram. However, the path between two successive IP addresses may include any number of routers. Figure 6.20 shows the comparison between strict and loose source routing.

Figure 6.19 Loose source routing.

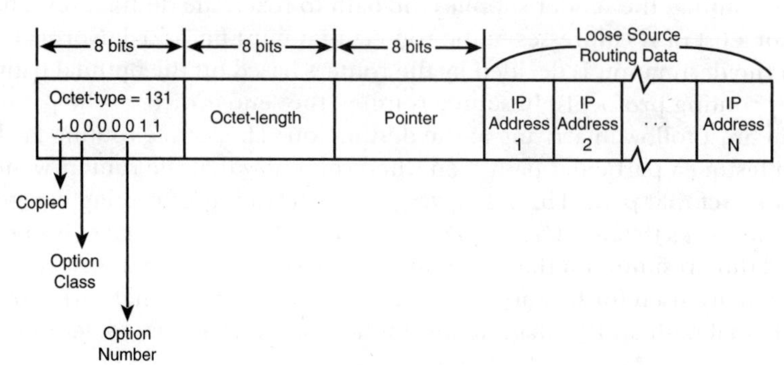

Figure 6.20 Strict versus loose source routing.

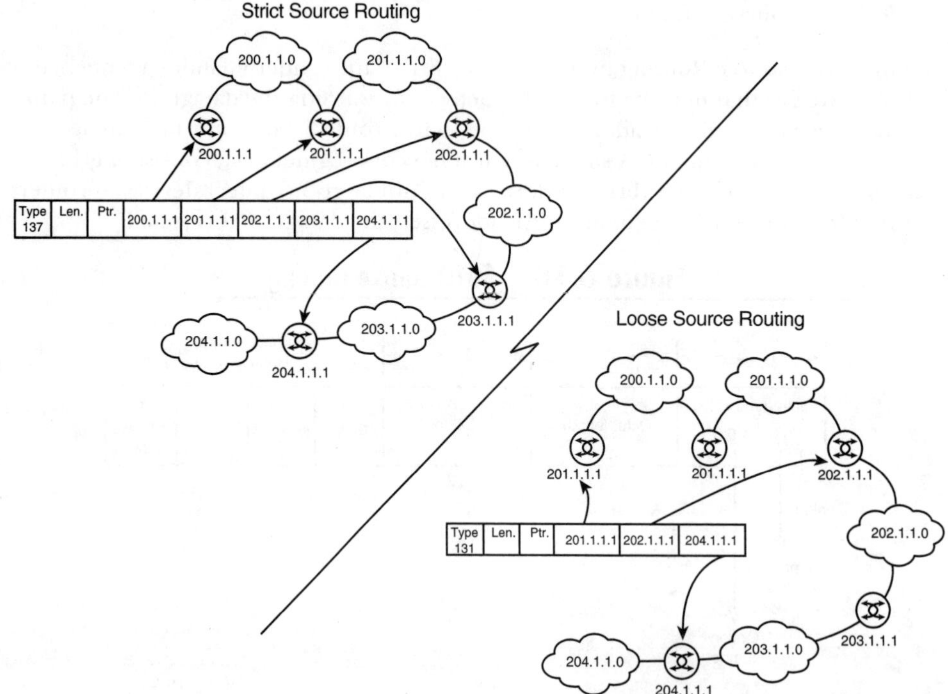

In both the Strict and Loose Source Routing options, the routers overwrite the source address in the option with their local IP addresses. When a datagram arrives at its destination, the IP address list contains the actual route that was taken. This list is like the one produced by the Record Route option. For this reason the Loose Source Routing option is also called the *Loose Source and Record Route* (LSRR) option, and the Strict Source Routing option is called the *Strict Source and Record Route* (SSRR) option.

As you examine the formats of the record route, strict source routing, and loose source routing in figures 6.17, 6.18, and 6.19, notice that the option format is very similar. The Pointer field acts like an index into the IP address list. The Octet-length field indicates the number of IP address slots. When a route finishes processing an IP address, it advances the Pointer index to the next available IP address slot. Since IP addresses are 4 octets long, the Pointer field value is incremented by 4 to advance it to the next IP address slot.

When the Pointer field value is greater than the Octet-length field value, the IP address list has been processed or exhausted. In this case, the IP datagram is forwarded as usual by information in the router's routing table, without the help of the information in the IP option fields. If the Pointer is not greater than the Octet-length field value, the IP address list has not been fully processed (see fig. 6.21). In this case, the router uses the Pointer field index to obtain the value of the next router address to which it must forward the datagram. Additionally, the router then places the IP address of the network interface through which the datagram is forwarded in the IP address slot pointed to by the Pointer field index. This is done for the purpose of recording the actual route that was taken. The Pointer field index is advanced to the next IP address slot by incrementing it by 4.

Figure 6.21 Use of Pointer and Octet-length field.

Octet-type	Octet-length 15	Pointer 4	IP Address 1	IP Address 2	IP Address 3
1 octet	1 octet	1 octet	4 octets	4 octets	4 octets

Pointer ≤ Octet-length

Octet-type	Octet-length 15	Pointer 16	IP Address 1	IP Address 2	IP Address 3
1 octet	1 octet	1 octet	4 octets	4 octets	4 octets

Pointer > Octet-length

The Route Data field consists of a series of IP addresses. Each IP address is 4 octets long. If the Pointer value is greater than the Octet-length field, the source route is empty and the recorded route is full. The routing is based on the destination address field of the IP datagram.

Internet Timestamp

The Internet Timestamp option is used to record the timestamps at which the IP datagram is received at each router. The router's IP address and time at which the IP datagram is received by a router is recorded. The timestamps are measured as the number of milliseconds since midnight, Universal Time Coordinated (m). UTC was formerly called Greenwich Mean Time (GMT) and is the time at 0 degrees longitude.

In addition to timestamps, the IP addresses of the router can also be recorded using the Internet Timestamp option. Figure 6.22 shows the format of the Internet Timestamp option.

Figure 6.22 Internet Timestamp option.

0 1 2 3 4 5 6 7 8 9 10 11 12 13 14 15 16 17 18 19 20 21 22 23 24 25 26 27 28 29 30 31

01000100 Octet-type (68) | Octet-length | Pointer | Overflow | Flags

IP Address 1

Timestamp 1

• • •

Data Field

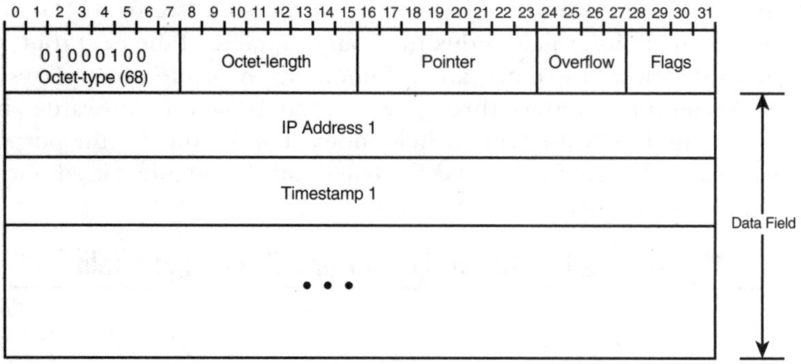

The Option-type is 68, and the Option-length is the number of octets in the option counting all the fields. Each entry in the data field of the Timestamp option contains two 32-bit values: the IP address of the router and the timestamp that it recorded.

The Octet-length specifies the amount of space reserved in the data field for the IP addresses and timestamps. The Pointer field is an index into the data field and points to the next unused slot. The index value in the Pointer field is measured from the beginning of the option. The smallest legal value of the Pointer field is 5. When the Pointer value is greater than the Octet-length field value, the timestamp area is full. The sender must create the Timestamp option with a large enough data area to hold all the timestamp information expected. The size of this option is not changed when the IP datagram is in transit. The sender must initialize the data area with zero values.

The Overflow field is 4 bits long and contains the number of routers that could not supply the timestamp because the data field was too small. The maximum value in the

Overflow field is 15 routers. If there is insufficient room for a full timestamp to be inserted in the data area, or the overflow count exceeds 15, then the IP datagram is considered to be in error and is discarded. In either case an ICMP parameter problem message is sent to the sender.

The Flags field controls the format of the information in the data field. It can have three values whose codes are described in table 6.9.

TABLE 6.9
IP Timestamp Option Flag Values

Flag Value	Meaning
0	Timestamps only, stored in consecutive 32-bit words. IP addresses are omitted.
1	Each timestamp is preceded with the IP address of the registering entity (router). This format is shown in figure 6.20.
3	The IP address fields are specified by the sender. An IP module (router) only registers its timestamp if its IP address matches the next specified IP address.

The Timestamp values are right-justified, with 32-bit values measured in milliseconds since midnight UTC. If the time is not available in milliseconds or cannot be provided with respect to midnight UTC, then any time value, such as local time, may be inserted in the Timestamp field provided the high-order bit of the Timestamp field is set to 1. Setting the high order bit of the Timestamp field to 1 indicates the use of a nonstandard value.

Routers may be set to the local time, and their clocks may not be synchronized. Because of differences in the routers' clock values, the Timestamp values should be treated as approximate values.

The Timestamp option is not copied upon fragmentation and is carried only in the first IP datagram fragment.

Network Byte Order

The Physical layer transmits the bits in the order in which they are received from the upper layers. The bits that constitute the transmitted data may be stored in a different way on each computer. For example, not all computers store 32-bit integer values (such as IP addresses) in the same way. Some computers store the low-order bytes of the 32-bit integer in lower-memory addresses. This storage method is called *little endian,* and the computers are called little endian computers. The other method is the *big endian* method in which the high-order bytes are stored in lower-memory addresses.

Some computers, especially the older 16-bit computers, store data in units of 16 bits with lower-order bytes stored in lower-memory addresses, but with the bytes swapped in the 16-bit word.

Because of differences in storage of data bytes, you cannot directly copy the data from one IP node to another. The TCP/IP protocols define a *network standard byte order* that is used for storing binary fields in internet packets. All IP nodes must represent the data in packets using this network standard byte order. Before sending a packet, an IP node converts its local data representation to the network standard byte order. On receiving the IP packet, an IP node converts the network standard byte order to the local data representation for that IP node. In most TCP/IP implementations, conversion between the network standard byte order to the node-specific representation is handled by the TCP/IP application programming interfaces and support routines.

The network standard byte order specifies that integers with the most significant byte are sent first; this is the *big endian* style. This means that if you examine an internet packet header field in transit, you see integer values with the most significant byte nearer the beginning of the packet and the least significant byte near the end of the packet.

TCP/IP protocol headers are often laid out as 32-bit words (refer to fig. 6.5). The order of transmission of the octets in the header is the normal order in which they are read in English (from left to right). For example, in figure 6.23 the octets are transmitted in the order in which they are numbered.

Figure 6.23 Transmission order of bytes.

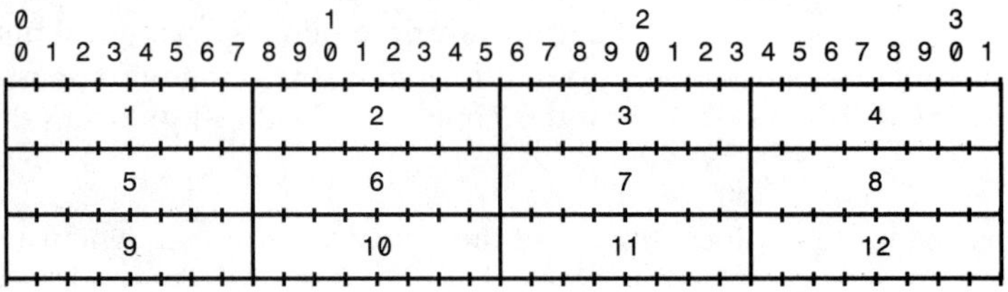

```
 0                   1                   2                   3
 0 1 2 3 4 5 6 7 8 9 0 1 2 3 4 5 6 7 8 9 0 1 2 3 4 5 6 7 8 9 0 1
+-+-+-+-+-+-+-+-+-+-+-+-+-+-+-+-+-+-+-+-+-+-+-+-+-+-+-+-+-+-+-+-+
|       1       |       2       |       3       |       4       |
+-+-+-+-+-+-+-+-+-+-+-+-+-+-+-+-+-+-+-+-+-+-+-+-+-+-+-+-+-+-+-+-+
|       5       |       6       |       7       |       8       |
+-+-+-+-+-+-+-+-+-+-+-+-+-+-+-+-+-+-+-+-+-+-+-+-+-+-+-+-+-+-+-+-+
|       9       |      10       |      11       |      12       |
+-+-+-+-+-+-+-+-+-+-+-+-+-+-+-+-+-+-+-+-+-+-+-+-+-+-+-+-+-+-+-+-+
```

Whenever an octet represents a numeric value, the left-most bit in the diagram is the high-order or most significant bit (MSB). That is, the bit labeled 0 is the most significant bit. For example, figure 6.24 represents the value 170 (decimal).

Figure 6.24 Significance of bits.

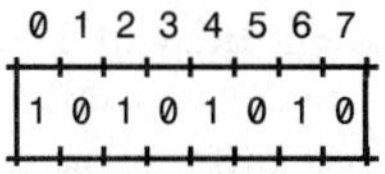

```
 0 1 2 3 4 5 6 7
+-+-+-+-+-+-+-+-+
|1 0 1 0 1 0 1 0|
+-+-+-+-+-+-+-+-+
```

Whenever a multi-octet field represents a numeric quantity, the left-most bit of the entire field is the most significant bit. When a multi-octet quantity is transmitted, the most significant octet is transmitted first.

IP Trace

The following sections present you with protocol decodes of IP packets captured on a real life network. You should study this protocol decode after briefly reviewing the previous sections that describe the meaning of the IP fields. Figure 6.25 shows the summary protocol trace of the first 50 packets captured in a Telnet session. Since this chapter discusses only the IP protocol, only selected packets in this Telnet trace will be discussed.

Figure 6.25 Telnet trace.

No.	Source	Destination	Layer	Size	Summary
1	0000C024282D	FFFFFFFFFFFF	arp	0064	Req by 144.19.74.44 for 144.19.74
2	0000C024282D	FFFFFFFFFFFF	arp	0064	Req by 144.19.74.44 for 144.19.74
3	0000C0A20F8E	0000C024282D	arp	0064	Reply 144.19.74.201=0000C0A20F8E
4	0000C024282D	0000C0A20F8E	tcp	0064	Port:6295 ---> TELNET SYN
5	0000C0A20F8E	0000C024282D	tcp	0064	Port:TELNET ---> 6295 ACK SYN
6	0000C024282D	0000C0A20F8E	telnt	0069	Cmd=Do; Code=Echo; Cmd=Do; Code=S
7	0000C0A20F8E	0000C024282D	tcp	0064	Port:TELNET ---> 6295 ACK
8	0000C0A20F8E	0000C024282D	telnt	0064	Cmd=Do; Code=;
9	0000C024282D	0000C0A20F8E	telnt	0064	Cmd=Won't; Code=;
10	0000C0A20F8E	0000C024282D	telnt	0067	Cmd=Will; Code=Echo; Cmd=Will; Co
11	0000C0A20F8E	0000C024282D	tcp	0064	Port:TELNET ---> 6295 ACK
12	0000C024282D	0000C0A20F8E	telnt	0072	Cmd=Do; Code=Suppress Go Ahead; C
13	0000C0A20F8E	0000C024282D	telnt	0070	Cmd=Do; Code=Terminal Type; Cmd=D
14	0000C0A20F8E	0000C024282D	tcp	0064	Port:TELNET ---> 6295 ACK
15	0000C024282D	0000C0A20F8E	telnt	0072	Cmd=Will; Code=Terminal Type; Cmd
16	0000C0A20F8E	0000C024282D	tcp	0064	Port:TELNET ---> 6295 ACK
17	0000C0A20F8E	0000C024282D	telnt	0064	Cmd=Subnegotiation Begin; Code=Te
18	0000C024282D	0000C0A20F8E	telnt	0071	Cmd=Subnegotiation Begin; Code=Te
19	0000C0A20F8E	0000C024282D	tcp	0064	Port:TELNET ---> 6295 ACK
20	0000C0A20F8E	0000C024282D	telnt	0067	Cmd=Do; Code=Echo; Cmd=Will; Code
21	0000C024282D	0000C0A20F8E	telnt	0069	Cmd=Won't; Code=Echo; Cmd=Don't;
22	0000C0A20F8E	0000C024282D	tcp	0064	Port:TELNET ---> 6295 ACK
23	0000C0A20F8E	0000C024282D	telnt	0104	Data=..Linux 1.3.50 (ltreec1.ltre
24	0000C024282D	0000C0A20F8E	tcp	0064	Port:6295 ---> TELNET ACK
25	0000C0A20F8E	0000C024282D	telnt	0064	Data=..
26	0000C024282D	0000C0A20F8E	tcp	0064	Port:6295 ---> TELNET ACK
27	0000C0A20F8E	0000C024282D	telnt	0073	Data=ltreec1 login:
28	0000C024282D	0000C0A20F8E	tcp	0064	Port:6295 ---> TELNET ACK
29	0000C024282D	0000C0A20F8E	telnt	0064	Data=u
30	0000C0A20F8E	0000C024282D	tcp	0064	Port:TELNET ---> 6295 ACK
31	0000C0A20F8E	0000C024282D	telnt	0064	Data=u
32	0000C024282D	0000C0A20F8E	tcp	0064	Port:6295 ---> TELNET ACK
33	0000C024282D	0000C0A20F8E	telnt	0064	Data=s
34	0000C0A20F8E	0000C024282D	tcp	0064	Port:TELNET ---> 6295 ACK
35	0000C0A20F8E	0000C024282D	telnt	0064	Data=s
36	0000C024282D	0000C0A20F8E	tcp	0064	Port:6295 ---> TELNET ACK
37	0000C024282D	0000C0A20F8E	telnt	0064	Data=e
38	0000C0A20F8E	0000C024282D	tcp	0064	Port:TELNET ---> 6295 ACK
39	0000C0A20F8E	0000C024282D	telnt	0064	Data=e
40	0000C024282D	0000C0A20F8E	tcp	0064	Port:6295 ---> TELNET ACK
41	0000C024282D	0000C0A20F8E	telnt	0064	Data=r
42	0000C0A20F8E	0000C024282D	tcp	0064	Port:TELNET ---> 6295 ACK
43	0000C0A20F8E	0000C024282D	telnt	0064	Data=r
44	0000C024282D	0000C0A20F8E	tcp	0064	Port:6295 ---> TELNET ACK
45	0000C024282D	0000C0A20F8E	telnt	0064	Data=1
46	0000C0A20F8E	0000C024282D	tcp	0064	Port:TELNET ---> 6295 ACK
47	0000C0A20F8E	0000C024282D	telnt	0064	Data=1
48	0000C024282D	0000C0A20F8E	tcp	0064	Port:6295 ---> TELNET ACK
49	0000C024282D	0000C0A20F8E	telnt	0064	Data=..
50	0000C0A20F8E	0000C024282D	tcp	0064	Port:TELNET ---> 6295 ACK

Notice that the first three packets of this Telnet trace are ARP packets. The use of ARP to resolve hardware addresses is discussed in Chapter 5, "Address Resolution Protocols."

The Ethernet header for all the IP datagrams contains an EtherType value of 800 hex. This EtherType value indicates that the Ethernet frame encapsulates an IP datagram.

The Protocol field in the IP headers of all the datagrams has a value of 6. This indicates that the IP datagram encapsulates a TCP packet.

IP Datagram #1: IP Packet with Flags = 0, MF = 0, DF = 0

Figure 6.26 shows the first IP datagram (packet # 4 in fig. 6.25) sent from the source at 199.245.180.44 to the Telnet host at 199.245.180.201. As you examine the IP header, you will notice the following parameter values:

Version: 4

Header Length (32 bit words): 5

TOS: 0 (Precedence: Routine, Normal Delay, Normal Throughput, Normal Reliability)

Total length: 44

Identification: 1

Flags: 0, DF = 0, MF = 0 (Fragmentation allowed, Last fragment)

Fragment Offset: 0

Time to Live: 100 seconds

Protocol: 6 (TCP)

Checksum: 0xA1AF(Valid)

Source IP address: 144.19.74.44

Destination IP address: 144.19.74.201

Figure 6.26 IP datagram 1.

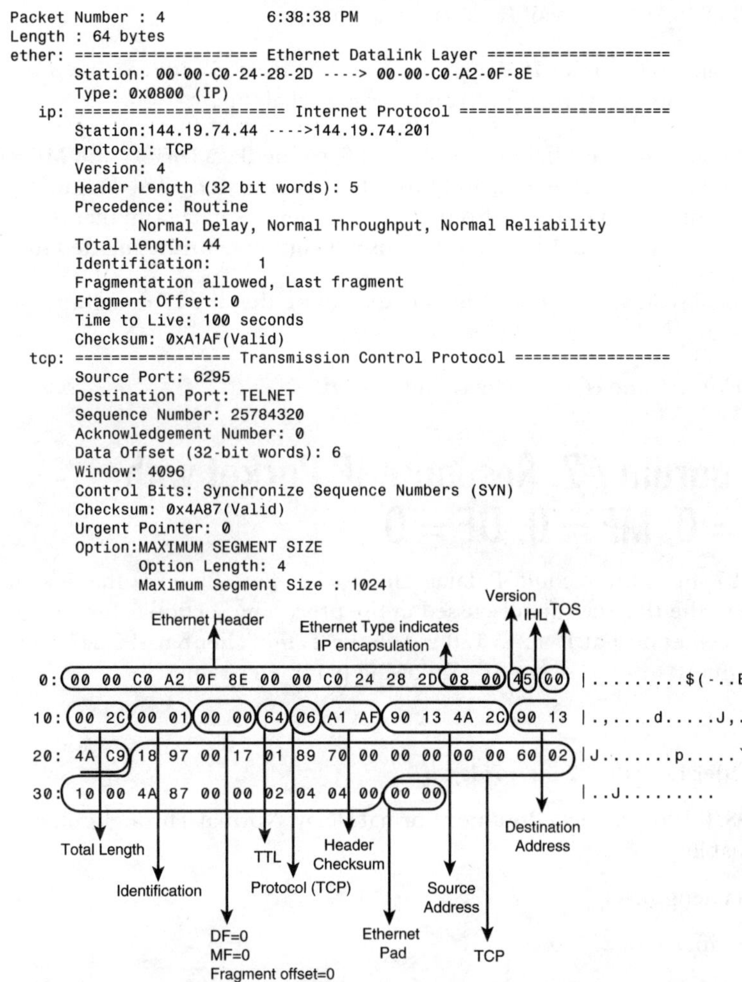

```
Packet Number : 4            6:38:38 PM
Length : 64 bytes
ether: =================== Ethernet Datalink Layer ===================
       Station: 00-00-C0-24-28-2D ----> 00-00-C0-A2-0F-8E
       Type: 0x0800 (IP)
   ip: ====================== Internet Protocol ======================
       Station:144.19.74.44 ---->144.19.74.201
       Protocol: TCP
       Version: 4
       Header Length (32 bit words): 5
       Precedence: Routine
              Normal Delay, Normal Throughput, Normal Reliability
       Total length: 44
       Identification:     1
       Fragmentation allowed, Last fragment
       Fragment Offset: 0
       Time to Live: 100 seconds
       Checksum: 0xA1AF(Valid)
  tcp: ================= Transmission Control Protocol =================
       Source Port: 6295
       Destination Port: TELNET
       Sequence Number: 25784320
       Acknowledgement Number: 0
       Data Offset (32-bit words): 6
       Window: 4096
       Control Bits: Synchronize Sequence Numbers (SYN)
       Checksum: 0x4A87(Valid)
       Urgent Pointer: 0
       Option:MAXIMUM SEGMENT SIZE
              Option Length: 4
              Maximum Segment Size : 1024

 0: 00 00 C0 A2 0F 8E 00 00 C0 24 28 2D 08 00 45 00  |.........$(-..E.
10: 00 2C 00 01 00 00 64 06 A1 AF 90 13 4A 2C 90 13  |.,....d.....J,..
20: 4A C9 18 97 00 17 01 89 70 00 00 00 00 00 60 02  |J.......p.....`.
30: 10 00 4A 87 00 00 02 04 04 00 00 00              |..J.........
```


The Version field value is 4, so the format of the IP datagram is IPv4.

The Header Length is 5 words (20 octets). This is the minimum size of the IP datagram, so there are no IP options.

The Total Length of this IP datagram is 44 octets. The Ethernet header and CRC checksum is 18 octets long. Adding these two gives an Ethernet packet size of 62 octets. An additional 2 octets of pad are added to bring the total Ethernet frame size to 64 octets.

This IP datagram has an Identification field value of 1 and a TTL value of 100 seconds. The TTL value of 100 seconds is the default TTL value that is used by the host at 199.245.180.44 for all IP datagrams that it sends.

The TOS value is 0, so this IP datagram should be treated with routine precedence, normal delay, normal throughput, and normal reliability.

The fragmentation Flags field has a value of 0, so the flags DF = 0, and MF = 0. This datagram could be fragmented, and this is the last fragment. The Fragment Offset value of 0 indicates that this is also the first fragment. A datagram that is the first and last fragment has no other fragments—this is a complete unfragmented datagram.

The Protocol field value has a code of 6, indicating that the IP datagram is carrying a TCP message.

The Checksum value is A1AF (hex) and is valid.

IP Datagram #2: Response IP Packet with Flags = 0, MF = 0, DF = 0

Figure 6.27 shows the second IP datagram (packet #5 in fig 6.25) that is sent in response to the IP datagram discussed in the preceding section. This datagram is sent from the Telnet host at 199.245.180.201 to the Telnet client at 199.245.180.44. As you examine the IP header, notice the following parameter values:

Version: 4

Header Length (32 bit words): 5

TOS: 0 (Precedence: Routine, Normal Delay, Normal Throughput, Normal Reliability)

Total length: 44

Identification: 21410

Flags: 0, DF = 0, MF = 0 (Fragmentation allowed, Last fragment)

Fragment Offset: 0

Time to Live: 64 seconds

Protocol: 6 (TCP)

Checksum: 0x720E (Valid)

Source IP address: 144.19.74.201

Destination IP address: 144.19.74.44

Figure 6.27 IP datagram 2.

```
Packet Number : 5            6:38:38 PM
Length : 64 bytes
ether: =================== Ethernet Datalink Layer ===================
       Station: 00-00-C0-A2-0F-8E ----> 00-00-C0-24-28-2D
       Type: 0x0800 (IP)
   ip: ====================== Internet Protocol ======================
       Station:144.19.74.201 ---->144.19.74.44
       Protocol: TCP
       Version: 4
       Header Length (32 bit words): 5
       Precedence: Routine
              Normal Delay, Normal Throughput, Normal Reliability
       Total length: 44
       Identification: 21410
       Fragmentation allowed, Last fragment
       Fragment Offset: 0
       Time to Live: 64  seconds
       Checksum: 0x720E(Valid)
  tcp: ================= Transmission Control Protocol =================
       Source Port: TELNET
       Destination Port: 6295
       Sequence Number: 1508167651
       Acknowledgement Number: 25784321
       Data Offset (32-bit words): 6
       Window: 30719
       Control Bits: Acknowledgement Field is Valid (ACK)
              Synchronize Sequence Numbers (SYN)
       Checksum: 0xB8AE(Valid)
       Urgent Pointer: 0
       Option:MAXIMUM SEGMENT SIZE
              Option Length: 4
              Maximum Segment Size : 1024
```

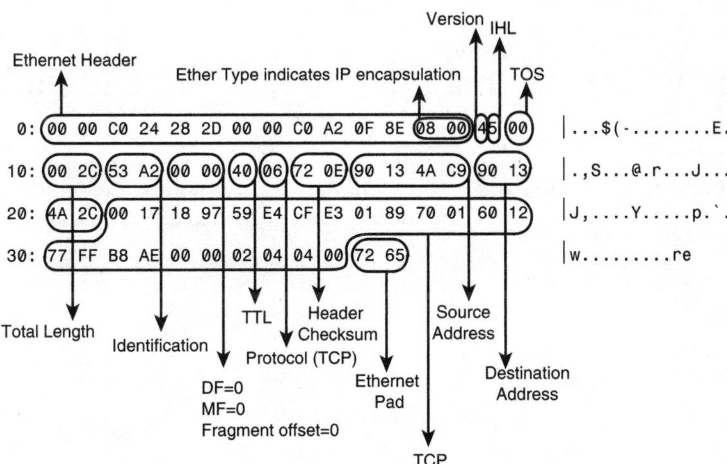

The Version field value is 4, so the format of the IP datagram is IPv4.

The Header Length is 5 words (20 octets). This is the minimum size of the IP datagram, so there are no IP options.

The Total Length of this IP datagram is 44 octets. The Ethernet header and CRC checksum is 18 octets long. Adding these two gives an Ethernet packet size of 62 octets. An additional 2 octets of pad are added to bring the total Ethernet frame size to 64 octets.

This IP datagram has an Identification field value of 21410. Notice that this Identification value is different from that sent by the Telnet client. The Identification value starts from a large number because the Telnet host has sent many IP datagrams prior to this session.

Another interesting item to note is that the TTL value is 64 seconds. This is the default TTL value that is used by the Telnet host at 199.245.180.201 for all IP datagrams that it sends. Notice that this TTL value is different from that sent by 199.245.180.44. Different TCP/IP implementations use different initial TTL values.

The TOS value is 0, and this indicates that this IP datagram should be treated with routine precedence, normal delay, normal throughput, and normal reliability.

The fragmentation Flags field has a value of 0, so the flags DF = 0, and MF = 0. This datagram could be fragmented, and this is the last fragment. The Fragment Offset value of 0 indicates that this is also the first fragment. A datagram that is the first and last fragment has no other fragments—this is a complete unfragmented datagram.

The Protocol field value has a code of 6, so the IP datagram is carrying a TCP message.

The Checksum value is 720E (hex) and is valid.

IP Datagrams #3 and #4: Observing the Identification Field

Figures 6.28 and 6.29 show the next two IP datagrams that are exchanged between the Telnet client at 199.245.180.44 and the Telnet host at 199.245.180.201.

Figure 6.28 IP datagram 3.

```
Packet Number : 6           6:38:38 PM
Length : 69 bytes
ether: ==================== Ethernet Datalink Layer ====================
       Station: 00-00-C0-24-28-2D ----> 00-00-C0-A2-0F-8E
       Type: 0x0800 (IP)
   ip: ====================== Internet Protocol ======================
       Station:144.19.74.44 ---->144.19.74.201
       Protocol: TCP
       Version: 4
       Header Length (32 bit words): 5
       Precedence: Routine
              Normal Delay, Normal Throughput, Normal Reliability
       Total length: 49
       Identification:     2
       Fragmentation allowed, Last fragment
       Fragment Offset: 0
       Time to Live: 100 seconds
       Checksum: 0xA1A9(Valid)
  tcp: ================= Transmission Control Protocol =================
       Source Port: 6295
       Destination Port: TELNET
       Sequence Number: 25784321
       Acknowledgement Number: 1508167652
       Data Offset (32-bit words): 5
       Window: 4096
       Control Bits: Acknowledgement Field is Valid (ACK)
              Push Function Requested (PSH)
       Checksum: 0x18A9(Valid)
       Urgent Pointer: 0
telnt: ======================= Telnet Protocol =======================
       Command: Do
       Option Code: Echo
       Command: Do
       Option Code: Suppress Go Ahead
       Command: Will
       Option Code:
```

```
 0: 00 00 C0 A2 0F 8E 00 00 C0 24 28 2D 08 00 45 00   |.........$(-..E.
10: 00 31 00 02 00 00 64 06 A1 A9 90 13 4A 2C 90 13   |.1....d.....J,..
20: 4A C9 18 97 00 17 01 89 70 01 59 E4 CF E4 50 18   |J.......p.Y...P.
30: 10 00 18 A9 00 00 FF FD 01 FF FD 03 FF FB 1F 00   |................
40: 00                                                |.
```

Figure 6.29 IP datagram 4.

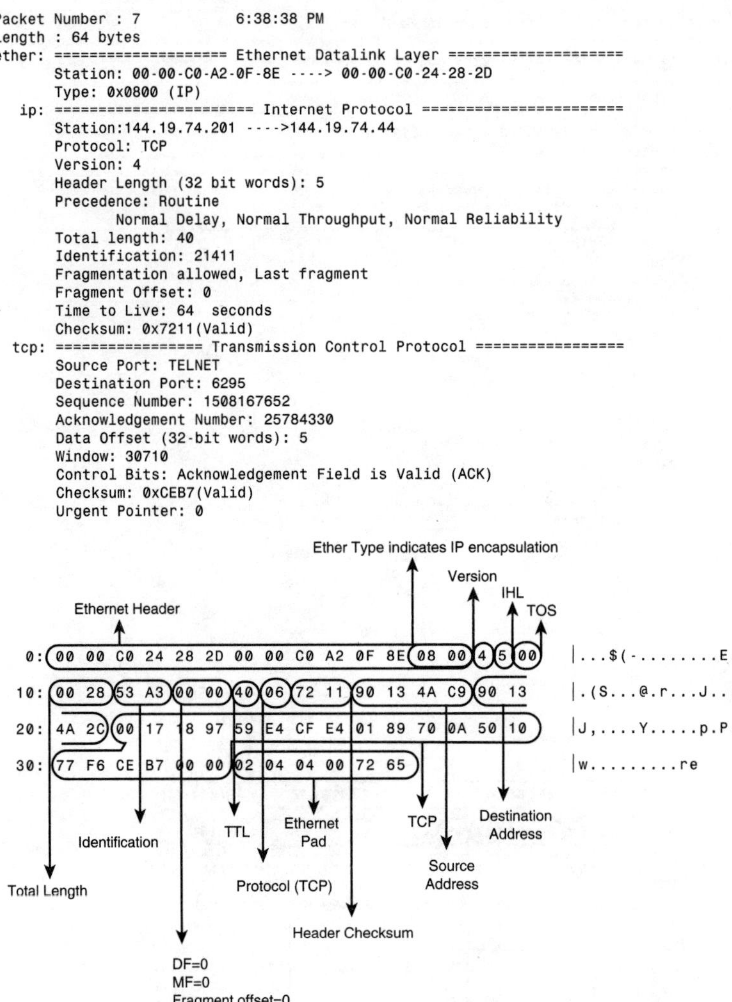

```
Packet Number : 7              6:38:38 PM
Length : 64 bytes
ether: ==================== Ethernet Datalink Layer ====================
       Station: 00-00-C0-A2-0F-8E ----> 00-00-C0-24-28-2D
       Type: 0x0800 (IP)
   ip: ====================== Internet Protocol ======================
       Station:144.19.74.201 ---->144.19.74.44
       Protocol: TCP
       Version: 4
       Header Length (32 bit words): 5
       Precedence: Routine
              Normal Delay, Normal Throughput, Normal Reliability
       Total length: 40
       Identification: 21411
       Fragmentation allowed, Last fragment
       Fragment Offset: 0
       Time to Live: 64  seconds
       Checksum: 0x7211(Valid)
  tcp: ================= Transmission Control Protocol =================
       Source Port: TELNET
       Destination Port: 6295
       Sequence Number: 1508167652
       Acknowledgement Number: 25784330
       Data Offset (32-bit words): 5
       Window: 30710
       Control Bits: Acknowledgement Field is Valid (ACK)
       Checksum: 0xCEB7(Valid)
       Urgent Pointer: 0

 0: 00 00 C0 24 28 2D 00 00 C0 A2 0F 8E 08 00 45 00   |...$(-........E.
10: 00 28 53 A3 00 00 40 06 72 11 90 13 4A C9 90 13   |.(S...@.r...J...
20: 4A 2C 00 17 18 97 59 E4 CF E4 01 89 70 0A 50 10   |J,....Y.....p.P.
30: 77 F6 CE B7 00 00 02 04 04 00 72 65               |w.........re
```


It is instructive to examine the Identification field value in these datagrams. The datagram in figure 6.28 is the second datagram sent from the Telnet client to the Telnet host. The identification field in this datagram is 2, which is one more than that of the datagram sent in figure 6.26. The datagram in figure 6.28 is the second datagram sent from the Telnet host to the Telnet client. The identification field in this datagram is 21411, which is one more than that of the previous datagram sent in figure 6.27. This example shows that the Identification fields are maintained separately by each sending side.

IP Datagram #5: Datagram with DF = 1

Figure 6.30 shows an IP datagram that is sent from the Telnet host at 199.245.180.201 to the Telnet client at 199.245.180.44. As you examine the IP header, notice the following parameter values:

Version: 4

Header Length (32-bit words): 5

TOS: 0 (Precedence: Routine, Normal Delay, Normal Throughput, Normal Reliability)

Total length: 43

Identification: 21412

Flags: 0, DF = 1, MF = 0 (Fragmentation not allowed, Last fragment)

Fragment Offset: 0

Time to Live: 64 seconds

Protocol: 6 (TCP)

Checksum: 0x320D (Valid)

Source IP address: 144.19.74.201

Destination IP address: 144.19.74.44

The field values are similar to those discussed in earlier IP datagrams. The difference is in the fragmentation Flags field, which has the DF flag set to 1. This means that the Telnet host is requesting that this datagram should not be fragmented.

Figure 6.30 IP datagram 5.

```
Packet Number : 8           6:38:39 PM
Length : 64 bytes
ether: ==================== Ethernet Datalink Layer ====================
       Station: 00-00-C0-A2-0F-8E ----> 00-00-C0-24-28-2D
       Type: 0x0800 (IP)
   ip: ====================== Internet Protocol ======================
       Station:144.19.74.201 ---->144.19.74.44
       Protocol: TCP
       Version: 4
       Header Length (32 bit words): 5
       Precedence: Routine
            Normal Delay, Normal Throughput, Normal Reliability
       Total length: 43
       Identification: 21412
       Fragmentation not allowed, Last fragment
       Fragment Offset: 0
       Time to Live: 64  seconds
       Checksum: 0x320D(Valid)
  tcp: ================= Transmission Control Protocol =================
       Source Port: TELNET
       Destination Port: 6295
       Sequence Number: 1508167652
       Acknowledgement Number: 25784330
       Data Offset (32-bit words): 5
       Window: 30710
       Control Bits: Acknowledgement Field is Valid (ACK)
            Push Function Requested (PSH)
       Checksum: 0xA9AE(Valid)
       Urgent Pointer: 0
telnt: ======================= Telnet Protocol =======================
       Command: Do
       Option Code:
```

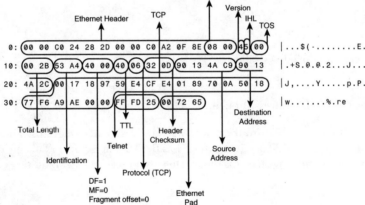

```
 0: 00 00 C0 24 28 2D 00 00 C0 A2 0F 8E 08 00 45 00  |...$(-........E.
10: 00 2B 53 A4 40 00 40 06 32 0D 90 13 4A C9 90 13  |.+S.@.@.2...J...
20: 4A 2C 00 17 18 97 59 E4 CF E4 01 89 70 0A 50 18  |J,....Y.....p.P.
30: 77 F6 A9 AE 00 00 FF FD 25 00 72 65              |w.......%.re
```


Summary

The Internet Protocol provides a logical view of the network regardless of the different network technologies used to build the physical network. The logical network is independent of physical layer addresses, MTU size, and any other differences. Upper-layer protocols, such as the TCP and UDP, treat the network as an IP only network. The IP network provides connectionless services to upper-layer services. The connectionless service is implemented using datagrams that contain the source and destination IP addresses and other parameters needed for IP operation. An important aspect of IP operation is that datagrams in transit are fragmented as needed by routers to ensure that the datagrams can be transmitted in the packet size of the underlying networks. When IP fragmentation takes place, the receiver is responsible for assembling the IP datagram fragments into the original datagram.

Test Yourself

1. Describe some of the characteristics of a logical IP network.
2. Does the IP network attempt to order the datagrams that may arrive out of sequence? Who is responsible for sequencing the IP datagrams?
3. Is a pure IP network a reliable network? What must a TCP/IP application do to ensure reliability of transmission?
4. Draw a diagram of an IPv4 header. Label each field and give a one- or two-line description of each field.
5. What is the minimum size of an IP header? What causes the IP header size to be variable?
6. Given that the IP datagram size is 100 octets, what is the protocol overhead of the Data Link and Network layers assuming that the IP datagram is sent on an Ethernet network?
7. The IP datagram length is 44 octets. If this datagram is sent in an Ethernet frame, is padding necessary? If so, how many octets of padding are required?
8. If IP software can only process version 4 datagrams, what happens if it receives datagrams with a different Version field value?
9. What is the maximum size of the IPv4 header? Prove your answer. For this maximum size, how many octets are used up for specifying IP options?
10. What are the different categories of Precedence values? What is the normal Precedence value in most IP datagrams that are generated by commercial TCP/IP applications?
11. How can the TOS field in IP datagrams be used by routing algorithms?
12. For applications that need to send interactive data, what TOS code would you assign in the IP datagrams?
13. For applications that need to send large file transfers, what TOS code would you assign in the IP datagrams?
14. For applications that need to send data with the least cost, what TOS code would you assign in the IP datagrams?

15. What is the minimum and maximum size of an IP datagram? Is the minimum IP datagram size likely to be encountered for TCP/IP applications? What are the problems associated with sending an IP datagram with the maximum size?
16. What is the minimum IP datagram size all IP nodes must be able to handle?
17. What is the purpose of the Identification field?
18. Under what circumstances might an IP datagram be sent with a DF flag set to 1?
19. If an IP datagram is sent with a DF flag set to 1, and a router finds that it is unable to forward this datagram because the MTU size of the network is less than the IP datagram size, what happens?
20. How might the TTL field in an IP datagram be useful?
21. Study the IP header format and explain why fragment sizes start at offsets that are multiples of 8.
22. How does a receiver know that the last fragment has been received?
23. How can a receiver know that an IP datagram fragment is the first fragment?
24. What are the DF and MF flag values for an unfragmented IP datagram?
25. An IP datagram is received with fragment offset of 0 and the MF flag set to 1. What conclusion can you draw from this information?
26. What are the disadvantages of excessive IP datagram fragmentation?
27. When an IP fragment is lost, what action occurs at the receiver?
28. An IP datagram is received with fragment offset of 0 and the MF flag set to 0. What conclusion can you draw from this information?
29. An IP datagram is received with fragment offset of 200 and the MF flag set to 1. What conclusion can you draw from this information?
30. An IP datagram is received with fragment offset of 600 and the MF flag set to 0. What conclusion can you draw from this information?
31. An IP datagram with a size of 1500 octets is sent with the DF flag set to 1 on a network with an MTU size of 1500 octets. The path to the destination node is across networks with an MTU size of 2000 and 4470 octets. Will fragmentation take place? Will IP be able to deliver the datagram to the destination?
32. An IP datagram of size 1500 octets and an Identification field value of 100 is sent with the DF flag set to 0 on a network with an MTU size of 1500 octets. The path to the destination node is across a network with an MTU size of 2000. The destination network has an MTU size of 1500 octets. Will fragmentation take place? If so, list the fragments with the values of the Identification, MF, DF, and Fragment Offset fields.

33. An IP datagram of size 1500 octets and an Identification field value of 100 is sent with the DF flag set to 0 on a network with an MTU size of 1500 octets. The path to the destination node is across a network with an MTU size of 625. The destination network has an MTU size of 1500 octets. Will fragmentation take place? If so, list the fragments with the values of the Identification, MF, DF, and Fragment Offset fields. Try to figure out the algorithm that the receiver could use to reassemble the IP fragments.

34. An IP datagram of size 1500 octets and an Identification field value of 100 is sent with the DF flag set to 0 on a network with an MTU size of 1500 octets. The path to the destination node is across a network with an MTU size of 625. The destination network has an MTU size of 525 octets. Will fragmentation take place? If so, list the fragments at each router between the networks. For each fragment show the value of the Identification, MF, DF, and Fragment Offset fields.

35. If there is insufficient room for a full timestamp to be inserted in the data area of the IP Timestamp option, what happens?

36. If the IP Timestamp option overflows, what happens?

37. Given an IP address of 199.245.201.33, show the network standard byte order for transmitting this value across the network. Number the bytes of this address from 1 to 4 to indicate the order in which they will be transmitted. Number the bits in each octet starting from 0 for the most significant bit, and specify the order in which the bits in the octets will be transmitted.

38. Given an integer value of 171 that is one octet long and is the value of a TCP/IP protocol field, specify the bit order in which the bits will be transmitted.

39. Describe the differences between strict and loose source routing.

40. In the source routing option, how are the Pointer and Octet-length field used to determine if the routing data has been processed?

41. What is the Internet Timestamp option used for?

42. Given the following hexadecimal dump of an IP datagram encapsulated in an Ethernet frame, decode the values of the IP header. Draw a sketch of an IP header and place the decoded values in the IP header fields.

```
 0: 00 00 C0 24 28 2D 00 00 C0 A2 0F 8E 08 00 45 00 ¦...$(-........E.
10: 00 29 53 B2 40 00 40 06 32 01 90 13 4A C9 90 13 ¦.)S.@.@.2...J...
20: 4A 2C 00 17 18 97 59 E4 D0 4A 01 89 70 3A 50 18 ¦J,....Y..J..p:P.
30: 77 FF 59 0F 00 00 75 74 72 65 65 63             ¦w.Y...utreec
```

43. Given the following hexadecimal dump of an IP datagram encapsulated in an Ethernet frame, decode the values of the IP header. Draw a sketch of an IP header and place the decoded values in the IP header fields.

```
 0: 00 00 C0 A2 0F 8E 00 00 C0 24 28 2D 08 00 45 00 ¦.........$(-..E.
10: 00 28 00 0C 00 00 64 06 A1 A8 90 13 4A 2C 90 13 ¦.(....d.....J,..
20: 4A C9 18 97 00 17 01 89 70 3A 59 E4 D0 4B 50 10 ¦J.......p:Y..KP.
30: 10 00 36 17 00 00 00 00 00 FF FE 05             ¦..6.........
```

44. Given the following partial hexadecimal dump of an IP datagram fragment encapsulated in an Ethernet frame, decode the values of the IP header. Draw a sketch of an IP header and place the decoded values in the IP header fields. What is the upper-layer protocol encapsulated by the IP datagram header?

```
 0: 00 00 C0 DD 14 5C 00 A0 24 AB D1 E6 08 00 45 00 ¦.....\..$.....E.
10: 05 DC 3A 01 20 00 20 01 43 16 C7 F5 B4 14 C7 F5 ¦..:. . .C.......
20: B4 0A 08 00 EA FB 01 00 07 00 61 62 63 64 65 66 ¦..........abcdef
30: 67 68 69 6A 6B 6C 6D 6E 6F 70 71 72 73 74 75 76 ¦ghijklmnopqrstuv
40: 77 61 62 63 64 65 66 67 68 69 6A 6B 6C 6D 6E 6F ¦wabcdefghijklmno
50: 70 71 72 73 74 75 76 77 61 62 63 64 65 66 67 68 ¦pqrstuvwabcdefgh
```

CHAPTER 7

IP Routing Concepts

You can use IP to build arbitrarily complex networks. These complex networks can extend the range of networks to span large distances. Complex IP networks are joined together by using relay devices called *routers*. IP routers understand the format of the IP header and can forward IP datagrams based on the information in the IP header. The forwarding of IP datagrams to their destinations is called *routing*. The routers act as packet-switching devices, which select one path over another based on specified criteria. Most commercial IP routers are not pure IP routers because you can configure the commercial routers to route other protocols.

Understanding Basic Routing Concepts

As explained in Chapter 3, "Network Support for TCP/IP," routers are OSI layer-3 devices. Layer 3 in the OSI model is concerned with routing functions. Figure 7.1 shows a simplified model for a router.

Figure 7.1 A simplified router model.

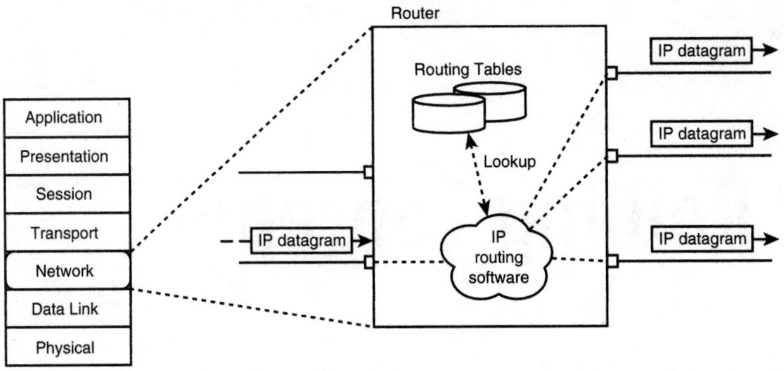

A router has multiple ports, but it must have a minimum of two ports. IP datagrams arrive at the router's port. The IP routing software examines the header of the IP datagram to determine how the datagram should be forwarded. The most important piece of information the routing software examines is the destination address of the IP datagram. The routing software consults the routing table in the router and forwards the datagram through one of the router's ports.

Static Versus Dynamic Routing

The routing table contains a list of destination networks and hosts; the table also contains information on the best way to reach these destinations. The way the information is set up in the routing table is determined by the following two methods of initializing a router's routing table:

- Static method
- Dynamic method

The static method requires you to manually enter the information in the routing table. In the dynamic method, the router can dynamically learn information about how to route to other networks and hosts. The router learns this information via *routing protocols.*

Modern networks typically use the Dynamic method. The Static method can be used for simple networks whose topology does not change, or for troubleshooting where manual corrections to the routing table may be required.

Defining Routing Protocols

Routing protocols define how routers exchange information among themselves to learn the best route to destinations on the Internet. Because routing protocols need to exchange messages in an IP network, the routing protocols are carried in IP datagrams. Routing protocols can run directly on top of IP, as in the case of OSPF (Open Shortest Path First); they can run on top of the UDP Transport layer protocol, as in the case of RIP (Routing Information protocol); or they can run on top of the TCP Transport layer protocol, as in the case of BGP (Border Gateway protocol).

Because routing protocols are clients of IP, TCP, or UDP, they can be treated as a class of special Application layer protocols.

Router Configuration Issues

Regardless of the routing protocol that a router uses, you always need to do some manual configuration to a router before it can be operated in a network because a router is an OSI layer-3 device whose network interfaces are identified by IP addresses. Therefore, you need to manually configure the IP addresses and related parameters for each network interface of the router. In some commercial routers, you can set up the configuration parameters in a file that can then be downloaded from a local or network device. By using configuration files, you can automate the setup of routers, but you still need to manually set up the configuration file in the proper way.

Traditionally, many routers were application hosts, such as Unix computers, that also performed routing functions. In fact, many Unix systems automatically act as routers, by default, if they have more than one network interface (*multihomed hosts*). Many PC-based network operating systems can also be configured as routers.

If a server or application host is configured to act as a router, it has to perform the dual job of providing routing and application services. Because each IP datagram needs to be routed separately, the routing algorithm can consume a substantial amount of the server's or application host's processor time on a busy network. This use of processing time can seriously affect the performance of the computer as an application server. For this reason, router vendors sell dedicated hardware devices that perform only routing functions. By using dedicated hardware devices that contain specialized hardware designed to speed routing functions, you can more easily separate the communications and applications functions. This separation leads to easier management of communications and applications and avoids conflict of interest.

Although a general-purpose application host can act as a router, you can assume (for the purpose of the discussion in this chapter) that hosts are computers that run such TCP/IP applications as Telnet, FTP, NFS, SNMP, HTTP, and so on. Routers are assumed to be specialized devices with two or more connections and that perform routing functions only.

Datagram Delivery

Both hosts and routers participate in the process of routing an IP datagram. IP datagrams are generated by a sending host that wants to contact services at another host. Figure 7.2 shows a network that has hosts and routers. The routers provide connections to outside networks.

Figure 7.2 Hosts and routers.

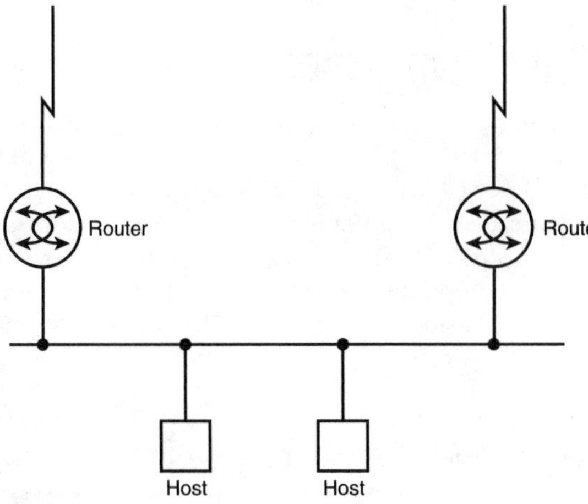

When the sending host sends an IP datagram, the host must make a decision about whether to send the datagram directly to a host on the network or to forward the datagram to one of the routers on that network. This decision is the routing that is performed at each host.

Although a router's ports are connected to the network, the router will forward only IP datagrams that are sent to the router port. The sending host is responsible for forwarding the IP datagram specifically to a router port. In the example in figure 7.2, the sender host forwards the datagram by discovering the hardware address of the router port that is connected to the network and by using the hardware address of the router port in the destination address field of the Data Link layer frame. In a broadcast network, a protocol such as ARP (refer to Chapter 5, "Address Resolution Protocols") is used to discover the hardware address of the router port.

Types of Datagram Delivery

An IP datagram can be delivered to the destination by the following two methods:

- Direct delivery
- Indirect delivery

The routing of an IP datagram in a complex network involves a combination of both methods.

The direct-delivery situation occurs when the sender and receiver are on the same physical network. The sender can send the IP datagram directly to the receiver without the involvement of any routers (see fig. 7.3). The underlying physical-transmission method of the network is used to perform the datagram delivery.

Figure 7.3 Direct datagram delivery.

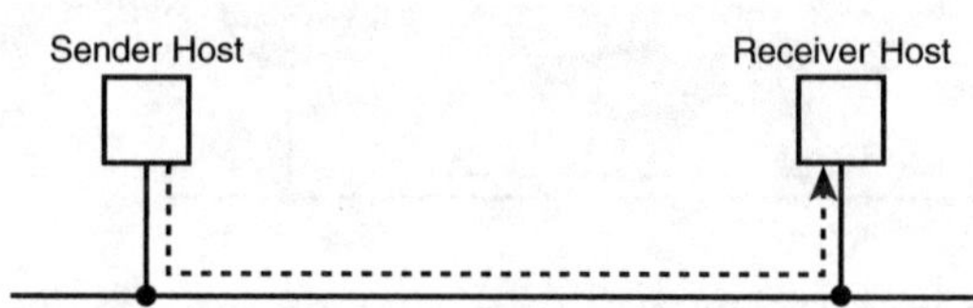

In a broadcast network such as a LAN, the IP datagram delivery may be preceded by ARP packets such as an ARP request from the sender to discover the hardware address of the receiver and by an ARP reply from the receiver that contains the receiver's hardware address. After the hardware address of the receiver is known, direct delivery of the datagram is made by placing the hardware address of the receiver in the destination address field of the Data Link layer frame and by sending the Data Link frame.

In indirect delivery, the receiver is not on the same physical network as the sender (see fig. 7.4). The sender must then forward the IP datagram through one of the routers connected to its physical network. Because more than one router may be involved, this process is called indirect delivery of the IP datagram.

Figure 7.4 Indirect datagram delivery.

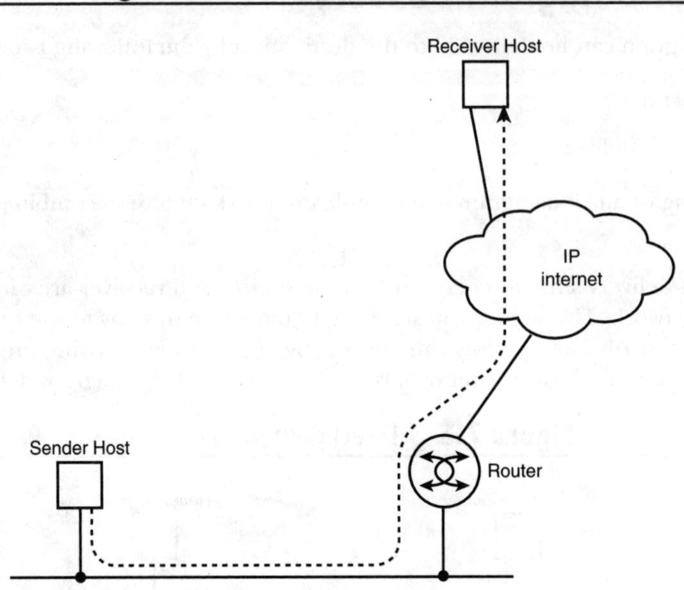

The example in figure 7.5 shows that IP datagram delivery across a complex network involves a combination of direct and indirect datagram delivery.

Figure 7.5 Delivery of an IP datagram in a complex network.

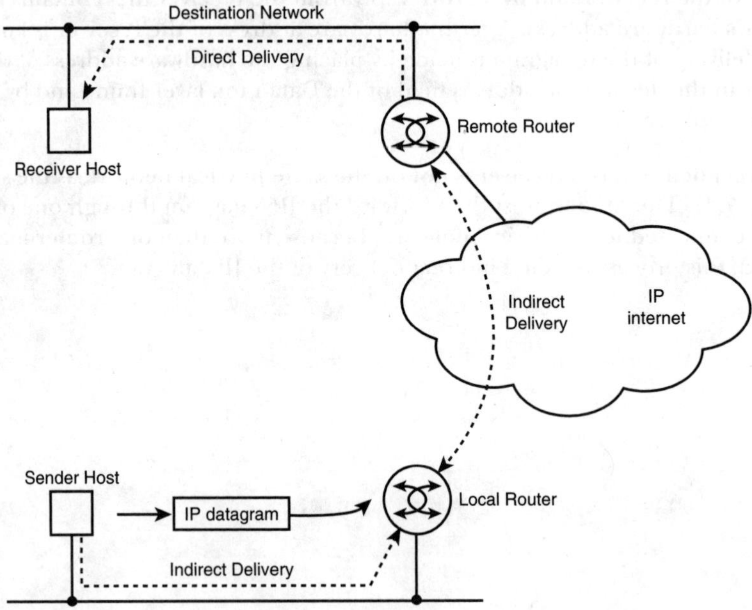

The indirect delivery is from the sender host to the local router, and from the local router to the remote router. The direct delivery is from the remote router to the receiver. If the destination network is a broadcast network such as a LAN, the remote router will use the ARP protocol to discover the hardware address of the receiver host before forwarding the IP datagram.

Direct and Indirect Delivery Illustrated

You can learn a great deal by looking at the sequence of events that is needed to send the IP datagram to the receiver host in the example in figure 7.5. Assume that the source and destination networks are Ethernet LANs. The following table contains the parameters for the devices in figure 7.5.

Address	Parameter
Sender IP address	199.245.180.1
Sender hardware address	08000034AD01
Local router IP address	199.245.180.99
Local router hardware address	0004DAC0031A
Destination IP address	200.1.1.1
Destination hardware address	0000C000CDA4
Remote router IP address	200.1.1.50
Remote router hardware address	0004DAC006AA

The sender, as part of its routing logic, determines that the destination IP address is not on the local network; therefore, the sender needs to forward the datagram to the local router. Before the sender can forward the IP datagram, however, the sender must learn the hardware address of the local router port because the datagram can be sent only to the local router port that uses the underlying Ethernet LAN. The hardware address of the local router port must be placed in the destination address field of the Ethernet frame. The sender uses the ARP protocol to discover the hardware address of the local router port. In other words, the sender uses ARP to bind the IP address of the local router port to its hardware address. The typical ARP exchange sequence is an ARP request broadcast and an ARP reply. Therefore the first two packets are as follows (see tables 7.1 and 7.2).

TABLE 7.1
Packet 1: ARP Request Broadcast

Field	Value
	Ethernet frame
Ethernet DA	FFFFFFFFFFFF
Ethernet SA	08000034AD01
Ethernet type	0806 hex
	ARP header
Hardware type	1
Protocol type	800 hex
Hlen	= 6
Plen	4
Operation	1 (ARP request)
Sender HA	= 08000034AD01
Sender IP	199.245.180.1
Destination HA	*xxxx* (value being determined)
Destination IP	199.245.180.99

TABLE 7.2
Packet 2: ARP Reply

Field	Value
	Ethernet frame
Ethernet DA	08000034AD01
Ethernet SA	0004DAC0031A
Ethernet type	0806 hex

Field	Value
ARP header	
Hardware type	1
Protocol type	800 hex
Hlen	6
Plen	4
Operation	2 (ARP reply)
Sender HA	0004DAC0031A ← *Answer*
Sender IP	199.245.180.99
Destination HA	08000034AD01
Destination IP	199.245.180.1

After binding the local router IP address to its hardware address, the sender forwards the datagram to the local router port by using an Ethernet frame. This sequence is an example of a direct delivery of the IP datagram to the local router port. The following frame is typically packet number 3 (see table 7.3).

TABLE 7.3
Packet 3: Direct Delivery of IP Datagram to Local Router Port

Field	Value
Ethernet frame	
Ethernet DA	08000034AD01
Ethernet SA	0004DAC0031A
Ethernet type	0800 hex

TABLE 7.3, CONTINUED
Packet 3: Direct Delivery of IP Datagram to Local Router Port

Field	Value
	IP header
Version	4
Header length (32 bit words)	5
TOS	0 (Precedence: Routine, NormalDelay, Normal Throughput, Normal Reliability)
Total length	*xxxx* (depends on size of upper-layer protocol data)
Identification	1 (actual value depends on prior IP datagrams that were sent)
Flags	0, DF = 0, MF = 0 (fragmentation allowed, last fragment)
Fragment offset	0
Time to live	64 seconds (actual value dependson IP implementation of sender host)
Protocol	6 (TCP upper layer protocol)
Checksum	*xxxx* (actual value depends onupper layer protocol data)
Source IP address	199.245.180.1
Destination IP address	200.1.1.1

The local router consults its table and forwards the IP datagram to the next router. This process is repeated until the IP datagram arrives at the remote router. The TTL field in the IP datagram is decremented at each router. For example, assume that the IP datagram is handled by five routers, and each router decrements the TTL field by one second. The TTL field value of the IP datagram before it leaves the remote router is then 64 – 5 = 59 seconds.

After the IP datagram arrives at the remote router, the routing logic at the remote router determines that the destination IP address of 200.1.1.1 can be reached through the remote router port IP address of 200.1.1.50. Before the remote router can forward the IP datagram to the destination IP address of 200.1.1.1, the remote router must discover the hardware address of the host at 200.1.1.1. Again, the reason for this discovery is that the IP datagram must be sent by using the underlying networking technology on the destination network, which is Ethernet. The hardware address of the destination host, 200.1.1.1, must be placed in the destination address field of the Ethernet frame that has been sent from the remote router port to the final destination. Again, the ARP protocol is used to discover the binding of the IP address 200.1.1.1 to its hardware address. An ARP request is sent by the remote router port (see table 7.4), and an ARP reply that contains the hardware address of 200.1.1.1 is received (see table 7.5).

TABLE 7.4
Packet 4: ARP Request Broadcast

Field	Value
	Ethernet frame
Ethernet DA	FFFFFFFFFFFF
Ethernet SA	0004DAC006AA
Ethernet type	0806 hex
	ARP header
Hardware type	1
Protocol type	800 hex
Hlen	6
Plen	4
Operation	1 (ARP request)
Sender HA	0004DAC006AA
Sender IP	200.1.1.50
Destination HA	*xxxx* (value being determined)
Destination IP	200.1.1.1

TABLE 7.5
Packet 5: ARP Reply

Field	*Value*
	Ethernet frame
Ethernet DA	0004DAC006AA
Ethernet SA	0000C000CDA4
Ethernet type	0806 hex
	ARP header
Hardware type	1
Protocol type	800 hex
Hlen	6
Plen	4
Operation	2 (ARP reply)
Sender HA	0000C000CDA4 ← *Answer*
Sender IP	200.1.1.1
Destination HA	0004DAC006AA
Destination IP	200.1.1.50

After binding the destination IP address to its hardware address, the remote router forwards the datagram through its network interface at 200.1.1.50. The IP datagram is encapsulated by using an Ethernet frame. Packet 6 is an example of a direct delivery of the IP datagram to the destination host from the remote router port (see table 7.6).

TABLE 7.6
Packet 6: Direct Delivery of IP Datagram to Destination Host from Remote Router Port

Field	Value
	Ethernet frame
Ethernet DA	0000C000CDA4
Ethernet SA	0004DAC006AA
Ethernet type	0800 hex
	IP header
Version	4
Header length (32 bit words)	= 5
TOS	0 (Precedence: Routine, Normal Delay, Normal Throughput, Normal Reliability)
Total length	*XXX* (depends on size of upper layer protocol data)
Identification	1 (actual value depends on prior IP datagrams that were sent)
Flags	0, DF = 0, MF = 0 (fragmentation allowed, last fragment)
Fragment offset	0
Time to live	59 seconds (actual value depends on IP implementation of sender host)
Protocol	6 (TCP upper layer protocol)
Checksum	*xxxx* (actual value depends on upper layer protocol data)
Source IP address	199.245.180.1
Destination IP address	200.1.1.1

Direct and Indirect Delivery Analyzed

When you look at the IP datagram in packets 3 and 6, notice that the IP datagram source and the destination IP address have not changed, even though the packet was handled by a series of routers. The TTL value was decreased to reflect the amount of time spent on the network, but no other substantial changes were made. However, if you compare the Ethernet headers of packets 3 and 6, you will notice that the source and destination addresses in the Ethernet frame are quite different. This difference is to be expected because Data Link layer addresses are used in packets within a physical network segment. These addresses are typically not used in protocols outside a physical network segment. In the case of packet 3, the Ethernet source and destination addresses were that of the sender host and local router port on the sender network. In packet 6, the Ethernet source and destination addresses were that of the remote router port and destination host on the destination network. The Ethernet address information is never sent outside the Ethernet network. IP datagrams and most upper layer protocols have no place to carry Ethernet addresses.

In figure 7.5, the transport of the IP datagram from the local router to the remote router is described as an example of indirect delivery. However, even indirect delivery consists of a sequence of direct deliveries. Consider the example shown in figure 7.6, which has three routers between the local and remote routers that are involved in the transport of the IP datagram. The local router consults its routing table and determines that the best path for the IP datagram involves forwarding the IP datagram to router R2. The local router and router R2 are connected to the same physical network segment. Therefore, the transport of the datagram from the local router to router R2 is an example of direct delivery. The Data Link layer protocol of the underlying network is used to transport the IP datagram. For example, you can use the Point to Point protocol (PPP) to send the IP datagram from the local router port to router R2.

Similarly, the transport of the IP datagram from R2 to R3, from R3 to R4, and from R4 to the remote router are each examples of direct deliveries.

In summary, all indirect deliveries of an IP datagram actually consist of a sequence of direct deliveries of the datagram.

Figure 7.6 Indirect delivery consists of a series of direct deliveries.

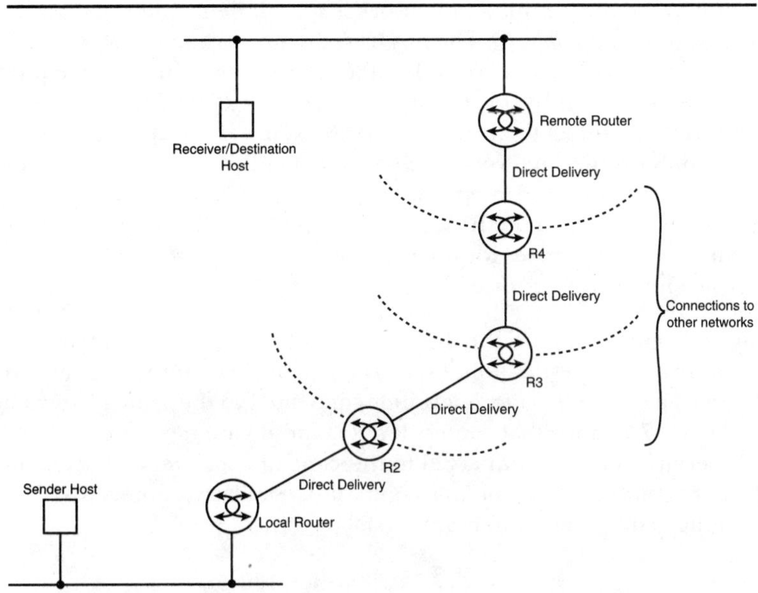

Host and Router Routing Tables

Both hosts and routers have IP routing tables. The routing table consists of information about destinations and how to reach the destination. Hosts and routers consult their routing tables to determine how to route a datagram.

In the case of hosts, the IP module consults the host routing table for outgoing datagrams that need indirect deliveries. You should remember from the preceding section that indirect deliveries must be used when the destination and source are not on the same network. Routers consult their routing tables for incoming datagrams, and they subsequently create a route based on information in their routing table.

What kind of information on destinations is kept in the routing table? If the routing table listed every possible destination host, the table would be too large to be manageable because it would contain an entry for every possible IP address destination. And you have a possibility of four billion IPv4 addresses. Therefore, in a completely connected Internet, the routing tables would have four billion entries! Computers would quickly run out of memory space to store the routing tables, and network managers would run out of patience in managing such large tables. Clearly, a more manageable solution is needed.

The IP routing table is designed so that routing can be performed with a minimum of information in the table. Instead of storing the IP address of every reachable host, the network number of the destination network is stored. Remember that an IP address consists of a *net ID* and a *host ID*. The net ID is the network number, which is the same for all hosts that are on that network. In other words, hosts on the same physical network share a common IP address prefix called the net ID. Instead of storing routing information on all the hosts on a network, it is more efficient to store the information only on their network number. The net ID vastly reduces the number of entries in a routing table and keeps the routing table small. For example, suppose that you have H host bits in the IP address for a network. By using a network number rather than the host addresses for the destination network, you reduce the number of routing table entries by a factor of 2^H.

A routing table entry contains the destination and the next-hop router to forward the datagram to reach the destination. (The traversal of a datagram through a router is called a *hop*.) The *next-hop router* is a router connected to the same physical network segment. Figure 7.7 shows that routers R1, R2, and R3 are next-hop routers for the router R0 because they are connected to the same physical network segment. Routers R0 and R1 are connected by a point-to-point link. Similarly, routers R0, R2 and R0, R3 are also connected by a point-to-point link.

Figure 7.7 Next-hop router.

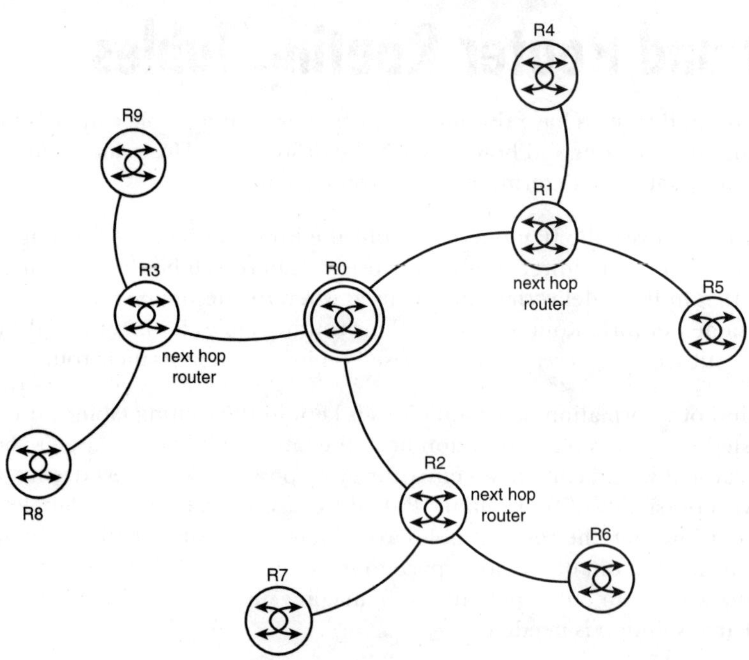

It is important to realize that the routing table points only to the next router on the same physical network and does not contain the complete path to the destination. In other words, the routing entry does not contain a list of all routers that a datagram must travel through. In the example of figure 7.7, the routing table for router R0 contains only the entries for R1, R2, and R3. The routing table for R0 does not list routers R4, R5, R6, R7, and R8 because they are not next-hop routers with respect to router R0.

The next-hop router is selected so that it represents a minimum cost to reach the destination. The minimum cost is measured in terms of time delays, monetary cost, or hop count. The routing protocol that is used by the routers to communicate routing information specifies how the minimum cost should be determined. The cost associated with sending a datagram through a particular next-hop router represents a global awareness of the topology of the network. However, the next-hop router represents only an awareness of the local network topology.

Because the routing table contains information only on the neighboring routers, the routing table is kept simple. The routing table needs to keep track of the neighbor routers. The routing protocol is responsible for computing the cost of selecting a particular neighbor router.

Using the network suffix in the routing table rather than the IP address of hosts reduces the size of the routing table but leads to other consequences. All hosts for a particular network have only one entry in the routing table and, therefore, only one path. In this simple model of the routing table, no provision for account delay, priority, or throughput of network traffic has been made.

Some routing protocols attempt to take into account these factors by associating a cost for each route in the routing table. The destination host is reached by a series of direct deliveries from the sender to final router. Until the final router attempts to deliver the datagram to the destination host, there is no way of knowing that the destination host exists. If the final router in the chain is not able to deliver the datagram, the final router sends an error report in the form of an ICMP (Internet Control Message Protocol) message to the sender. If the destination host is on a broadcast network, such as an Ethernet LAN, the final router attempts to deliver the datagram by using ARP to bind the destination IP address to its hardware address. If the ARP binding fails, the final router assumes that the destination host is not reachable.

The routing table for a host is similar to that for a router. The difference is that hosts route only IP datagrams that originate from that host; they do not forward datagrams received from other IP nodes. Routers, on the other hand, forward IP datagrams received from other IP nodes.

The following sections explain pratical examples of host and router routing tables.

Example of a Host Routing Table

Figure 7.8 shows the routing table for a host. The network contains three routers. Host A can choose any of the routers, but it does not make this selection in an arbitrary manner. The host consults its routing table to determine how to send an IP datagram. The routing table for host A contains the following entries:

Destination	Next-Hop Router
200.1.1.0	Directly connected
201.12.5.0	200.1.1.10
202.10.10.0	200.1.1.11
203.4.5.0	200.1.1.12

Figure 7.8 Host routing table example.

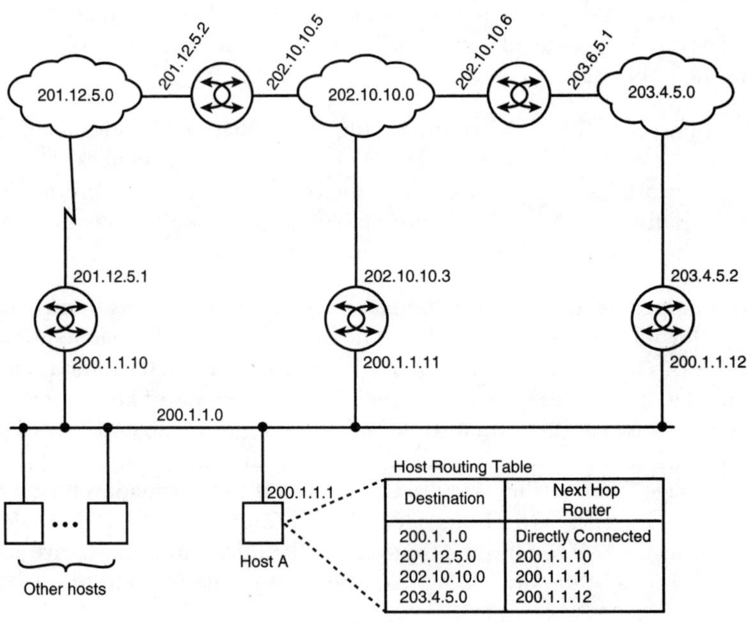

The first entry in the routing table is for the local network 200.1.1.0. The next router-hop column indicates that it is a directly connected network, which means that the host can use direct delivery to reach the destination and that any datagrams destined for the local network 200.1.1.0 do not have to be forwarded. The host uses the physical transport mechanism to forward the datagram to any host on network 200.1.1.0. For a broadcast network such as Ethernet, forwarding the datagram may involve using ARP to discover the hardware address of the local destination host before sending the IP datagram.

The second entry in the routing table says that all datagrams for network 201.12.5.0 should be forwarded to the router port 200.1.1.10. Note that network 201.12.5.0 can be reached through other local routers, but the path would involve traversing other networks, such as 202.10.10.0 and 203.4.5.0. The routing protocol is smart enough to figure out that the optimal path to reach network 201.12.5.0 is through the router at 201.1.1.10, based on additional information such as the cost of each path. If the router at 201.1.1.10 is down, the routing entry for destination 201.12.5.0 will indicate other routers to reach the destination.

The third entry in the routing table says that all datagrams for network 202.10.10.0 should be forwarded to the router port 200.1.1.11. Again, note that network 202.10.10.0 can be reached through other local routers, but the path would involve traversing other networks, such as 201.12.5.0 and 203.4.5.0. The routing protocol is smart enough to figure out that the optimal path to reach network 202.10.10.0 is through the router at 201.1.1.11. If the router at 201.1.1.11 is down, the routing entry for destination 202.10.10.0 will indicate other routers to reach the destination.

The last entry in the routing table says that all datagrams for network 203.4.5.0 should be forwarded to the router port 200.1.1.12. Again, note that the network 203.4.5.0 can be reached through other local routers, but the path would involve traversing other networks, such as 201.12.5.0 and 202.10.10.0. The routing protocol is smart enough to figure out that the optimal path to reach network 203.4.5.0 is through the router at 201.1.1.12. If the router at 201.1.1.12 is down, the routing entry for destination 203.4.15.0 will indicate other routers to reach the destination.

If you examine the next-hop router IP addresses, you will notice that the port connected to the local network has the same IP address prefix of 200.1.1. Moreover, this network prefix is the same as that of the local network and all hosts connected to the local network 200.1.1.0. It is important to remember that next-hop routers share a common network prefix with the network to which their ports are connected. Because the routers must have more than one port, the other ports also must have the same network prefix as the port they connect to (refer to figure 7.8).

Example of a Router Routing Table

Unlike hosts, routers can forward IP datagrams received from other IP nodes. Figure 7.9 shows the routing table for the R0 router in an inter-network consisting of five networks and five routers. The routing table for the R0 router contains the following entries:

Destination	Next-Hop Router	Interface
136.1.0.0	Directly connected	P1
138.9.0.0	Directly connected	P2
137.5.0.0	136.1.2.5	P1
135.12.0.0	136.1.2.3	P1
140.33.0.0	138.9.1.2	P2

Figure 7.9 Router routing table example.

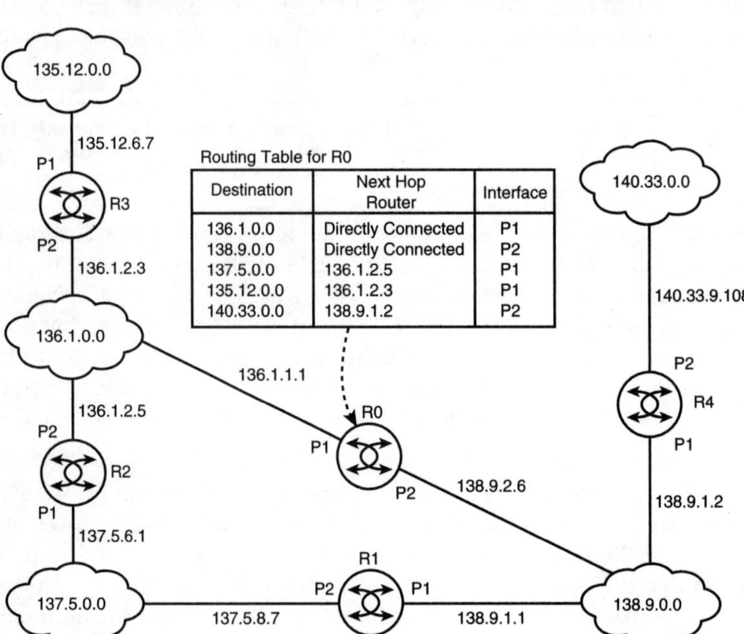

Destination	Next Hop Router	Interface
136.1.0.0	Directly Connected	P1
138.9.0.0	Directly Connected	P2
137.5.0.0	136.1.2.5	P1
135.12.0.0	136.1.2.3	P1
140.33.0.0	138.9.1.2	P2

The first and second entries in the routing table are for the locally connected networks 136.1.0.0 and 138.9.0.0. Because routers have more than one port, routers label each port internally with an interface label. In the example in figure 7.9, the router interfaces are labeled P1 and P2. A router implementation can use any scheme for labeling its interfaces. The next-hop router for the locally connected networks indicates that these networks are directly connected; therefore, direct delivery can be used to reach a host on these networks. A third column shows the interface number for the router port through which the destination can be reached. Directly connected network 136.1.0.0 can be reached through port P1, and directly connected network 138.9.0.0 can be reached through port P2.

The third entry in the routing table indicates that the network 137.5.0.0 can be reached by forwarding the datagram to the router at 136.1.2.5 via port P1. Note that the IP address of port P1 is 136.1.1.1 and that the address of the router port is 136.1.2.5. Is the router at 136.1.2.5 a next-hop router for R0? The answer is "Yes" because the routers share the same network prefix of 136.1 for the class B network 136.1.0.0.

The fourth entry in the routing table indicates that the network 135.12.0.0 can be reached by forwarding the datagram to the router at 136.1.2.3 via port P1. Note that the IP address of port P1 is 136.1.1.1 and that the address of the router port is 136.1.2.3. The router at 136.1.2.5 is a next-hop router for R0 because the routers share the same network prefix of 136.1 for the class B network 136.1.0.0.

The fifth entry in the routing table indicates that the network 140.33.0.0 can be reached by forwarding the datagram to the router at 138.9.1.2 via port P2. Note that the IP address of port P2 is 138.9.2.6 and that the address of the router port is 138.9.1.2. The router at 138.9.1.2 is a next-hop router for R0 because the routers share the same network prefix of 138.9 for the class B network 138.9.0.0.

As previously noted, the next-hop router IP addresses must have the same IP address prefix as that of the port used to forward the IP datagram. This prefix enables direct delivery to be used in forwarding the IP datagram to the next-hop router.

Host-Specific Routes

Most routing entries specify the network number as their destination. However, many implementations include a provision for specifying a host IP address as the destination. When the host IP address is used as the destination in a routing table, you have more control over how a host should be reached because you can specify the next-hop router on a host IP address basis rather than on a network number basis. The capability of specifying a particular next-hop router is very useful in testing and debugging. Consider the network in figure 7.10, which shows the routing table for a host as follows:

Destination	Next-Hop Router	
200.1.1.0	Directly connected	
201.12.5.27	200.1.1.11	← *Host-specific route*
202.10.10.33	200.1.1.12	←*Host-specific route*
201.12.5.0	200.1.1.10	
202.10.10.0	200.1.1.11	
203.4.5.0	200.1.1.12	

Figure 7.10 Host-specific route.

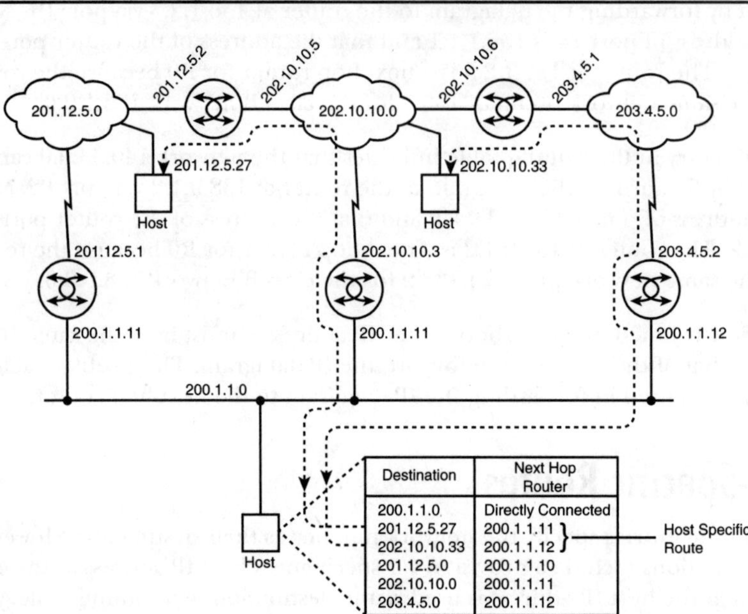

The example in figure 7.10 is similar to the one in figure 7.8 except that destination hosts 201.12.5.27 and 202.10.10.33 are specified as having host-specific routes in the routing table for host A.

Without the host-specific route, destination 201.12.5.27 would be reached via the router 200.1.1.11 that is specified for the destination network 201.12.5.0. Similarly, without the host-specific route, destination 202.10.10.3 would be reached via the router 200.1.1.11 that is specified for the destination network 201.12.5.0. For debugging and testing purposes, you may want to send the data for a destination host through a specific next-hop router. You can send the data in this way by using the host-specific routes that are illustrated in figure 7.10.

Default Routes

If a network has only one next-hop router, all remote destinations must be reached through this next-hop router (see fig. 7.11). In this case, you do not have to specify each destination explicitly; instead, you should specify a default route that is a catchall for all destinations. The router specified by this default route is called the *default router.*

Figure 7.11 Single next-hop router.

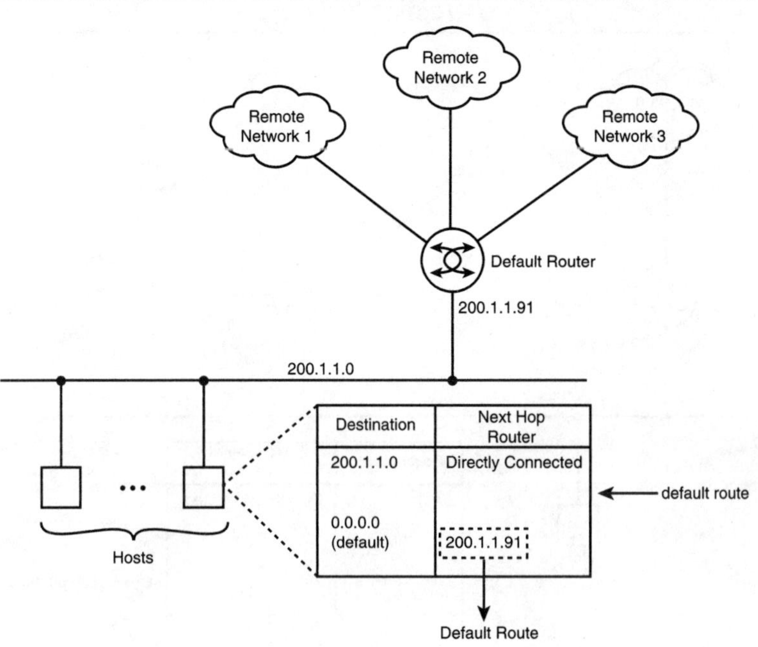

In figure 7.11, the router table for the hosts consists of only two entries: one for the local network and the other for the default route. The routing software has to make only two tests to determine how to route the IP datagram.

In general, the default route is useful in keeping the routing table small, where many destinations need to be reached through the same next-hop router (see fig. 7.12). The routing software searches the routing table for an exact match for the destination. If a match cannot be found, the default route is used. The default route is represented in the routing table with a special destination value of 0.0.0.0.

Figure 7.12 **Use of default route to minimize size of routing table.**

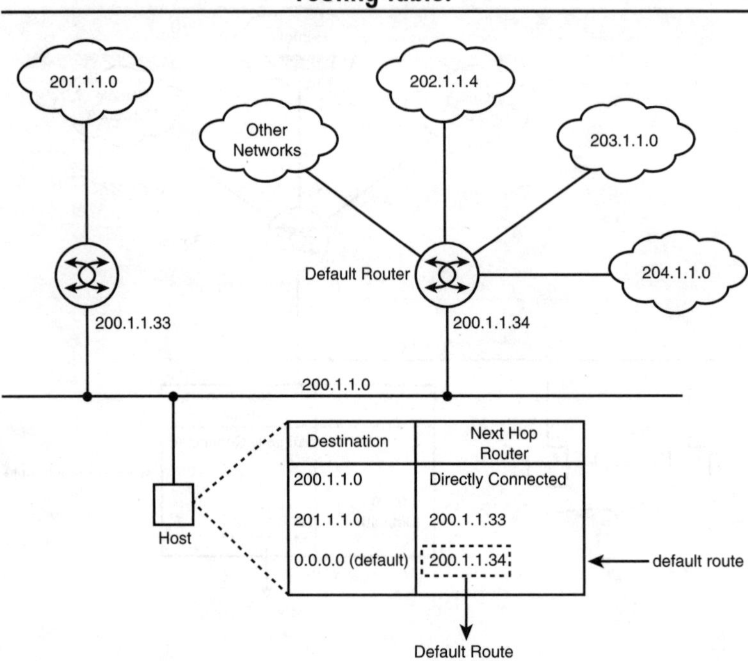

In figure 7.12, the routing table for a host can be written as follows without using default routes:

Destination	Next-Hop Router
200.1.1.0	Directly connected
201.1.1.0	200.1.1.33
202.1.1.0	200.1.1.34
203.1.1.0	200.1.1.34
204.1.1.0	200.1.1.34

This routing table has five route entries. By using a default route, you can consolidate the last three route entries into a single route, as shown in the following routing table (which is equivalent to the preceding routing table):

Destination	Next-hop Router	
200.1.1.0	Directly connected	
201.1.1.0	200.1.1.33	
0.0.0.0	200.1.1.34	←*default route*

The IP Routing Algorithm

The examples on routing given so far have explained portions of the routing process. The routing process is more formally described in the following routing algorithm. The IP routing algorithm is described by the following steps (this algorithm does not discuss the use of subnet masks, which are introduced in Chapter 10, "IP Routing Protocols," and Chapter 11, "Transfer Protocols"):

1. Go to DestIPAddr, the destination address field, of the IP datagram. From the DestIPAddr field, determine the NetSuffix, the network suffix. For a class A network, the NetSuffix is the first byte of the DestIPAddr. For a class B network, the NetSuffix is the first two bytes of the DestIPAddr. For a class C network, the NetSuffix is the first three bytes of the DestIPAddr.
2. If NetSuffix matches the net ID of any directly connected network, the destination host is on the directly connected network. In this case, perform direct delivery of the IP datagram. Direct delivery may involve binding DestIPAddr to its physical address by using a protocol such as ARP. The IP datagram is encapsulated by the Data Link layer frame and sent on the directly attached network.
3. If you have no match in Step 2, examine the routing table for a host-specific entry for DestIPAddr. If you find such an entry, forward the IP datagram as indicated by the corresponding next-hop router entry.
4. If you have no match in Step 3, examine the routing table for a network entry for NetSuffix. If you find such an entry, forward the IP datagram as indicated by the corresponding next-hop router entry.
5. If you have no match in Step 4, examine the routing table for 0.0.0.0, the default entry. If you find such an entry, forward the IP datagram as indicated by the corresponding default router entry.
6. If you have no match in Step 5, the IP datagram cannot be routed. Report a routing error to the upper layer protocols.

Processing of Incoming Datagrams

The discussion in the previous sections has been confined to outgoing datagrams from a host or a router. This section describes how incoming datagrams are processed. When a host or router receives a datagram, a series of events must take place for the datagram to be handled properly. These events are described here.

The host/router checks the destination IP address in the datagram and compares it with its own IP address. If the host/router finds a match, it accepts the IP datagram and passes it to upper layer protocols for processing. In the case of hosts, the upper layer protocols are the transport and application protocols that handle the datagram. In the case of routers, the routing module handles the incoming datagram and forwards the datagram. Keep in mind that the datagram may not be destined for the routing module but for an upper layer management protocol module in the router. An example of this situation is datagrams that are sent to the SNMP agent module that runs on the router. The protocol demultiplexing that takes place at the IP and Transport layers determines which application module should handle the IP datagram.

If an IP address match does not take place, the host must discard the IP datagram. Hosts, by definition, cannot accept datagrams or attempt to forward datagrams that are not destined for it. Routers, on the other hand, are designed to forward datagrams that are not directly addressed to them. Routers forward datagrams based on the information in their routing tables.

The process of determining an IP address match is simple when the IP node, such as a host, has a single network interface. In this case, the destination IP address in the datagram must be compared with the IP address of a single network connection.

Routers must have at least two network connections. Multihomed hosts can also have more than one network connection. When an IP node has more than one network connection, the process of determining an IP address match is not so simple because the destination IP address must be compared with the IP address of each of the network interfaces. This situation occurs because an IP datagram addressed to one of the network interfaces may be received on any of the other network interfaces for the IP node (see fig. 7.13). If the destination IP address in the datagram matches that of one of the network interfaces, the IP node keeps the datagram and sends it to the appropriate module for processing.

Figure 7.13 Addressing a network interface in a router/ multihomed host.

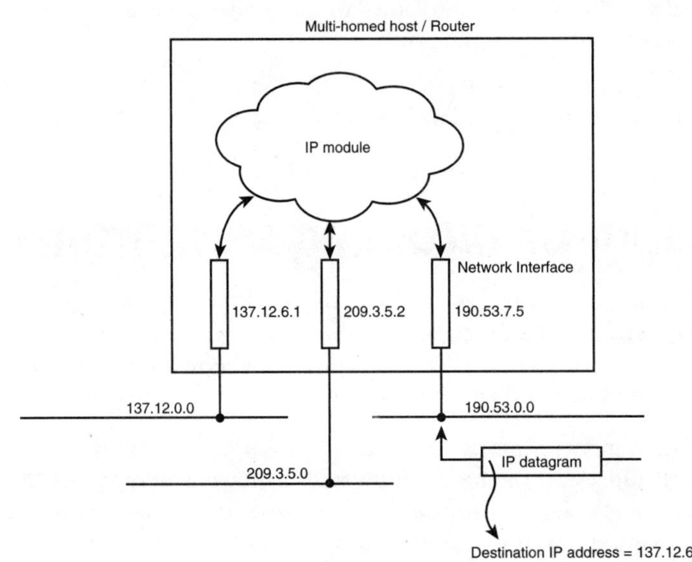

The IP node must also accept datagrams that were received as a broadcast on any of its network interfaces. Broadcasts can be limited broadcast (255.255.255.255) or directed broadcast to a network or subnet. The IP node must also accept multicasts, which are class D addresses. Broadcast and multicast addresses are discussed in Chapter 4, "IP Addressing."

If a router decides to forward a datagram, the router must decrement the TTL field in the IP header. If the TTL field value is zero, the datagram is discarded, and the router sends an ICMP message informing the sender that the TTL has expired.

After determining the network interface on which the datagram must be forwarded, the router then determines whether the datagram must be fragmented. Recall that fragmentation of the datagram occurs if the datagram size exceeds the MTU size on the network interface on which the datagram is to be forwarded. If the datagram is to be fragmented, the IP header fragmentation flags DF, MF; and the Fragmentation Offset must be set appropriately, even as new IP datagram fragments are issued. Because the TTL field changes after the router processes a datagram, the Checksum field must be recomputed at every router.

Summary

IP provides an amazing degree of flexibility in building arbitrarily complex networks. You can use router devices to extend the range of networks to span large distances. Datagrams are delivered to remote destinations by indirect delivery. Indirect delivery consists of a series of direct delivery steps as the datagram is forwarded from router to router and eventually to the destination. Routing takes place at both hosts and routers.

Hosts use route outgoing datagrams only. Hosts do not normally route (forward) incoming datagrams unless the hosts are deliberately configured to act as routers. Routers, on the other hand, are designed to accept incoming datagrams and forward them.

Both hosts and routers use a routing table. The routing table consists of routing entries that specify the destination and the next-hop router through which the datagram should be forwarded to reach the destination.

Test Yourself

1. Draw a diagram showing the model of a router. Label each part of this model and briefly explain the behavior of the router.
2. What is the difference between static and dynamic routing?
3. How do routers keep their routing tables updated in dynamic routing?
4. What are routing protocols? Give a few example of routing protocols.
5. Why do routers need to be configured before they can be operated in a network?
6. What are the two methods of datagram delivery?
7. When is direct delivery used?
8. When is indirect delivery used?
9. Give an example that illustrates when the indirect delivery of a datagram consists of a series of direct deliveries.
10. Before direct delivery is used in a broadcast network, what protocol is typically used?
11. Given a host at IP address 20.10.22.11 and a destination of 20.200.122.122.11, would direct delivery be used (assuming that the network is not subnetted)?
12. Given a host at IP address 134.100.122.111 and a destination of 134.100.222.1, would direct delivery be used (assuming that the network is not subnetted)?
13. Given a host at IP address 212.144.108.18 and a destination of 212.144.108.99, would direct delivery be used (assuming that the network is not subnetted)?
14. Given a host at IP address 144.144.108.18 and a destination of 144.145.108.18, would direct delivery be used (assuming that the network is not subnetted)?
15. Given a host at IP address 144.144.108.18 and a destination of 201.144.108.18, would direct delivery be used (assuming that the network is not subnetted)?
16. Networks 202.34.56.0 and 202.34.57.0 are Ethernet LANs connected by a router whose two network interfaces are configured with the IP addresses 202.34.56.100 and 202.34.57.100. Host 202.34.56.1 is connected to 202.34.56.0 and sends an IP datagram to 202.34.57.1 on 202.34.57.0. Assuming that this event is the first time 202.34.56.1 has attempted to communicate outside the network, show the sequence of packets that you can expect to see for the datagram to reach its destination. Assume that the default TTL value is 64 seconds. What TTL value can you expect when the datagram reaches its destination?

17. For this question, assume that the hardware addresses of the network interfaces are as follows:

    HA of 202.34.56.1 is 0000AA000033

    HA of 202.34.56.100 is 00000C00ACB7

    HA of 202.34.57.100 is 00000C00BCD9

    HA of 202.34.57.1 is 0000AA0023C9

    Assume also that the Identification value of the datagram is 33, the Protocol field is 17, and the IP datagram Checksum value is 33DA hex. Show the header values of all packets that you can expect on the network.

18. A host at 221.3.4.3 routing table contains the following entries:

Destination	Next-Hop Router
221.3.4.0	Directly connected
221.12.5.0	221.3.4.100
222.10.10.0	221.3.4.110
223.4.5.0	221.3.4.109
221.22.1.0	221.3.4.100

    For each of the following destinations, specify whether the destination can be routed from the host. Also specify the next-hop router value selected to reach the destination.

    221.3.4.1

    221.10.10.44

    221.10.11.44

    222.10.10.7

    221.22.1.9

    223.4.5.7

    220.1.1.1

19. A host at 100.3.4.3 routing table contains the following entries:

Destination	Next-Hop Router
100.0.0.0	Directly connected
22.0.0.0	100.3.5.9
222.0.44.0	100.45.22.224
134.6.0.0	100.56.45.66
199.22.1.0	100.99.99.99

For each of the following destinations, specify whether the destination can be routed from the host. Also specify the next-hop router value selected to reach the destination.

221.3.4.1

221.10.10.44

100.66.85.66

199.22.1.9

222.10.10.7

221.22.1.9

222.0.44.44

22.55.44.56

20. In the following routing table, suggest how you can use a default route to consolidate routing entries and minimize the size of the routing table.

Destination	Next-Hop Router
210.1.1.0	Directly connected
133.1.1.0	210.1.1.3
134.1.1.0	210.1.1.4
135.1.1.0	210.1.1.4
136.1.1.0	210.1.1.4

21. What are the advantages/disadvantages of a multihomed host acting as a router?
22. If a multihomed host not designated as a router receives an IP datagram not destined for the host, should it forward the datagram if it is capable of routing the datagram? Your answer should include advantages/disadvantages (if any) of forwarding the datagram.
23. When would you want to use host-specific routes? Does the use of host-specific routes minimize or increase the size of the routing table?
24. What is the advantage, if any, of using a default route?

CHAPTER 8

The ICMP Protocol

The Internet Protocol provides a connectionless datagram delivery service. IP does not attempt to guarantee reliable delivery of datagrams; this is a job best left to the upper-layer protocols, such as the transport layer protocol (TCP). However, IP does provide a facility to send alert and diagnostic messages through the Internet Control Message Protocol (ICMP) module. These messages can be used by the network administrator in detecting problems or potential problems on the network.

Overview of ICMP

Because the IP protocol is kept simple, there are several situations where errors are encountered in the transmission of an IP datagram. The sender sends the datagram and trusts the underlying network (OSI layers 3, 2, and 1) to deliver the datagram. The sender has no way of knowing potential problems that may occur in datagram transmission.

Errors in datagram transmission are typically detected at some intermediate router. For example, the last router in the chain of routers on the datagram path may detect that the destination host does not exist. If the destination network is a broadcast LAN, such as Ethernet, the router detects the unavailability of the host when it uses ARP to bind the IP address of the destination host and its hardware address. The router, in this case, attempts to inform the sender by sending an Internet Control Message Protocol (ICMP) message concerning the unavailability of the destination host.

Other problems that may be encountered include the following:

- Expiration of the Time to Live (TTL) parameter in the datagram because of a routing loop error
- Non-delivery of a datagram because of the loss of a datagram fragment
- Unavailability of a protocol, service, or host
- Inability to forward a datagram because fragmentation is not permitted, and the datagram size is too big for intermediate networks
- Congestion of network traffic at a router prevents the router from handling incoming datagrams

In each of these cases, ICMP is used to alert the sender of a problem on the network. The IP protocol itself does not contain any mechanism to alert the network of these problems. The designers of IP specified a special purpose protocol to be used in conjunction with IP to alert the network of unexpected errors, test the network, and obtain information on the network. This special purpose protocol is ICMP.

All IP implementations are required to support ICMP, although they, unfortunately, differ in the degree to which they support ICMP. Some implementations of ICMP do not return any error message when encountering a specific problem, while others generate the wrong messages. Although ICMP messages are generated, they may not always be acted upon by the IP implementation on a host that receives the ICMP message.

Any IP implementation can generate an ICMP message. Specifically, both routers and hosts can generate ICMP messages. Routers generate ICMP error messages when they encounter a forwarding problem, whereas hosts generate ICMP error messages when they encounter a delivery problem to a particular protocol or application. Not all ICMP messages deal with error conditions. There are ICMP messages that are specifically used for testing a network and obtaining information on the network.

Here are some important aspects of ICMP that you should be aware of:

- All IP implementations must also implement ICMP.
- ICMP runs on top of IP. That is, ICMP is a "client" of IP even though ICMP is implemented in the IP module.
- ICMP reports on error conditions. It does not make IP more reliable.
- ICMP reports errors only on the first IP datagram fragment. This is the IP datagram fragment with its Fragment Offset field set to 0. The purpose of this is to avoid sending ICMP messages on each of the remaining datagram fragments.
- ICMP is an error reporting mechanism on IP datagrams. ICMP does not generate error messages on problems with ICMP datagrams.

In addition to the preceding instances, ICMP must not report problems caused by the following:

- Routing or delivery of ICMP messages. If ICMP error messages were generated on ICMP error messages, they would multiply in number and add to the network traffic.
- IP Broadcast or multicast datagrams. If ICMP error messages were generated for IP broadcast or multicast, each node receiving the broadcast/multicast datagram would generate an ICMP message and add to the network traffic.
- Data Link layer broadcast or multicast. If ICMP error messages were generated for Data Link broadcast or multicast, each node receiving the broadcast/multicast datagram would generate an ICMP message and add to the network traffic.
- Datagrams with source addresses that do not identify a unique IP node, such as the loopback addresses 127.x.x.x or 0.0.0.0, or an address with a 0 network prefix. The network prefix is the bits in the IP address that identify the network uniquely.

The following sections describe ICMP behavior in greater detail.

ICMP-Related RFCs

Information on ICMPs is distributed across several RFCs. This section lists some of the relevant RFCs for ICMP.

ICMP is a standard protocol (STD 5) and is documented in RFC 792 on "Internet Control Message Protocol," with subnet extensions in RFC 950 on "Internet standard subnetting procedure." RFC 1812 on "Requirements for IP Version 4 Routers" contains information on ICMP message types 13, 14, and 15. RFC 1122 on "Requirements for Internet Hosts—Communication Layers" contains advice on ICMP message handling issues for hosts. RFC 1256 on "ICMP Router Discovery Messages" contains information on ICMP Types 9 and 10 that are used to implement the router discovery protocol. RFC 1191 on "Path MTU Discovery" contains extensions to the ICMP Type 4 messages.

ICMP Error Detection

As pointed out in the previous section, ICMP is an error reporting mechanism on IP datagrams. ICMP error messages on the IP datagram are sent to the originator of the datagram. However, while the ICMP specification mentions the intended use of the IP datagram, it does not completely specify the actions that must be taken. It is up to the originator that receives the ICMP message to take appropriate action.

ICMP messages are sent to the originator of the IP datagram. This is based on the assumption that the originator of the IP datagram would know how to handle the problem. This is true in most situations, but not always so. Consider the situation in figure 8.1 where datagram sent from source A to destination B follows a path that includes routers R1, R2, R3.

Figure 8.1 ICMP message example.

B
R3
R3 cannot deliver
datagram to B
because of bad
routing table
R4
R2
ICMP message
sent to original
source A
R1
A

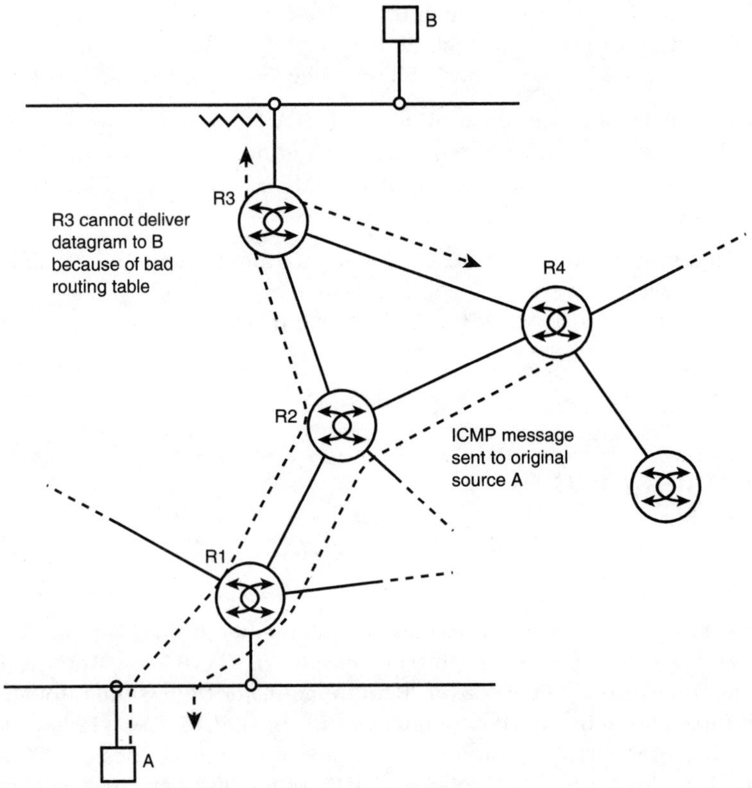

Assume that router R3 has incorrect information about the destination in its routing table, and according to this information the datagram should be routed to the router R4, instead of to destination B. In that case, the datagram will be forwarded to R4 instead of destination B. R4 can send an ICMP message about the incorrect route, but it cannot send the message to router R3, the cause of the problem. Instead, it sends the ICMP message to source A, which is not the cause of the problem and does not have responsibility for router R4. In most cases, the source, on receiving the ICMP message, cannot determine the router that was the cause of the problem. Why is ICMP restricted to sending messages to the original source? The reason for this is that the IP header of the datagram has only two address fields: the original source IP address and the final destination IP address. The IP addresses of the intermediate routers are not recorded in the IP header field unless the IP record route option is enabled by the original source. Most IP datagrams are sent without IP options. It is not normal to use the record route IP option because of the additional processing needed to record the route at each router, and the increased IP header size overhead.

When router R4 wants to send the ICMP message back, it has knowledge of only the initial source and final destination IP addresses. Router R4 does not know of the intermediate routers that handled the datagram, so it cannot send the ICMP messages to them. It is not reasonable for router R4 to send the ICMP message to the destination, as the original datagram most likely had a problem reaching the destination. Also the destination is not the cause of the problem—it is the source or one of the intervening routers. Sending the ICMP message to the source is the only reasonable choice.

Sending an ICMP message back to the source is better than not sending any message back at all. If no ICMP message is sent, the network administrator does not have sufficient information about the cause of the problem. With the ICMP message sent back to the source, there is the possibility that a knowledgeable network administrator can locate and correct the problem.

ICMP Encapsulation

Because ICMP message must be carried across the internet and across routers, the ICMP message must be encapsulated by IP. Recall that without IP, upper-layer protocol data cannot cross a router boundary. This means that the ICMP message is included in the data portion of the IP datagram. The IP header of this datagram contains the Protocol field value of 1, which is assigned to ICMP.

The receiving IP module demultiplexes the IP datagram data based on the Protocol field value and sends the data to the ICMP module. Figure 8.2 shows the protocol layering of ICMP and IP. It also shows that the ICMP module is implemented as part of the IP module. Figure 8.3 shows the encapsulation of ICMP inside an IP header.

Figure 8.2 ICMP and IP relationship.

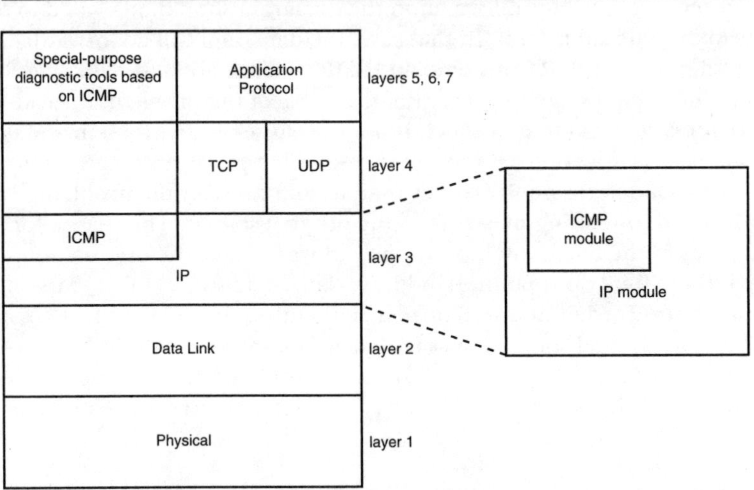

Figure 8.3 ICMP encpasulation.

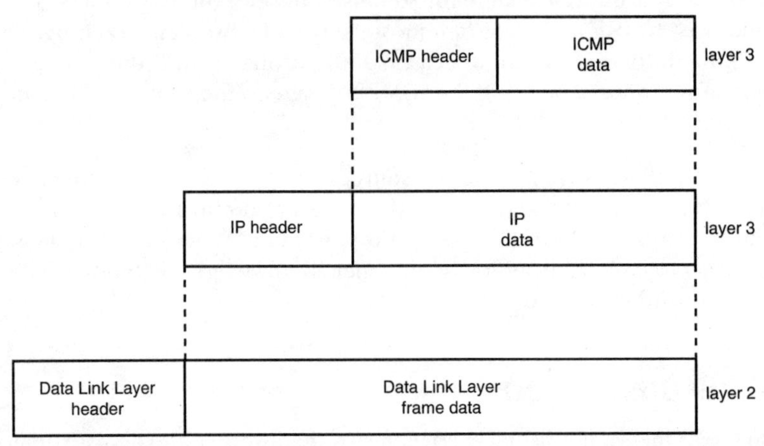

Figure 8.2 also shows that even though ICMP message is encapsulated by IP, ICMP is not considered to be an upper-layer protocol. ICMP is a required part of IP. It is possible to build special purpose applications, utilities, and diagnostic tools that use ICMP. These special purpose applications can be considered as part of the application layer.

An example of the special purpose diagnostic tool that uses ICMP is the PING utility, which is available on many TCP/IP systems. The PING utility is used to send an echo request message to a destination. If the echo request message reaches a remote IP module, that module is obliged to send back an echo reply message. Reception of the echo message implies that the remote IP node is reachable up to the IP layer. You will learn more about the ICMP messages that are used to implement the PING utility later in this chapter. In some IP implementations direct access to the ICMP module is not available to applications. In this case, applications such as PING mimic the behavior of ICMP in generating ICMP messages.

The IP header used to carry an ICMP message is shown as follows:

Version	4
Header Length (32 bit words)	Usually set to 5 unless IP options are in use
TOS	0 (Precedence: Routine, Normal Delay, Normal Throughput, Normal Reliability)
Total length	Depends on size of ICMP message
Identification	Depends on previous datagrams sent
Flags	Set to indicate possible fragmentation. Normally datagrams containing ICMP messages are short, and you should not see datagram fragmentation.
Fragment Offset	Depends on fragmentation flag. Normally 0.
Time to Live	Implementation dependent. Should be large enough for the datagram to reach its destination.
Protocol	1 (Indicates ICMP message)
Checksum	Depends on actual data
Source IP address	The IP address of the router or host that composes the ICMP message. This address can be any of the router's port addresses.
Destination IP address	The IP address of the router or host to which the message should be sent.

Note that the IP header does not indicate any special priority for delivering ICMP messages. IP datagrams containing ICMP messages are treated by IP nodes (such as hosts and routers) in a routine fashion like any other datagrams.

Because IP does not guarantee delivery of messages, it is possible for the ICMP messages to get lost or discarded because of router congestion. Also in a network that is already congested, generation of ICMP messages due to congestion adds to the congestion.

What if the IP datagram carrying an ICMP message encounters an error? Should an ICMP message be generated on the IP datagram carrying an ICMP message? The answer is that an exception is made in these circumstances, and no ICMP message is generated for errors encountered in processing IP datagrams that contain ICMP messages. This does make sense because generating error messages on the ICMP messages would add to the network traffic and be of little value to the network administrator, who is trying to locate the source of the problem.

ICMP Services

ICMP provides a variety of error message, information, and diagnostic services (see fig. 8.4).

Figure 8.4 ICMP services. (Courtesy Learning Tree)

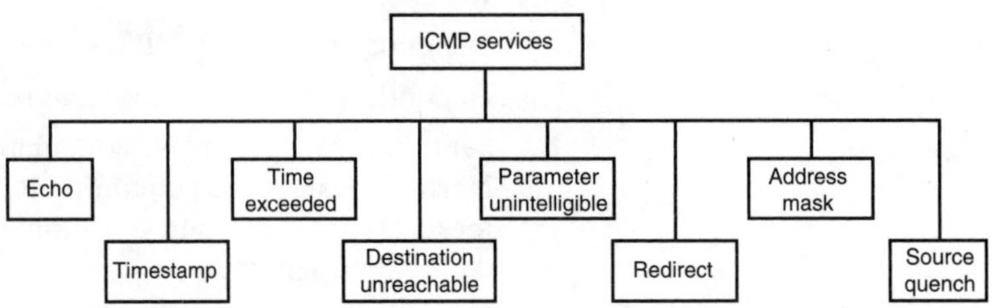

• Internet Control Message Protocol (ICMP) carries errors on IP datagrams

• ICMP does not make IP more reliable

The main ICMP services are the following:

- **Echo.** This is used as a diagnostic to determine the reachability of an IP node.
- **Destination unreachable.** Used to indicate that a destination IP node is not reachable.
- **Source quench.** Used to indicate a congestion problem to the source.
- **Redirect.** Used by routers to inform of an alternate route.
- **Time exceeded.** Used to indicate the expiration of the IP header TTL field value.
- **Parameter problem.** Used to indicate a problem in an IP datagram.
- **Timestamp.** Used for time measurements on an internet.
- **Address mask.** Used to obtain subnet mask information for the network.

Regardless of the ICMP message, the formats are very similar and are described in figure 8.5. The first octet in the ICMP header, the Type field, indicates the type of ICMP service. The following octet contains a Code value that further describes the nature of the message type. Both Type and Code field values must be considered for determining the actual ICMP message.

Figure 8.5 General ICMP message structure. (Courtesy Learning Tree)

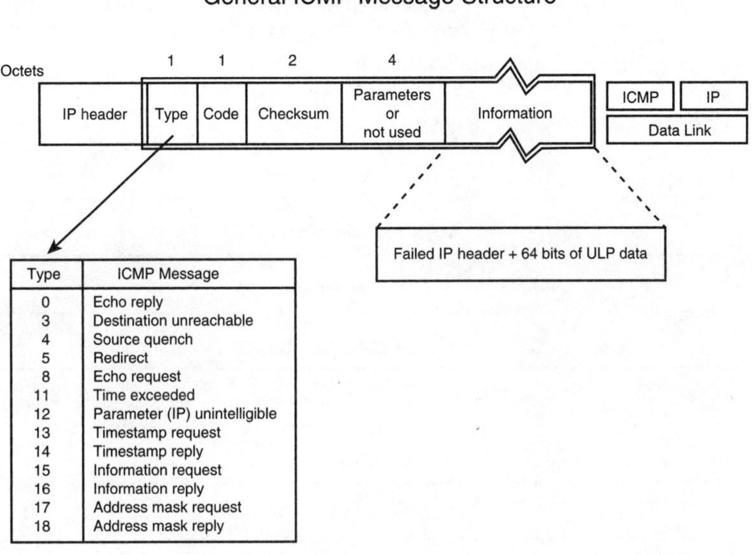

Table 8.1 shows the assigned ICMP type values, and table 8.2 shows the assigned code values for the corresponding types. Some of the type values are assigned for experimental protocols, and their code values are not listed as they are subject to change.

TABLE 8.1
ICMP Type Fields

Type Value	Meaning
0	Echo Reply
1	Unassigned
2	Unassigned
3	Destination Unreachable
4	Source Quench

continues

Table 8.1, Continued
ICMP Type Fields

Type Value	Meaning
5	Redirect
6	Alternate Host Address
7	Unassigned
8	Echo
9	Router Advertisement
10	Router Selection
11	Time Exceeded
12	Parameter Problem
13	Timestamp
14	Timestamp Reply
15	Information Request
16	Information Reply
17	Address Mask Request
18	Address Mask Reply
19	Reserved (for Security)
20–29	Reserved (for Robustness Experiment)
30	Traceroute
31	Datagram Conversion Error
32	Mobile Host Redirect
33	IPv6 Where-Are-You
34	IPv6 I-Am-Here
35	Mobile Registration Request

Type Value	Meaning
36	Mobile Registration Reply
37–255	Reserved

TABLE 8.2
ICMP Code Fields

Type	Codes	Meaning
0 (Echo Reply)	0	No Code
1 (Unassigned)		
2 (Unassigned)		
3 (Destination Unreachable)	0	Net Unreachable
	1	Host Unreachable
	2	Protocol Unreachable
	3	Port Unreachable
	4	Fragmentation Needed and Don't Fragment was Set
	5	Source Route Failed
	6	Destination Network Unknown
	7	Destination Host Unknown
	8	Source Host Isolated
	9	Communication with Destination Network is Administratively Prohibited
	10	Communication with Destination Host is Administratively Prohibited
	11	Destination Network Unreachable for Type of Service

continues

TABLE 8.2, CONTINUED
ICMP Code Fields

Type	Codes	Meaning
	12	Destination Host Unreachable for Type of Service
4 (Source Quench)	0	No Code
5 (Redirect)	0	Redirect Datagram for the Network (or subnet)
	1	Redirect Datagram for the Host
	2	Redirect Datagram for the Type of Service and Network
	3	Redirect Datagram for the Type of Service and Host
6 (Alternate) Host Address	0	Alternate Address for Host
7 (Unassigned)		
8 (Echo)	0	No Code
9 (Router Advertisement)	0	No Code
10 (Router Selection)	0	No Code
11 (Time Exceeded)	0	Time to Live exceeded in Transit
	1	Fragment Reassembly Time Exceeded
12 (Parameter Problem)	0	Pointer indicates the error
	1	Missing a Required Option
	2	Bad Length
13 (Timestamp)	0	No Code
14 (Timestamp Reply)	0	No Code

Type	Codes	Meaning
15 (Information Request)	0	No Code
16 (Information Reply)	0	No Code
17 (Address Mask Request)	0	No Code
18 (Address Mask Reply)	0	No Code
19 (Reserved for Security)		

The next two octets are a Checksum field. The Checksum field is only over the ICMP message and does not include the IP header of the encapsulating datagram. The actual checksum algorithm is the same checksum algorithm that is used for IP (refer to Chapter 7, "IP Routing Concepts"). An implementation may set the ICMP Checksum field to 0 to indicate that this value is not calculated. Recall that the IP header also has a checksum field that includes the ICMP message in its checksum because ICMP is encapsulated by IP. Also, the Data Link layer frame may also provide a frame checksum field. Under these circumstances, calculating an ICMP checksum is an extra precaution that may not be needed because errors in ICMP messages are detected by the IP checksum or Data Link Layer frame checksum.

The next 4 octets include optional parameters. The actual parameters that are used depends on the ICMP message. This field is optional and may not be included for some ICMP message types. The Information field, which is used by ICMP messages that indicate errors, includes the IP header plus 64 bits of upper-layer protocol data in the datagram causing the problem.

Inclusion of information on the datagram causing the problem is very valuable as this can be used to determine which datagram caused the problem. The IP header is included so you can determine the sender and destination IP address. This tells you who sent the datagram and where it was being sent. The 64 bits (8 octets) of upper-layer data include part of the TCP header or the full UDP header.

You will learn later on that the minimum size of a TCP header is 20 octets. Since only 8 octets of the upper-layer protocol are sent in the ICMP message, only part of the TCP header is reported. However, the first 8 octets of the TCP header contain source and destination port numbers and the sequence number field. The port numbers identify the applications that are involved in the TCP session. On the other hand, if UDP is being used as the transport layer protocol, the full UDP header is reported because the UDP header size is only 8 octets.

The individual ICMP messages are described in the upcoming sections.

ICMP Types 0 and 8—Echo/PING

Perhaps the most widely used ICMP messages are the Echo types 0 and 8. These messages are used for diagnostic purposes by the PING (Packet Internet Groper) utility that is available on most TCP/IP systems. The PING utility is used to check if an IP node is "alive" and reachable. The PING utility sends an ICMP Echo Request Type (8) message to an IP node. The IP node, on receiving this message, sends back an ICMP Echo Reply (0) message. The Echo Reply message contains a copy of the data that was sent in the Echo Request message. Successful receipt of an Echo Reply message verifies that the IP layer (and lower layers) in the transport system are working between the source and the destination. If there are any intervening routers between the source and destination, the Echo Reply message also implies that the routers are able to route between the source and destination.

The IP node is typically a host or a router. Figure 8.6 shows how the PING utility might be used.

Figure 8.6 Using ICMP Echo Request/Reply messages.

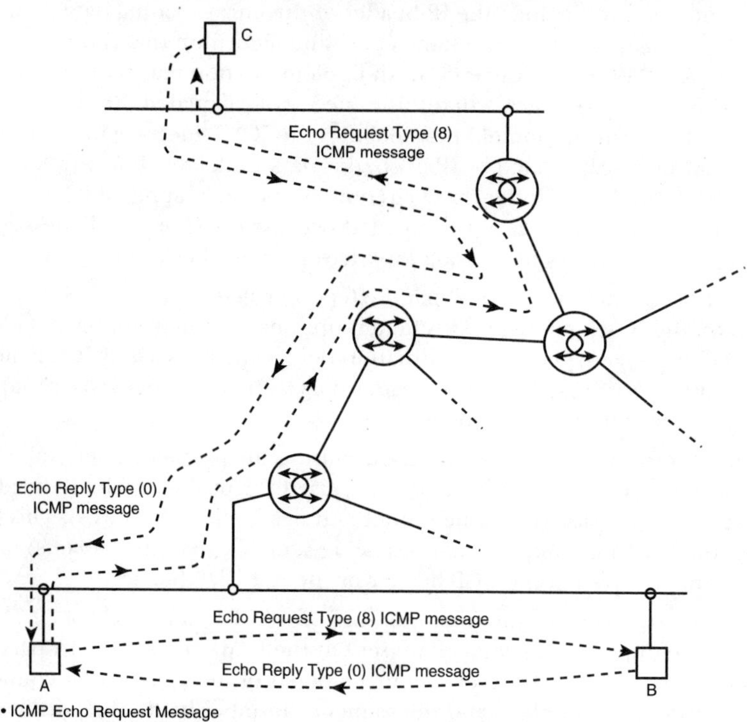

This figure shows the situation where PING can be used to test reachability of local and remote hosts. In figure 8.6, host B is local to host A, and host C is remote from host A. The ICMP messages sent between A and C are treated as normal IP datagrams by the intervening routers and do not get any special consideration. If ICMP messages get lost, no attempt is made to resend the ICMP message.

The PING utility is used to generate the ICMP Echo Request message. The IP module running on the destination node responds to ICMP messages automatically. There is no need to run any special software on destination nodes to generate the ICMP Echo Response. This means that all IP nodes on an internet are capable of responding to ICMP Echo Request messages generated by the PING utility.

There is no standard for the options and capabilities provided by the PING utility, although most implementations provide similar services. The actual syntax for invoking the PING utility is operating system dependent, though similarities do exist between many operating systems, especially the Unix operating systems. Most operating system implementations provide a command line version of the PING utility that is appropriately called *ping*, although graphical implementations may also be available. Most implementations of the PING utility give an estimated round trip delay measured in seconds and statistics about datagram loss. There are also a number of options available with some implementations of the PING utility. For example, you can use options to send various sizes of data in each ICMP Echo Request message, and control the time interval between Echo Requests. Some PING utilities enable you to send different IP options—such as the IP source route option, which can be used to control the path taken by the ICMP message.

The format of the ICMP Echo Request and Echo Reply messages are shown in figure 8.7.

Figure 8.7 ICMP Echo Request/Reply format.

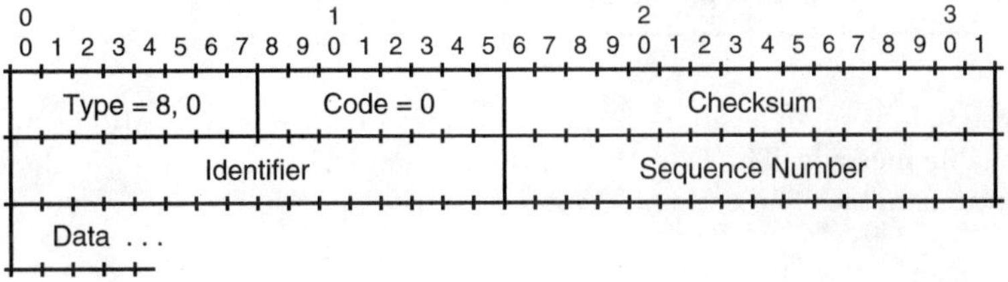

```
 0                   1                   2                   3
 0 1 2 3 4 5 6 7 8 9 0 1 2 3 4 5 6 7 8 9 0 1 2 3 4 5 6 7 8 9 0 1
+-+-+-+-+-+-+-+-+-+-+-+-+-+-+-+-+-+-+-+-+-+-+-+-+-+-+-+-+-+-+-+-+
|  Type = 8, 0  |   Code = 0    |           Checksum            |
+-+-+-+-+-+-+-+-+-+-+-+-+-+-+-+-+-+-+-+-+-+-+-+-+-+-+-+-+-+-+-+-+
|          Identifier           |        Sequence Number        |
+-+-+-+-+-+-+-+-+-+-+-+-+-+-+-+-+-+-+-+-+-+-+-+-+-+-+-+-+-+-+-+-+
|  Data ...
+-+-+-+-+-
```

The Type field has a value of 8 for Echo Request and a value of 0 for Echo Reply. The Code field is set to 0 for both Echo Request and Echo Reply message types. The Checksum field is common to all ICMP message types and was described earlier.

The Identifier and Sequence Number fields are used for the ICMP Echo Request and Echo Reply messages uniquely so that they can be properly matched. Matching is necessary because the IP network makes no guarantees that the ICMP Echo Reply messages will be sent in the correct order.

The Data field is provided so that arbitrary size messages can be sent. This is very useful in testing the capacity of a network to carry large datagrams. For example, a router or host may properly handle small sized datagrams but not large datagrams. By using PING to send large data fields, this problem can be detected.

The Echo Reply message sends the same data that was received from the Echo Request.

ICMP Type 3—Destination Unreachable

The IP network provides a best-efforts service and may not always be able to deliver the IP datagram. Non-delivery of datagrams is usually detected by routers, especially the last router in the chain of routers used to deliver the datagram to the destination.

When a router is unable to deliver a datagram, it alerts the sender with an ICMP destination unreachable message. Upper-layer protocols, such as TCP, transmit the lost message without knowing the cause of the failed delivery. The ICMP message is an attempt to give the sender the cause of the failed delivery.

The format of the ICMP destination unreachable message is shown in figure 8.8.

Figure 8.8 **ICMP Destination Unreachable message.**

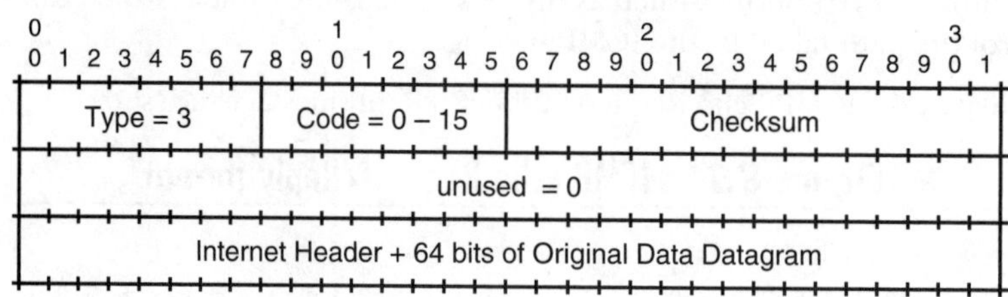

The Type field is set to a value of 3 and indicates that this is an ICMP destination unreachable message. The Code field gives further information on *why* the destination is unreachable. The code field values are listed in table 8.3.

TABLE 8.3
Code for ICMP Destination Unreachable

Code	Meaning
0	Net Unreachable
1	Host Unreachable
2	Protocol Unreachable

Code	Meaning
3	Port Unreachable
4	Fragmentation Needed and Don't Fragment was Set
5	Source Route Failed
6	Destination Network Unknown
7	Destination Host Unknown
8	Source Host Isolated
9	Communication with Destination Network is Administratively Prohibited
10	Communication with Destination Host is Administratively Prohibited
11	Destination Network Unreachable for Type of Service
12	Destination Host Unreachable for Type of Service
13	Communication Administratively prohibited because of firewalls
14	Host Precedence Violation
15	Precedence cut-off in effect

The following sections cover each of the codes in greater detail.

ICMP Type 3, Code 0—Net Unreachable

The code value of 0 (Net Unreachable) is generated when the network specified in the IP destination address cannot be found. This error message is generated only by routers. This could be caused by a mistake made in specifying the IP destination address or by an error in the routing table for the router generating the ICMP message. The source address in the IP header that carries this ICMP message identifies the router that generated this error. The next step is to examine the routing tables for the router that generates this message.

ICMP Type 3, Code 1—Host Unreachable

The code value of 1 (Host Unreachable) is generated by the router that directly connects to the destination network. It indicates that the datagram was delivered successfully by the routers, but the last router cannot communicate with the host. This could be because the ARP binding attempt made by the router to find the hardware address of the destination is unsuccessful. The host may not be reachable because it is down, misconfigured, or an incorrect IP address was specified. The source address in the IP header that carries this ICMP message identifies the router that generated this error. Host Unreachable ICMP error messages imply delivery failure, whereas the Network Unreachable ICMP error messages imply routing failures.

ICMP Type 3, Code 2—Protocol Unreachable

The code value of 2 (Protocol Unreachable) is generated by the destination host. This message implies that the datagram reached the destination host, but the upper protocol carried by the IP datagram, identified by the Protocol field in the IP header, is not available. The protocols carried by IP are listed in table 6.5 in Chapter 6, "The Internet Protocol." Common upper-layer protocols that are implemented in most TCP/IP hosts are TCP, UDP, OSPF. Most TCP/IP hosts are expected to support at least TCP and UDP. You should not see an ICMP error message caused by these protocols not being available, unless there is a major configuration problem at the host. It is possible for an application to try to access one of the other protocols listed in table 6.5 and find that this protocol is not available. The ICMP module at the destination host then sends an ICMP Type 3, Code 2, Protocol Unreachable message.

Many TCP/IP systems contain special configuration data—such as the /etc/protocols file in Unix systems—that identify the protocols supported by IP. This configuration data should be checked at the destination host for correctness if a Protocol Unreachable message is reached.

ICMP Type 3, Code 3—Port Unreachable

The code value of 3 (Port Unreachable) is generated when the designated transport layer protocol (TCP or UDP) is unable to demultiplex the datagram and has no other protocol mechanism to inform the sender. The transport layer protocol may be unable to demultiplex the datagram because of the absence of a specific application service at the destination host.

Application services are identified by TCP and UDP port numbers. On many systems, application services are started by reading configuration data about the application services—such as the /etc/inetd.conf file in Unix systems—when the TCP/IP system is initialized.

If a Type 3, Code 3 message is received, it implies that the application service that was being reached is not available. You should check the configuration data area for application services to see if the service is listed. Additionally, you should check the mechanism used to initialize and start an application service at the destination host. For example, many systems, particularly Unix, use the concept of a server process (called the *inetd* super daemon) that listens for requests on application service port numbers. If the server process is not active, the application services may be unreachable.

ICMP Type 3, Code 4—Fragmentation Needed and Don't Fragment Was Set

The code value of 4 (Fragmentation Needed and Don't Fragment was Set) is generated by routers that need to fragment the datagram because the MTU size of the network interface through which the datagram is to be forwarded is smaller than the size of the datagram. However, if the IP header of the datagram has the Don't Fragment (DF) flag set to 1, the router cannot fragment the datagram. Under these circumstances, the router cannot forward the datagram and therefore must discard it. The router sends an ICMP type 4 message to the sender informing it that the datagram could not be sent, and the code value of 4 indicates the reason why.

Note The DF flag is set to 1 by diskless workstations performing a Trivial File Transfer Protocol (TFTP) file transfer to download the system boot image. TFTP sends data in blocks of 512 octets. Adding the overhead for the IP header (20 octets) and UDP header (8 octets), and the transport protocol used by TFTP, the average message size is 540 octets. According to RFC 791 on the Internet Protocol, all hosts/routers should be prepared to accept an IP datagram of 576 octets. Since the TFTP IP datagram size is 540 octets, the datagram should never need to be fragmented, unless the host/router does not comply with the 576 octet minimum size requirement, or the MTU size for a network interface is smaller than 540 octets.

RFC 1191 on "Path MTU Discovery" describes a slight modification in the form of Code 4 Destination Unreachable messages. RFC 1812 on "Requirements for IP Version 4 Routers" states that a router must use this modified form when originating Code 4 Destination Unreachable messages. Figure 8.9 describes the modified form of this message.

Figure 8.9 Modified Type 3, Code 4 message as per RFC 1812.

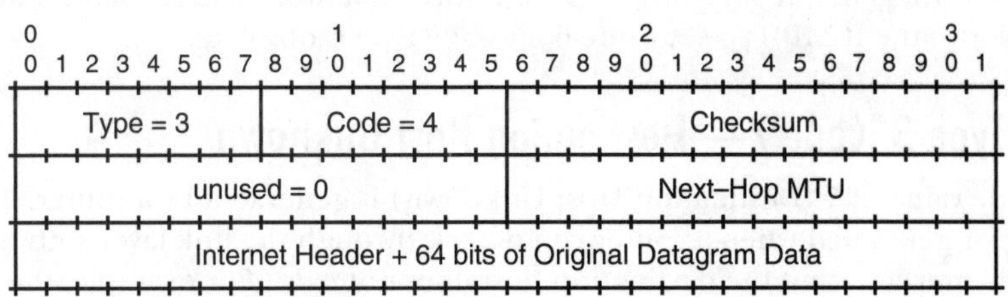

The modified Code 4 format is required to support the Path MTU Discovery technique specified in RFC 1191. The router must include the MTU of that next hop network in the low-order 16 bits of the ICMP header field, which is labeled "unused" in figure 8.8. The high-order 16 bits remain unused, and must be set to zero.

The value carried in the Next Hop MTU field is the size in octets of the largest datagram that could be forwarded along the path of the original datagram, without being fragmented at this router. The size includes the IP header and IP data but does not include any lower-level headers, such as the Data Link and Physical layer headers.

ICMP Type 3, Code 5—Source Route Failed

The code value of 5 (Source route failed) is generated by a router. This message is generated for IP datagrams that are using the IP source route option (refer to Chapter 6). The IP source route option specifies the complete path of router addresses that should be used to forward the datagram.

If a router is unable to forward the datagram based on the source route path, it must discard the datagram. The router sends an ICMP Type 3, Code 5 message to the sender to indicate that the source route failed. The identity of the router that generates this ICMP message can be discovered by examining the source address field in the IP header of the ICMP message.

The ICMP Source route failed message should contain a source route option of the same type (strict or loose), created by reversing the portion before the pointer of the route recorded in the source route option of the original datagram (the datagram that results in the ICMP message). The only time the source route fields of the failed IP datagram are not used is when an ICMP Parameter Problem about a source route option in the original packet is issued, or the router is aware of policy that would prevent the delivery of the ICMP error message using the source route information in the original datagram.

ICMP Type 3, Code 6—Destination Network Unknown

The code value of 6 (Destination Network Unknown) was meant to be generated by a router when it could detect through its routing table that the destination network is unknown. Actually, this message will not be generated in real-life networks, because the router will generate an ICMP Type 3, Code 0 (Network Unreachable), instead. In other works, the ICMP Type 3, Code 6 message type is obsolete.

ICMP Type 3, Code 7—Destination Host Unknown

The code value of 7 (Destination Host Unknown) is generated by a router. This message is generated when a router can detect, through the link layer software at its network interface, that the destination host does not exist. For example, the router's link layer software can detect that a host does not exist if it is connected to the host using a point-to-point link. The Data Link layer protocol for point-to-point links can detect the existence of devices at either end of the link.

If a router is connected to the destination host through a broadcast LAN, such as Ethernet, the router cannot determine that the host does not exist. For a LAN, the router sends an ARP request to find the hardware address, and if there is no ARP reply, it assumes that the destination host is unreachable. The router cannot assume, from the absence of an ARP reply, that the host does not exist. The host may exist but may be misconfigured.

Routers must use Host Unreachable (Code 1) or Destination Host Unknown (Code 7) codes whenever other hosts on the same destination network might be reachable; otherwise, the sender may erroneously conclude that all hosts on the network are unreachable, which may not be the case.

ICMP Type 3, Code 8—Source Host Isolated

STD3, which is described by RFC 1122 on "Requirements for Internet Hosts—Communication Layers," defines a code 8 message. This message is generated if a router can detect that the host is isolated from the rest of the network. However, RFC 1812 on "Requirements for IP Version 4 Routers" states that routers should not generate Code 8 messages. Instead, they should generate either a Network Unreachable (Code 0) or a Host Unreachable (Code 1) message, as appropriate. Therefore, a Code 8 message is of historical interest only.

ICMP Type 3, Codes 9 and 10—Communication with Destination Network/Host Administratively Prohibited

Many routers enable the administrator to prohibit routing to specific destinations, even though the router may otherwise be able to route to these destinations. This may be done as part of the network policy for an organization. There are many factors that influence network policy, such as political/administrative reasons, network cost, and security.

A Code field value of 9 indicates that communication with the destination network is administratively prohibited, whereas a code value of 10 indicates that communication with the destination host is administratively prohibited.

Codes 9 and 10 were intended for use by end-to-end encryption devices used by U.S. military agencies. RFC 1812 states that routers should use the newly defined Code 13 (Communication Administratively Prohibited) if they administratively filter packets.

ICMP Type 3, Codes 11 and 12—Destination Network/Host Unreachable for Type of Service

These message types are generated if a router cannot forward the datagram to a destination network or host because the routes in its routing table cannot match the type of service (TOS) value requested or the default TOS value. The TOS field value is specified in the IP header of the datagram and enables the specification of precedence, delay, throughput, and cost for the path taken by the datagram (refer to Chapter 6).

A Code field value of 11 indicates that the destination network is unreachable, whereas a code value of 12 indicates that a destination host is unreachable for the given TOS value.

ICMP Type 3, Codes 13—Communication Administratively Prohibited Because of Firewalls

Many modern routers contain packet filtering software, which can set up filter rules to disenable forwarding of packets based on IP addresses, protocol types, port numbers, and so on. This is done for reasons of security and as a first line of defense against hostile users.

A router implementation may send ICMP messages indicating that the datagram could not be forwarded for administrative reasons. Routers may have a configuration option causing Code 13 messages not to be generated. If this option is enabled, no ICMP error message is sent in response to a dropped packet because its forwarding is administratively prohibited. Such an option is useful because it does not make sense to give additional information to a hostile user generating packets to penetrate the network.

ICMP Type 3, Code 14—Host Precedence Violation

This ICMP message is generated by the first hop router to the sender host. The first hop router is the first router that the datagram must cross to reach its destination. This ICMP message is generated to indicate that the requested precedence is not permissible for the specified source/destination addresses, upper-layer protocol (such as TCP and UDP) and source/destination port numbers.

A router may have a configuration option that causes Code 14 messages not to be generated. If this option is enabled, no ICMP error message is sent in response to a packet that is dropped because of a host precedence violation.

ICMP Type 3, Code 15—Precedence Cut-Off in Effect

This ICMP message is generated by a router. A network administrator can specify a minimum precedence level that may be required for a specific route in the router's routing table. If the datagram was sent with a lower precedence value, the datagram cannot be forwarded using this route. If the datagram must be discarded, a Type 3, Code 15 ICMP message is sent to the sender.

A router may have a configuration option that causes Code 15 messages not to be generated. If this option is enabled, no ICMP error message is sent in response to a dropped packet because of a precedence cut-off in effect.

ICMP Type 4—Source Quench

The IP network is connectionless. Routers in an IP network forward IP datagrams on an individual basis and do not reserve memory for datagrams for a particular session. In fact there is no notion of a session when routing datagrams. It is, therefore, possible for routers to get temporarily congested.

What is congestion in a router? It is a state where there is no more memory or buffer capacity in the router to store incoming datagrams. Why does this happen? Because of an increase in network traffic that exceeds the storage capacity of the network, particularly the routers. When congestion takes place, more than one router on the network can be affected. Incoming datagrams in a router may not be processed immediately because the router is busy processing other datagrams. Memory buffers are used in routers to temporarily store datagrams before they can be processed and forwarded using the routing algorithm.

Typically, routers tied to slow links are affected by network congestion. However, routers with small memory or low processing power can also experience congestion. When a router experiences congestion and its memory buffers are full, it must discard additional incoming datagrams. The router uses the ICMP Source Quench message to inform senders to slow down (reduce their current rate of datagram transmission). The ICMP Source Quench message is an attempt to implement flow control so that the routers do not get overrun with incoming datagrams.

How often should the ICMP Source Quench message be sent? A simplistic implementation may attempt to send a source quench message for every datagram the router must discard because its memory buffers are full. This approach is not particularly good because the additional ICMP source quench message increases the congestion in the network and affects other routers. More sophisticated router implementations may monitor the datagram rates from different sources and send ICMP Source Quench messages to those sources generating the most datagrams. A router implementation may also start sending ICMP Source Quench messages when its memory buffers are getting full so that it can prevent overflow of its buffers, rather than waiting to send ICMP Source Quench messages until after its buffers are full.

How does the source know when the congestion problem is over and when it can increase its transmission rate? Unfortunately there is no ICMP message to cancel or reverse the Source Quench message and indicate that the congestion problem is over, at least for the time being. This poses an interesting design problem for the sender. How does the sender know when to start increasing the data rate? The answer is that at the IP level, the source is not aware of when to increase the transmission rate, but it is aware of when to increase the transmission rate at the TCP protocol level. This is because TCP implements sophisticated flow control mechanism that can detect congestion and reduce data transmission rates and also increase transmission rates when the network appears to no longer be congested. In fact, the flow control problem is best handled by the transport layer protocols, such as TCP, which are responsible for reliable data delivery. In fact RFC 1122 on "Requirements for Internet hosts—communication layers" states that the ICMP Source Quench message must be reported to the transport layer, which should implement a mechanism to respond to the source quench.

RFC 1106 on "Something a Host Could Do with Source Quench: The Source Quench Introduced Delay (SQUID)" describes a mechanism for handling Source Quench messages, but this approach is not widely implemented.

Experience has also shown that ICMP source quench messages, in many situations, do little to improve the performance of a congested network, but could actually worsen network congestion and the communications processing load to handle these messages. Many implementations, therefore, simply ignore the ICMP Source Quench messages.

RFC1812, which is a proposed standard on "Requirements for IP Version 4 Routers," actually states that routers should not send ICMP Source Quench messages. Hosts are obliged to receive any ICMP messages sent to them, but need not take any action.

The format of the ICMP source message is shown in figure 8.10.

Figure 8.10 ICMP source quench message.

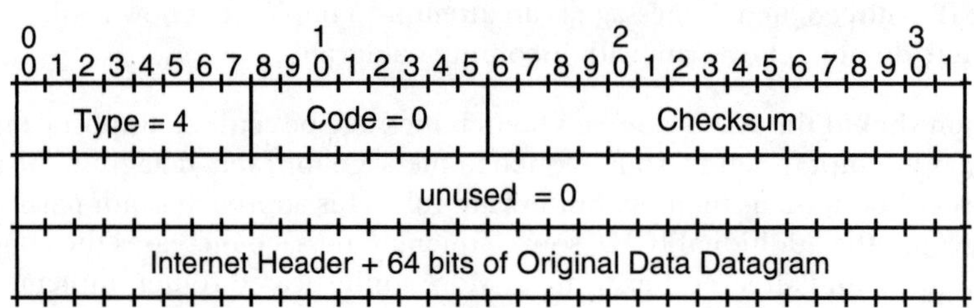

The Type field is set to 4, which indicates that this is an ICMP Source Quench message. The Code field is set to 0. The 4-octet Parameter field after the Checksum field is not used, and is set to 0.

ICMP Type 5—Redirect

An ICMP Redirect message is sent by a router whenever it detects that another router has a more optimal path for the datagram. Routers communicate routing information on the network with each other using a routing protocol. At any given time, routers have either optimal information or close to optimal information about the routes for the network. Hosts, on the other hand, are programmed with minimal routing information. A host is typically programmed with knowledge of only a few networks, and the next hop router used to get to these networks. The next hop routers are the routers that are one hop away from the source host; that is, the source host and next hop routers are directly connected (refer to Chapter 7). Hosts, typically, also have a default router, which is used to forward datagrams for all destinations not explicitly listed in the host routing table.

Hosts typically initialize their routing tables on system startup. The routing table information is kept in a configuration data area on the host, such as a file. If the network topology changes, the routers learn about the new routes to reach the destination because they participate in the routing protocols used to exchange information about the changes in the network topology. Typically, hosts are not configured to participate directly in the routing protocol exchanges. As a result, the hosts are not aware of the changed topology, and their routing tables may not contain the optimal information for reaching a destination.

Figure 8.11 shows a situation where a new router has been added to the network. This new router, R2, contains a more optimal path to reach the destination host B, but the host A is still configured to forward datagrams through router R1. If router R1 detects that router R2 has a more optimal path to the destination, it sends an ICMP Redirect message to the sender, and also forwards the datagram to the more optimal router, R2.

Figure 8.11 Example of ICMP Redirect messages.

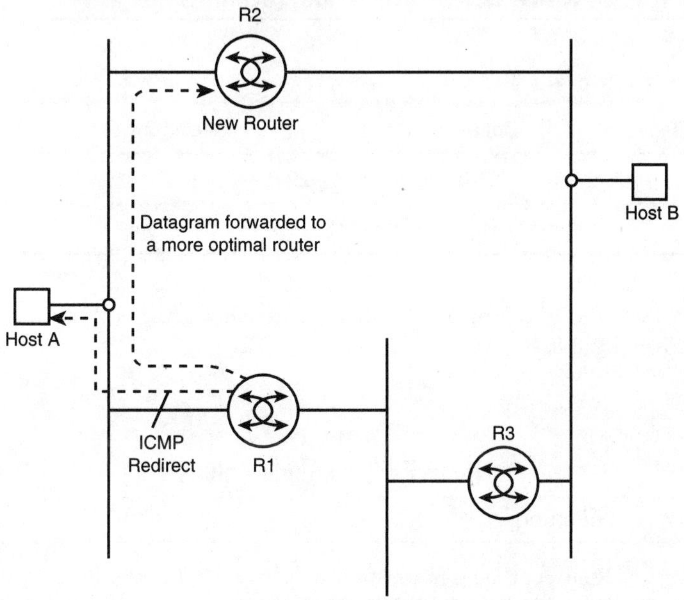

Upon receiving an ICMP Redirect message, hosts should update their routing table with the information about the new router for reaching the destination. The next datagram sent to the same destination should use the more optimal route received from the ICMP Redirect message. However, some host TCP/IP implementations simply ignore the ICMP Redirect messages. This results in extra network traffic being generated with each datagram sent to the non-optimal router generating an ICMP Redirect message to the source.

The router that generates the ICMP Redirect message also forwards the datagram to the more optimal router. Because this forwarding may be done through the same network on which the datagram was received this doubles the number of datagrams that are transmitted (refer to fig. 8.11).

The presence of ICMP Redirect messages should alert the network administrator of the possibility of non-optimal routes. If the ICMP Redirect messages persist for a long period of time, the host routing tables should be checked for inefficiencies. If ICMP Redirect messages are continuously sent to particular hosts, the TCP/IP software on these hosts needs to be updated because hosts should not ignore ICMP Redirect messages.

Routers should also implement a rate limit parameter that controls the number of ICMP Redirect messages that should be sent to the same host. This rate limit parameter should be configurable as part of the router configuration.

Figure 8.12 shows the format of the ICMP Redirect message.

Figure 8.12 ICMP Redirect message.

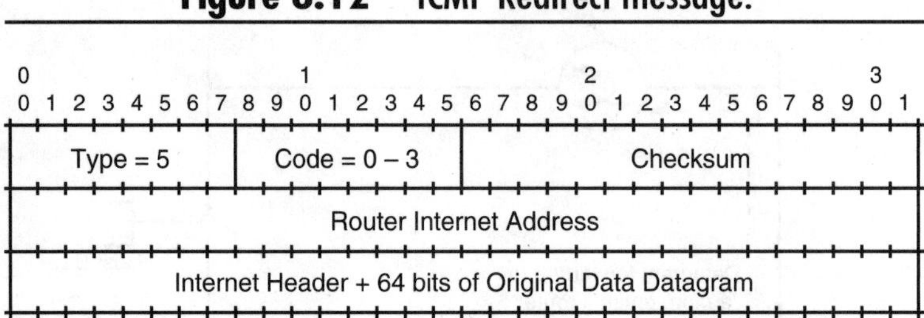

The Type field is set to 5 to indicate an ICMP Redirect messages. The Code field values are shown in table 8.4.

TABLE 8.4
ICMP Redirect Code Values

Code	Meaning
0	Redirect Datagram for the Network (or subnet)
1	Redirect Datagram for the Host
2	Redirect Datagram for the Type of Service and Network
3	Redirect Datagram for the Type of Service and Host

The address of the more optimal router is placed in the Router Internet Address field.

RFC 1812 states that routers must not generate the Redirect Datagram for Network (Code 0) or Redirect Datagram for Type of Service and Network (Code 2) messages. Instead, routers must be able to generate the Redirect Datagram for Host message (Code 1) and should be able to generate the Redirect Datagram for Type of Service and Host message (Code 3).

Code 0 and Code 2 messages apply to all hosts on the specified network; this is more economical than using Code 1 and Code 3 messages that are for specific hosts. In the case of subnetted networks, Code 0 and Code 2 messages are difficult to handle because of the ambiguity about the subnet mask used to interpret a network redirect message. In a Classless Internet Domain Routing (CIDR) environment, it is difficult to specify precisely the cases in which network Redirects can be used.

The Code 3 (Redirect Datagram for Host and Type of Service) message is generated when the packet provoking the ICMP Redirect message is to be sent via a path that would depend, in part, on the TOS requested. Routers that can generate Code 3 redirects must have a configuration option, which defaults to on to enable Code 1 redirects to be substituted for Code 3 redirects. If a router is not able to generate Code 3 Redirects, then it must generate Code 1 Redirects in situations where a Code 3 Redirect is called for.

Routers must not generate a Redirect message unless all the following conditions are met:

- The datagram is being forwarded out through the same physical interface that it was received from.
- The IP source address in the packet is on the same Logical IP (sub)network as the next hop IP address.
- The datagram does not contain an IP source route option.

The source IP address used in the ICMP Redirect must belong to the same logical subnet as the destination address. A router not using static routes and using a routing protocol must not consider paths learned from ICMP Redirects when forwarding a packet. The reason behind this is that the ICMP Redirects are designed to convey routing information to hosts. Routers use more efficient and effective mechanisms, such as routing protocols, to learn routing information. Also, if ICMP Redirect messages are believed, it is possible for correct routing information in the router's routing table to be replaced with incorrect information supplied by ICMP redirects. This could cause routing loops and other problems. Believing in ICMP Redirect messages also makes routers susceptible to attacks by malicious users who could send bogus ICMP Redirect messages to disrupt the network.

However, if a router is not using a routing protocol, it may be configured to enable the router to consider routes learned through ICMP Redirects when forwarding packets.

ICMP Types 9 and 10—Router Advertisement and Router Selection

ICMP Types 9 and 10 are used to implement the ICMP router discovery mechanism that can dynamically enable hosts to discover all routers on the directly connected network.

Prior to the introduction of these new ICMP types, hosts had to rely on static routing entries, ICMP redirects, or running a Routing Information Protocol (RIP) listening process that would monitor RIP advertisements on the directly connected network.

By using ICMP Router Discovery, hosts do not have to depend on static or manual configuration of their routing tables. Instead they can find all routers that are available to them in a manner that is independent of the routing protocol used by the routers. For example, there is no requirement to run the RIP listening process at the host. The ICMP Router Discovery is used for discovering local routers on the directly connected network; it is not a general router-to-router protocol.

In ICMP router discovery, ICMP Type 9 (Router Advertisement) messages are sent by routers at periodic intervals that vary from 7 to 10 minutes. The ICMP Router Advertisement message can also be sent in response to a router solicitation request from a host. A host issues a router solicitation request by sending an ICMP Router Selection (Type 10) message.

ICMP Router Advertisement messages are not broadcast; instead, they are multicast to the class D address of 224.0.0.1. This makes them more efficient than broadcast messages because multicast messages are processed by members of the multicast group instead of by all nodes on the network. Figure 8.13 shows the format of an ICMP Router Advertisement message.

Figure 8.13 ICMP Router Advertisement message.

```
 0                   1                   2                   3
 0 1 2 3 4 5 6 7 8 9 0 1 2 3 4 5 6 7 8 9 0 1 2 3 4 5 6 7 8 9 0 1
+-+-+-+-+-+-+-+-+-+-+-+-+-+-+-+-+-+-+-+-+-+-+-+-+-+-+-+-+-+-+-+-+
|   Type = 9    |   Code = 0    |           Checksum            |
+-+-+-+-+-+-+-+-+-+-+-+-+-+-+-+-+-+-+-+-+-+-+-+-+-+-+-+-+-+-+-+-+
|   Num Addrs   |Addr Entry Size|           Lifetime            |
+-+-+-+-+-+-+-+-+-+-+-+-+-+-+-+-+-+-+-+-+-+-+-+-+-+-+-+-+-+-+-+-+
|                       Router Address [1]                      |
+-+-+-+-+-+-+-+-+-+-+-+-+-+-+-+-+-+-+-+-+-+-+-+-+-+-+-+-+-+-+-+-+
|                      Preference Level [1]                     |
+-+-+-+-+-+-+-+-+-+-+-+-+-+-+-+-+-+-+-+-+-+-+-+-+-+-+-+-+-+-+-+-+
|                       Router Address [2]                      |
+-+-+-+-+-+-+-+-+-+-+-+-+-+-+-+-+-+-+-+-+-+-+-+-+-+-+-+-+-+-+-+-+
|                      Preference Level [2]                     |
+-+-+-+-+-+-+-+-+-+-+-+-+-+-+-+-+-+-+-+-+-+-+-+-+-+-+-+-+-+-+-+-+
|                               .                               |
|                               .                               |
|                               .                               |
```

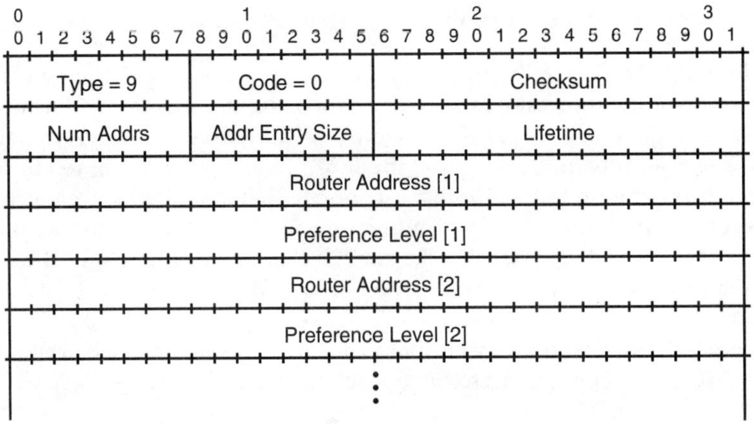

The Type field is set to 9 for an ICMP message to identify it as a Router Advertisement message. The Code field is set to 0. The Checksum is the usual 16-bit one's complement of the one's complement sum of the ICMP message.

After the Checksum field is the Num Addrs field, which contains the number of router addresses advertised in this message. The Addr Entry Size is the number of 32-bit words of information per each router address. This value is 2 in the version of the protocol described here. The Lifetime field contains the maximum number of seconds that the router addresses may be considered valid. After the expiration of this interval, the hosts must discard these router addresses. The Router Address[i] fields for $i = 1$ to Num Addrs identifies the interface from which this message is sent. The Preference Level[i] for $i = 1$ to Num Addrs is the preferability value for each Router Address[i]. A higher value indicates that the router address is more preferable. The format of the value is a signed 2's complement.

The ICMP Router Selection message can be sent by a host at any time. When the host starts up, it is sent to discover routers on the directly connected network. The ICMP Router Selection message is multicast to the class D address of 224.0.0.2.

Upon receiving the ICMP Router Selection message, routers respond with an ICMP Router Advertisement message. The hosts also receive unsolicited ICMP Router Advertisement messages every 7 to 10 minutes. Figure 8.14 shows the format of an ICMP Router Selection message.

Figure 8.14 ICMP Router Selection message.

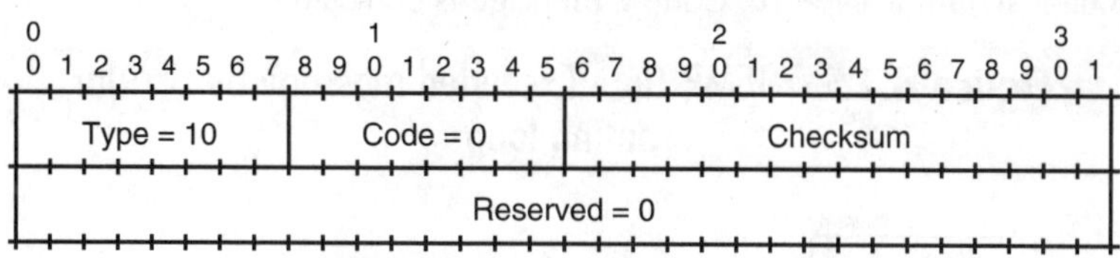

The Type field for an ICMP message is set to 10 to identify it as a Router Selection message. The Code field is set to 0. The Checksum is the usual 16-bit one's complement of the one's complement sum of the ICMP message. The Reserved field value is set to 0 and ignored on reception.

The TTL field value for the IP header carrying the ICMP Router Advertisement and Router Solicitation messages is set to 1 for the destination multicast address. This ensures that the ICMP messages do not go beyond the local network because the routers will decrease the value of the TTL field by at least 1; when this value becomes 0, the datagram will be silently discarded. Recall that no ICMP messages are generated when multicast datagrams are discarded.

ICMP Type 11—Time Exceeded

The ICMP Time Exceeded message is generated in the following situations:

- By routers to indicate that the TTL field value in the IP header has been decremented to 0. The Code value for this message is set to 0. The datagram is discarded before it can reach its destination. This could occur if the original setting in the TTL field is too low, or if there is a circular or excessively long loop that the datagram is required to traverse. A circular loop can be formed if certain links in the network are down, or by errors in the routing tables. In a circular loop, the chain of routers that forward the datagram form a closed loop, as illustrated in figure 8.15. Each time a router sees the datagram, it must decrease the TTL field by at least 1. If a datagram enters a loop, the TTL field eventually decreases to 0, at which time the datagram must be discarded. The ICMP Type 11, Code 0 message indicates the reason why the datagram was discarded. The router that discards the datagram can be identified by examining the source address in the IP header for the ICMP message.
- By Hosts to indicate that a datagram fragment is missing. The Code value for this message is set to 1. Recall that when a datagram is fragmented, the end node (host) is responsible for assembling the fragments into the original datagram. Each fragment is routed independently. If any fragment is lost, the host cannot reassemble the datagram, but must discard the complete datagram. The host usually maintains an internal reassembly timer, which it starts on receiving the first datagram fragment. If the rest of the datagram fragments do not arrive within the reassembly time-out, the datagram fragments are assumed to be lost, and a Type 10, Code 1 message is generated.

Figure 8.15 ICMP Time Exceeded message by circular routing loop.

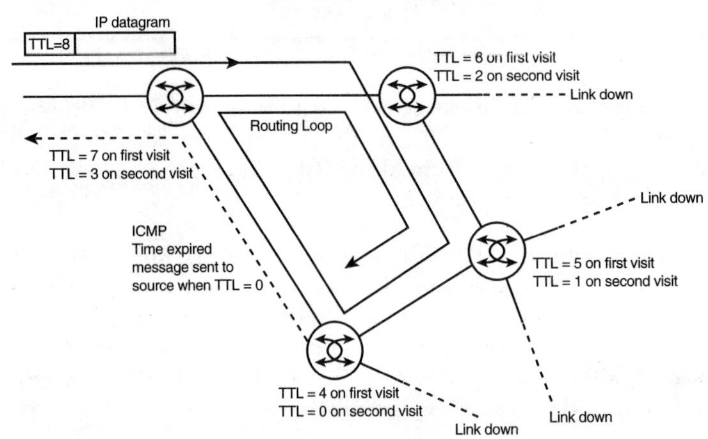

Generally speaking, a router must generate a Time Exceeded message (Code 0) (In Transit) when it discards a packet due to an expired TTL field. However, a router implementation may have a per interface option to disable the generation of Time Exceeded messages on that interface. The default for this option must be set to enable the generation of ICMP Time Exceeded messages.

Figure 8.16 shows the format of an ICMP Time Exceeded message.

Figure 8.16 ICMP Time Exceeded message.

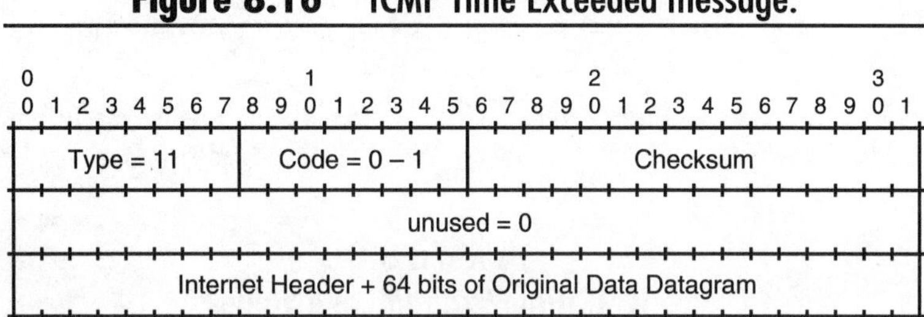

The Type field for an ICMP message is set to 11 to identify it as a Time Expired message. The Code field is set to 0 or 1 as indicated in table 8.5.

TABLE 8.5
ICMP Time Expired Code Values

Code	Meaning
0	Time to Live exceeded in Transit (generated by router)
1	Fragment Reassembly Time Exceeded (generated by host)

The Checksum is the usual 16-bit one's complement of the one's complement sum of the ICMP message. The Unused field value is set to 0 and ignored on reception.

ICMP Type 12—Parameter Problem

If the router or host finds a problem with the IP header parameters that prevents it from completely processing the datagram, it must discard the datagram and send an ICMP Type 12 (Parameter Problem) message. It is rare to find problems with one of the fields in the IP header, unless there is a bug in the IP module implementation. Instead, the incorrect argument in an IP option is a more common source of Parameter Problem errors.

The ICMP Parameter Problem can be generated by both hosts and routers. A pointer in the message identifies the octet where the problem was encountered. Figure 8.17 shows the format of the ICMP Parameter Problem message.

Figure 8.17 ICMP Parameter Problem message.

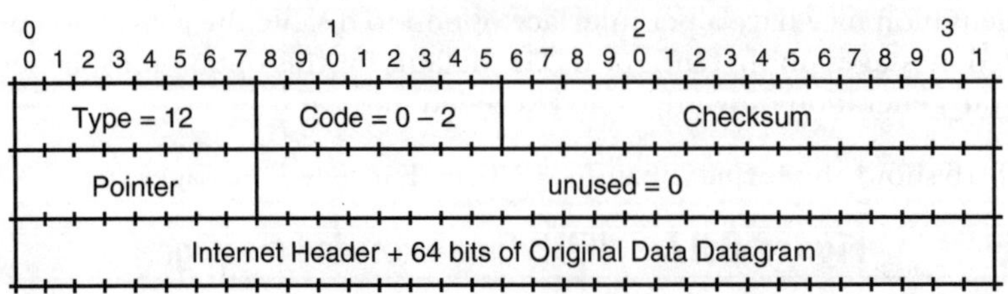

The Type field for an ICMP message is set to 12 to identify it as a Parameter Problem message. The Code field is set to 0, 1, or 2, as indicated in table 8.6.

TABLE 8.6
ICMP Time Expired Code Values

Code	Meaning
0	Pointer indicates the error
1	Missing a Required Option
2	Bad Length

When a Code 1 message is sent, the Pointer field is not used. Code 1 is used in military networks to indicate a missing security option.

The Pointer field identifies the octet of the original datagram's header where the error was detected. It is measured as an offset from the beginning of the IP header. For example, 1 indicates something is wrong with the Type of Service field (the second octet from start of IP header), and a value of –20 indicates something is wrong with the type code for the first option.

An incoming ICMP Parameter Problem message must be passed to the transport layer, and may be reported optionally to the user. In general, the ICMP Parameter Problem message is sent to the source host for any problem not specifically covered by another ICMP message. Receipt of a Parameter Problem message generally indicates some local or remote implementation error.

This ICMP message is only sent if the parameter problem caused the datagram to be discarded. If the IP node can continue with the processing of the datagram, no ICMP Parameter Problem message is generated.

ICMP Type 13, 14—Timestamp Request, Timestamp Reply

IP nodes maintain their own internal clocks. The ICMP Type 13 and 14 messages are used to obtain the time from a remote IP node. The returned times can be used for synchronizing the clocks on the IP node. There are a number of other more sophisticated protocols, such as Network Time Protocol (NTP), that can be used for synchronizing clocks on the Internet, but one of the simplest is the ICMP Type 13 and 14 messages. RFC 778 on "DECNET Internet Clock Service" discusses an implementation of an Internet Clock service using ICMP Timestamp messages. ICMP Type 13 and 14 messages can also be used for gathering performance statistics on network connections and transit times for datagrams.

ICMP Type 13 is a Time Request to a remote machine. ICMP Type 14 contains the reply from the remote machine. Figure 8.18 shows the format of the ICMP Type 13 and 14 messages.

Figure 8.18 **ICMP Time Request and Time Reply messages.**

Bits 0–7	Bits 8–15	Bits 16–31
Type = 13 – 14	Code = 0	Checksum
Identifier		Sequence Number
Originate Timestamp		
Receive Timestamp		
Transit Timestamp		

The Type field for ICMP message is set to 13 for Time Request and 14 for the Time Reply message. The Code field is set to 0. The Checksum is the usual 16-bit one's complement of the one's complement sum of the ICMP message. The Identifier and Sequence Number fields are used to match Timestamp Request and Replies.

The time stamp fields are 32 bits long, and are measured in milliseconds since midnight Universal Time. The Originate Timestamp is filled by the sender and contains the time the sender last processed the message before transmission. The Receive Timestamp is filled by the receiver and contains the time the message was received. The Transmit Timestamp is filled by the receiver just before the ICMP Timestamp reply message is sent. Figure 8.19 describes the use of the time stamp fields.

Figure 8.19 ICMP Type 13, 14 Timestamp fields. (Courtesy Learning Tree)

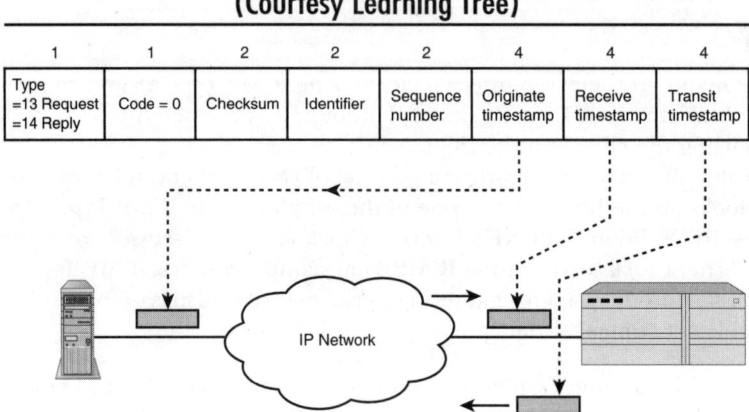

If the time is not available in milliseconds or cannot be provided with respect to midnight UT, then any time can be inserted in a time stamp provided the high-order bit of the time stamp is also set to indicate this non-standard value.

ICMP Types 15, 16—Information Request, Information Reply

ICMP Type 15 was intended for obtaining the IP address of the requesting host, and Type 16 is used to return the reply. Figure 8.20 shows the format of these messages.

Figure 8.20 ICMP Types 15, 16—Information Request/ Information Reply. (Courtesy Learning Tree)

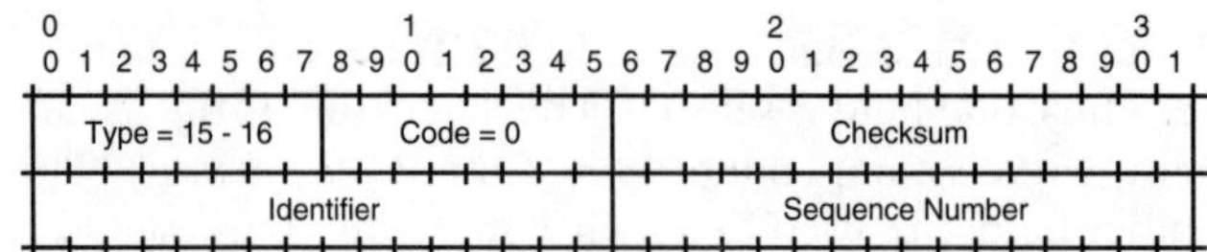

The source address of the IP header that carries the ICMP message has a value of 0.0.0.0 to indicate "this network." The reply contains the requested address.

The use of these ICMP types is now of obsolete and historical interest. In fact RFC 1122 advises that a host should not implement these messages because they were originally intended to support self-configuring systems, such as diskless workstations, enabling them to discover their IP addresses at boot time. The RARP, BOOTP, and DHCP protocols provide superior mechanisms for a host to discover its own IP address, and should be used instead.

ICMP Types 17, 18—Address Mask Request, Address Mask Reply

ICMP Type 17 is used to obtain the subnet mask for the requesting host, and Type 18 is used to return the reply. Subnet masks are used to indicate the format of the IP address in terms of the number of bits used for network identification, and the number of bits used for host identification. It is possible to use a portion of the host number field to extend the bits used for network identification and have more networks than enabled by the original format (class A, B, C) of the IP address. The number of additional bits used from the host number field is indicated by the subnet mask. You will learn more about subnet masks in Chapter 10, "IP Routing Protocols."

ICMP Types 17 and 18 are intended to support self-configuring systems, such as diskless workstations, to enable them to discover their subnet mask at boot time. From the discussion in Chapter 5, "Address Resolution Protocols," you learned that the RARP protocol can be used to obtain IP addresses. In addition to RARP, the ICMP Types 17 and 18 can be used to obtain the subnet mask.

There are other alternatives to discovering IP addresses and subnet masks using a single protocol. These are the BOOTP and DHCP protocols.

Figure 8.21 shows the format of the Address Mask Request/Address Mask Reply messages.

Figure 8.21 ICMP Types 17, 18—Address Mask Request/ Address Mask Reply.

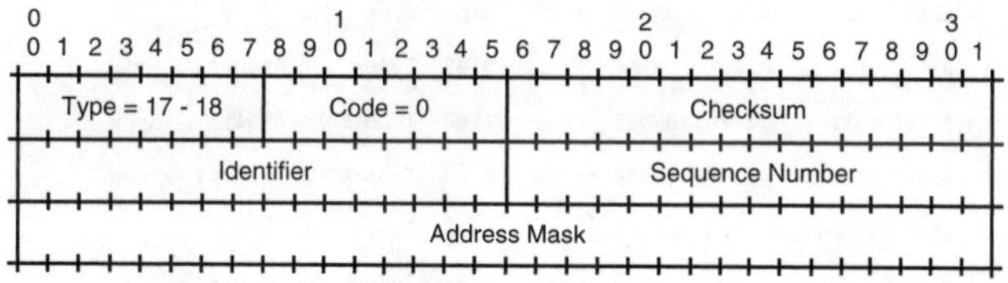

The IP node making the Address Mask Request can send the request directly to a router if it knows the address, or broadcast it on the network. Only authorized agents, such as routers and some special hosts, running software to reply to address mask requests, should send address mask replies. A host uses the first address mask reply that it receives, and silently ignores all other address mask replies. If there is no address mask reply, the host should assume an unsubnetted network and set its address mask appropriately.

The Type field for an ICMP message is set to 17 for Address Mask Request and 18 for the Address Mask Reply message. The Code field is set to 0. The Checksum is the usual 16-bit one's complement of the one's complement sum of the ICMP message. The Address Mask field in the ICMP Type 18 message contains the address mask value.

ICMP Traces

The following sections present you with protocol decodes of ICMP packet traces captured on a real-life network. You should study this protocol decode after briefly reviewing the previous sections that describe the meaning of the ICMP fields.

ICMP Echo/Reply Traces

Figure 8.22 shows the packets generated by the use of the PING utility. This figure shows that ten ICMP Echo/Request Reply pairs were sent.

Figure 8.22 Echo Request/Reply packet traces.

No.	Source	Destination	Layer	Size	Summary
1	0080C72DFD05	FFFFFFFFFFFF	arp	0064	Req by 199.245.180.9 for 199.245.
2	080020719BFA	0080C72DFD05	arp	0064	Reply 199.245.180.33=080020719BFA
3	0080C72DFD05	080020719BFA	icmp	0102	Type=Echo Request
4	080020719BFA	0080C72DFD05	icmp	0102	Type=Echo Reply
5	0080C72DFD05	080020719BFA	icmp	0102	Type=Echo Request
6	080020719BFA	0080C72DFD05	icmp	0102	Type=Echo Reply
7	0080C72DFD05	080020719BFA	icmp	0102	Type=Echo Request
8	080020719BFA	0080C72DFD05	icmp	0102	Type=Echo Reply
9	0080C72DFD05	080020719BFA	icmp	0102	Type=Echo Request
10	080020719BFA	0080C72DFD05	icmp	0102	Type=Echo Reply
11	0080C72DFD05	080020719BFA	icmp	0102	Type=Echo Request
12	080020719BFA	0080C72DFD05	icmp	0102	Type=Echo Reply
13	0080C72DFD05	080020719BFA	icmp	0102	Type=Echo Request
14	080020719BFA	0080C72DFD05	icmp	0102	Type=Echo Reply
15	0080C72DFD05	080020719BFA	icmp	0102	Type=Echo Request
16	080020719BFA	0080C72DFD05	icmp	0102	Type=Echo Reply
17	0080C72DFD05	080020719BFA	icmp	0102	Type=Echo Request
18	080020719BFA	0080C72DFD05	icmp	0102	Type=Echo Reply
19	0080C72DFD05	080020719BFA	icmp	0102	Type=Echo Request
20	080020719BFA	0080C72DFD05	icmp	0102	Type=Echo Reply
21	0080C72DFD05	080020719BFA	icmp	0102	Type=Echo Request
22	080020719BFA	0080C72DFD05	icmp	0102	Type=Echo Reply

The first two packets are the ARP Request and ARP Reply packets used to discover the hardware address of the destination being contacted.

Packet 3 is the first ICMP Echo Request, and packet 4 is the corresponding reply. Figures 8.23 and 8.24 show the protocol decode of these packets.

Figure 8.23 Packet 3—ICMP Echo Request.

```
Packet Number : 3             3:55:17 PM
Length : 102 bytes
ether: ==================== Ethernet Datalink Layer ====================
       Station: 00-80-C7-2D-FD-05 ----> 08-00-20-71-9B-FA
       Type: 0x0800 (IP)
   ip: ======================= Internet Protocol =======================
       Station:199.245.180.9 ---->199.245.180.33
       Protocol: ICMP
       Version: 4
       Header Length (32 bit words): 5
       Precedence: Routine
              Normal Delay, Normal Throughput, Normal Reliability
       Total length: 84
       Identification:   121
       Fragmentation allowed, Last fragment
       Fragment Offset: 0
       Time to Live: 255 seconds
       Checksum: 0xC319(Valid)
 icmp: =============== Internet Control Message Protocol ===============
       Type: Echo Request
       Checksum: 0x8B5E(Valid)
       Code: 0
       Identifier: 46080
       Sequence Number: 0
Data:
  0: 7C 09 8D 33 B9 60 0B 00 08 09 0A 0B 0C 0D 0E 0F ||..3.`..........
 10: 10 11 12 13 14 15 16 17 18 19 1A 1B 1C 1D 1E 1F |................
 20: 20 21 22 23 24 25 26 27 28 29 2A 2B 2C 2D 2E 2F | !"#$%&'()*+,-./
 30: 30 31 32 33 34 35 36 37                         |01234567
```

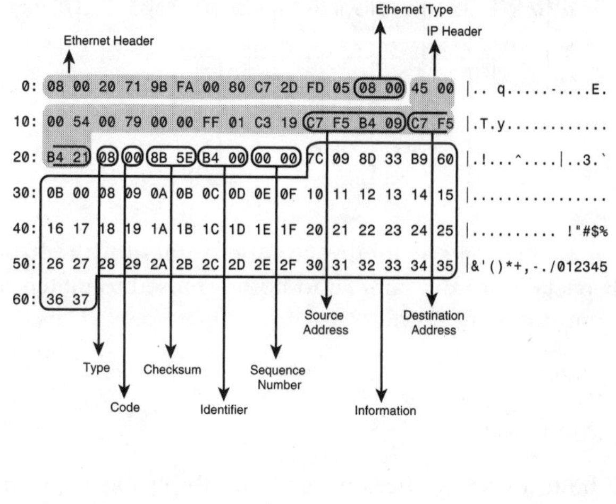

Figure 8.24 Packet 4—ICMP Echo Reply.

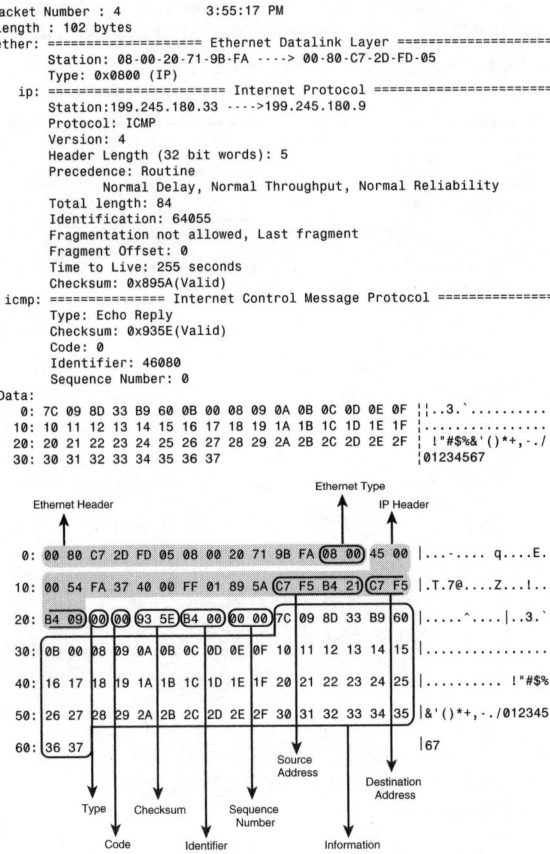

```
Packet Number : 4              3:55:17 PM
Length : 102 bytes
ether: ==================== Ethernet Datalink Layer ====================
         Station: 08-00-20-71-9B-FA ----> 00-80-C7-2D-FD-05
         Type: 0x0800 (IP)
   ip: ====================== Internet Protocol ======================
         Station:199.245.180.33 ---->199.245.180.9
         Protocol: ICMP
         Version: 4
         Header Length (32 bit words): 5
         Precedence: Routine
                  Normal Delay, Normal Throughput, Normal Reliability
         Total length: 84
         Identification: 64055
         Fragmentation not allowed, Last fragment
         Fragment Offset: 0
         Time to Live: 255 seconds
         Checksum: 0x895A(Valid)
 icmp: =============== Internet Control Message Protocol ===============
         Type: Echo Reply
         Checksum: 0x935E(Valid)
         Code: 0
         Identifier: 46080
         Sequence Number: 0
Data:
   0: 7C 09 8D 33 B9 60 0B 00 08 09 0A 0B 0C 0D 0E 0F ¦¦..3.`..........
  10: 10 11 12 13 14 15 16 17 18 19 1A 1B 1C 1D 1E 1F ¦................
  20: 20 21 22 23 24 25 26 27 28 29 2A 2B 2C 2D 2E 2F ¦ !"#$%&'()*+,-./
  30: 30 31 32 33 34 35 36 37                         ¦01234567
```


Notice that the Identifier and Sequence Number values for the ICMP Echo Request and Echo Reply packets are the same, and both are used to match the Echo Request with the corresponding Echo Reply:

Identifier: 46080

Sequence Number: 0

Also, note that the Information field in the Echo Reply message contains the same 56 octets of data sent in the Echo Request message:

```
 0: 7C 09 8D 33 B9 60 0B 00 08 09 0A 0B 0C 0D 0E 0F ¦¦..3.'..........
10: 10 11 12 13 14 15 16 17 18 19 1A 1B 1C 1D 1E 1F ¦................
20: 20 21 22 23 24 25 26 27 28 29 2A 2B 2C 2D 2E 2F ¦ !"#$%&'()*+,-./
30: 30 31 32 33 34 35 36 37                         ¦01234567
```

Figures 8.25 and 8.26 are a repeat of the ICMP Echo Request and Reply messages sent as packets 5 and 6. The same data was sent in the ICMP Echo Request. Upon examination of the Identifier and Sequence Number values, notice the following values:

Identifier: 46080

Sequence Number: 256

This particular implementation increments the Sequence Number value in increments of 256.

Figure 8.25 Packet 5—ICMP Echo Request.

```
Packet Number : 5           3:55:18 PM
Length : 102 bytes
ether: ==================== Ethernet Datalink Layer ====================
       Station: 00-80-C7-2D-FD-05 ----> 08-00-20-71-9B-FA
       Type: 0x0800 (IP)
   ip: ====================== Internet Protocol ======================
       Station:199.245.180.9 ---->199.245.180.33
       Protocol: ICMP
       Version: 4
       Header Length (32 bit words): 5
       Precedence: Routine
             Normal Delay, Normal Throughput, Normal Reliability
       Total length: 84
       Identification:   122
       Fragmentation allowed, Last fragment
       Fragment Offset: 0
       Time to Live: 255 seconds
       Checksum: 0xC318(Valid)
 icmp: =============== Internet Control Message Protocol ===============
       Type: Echo Request
       Checksum: 0xCD72(Valid)
       Code: 0
       Identifier: 46080
       Sequence Number: 256
Data:
    0: 7D 09 8D 33 75 4C 0B 00 08 09 0A 0B 0C 0D 0E 0F |}..3uL..........
   10: 10 11 12 13 14 15 16 17 18 19 1A 1B 1C 1D 1E 1F |................
   20: 20 21 22 23 24 25 26 27 28 29 2A 2B 2C 2D 2E 2F | !"#$%&'()*+,-./
   30: 30 31 32 33 34 35 36 37                         |01234567
```

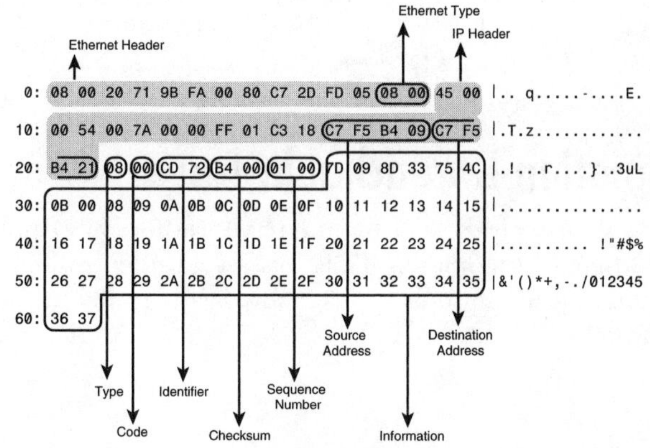

```
 0: 08 00 20 71 9B FA 00 80 C7 2D FD 05 08 00 45 00 |.. q.....-....E.
10: 00 54 00 7A 00 00 FF 01 C3 18 C7 F5 B4 09 C7 F5 |.T.z............
20: B4 21 08 00 CD 72 B4 00 01 00 7D 09 8D 33 75 4C |.!...r....}..3uL
30: 0B 00 08 09 0A 0B 0C 0D 0E 0F 10 11 12 13 14 15 |................
40: 16 17 18 19 1A 1B 1C 1D 1E 1F 20 21 22 23 24 25 |.......... !"#$%
50: 26 27 28 29 2A 2B 2C 2D 2E 2F 30 31 32 33 34 35 |&'()*+,-./012345
60: 36 37
```

Figure 8.26 Packet 6—ICMP Echo Reply.

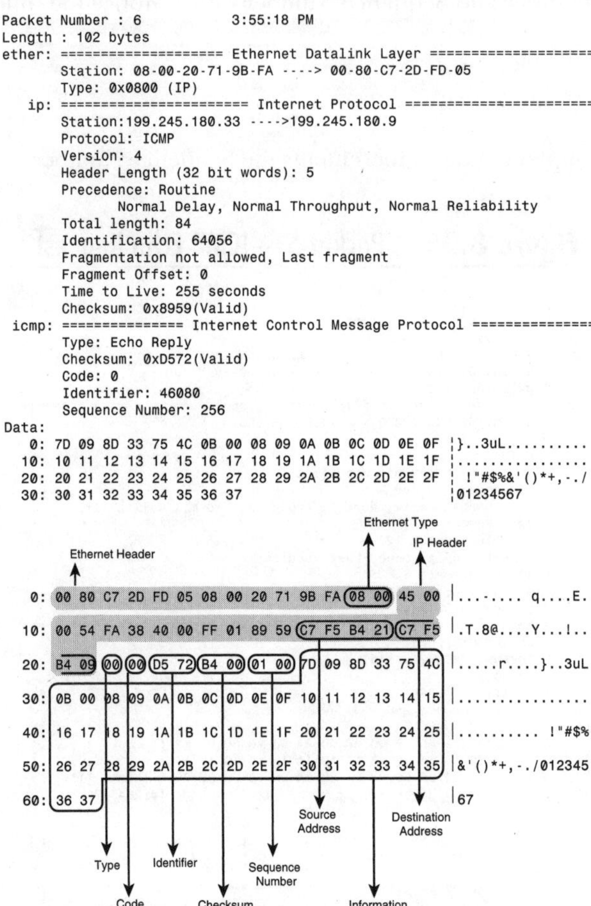

```
Packet Number : 6          3:55:18 PM
Length : 102 bytes
ether: =================== Ethernet Datalink Layer ===================
       Station: 08-00-20-71-9B-FA ----> 00-80-C7-2D-FD-05
       Type: 0x0800 (IP)
   ip: ====================== Internet Protocol ======================
       Station:199.245.180.33 ---->199.245.180.9
       Protocol: ICMP
       Version: 4
       Header Length (32 bit words): 5
       Precedence: Routine
             Normal Delay, Normal Throughput, Normal Reliability
       Total length: 84
       Identification: 64056
       Fragmentation not allowed, Last fragment
       Fragment Offset: 0
       Time to Live: 255 seconds
       Checksum: 0x8959(Valid)
 icmp: ============== Internet Control Message Protocol ==============
       Type: Echo Reply
       Checksum: 0xD572(Valid)
       Code: 0
       Identifier: 46080
       Sequence Number: 256
Data:
   0: 7D 09 8D 33 75 4C 0B 00 08 09 0A 0B 0C 0D 0E 0F ¦}..3uL.........
  10: 10 11 12 13 14 15 16 17 18 19 1A 1B 1C 1D 1E 1F ¦................
  20: 20 21 22 23 24 25 26 27 28 29 2A 2B 2C 2D 2E 2F ¦ !"#$%&'()*+,-./
  30: 30 31 32 33 34 35 36 37                         ¦01234567
```


ICMP Destination Unreachable Traces

Figure 8.27 shows a packet trace showing the ICMP Destination Unreachable messages generated when an attempt was made to start a Telnet session with the host 200.1.1.1. That host was found to be unreachable by the router at 199.245.180.10 (see fig. 8.28).

Figure 8.27 ICMP Destination Unreachable messages.

No.	Source	Destination	Layer	Size	Summary
1	0080C72DFD05	FFFFFFFFFFFF	arp	0064	Req by 199.245.180.9 for 199.245.
2	0000C0DD145C	0080C72DFD05	arp	0064	Reply 199.245.180.10=0000C0DD145C
3	0080C72DFD05	0000C0DD145C	tcp	0078	Port:1027 ---> TELNET SYN
4	0000C0DD145C	0080C72DFD05	icmp	0074	Type=Destination Unreachable
5	0080C72DFD05	0000C0DD145C	tcp	0078	Port:1027 ---> TELNET SYN
6	0000C0DD145C	0080C72DFD05	icmp	0074	Type=Destination Unreachable

Figure 8.28 Unsuccessful attempt to reach a host.

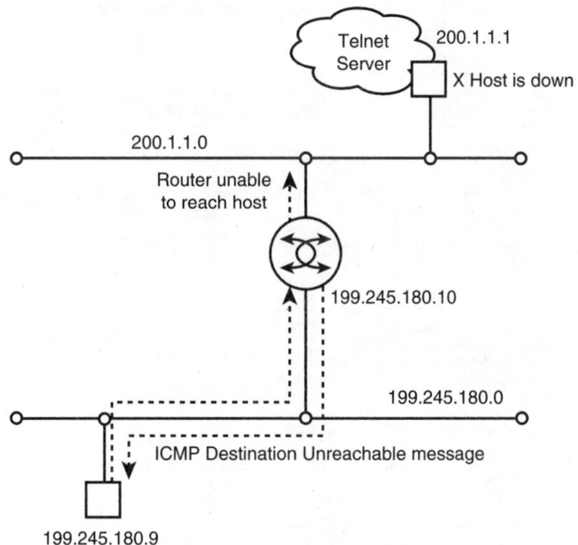

Packets 1 and 2 contain the ARP Request and ARP Reply messages that are used to find the hardware address of the router 199.245.180.10, through which the datagrams of the Telnet session are to be forwarded. Packet 3 contains an attempt to start a Telnet session. Packet 4 is the ICMP Destination Unreachable message sent by the router for packet 4. Packets 5 and 6 are a repeat of packets 3 and 4, and represent a second attempt to start the Telnet session.

Figure 8.29 shows the decode of packet 4, which contains the ICMP Destination Unreachable message.

Figure 8.29 Packet 4—ICMP Destination Unreachable.

```
Packet Number : 4           4:24:14 PM
Length : 74 bytes
ether: ==================== Ethernet Datalink Layer ====================
       Station: 00-00-C0-DD-14-5C ----> 00-80-C7-2D-FD-05
       Type: 0x0800 (IP)
   ip: ======================= Internet Protocol =======================
       Station:199.245.180.10 ---->199.245.180.9
       Protocol: ICMP
       Version: 4
       Header Length (32 bit words): 5
       Precedence: Routine
             Normal Delay, Normal Throughput, Normal Reliability
       Total length: 56
       Identification:  8288
       Fragmentation allowed, Last fragment
       Fragment Offset: 0
       Time to Live: 128 seconds
       Checksum: 0x2266(Valid)
 icmp: =============== Internet Control Message Protocol ===============
       Type: Destination Unreachable
       Checksum: 0x1800(Valid)
       Code: Host Unreachable
ORIGINAL IP PACKET HEADER
   ip: ======================= Internet Protocol ======================
       Station:199.245.180.9 ---->200.1.1.1
       Protocol: TCP
       Version: 4
       Header Length (32 bit words): 5
       Precedence: Routine
             Low Delay, Normal Throughput, Normal Reliability
       Total length: 60
       Identification:   226
       Fragmentation allowed, Last fragment
       Fragment Offset: 0
       Time to Live: 64  seconds
       Checksum: 0x34C9(Valid)
  tcp: ================ Transmission Control Protocol ================
       Source Port: 1027
       Destination Port: TELNET
       OUT OF DATA. DECODE ABORTED.
```

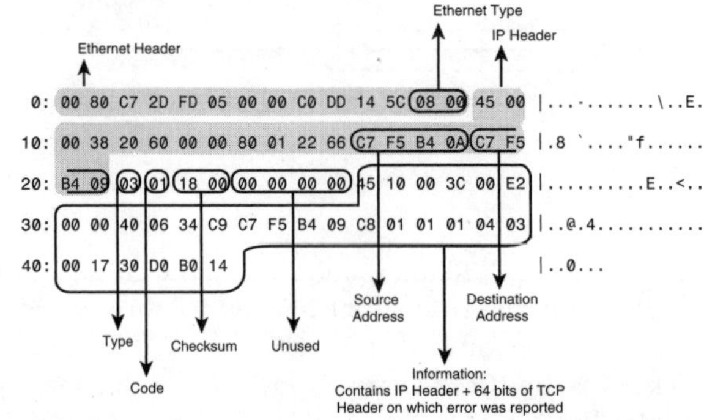
Ethernet Type
IP Header
Ethernet Header
0: 00 80 C7 2D FD 05 00 00 C0 DD 14 5C 08 00 45 00 |...-.......\..E.
10: 00 38 20 60 00 00 80 01 22 66 C7 F5 B4 0A C7 F5 |.8 `...."f......
20: B4 09 03 01 18 00 00 00 00 00 45 10 00 3C 00 E2 |..........E..<..
30: 00 00 40 06 34 C9 C7 F5 B4 09 C8 01 01 01 04 03 |..@.4...........
40: 00 17 30 D0 B0 14 |..0...
Source Address
Destination Address
Type
Checksum
Unused
Code
Information:
Contains IP Header + 64 bits of TCP
Header on which error was reported

Notice that the decode of packet 4 shows an ICMP Type 3, Code 1, which indicates that the host is unreachable. The Information field contains the IP header and the first 64 bits of the upper-layer protocol that caused the error (TCP, in this case). The full decode of the TCP header could not be shown because there were only 64 bits of the header. There was sufficient information in the TCP header to identify the source and destination port numbers, which are 1027 and 23 (Telnet), respectively. The IP header that was reported in the Information field showed that the error was sent by the datagram sent from 199.245.180.10 to 200.1.1.1. If you examine the IP header of the ICMP message itself, you can see that the ICMP message was sent from the router at 199.245.180.10 to the source host at 199.245.180.9.

ICMP Timestamp Traces

Figure 8.30 shows a packet trace that shows the ICMP Timestamp Request/Reply messages that were generated to obtain the time stamp for host 199.245.180.201.

Figure 8.30 ICMP Timestamp messages.

No.	Source	Destination	Layer	Size	Summary
1	0080C72DFD05	0000C0A20F8E	icmp	0066	Type=Timestamp Request
2	0000C0A20F8E	0080C72DFD05	icmp	0064	Type=Timestamp Reply
3	0080C72DFD05	0000C0A20F8E	icmp	0066	Type=Timestamp Request
4	0000C0A20F8E	0080C72DFD05	icmp	0064	Type=Timestamp Reply
5	0080C72DFD05	0000C0A20F8E	icmp	0066	Type=Timestamp Request
6	0000C0A20F8E	0080C72DFD05	icmp	0064	Type=Timestamp Reply
7	0080C72DFD05	0000C0A20F8E	icmp	0066	Type=Timestamp Request
8	0000C0A20F8E	0080C72DFD05	icmp	0064	Type=Timestamp Reply
9	0080C72DFD05	0000C0A20F8E	icmp	0066	Type=Timestamp Request
10	0000C0A20F8E	0080C72DFD05	icmp	0064	Type=Timestamp Reply
11	0080C72DFD05	0000C0A20F8E	icmp	0066	Type=Timestamp Request
12	0000C0A20F8E	0080C72DFD05	icmp	0064	Type=Timestamp Reply
13	0080C72DFD05	0000C0A20F8E	icmp	0066	Type=Timestamp Request
14	0000C0A20F8E	0080C72DFD05	icmp	0064	Type=Timestamp Reply
15	0080C72DFD05	0000C0A20F8E	icmp	0066	Type=Timestamp Request
16	0000C0A20F8E	0080C72DFD05	icmp	0064	Type=Timestamp Reply
17	0080C72DFD05	0000C0A20F8E	icmp	0066	Type=Timestamp Request
18	0000C0A20F8E	0080C72DFD05	icmp	0064	Type=Timestamp Reply
19	0080C72DFD05	0000C0A20F8E	icmp	0066	Type=Timestamp Request
20	0000C0A20F8E	0080C72DFD05	icmp	0064	Type=Timestamp Reply
21	0080C72DFD05	0000C0A20F8E	icmp	0066	Type=Timestamp Request
22	0000C0A20F8E	0080C72DFD05	icmp	0064	Type=Timestamp Reply
23	0080C72DFD05	0000C0A20F8E	icmp	0066	Type=Timestamp Request
24	0000C0A20F8E	0080C72DFD05	icmp	0064	Type=Timestamp Reply
25	0080C72DFD05	0000C0A20F8E	icmp	0066	Type=Timestamp Request

continues

```
26 0000C0A20F8E  0080C72DFD05  icmp   0064  Type=Timestamp Reply
27 0080C72DFD05  0000C0A20F8E  icmp   0066  Type=Timestamp Request
28 0000C0A20F8E  0080C72DFD05  icmp   0064  Type=Timestamp Reply
29 0080C72DFD05  0000C0A20F8E  icmp   0066  Type=Timestamp Request
30 0000C0A20F8E  0080C72DFD05  icmp   0064  Type=Timestamp Reply
31 0080C72DFD05  0000C0A20F8E  icmp   0066  Type=Timestamp Request
32 0000C0A20F8E  0080C72DFD05  icmp   0064  Type=Timestamp Reply
```

Figures 8.31 and 8.32 show the protocol decodes for packets 1 and 2 that are the ICMP Timestamp Request and the corresponding ICMP Timestamp Reply message. The other packets are a repeat of these Timestamp Request/Reply messages.

Figure 8.31 Packet 1—ICMP Timestamp request.

```
Packet Number : 1          5:42:12 PM
 Length : 66 bytes
 ether: ==================== Ethernet Datalink Layer ====================
        Station: 00-80-C7-2D-FD-05 ----> 00-00-C0-A2-0F-8E
        Type: 0x0800 (IP)
    ip: ====================== Internet Protocol ======================
        Station:199.245.180.9 ---->199.245.180.201
        Protocol: ICMP
        Version: 4
        Header Length (32 bit words): 5
        Precedence: Routine
               Normal Delay, Normal Throughput, Normal Reliability
        Total length: 48
        Identification:   319
        Fragmentation allowed, Last fragment
        Fragment Offset: 0
        Time to Live: 255 seconds
        Checksum: 0xC1CF(Valid)
  icmp: ============== Internet Control Message Protocol ==============
        Type: Timestamp Request
        Checksum: 0xC52D(Valid)
        Code: 0
        Identifier: 62976
        Sequence Number: 0
        Originate Timestamp: 6:30:35.7
        Receive Timestamp: 0:0:0.0
        Transmit Timestamp: 0:0:0.0
Data:
   0: 00 00 00 00 00 00 00 00 9B 6C 02 A0           |.........l..
```

```
   0: 00 00 C0 A2 0F 8E 00 80 C7 2D FD 05 08 00 45 00 |.........-....E.
  10: 00 30 01 3F 00 00 FF 01 C1 CF C7 F5 B4 09 C7 F5 |.0.?...........
  20: B4 C9 0D 00 C5 2D F6 00 00 00 01 65 98 5F 00 00 |.....-.....e._..
  30: 00 00 00 00 00 00 00 00 00 00 9B 6C 02 A0       |...........l..
```

Figure 8.32 Packet 2—ICMP Timestamp reply.

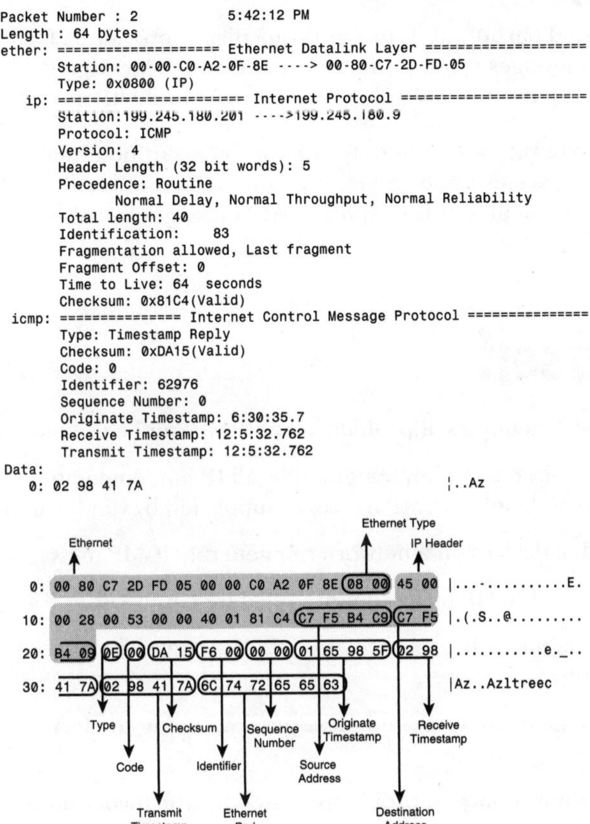

```
Packet Number : 2           5:42:12 PM
Length : 64 bytes
ether: ==================== Ethernet Datalink Layer ====================
       Station: 00-00-C0-A2-0F-8E ----> 00-80-C7-2D-FD-05
       Type: 0x0800 (IP)
   ip: ======================= Internet Protocol =======================
       Station:199.245.180.201 ---->199.245.180.9
       Protocol: ICMP
       Version: 4
       Header Length (32 bit words): 5
       Precedence: Routine
              Normal Delay, Normal Throughput, Normal Reliability
       Total length: 40
       Identification:    83
       Fragmentation allowed, Last fragment
       Fragment Offset: 0
       Time to Live: 64  seconds
       Checksum: 0x81C4(Valid)
 icmp: =============== Internet Control Message Protocol ===============
       Type: Timestamp Reply
       Checksum: 0xDA15(Valid)
       Code: 0
       Identifier: 62976
       Sequence Number: 0
       Originate Timestamp: 6:30:35.7
       Receive Timestamp: 12:5:32.762
       Transmit Timestamp: 12:5:32.762
Data:
   0: 02 98 41 7A                                          |..Az

   0: 00 80 C7 2D FD 05 00 00 C0 A2 0F 8E 08 00 45 00  |..-.........E.
  10: 00 28 00 53 00 00 40 01 81 C4 C7 F5 B4 C9 C7 F5  |.(.S..@.........
  20: B4 09 0E 00 DA 15 F6 00 00 00 01 65 98 5F 02 98  |..........e._..
  30: 41 7A 02 98 41 7A 6C 74 72 65 65 63              |Az..Azltreec
```


Packet 1 has a Type of 13, which identifies it as an ICMP Timestamp Request. The Identifier and Sequence fields are 62976 and 0, respectively. Notice that the Originate Timestamp field is filled by the sender and shows a time of 6:30:35.7 UT (0165985F hex milliseconds since midnight UTC). The Receive Timestamp and Transmit Timestamp are filled with zeros in the Timestamp Request.

Packet 2 has a Type of 14, which identifies it as an ICMP Timestamp Reply. The Identifier and Sequence fields are respectively 62976 and 0, which are the same as that in the ICMP Timestamp Request. Notice that the Originate Timestamp field was already filled by the sender with the time of 6:30:35.7. The Receive Timestamp and Transmit Timestamp are filled by the host at 199.245.180.201 with the following values:

Originate Timestamp: 6:30:35.7

Receive Timestamp: 12:5:32.762

Transmit Timestamp: 12:5:32.762

Summary

ICMP is a required part of the Internet Protocol and provides a facility to send alert and diagnostic messages through the Internet Control Message Protocol (ICMP) module. The ICMP module is implemented as part of the IP module.

ICMP messages are very useful in detecting problems or potential problems on the network. ICMP messages can be generated for a variety of error conditions that have been examined in detail in this chapter. ICMP messages can also be used for network diagnostics and statistics.

Test Yourself

1. List at least 5 examples of problems that ICMP can be used to report upon.
2. Is ICMP required to be implemented by all IP implementations? Comment on the degree of detail of ICMP messages supported by vendor implementations.
3. What kind of devices on a network can generate ICMP messages?
4. Does the use of ICMP make IP more reliable? Give reasons for your answer.
5. If an IP datagram is fragmented, are ICMP messages generated for each fragment? Justify your answer.
6. Does ICMP generate errors on messages containing the ICMP message? Justify your answer.
7. ICMP does not report on problems caused by which conditions?
8. Given an ICMP message, how can you determine the device responsible for generating this message? How can you determine the type of problem reported by the ICMP message?
9. Why are ICMP messages sent to the originator of the datagram that is being reported on? If an error in a router's routing table is responsible for generation of the ICMP message, why can't the ICMP message be sent to the router itself?
10. ICMP is encapsulated by which protocol? Does ICMP encapsulate another protocol? Draw a diagram showing all the layers of ICMP encapsulation on an ethernet network.
11. Outline the values that must be placed in the IP header fields for sending an ICMP message.
12. Are ICMP messages guaranteed to be delivered? Discuss your answer.
13. Draw a diagram showing the general format of ICMP messages. Label the components/fields in this diagram.

14. What is the purpose of the Type and Code fields in an ICMP message?
15. What is the purpose of the Checksum field in an ICMP message?
16. What is the purpose of the Identification and Sequence Number fields in an ICMP message? Give examples of ICMP messages where these fields are used.
17. When can the ICMP Checksum field be set to 0? What is its meaning?
18. What kind of information is contained in the Information field of an ICMP message?
19. Discuss the kind of information on the transport protocols TCP and UDP is reported in the ICMP message. Is this information complete? How many additional (if any) octets should the ICMP message carry in its information field to give a complete report on the transport layer header?
20. Discuss the use of the ICMP Type 8 and 0 messages in troubleshooting a network.
21. What kinds of options are available in most PING utilities for troubleshooting a network?
22. List the different types of error/network conditions that can be detected by an ICMP Type 3 message.
23. When would an ICMP Type 3, Protocol unreachable message be sent?
24. When would an ICMP Type 3, Port unreachable message be sent?
25. When would an ICMP Type 3, Fragmentation Needed and Don't Fragment was Set be sent?
26. Discuss how the ICMP Type 3, Fragmentation Needed and Don't Fragment message be used for estimating the minimum MTU size of the path to a destination.
27. When would an ICMP Type 3, source route failed message be sent? Does this type of message include IP source route options?
28. When would an ICMP Type 3, Communication Administratively Prohibited because of firewalls message be sent?
29. When would an ICMP Type 4, Source Quench message be sent? Why does current thinking recommend that this message not be sent by routers? What OSI layer is best suited for handling the problem being detected by the Source Quench message?
30. Should the ICMP error message be reported to the transport layer?
31. What could cause congestion in a router?
32. Discuss the purpose of sending an ICMP Redirect message.
33. Routers must not generate ICMP messages unless what conditions are met?

34. Discuss the ICMP messages used for router discovery. What advantages does this method have over other techniques?

35. When would an ICMP Time exceeded message be sent?

36. When would an ICMP Parameter Problem message be sent?

37. What is the purpose of the ICMP Types 13 and 14 messages?

38. Why is the ICMP Information Request/Reply not used? What other protocols can be used for this purpose?

39. What is the purpose of the ICMP Address Mask Request/Reply messages? What other protocols can be used for this purpose?

40. If no reply is received for an ICMP Address Mask Request, what should a host do?

41. Decode the following hexadecimal dump. Label the fields of the highest-layer protocol in this packet. Describe what this packet does.

```
 0: 00 00 C0 A2 0F 8E 00 80 C7 2D FD 05 08 00 45 00 ¦.........-....E.
10: 00 30 01 4E 00 00 FF 01 C1 C0 C7 F5 B4 09 C7 F5 ¦.0.N............
20: B4 C9 0D 00 2E FF F6 00 96 00 01 65 98 8D 00 00 ¦...........e....
30: 00 00 00 00 00 00 00 00 00 00 9B 6C 02 A0       ¦...........l..
```

42. Decode the following hexadecimal dump. Label the fields of the highest-layer protocol in this packet. Describe what this packet does.

```
 0: 00 80 C7 2D FD 05 00 00 C0 A2 0F 8E 08 00 45 00 ¦...-..........E.
10: 00 28 00 62 00 00 40 01 81 B5 C7 F5 B4 C9 C7 F5 ¦.(.b..@.........
20: B4 09 0E 00 43 8B F6 00 96 00 01 65 98 8D 02 98 ¦....C......e....
30: 41 A8 02 98 41 A8 6C 74 72 65 65 63             ¦A...A.ltreec
```

43. Decode the following hexadecimal dump. Label the fields of the highest-layer protocol in this packet. Describe what this packet does.

```
 0: 00 80 C7 2D FD 05 00 00 C0 DD 14 5C 08 00 45 00 ¦...-.......\..E.
10: 00 38 20 61 00 00 80 01 22 65 C7 F5 B4 0A C7 F5 ¦.8 a...."e......
20: B4 09 03 01 18 00 00 00 00 00 45 10 00 3C 00 E3 ¦..........E..<..
30: 00 00 40 06 34 C8 C7 F5 B4 09 C8 01 01 01 04 03 ¦..@.4...........
40: 00 17 30 D0 B0 14                               ¦..0...
```

44. Decode the following hexadecimal dump. Label the fields of the highest-layer protocol in this packet. Describe what this packet does.

```
 0: 01 00 5E 00 00 01 00 00 C0 DD 14 5C 08 00 45 00 ¦..^........\..E.
10: 00 24 ED AD 00 00 01 01 70 2A C7 F5 B4 0A E0 00 ¦.$......p*......
20: 00 01 09 00 72 F5 01 02 07 08 C7 F5 B4 0A 00 00 ¦....r...........
30: 00 00 00 00 11 02 00 F0 00 00 99 00             ¦............
```

CHAPTER 9

IP Subnetting and Supernetting

The IPv4 address formats were designed for accommodating networks of different sizes. These address formats worked well in the initial stages of the Internet. As the Internet began to grow in size, however, several weaknesses in the IP address formats became apparent. The primary weakness in the IP address formats was the wasted address space in the design of an internet.

To solve the wasted IP address space problem, the concept of the subnet was designed and formalized in RFC 950, "Internet Standard Subnetting Procedure," in 1985. Subnets enabled the use of a single network number to build several interconnected networks. The network number prefix was shared among the interconnected networks, which are called subnets. *Subnetting* is commonly used in situations where the same network number is used for a number of interconnected networks.

More recently, the concept of supernetting has been introduced under the name of Classless Internet Domain Routing (CIDR). *Supernetting* is the combining of several network numbers into a single logical network number, which you can use to build a much larger network. Supernetting is commonly used in connection with combining several class C addresses to form a logical class that is larger than a class C address, but usually smaller than a class B address in terms of the number of IP nodes that can be connected.

Subnetting

In the IPv4 addressing scheme, a 32-bit number is selected for any IP address. The IP address is divided into the following two parts:

- Network address (also called network identification, network ID net Id, or netid field)
- Host address (also called host identification, host ID, or hostid field)

The network address is common to all hosts within a given network. Typically, the network designer assigns a unique network address to a given network, and the hosts are then assigned values for the host part of the IP address. This setup results in all hosts within the network having a common network address prefix.

The number of bits used in the network address prefix depends on the format of the IP address. For a class A address format, 8 bits are used for the network address, and 24 bits are used for the host address. For a class B address format, 16 bits are used for the network address, and 16 bits are used for the host address. For a class C address format, 24 bits are used for the network address, and 8 bits are used for the host address. The class D address format is used for multicasting, and class E is reserved for future use.

The advantage of using a two-part scheme of network address and host address for IP addresses has the advantage of minimizing the number of entries in a router's routing table. Instead of having a routing table entry for each host on a network, you can now summarize all the hosts in a network by using a single routing table entry. This routing table entry contains only the network address part, which is the common prefix for all hosts on the network. Routers match the common prefix of destination networks in their routing table with the prefix for the destination addresses of the IP datagrams to be routed. A match results in the selection of that particular route for routing the datagram.

The sections that follow explain the subnetting technique, which extends the notion of the common prefix for hosts on a network to permit subdivision of networks.

The Motivation for Subnets

When a router sends a datagram to a network, the router examines only the network part of the datagram's destination IP address. The router does not examine the host part of the destination IP address. This action means that for a class A address, the router examines only the first octet of the IP address; for a class B address, the router examines the first two octets of the IP address; and for a class C address, the router examines only the first three octets of the IP address.

Consider an IP network number of 149.108.0.0, which has 16 bits that are assignable. These 16 bits give a total of 2^{16} possible host number combinations, which is equal to 65,536. Out of 65,536 combinations, you cannot use the pattern consisting of all 1s (ones) because this pattern is reserved for the broadcast address. Also, you cannot use the pattern consisting of all 0s (zeros) for host number assignments because this pattern is reserved for the network itself. Thus, from a total of 65,536 host numbers, you cannot use only two host numbers, which still leaves the possibility of 65,534 hosts (see table 2.12).

Now, consider the example of a class B network, such as that shown in figure 9.1, where the network number 149.108.0.0 (called network 1) connects to the Internet by using a router. All traffic for network number 149.108.0.0 is sent to the router for that network. You can have 65,534 hosts on the network. If the network is to be inside a building, however, it will probably have fewer than 65,534 hosts on the same physical network. Keep in mind that the network does have the capacity to grow up to 65,534 hosts, even though this number may not be practical.

Figure 9.1 A class B network connected to the Internet.

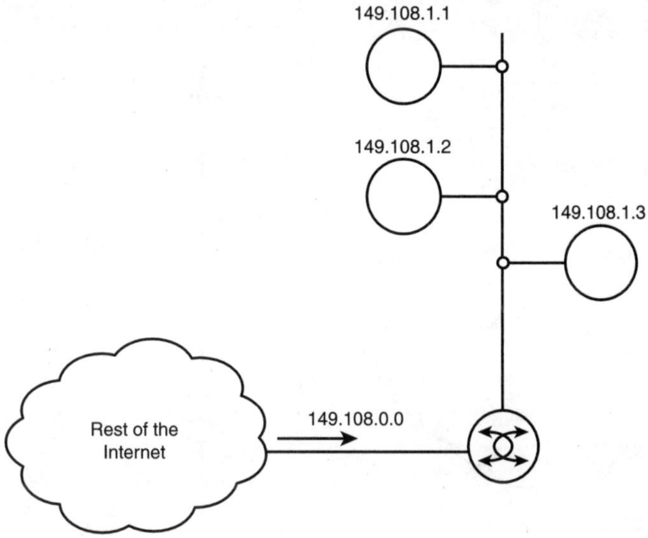

Suppose that the organization decides to build a second network, perhaps in a separate building, and decides to connect this new network to the Internet. What network number should the organization use? If it uses the network number of 149.108.0.0 for the second network, then the IP router cannot distinguish between the two networks by examining the netid field of the IP address for a host on these networks. A different network number assignment that belongs to class A, B, or C could be used, but this involves applying for a new network number assignment, even though there are many *hostid* bit patterns on network 1 that are not in use and may never be used. Indeed, if a different network number were assigned for a second network, it would be a very inefficient use of the IP address allocation space.

A better way is to use some of the bits in the hostid field to distinguish between the two networks and leave the rest for the host number assignments. This scheme is called *subnetting*, and the resulting networks are called *subnets*. The scheme for subnetting has been documented in RFC 950.

Figure 9.2 shows that a second network (network 2) can be connected to the first network and to the rest of the Internet by using the same router that was used in figure 9.1, provided that the router has an extra unused port. In figure 9.2, the first octet of the hostid field is used to distinguish between the two networks. In the hostid field, the bits that are used to distinguish between the two networks are called *subnet numbers*. Therefore, network 1 has been given a subnet number value of 1, and network 2 has been given a subnet number value of 2.

Figure 9.2 A class B network connected to the Internet by using subnets.

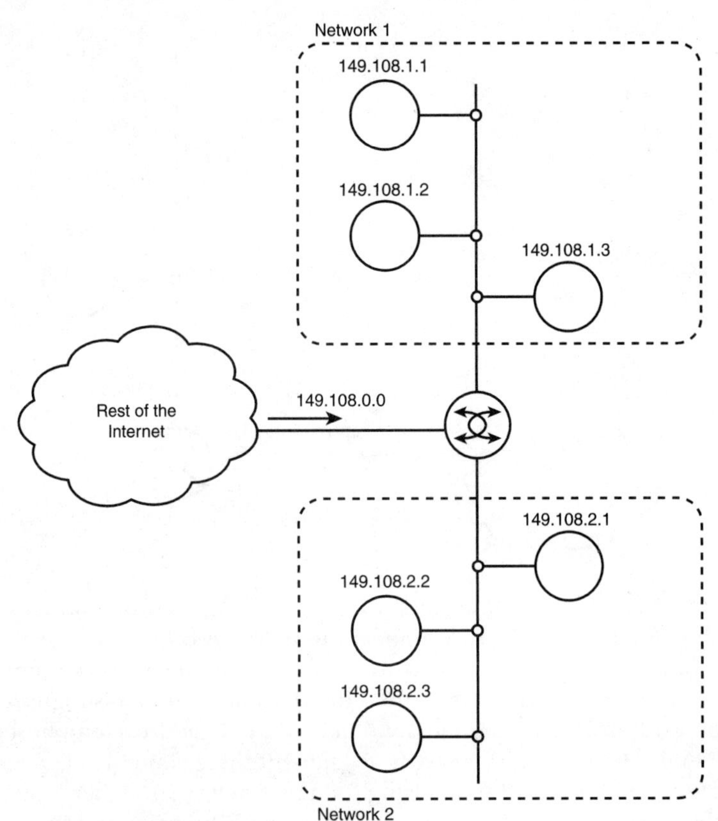

Defining Subnetting and Its Advantages

Subnetting is a scheme that enables you to break a network into smaller networks by using the same network number assignment. The advantages of subnetting (besides, of course, the more efficient use of IP address allocation space) include the following:

- Simplifying administration
- Restructuring an internal network without affecting external networks
- Improving security

Simplified administration results from using routers to partition networks by using logical boundaries. This partitioning often enables the smaller networks to be administered independently and more efficiently. The smaller networks can even be managed by their own independent network administration staff. This arrangement can even avoid or eliminate certain types of political problems among department staffs that may desire to have greater control over their network.

Using subnets enables the network to be structured internally without the rest of the connected network's being aware of changes in the internal network. In figure 9.2, the internal network has been divided into two subnets, but external traffic coming from the internal network is still sent to the network address 149.108.0.0. The router that belongs to the organization must make a further distinction between IP addresses belonging to its subnets. A very important aspect of the "invisibility" of internal networks is that an organization can achieve this internal restructuring without having to obtain an additional network number. With the inter-network running out of network numbers, this capability is a great advantage.

Because the structure of the internal subnetworks is not visible to external networks, use of subnets results in an indirect improvement in network security.

Figure 9.3 shows the relationship among the different fields of an IP address and the subnetworks. If the subnets in figure 9.3 are connected, routers must be used between them. Moreover, the routers must understand that subnetting is being used, and they must understand how many bits of the hostid field are being used for subnets.

Figure 9.3 Subnets and subnet numbers.

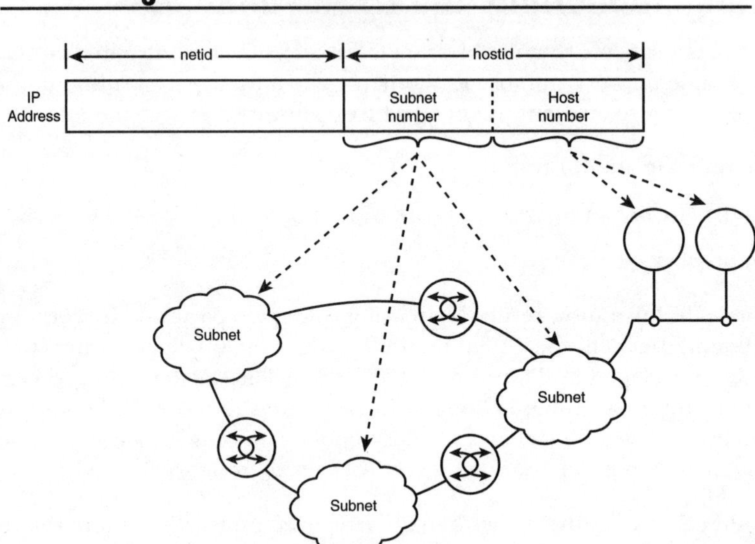

The router in the example of figure 9.3 must be made to understand that the hostid field of the IP address is to be treated in a special way; that is, a part of the field will be used for the subnet number, and the remaining part for the host number. This information is typically represented to the router as the *subnet mask.*

Subnet Mask

The subnet mask is used by routers and hosts on subnets to interpret the hostid field in such a way that the routers and hosts can determine how many bits are being used for subnetting. The subnet mask divides the hostid field into the subnet number and the host number. The subnet mask is a 32-bit number whose value is formed by using the following rules:

- Ones (1s) in the subnet mask correspond to the position of the net ID and the subnet number in the IP address.
- Zeros (0s) in the subnet mask correspond to the position of the host number in the IP address.

Figure 9.4 shows an application of these rules. This figure shows a class B network number that is used for subnetting. Eight bits of the hostid field are being used for the subnet number. The resulting subnet mask is also shown in figure 9.4. The subnet mask is a 32-bit pattern and is conventionally written in a dotted-decimal notation form. Because a group of eight 1s corresponds to a decimal value of 255, the subnet mask of figure 9.4 can be written in the following manner:

255.255.255.0

Figure 9.4 Subnet mask representation. (Courtesy Learning Tree)

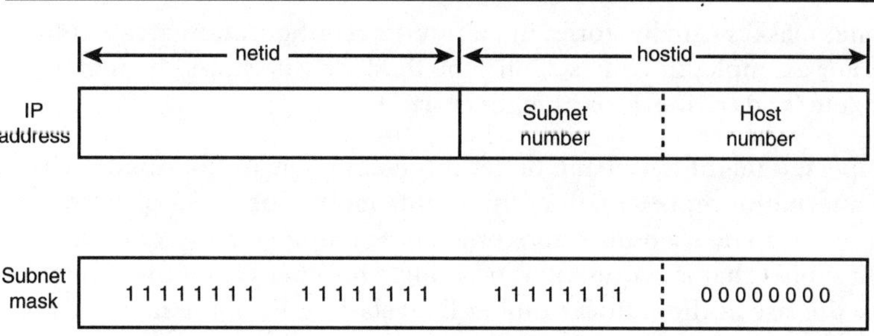
netid
hostid
IP address
Subnet number
Host number
Subnet mask
11111111 11111111 11111111 00000000
1s in the subnet mask correspond to the *netid* and *subnet number* in the IP address
0s in the subnet mask correspond to *host number* in the IP address

If a subnet mask value of 255.255.0.0 is used for a class B address, this value indicates that no subnetting is being used. A class B address has 16 bits of netid field. This netid field is accounted for by the first two 255s (255.255) in the 255.255.0.0 subnet mask value. The remaining value of 0.0 must correspond to the host number. Because no 1s are in the subnet mask for the subnet number field, no subnetting is being used.

If the same subnet mask value of 255.255.0.0 is used for a class A address, the value would indicate that subnetting is being used. A class A address has 8 bits of netid field. This netid field is accounted for by the first 255 in the 255.255.0.0 subnet mask value. The remaining 255 must correspond to the subnet number, which is 8 bits long.

If a subnet mask value of 255.255.255.0 is used for a class C address, the value indicates that no subnetting is being used. A class C address has 24 bits of netid field. This netid field is accounted for by the first three 255s (255.255.255) in the 255.255.255.0 subnet mask value. The remaining value of 0 must correspond to the host number. Because no 1s are in the subnet mask for the subnet number field, no subnetting is being used.

You cannot use a subnet mask value of 255.255.0.0 for a class C address because this value is illegal for subnet masks (you will learn later that this value is legal for creating supernets). A class C address has 24 bits of netid field, but the first two 255s in the 255.255.0.0 value account for only 16 bits of the netid field. You should have at least another 255 to cover the remaining 8 bits of netid field.

The subnet mask value is usually required at the time you specify the IP address for a host or router. The value can be expressed as the dotted-decimal notation value seen in earlier examples. An alternative form used by some TCP/IP software is a hexadecimal pattern or a dotted-hexadecimal notation. Therefore, a subnet mask of 255.255.255.0 can be alternatively expressed in the following ways:

FFFFFF00	(hex pattern)
0xFF.0xFF.0xFF.0xFF.0x00	(a dotted-hexadecimal notation)

A subnet number value (a portion of the hostid field designated for subnetting) of all 0 bits or all 1 bits is not permitted.

The subnet mask is usually stored in an internal configuration area in most operating systems. For example, in Unix systems, the mask may be stored in /etc/rc.local, /etc/netd.cf, /etc/rc.d/rc.inetl, or /etc/netstart files.

In retrospect, it might have been better if the designers of the subnet scheme had used an alternative representation different from the subnet mask to specify the number of bits to be used for subnetting. For example, the designers could have created a subnet that is represented by a single number called the subnet bit. This bit would be the size of the subnet number field starting from the most significant part of the hostid field. In fact, some TCP/IP implementations enable you to specify subnetting in precisely this manner. The TCP/IP software could then figure out the subnet mask values based on this information.

This design may have prevented several generations of network administrators from becoming confused about subnet masks. The problem with subnet masks is that they often require network administrators to work with bit (or hex) patterns that most administrators are unfamiliar with. For a systems programmer working in assembly or C/C++ languages, working with bit patterns is natural and easy, but for ordinary mortals, such as network administrators, it can be a daunting task.

If you are having difficulties grasping subnet masks, do not despair. The basic idea is simple—it is just working with bits that may be unfamiliar. Use the examples in this chapter as practice to further your understanding.

Subnet Masks in RFC Literature

Subnet masks are represented as a "3-tuple" (three components) in the RFC literature:

{<network number>, <subnet number>, <host number>}

A –1 value is used to represent all 1s. For example, the subnet mask of 255.255.255.0 for a class B network is represented as the following:

{–1, –1, 0}

The first –1 corresponds to all 1s for the <network number> value. The second –1 corresponds to all 1s for the <subnet number> value. The last 0 corresponds to all 0s for the <host number> value.

Conversion Between Decimal and Binary Numbers

As you work through the examples of subnet masks and IP addresses that you encounter in real life, you may come across situations where you need to convert between decimal numbers and their binary values. This section is a short tutorial in performing these conversions.

First, you will examine the problem of converting a binary number to a decimal value. You will later learn how to convert a decimal number to its binary form.

Consider an 8-bit binary pattern of 10101000, whose decimal value you need to find out in order to solve an IP address problem. Because IP addresses are typically represented in a dotted-decimal notation, where 8 bits of the IP address are converted to a decimal value, only 8-bit patterns will be discussed in this section.

The binary number of 10101000 uses a base-2 system, just as a decimal number, such as 143, uses a base-10 system. In fact, the word *bit,* which is commonly used to describe a 1 or a 0, is a contraction of the words *bi*nary digi*t*. *Binary* means a value of 2; therefore, bit patterns use a base-2 system, just as decimal numbers use a base-10 system.

In a decimal number such as 143, the 1 represents the 100's position; the 4 represents the 10's position; and the 3 represents the 1's position. The digit 1 represents the 100's position because two digits are to the right of it. These two digits correspond to a magnitude of 10 to the power of 2 (10^2), or 100. Similarly, the digit 4 in the number 143 represents the 10's position because one digit is to the right of it. This digit corresponds to a magnitude of 10 to the power of 1, or 10. Finally, the digit 3 in the number 143 represents the 1's position because no digits are to the right of it. The 0 digit to the right of 4 corresponds to a magnitude of 10 to the power of 0, or 1.

Now consider again the bit pattern of 10101000. The 1 in the leftmost position of this bit pattern has seven bits to the right of it. This 1 must correspond to a magnitude of 2 to the power of 7, or 2^7. The value of 2^7 is 128. You can use table 9.1 to find the decimal value for the powers of 2 up to 8, or you can use a simple mathematical trick to find out the decimal value. 2^7 can be expressed as a product of 2^3, 2^3, and 2, as shown in the following example.

$$
\begin{aligned}
2^7 &= 2^{(3+3+1)} \\
&= 2^3 \times 2^3 \times 2^1 \\
&= 8 \times 8 \times 2 = 128
\end{aligned}
$$

In the preceding equation, the index 7 has been expressed as the sum of 3 + 3 + 1.

The next 1 in the bit pattern of 10101000 has five bits to the right of it. Its magnitude is 2^5, or 32 (see table 9.1). The remaining 1 in the bit pattern of 10101000 has three bits to the right of it. Its magnitude is 2^3, or 8. You can write the bit pattern of 10101000 in the following form:

$$\begin{aligned} 10101000 &= 1 \times 2^7 + 0 \times 2^6 + 1 \times 2^5 + 0 \times 2^4 \\ &+ 1 \times 2^3 + 0 \times 2^2 + 0 \times 2 + 0 \times 1 \\ &= 128 + 32 + 8 \\ &= 168 \end{aligned}$$

TABLE 9.1
Powers of 2 Table

Power of 2	Decimal Value
2^0	1
2^1	2
2^2	4
2^3	8
2^4	16
2^5	32
2^6	64
2^7	128
2^8	256

Now consider the problem of converting the number 145 to a binary 8-bit pattern. One way of performing this conversion is to use entries in table 9.1 and then express 145 as the sum of the powers of 2. You can do this computation as follows:

$$\begin{aligned} 145 &= 128 + 16 + 1 \\ &= 2^7 + 2^4 + 2^0 \end{aligned}$$

From the preceding discussion, 2^7 consists of a binary pattern of 1 with seven 0s after it; 2^4 consists of a binary pattern of 1 with four 0s after it; and 2^0 consists of a binary pattern of 1 with no 0s after it.

$$2^7 = 10000000$$

$$2^4 = 00010000$$

$$2^0 = 00000001$$

Adding up these bit patterns gives the following answer:

145 $= 128 + 16 + 1$
$= 2^7 + 2^4 + 2^0$
= 10010001 (binary pattern)

You can use table 9.1 to perform the conversion of a decimal value to a binary pattern, or you can use an alternative technique, which includes these steps:

1. Divide the number by 2. Call the quotient (whole number) of the division Q, and call the remainder R.
2. Place the remainder R in the binary pattern. The placement of the remainder (0 or 1 because you are dividing by 2) starts with the rightmost position and gradually works its way to the left.
3. Use the quotient Q as the number to divide in Step 1. Repeat this process until the quotient becomes a zero.

You can apply these rules of conversion to convert 145 to a binary pattern as follows:

Round 1:

Divide 145 by 2.

Quotient is 72.

Remainder is 1.

Bit pattern is 1.

Round 2:

Divide 72 by 2.

Quotient is 36.

Remainder is 0.

Bit pattern is 01.

Round 3:

Divide 36 by 2.

Quotient is 18.

Remainder is 0.

Bit pattern is 001.

Round 4:

Divide 18 by 2.

Quotient is 9.

Remainder is 0.

Bit pattern is 0001.

Round 5:

Divide 9 by 2.

Quotient is 4.

Remainder is 1.

Bit pattern is 10001.

Round 6:

Divide 4 by 2.

Quotient is 2.

Remainder is 0.

Bit pattern is 010001.

Round 7:

Divide 2 by 2.

Quotient is 1.

Remainder is 0.

Bit pattern is 0010001.

Round 8:

Divide 1 by 2.

Quotient is 0 (stop the algorithm).

Remainder is 1.

Bit pattern is 10010001.

Because the quotient is a 0, you stop the conversion. The resulting bit pattern of 10010001 is the answer you want.

Now, practice converting 11001001 and 11110000 to their decimal values. Verify your answer by converting the decimal values back to their binary pattern.

Also, practice converting 212 and 254 to their 8-bit binary values. Verify your answer by converting the binary values back to their decimal values.

The following sections present several examples that will help you understand the use of subnets.

Subnet Example Problem: Using a Class B Address with a Subnet Mask on a Byte Boundary

Use these IP address and subnet mask values as givens for the question that follows:

IP address = 128.12.34.71

Subnet mask = 255.255.255.0

What is the value of the following?

Subnet number = ?

Host number = ?

Directed broadcast address = ?

On examining the subnet mask of 255.255.255.0, you can see that the division of 1s and 0s in the subnet mask falls on a byte boundary. The byte boundary simplifies the calculation.

The IP address 128.12.34.71 is a class B address because 128 is between 128 and 191 (see table 9.1). The first two 255s of the subnet mask of 255.255.255.0 correspond to the 16 bits of a class B's netid field. The remaining 255 must then correspond to the subnet number on the IP address. Therefore, the subnet number is 34, which is expressed in dotted-decimal notation as follows:

Subnet number = 0.0.34.0

The 0 in the subnet mask of 255.255.255.0 corresponds to the host number. The host number in the IP address must be 71, which is expressed in dotted-decimal notation as follows:

Host number = 0.0.0.71

The directed broadcast for the network must have all 1s in the host number field. Therefore, the last byte of the subnet must have all 1s, which is expressed in dotted-decimal notation as follows:

Directed broadcast address = 128.12.34.255

Subnet Example Problem: Using a Class C Address with a Subnet Mask on a Non-Byte Boundary

Use these IP address and subnet mask values as givens for the question that follows:

IP address = 192.55.12.120

Subnet mask = 255.255.255.240

What are the values of the following?

Subnet number = ?

Host number = ?

Directed broadcast address = ?

On examining the subnet mask of 255.255.255.240, you can see that the division of 1s and 0s in the subnet mask is in the last byte on a bit boundary. The bit boundary complicates the calculation. As an aid to computing the desired values, the bit patterns for the various values to be computed are also shown in figure 9.5.

Figure 9.5 Subnet example solution. (Courtesy Learning Tree)

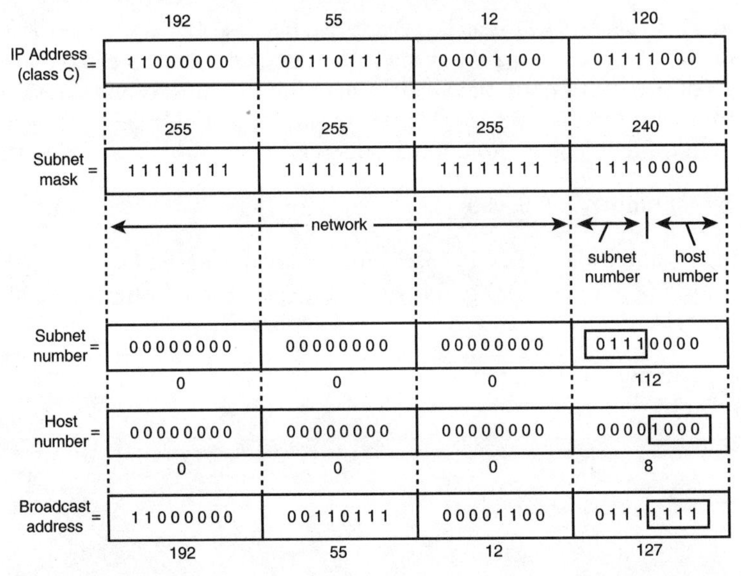

	192	55	12	120
IP Address (class C) =	11000000	00110111	00001100	01111000
	255	255	255	240
Subnet mask =	11111111	11111111	11111111	11110000
	← network →			subnet number / host number
Subnet number =	00000000	00000000	00000000	0111 0000
	0	0	0	112
Host number =	00000000	00000000	00000000	0000 1000
	0	0	0	8
Broadcast address =	11000000	00110111	00001100	0111 1111
	192	55	12	127

The IP address 192.55.12.120 is a class C address because 192 is between 192 and 223 (see table 9.1). The first three 255s of the subnet mask of 255.255.255.240 correspond to the 24 bits of a class C netid field. The remaining 240 must therefore correspond to the subnet number on the IP address. The decimal value of 240 has a bit pattern of 1110000. The following is the subnet mask represented as a bit pattern:

11111111 11111111 11111111 11110000

The last four 1s correspond to the subnet number field in the IP address. The following is the bit pattern representation of the IP address with the subnet field highlighted in bold:

11000000 00110111 00001100 **0111**1000

The subnet number field bit pattern of 0111 has a decimal value of 7, but this value is part of the last 8-bit value of the IP address. This subnet number expressed as a bit pattern is as follows:

00000000 00000000 00000000 01110000

This subnet number expressed in dotted-decimal notation is as follows:

Subnet number = 0.0.0.112

The 0 in the subnet mask of 255.255.255.240 corresponds to the host number. The host number in the IP address is shown in bold in the following IP address pattern:

11000000 00110111 00001100 0111**1000**

This host number expressed as a bit pattern is as follows:

00000000 00000000 00000000 00001000

This host number expressed in dotted-decimal notation is as follows:

Subnet number = 0.0.0.8

The directed broadcast for the network must have all 1s in the host number field. Therefore the last four bits of the subnet must have all 1s.

This directed broadcast address expressed as a bit pattern is as follows:

11000000 00110111 00001100 0111**1111**

The bold 1s represent the 1s used in the host number fields that form the directed broadcast address. This directed broadcast address expressed in dotted-decimal notation is as follows:

Directed broadcast address = 192.55.12.127

Non-Byte Boundary Subnet Masks

The preceding example used a subnet mask of 255.255.255.240. The last decimal number 240 translated into a bit pattern of 11110000. In general, you should know the bit pattern representations when a subnet number field of 1 to 7 bits is used. Table 9.2 shows the decimal subnet size and the decimal values in the subnet mask. The table assumes that the subnet number bits are all *contiguous* (grouped together without any gaps), and this scenario is normally true for most real-world networks. The RFCs, however, do not prohibit the subnet numbers from being noncontiguous; in other words, you can actually have a subnet mask where the subnet number bits and host number bits can alternate. For example, you can have the following subnet mask for a class B address:

11111111 11111111 **10110101 00001111**

or

255.255.171.15

In this subnet mask, you can see nine subnet number bits (bold in the bit pattern), but they are interspersed with the host number bits. Even though RFC 950 may allow such monstrosities, most TCP/IP software will not function with noncontiguous subnet number bits. No useful purpose is served in using such subnet masks except to confound future network administrators.

TABLE 9.2
Subnet Size and Decimal Values

Subnet Size (Bits)	Bit Pattern	Decimal value
1	10000000	128
2	11000000	192
3	11100000	224
4	11110000	240
5	11111000	248

Subnet Size (Bits)	Bit Pattern	Decimal value
6	**11111100**	**252**
7	11111110	254

Wasted Address Space with a Single Subnet Mask

Using a single subnet mask can result in wasted address space for a network when the subnets do not support the same number of nodes on a network. A classic example of this scenario is the separation of two subnets by a point-to-point link, as shown in figure 9.6.

Figure 9.6 Subnets separated by point-to-point link.

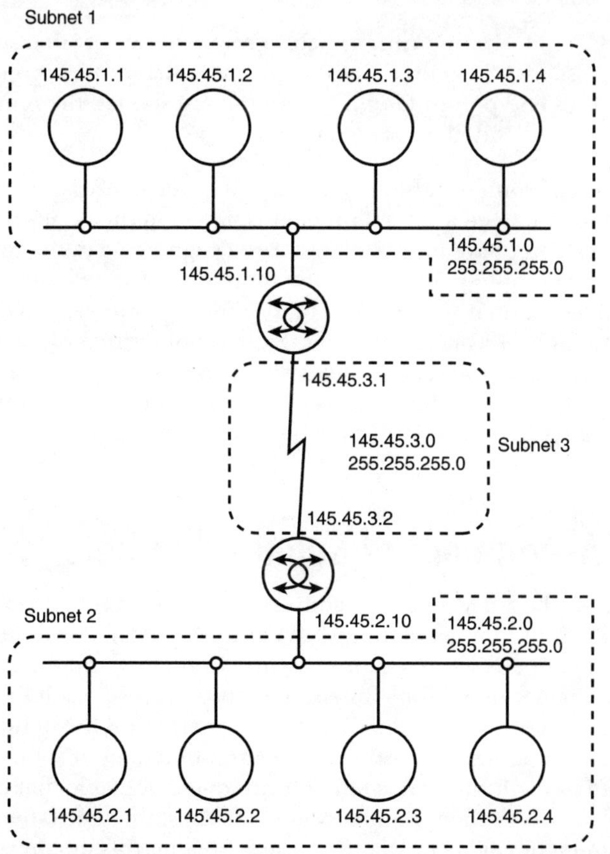

This figure shows a subnet mask of 255.255.255.0 being used for the class B network number that is divided into the following three subnets:

Subnet 1:	145.45.1.0
Subnet 2:	145.45.2.0
Subnet 3:	145.45.3.0

You may be surprised to learn that subnet 2 has been assigned to a point-to-point link that needs only two IP addresses assigned to its points. Unless a router uses special internal methods to recognize this point-to-point link, a unique network identification needs to be assigned to this subnet so that the routers can send datagrams through this point-to-point link.

Each of the subnetworks can support up to 254 hosts. These are the 2^8 hosts that are represented by the 8 bits, minus all the 0s and all the 1s (patterns for the hostid field) that are not to be assigned to hosts.

Subnets 1 and 2 are LANs and can probably grow to a capacity that supports 254 hosts. However, subnet 3 is a point-to-point network that can have only two IP address assignments for its end points. On this point-to-point subnet, the remaining 252 addresses are unused and, therefore, wasted.

Several commercial routers have internal logic that recognizes this point-to-point link. These routers do not need a subnet number assigned to the point-to-point link, which means that you do not have to make IP address assignments to the router ports connected to the point-to-point links. This approach conserves subnet numbers and IP addresses that can then be used for other subnets. However, one disadvantage of not having IP addresses assigned to point-to-point links is that you cannot use such utilities as PING to perform reachability tests on the router ports connected to the point-to-point links. This problem exists because the router ports connected to the point-to-point links cannot be identified by using an IP address if no IP address is assigned to them.

Efficient Assignment of Subnet Numbers

In subnetting, the host part of the IP address is subdivided into two fields: the subnet number and the host number. This division gives the IP address a third level of hierarchy. Although this setup results in savings in routing and the reuse of a common network number prefix for subnets, the setup can also result in inefficiency in the allocation of addresses. The inefficiency originates with the network administrator, who selects a subnet size to estimate the largest number of subnets and hosts that may be needed in the future. However, a technique is available that enables an administrator to select subnet number values and host number values in order to provide maximum flexibility in changing the subnet mask—should you need to do so in the future—with a minimum impact on changing IP address assignments at each host in the subnets.

To get an intuitive understanding of this technique, consider figure 9.7, in which the dotted line shows the boundary between the host number and the subnet number. This boundary is labeled as the *subnet mask boundary*. To the left of this boundary, the subnet mask consists of 1s; and to the right of this boundary, the mask consists of 0s. If the subnet number and host number assignment is selected so that zeros are near the subnet mask boundary, then moving the subnet mask boundary to the left or right will not alter the subnet and host number assignment; only the subnet mask will change. In fact, the subnet boundary mask can be moved as far left or as far right as possible, without changing the subnet and host number, until a value of 1 is encountered in the subnet or host number. Therefore, subnet numbers should be assigned with 1s in their leftmost position, and host numbers should be assigned with 1s in their rightmost position. The central region should be filled with zeros as far as possible.

Figure 9.7 Efficient subnet mask assignment.

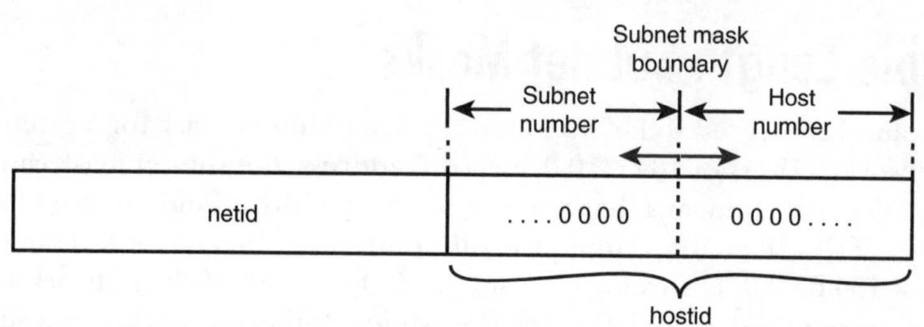

This assignment of subnet and host numbers is called *mirror image counting* because the subnet numbers and host numbers are like mirror images of each other.

Consider the following bit patterns for subnet number and host number assignment:

Subnet number assignment:

```
0      (reserved to mean "this subnet")
10
01
110
001
101
 :
 :
011...11
111...11    (reserved to mean "all subnets")
```

Host number assignment:

```
        0    (reserved to mean "this host")
       01
       10
      011
      100
      101
        :
        :
  11...1110
  11...1111    (reserved to mean "all hosts")
```

The technique on flexibility in assigning subnet numbers is described in detail in RFC 1219 on "On the Assignment of Subnet Numbers."

Variable Length Subnet Masks

In the examples covered so far, you used the same subnet mask for a given network. For a network address of 134.65.0.0, a class B address, the subnet mask can be 255.255.255.0, which means that 8 bits of the host address field are used for subnetting. TCP/IP enables you to use different subnet masks for the same network address of 134.65.0.0. For example, a subdivided network of the network 134.65.0.0 can use a subnet mask of 255.255.255.192, while another network uses a subnet mask of 255.255.255.0. When different subnet masks are used, restrictions exist about what combinations of host IP addresses and subnet masks you can use.

Suppose that you want to divide a class C network 216.144.108.0 into three subnets with a maximum of 120 hosts on one subnet and a maximum of 60 hosts each on the other two subnets. What subnet mask can you use? The total number of hosts on the three subnets is 120 + 60 + 60 = 240 hosts. You can have 254 hosts in a class C network. This number is computed as 256 – 2 = 254; you subtract 2 for the reserved addresses of all 0s and all 1s. It is possible to have 240 hosts on a class C network. But when you decide to use a single subnet mask, you must accommodate the largest subnet possible, which, in this case, is the subnet with 120 hosts. You can have only one subnet mask for such a subnet:

11111111 11111111 11111111 **1 0000000**

255.255.255.128

The subnet number is the **1** in bold, and the host number is the seven zeros in bold, **0000000**. With seven host bits, two subnets are possible, each with a size of $2^7 - 2 = 126$ hosts. This type of subnet division can accommodate the subnet with 120 hosts, and it can accommodate one other subnet with 60 hosts; but it cannot accommodate the remaining 60 host subnets. This situation exists because three subnets are needed and only two subnets are available. Actually, if you examine the subnet mask of 255.255.255.128, this is not legal as per the RFCs, even though many commercial routers will permit this subnet. 255.255.255.128 is illegal for a class C network because the subnet number is 0 or 1—that is, all 0s or all 1s. All 0s and all 1s are not permitted for subnet numbers. As pointed out earlier, however, many commercial routers permit this subnet mask.

Suppose that you use two bits for the subnet number, which then permits $2^2 = 4$ subnets. The subnet mask then becomes the following:

11111111 11111111 11111111 **11 000000**

255.255.255.192

The subnet number is the **11** in bold, and the host number is the six zeros in bold, **000000**. With six host bits, you can have four possible subnets, each with a size of $2^6 - 2 = 62$ hosts. This type of subnet division can accommodate the two subnets with 60 hosts each. But this subdivision cannot accommodate the remaining subnet with 120 hosts. This situation exists because the subnet mask of 255.255.255.192 can accommodate only 62 hosts, which is much less than the desired 120 hosts on the subnet.

The preceding example shows that a single subnet mask cannot be used for the class C network in some situations. What is needed is a way of dividing the class C network into subnets with 126 hosts and then further dividing one of these subnets into two subnets of $2^6 - 2 = 62$ hosts each. This technique is called *Variable Subnet Length Mask (VLSM)* and is discussed in RFC 1878 on "Variable Length Subnet Table For Ipv4."

Figure 9.8 shows an example of how you can use variable length subnet masks. In this example, you use the subnet mask 255.255.255.128 to divide the class C network into two subnets of 126 hosts each. Then you use the subnet mask 255.255.255.192 to divide one of the subnets into two subnets with 62 hosts each.

Figure 9.8 VLSM subnet mask example.

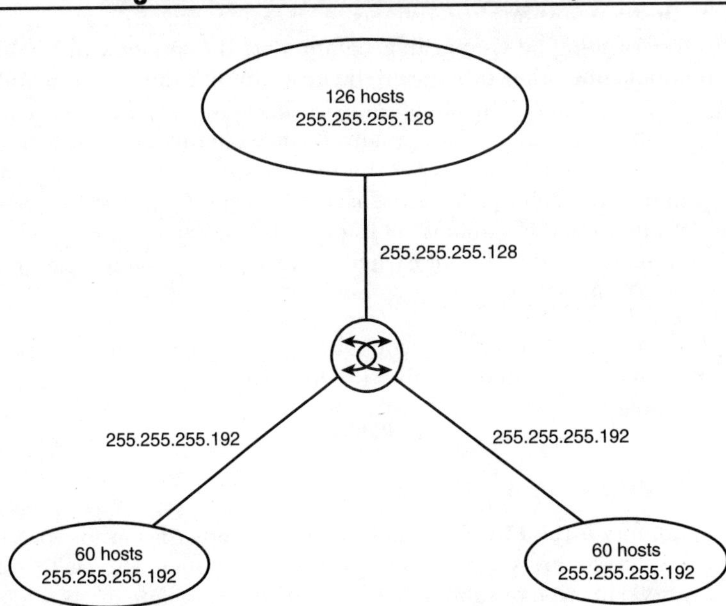

For your reference, table 9.3 lists the number of hosts and subnets provided by commercial routers. Note that the Number of Subnets column includes the all 0s and all 1s combination, which is prohibited by RFCs but permitted by many commercial routers.

TABLE 9.3
Capacity of Subnets for Class C Networks Permitted by Commercial Routers

Subnet Mask	Number of Subnets	Number of Hosts
255.255.255.128	2	126
255.255.255.192	4	62
255.255.255.224	8	30
255.255.255.240	16	14
255.255.255.248	32	6
255.255.255.252	64	2

Not all routing protocols can handle all the different subnet masks that are used in a network. For example, the RIP (Routing Information Protocol) version 1 routing protocol does not handle a mix of different subnet masks for the same network address, and RIP cannot be used in conjunction with variable subnet masks. If you were to use RIP with variable subnet masks, the network topology reported by RIP would not accurately reflect the network topology that you have set up. This is because the RIP packet format does not include a field to communicate subnet masks to other routers. On the other hand, such routing protocols as OSPF (Open Shortest Path First), RIP version 2, ISIS (Intermediate System-to-Intermediate System) enable routers to exchange subnet mask information for the interconnected networks and can be used to support a mix of different subnet masks. However, despite the use of these protocols, VLSM is not as widely used for the following reasons:

- IP address assignments for subnets need to be grouped into blocks indicated by the VLSMs. Older IP address assignments need to be changed, and making this change is not always easy.
- Some older networks are using RIP version 1, which cannot support VLSM. You should use a more modern protocol that enables subnet mask information to be exchanged.
- The VLSM technique is not well understood by network administrators. Many administrators have difficulty coping with subnet masks and subnetting. Better training and books, such as this one, will hopefully address this problem.

Routing for Subnets

Chapter 7, "IP Routing Concepts," discussed the IP routing algorithm that is used by routers and hosts. However, this routing algorithm did not take into account subnet masks. The basic information in a routing table (not taking subnet masks into account) consists of the following entries:

(destination address, next-hop address)

The *destination address* is a network address or host address that is specified in the routing table as an explicit route. The *next-hop address* is not the complete path to reach the destination, but it is the next router (neighbor router) to whom the datagram should be forwarded. The *next-hop address* is always on the directly connected network. By definition, you cannot have any additional routers between the host/router under consideration and the *next-hop address* router.

The following sections illustrate the use of subnet masks in routing tables.

Use of Subnet Masks in the Routing Table

The IP routing algorithm in Chapter 7 compares the network portion of the destination address in the IP datagram with the destination address in the routing table entry. If a match is found, the next-hop address is selected for forwarding the datagram. If no match is found, a comparison is made with the next routing table entry. The default entry (destination address 0.0.0.0) is considered to match all destination addresses, and it is selected if no other destination address matches. How does this routing algorithm know how to determine the network portion of an IP address? By looking at the most significant bits of the destination IP address to determine the format of the IP address: class A, B, C, or D (multicast).

When subnets are used, you cannot determine the network portion of an IP address just by its address format. For example, the IP address format may be class B with the first two octets used for the network identifier. But if a subnet mask of 255.255.255.0 is used, the routing algorithm must use the third octet as well for determining the network portion. The routing table that takes subnets into account must, therefore, have an additional entry in each routing table entry for subnet masks, as shown in the following example:

(destination address, subnet mask, next-hop address)

When subnets are in use, the routing algorithm must use the subnet mask listed in the routing table entry to extract the network portion. The algorithm does this by using a bitwise AND operation, using the destination address in the IP datagram and the subnet mask entry. Then the algorithm checks to see whether this result matches the destination address entry in the routing table entry. If a match is found, the corresponding next-hop address is used to route the datagram. If no match is found, the next routing table entry is tried. The bitwise AND operation to extract the network portion can be described by using the following equation:

Extracted network portion = *destination IP address*
bitwise AND
subnet mask

As an example of the application of this operation, consider the following routing table entry:

(144.19.74.0, 255.255.255.0, 144.19.74.91)

Consider two datagrams with the following destination IP addresses:

144.19.74.12

144.19.75.21

The network portion of theses IP addresses can be computed as follows:

Extracted network
portion of 144.19.74.12 = 144.19.74.12
bitwise AND
255.255.255.0
= 144.19.74.0

Extracted network
portion of 144.19.75.21 = 144.19.75.21
bitwise AND
255.255.255.0
= 144.19.75.0

When the network portion is compared with the routing table entry, a match occurs for 144.19.74.12. No match is found for 144.19.75.12.

The example of the routing table entry contains a network destination address of 144.19.74.0. How are host-specific addresses and default routes represented by using subnet masks? Host-specific routes have a subnet mask of 255.255.255.255 (all 1s) in their routing table entry, and default routes have a subnet mask of 0.0.0.0 (all 0s). As you examine the use of the subnet mask in the preceding example, you will notice that the presence of a 1 in the subnet mask means that the corresponding bit in the destination IP address is significant for routing purposes. A 0 in the subnet mask means that the corresponding bit in the destination IP address is *not* significant for routing purposes. All 1s (255.255.255.255) in the subnet mask means that all bits in the destination address are used, and this example represents a host-specific route. All 0s (0.0.0.0) in the subnet mask means that no bits in the destination address are used, and a match will occur for any destination IP address. Consider the following routing table that contains host specific and default routes:

Destination	Subnet Mask	Next-Hop Address
144.19.74.0	255.255.255.0	144.19.74.91
145.12.2.101	255.255.255.255	144.19.74.92
202.33.23.3	255.255.255.255	144.19.74.93
0.0.0.0	0.0.0.0	144.19.74.91
0.0.0.0	0.0.0.0	144.19.74.94

There are two host-specific routes for the destination addresses 145.12.2.101 and 202.33.23.3. You can recognize these addresses by the presence of the subnet mask of 255.255.255.255 in the routing table entry. Similarly, there are two default routes that point to next-hop address routers 144.19.74.91 and 144.19.74.94.

Consider an IP datagram with a destination address of 202.33.23.3. When you use the preceding routing table, the extracted network portion used for the third routing table entry is as follows:

Extracted network portion of 202.33.23.3	= 202.33.23.3
	bitwise AND
	255.255.255.255
	= 202.33.23.3

The value of 202.33.23.3 results in a match with the third routing table entry:

(202.33.23.3, 255.255.255.255, 144.19.74.93)

Consider another IP datagram with a destination address of 201.3.3.3. When you use the preceding routing table, no match is found until the first default route is considered. The extracted network portion used for the first default route is as follows:

Extracted network portion of 201.3.3.3	= 201.3.3.3
	bitwise AND
	0.0.0.0
	= 0.0.0.0

The value of 0.0.0.0 results in a match with the first default route, as follows:

(0.0.0.0, 0.0.0.0, 144.19.74.91)

Because of the 0.0.0.0 mask value, the bitwise AND operation with this mask value will always result in a 0.0.0.0 value, which matches the destination value of 0.0.0.0.

If you always have a match with the first default route, what is the value of having a second default route that will never be selected? The answer is that you can select the second default route if the first default route is down. In many commercial routers, the network administrator can specify a down value for a particular router port. This down value can disable routes in the routing table. Other techniques—such as the judicious use of the ICMP echo/reply packets and communication with the Transport layer protocol at a host—can also determine whether a particular route is down.

If the first default route is down, the routing logic at the host/router can then select the other default routes. Although RFC 1122 on "Requirements for Internet Hosts—Communication Layers" suggests the use of several default routes, many TCP/IP implementations provide the use of only one default route.

The Complete IP Routing Algorithm Taking into Account Subnets

The IP routing algorithm that takes subnets into account is described by the following steps:

1. Go to DestIPAddr, the destination address field, of the IP datagram. From the DestIPAddr field, determine the network portion NetPrefix by doing a bitwise AND with the subnet mask listed in the routing table entry.
2. If NetPrefix matches the net ID of any directly connected network, the destination host is on the directly connected network. In this case, perform direct delivery of the IP datagram. Direct delivery may involve binding DestIPAddr to its physical address by using a protocol such as ARP. The IP datagram is encapsulated by the Data Link layer frame and sent on the directly attached network.
3. If you have no match in Step 2, examine the routing table for a destination entry for NetPrefix. If you find such an entry, forward the IP datagram as indicated by the corresponding next-hop router entry.
4. If you have no match in Step 3, examine the routing table for a default entry, 0.0.0.0. If you find such an entry, forward the IP datagram as indicated by the corresponding default router entry.
5. If you have no match in Step 4, the IP datagram cannot be routed. Report a routing error to the upper layer protocols.

Other Subnetting Techniques

Prior to 1985, the subnetting technique described in this chapter was not in use. Subnetting was introduced to avoid the depletion of network numbers because of inefficient address allocation caused by using strictly the class A, B, and C address formats.

After subnetting was introduced in 1985, it became a requirement for all new TCP/IP implementations. Older TCP/IP software, however, continued to exist and did not incorporate subnetting. The technique of proxy ARP was introduced to handle the coexistence of subnets with older style networks that did not understand subnets. Another technique called transparent routing was used to extend an address, such as a class A address, beyond a router boundary. These techniques are discussed in the next sections.

Proxy ARP

Proxy ARP is used in broadcast networks to enable the coexistence of hosts that do not understand subnets with other hosts that do understand subnets. Figure 9.9 illustrates the use of this technique for a network consisting of two subnets:

Subnet 1:

network = 144.19.74.0

net mask = 255.255.255.0

Subnet 2:

network = 144.19.75.0

net mask = 255.255.255.0

Figure 9.9 Proxy ARP example.

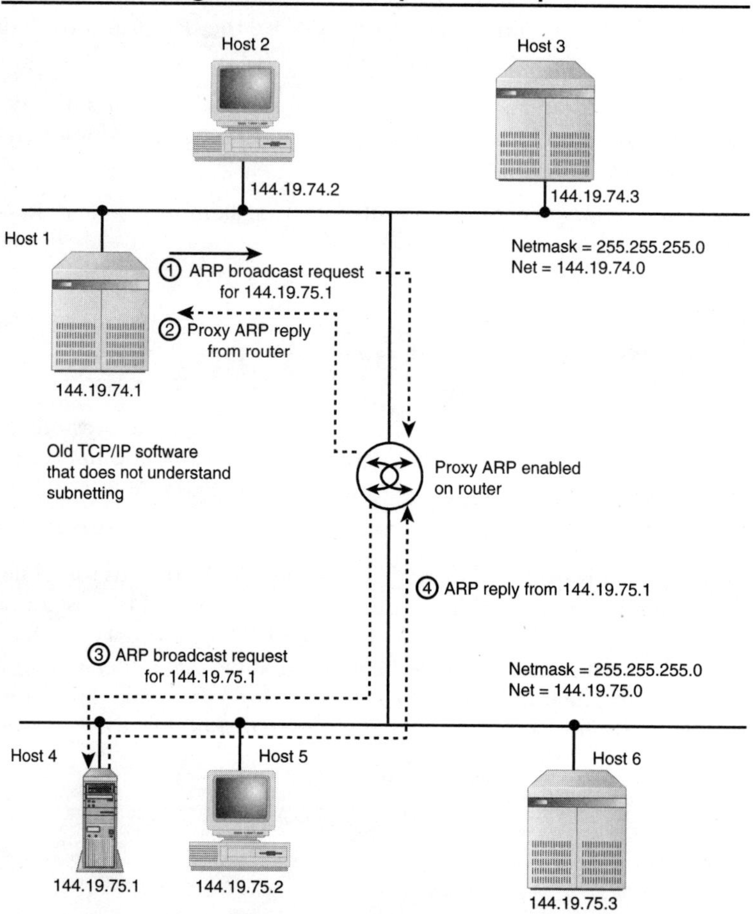

In this figure, host 1 at 144.19.74.1 wants to communicate with host 4 at 144.19.75.1. These hosts are on two separate networks. If host 1 is using TCP/IP software that understands subnets, the host routing logic at host 1 can detect that host 4 is on a separate network and forward the datagrams for host 4 to the router. In this example, however, you can assume that host 1 is using older TCP/IP software that does not understand subnets. Such a host assumes that the directly connected network is 144.19.0.0 and has the subnet mask of 255.255.0.0.

If a datagram needs to be sent to 144.19.75.1, the host assumes that this destination host is on the directly connected network 144.19.0.0. Because this is a broadcast network, it sends an ARP broadcast request to 144.19.75.1 for its hardware address. Host 144.19.75.1 is on a different network across a router boundary. Recall that Data Link layer broadcasts, such as the one used by the ARP request, do not cross router boundaries, so the ARP request does not reach the host at 144.19.75.1. Therefore, host 144.19.75.1 does not reply to the ARP request, and host 1 will time out waiting for an ARP reply, unless the router is configured to use proxy ARP.

If the router is enabled to use proxy ARP, it detects that host 1 is asking for the hardware address of a node that is on the other subnet. The router responds to the ARP request with its hardware address: that is, the hardware address of the router port on network 144.19.74.0. Host 1 assumes that the ARP reply is returned from host 144.19.75.1 and is unaware that the ARP reply contains the hardware address of the router port. Host 1 sends all datagrams to 144.19.75.1 to the router port. The router knows that the datagram is to be sent to the directly connected network 144.19.75.0. The router accepts these datagrams and forwards them to the host at 144.19.75.1 on the network 144.19.75.0.

Note that if the network 144.19.75.0 is a broadcast network, the router performs a normal ARP binding to discover the hardware address of 144.19.75.1 before forwarding the datagram to 144.19.75.1.

The proxy ARP software running on the router returns a proxy ARP reply for all hosts that are not aware of subnets. In the example in figure 9.9, if all the hosts are running TCP/IP software that is not aware of subnets, the proxy ARP service will be used for all datagrams that need to be sent to the other subnet.

From the preceding discussion, you may have noticed that the router replies with its hardware address for a number of hosts on the other subnet. This means that the ARP cache tables of hosts that do not understand subnetting will be populated with several entries for IP addresses that map to the same hardware address (the router port address). Some ARP implementations may not complain about this situation; whereas, others may suspect that a host—in this case, the router—is attempting to masquerade as several other nodes by changing its IP address. This situation may lead to a legitimate security risk called *spoofing*, where a host that comes online tries to masquerade as another host. ARP software that is designed to alert the network administrator about spoofing will send an alert message when it finds several ARP cache entries that are using the same hardware address. If proxy ARP is being used, it results in frequent warning messages about spoofing from hosts that meet the following conditions:

- If the host uses old TCP/IP software that does not understand subnets
- If the host's ARP implementation warns about spoofing
- If the host is sending datagrams to more than one node that is on the other subnet

Proxy ARP assumes that the networks that are to be connected use ARP to resolve the binding between IP addresses and hardware addresses; therefore, the networks must be broadcast networks. If multiple routers are connected to the same network, only one router should be configured with proxy ARP software. Why? Because if more than one router responds to an ARP request for an IP address, you have a situation similar to that of duplicate IP addresses, where two nodes with the same IP address respond to an ARP request that contains the IP address.

Proxy ARP is also called the *ARP hack* or *promiscuous ARP* and is described in RFC 1027, "Using ARP to Implement Transparent Subnet Gateways."

Transparent Routers

Using transparent routers is a technique that has evolved from the original ARPANET, where a class A address is extended beyond a router, as illustrated in figure 9.10.

In figure 9.10, the transparent router makes the hosts on the LAN appear as if they were hosts connected to the WAN. Hosts sending datagrams to the hosts on the WAN do not know of the existence of the transparent router. As its name implies, the transparent router connects the LAN and the WAN transparently, as if they were part of the same network. Both the WAN and the LAN share the same network prefix. In some ways, this situation is similar to the subnet scheme, where the subnets share the same net ID but have different subnet numbers.

The transparent router can use a table of addresses for the hosts on the LAN to determine which host on the LAN should receive the datagram.

Figure 9.10 Using a transparent router.

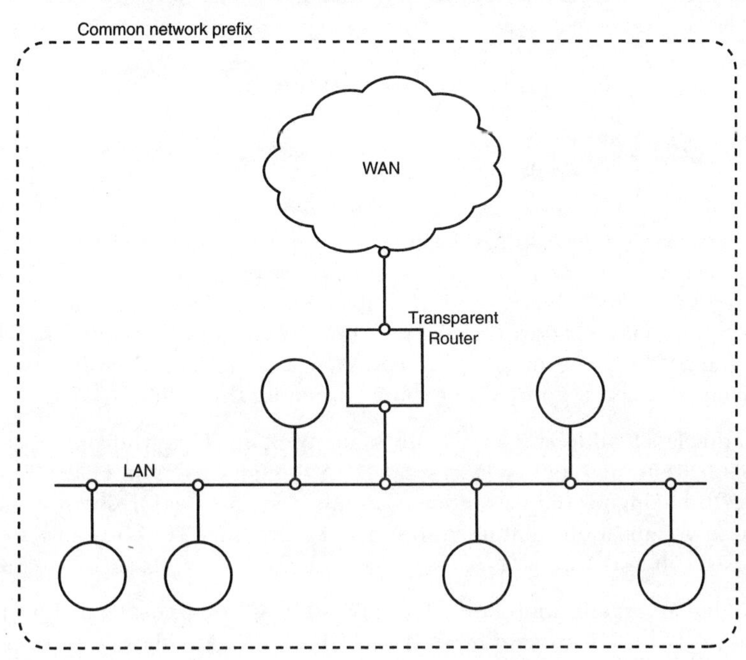

In regard to the ARPANET, the transparent routers use parts of the IP address to encode the information for demultiplexing the datagram to the appropriate host. The ARPANET uses a class A network address of 10.0.0.0. An address on this network is interpreted as follows:

10.P.U.I

The 10 refers to the network address—in this case, the class A address assigned to the ARPANET. The *P* refers to the port number on the destination packet switch node (PSN), designated by *I,* the last octet. Octet *U* is not interpreted by PSNs but is interpreted by transparent routers to determine which host on the LAN should receive the datagram.

For example, consider the IP addresses 10.4.1.40 and 10.4.2.40. Both addresses refer to PSN 40. Both addresses also refer to port number 4 on the PSN. A transparent router can be connected to this port. The third octet, *U,* is used by the transparent router to decide which host should receive the datagram.

Because transparent routers are "transparent they cannot host services that can be accessed as they are in a conventional router. Why? Because transparent routers do not have an IP address that can be used to access these services. For example, conventional routers can provide services for network management protocols such as SNMP.

These routers can also provide services for remote login by using TELNET and for diagnostic capability that can be accessed by ICMP. These services are not provided by transparent routers because you have no easy way of accessing them from a remote location.

Supernetting

The subnetting technique was devised in 1985 to make efficient use of IP address allocation for large networks. Subnetting works quite well for networks with large address space, such as class A and class B, but these network address formats are very popular and are rapidly being used up. Subnetting can also be used for class C addresses, but a class C address can support only 254 hosts. In many networks, subdividing a class C network may not be practical, especially when the number of hosts that need to be supported per subnet are more than 126.

Class A and class B addresses are rapidly being used up. This syndrome is called ROADS, for Running Out of ADdress Space. Although class A and class B network addresses are being used up, a sufficient number of class C addresses are still available. Large organizations that need to support more than 245 hosts have to use several class C network addresses.

Suppose that an organization needs a class B address to support 65,534 hosts. If a class B address is not forthcoming from the NIC, how many class C addresses would you need to support 65,534 hosts? The answer is about 256. These 256 class C addresses can be assigned as a block. For example, the following class C address range supports the same number of addresses as a single class B address:

202.100.0.0 to 202.100.255.255

If you examine the range of bits that can vary in this class C address, you will see that there are 16 lower-order bits, the same number as you need for a class B address.

In supernetting or supernet addressing, a block of class C addresses is assigned rather than a single class B network address to create a virtual address class that is somewhere between a class C and a class B address class. This setup has the advantage of better address utilization. For example, if an organization needs to have a network of 8,000 hosts, it is better to assign a block of 32 class C addresses rather than a single class B address. A class B address can support up to 65,534 hosts; but in this example, 65,534 – 8,000 = 57,535 addresses are not utilized.

The supernetting technique is designed to be used by inter-network service providers (ISPs) for Internet connectivity. Typically, only ISPs are allowed to obtain large address blocks of class C addresses. ISPs can then allocate smaller blocks of these class C addresses to other organizations that want to connect a large number of their computers to the Internet. Many commercial organizations that have been assigned class C address blocks use supernetting as well. Supernetting also reduces the size of the routing tables.

Classless Internet Domain Routing (CIDR)

Allocating blocks of class C addresses prevents the rapid depletion of class B addresses. However, this class C allocation requires additional routing table entries to be stored in routers. Because you need a block of 256 class C addresses to support the same address space as a single class B address, a routing table must have 256 network address entries for each of the class C networks. This size represents an increase in the number of routing table entries by a factor of 256. If a router has 2MB of memory for its routing table that uses class B addresses, then replacing these addresses with class C addresses will require a memory of 2×256 = 512MB!

The Classless Internet Domain Routing (CIDR) technique is used to summarize a block of class C addresses into a single routing table entry. This consolidation results in a reduction in the number of separate routing table entries. The block of class C addresses are consolidated by a routing table entry that consists of the following:

(lowest address in block, supernet mask)

The lowest address in block is the start of the address block, and the supernet mask specifies the number of class C addresses in the block. The supernet mask, also called the *CIDR mask,* contains 1s for the common prefix for all the class C addresses, and 0s for the parts of the class C addresses that have different values. Consider the following CIDR routing table entry:

(200.1.160.0, 255.255.224.0)

The 200.1.160.0 and the CIDR mask 255.255.224.0 have the following bit representations:

11001000 00000001 10100000 00000000

11111111 11111111 11100000 00000000

The 1s in the CIDR mask correspond to the following common prefix:

11001000 00000001 101

The 0s in the CIDR mask correspond to the varying part of the block of class C addresses; therefore, the range of class C addresses is between the following lower- and upper-class C addresses:

11001000 00000001 10100000 00000000 = 200.1.160.0

11001000 00000001 10111111 11111111 = 200.1.191.255

Figure 9.11 illustrates the preceding CIDR block of addresses.

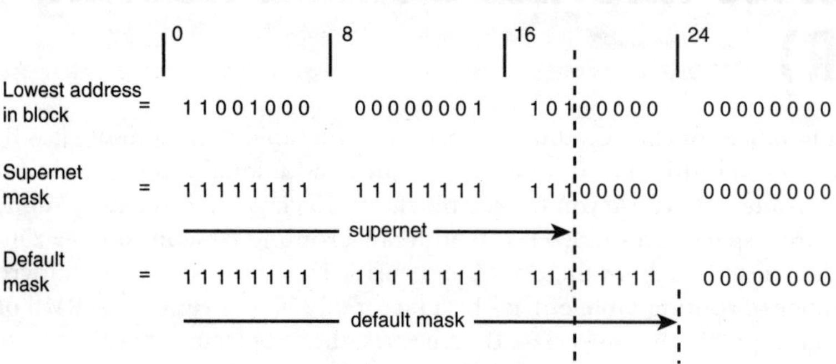

How many class C addresses are there in this block of class C addresses? You can determine this number by looking in the network portion of the class C address and noting the number of bits that can vary in the address range. Five such bits are shown in bold in the following CIDR mask:

11111111 11111111 111**00000** 00000000

Therefore, the number of class C addresses in the range is $2^5 = 32$. Routes in a CIDR block can be summarized in a single router advertisement called an *aggregate.*

Table 9.4 shows the number of contiguous class C addresses that need to be assigned for a given size of the network by using CIDR. The number of contiguous class C addresses for CIDR must be a power of 2.

Table 9.4
Number of Class C Addresses in CIDR for a Given Network Size

Network Size (Number of Hosts)	Number of Class C Addresses
254	1
255–508	2
509–1016	4
1017–2032	8

Network Size (Number of Hosts)	Number of Class C Addresses
2033–4064	16
4065–8128	32
8129–16,256	64

Another notation that you can use for CIDR blocks is the following:

lowest address in block/number of common prefix bits

The number of common prefix bits is the number of 1s in the supernet mask; thus, the following examples are equivalent representations of the CIDR block:

(200.1.160.0, 255.255.224.0)

200.1.1.160.0/19

The default subnet mask of a class C address is 255.255.255.0, which indicates that hosts in a single class C address have 24 common prefix bits. Whenever the number of common prefix bits is less than 24 for a class C address, supernetting is being used.

Networks that are subsets of a CIDR block are said to be *more specific* relative to the CIDR block. The common prefix length of more specific addresses is greater than that of the CIDR block. The following shows an example of a CIDR block and a more specific route:

199.22.0.0/16—CIDR block with prefix length 16

199.22.176.0/20—more specific prefix of length 20

Routers that understand CIDR use the longest match to select a route. The CIDR mask is used to determine the number of prefix bits that are to be considered in the match. But if more than one route to the destination is available, the router selects the route with the longest prefix. Consider the example of the network shown in figure 9.12. The network has router R1, which receives two routing updates:

199.22.0.0/16 from router R2

199.22.176.0/20 from router R3

Router Rl selects the path through router R3 because it is the path with the longest prefix.

RFC 1519, "Classless Inter-Domain Routing (CIDR): An Address Assignment and Aggregation Strategy," discusses the CIDR technique.

Figure 9.12 Longest match routing prefix.

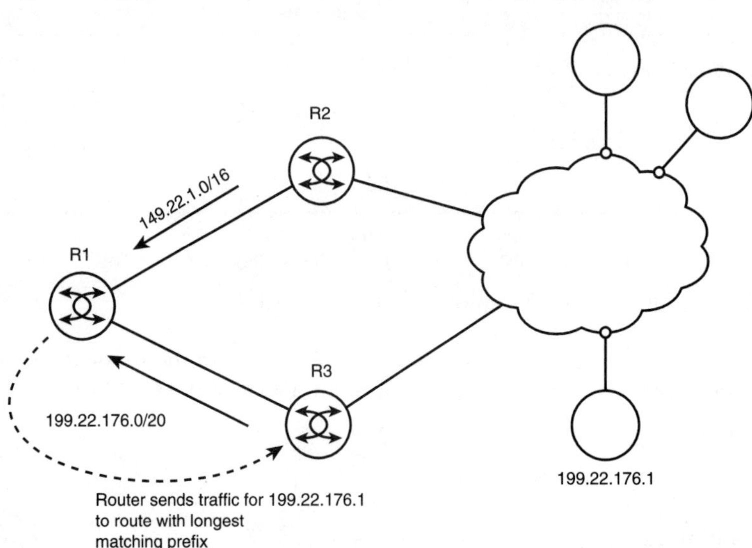
R2
149.22.1.0/16
R1
R3
199.22.176.0/20
199.22.176.1
Router sends traffic for 199.22.176.1
to route with longest
matching prefix

Broadcasting and Multicasting

Broadcasting is the process of sending a copy of the datagram to all nodes on a network. *Multicasting* is the process of sending a copy of the datagram to a group of nodes on the network. The presence of subnets can complicate broadcasting and multicasting.

Broadcasting can be an efficient way of communicating the same information to all nodes on a network. However, if all nodes on the network do not need this information, broadcasting is inefficient and leads to additional network traffic and processing overhead by nodes that do not need the broadcast information. Multicasting is more efficient than broadcasting for sending information to a select group of nodes on networks. If multicasts are to be delivered efficiently to a network, the Data Link layer facility on that network must have a Data Link level multicast capability. IEEE LANs provide multicast capability at the Data Link layer.

Broadcasting for Subnets

A broadcast is indicated by the presence of all 1s in the host portion of the destination address. This type of broadcast is called the *directed broadcast* and must be sent to all nodes on the network. The broadcast address can be represented as the following:

{network number, –1}

The *network number* is the network number portion of the class A, B, or C network address. The –1 represents all 1s. When subnets are used, a broadcast to a specific subnet is represented by the following:

{network number, subnet number, –1}

The *subnet number* is the subnet portion of the network address. If a broadcast is to be delivered to all subnets of a given network, the broadcast address is represented as the following:

{network number, –1, –1}

For broadcasts to be delivered within subnets, the routers connecting the subnets must agree to propagate the datagram to all physical networks. A potential problem that arises is when a broadcast datagram gets into a routing loop. This problem can occur in a poorly implemented router that sends a broadcast datagram blindly on all its ports.

Figure 9.13 shows a scenario with broadcast routing loops where routers blindly forward the broadcast datagram on all interfaces that share a common network number prefix of 132.27. As a rule, routers do not forward broadcasts unless they have been configured to do so. In this example, we are assuming that the the routers have been configured to forward broadcasts. Note that these routers do not discriminate about whether they have received a broadcast before. This lack of discrimination can result in a broadcast loop. As a result, the physical subnets will receive multiple broadcasts. Eventually, the TTL field in the IP header of the broadcast datagrams will be reduced to zero, and the broadcast datagrams will be removed from the network, but not before they have caused multiple broadcasts and additional network traffic.

To prevent broadcast routing loops, routers are required to use reverse path forwarding. In this technique, routers consult their routing table to see which port should be used to send a datagram to the source address in the broadcast datagram. The router accepts the broadcast datagram only if it comes from this port; the router discards all broadcast datagrams that come from other ports. In the example in figure 9.13, the routing table for router R1 reveals that the source of the broadcast datagram can be reached through port P1. Therefore, the router ignores broadcast datagrams that are received on ports P2 and P3 from the source.

When the same subnet mask is used for all the subnets of a network, no ambiguity exists in interpreting a broadcast address. However, when different subnet masks are used, you have no guarantee that a given router implementation will correctly interpret the broadcast address in the datagram.

Broadcasting for subnets is described in RFC 922 (STD 5) on "Broadcasting Internet Datagrams in the Presence of Subnets."

Figure 9.13 Broadcast routing loop.

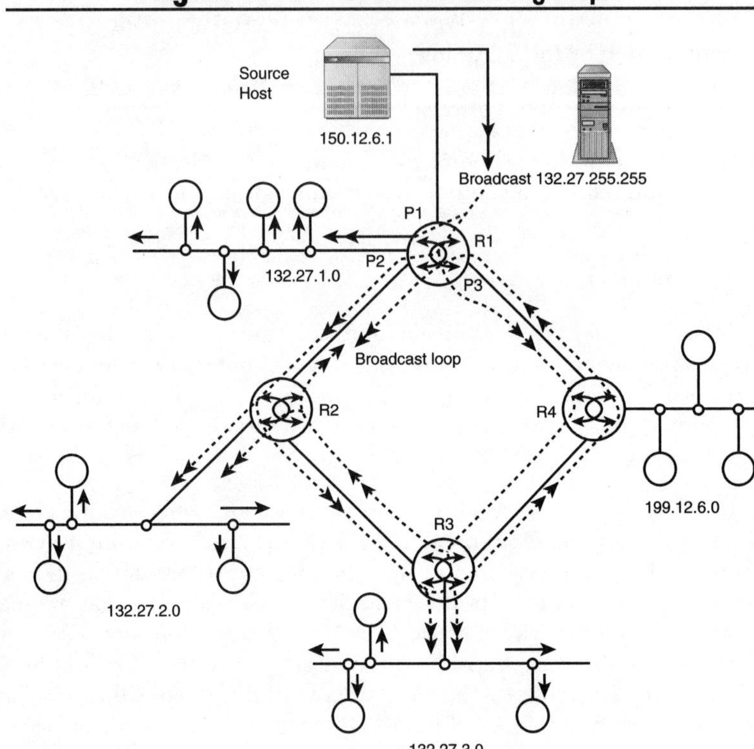

Multicasting

You use IP multicasting to send a datagram to a select group of nodes. The class D address format is reserved for multicasts. The members of a multicast group join the group dynamically and can leave the group at any time. A multicast address is similar to a radio channel that operates at a particular frequency. Radio receivers can tune into the channel frequency and hear the radio broadcast at that frequency, and they can also tune out. In IP networks this radio frequency is identified by a specific class D address.

Membership in a multicast group is required to receive a multicast datagram sent to the group's multicast class D address. A host can simultaneously be a member of several multicast groups. Any host can send a multicast to a multicast group address. A host does not need to be a member of a multicast group to send a multicast.

Some multicast class D addresses are assigned by IANA and are well known. These addresses are listed in Chapter 4, "IP Addressing" in table 4.5. Multicast addresses that are available for temporary use are called *transient multicast groups.*

To send a multicast on subnets or networks connected by routers requires that the routers be able to forward multicast datagrams. Conventional routers that are enabled for multicasting can be used to forward multicast datagrams. When the multicast is delivered to the physical network, the underlying hardware capability of the physical network is used to send the multicast on that physical network. The mapping of multicast addresses to Physical layer multicast addresses for Ethernet is discussed in Chapter 4.

An IP node can participate in multicasting at three levels:

- **Level 0.** The IP node cannot send or receive an IP multicast.
- **Level 1.** The IP node can send but not receive an IP multicast.
- **Level 2.** The IP node can send and receive an IP multicast.

Most IP implementations can operate at levels 0 and 1. Level 2 operation requires that the IP node have the capability to receive multicasts and is the subject of discussion in the next section.

The Internet Group Management Protocol (IGMP)

A host joins or leaves membership of a multicast group on a per-network interface basis. Therefore, a multihomed host with several network connections can join a multicast group on some network interfaces but not on others. Usually a client of the IP layer, such as a routing protocol or another high-level application, makes a request to join or leave a multicast group on a specific network interface. A network interface is specified because the application may want to send multicasts to nodes on one network but not on others.

Hosts that join or leave a multicast group use the Internet Group Management Protocol (IGMP) to report their group memberships to neighboring routers. IGMP is implemented by the IP module, but it uses IP to carry messages. In that sense, IGMP is similar to ICMP (see fig. 9.14).

Figure 9.14 Conceptual view of IGMP layering.

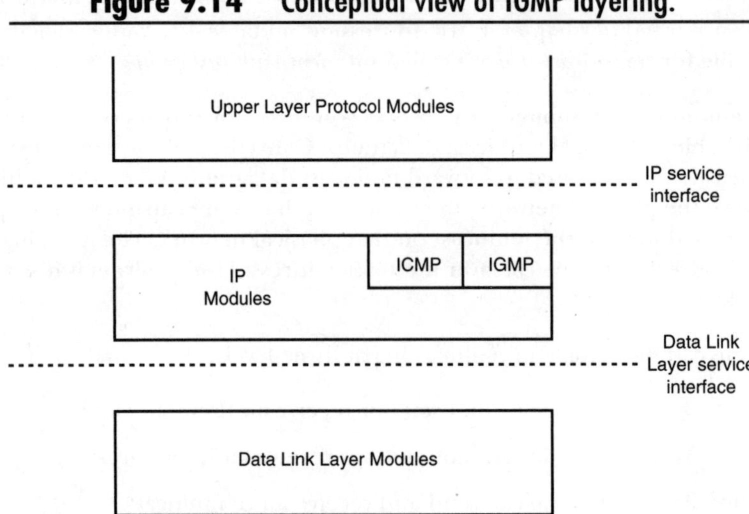

The IGMP message format is shown in figure 9.15.

Figure 9.15 IGMP message format.

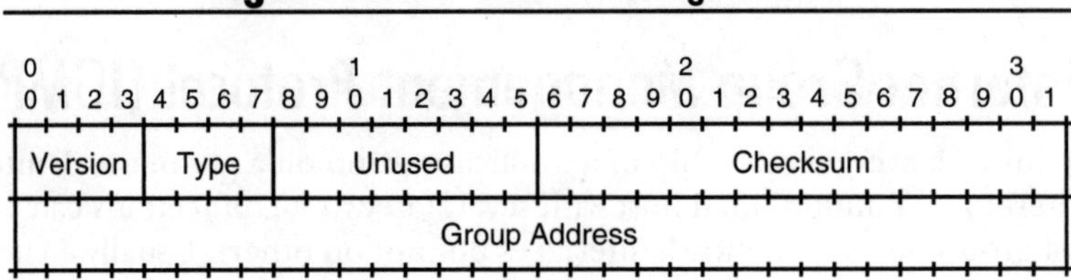

The Version field is the version number of the protocol and is currently set to 1. The Type field identifies whether the IGMP message is a query sent by a multicast router or a response sent by a host to a multicast router query:

1 = Host Membership Query

2 = Host Membership Report (Response)

The Unused field must be set to 0 upon sending and is ignored upon reception. As the name indicates, this field is not used.

The checksum field is the usual 16-bit one's complement of the one's complement sum of the 8-octet IGMP message.

In a host membership query message, the Group Address field is at 0 when it is sent, and it is ignored when it is received. In a host membership report message, the Group Address field holds the IP host group address of the group being reported.

Multicast routers send host membership query messages on their network interfaces to discover which class D addresses have members. The IGMP host membership query is sent to the multicast group address 224.0.0.1 in an IP header with a TTL value of 1. Hosts respond to this query by sending an IGMP host membership report message. The response message reports each multicast group address for which the host is a member on the network interface from which the query was received. To avoid simultaneous response messages and to reduce the number of response messages, the following technique is used:

- When a host receives an IGMP host membership query, the host does not send an IGMP host membership report message immediately. Instead, the host starts a report delay timer for each of its group memberships on the network interface of the incoming query. Timer values are selected randomly from 0 to *D* seconds (typically, 10 seconds). When a timer expires, a response message for the corresponding multicast group is sent.
- A response message is sent with an IP destination address equal to the host group address being reported and with an IP TTL of 1. This address ensures that other members of the same multicast group on the same network can receive the response message. If a host receives a response message for a group to which the host belongs on that network, the host stops its own timer for that group and does not generate a response for that group.

Typically, only one IGMP host membership report message will be generated for each group present on the network. This message is generated by the host whose delay timer expires first. A multicast router does not have to know which hosts belong to a particular multicast group; it is sufficient that multicast routers know whether at least one host belongs to a group on a particular network. Multicast routers receive all IP multicast datagrams; therefore, these routers need not be addressed explicitly.

Summary

The IPv4 address formats were designed for accommodating networks of different sizes. In the early history of the Internet, these address formats worked well. But as the Internet began to grow in size, a number of weaknesses in the IP address formats became apparent.

The concept of the subnet was designed and formalized to enable a single class A, B, or C network number to be subdivided by using a process called subnetting. The resulting subnets share a common network prefix. The number of bits used in the host portion of an IP address to identify the subnet is called a subnet number. Typically, the same number of host bits are used for the subnet number in all subnets, which results in a uniform subnet mask. The supernetting technique can be used to combine several class C addresses into a single address.

Instead of assigning separate class C addresses that can use up a considerable number of router entries, a technique of aggregating route information called Classless Internet Domain Routing (CIDR) can be used. CIDR is an implementation of the supernetting technique.

The role of multicasting in networks that are subnetted or supernetted was discussed. IGMP is used to define membership in a multicast group.

Test Yourself

1. What is the network address of a TCP/IP host that has an IP address of 203.23.32.34?
2. What is the node (or host) address of a TCP/IP host that has an IP address of 182.23.32.34?
3. Convert the following IP address to its equivalent dotted-decimal notation:

   10110101 01011100 10000100 11001100

   How many different subnet masks are possible for the network that contains this IP address?
4. What is the subnet mask for 184.231.0.0, if the first ten bits of node address are used for subnetting?
5. What are the advantages of subnetting? What are its disadvantages?
6. Describe the rule(s) used to form the value of a subnet mask.
7. What are the subnet masks for class A, B, and C address formats that indicate that subnetting is not being used?
8. Suppose that you are reading an RFC that uses the following to describe a subnet mask for a class B address:

   {–1, –1, 0}

   Using the dotted-decimal notation, what is the equivalent subnet mask representation if three host bits are being used for subnets?
9. For this question, assume that the IP address and subnet mask values are as follows:

   IP address = 128.12.34.71

   Subnet mask = 255.255.240.0

What is the value of the following?

Subnet number = ?

Host number = ?

Directed broadcast address = ?

Limited broadcast address for any subnet = ?

10. For this question, assume that the IP address and subnet mask values are as follows:

    IP address = 108.77.51.70

    Subnet mask = 255.255.128.0

    What is the value of the following?

    Subnet number = ?

    Host number = ?

    Directed broadcast address = ?

    Limited broadcast address for any subnet = ?

11. An organization has been given a network number assignment of 144.19.0.0. The organization has three sites in Los Angeles, New York, and Munich. These sites need to be connected to each other by using point-to-point WAN links. Each site is expected to have no more than a 1,000 TCP/IP nodes. Discuss how you would use subnets for the given network number assignment for the organization. If you are using a uniform subnet mask for the entire organization, what would be the subnet mask? How many subnetworks are needed? Show the IP address assignments for the router ports and for at least two hosts on each network. How can you eliminate the need for assigning subnet numbers for point-to-point links?

12. Which of the following hosts must use a router to communicate with the host 129.23.144.10 if the subnet mask is 255.255.192.0?

    129.23.191.21

    129.23.127.222

    129.23.130.33

    129.23.148.127

13. Which of the following IP addresses is located on the same subnet as 130.12.127.231 if the subnet mask is 255.255.192.0?

    130.45.130.1

    130.22.130.1

    130.12.64.23

    130.12.167.127

14. An organization has applied for and received a network number of 133.24.0.0. The organization plans on using subnetworks with each network limited to a maximum of 1,000 TCP/IP nodes. What is the subnet mask that will permit the maximum number of subnetworks? Show the reasoning behind your answer.

15. An organization has applied for and received a network number of 181.255.0.0. The organization plans on using subnetworks with each network limited to a maximum of 2,000 TCP/IP nodes. What is the subnet mask that will permit the maximum number of subnetworks? What is the maximum number of subnetworks? Show the reasoning behind your answer.

16. An organization has applied for and received a network number of 190.240.0.0. The organization plans on using subnetworks with each network limited to a maximum of 500 TCP/IP nodes. What is the subnet mask that will permit the maximum number of subnetworks? What is the maximum number of subnetworks? Show the reasoning behind your answer.

17. An organization has applied for and received a network number of 27.0.0.0. The organization plans on using subnetworks with each network limited to a maximum of 5,000 TCP/IP nodes. What is the subnet mask that will permit the maximum number of subnetworks? What is the maximum number of subnetworks? Show the reasoning behind your answer.

18. An organization has applied for and received a network number of 202.7.17.0. The organization plans on using subnetworks with each network limited to a maximum of 64 TCP/IP nodes. What is the subnet mask that will permit the maximum number of subnetworks? What is the maximum number of subnetworks? Show the reasoning behind your answer.

19. Given a network address of 184.84.0.0, which needs to be divided into nine subnets, show the subnet number and host number assignments that will give you maximum flexibility in case you need to change the subnet mask in the future.

20. A network address of 199.233.18.0 has four host bits that are used for the subnet number. Currently, only ten subnets are to be built. Show the subnet number and host number assignments that will give you maximum flexibility in case you need to change the subnet mask in the future.

21. Suppose that you want to divide a class C network 199.200.30.0 into three subnets with a maximum of 100 hosts on one subnet and a maximum of 50 hosts each on the other two subnets. What subnet mask can you use? If you decide to use VLSM, what are the subnet masks for the three subnets?
22. Why are VLSMs not widely used?
23. What are the values of subnet masks in a routing table for a host-specific route and a default route? Why are these values used?
24. If multiple routers are connected to the same network, only one router should be configured with proxy ARP software. Why?
25. Suppose that you are using old TCP/IP software on some hosts on an Ethernet network. If this TCP/IP software does not use subnetting, how can you send datagrams from these hosts to other hosts on a different subnet?
26. What are the advantages and disadvantages of using proxy ARP?
27. The number of contiguous class C addresses for CIDR must be a power of 2. Why?
28. A CIDR block is described by the following parameters:

    (200.1.160.0, 255.255.224.0)

    How many class C addresses are described by this CIDR block?
29. A CIDR block is described by the following parameters:

    203.11.192.0/20

    How many class C addresses are described by this CIDR block?
30. A CIDR block has the following range of addresses:

    204.23.128.0 – 204.23.255.255

    How many bits are used for the common network prefix? What is the supernet mask for this CIDR block?
31. Show an example of how you can use CIDR to minimize the number of route aggregates that need to be advertised.
32. For each of the following number of hosts that need to be in a network, give the CIDR block size in terms of the number of class C addresses:

    1,000 hosts

    2,000 hosts

    3,000 hosts

    4,000 hosts

    5,000 hosts

33. Name the technique that is used to prevent routing loops for processing broadcast datagrams. Give an example of how you can use this technique to prevent routing loops.
34. In what three levels can an IP node participate in a multicast group?
35. Why does a host join or leave membership of a multicast group on a per-network interface basis?
36. What is the purpose of IGMP? Describe the IGMP message format.
37. Describe the techniques used to reduce the amount of traffic in response to an IGMP host query message.
38. Why is it not essential that a multicast router know which hosts are a member of a multicast group on a particular network?
39. Why is the TTL set to 1 in the IP header for IGMP messages? Will an ICMP message be generated when the TTL value expires?

CHAPTER 10

IP Routing Protocols

Earlier chapters have discussed routing principles and the routing algorithms used at the host and the router. In this chapter, you will learn about the routing protocols used by routers to exchange information. The concept of autonomous systems and Interior Gateway Protocols (IGPs) that are used in autonomous systems is introduced in this chapter. The Vector Distance and Link State routing protocol mechanisms are discussed in relationship to the Routing Information Protocol (RIP) and OSPF (open shortest path first) IGPs.

Autonomous Systems

An internet system consists of a number of connected networks. Some of these networks are managed by separate organizations. This is definitely true for the Internet, in which different network service providers connect to its core backbone. The network service providers and the organizations that connect to them and the Internet core backbone are all managed separately. In large organizations, parts of the network may have to be managed separately for a variety of reasons, such as the following:

- ◆ Different departments are responsible for parts of the network.
- ◆ Easier management of smaller networks.
- ◆ Political reasons.

To model the reality of separately managed networks, the Internet architecture defines the concept of *Autonomous systems* (AS), which consist of independently managed networks connected to a backbone network (see fig. 10.1). Internally, an AS system may be further subdivided (subnetted) for ease of administration, but an AS appears as one logical network to outside networks.

Figure 10.1 Autonomous systems. (Courtesy Learning Tree)

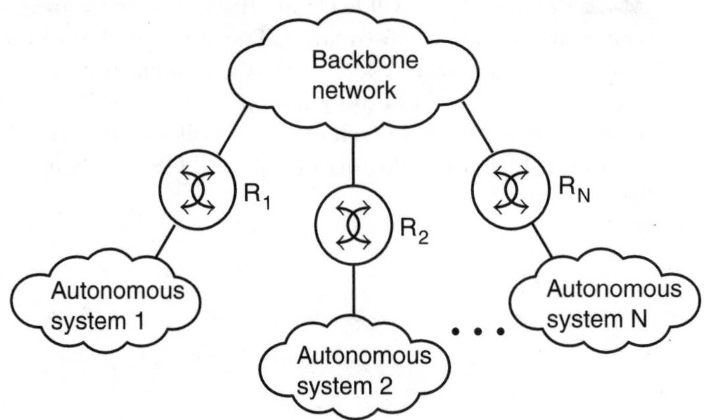

The backbone network also forms an Autonomous System. The routers between Autonomous Systems are called *boundary routers* because they are at the boundary between Autonomous Systems.

Each Autonomous System can select its own routing protocols depending on the nature of its topology, availability of existing equipment, and any other local factors. An Autonomous System is free to change its routing protocols any time without affecting other Autonomous Systems. The Internet backbone system has in fact changed its routing protocols a few times without affecting the Autonomous Systems that connect to it.

At different times, the routing protocols on the Internet have been Gateway to Gateway Protocol (GGP), Exterior Gateway Protocol (EGP), and SPREAD, a Shortest Path First (SPF) protocol implemented by BBN, Inc. GGP and EGP are not in common use today and are not discussed in this chapter. For your reference, RFC 823 contains some details on the GGP protocol, and RFC 904 contains a formal specification of the EGP protocol. The SPREAD protocol is not documented in the RFC literature. Commercial routers do not implement SPREAD as this protocol is implemented on special processors built by BBN, Inc.

The routers within an Autonomous System are said to be interior to the router system. The routing protocols used by interior routers are called *interior gateway protocols* (IGPs). Routing protocols between Autonomous Systems are called *exterior gateway protocols* (EGPs). The acronym EGP is a little confusing because it also refers to an actual implementation of an exterior gateway protocol that is now obsolete. Depending on the context, EGP could be a generic name for AS-to-AS protocols or the name of the historical EGP protocol. The term Inter-AS protocol is used in RFC 1058 to describe the notion of an AS-to-AS protocol.

The focus of this chapter is on the following interior gateway protocols in an Autonomous System:

- RIP (Routing Information Protocol)
- OSPF (Open Shortest Path First)

Routing Information Protocol (RIP)

The RIP protocol is an example of a class of protocols called *Vector Distance protocols.* In Vector Distance protocols, the router maintains a list of all known routes in its routing table and periodically broadcasts the contents of its routing table. Each route entry in the routing table consists of the following: destination, distance and next hop router.

The *destination* has the usual meaning of a destination network or destination host. The *next hop router* represents the directly connected router that will be used to forward the datagram to the *destination*. The *distance* is a measure of the cost associated with the route, and is measured as hops for the RIP protocol (the path through one router counts as one hop). Other Vector Distance protocols may use other measures of cost, such as time or economic cost, or a combination of factors. For example, the HELLO protocol that was widely deployed as the IGP on the NSFNET Internet backbone Internet used milliseconds to a destination as a measure of the distance. HELLO is not widely implemented today, and is of historical interest only.

Many Vector Distance protocols use a zero distance cost to reach a directly connected network. RIP uses a hop count of 1 to reach a directly connected network, a hop count of 2 for a network that is reached through one router, and so on.

When a router running a Vector Distance protocol receives a routing table broadcast from a neighbor, it recomputes its routing table based on the new information. The router does this by adding the cost to reach the neighbor router to the cost to reach the destination from the neighbor. Then the router compares this calculated cost with the current cost in its routing table. If the new cost is lower, the current route is replaced by the new route. As an example, assume that a router receives the following information from a neighbor, *K*, that is *Nk* distance away:

(Net1, D1)

The calculated route based on this information is the following:

(Net1, D1+Nk, K)

The calculated route says that *Net1* can be reached via router *K* at a cost of *D1+Nk*. If there is no entry for *Net1* in the routing table, this entry is added. If there is already an entry in the routing table, a comparison is done between the old cost and the new cost. Suppose the existing entry is the following:

(Net1, C, R)

If cost *D1+Nk* is less than *C*, the new route is used; otherwise, the cost is left unmodified.

The following is a more concrete example of a how the routing table is calculated for a number of route entries. To begin with, a routing table will only have entries for the directly connected network.

Destination	Distance	Next hop router
144.19.0.0	1	(directly connected)
130.21.0.0	1	(directly connected)

A distance of 1 is shown for the directly connected network (this is true for RIP). After receiving routing updates from neighbor routers, the routing table is populated with other entries. The following is an example of how the routing table may look after some time:

Destination	Distance	Next hop router
144.19.0.0	1	(directly connected)
130.21.0.0	1	(directly connected)
200.1.1.0	5	144.19.1.100
200.2.5.0	3	144.19.1.101
199.23.3.0	4	130.21.5.30
131.200.0.0	7	130.21.5.32

Now consider how the routing table is affected by a routing update broadcast from the router at 144.19.1.102 that contains the following information:

Destination	Distance
144.19.0.0	2
200.1.1.0	3
200.2.5.0	1
199.23.3.0	5
131.200.0.0	8

The preceding information is routing information from a neighbor. Since a neighbor is one hop away from the router that receives this update, the computed routes are one hop greater than the values in the routing update:

Destination	Distance
144.19.0.0	3
200.1.1.0	4 (Better route)
200.2.5.0	2 (Better route)
199.23.3.0	6
131.200.0.0	9

Note that the following routes in the preceding update are better than the current information in the routing table:

200.1.1.0	4
200.2.5.0	2

The Vector Distance protocol updates the routing table with these better routes. The routing table now appears as follows:

Destination	Distance	Next hop router
144.19.0.0	1	(directly connected)
130.21.0.0	1	(directly connected)
200.1.1.0	4	144.19.1.102 (Update route)
200.2.5.0	2	144.19.1.102 (Update route)
199.23.3.0	4	130.21.5.30
131.200.0.0	7	130.21.5.32

Vector Distance protocols communicate information only on a periodic basis. As a result, there may be delays before the route updates are communicated to all routers on the network. The following is a list of potential problems with Vector Distance protocols:

- When routes change rapidly, the route computations may not stabilize.
- Because of rapid changes in the network and a slow propagation rate, the routers may have incorrect information. This leads to inefficient routes or lost packets.
- Route computation is based on second hand information. Bad information on a route can get propagated in the same manner as good information, which leads to inefficient or wrong routes.
- The entire routing table is exchanged. As the number of networks increase, so does the size of the route information packets. Also, each router sends its routing information periodically. As the number of routers increase so do the number of packets that exchange routing information. Because of these issues, Vector Distance protocols do not scale well to large scale networks, and network traffic increases due to an increase in routing information.

The algorithm for computing the routing table in Vector distance protocols is sometimes called the Ford-Fulkerson algorithm, after the names of the researchers. The term Bellman-Ford recently has been used to describe this algorithm because the formulation of computing the routing table is an application of Bellman's equation in the field of applied mathematics called *Dynamic Programming*.

In the literature, the term Distance Vector is also used to describe the Vector Distance protocol. The Bellman-Ford algorithm is also referred to as the Distance Vector Algorithm (DVA). The following sections discuss RIP implementation issues.

Routing Protocol Implementations

The TCP/IP RIP protocol, though old, is still often used as an IGP protocol. The RIP protocol evolved from the work done by Xerox Corporation's Palo Alto Research Center (PARC) in the development of a routing protocol—also called RIP—for the Xerox Network Systems protocol suite. The XNS RIP became the basis of development for many routing protocols that were also called RIP. In the early 1980s, a number of Network Operating System vendors—such as 3COM, Banyan, and Novell—developed routing protocols also based on XNS RIP. Even though these derived routing protocols were a little different from the original XNS RIP, they were still called RIP.

When TCP/IP was being integrated into the kernel of the Berkeley Software Distribution Unix (BSD Unix), the developers included an implementation of XNS RIP modified for IP. The software module that implemented the RIP protocol in BSD Unix was called *routed* (pronounced as *route-dee*). The implementation of routed became the standard implementation of RIP on many other TCP/IP platforms. Network administrators began deploying RIP as an IGP on local TCP/IP LANs. As the networks began to grow in size, the network administrators continued using RIP without any consideration as to whether it was suited for large scale networks. Many organizations adopted RIP and continued to use it until better routing protocols such as OSPF became commonly available. Perhaps this explains the widespread use of RIP.

TCP/IP RIP is interesting because it was adopted before an RFC for the protocol was proposed. It was adopted as a de facto protocol because of the widespread distribution of the BSD Unix source software. For a long time, the only definition of TCP/IP RIP was the reference implementation of the protocol in the BSD Unix source code. Because of this, a number of interoperability problems surfaced with RIP on other platforms because of programmers' limited understanding of the original code. Finally, in 1988, the RFC 1058 (STD 34) on "Routing Information Protocol" was issued as a specification of the RIP protocol to help eliminate the interoperability problems. This points out the value of a having a protocol specification to help resolve misunderstandings about protocol implementation.

In some Unix implementations, a program called *gated* (pronounced *gate-dee*) is used instead of the routed program. The gated program implements multiple routing protocols—RIP, HELLO and EGP. Because the metrics used by each of these routing protocols are different, a conversion factor must be specified in networks that use these protocols to convert the routing cost from one system to another. Typically, the configuration files for gated and routed are kept in /etc/gated.conf and etc/routed.conf, respectively.

Active and Passive RIP Routers

RIP routers are classified as *active* or *passive.* Active routers are those that can advertise routes as well as receive routes. Passive routers can only receive routing information; they do not advertise routes. Passive routers only listen for routes, and based on the information they receive, they compute their routing tables. They do not share the results of their computation (the new routing table) with other routers. Only router devices can act as active routers. Hosts typically do not act as active routers (see fig. 10.2).

Figure 10.2 Active and Passive routers.

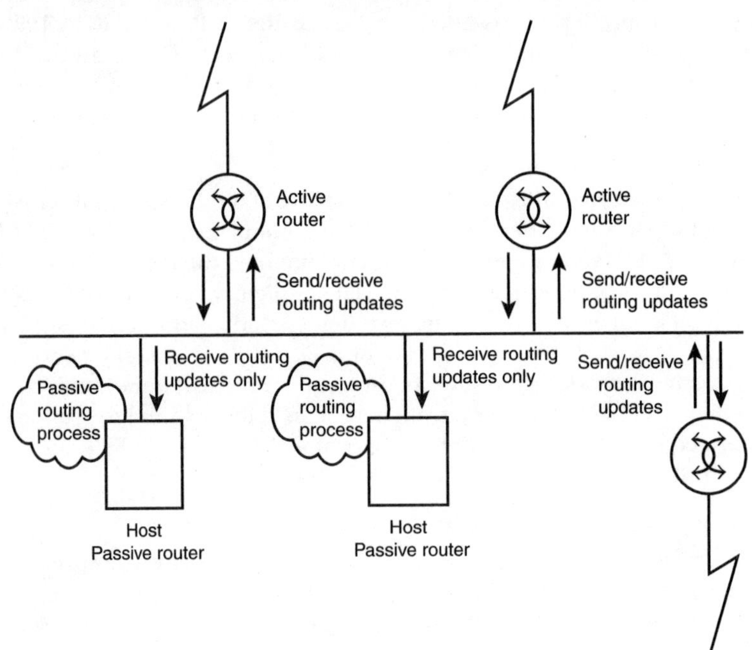

If hosts act as routers, they are performing the functions of a router. Chapter 7, "IP Routing Concepts," discusses the issues of hosts acting as routers.

An Active RIP router broadcasts routing information every 30 seconds. In many implementations the interval between broadcasts is a configurable parameter. Usually, some multiple of the 30-second broadcast interval is used to set the actual broadcast interval. Each RIP broadcast contains pairs of network address and hop count.

Normally, if a routing update is not received in three broadcast intervals (90 seconds if the broadcast interval is 30 seconds), the network is assumed to be non-reachable, and the routing entry is purged.

Problems with the Hop Count Metric

Route path costs based on hop metrics may be less than optimal. Why? Because hop counts count only the number of routers required to reach a destination and do not consider other factors—such as cost of link, delay, reliability, speed of link, and so on. Consider figure 10.3, which shows two possible paths between routers R1 and R3. The direct path from R1 to R3 is over a low speed link and has a cost of 1 hop.

Figure 10.3 Selection of less optimal path based on hop count. (Courtesy Learning Tree)

- Router paths based on hop metric may be less than optimal

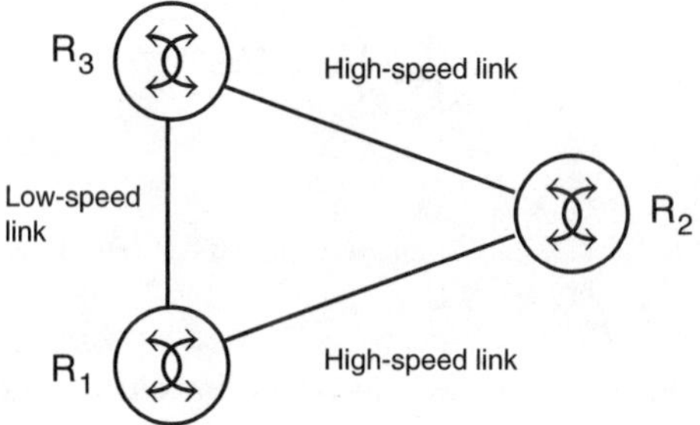

- Using hop count as route path cost, direct path between R_1 and R_3 will be selected
- Alternate route paths not available

The path from R1 to R3 via R2 is over a high speed link but costs 2 hops. In this case the low-cost path of 1 hop, the direct path from R1 to R3, is selected over the high-speed link. This is unfortunate as it is desirable in many instances to select the high-speed links over the low-speed link.

To solve the problem of a less optimal path being selected based solely on hop count, many RIP implementations such as those in Unix enable an artificially high hop count to be assigned to undesirable paths. Figure 10.4, for example, shows that the low-speed link has been artificially assigned a hop count of 3. This hop count is now greater than the hop count cost of 2 for the high-speed link.

Figure 10.4 Using an artificially high hop count to select optional paths. (Courtesy Learning Tree)

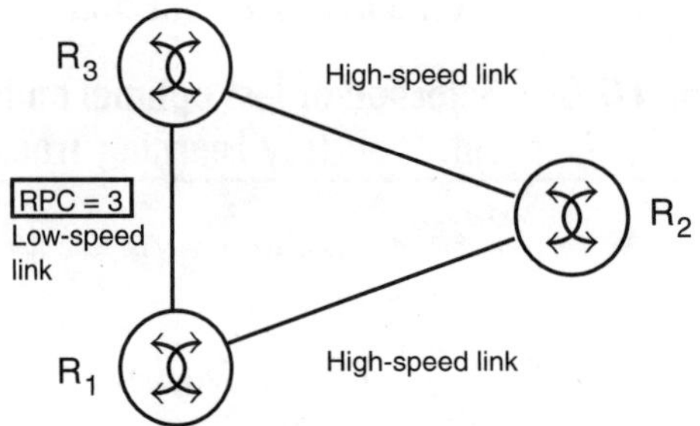
• Router path cost for slower links can be assigned artificially
R3
High-speed link
RPC = 3
Low-speed link
R2
R1
High-speed link
- Set path cost for low-speed link higher than path cost through R2

When RIP has to select between two paths that have the same hop count, RIP arbitrarily selects any one of the paths with equal hop counts.

Slow Convergence in RIP

When RIP receives a route update and updates routing table entries, it starts a timer for the updated route. If a routing update fails to arrive within a specified timeout value, the routing entry is removed from the routing table. If a routing update arrives for a specific route, the timer is restarted.

In RIP, changes in routing tables may take several update cycles before all routers are receive these changes. This is because RIP has a very slow convergence rate.The process of finalization of the routing table changes caused by network changes is caused by convergence. The slow convergence of RIP is a characteristic of all Vector Distance protocols.

Figure 10.5 illustrates the problems associated with slow convergence in RIP. This figure (see fig. 10.5a) shows network Net1 connected to router R1. Router R2 connects to router R1, and router R3 connects to router R2. Figure 10.5b shows a break in the link between R1 and Net1. When R1 detects that the link to Net1 is down, it sets the value of the hop count to Net1 to 16. In RIP, a hop count of 16 is regarded as "infinity" and indicates that the corresponding destination is unreachable.

Figure 10.5 Slow Convergence problem illustrated for RIP. (Courtesy Learning Tree)

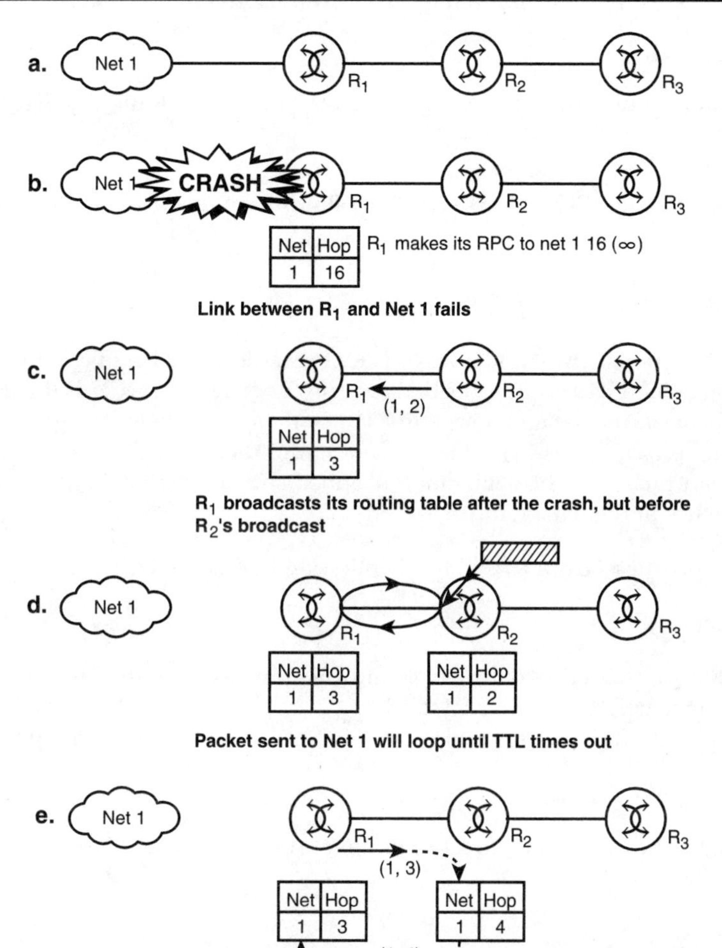

Normally, router R1 would eventually broadcast its routing table to its neighbor R2 on its broadcast interval. However, R2's broadcast interval may come up before router R1 can send its routing update. R2 was originally 2 hops away from Net1 before the link between Net1 and R2 went down. If R2 sends its update before R1, then R1 receives the following update:

(Net1, 2)

Router R1, at this point, computes the routing table information. If neighbor router R2 is 2 hops away from Net1, then R1 must be 2+1=3 hops away from Net1. A hop count of 3 is less than the following current route entry for Net1 at R1:

(Net1, 16)

The previous route entry is, therefore, replaced by the following (see fig. 10.5c):

(Net1, 3)

At this point routers R2 and R3 have the following route entries for Net1:

Router R1:	(Net1, 2)
Router R2:	(Net1, 2)

If an IP datagram arrives at R2 for Net1, R2 forwards it to R1 thinking that Net1 is 2 hops away. When R1 receives this IP datagram for Net1, R1 forwards the datagram to R2. R2 forwards the datagram back to R1. The datagram, therefore, gets into a routing loop (see fig. 10.5d). This continues until the TTL field in the IP header expires, at which time the datagram is dropped and an ICMP message sent to the source that sent the datagram.

The next broadcast from R1 sends the following update to R2:

(Net1, 3)

Router R2 computes the routing table information based on the previous routing update. Since neighbor router R1 is 3 hops away from Net1, R2 must be 3+1=4 hops away from Net1. The routing table entry for Net1 at R2 then becomes the following:

(Net1, 4)

R2 sends the previous route to R1 in its next broadcast. R1 updates its routing table to be the following:

(Net1, 5)

This process of increasing the hop count continues indefinitely with each router counting to infinity. For this reason, this problem is called the "count-to-infinity" problem (see fig. 10.5e).

The designers of RIP set an artificial ceiling of a hop count of 16 to prevent the routers from counting indefinitely. When a count of 16 is reached, the counting to infinity is stopped, and the destination is declared to be unreachable. The maximum hop count of 16 indicates that RIP can be used to compute routes with only 15 routers between any two points.

The next section discusses a number of techniques used for the elimination of slow convergence.

Eliminating Slow Convergence in RIP

A number of techniques have evolved to eliminate the slow convergence of RIP. These techniques include the following:

- Split horizon update
- Hold down
- Poison reverse

Split Horizon Update

In the *split horizon update* technique, the router records the interface over which a new route is received. The interface over which particular route update information is received is regarded as the *source interface* because it is the source of the route information. The router does not send route information on the source interface. Consider the cause of the problem of slow convergence in figure 10.5. Router R2 sends a route update for Net1 to R1, regardless of the fact that R2 obtained its route information about Net1 from R1. When route R1 receives an update from R2, it trusts this information even though this information is bogus—the only route to Net1 is through R1 and the link between R1 and Net1 is down.

By preventing route information from being sent through the source intraface, the problem illustrated in figure 10.5 cannot escalate (see fig. 10.6).

Figure 10.6 Split horizon update. (Courtesy Learning Tree)

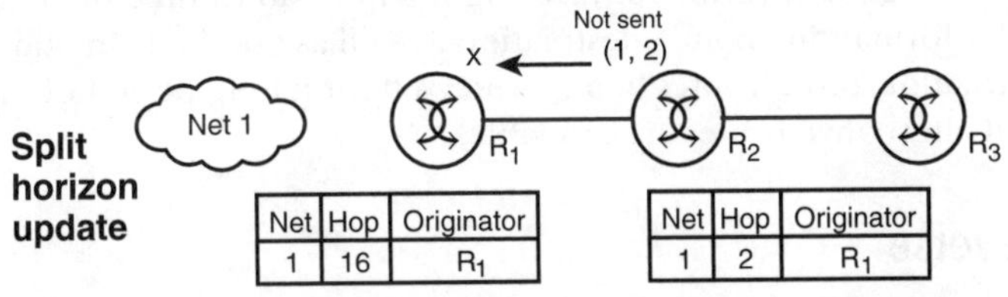

In split horizon, when the link between R1 and Net1 goes down, router R1 stops advertising the route about R1. When other routers on the network do not receive information about Net1 for three update cycles (90 seconds, if broadcast interval is 30 seconds), they removes the entry for Net1 from their routing tables. If a router meanwhile receives another route to Net1, it uses this alternative route. However, it is possible that this route information about Net1 depended on the route that just disappeared. The router advertising the bad route would have to discover that the route is no longer valid, and stop advertising this route before other routers stop reacting to this bad route information.

Typically, after several update cycles in RIP, all routers on the network become aware of the change in the network topology.

Hold Down

In the *hold down* technique, routers ignore routing information about a destination for an interval time when they receive a message that the destination is no longer reachable (see fig. 10.7).

Figure 10.7 Hold down. (Courtesy Learning Tree)

The interval of time that the routers ignore messages about a destination is called the *hold down time.* The hold down time is typically set to two update intervals (60 seconds). The hold down time permits most routers to receive information about bad routes. All routers use the same hold down time interval.

One of the problems with the hold down technique is that it does not discriminate between bad and good information. During the hold down time interval, the router ignores bad information about a destination as well as good information. This results in bad information about routes being preserved for a long period of time even though valid alternative routes are available.

Poison Reverse

In the *poison reverse* technique, the router advertising the unavailability of a link does so for several broadcast intervals (see fig. 10.8). When a destination becomes unreachable because of the unavailability of a link, RIP sends a hop count cost of 16 ("infinity" in RIP) for that destination. This is equivalent to saying that the route to the destination through a particular router is "poison."

Continually advertising an infinite route cost for a destination ensures that all routers eventually receives the message about the destination being unreachable.

Figure 10.8 Poison reverse. (Courtesy Learning Tree)

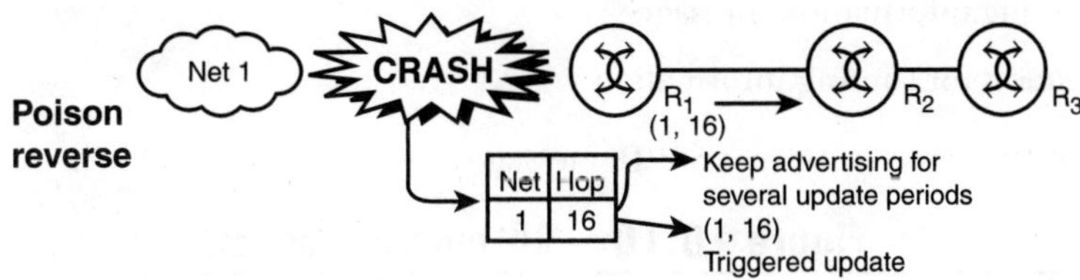

A variation of the poison reverse technique is *poison reverse with triggered update.* In triggered update, the router does not wait for its next broadcast interval to advertise that a destination is unreachable. Triggered update forces a router to send a route update immediately when it detects that a destination is unreachable. The motivation for this technique is to not wait till the broadcast interval. For example, in the situation of figure 10.5, if triggered update was in use, the router R1 would not have to wait till the end of the broadcast interval to send its broadcast. R2 would receive the broadcast and update its routing table.

In some networks, the use of triggered update can create a broadcast storm. A triggered update could cause receiving routers to change their routing tables immediately. If the receiving routers are using triggered updates, they could then send triggered updates to other routers, which would then send triggered updates, and so on. As you can see, this could result in a broadcast storm of triggered updates.

RIP Message Format

RIP uses UDP as its transport protocol. RIP routers send and receive routing information updates and requests on UDP port number 520 (see fig. 10.9).

Figure 10.9 RIP and its transport mechanism.

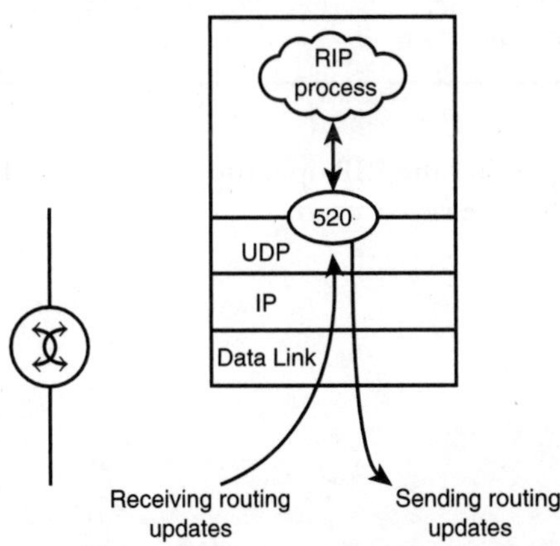

RIP messages are essentially of two types:

- Routing information message
- Request for routing information

Figure 10.10 shows the format of RIP messages.

Figure 10.10 RIP message format.

0 1 2 3 4 5 6 7	8 9 0 1 2 3 4 5 (1)	6 7 8 9 0 1 2 3 4 5 6 7 8 9 0 1 (2, 3)
command (1)	version (1)	must be zero (2)
address family identifier (2)		must be zero (2)
IP address (4)		
must be zero (4)		
must be zero (4)		
metric (4)		
address family identifier (2)		must be zero (2)
IP address (4)		
must be zero (4)		
must be zero (4)		
metric (4)		
• • • Other routing entries • • •		

The command field specifies the RIP operation type. Table 10.1 shows the different RIP operation types that are recognized.

TABLE 10.1
RIP Command Field Types

Command Type	Description
RIP request	A request for the responding system to send all or part of its routing table.
RIP response	A message containing all or part of the sender's routing table. This message may be sent in response to a request or poll, or it may be an update message generated by the sender.
Trace on	Now obsolete. Messages containing this command are to be ignored.
Trace off	Now obsolete. Messages containing this command are to be ignored.
Reserved	This value is used by Sun Microsystems for its own purposes. If new commands are added in any succeeding version, they should begin with 6. Messages containing this command may safely be ignored by implementations that do not choose to respond to it.

While both active and passive routers can request specific information, they usually receive information through unsolicited broadcast messages from other routers.

The version field describes the version of the RIP protocol which is set to 1.

The rest of the datagram contains a list of destinations and their metric costs. Figure 10.10 shows only two route entries, but these entries are repeated for each destination. Recall that a destination can be either a network or a specific host. Four octets are used for the destination, and the following 8 octets are zero. This packet format is intended to allow RIP to carry routing information for several different protocols. Recall from our earlier description that RIP was derived from XNS RIP.

In XNS RIP destinations can have up to 14 octet addresses. Each entry is preceded by an address family identifier to indicate what type of address is specified in that entry, and this if followed by 14 octets reserved for address values. The address family identifier for IP is 2. The IP address is the usual Internet address, stored as 4 octets in network order and is the address of the destination. The IP address is aligned on a 32-bit boundary which explains why the two address octets immediately following the address family identifier is set to zero for the IP. The metric field must contain a value between 1 and 15 inclusive, and represents the cost to reach the specified destination. A value of 16 indicates that the destination is not reachable.

By convention, an IP address value of 0.0.0.0 in the address field indicates a default route. If several routers on a network advertise default routes, other routers/hosts can use this to set up default route entries. The default route with the lowest metric is used as the primary default route, and other routes are used as backup routes (see fig. 10.11). This assumes that the routers/hosts are capable of handling more than one default route. This may not be the case with some TCP/IP implementations.

Figure 10.11 Default route advertised by RIP.

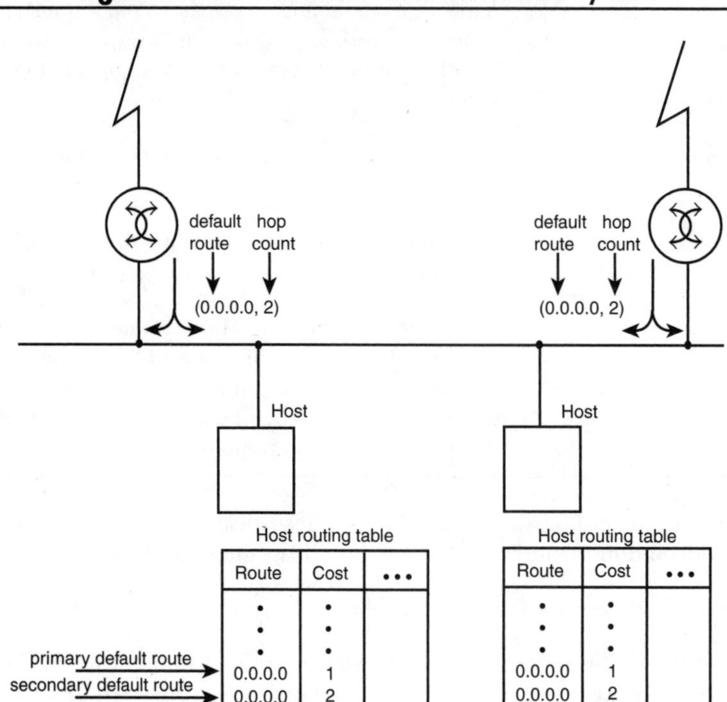

The maximum RIP message size is 512 octets. This includes only the RIP message described in figure 10.10 and not the IP or UDP headers that encapsulate the RIP message. If the RIP message routing information is too large to be accommodated in a single message, the information is spread across several RIP messages. There is no need for special provisions for continuations for RIP messages since each RIP message can be treated independently, and correct results are obtained if the RIP messages are processed individually.

When routing a datagram there is a certain order in which the RIP router checks the destination address in the datagram for a match:

1. First, the destination address must be checked against the list of host addresses.
2. Next, the destination address must be checked to see whether it matches any known subnet or network number.
3. Finally, if none of these match, the default route is used.

When a host receives route updates via RIP, its interpretation of an address depends upon whether it knows the subnet mask that applies to the net. If the host knows the subnet mask to the interface for the directly connected network, it can determine the meaning of the address. For example, consider that the host receives the following route information:

(134.3,0.0, 2)

If the host has a subnet mask of 255.255.255.0, then 134.3 is a network number. If an address of 134.3.5.0 is received, then the subnet number is 0.0.5.0. If an address of 134.3.5.2 is received then 134.3.5.2 is a host address.

If the host does not know the subnet mask, evaluation of an address may be ambiguous. If there is a non-zero host part, there is no clear way to determine whether the address represents a subnet number or a host address. In the absence of a subnet mask, addresses that have a non-zero host part are assumed to represent host addresses.

RIP Message Trace

This section shows protocol decodes of several RIP messages. Understanding protocol decodes helps you to understand the RIP message format.

Figure 10.12 shows a packet decode of a RIP message request, and figure 10.13 shows the packet decode of a RIP message broadcast.

Figure 10.12 RIP request message.

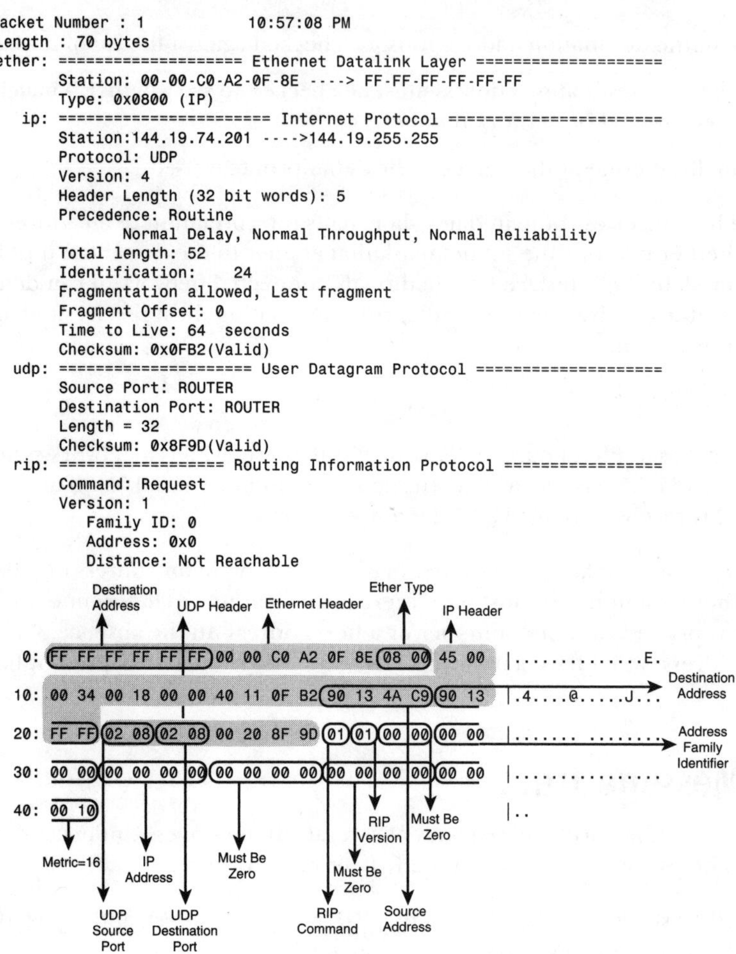

```
Packet Number : 1            10:57:08 PM
Length : 70 bytes
ether: ==================== Ethernet Datalink Layer ====================
       Station: 00-00-C0-A2-0F-8E ----> FF-FF-FF-FF-FF-FF
       Type: 0x0800 (IP)
   ip: ====================== Internet Protocol ======================
       Station:144.19.74.201 ---->144.19.255.255
       Protocol: UDP
       Version: 4
       Header Length (32 bit words): 5
       Precedence: Routine
              Normal Delay, Normal Throughput, Normal Reliability
       Total length: 52
       Identification:    24
       Fragmentation allowed, Last fragment
       Fragment Offset: 0
       Time to Live: 64  seconds
       Checksum: 0x0FB2(Valid)
  udp: ==================== User Datagram Protocol ====================
       Source Port: ROUTER
       Destination Port: ROUTER
       Length = 32
       Checksum: 0x8F9D(Valid)
  rip: ================== Routing Information Protocol =================
       Command: Request
       Version: 1
          Family ID: 0
          Address: 0x0
          Distance: Not Reachable

  0: FF FF FF FF FF FF 00 00 C0 A2 0F 8E 08 00 45 00   |..............E.
 10: 00 34 00 18 00 00 40 11 0F B2 90 13 4A C9 90 13   |.4....@.....J...
 20: FF FF 02 08 02 08 00 20 8F 9D 01 01 00 00 00 00   |....... ........
 30: 00 00 00 00 00 00 00 00 00 00 00 00 00 00 00 00   |................
 40: 00 10                                             |..
```

Figure 10.13 RIP response message.

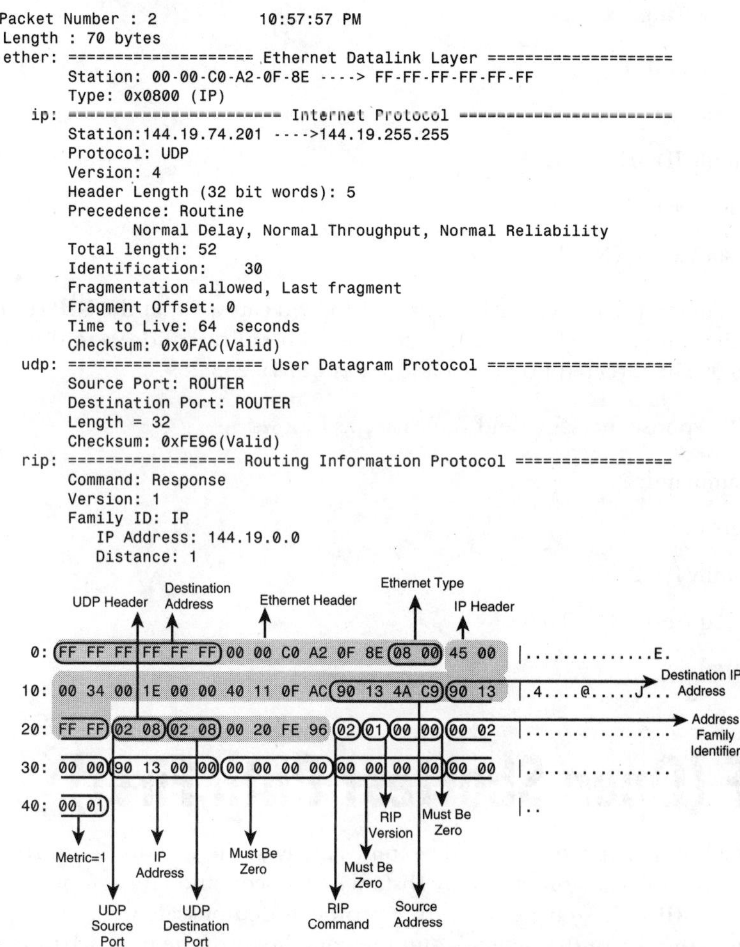

```
Packet Number : 2           10:57:57 PM
 Length : 70 bytes
 ether: ==================== Ethernet Datalink Layer ====================
        Station: 00-00-C0-A2-0F-8E ----> FF-FF-FF-FF-FF-FF
        Type: 0x0800 (IP)
    ip: ======================= Internet Protocol =======================
        Station:144.19.74.201 ---->144.19.255.255
        Protocol: UDP
        Version: 4
        Header Length (32 bit words): 5
        Precedence: Routine
               Normal Delay, Normal Throughput, Normal Reliability
        Total length: 52
        Identification:    30
        Fragmentation allowed, Last fragment
        Fragment Offset: 0
        Time to Live: 64  seconds
        Checksum: 0x0FAC(Valid)
   udp: ==================== User Datagram Protocol ====================
        Source Port: ROUTER
        Destination Port: ROUTER
        Length = 32
        Checksum: 0xFE96(Valid)
   rip: ================== Routing Information Protocol =================
        Command: Response
        Version: 1
        Family ID: IP
           IP Address: 144.19.0.0
           Distance: 1

 0: FF FF FF FF FF FF 00 00 C0 A2 0F 8E 08 00 45 00  |..............E.
10: 00 34 00 1E 00 00 40 11 0F AC 90 13 4A C9 90 13  |.4....@.....J...
20: FF FF 02 08 02 08 00 20 FE 96 02 01 00 00 00 02  |....... .......
30: 00 00 90 13 00 00 00 00 00 00 00 00 00 00 00 00  |................
40: 00 01                                            |..
```


Notice that as discussed earlier, RIP messages are encapsulated in UDP headers. (Chapter 12, "Automatic Configuration," discusses the decode of UDP headers.) A UDP header has a size of 8 octets. The first two octets of the UDP header are the source port number, and the next two octets are the destination port number. In both RIP request and response broadcast messages (refer to figs.10.12 and 10.13), you can see that the UDP source and destination ports are set to 520. This is the well known UDP port number assigned to RIP.

You can see that the RIP request (refer to fig. 10.12) contains a general request to get all possible routes. As you examine the IP header of this message you can see that the

RIP request is sent by 144.19.74.201 as a broadcast on network 144.19.0.0. The directed broadcast address is 144.19.255.255. The RIP request message field values are the following:

Command: 1

Version: 1

Family ID: 0

Address: 0x0

Distance: 16 (Not Reachable)

As you examine the IP header in figure 10.13, you can see that the RIP response is sent by the router at 144.19.74.201 as a directed broadcast address to the network 144.19.0.0. The directed broadcast address is 144.19.255.255.

The RIP response message field values are as follows:

Command: 2

Version: 1

Family ID: 2

IP Address: 144.19.0.0

Distance: 1

OSPF (Open Shortest Path First)

OSPF is a link state protocol that overcomes many of the weaknesses of RIP. As seen in the previous discussion of Vector Distance protocols and an example of its implementation (RIP), these types of routing protocols do not scale well. As there is an increase in the size of the network and the complexity of the network topology, Vector Distance protocols begin to show weaknesses. The routing message size is proportional to the number of networks. The number of routing messages also increase with an increase in the number of routers.

An alternative technique to Vector Distance protocol that is widely implemented is the link state routing protocols, which are explained in the sections that follow.

Link State Protocols

Link state protocols are also called Shortest Path First (SPF). SPF is a reference to the Shortest Path First algorithm that each router uses to compute the routing table. The SPF algorithm was created by Dijkstra, a Dutch computer scientist.

The SPF algorithm is used by each router to compute an internal topology map of the entire network. This topology map contains information on all routers and connected networks. Figure 10.14 shows an example of this topology map. Every router has a complete topological map of the network. This map is represented as a graph in which routers correspond to the nodes, and the networks are arcs or links between the nodes. Routers are neighbors if they share the same link. Thus in figure 10.14, the neighbors of router R1 are R2, R3 and R4 across links Net 1, Net 5, and Net 2.

Figure 10.14 Topological map of network. (Courtesy Learning Tree)

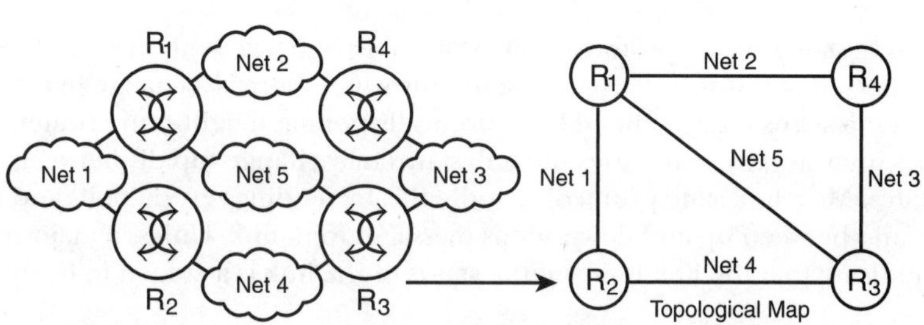

Routers periodically exchange information about the status of their links (see fig. 10.15). The link status can be *up* or *down* to indicate that a link is operational or inoperational. The link status messages are propagated throughout the network so that every router is aware of the same status information. Unlike the case of vector distance protocols, the link information is received from the original source and not as a result of some intermediate computation by another router. In other words, link status messages are received unmodified by all routers. Thus the possibility of a router incorrectly handling the message is reduced in link state routing protocols. Also, it is easier to debug problems that may cause incorrect entries in routing tables.

Figure 10.15 Determining link status. (Courtesy Learning Tree)

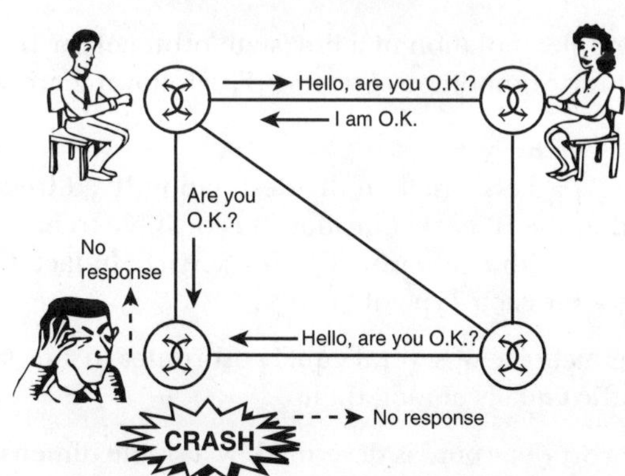

Link status messages carry information about direct connections to a particular router; they do not carry information about indirect connections. Therefore the size of a link status message depends on the number of direct connections that a router has, and not on the size of the network. This makes link state routing protocols more scalable than vector distance protocols.

Typically, most link state protocols do not broadcast the link status messages; instead they use a class D multicast address which is more efficient. If the underlying Data Link layer hardware does not support broadcast or multicast, as in the case of point-to-point links, a copy of the link status message is individually forwarded to all participating routers.

In some link state routing protocols, link status messages are sent on a periodic basis; and in others, link status messages are sent only when there is a change in the status of the link. Link status is determined by periodically polling neighboring routers through a router's interface. In some cases the link status may change rapidly between up and down states. Most link state protocols handle this by sending several polls and measuring the ratio between up and down status messages for a link. Unless a majority of the replies indicate that the link is down, the status of the link is assumed to be up.

It is important to realize that the actual information exchanged by link state routers are not the actual routes, but a status of the links. The status of the links informs routers if there is a direct communication path between two routers. Link status routing protocols compute their routing tables from the link status messages. Routers maintain a topological map of the network, and update this map based on the link status messages that they receive. Whenever there is a change in the link status, the topological map is adjusted, and the routing table is computed using the SPF algorithm. The SPF algorithm computes the shortest path to destinations on the network from the router on which this computation is performed. The SPF algorithm is executed on each router, and there is no dependence on computations performed on other routers. As a result, the SPF algorithm can converge rapidly.

OSPF Features

OSPF is a popular implementation of a link state protocol for IP networks. OSPF is designed as an IGP for Autonomous Systems. The following are some of the features of OSPF:

- OSPF routes IP packets based on the destination IP address and IP Type of Service found in the IP packet header. It is possible to have multiple routes to a destination, each with a different Type of Service. In fact, OSPF calculates separate routes for each Type of Service.
- When there is a choice of several equal-cost routes to a destination, OSPF can distribute traffic equally among them.
- In OSPF, the cost of a route is described by a single dimensionless metric.

- OSPF enables sets of networks to be grouped together into an *area*. The topology of an *area* is hidden from the rest of the Autonomous System. Hiding information enables reduction of routing traffic. Using area routing has the advantage that bad information does not go beyond an area.
- OSPF enables the flexible configuration of IP subnets. Routes distributed by OSPF include subnet masks. It is possible to use Variable Length Subnet Masks (VLSMs) with OSPF. With VLSM, a packet is routed using the longest or most specific match. Host-specific routes are specified with all *1s* in the subnet mask.
- OSPF uses a simple password scheme for authentication. However, authentication is weak as it is based on passwords sent in the clear (without any encryption).
- Routes learned from inter-AS protocols can be passed transparently through the Autonomous System. This externally derived data is kept separate from the OSPF protocol's link state data. External routes are tagged with the advertising route. This enables routers on boundaries of the Autonomous System to pass information through the Autonomous System.
- OSPF allows the network administrator to create virtual network topologies. For example, a virtual link can be set up between two routers even if they are not neighbor routers.
- In OSPF, each multi-access network that has at least two attached routers has a Designated Router. The Designated Router sends link status messages for all links on the network to routers connected to the network. Because only the designated router sends a link status message, this reduces the amount of routing traffic and the size of the topological database.

OSPF Message Format

All OSPF packets have a common 24 octet header. This fixed header contains the information needed to determine how to process the packet. Figure 10.16 shows the common OSPF header.

Figure 10.16 **Fixed OSPF header.**

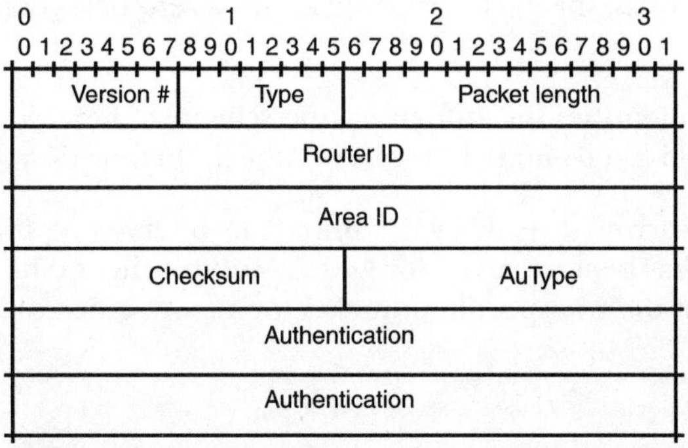

0 1 2 3
0 1 2 3 4 5 6 7 8 9 0 1 2 3 4 5 6 7 8 9 0 1 2 3 4 5 6 7 8 9 0 1

Bits 0–7	Bits 8–15	Bits 16–31
Version #	Type	Packet length
Router ID		
Area ID		
Checksum		AuType
Authentication		
Authentication		

The Version # field specifies the version number of the OSPF protocol. The current OSPF version number is 2.

The Type field describes the format of each of these packet types. Table 10.2 describes the OSPF Type field values.

TABLE 10.2
OSPF Type Field Values

Type	Description
1	Hello
2	Database Description
3	Link State Request
4	Link State Update
5	Link State Acknowledgment

The Packet length field is the length of the protocol packet in octets. This length includes the fixed OSPF header.

The Router ID is a 32-bit identification of the packet's source.

The Area ID is a 32-bit number identifying the area that this OSPF packet belongs to. All OSPF packets are associated with a single area. Typically, OSPF packets travel only over a single hop. Packets that travel over a virtual link are labeled with the backbone Area ID of 0.0.0.0.

The Checksum field is the standard IP checksum of the entire contents of the OSPF packet, but excluding the 64-bit authentication field. The checksum is calculated as the 16-bit one's complement of the one's complement sum of all the 16-bit words in the packet, excluding the authentication field. If the packet's length is not an integral number of 16-bit words, the packet is padded with a zero octet before performing the checksum.

The AuType field identifies the authentication scheme to be used for the packet. The Authentication field is a 64-bit field for use by the authentication scheme.

OSPF packets are carried directly by IP without any intervening transport layer. A protocol ID of 89 has been reserved for OSPF. Multiplexing OSPF packets at the IP layer rather than at the transport layer makes for a more efficient implementation.

OSPF Hello Packet

OSPF Hello packets are of OSPF packet type 1 and are sent in order to determine the status of the directly connected links. Hello OSPF packets are multicast/broadcast of the underlying hardware supports multicast/broadcast. Figure 10.17 shows the Hello message format.

Figure 10.17 OSPF Hello message format.

0 1 2 3 4 5 6 7	8 9 0 1 2 3 4 5	6 7 8 9 0 1 2 3	4 5 6 7 8 9 0 1
Version #	1	Packet length	
Router ID			
Area ID			
Checksum		AuType	
Authentication			
Authentication			
Network Mask			
Hello Interval		Options	Rtr Pri
RouterDeadInterval			
Designated Router			
Backup Designated Router			
Neighbor			
...			

The Network mask is the subnet mask for the interface over which the Hello packet is sent.

The HelloInterval is the number of seconds between this router's Hello packets.

The Options field describes optional capabilities supported by the router.

The Rtr Pri field is this router's Router Priority. This field is used in Designated Router election. When set to 0, the router is ineligible to become a Designated Router.

The RouterDeadInterval is the number of seconds before assuming that a silent router is down.

The Designated Router field is used to identify the Designated Router for this network, as seen by the advertising router. This field value is identified by its IP interface address on the network. When set to 0.0.0.0, it indicates that there is no Designated Router.

The Backup Designated Router field identifies the IP address of the Backup Designated Router for this network. It is set to 0.0.0.0 if there is no Backup Designated Router.

The Neighbor field identifies the Router IDs of each router from which valid Hello packets have been seen recently (since the last RouterDeadInterval seconds) on the network.

OSPF Database Description Packet

The OSPF Database Description packets have an OSPF packet type value of 2. The OSPF Database Description packets are exchanged when a router initializes itself from a router which serves as a master for the contents of the topological database. Because of the large size of the topological database, multiple packets may be used to describe the database. Figure 10.18 shows the OSPF The Database Description packet.

Figure 10.18 OSPF The Database Description packet.

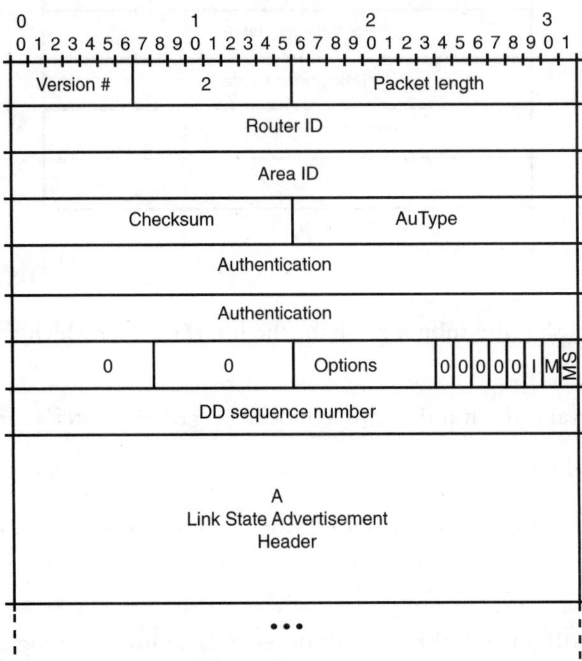

Figure 10.18 shows that the main part of the message is a list of link state advertisement headers.

The Options field describes capabilities supported by the router.

The I-bit field is the Init bit. When set to 1, this packet is the first in the sequence of Database Description packets. The M-bit field is the More bit. When set to 1, it indicates that more Database Description Packets are to follow. Together, the I-bit and M-bit fields control the division of a large topological database description into multiple messages.

The MS-bit is the Master/Slave bit. When set to 1, it indicates that the router is the master during the Database Exchange process. When set to 0, it indicates that the router is a slave.

The DD sequence number is used to properly sequence the collection of Database Description packets so that the slave router can tell if a message is missing. The initial value of this field should be unique. The DD sequence number is incremented until the complete database description has been sent.

The rest of the packet consists of a list of link state advertisements.

Each link state advertisement is described by its link state advertisement header. The link state advertisement is documented in the section "Link State Advertisement Format."

OSPF Link State Request Packet

The OSPF Link State Request packets are OSPF packet type 3. After initializing itself using the OSPF Database Description messages from a master router, a router may detect that parts of its topological database are out of date. The Link State Request packet is used to request the pieces of a neighbor router's database that are more up to date. A router can send multiple Link State Request packets. The requested link status is defined uniquely by the LS sequence number, LS checksum, and LS age. Figure 10.19 shows the format of the Link State Request packet.

Figure 10.19 OSPF Link State Request packet.

0–7	8–15	16–31
Version #	3	Packet length
Router ID		
Area ID		
Checksum		AuType
Authentication		
Authentication		
LS type		
Link State ID		
Advertising Router		
...		

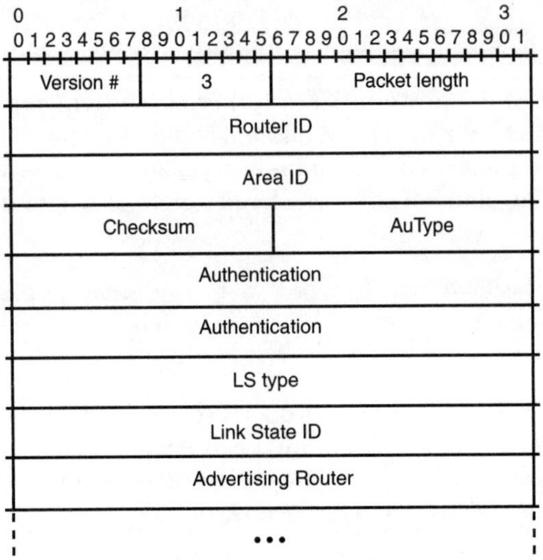

Each link state that is requested is specified by its LS type, Link State ID, and Advertising Router. These values uniquely identify the link state advertisement. The Link State Request packets are requests for the most recent state.

OSPF Link State Update Packet

The OSPF Link State Update packets are of OSPF packet type 4. These packets are used to flood the network with link state advertisements. Several link state advertisements may be included in a single packet. Each Link State Update packet carries a collection of link state advertisements one hop further from its origin.

Link State Update packets (see fig. 10.20) are multicast/broadcast on networks that support multicast/broadcast at the Data Link layer. Link State Update packets are acknowledged in Link State Acknowledgment packets. If Link State Updates are not received by a particular router, they are retransmitted by using unicast Link State Update packets.

Figure 10.20 OSPF Link State Update packet.

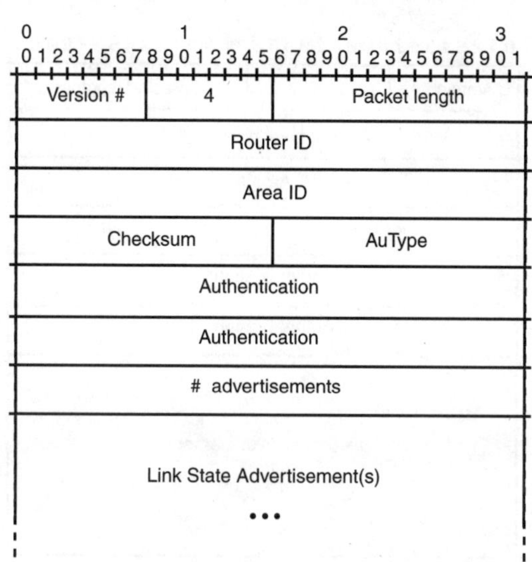

The # advertisements field is the number of link state advertisements included in this update.

The rest of the Link State Update packet consists of a list of link state advertisements. Each link state advertisement is described by its link state advertisement header. The link state advertisement is documented in the section "Link State Advertisement Format."

OSPF Link State Acknowledgment Packet

The OSPF Link State Acknowledgment packets are of OSPF packet type 5. This packet is used to acknowledge a Link State Update packet. Its primary purpose is to make the flooding of link state advertisements reliable. Multiple link state advertisements can be acknowledged in a single Link State Acknowledgment packet.

Figure 10.21 shows the format of a Link State Acknowledgment packet.

Figure 10.21 OSPF Link State Acknowledgment packet.

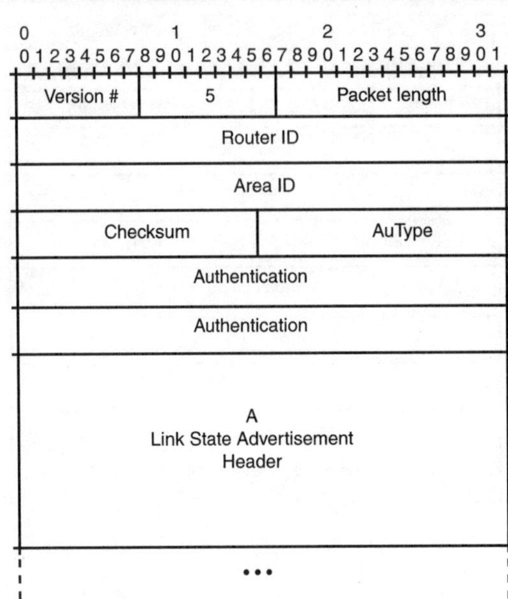

The body of a Link State Acknowledgment packet is simply a list of acknowledged link state advertisement headers. Each link state advertisement is described by its link state advertisement header. The link state advertisement is documented in the following section.

Link State Advertisement Format

There are five types of link state advertisements. Each type begins with a standard 20-octet link state advertisement header. Each link state advertisement describes a part of the OSPF routing domain. Every router sends a router links advertisement. Whenever the router is elected Designated Router, it sends a network links advertisement. All link state advertisements are then flooded throughout the OSPF routing domain. This collection of advertisements is called the *link state topological database.* The link state topological database is used by each router to construct the shortest path tree with the router as root. The node values of this tree yields a routing table.

Figure 10.22 describes the common 20-octet header used with link state advertisements.

Figure 10.22 Link State advertisement header.

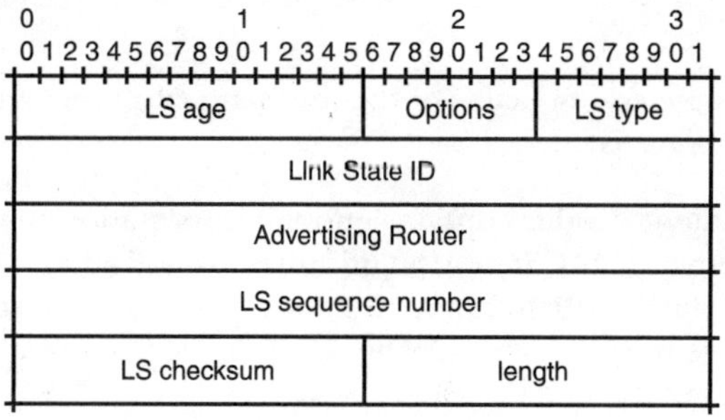

```
0                   1                   2                   3
0 1 2 3 4 5 6 7 8 9 0 1 2 3 4 5 6 7 8 9 0 1 2 3 4 5 6 7 8 9 0 1
+-+-+-+-+-+-+-+-+-+-+-+-+-+-+-+-+-+-+-+-+-+-+-+-+-+-+-+-+-+-+-+-+
|            LS age             |    Options    |    LS type    |
+-+-+-+-+-+-+-+-+-+-+-+-+-+-+-+-+-+-+-+-+-+-+-+-+-+-+-+-+-+-+-+-+
|                        Link State ID                          |
+-+-+-+-+-+-+-+-+-+-+-+-+-+-+-+-+-+-+-+-+-+-+-+-+-+-+-+-+-+-+-+-+
|                     Advertising Router                        |
+-+-+-+-+-+-+-+-+-+-+-+-+-+-+-+-+-+-+-+-+-+-+-+-+-+-+-+-+-+-+-+-+
|                     LS sequence number                        |
+-+-+-+-+-+-+-+-+-+-+-+-+-+-+-+-+-+-+-+-+-+-+-+-+-+-+-+-+-+-+-+-+
|         LS checksum           |             length            |
+-+-+-+-+-+-+-+-+-+-+-+-+-+-+-+-+-+-+-+-+-+-+-+-+-+-+-+-+-+-+-+-+
```

The LS age field is the time in seconds since the link state advertisement was sent.

The Options field indicates optional capabilities supported by the described portion of the routing domain.

The LS type is the type of the link state advertisement. Each link state type has a separate advertisement format (see table 10.3).

TABLE 10.3
OSPF Link Status Types

LS Type	Description
1	Router links
2	Network links
3	Summary link (IP network)
4	Summary link (ASBR)
5	AS external link

The Link State ID field identifies the portion of the internet environment that is described by the advertisement.

The Advertising Router field is the Router ID of the router that originated the link state advertisement.

The LS sequence number field detects old or duplicate link state advertisements. Successive instances of a link state advertisement are given successive LS sequence numbers.

The LS checksum field is a checksum of the complete contents of the link state advertisement, including the link state advertisement header but excepting the LS age field.

The length field is the size in octets of the link state advertisement, including the 20-octet link state advertisement header.

The link advertisement header contains enough information to uniquely identify the advertisement (LS type, Link State ID, and Advertising Router). If there are several instances of a link state advertisement, the most recent one is used by examining the LS age, LS sequence number, and LS checksum fields that are also contained in the link state advertisement header.

RFC 1583, "OSPF Version 2," describes the OSPF protocol in detail.

Router Table Model

In the discussion so far, only portions of the routing table that have been relevant to the discussion have been described. Typically, routers contain additional information in routing table entries. Until the emergence of Simple Network Management Protocol (SNMP) standards for describing the Management Information Base (MIB) for a router, there was no standard representation. Each router vendor designed its own representation of the routing table. Starting with the release of RFC 1213 on "Management Information Base for Network Management of TCP/IP-based internets: MIB-II," a formal MIB definition of the routing table was created. The following is the definition of the routing table MIB using the ASN.1 notation:

```
IpRouteEntry ::=
          SEQUENCE {
              ipRouteDest
                  IpAddress,
              ipRouteIfIndex
                  INTEGER,
              ipRouteMetric1
                  INTEGER,
              ipRouteMetric2
                  INTEGER,
              ipRouteMetric3
                  INTEGER,
              ipRouteMetric4
                  INTEGER,
              ipRouteNextHop
                  IpAddress,
              ipRouteType
                  INTEGER,
```

```
        ipRouteProto
            INTEGER,
        ipRouteAge
            INTEGER,
        ipRouteMask
            IpAddress,
        ipRouteMetric5
            INTEGER,
        ipRouteInfo
            OBJECT IDENTIFIER
    }
```

Figure 10.23 shows the previous information translated into the form of a routing table. As part of the router operation, route entries are added to this routing table. The columns describe the type of information carried for each route.

Figure 10.23 Information contained in a routing table.

ipRoute Dest	ipRoute If Index	ipRoute Metric 1 • • • ipRoute Metric 5	ipRoute Next Hop	ipRoute Type	ipRoute Proto	ipRoute Age	ipRoute Mask	ipRoute Info

The following is a summary of the meanings of these columns:

- **ipRouteDest.** The destination IP address of this route. An entry with a value of 0.0.0.0 is considered a default route. Multiple routes to a single destination can appear in the table, but access to such multiple entries is dependent on the table-access mechanisms defined by the network management protocol in use.
- **ipRouteIfIndex.** The index value which uniquely identifies the local interface through which the next hop of this route should be reached.

- **ipRouteMetric1.** The primary routing metric for this route. The semantics of this metric are determined by the routing protocol specified in the route's ipRouteProto value. If this metric is not used, its value should be set to –1.
- **ipRouteMetric2, ipRouteMetric3, ipRouteMetric4, ipRouteMetric5.** An alternate routing metric for this route. The semantics of this metric are determined by the routing protocol specified in the route's ipRouteProto value. If this metric is not used, its value should be set to –1.
- **ipRouteNextHop.** The IP address of the next hop of this route.
- **ipRouteType.** The type of route. Can be other(1), invalid(2), direct(3), indirect(4). The direct/indirect values refer to the notion of direct and indirect routing in the IP architecture. Setting this object to the value invalid(2) has the effect of invalidating the corresponding entry in the ipRouteTable object; that is, it effectively disassociates the destination from the route. It is an implementation-specific matter as to whether the agent removes an invalidated entry from the table.
- **ipRouteProto.** The routing mechanism via which this route was learned. Values include the following: other(1), which means manual configured entries and none of the following non-protocol information; local(2), which means entries set via a network; netmgmt(3), which means entry set by a management protocol; icmp(4), which means entry set by an ICMP message such as redirect; egp(5); ggp(6); hello(7); rip(8); is-is(9); es-is(10); ciscoIgrp(11); bbnSpfIgp(12); ospf(13); bgp(14).
- **ipRouteAge.** The number of seconds since this route was last updated or otherwise determined to be correct.
- **ipRouteMask.** Indicates the mask to be logical-ANDed with the destination address before being compared to the value in the ipRouteDest field. If the value of the ipRouteDest is 0.0.0.0 (a default route), then the mask value is also 0.0.0.0.
- **ipRouteInfo.** A reference to MIB definitions specific to the particular routing protocol that is responsible for this route.

Summary

This chapter focused on the protocols Routing Information Protocol (RIP) and Open Shortest Path First (OSPF) that are used within Autonomous Systems. Both are examples of Interior Gateway Protocols (IGPs) that are used within Autonomous Systems. RIP is a classic example of a Vector Distance protocol, and OSPF is a link state routing protocol that is a commonly implemented IGP for IP Autonomous Systems. The RIP protocol has gone through modifications to overcome some of its limitations. The new RIP protocol is called RIP version 2 (RIPv2). The version of RIP discussed in this chapter is RIP version 1, a commonly deployed protocol.

The preferred protocol for use between Autonomous Systems is Border Gateway Protocol (BGP4). Discussion on RIPv2 and BGP4 is planned in the sequel to this book titled "TCP/IP: The Professional Reference" by the same author and publisher, New Riders Publishing.

Test Yourself

1. For what reasons do organizations build their networks as Autonomous Systems?
2. List the differences between Vector Distance and Link State routing protocols.
3. Give examples of Vector Distance protocols.
4. Give examples of Link State protocols.
5. What is the metric count used in RIP? What is its minimum and maximum value?
6. Is it possible to build networks using RIP that have more than 15 routers?
7. Is it possible to build networks using RIP that have more than 15 routers between two nodes on a network?
8. An RIP router has the following entries in its routing table:

Destination	Distance	Next Hop Router
134.33.0.0	1	(directly connected)
145.108.0.0	1	(directly connected)

The following RIP update is received from the router at 145.108.0.0.

Destination	Distance
144.19.0.0	2
200.1.1.0	3
200.2.5.0	2
0.0.0.0	3

Show the new contents of the router table. What is the default route in the router table?

9. An RIP router has the following entries in its router table:

Destination	Distance	Next Hop Router
134.33.0.0	1	(directly connected)
145.108.0.0	1	(directly connected)
0.0.0.0	2	134.33.12.1

34.0.0.0	4	145.108.1.9
141.12.0.0	3	145.108.1.9

The following RIP update is received from the router at 134.33.12.1:

Destination	Distance
0.0.0.0	1
199.245.180.0	3
34.0.0.0	2
0.0.0.0	3
141.12.0.0	2

Show the new contents of the router table. What are the default route(s) in the routing table?

10. There is a chain of 16 networks connected by 15 routers. The routers use the RIP protocol. If adjacent time broadcast intervals for the routers are staggered by 15 seconds, how long will it take for a routing update to reach from one end of the network to the other end?
11. List the potential problems with RIP. Under what conditions might a network administrator select RIP?
12. Describe the difference between passive and active RIP routers. Give an example of each.
13. What are some of the problems associated with an RIP metric count?
14. Under what conditions does RIP converge slowly? Use an example network to illustrate your point.
15. Describe the "count-to-infinity" problem in RIP.
16. Describe the techniques used to eliminate slow convergence in RIP.
17. What, if any, is the potential problem with using the *poison reverse with triggered update* technique with RIP?
18. What are the typical RIP-type messages you can expect to see in a network?
19. When do you think an RIP request type message might be issued?
20. What RIP-type message is used by RIP to broadcast routes?
21. Why does RIP use a transport protocol? What are the port numbers used by RIP in connection with this transport protocol?
22. What is the maximum number of routes that can be carried in a single RIP message? Show how you arrived at your answer.

23. Can RIP be used on a network with Variable Length Subnet Masks? Give reasons for your answer.

24. Decode the following packet type:

```
 0: FF FF FF FF FF FF 00 00 C0 A2 0F 8E 08 00 45 00 ¦..............E.
10: 00 34 00 2C 00 00 40 11 0F 9E 90 13 4A C9 90 13 ¦.4.,..@.....J...
20: FF FF 02 08 02 08 00 20 FE 96 02 01 00 00 00 02 ¦....... ........
30: 00 00 90 13 00 00 00 00 00 00 00 00 00 00 00 00 ¦................
40: 00 01                                           ¦..
```

25. List some of the OSPF features.

26. Does OSPF use a transport protocol? Draw a diagram showing the protocol layers that are used with OSPF.

27. What is the purpose of an OSPF Hello packet?

28. What are the purposes of an OSPF Database Description packet?

29. What are the purposes of an OSPF Link State Request packet?

30. What are the purposes of an OSPF Link State Update packet?

31. How is reliable delivery of OSPF Link State Update packets done?

32. What OSPF packet type is used to perform flooding of link status messages?

CHAPTER 11

Transfer Protocols

The TCP/IP transport protocols correspond to the Transport layer of the OSI model. The TCP/IP protocol suite defines two standard transport protocols: TCP and UDP. TCP (Transmission Control protocol) implements a reliable data-stream protocol, whereas UDP (User Datagram protocol) implements an unreliable data-stream protocol.

Both TCP and UDP run on top of the Internet protocol and build on the services provided by IP (see fig. 11.1). IP provides a connectionless datagram service between two computers. By using TCP and UDP, you can deliver data not just to a remote computer, but to an application process running on the remote computer. These application processes are identified by port numbers. TCP can ensure that data is delivered reliably to the destination by providing a connection-oriented service. UDP, on the other hand, is connectionless and cannot guarantee delivery of data. However, UDP is useful in many applications, such as those where data needs to be sent to a particular application running on a machine, or in situations where application data needs to be broadcasted or multicasted.

Figure 11.1 TCP and UDP.

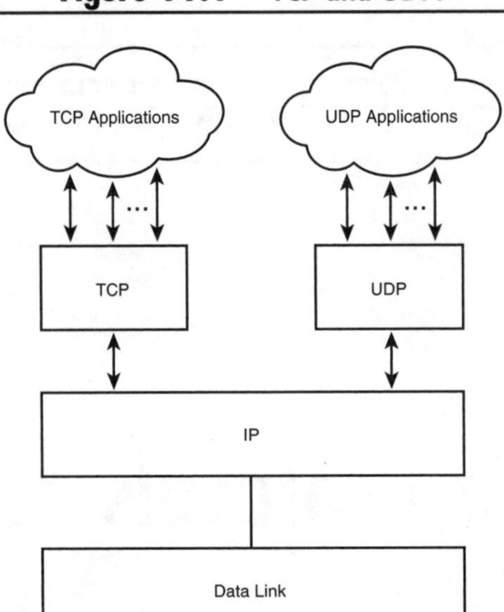

The Transmission Control Protocol (TCP)

The TCP protocol provides a very important service in the TCP/IP protocol suite because it provides a standard general-purpose method for reliable delivery of data. Rather than inventing their own transport protocol, applications typically use TCP to provide reliable delivery of data because the TCP protocol has reached considerable maturity and many improvements have been made to the protocol to improve its performance and reliability.

TCP provides end-to-end reliability between an application process running on one computer system to another application process running on another computer system (see fig. 11.2). TCP provides this reliability by adding services on top of IP. IP is connectionless and does not guarantee delivery of packets. TCP assumes that IP is inherently unreliable, so TCP adds services to ensure end-to-end delivery of data. Because TCP has very few expectations on the services provided by the network, TCP can run across a large variety of hardware. All that TCP asks for is that some kind of simple, unreliable datagram service be provided at the lower layer. Sometimes networks such as X.25 provide sophisticated connection-oriented services at the Network layer. In this case, the IP datagrams are transmitted on an X.25 virtual circuit, and the TCP protocol packets are encapsulated inside the IP datagrams.

TCP is the primary transport protocol used to provide reliable, full-duplex, virtual-circuit connections. The most common use of TCP is to run it over IPv4 or Ipv6, although several experimental projects have been done to run TCP on other Network layer protocols.

Figure 11.2 End-to-End TCP reliability.

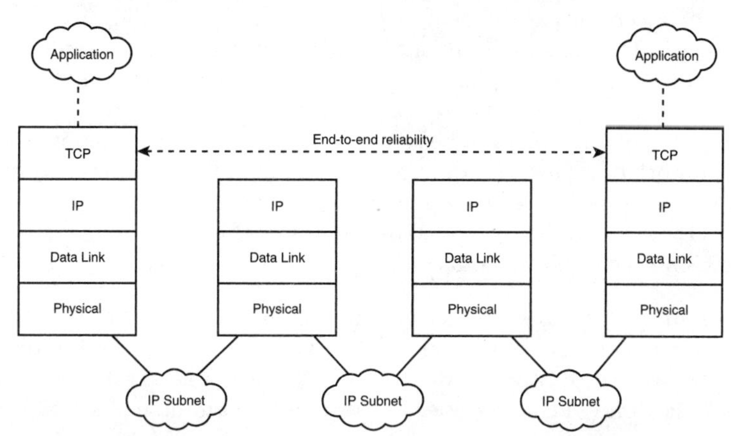

Although IP is implemented on hosts and routers, TCP is typically implemented on hosts only to provide reliable end-to-end data delivery. Today, many routers are not just routers—they also provide other services that make them easy to configure and manage. For example, many commercial routers can also implement TCP or UDP to provide remote login and network-management facilities. Even though TCP and UDP are implemented in routers, the transport protocols are not used by routing services and messages.

The TCP protocol is described in RFC 792 (STD 7), "Transmission Control Protocol." The UDP protocol is described in RFC 768 (STD 6), "User Datagram Protocol." RFC 1122 (STD 3), "Requirements for Internet Hosts—Communication Layers," contains important additions. Both the TCP and UDP protocol status is recommended. But in actual practice, all TCP/IP devices—unless they are pure routers—will implement TCP and UDP. In most implementations, UDP logic is embedded in the TCP module and is not separate from the TCP implementation.

The following section discusses the features of TCP.

TCP Features

TCP has the following noteworthy features:

- Basic data transfer
- Reliability
- Flow control
- Multiplexing
- Connections
- Precedence and security

Basic Data Transfer

Basic data transfer is the capability of TCP to transfer a continuous stream of octets in each direction. The octets are sent among application processes running on remote systems that use TCP. The application processes then group a set of bytes that need to be sent/received into a message *segment.* Message segments can be of arbitrary length. Ultimately, the messages have to be sent in IP datagrams that are limited by the MTU size of a network interface. However, at the TCP level, there is no real restriction on message size because the details of accommodating the message segments in IP datagrams is the task of the IP layer. For reasons of efficiency in managing messages, TCP connections typically negotiate a maximum segment size.

Messages sent by TCP have an octet stream orientation (see fig. 11.3). TCP keeps track of each octet that is sent/received. The TCP has no inherent notion of a block of data, unlike other transport protocols, which typically keep track of the Transport Protocol Data Unit (TPDU) number and not the octet number. TCP can be used to provide multiple virtual-circuit connections between two TCP hosts.

Figure 11.3 TCP octet stream orientation. (Courtesy Learning Tree)

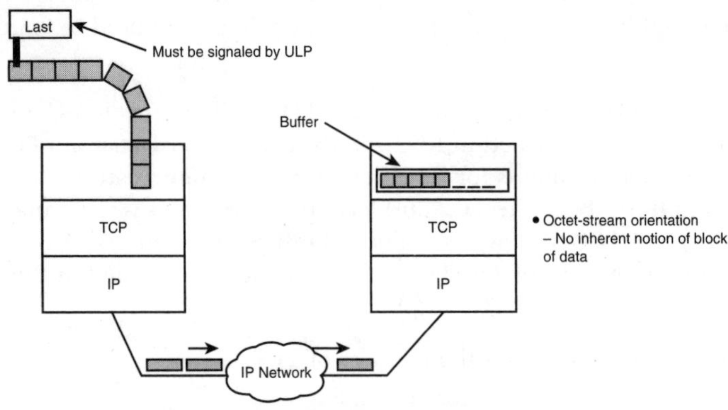

Application processes that use TCP send data in whatever size is convenient for sending. For example, an application can send data that is as little as one octet or as big as several kilo-octets. TCP numbers each octet that it sends. The octets are delivered to the application processes at the receiving end in the order in which they are sent. This process is called *sequencing* of octets.

An application can send data to TCP a few octets at a time. TCP buffers this data and sends these octets either as a single message or as several smaller message segments. All that TCP guarantees is that data arrives at the receiver in the order in which it was sent. For example, if an application sends 1,024 octets of data over a period of ten seconds, the data can be sent across the network in a single TCP packet of 1,024 octets, or in four TCP packets of 256 octets, or in any combination of octets.

Because TCP sends data as a stream of octets, there is no real end-of message marker in the data stream. To ensure that all the data submitted to the TCP module has been transmitted, a *push* function is required to be implemented by TCP. The push causes the TCP promptly to send any data that it has received from an application up to that point.

The actual data that is sent by TCP is treated as an unstructured stream of octets. TCP does not contain any facility to superimpose an application-dependent structure on the data. For example, you cannot tell TCP to treat the data as a set of records in a database and to send one record at a time. Any such structuring must be handled by the application processes that communicate by using TCP.

Reliability

One of the most important features of TCP is reliable end-to-end data delivery. In order to provide reliability, TCP must recover from data that is damaged, lost, duplicated, or delivered out of order by the Network layer. TCP uses the Positive Acknowledgment Retransmission (PAR) scheme for achieving reliability. Figure 11.4 shows the PAR scheme, where all data and acknowledgments are received as expected. This figure shows that data is sent only after previously sent data has been acknowledged. Figure 11.5 shows how the PAR scheme recovers from lost data.

Figure 11.4 PAR scheme under normal operation.

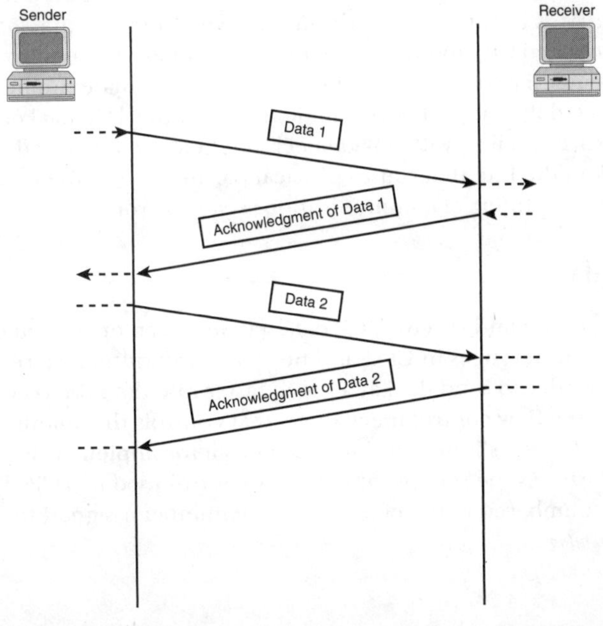

Figure 11.5 PAR scheme illustrating recovery from lost data.

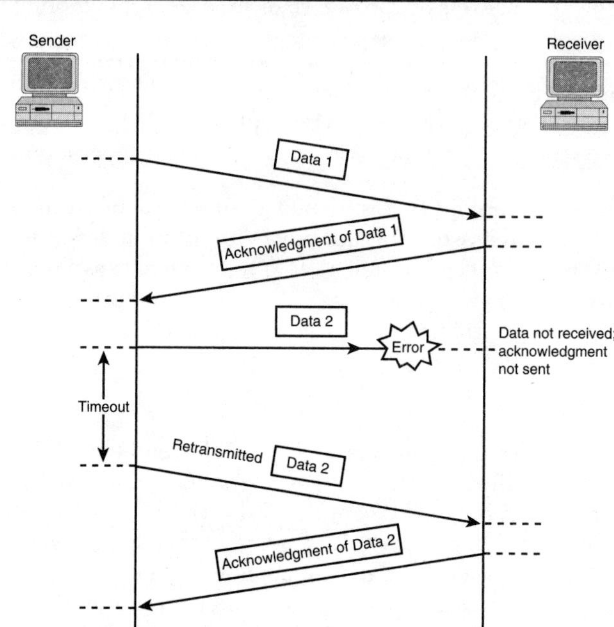

TCP implements PAR by assigning a sequence number to each octet that is transmitted and by requiring a positive acknowledgment (ACK) from the receiving TCP module. If the ACK is not received within a time-out interval, the data is retransmitted. At the receiver TCP module, the sequence numbers are used to correctly order segments that may have arrived out of order and to eliminate duplicates. Corruption of data is detected by using a checksum field filed in the TCP packet header. Data segments that are received with a bad checksum field are discarded. Unless there is a physical break in the link that causes physical partitioning of the network, TCP recovers from most Internet communications system errors.

Flow Control

Computers that send and receive TCP data segments can operate at different data rates because of differences in CPU and network bandwidth. As a result, it is quite possible for a sender to send data at a much faster rate than the receiver can handle. TCP implements a flow control mechanism that controls the amount of data sent by the sender. TCP uses a sliding window mechanism for implementing flow control. Figure 11.6 illustrates the sliding window flow control used in TCP. The stream of data in TCP is numbered at the octet level. The number assigned to an octet is called the *sequence number*.

Figure 11.6 TCP Sliding Window flow control. (Courtesy Learning Tree)

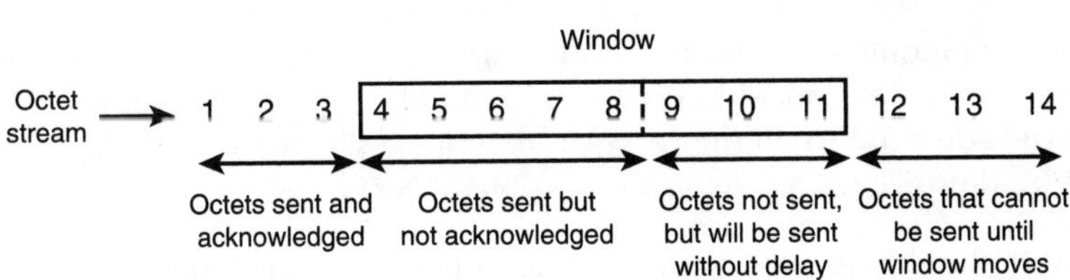

The receiver TCP module sends back to the sender an acknowledgment that indicates a range of acceptable sequence numbers beyond the last segment successfully received. This range of acceptable sequence numbers is called a *window.* The window, therefore, indicates the number of octets that the sender can transmit before receiving further permission.

In figure 11.6, the window range is from sequence numbers 4 through 11. In this example, octets 1 through 3 have been sent and acknowledged. Octets 4 through 11, which are in the window range, may have been sent or are waiting to be sent, but they have not been acknowledged yet. The sender TCP is not required to send a TCP segment that is equal to the window size. The window size indicates the maximum number of unacknowledged octets that TCP can send. In figure 11.6, octets 4 through 8 have been sent; octets 9 through 11, which are within the window range, have not been sent, but they can be sent without delay. Octets 12 and beyond cannot be sent because they are to the right of the window range. To summarize, the TCP flow control mechanism exhibits the following properties:

- Octets that are to the left of the window range have already been sent and acknowledged.
- Octets in the window range can be sent without any delay. Some of the octets in the window range may already have been sent, but they have not been acknowledged. Other octets may be waiting to be sent.
- Octets that are to the right of the window range have not been sent. These octets can be sent only when they fall in the window range.

The left edge of the window is the lowest numbered octet that has not been acknowledged. The window can advance; that is, the left edge of the window can move to the right when an acknowledgment is received for data that has been sent. The TCP packet containing the acknowledgment contains information about the window size that the sender should use.

The window size reflects the amount of buffer space available for new data at the receiver. If this buffer space size shrinks because the receiver is being overrun, the receiver will send back a smaller window size. In the extreme case, it is possible for the receiver to send a window size of only one octet, which means that only one octet can be sent. This situation is referred to as the *silly window syndrome,* and most TCP implementations take special measures to avoid it. See "Avoiding the Silly Window Syndrome," later in this chapter.

When a TCP module sends back a window size of zero, it indicates to the sender that its buffers are full and no additional data should be sent. TCP includes mechanisms to shrink window size when the receiver experiences congestion of data and to expand window size as the congestion problem clears.

The goal of the sliding window mechanism is to keep the channel full of data and to reduce to a minimum the delays experienced by waiting for acknowledgments.

Multiplexing

TCP enables many processes within a single computer to use the TCP communications services simultaneously; this is called TCP *multiplexing.* Because these processes may be communicating over the same network interface, they are identified by the IP address of the network interface. However, you need more than the IP address of the network interface to identify a process because all processes that are using the same network interface on a computer have a common IP address.

TCP associates a port number value for applications that use TCP. This association enables several connections to exist between application processes on remote computers because each connection uses a different pair of port numbers. Figure 11.7 shows several connections being multiplexed over TCP.

Figure 11.7 TCP Multiplexing.

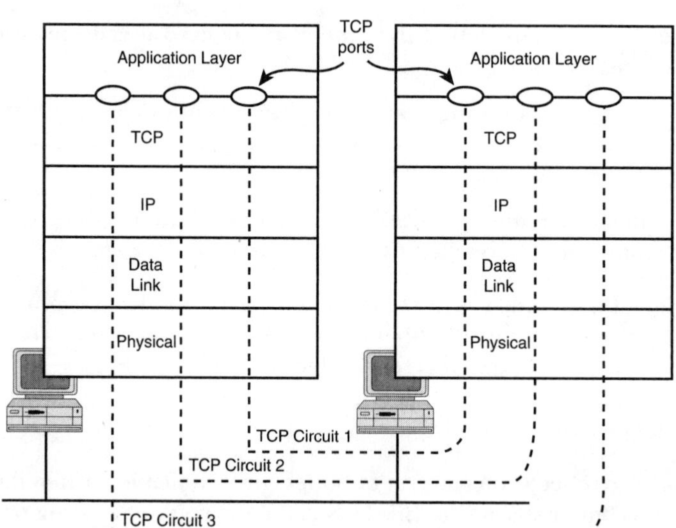

The binding of ports to application processes is handled independently by each computer. In many computer systems, a *logger* or *super daemon* process watches over the port numbers that are identified or well known to other computer systems.

Connections

Before application processes can send data by using TCP, they must establish a connection. The connections are made between the port numbers of the sender and the receiver nodes. A TCP connection identifies the end points involved in the connection. The end point (see fig. 11.8) is formally defined as a pair that includes the IP address and port number:

(IP address, port numbers)

The *IP address* is the inter-network address of the network interface over which the TCP/IP application communicates. The *port* number is the TCP port number that identifies the application. The *end point* contains both the IP address and port numbers because port identifiers are selected independently by each TCP, and they may not be unique. By concatenating the unique IP address with port numbers, a unique value for the end point is created.

Figure 11.8 TCP end point.

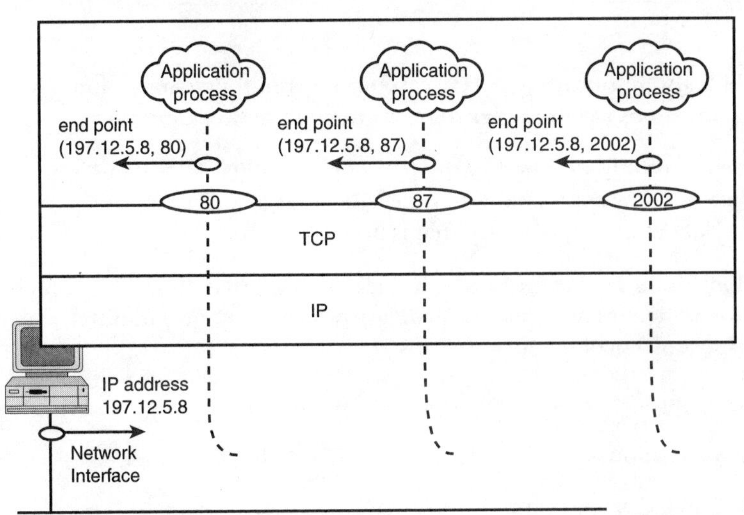

A TCP connection is established between two end points (see fig. 11.9). The TCP connection is identified by the parameters of both end points, as follows:

(IP address1, port number1, IP address2, port number2)

These parameters make it possible to have several application processes connect to the same remote end point. Figure 11.9 shows that there are several application processes that connect to the same remote end point (199.11.23.1, 2001). The TCP module at 199.11.23.1 can keep the different TCP connections separate because TCP uses both the local and remote end points to identify the connection. In figure 11.9, the end point (199.11.23.1, 2001) is the same, but the end points at the other end of the connection are different. This difference enables TCP to keep these connections separate.

Figure 11.9 TCP connection between end points. (Courtesy Learning Tree)

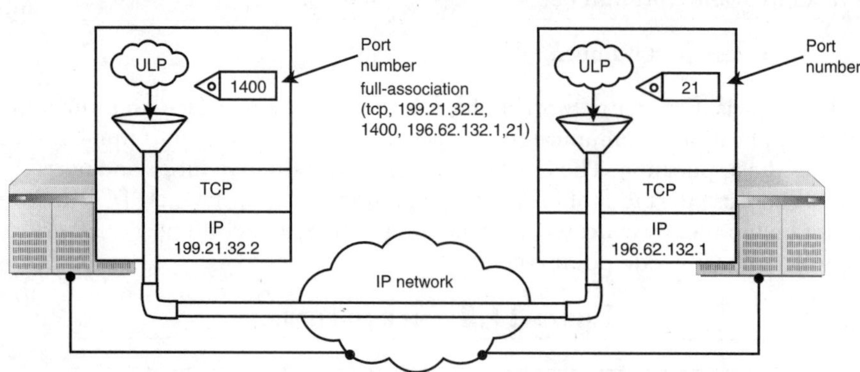

Figure 11.9 also illustrates that TCP can support multiple connections concurrently. These connections are multiplexed over the same network interface.

A connection is fully specified by the pair of end points. A local end point can participate in many connections to different foreign end points. A TCP connection can carry data in both directions; that is, it is *full duplex.*

In relationship to TCP connections, it is also helpful to define the notion of a half association and a full association. A *half association* is an end point that also includes the transport protocol name, as follows:

(TransportProtocol, IP address, port number)

The half associations in figure 11.9 are, therefore, the following:

(tcp, 199.21.32.2, 1400)

(tcp, 196.62.132.1, 21)

A *full association* consists of two half associations and is expressed by the following ordered pair:

(TransportProtocol, IP address1, port number1, IP address2, port number2)

The *TransportProtocol* is listed only once because it has to be the same on both parts of the half association. The concept of half- and full associations is useful when dealing with different transport protocols. As an example, the full association in figure 11.9 is listed as follows:

(tcp, 199.21.32.2, 1400, 196.62.132.1, 21)

A full association consisting of source and destination IP addresses, and source and destination port numbers uniquely identifies a TCP connection.

TCP Host Environment

TCP is implemented as a protocol module that interacts with the computer's operating system. In many operating systems, the TCP module is accessed like the file system of the operating system. The BSD Sockets interface that is implemented on Unix systems and the more recent Winsock interface implemented by Microsoft's proprietary operating systems are based on this file system model.

The TCP module depends on other operating system functions to manage its data structures and services. The actual interface to the network is typically controlled by a device driver module. TCP does not interact directly with the device driver module. Instead, TCP calls the IP module, which in turn calls on the device driver module (see fig. 11.10).

Figure 11.10 TCP module interaction with network.

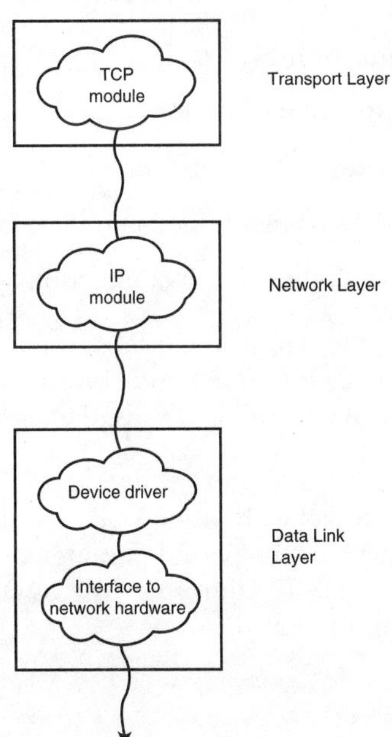

It is also possible to offload the processing of the TCP/IP protocol stack modules to a front-end processor. The front-end processor acts as a dedicated protocol communications device that executes the protocol modules (see fig. 11.11). There has to be a mechanism for communication between the host and its front-end processor. Typically, this mechanism is provided by a file system interface.

Figure 11.11 Offloading TCP processing.

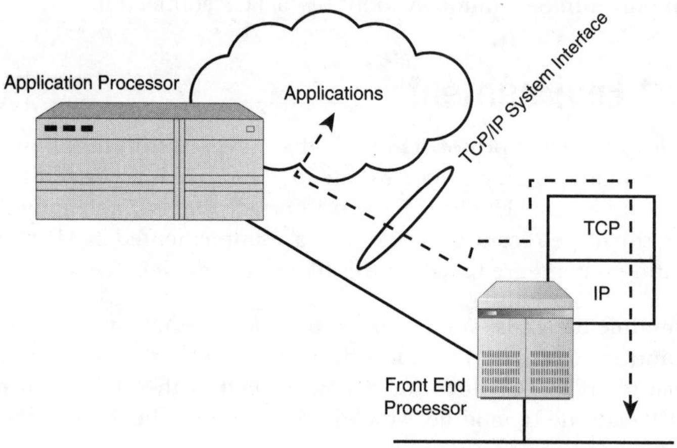

From an abstract viewpoint, applications will interface with the TCP module with the following system calls:

- ◆ OPEN to open a connection
- ◆ CLOSE to close a connection
- ◆ SEND to send data on an open connection
- ◆ RECEIVE to receive data from an open connection
- ◆ STATUS to find information about a connection

These system calls are implemented just like calls from user programs on the operating system. For example, the calls to open and close a connection are like the calls to open and close a file. The call to send or receive data is like the call to write or read from a file.

The TCP system calls can interact with other TCP modules anywhere on an internet system. The TCP system calls must be passed parameters for executing the system call. Examples of such parameters are IP addresses, type of service, precedence, security, application port number, and so on.

TCP Connection Opening and Closing

A connection is specified in the OPEN call on the local port. The parameters supplied are the destination end point. The return from the system call contains a short integer value called the *handle*, by which the user refers to the connection in subsequent calls. Information about the connection is stored in a data structure called a *Transmission Control Block* (TCB), and the handle is used to access the information in the TCB.

TCP identifies two types of OPEN calls:

- Active OPEN
- Passive OPEN

In an active OPEN call, the connection establishment is to be actively initiated. An active OPEN call translates to a TCP message that is generated to contact another end point.

A passive OPEN call signals an intent to receive an active OPEN connection; it does not generate any TCP message segment. A passive OPEN request means that the process wants to accept incoming connection requests rather than attempting to initiate a connection. Often the process requesting a passive OPEN call will accept a connection request from any caller. Alternatively, a passive OPEN call can specify that it can accept only a connection from a specific end point.

Processes that issue passive OPENs and wait for matching active OPENs from other processes can be informed by the TCP when connections have been established (see fig. 11.12).

If two processes issue active OPENs to each other at the same time, they will be correctly connected (see fig. 11.13). Using two active OPENs to set up a TCP connection is useful in distributed computing, where components can act asynchronously with respect to each other.

Figure 11.12 Active and passive OPENs for setting up TCP connections.

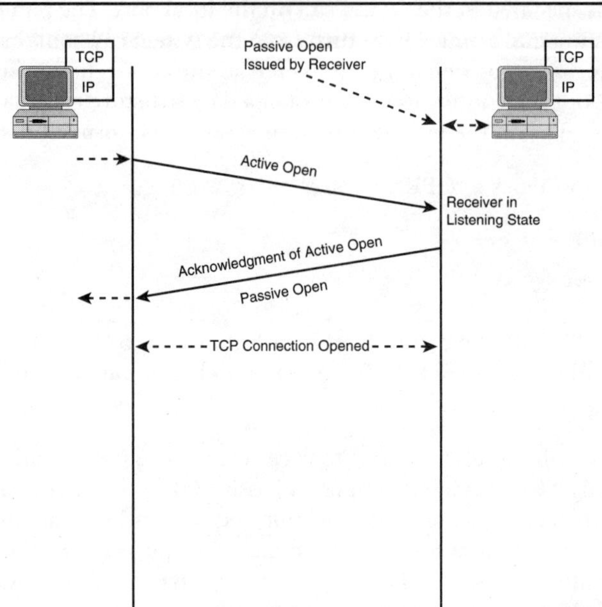

Figure 11.13 Using only active OPENs for setting up TCP connections.

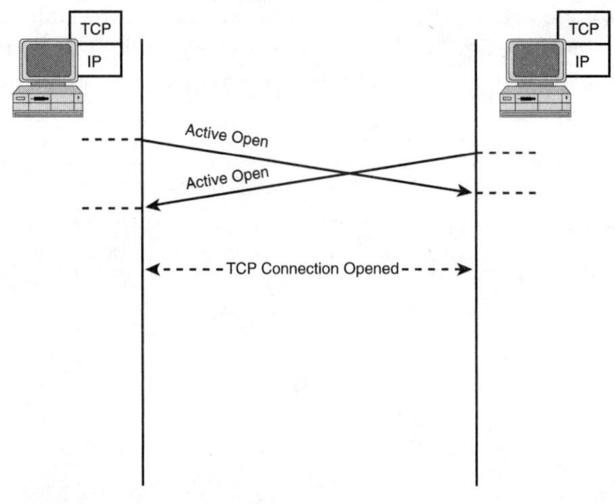

TCP Message Format

Figure 11.14 shows the TCP packet structure. Like most TCP/IP protocols, the TCP header is using a 32-bit word format.

Figure 11.14 TCP packet structure.

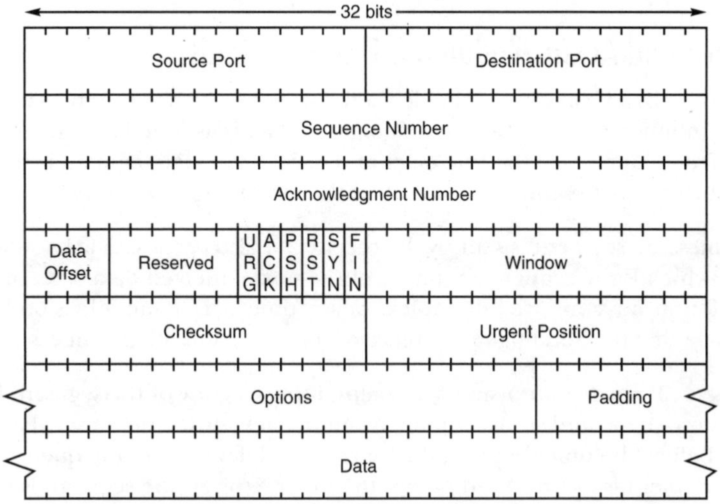

The following sections define the individual fields in the TCP header.

Source and Destination Port Number Fields

The Source Port and Destination Port number fields (refer to figure 11.14) are used to identify the end point processes in the TCP virtual circuit. Source- and Destination Port numbers are needed in defining associations between processes. Some port numbers are well-known port numbers, others have been registered, and still others are dynamically assigned.

The Assigned Number RFC, which is issued periodically as a different numbered RFC, contains a description of some of the well-known port numbers. Table 2.5 in Chapter 2, "TCP/IP Protocol Layering Concepts," shows some TCP port number assignments. Port numbers in the range of 0–1,023 are called *well-known port numbers* and are administered by IANA. Port numbers greater than 1,023 can be registered but are not controlled by IANA. These port numbers are, therefore, called *registered port numbers.* Not all port numbers at 1,024 and greater are registered. Some are assigned on an as-needed basis and are called *transient port numbers.* Transient port numbers are allocated within a TCP implementation. The actual algorithm used to allocate transient port numbers is implementation-dependent.

TCP modules are free to associate any port number with application processes, with the restriction that well-known ports are reserved for special applications. In many operating systems, application processes can "own" ports. These ports are allocated on a random basis as long as they are greater than 1,023. Some implementations use a hashing function that takes into account the process name when allocating port numbers. Typically, the high-order bits of the port number are associated with the process name.

Sequence and Acknowledgment Number Fields

Transmission by TCP is made reliable via the use of sequence numbers and acknowledgment numbers. Conceptually, each octet of data is assigned a sequence number. The sequence number of the first octet of data in a message segment is sent in the TCP header for that segment and is called the *segment sequence number.*

When a message segment is sent by the receiver, it also carries an acknowledgment number, which is the sequence number of the next expected data octet of transmission. TCP transmissions are full duplex. At any time, a TCP module is both a sender for the data that it is sending and a receiver for data from other senders.

When the TCP needs to transmit a segment, it puts a copy of the segment into its transmission queue and starts a timer. When the acknowledgment for that data is received before the timer expires, the segment is deleted from the queue. If the acknowledgment is not received before the timer expires, the segment is retransmitted from its copy in the transmission queue.

The 32-bit Sequence Number field (refer to figure 11.14) is the number of the first byte of data in the current message. If the SYN flag field is set to 1, this field defines the initial sequence number (ISN) to be used for that session, and the first data offset is ISN+1. A 32-bit value is used to avoid using old sequence numbers that already may have been assigned to data that is in transit on the network.

The Acknowledgment Number field is used to indicate the sequence number of the next byte expected by the receiver. TCP acknowledgments are cumulative. That is, a single acknowledgment can be used to acknowledge a number of prior TCP message segments. After a connection is established, the acknowledgment number is always sent.

An acknowledgment by TCP guarantees only that the TCP module has received the data. The acknowledgment does not guarantee that the data has been delivered to the application running on top of TCP. An acknowledgment indicates that the receiving TCP has taken the responsibility to deliver the data to the application. It is possible that other system errors in the TCP module and the application interface may prevent the data from being delivered to the application.

Data Offset Field

The Data Offset field is the number of 32-bit words in the TCP header (refer to figure 11.14). This field is needed because the TCP options field could be variable in length. Without TCP options, the Data Offset field is five words (20 octets). The TCP header, even if it includes options, is an integral number of 32 bits.

The only TCP option that has been defined is the Maximum Segment Size (MSS) option. This option is used at the start of a TCP connection. When this option has been specified, the Data Offset field value is six words (24 octets).

The Reserved fields that follow the Data Offset field must be set to 0.

The Flags Field

The Flags field in the TCP header (refer to figure 11.14) have the following meanings:

- When the ACK flag is set, it indicates that the Acknowledgment Number field is valid.
- The SYN flag is used to indicate the opening of a virtual-circuit connection.
- The FIN flag is used to terminate the connection.
- The RST bit is used to reset the virtual circuit due to unrecoverable errors. When an RST is received in a TCP segment, the receiver must respond by immediately terminating the connection. A reset causes both sides immediately to release the connection and all its resources. As a result, transfer of data ceases in both directions, which can result in loss of data that is in transit. A TCP RST is not the normal way to close a TCP connection; it indicates an abnormal condition. To close a TCP connection normally, use the FIN flag. The reason for a reset can be a host crash or delayed duplicate SYN packets.
- When the PSH flag is set, it tells TCP immediately to deliver data for this message to the upper-layer process.
- The URG flag is used to send out-of-band data without waiting for the receiver to process octets already in the stream.

TCP connections are opened by using the three-way-handshake procedure. The SYN and the ACK flags are used to indicate the following packets:

SYN = 1 and ACK = 0	Open connection packet
SYN = 1 and ACK = 1	Open connection acknowledgment
SYN = 0 and ACK = 1	Data packet or ACK packet

The procedures to establish connections utilize the synchronize (SYN) control flag and involves an exchange of three messages termed the three-way handshake (see fig. 11.15).

Figure 11.15 TCP SYN flag use. (Courtesy Learning Tree)

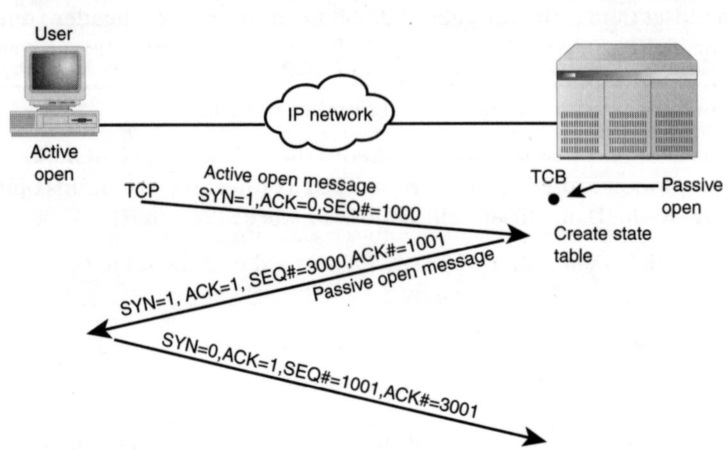

A connection is initiated by the rendezvous of an arriving segment containing a SYN and a waiting TCB entry. The arriving TCP segment is generated by an active OPEN, and the waiting TCB entry is created by a passive OPEN. The matching of an active- and a passive OPEN results in the creation of a connection. The SYN flag is set to 1 to indicate that sequence numbers have been synchronized in both directions. In figure 11.15, the active OPEN generates a TCP segment with the following flags:

***begin ULSYN =1, ACK = 0

When the receiving TCP that has issued a passive OPEN receives an active OPEN, it acknowledges this active OPEN with the following TCP flags:

SYN = 1, ACK = 1

This acknowledgment of the active OPEN packet is sometimes called the passive OPEN packet. The ACK = 1 flag indicates that the Acknowledgment Number field contains valid data.

Figure 11.16 illustrates the general mechanism of the three-way handshake.

Figure 11.16 Three-way handshake. (Courtesy Learning Tree)

Step 1	Step 2	Step 3
Source	Destination	Source
May I open? SEQ=X ACK=0 *Begin data transmission option* send Z octets	Yes. You may. SEQ=Y ACK=X+1+Z	SEQ=X+1+Z ACK=Y+1 *Continue data transmission*

In Step 1 (see figure 11.16), the active OPEN is sent with a Sequence Number value of *X*. As an option, additional data can be sent with the active OPEN packet. This additional data (Z octets) may contain authentication information, such as user name and password, for the service being requested. In most TCP/IP applications, authentication information is sent after the connection is established. But in some networks, such as those in which TCP/IP is run on X.25 networks, authentication information may be sent as part of the OPEN connection request. The Sequence- and Acknowledgment Number fields are set as follows:

Sequence Number = X

Acknowledgment Number = 0

In Step 2, the receiver responds with an Acknowledgment Number set to X+1+Z, the next expected octet number. The initial Sequence Number (Y), which is used by the destination, is also sent. The Sequence- and Acknowledgment Number fields are set as follows:

Sequence Number = Y

Acknowledgment Number = X + 1 + Z

In Step 3, the source acknowledges that it has received the Sequence Number value from the receiver. The Sequence- and Acknowledgment Number fields are set as follows:

Sequence Number = X + 1 + Z

Acknowledgment Number = Y + 1

Why is the third step necessary in the three-way handshake? This step is often a source of puzzlement and confusion. You use the third step to complete the handshake to inform the receiver that its initial sequence number has been received by the source that opens the TCP connection. Without this acknowledgment, there is no way to ensure that the sender knows about the initial receiver sequence number. The following summarizes the three steps involved in the three-way handshake:

- Step 1: Source sends its initial SEND sequence number (ISS).
- Step 2: Receiver acknowledges reception of ISS by sending an acknowledgment number that is 1 greater than ISS or the amount of data sent by the source. Receiver sends its initial RECEIVER sequence number (IRS).
- Step 3: Source sends an acknowledgment number to acknowledge that it has received the receiver ISN.

To ensure that TCP does not send a segment containing a sequence number that is the duplicate of an old segment on the network, TCP has the notion of a *maximum segment lifetime (MSL)*. MSL is the time that must elapse before assigning any sequence numbers upon starting up or recovering from a crash (in which memory of sequence numbers previously used was lost). In the TCP specification, MSL is taken to be two minutes. If a TCP implementation can retain memory of sequence numbers in use, then it need not wait for the MSL duration because it can start using sequence numbers larger than those recently used.

In TCP, because every octet is numbered, sequence numbers are consumed rapidly. If message octets are sent at the rate of 2 Mbps, it takes about 4.5 hours to use up 2^{32} octets of sequence numbers. Because the maximum segment lifetime in the net is not likely to exceed a few tens of seconds, this amount of time is adequate protection for rates that escalate to l0s of Mbps. At 100 megabits/sec, the MSL time is 5.4 minutes, which is still greater than the two minutes assumed by the TCP specification in RFC 793.

How is the value of an ISN selected? RFC 793 suggests the use of an initial sequence number (ISN) generator to select a new 32-bit ISN. One possibility is that this generator is bound to a 32-bit time clock whose low-order bit is incremented roughly every four microseconds. If this is the case, the ISN cycles approximately every 4.55 hours. It is unlikely that segments will stay in the network more than 4.55 hours; therefore, you can reasonably assume that ISNs will be unique.

After a TCP connection has been established, the ACK flag is always set to 1 to indicate that the Acknowledgment Number field is valid. Data transmission then takes place with messages being exchanged by both sides in a full-duplex fashion until the TCP connection is ready to be closed.

When a TCP connection is ready to close, the FIN control flag is issued. In TCP, a connection is not automatically closed when TCP sends a FIN flag. Both sides of the connection must send a FIN flag and agree to close the connection. This kind of FIN close is called a *graceful close* because it ensures that the connections are not abruptly closed. Consider what would happen if one side of the connection closed the connection without informing the other side. The other side may still continue sending data that is never acknowledged because the connection is closed. This scenario would result in the loss of data. The TCP graceful close mechanism illustrated in figure 11.17 prevents the loss of data due to premature closing of a TCP connection.

Figure 11.17 TCP FIN flag use (the graceful close). (Courtesy Learning Tree)

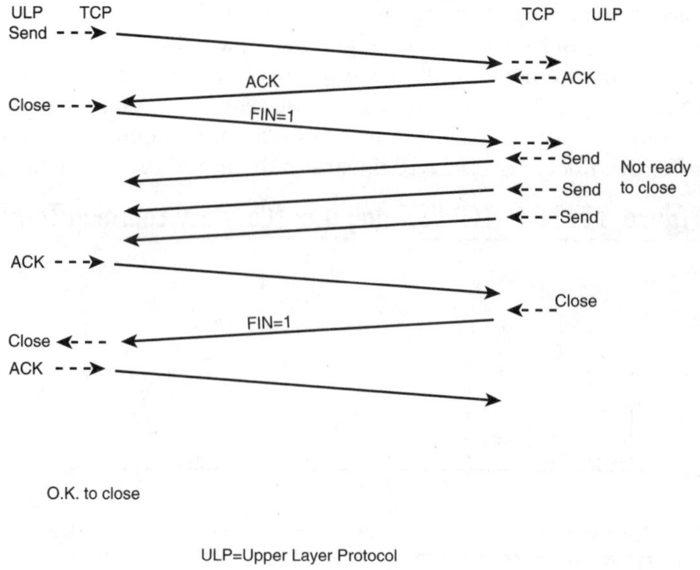

Another point to note about the use of TCP flags in sending messages is how the PSH flag is used. The PSH flag was initially designed to inform TCP that it must act upon the data that it has received so far. When an application issues a series of SEND calls without setting the PSH flag, the TCP can aggregate the data internally without sending it. Similarly, when a series of segments is received without the PSH bit, a TCP can queue the data internally without passing it to the receiving application. The PSH bit is not a record marker and is independent of segment boundaries. Some implementations incorrectly think of the PSH as a record marker, however. The transmitter should collapse successive PSH bits when it packetizes data to send the largest possible segment.

A TCP can implement PSH flags on SEND calls. If PSH flags are not implemented, then the sending TCP must do the following:

1. It must not buffer data indefinitely.
2. It must set the PSH bit in the last buffered segment (for example, when there is no more queued data to be sent).

RFC-793 erroneously implies that a received PSH flag must be passed to the Application layer. Passing a received PSH flag to the Application layer is now optional.

An application program is logically required to set the PSH flag in a SEND call whenever the program needs to force delivery of the data to avoid a communications deadlock. A TCP should send a maximum-size segment whenever possible to improve performance, however. This means that on the sender side, a PSH may not result in the segment's being immediately transmitted.

When the PSH flag is not implemented on SEND TCP calls (or when the application/TCP interface uses a pure streaming model), responsibility for aggregating any tiny data fragments to form reasonable-size segments is partially borne by the Application layer. Generally, an interactive application protocol must set the PSH flag, at least in the last SEND call in each command or response sequence. A bulk transfer protocol such as FTP should set the PSH flag on the last segment of a file or when necessary to prevent buffer deadlock. Figure 11.18 illustrates the use of the PSH flag.

Figure 11.18 TCP PSH flag use. (Courtesy Learning Tree)

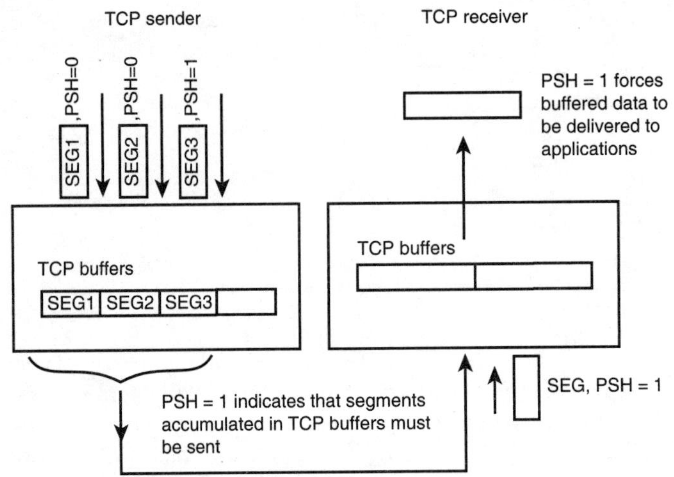

- A TCP sender should collapse successive PSH bits when it turns data into packets as per RFC 1122
- Interactive applications must set the PSH bit at the end of each command/response sequence
- Bulk transfer protocols such as FTP should set the PSH flag on the last segment of a file

At the receiver, the PSH bit forces buffered data to be delivered to the application (even if less than a full buffer has been received). Conversely, the lack of a PSH avoids unnecessary wake-up calls to the application process. Avoiding these calls can be an important performance optimization for large time-sharing hosts.

TCP contains a mechanism to send out of band data by using the URG flag. The URG flag is used in conjunction with the Urgent Pointer field to "jump the queue" for sending data and to communicate an important message to the receiver. This feature enables the sender to send interrupt signals to the receiver without these signals ending up in the normal data queue at the receiver.

Consider what would happen if such a mechanism did not exist. Suppose that you want to interrupt the processing of user data that is sent. If the urgent message ends up in the normal data queue for TCP at the receiver, it may never be read because data that is ahead of the urgent message in the queue will have to be processed before the urgent message is detected. In many cases, the urgent message may arrive too late. Also, the urgent message may never be read if the application process that is supposed to read the message is hung up.

When the URG flag is set, the Urgent Pointer field is valid (see fig. 11.19). RFC 1122 states that the urgent pointer points to the sequence number of the LAST octet (not LAST+1) in a sequence of urgent data, and that RFC 793 describes it incorrectly as LAST+1.

Figure 11.19 TCP URG flag. (Courtesy Learning Tree)

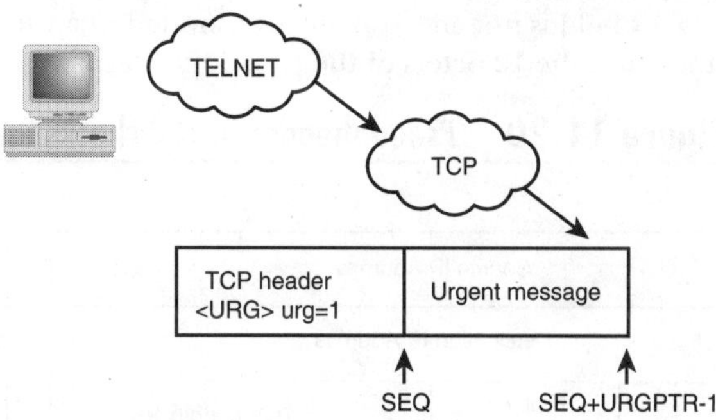
• Used for sending *out-of-band* data
- Without waiting for receiver to process octets already in the stream
• Has meaning only if URG=1
TELNET
TCP
TCP header
<URG> urg=1
Urgent message
SEQ
SEQ+URGPTR-1
• Urgent pointer indicates the last octet of the urgent message

A TCP implementation must support a sequence of urgent data of any length. A TCP layer must inform the Application layer asynchronously whenever the TCP layer receives an urgent pointer with no previous pending urgent data, or whenever the urgent pointer advances in the data stream. There must be a way for the application to learn how much urgent data remains to be read from the connection or at least to determine whether more urgent data remains to be read. Although the urgent mechanism may be used for any application, it is normally used to send interrupt-type commands to a Telnet program. The asynchronous, or out-of-band, notification enables the application to go into urgent mode by reading data from the TCP connection. This allows control commands to be sent to an application whose normal input buffers are full of unprocessed data.

Window Field

The Window field is used to implement flow control and is used by the receiver. The receiving TCP reports a "window" to the sending TCP. This window specifies the number of octets—starting with the acknowledgment number—that the receiving TCP is currently prepared to receive.

Checksum Field

The checksum field is 1's complement of the 1's complement sum of all the 16-bit words in the TCP packet. A 96-bit pseudoheader (see fig. 11.20) is prepended to the TCP header for checksum computation. The pseudoheader is used to identify whether the packet has arrived at the correct destination. The pseudoheader gives the TCP protection against misrouted segments. The pseudoheader has the protocol ID (6 for TCP), source, and destination IP address. Because the TCP header contains the source and destination port number, this describes the connection between the end points. Between the IP and TCP headers, there is sufficient information to identify completely the *full association* formed by the TCP connection.

The TCP Length field in the pseudoheader is the TCP header length plus the data length in octets. (This field is not an explicitly transmitted quantity; it is computed,) This field does not count the 12 octets of the pseudoheader.

Figure 11.20 Pseudoheader in TCP checksum.

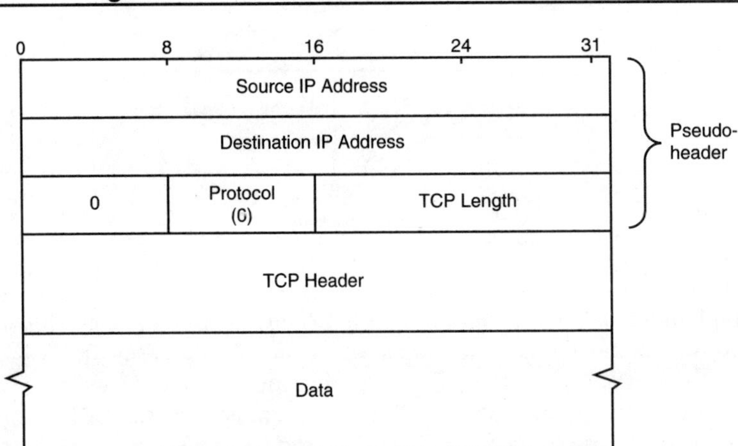

Options Field

The TCP Options field may occupy space at the end of the TCP header and is a multiple of eight bits in length. The Options field is included in the checksum. An option may begin on any octet boundary. There are two formats for an option:

- Case 1: A single octet of option-kind.
- Case 2: An octet of option-kind, an octet of option-length, and the actual option-data octets.

In Case 2, the option-length counts the two octets of option-kind and option-length as well as the option-data octets. The actual list of options may be shorter than the Data Offset field implies. The content of the header beyond the End-of-Option list must be zero padded.

Currently, the defined options include the following:

Kind	Length	Meaning
0	-	End-of-Option list
1	-	No-Operation
2	4	Maximum Segment Size

Options with the option-kind value of 0 (End-of-Option list) and 1 (No-Operation) are examples of the Case 1 format option. The TCP options are shown in figure 11.21.

Figure 11.21 TCP options.

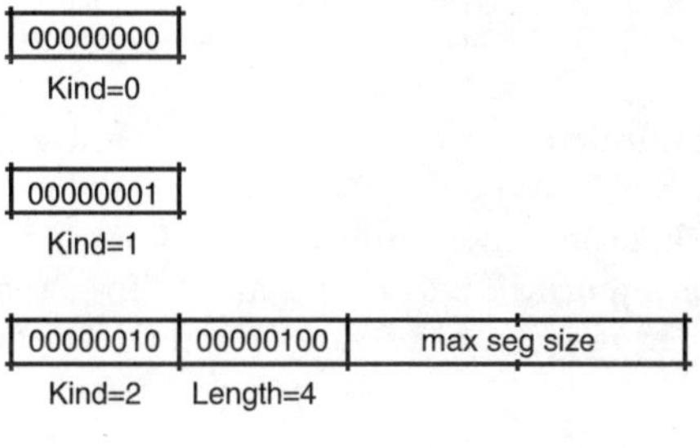

The End-of-Option list indicates the end of the option list that may not coincide with the end of the TCP header according to the Data Offset field. The End-of-Option list is used at the end of all options, but not at the end of each option. You need to use this option only if the end of the options would not otherwise coincide with the end of the TCP header.

The No-Operation option code may be used between options to align the beginning of a subsequent option on a word boundary. Because there is no guarantee that TCP senders will use this option, TCP receivers must be prepared to process options even if they do not begin on a word boundary.

Currently, the only specific option carrying any real information is the Maximum Segment Size (MSS). The MSS can be negotiated only at the start of the TCP connection when the sequence numbers are being synchronized. This synchronization occurs when the SYN flag is set to 1. Typically, each TCP sends a MSS option informing the remote TCP about its MSS. If the MSS option is not used, any segment size is allowed.

Cumulative ACKs in TCP

Compared to transport protocols in other protocol suites, TCP is unusual as far as the meaning of the sequence numbers is concerned. In most transport protocols, the sequence number refers to the number of a packet. Not so in TCP. In TCP, sequence numbers refer to octets. Every octet is numbered in TCP. TCP sends octets in segments of variable length. When an acknowledgment is not received, segments are retransmitted. There is no guarantee that a retransmitted segment will be exactly the same as the original transmission. A retransmitted segment may contain additional data because the sending application may have generated additional data since the original transmission. The acknowledgment number cannot, therefore, refer to the segment that was sent.

In TCP, the acknowledgment number indicates the position in the data stream up to which data has been received and acknowledged by the remote TCP module. More specifically, an acknowledgment number value refers to the next octet number that needs to be sent. The acknowledgment number corresponds to the left edge of the TCP window.

TCP acknowledgment numbers are cumulative in the sense that an acknowledgment number indicates how much of the data stream has been accumulated so far. It is possible for a single acknowledgment number to acknowledge octets received in multiple data segments. Figure 11.22 shows that the three segments sent by the sender are acknowledged by a single acknowledgment number.

Figure 11.22 Single acknowledgment for multiple data segments.

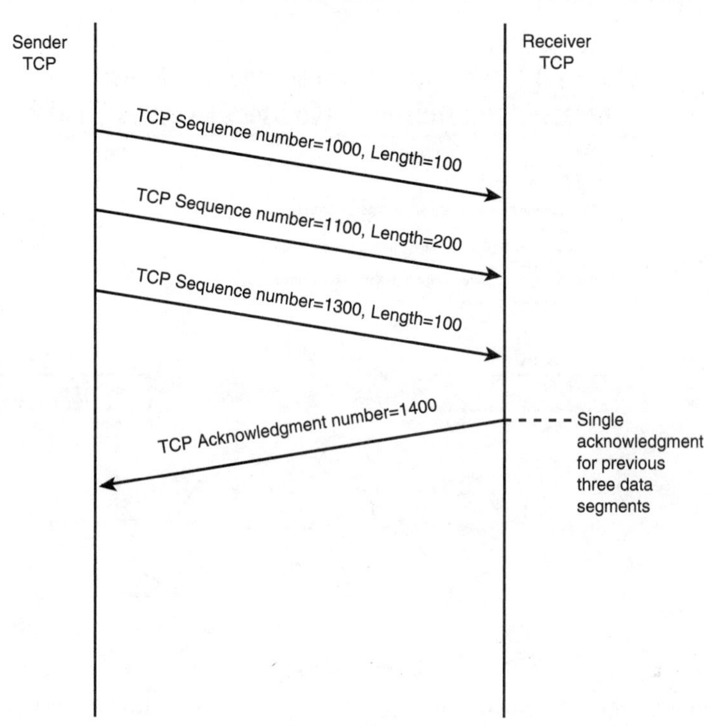

Many TCP implementations try to minimize the number of separate acknowledgment segments that need to be sent. For example, a TCP implementation may try to send a single acknowledgment for every two TCP data segments that are received.

Because TCP segments are ultimately encapsulated in IP datagrams, there is no guarantee that they will arrive in order at the destination. The receiver TCP uses the sequence numbers of the octets in the segments to construct a continuous stream of octets. The receiver acknowledges the longest continuous prefix octet stream that it has received so far. If there is a gap in the octet stream that represents data not received, the received TCP can acknowledge only data up to the gap.

Cumulative acknowledgments have the advantage in that lost acknowledgments do not force retransmission. Therefore, even if one acknowledgment is lost in transmission, subsequent acknowledgments will acknowledge all the data that has been received so far. However, cumulative acknowledgments are not efficient when there is a gap representing lost data and when data after the gap has been received. Data received after the gap cannot be acknowledged unless the missing data in the gap is received. The sender does not receive information about the successful transmission of data after the gap because the receiver can acknowledge only data prior to the gap. This situation is illustrated in figure 11.23. In this figure, segments SEG2 and SEG3 have been successfully received. However, segment SEG1 has been lost in transmission.

Figure 11.23 A TCP sender does not know about successful transmissions. (Courtesy Learning Tree)

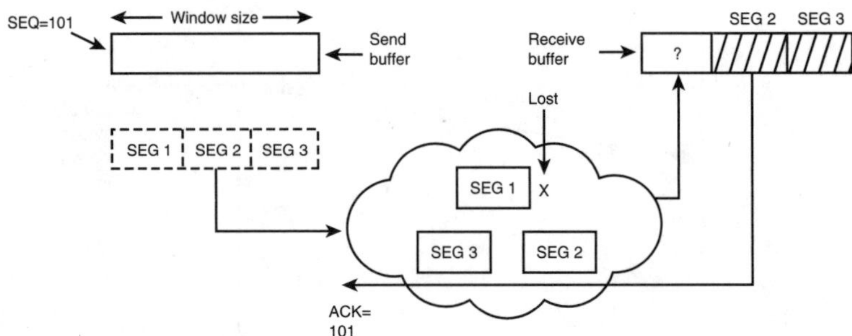

Even though segments SEG2 and SEG3 have been successfully received, the loss of segment SEG1 represents a gap in the data stream at the receiver. The sender cannot advance the window because it does not receive acknowledgment about SEG1. There is no mechanism for the receiver to tell the sender that it has received segments SEG2 and SEG3 successfully. At this point, the following two situations can arise:

1. The sender will time out and send segments SEG1, SEG2, and SEG3. In this case, segments SEG2 and SEG3 are sent needlessly because they were previously sent successfully. Retransmission of segments SEG2 and SEG3 is inefficient and adds to additional network traffic.

2. The sender will time out and send only segment SEG1 and wait for acknowledgment to come back before deciding on sending additional data. When the receiver receives SEG1, it sends a cumulative acknowledgment packet that acknowledges correct reception of segment SEG1 and the previously sent segments SEG2 and SEG3. Although this scenario may appear to be more efficient, you should take into account that the sender has to wait for an acknowledgment of SEG1 before sending SEG2 and SEG3. This wait means that the sender is not taking advantage of its large window size and is sending only a segment at a time.

Adaptive Time-Outs in TCP

TCP was originally designed to run over WAN links; later on, TCP adapted for LANs also. Therefore, TCP has an advantage over those protocols that have their origins in LANs only. This advantage means that TCP has sophisticated algorithms that adjust to the wide variance in time delays that are encountered in sending messages over WAN links. LANs, on the other hand, typically do not exhibit such wide variances in time delays.

An interesting fact to note about IP is that even if the IP layers send the same message over the same path at two different times, the time delay to reach the destination is probably different because of the following factors:

- WAN links typically send messages serially, one at a time. If the WAN link is busy sending other messages, the message has to wait in a queue. This process leads to uncertainties in time delay.
- Routers connecting the WAN links may be flooded with bursts of traffic. The IP datagrams that a router receives may have to wait in a queue until the time the router can resolve the route for the datagram. Even after its route is determined, the datagram may have to queue up for a network interface over which it is to be routed to become available. In the worst case, the datagrams arrive at a rate that fills the available router memory, in which case the router will have to drop datagrams that it cannot store in its memory. This scenario can happen because there is no pre-allocation of memory for individual TCP connections in an IP datagram network.

The IP layer is so designed that each IP datagram is routed independently. Successive TCP segments in a connection may not be sent on the same path and may experience different delays as they traverse different sets of routers and links.

When TCP sends a message, it waits for acknowledgments to come back before it can advance its window. How long should it wait? The time it should wait is called the *time-out interval.* Because of the wide variance in time delays between successive transmissions in TCP, it uses an adaptive time-out. The algorithm for this adaptive time-out is called the *adaptive retransmission algorithm.* This algorithm is described in the following steps:

1. Measure the elapsed time between sending a data octet with a particular sequence number and receiving an acknowledgment that covers that sequence number. This measured elapsed time is the round-trip time (RTT). Based on the RTT, compute a smoothed round-trip time (SRTT) as

   $$SRTT = (\alpha \times SRTT) + ((1 - \alpha) \times RTT)$$

   α is the weighting factor whose value is between 0 and 1 ($0 <= \alpha < 1$). The SRTT is an estimated time-out. The SRTT computation, therefore, takes into account its old SRTT value and the new RTT value and takes a weighted average of these two. When $\alpha = 0.5$, SRTT is just the simple average of old SRTT and the following RTT values:

SRTT = (SRTT + RTT) ÷ 2, when $\alpha = 0.5$

When α is less than 0.5, a greater weight is given to the actual round-trip time (RTT). When α is greater than 0.5, a greater weight is given to the preceding estimated smoothed round-trip time (SRTT).

When $\alpha = 0$ or almost 1, you have the two extremes. When $\alpha = 0$, SRTT is always set to RTT; and when α is almost 1, a fixed SRTT is used with little deference to the actual RTT. Needless to say, the two extremes are seldom used in actual practice, but they are useful for understanding the nature of the weighted average.

2. The SRTT is then used to compute the retransmission time-out (RTO) by using the following:

   RTO = min[UBOUND,max[LBOUND,(β × SRTT)]]

   UBOUND is an upper boundary on the time-out (for example., 1 minute), and LBOUND is a lower boundary on the time-out (for example 1 second). These values ensure that the RTO will fall between LBOUND and UBOUND. β is a delay variance factor that changes the sensitivity of the delay. If β is set to 1, RTO will be set to SRTT unless the SRTT value is below LBOUND or above UBOUND. This value ($\beta = 1$)will make TCP sensitive to packet loss and will not cause TCP to wait for a long time before retransmitting. However, small delays may cause unnecessary retransmissions. To make TCP less susceptible to small delays, a larger β value can be used. RFC 793 suggests using a value from 1.3 to 2.0.

In 1987, Karn and Partridge published a paper, "Improving Round-Trip Estimates in Reliable Transport Protocols," in the Proceedings of ACM SIGCOMM'87. Although not issued as an RFC, this paper influenced several TCP implementations, particularly the BSD Unix implementation of TCP. This algorithm has since become known as *Karn's algorithm.* RFC 1122 recommends that Karn's algorithm be used in conjunction with Van Jacobson's slow start algorithm for congested networks. Van Jacobson's slow start algorithm is discussed in the section "Minimizing Impact of Congestion in TCP" in this chapter. Karn's algorithm takes into account the fact of retransmitted segments and is described next.

When retransmissions take place in Karn's algorithm, the SRTT value is not adjusted. Instead, a backoff strategy is used to adjust the time-out by a factor. The idea is that if a retransmission takes place, something drastic happened on the network, and the time-out should be increased sharply to avoid further retransmissions. The timer backoff strategy is implemented by using a simple equation such as the following:

Backoff TIMEOUT = Γ × TIMEOUT

This equation is used until some previously decided upon upper boundary is reached. Typically, Γ is set to 2 so that this algorithm behaves like a binary exponential backoff algorithm. The Backoff TIMEOUT does not affect the SRTT that is used in normal computation. When an acknowledgment is received for a segment that does not require retransmission, TCP measures the RTT value and uses this value to com-pute the SRTT and the RTO values.

Minimizing Impact of Congestion in TCP

When congestion occurs in a network, TCP can respond with adjusting the time-out and retransmitting when acknowledgments are not received within the time-out interval. However, retransmissions can add to the problems of an already congested network by increasing the amount of data already being processed by the network. If retransmissions increase to a point that the retransmitted data being added to the network approaches the storage capacity of the network, then a condition called *congestion collapse* is imminent. When a network is experiencing congestion, a method is needed to stop or slow down additional data from being added to the network.

In 1988, Van Jacobson published a paper on "Congestion Avoidance and Control" in Proceedings ACM SIGCOMM'88. This paper outlines a technique for responding to congestion by reducing the amount of data sent by the sender. Recall that Chapter 8, "The ICMP Protocol," discussed the ICMP Type 4 Source Quench message that is an attempt to deal with congestion. Routers that detect congestion can send the ICMP Source Quench message to the sender. The sender passes this message to the TCP module, which is alerted to a congestion condition. As discussed in Chapter 8, there is no mechanism to cancel the ICMP Source Quench message. Techniques such as the Jacobson's slow start algorithm can deal successfully with congestion by adjusting the TCP window size dynamically.

Jacobson's slow start algorithm tries to avoid congestion by automatically adjusting the TCP window size, and it is implemented in all modern TCP implementations. In fact, Jacobson's algorithm, along with Karn's algorithm, is required to be implemented as per RFC 1122.

In Jacobson's slow start algorithm, TCP keeps track of a second limit called the *congestion window size.* The actual window size that is used is the smaller of the congestion window size and the TCP receiver window size.

Actual window size = min {congestion window size, TCP window size }

Under normal network conditions when there is no congestion, the congestion window size is the same as the TCP window size, which means that the actual window size is the same as the TCP window size. When congestion is detected, such as when there is a loss of segment, Jacobson's algorithm reduces the congestion window size by half. At every successive loss of a segment, the congestion window is again reduced by half. This process results in a rapid exponential decrease in window size. If the loss continues, the TCP window size is reduced to one segment, which means that only one datagram is transmitted at a time. At the same time, Karn's algorithm is used to double the time-out value before retransmitting. This dramatic reduction is called *exponential backoff* or *multiplicative decrease.*

Jacobson's algorithm uses a slow start to recover from congestion. If an acknowledgment is received for a segment, the algorithm increases the congestion window size by one segment. Because the initial window size for a severely congested network is 1, when an acknowledgment is received, the congestion window size becomes 2. This process means that TCP can now send two segments. If the acknowledgments for these segments come back, the congestion window size becomes 4, which enables TCP to send four segments. When the acknowledgments for these segments come back, the congestion window size becomes 8. This process continues until the congestion window size is equal to the receiver window size. Because of the exponential increase in congestion window size, it takes only $\log_2(N)$ successful transmissions before TCP can send N segments.

If the congestion window size increases too rapidly, it can add to network traffic before the network has completely recovered from congestion. If congestion is experienced again, the congestion window size will shrink rapidly. This alternating increase and decrease in congestion window size causes the congestion window size to oscillate rapidly. Jacobson's algorithm prevents too rapid an increase in congestion window size by using the *congestion avoidance* technique. In this technique, when the congestion window size becomes one-half the original TCP window size, the congestion window size is increased by one segment only if all the segments sent so far have been acknowledged.

Avoiding the Silly Window Syndrome

Early TCP implementations exhibited a pathological condition called the *Silly Window Syndrome (SWS)*. This condition was so named because the TCP transmission took place one octet at a time under certain conditions. Therefore, a TCP segment consists of one octet only, and each octet is individually acknowledged. The SWS can occur when any of the following is true:

- ◆ The application at the receiver reads data one octet at a time from a buffer that is full, and the receiver TCP sends a window size of 1 in an acknowledgment to the sender (see fig. 11.24).
- ◆ The application at the sender generates data one octet at a time, and the sender TCP sends this data immediately (see fig. 11.25).

Figure 11.24 Silly Window Syndrome caused by receiver.

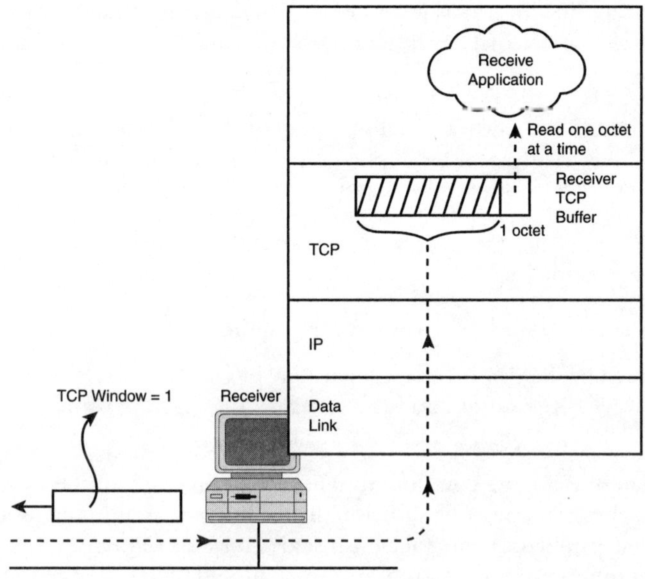

Figure 11.25 Silly Window Syndrome caused by sender.

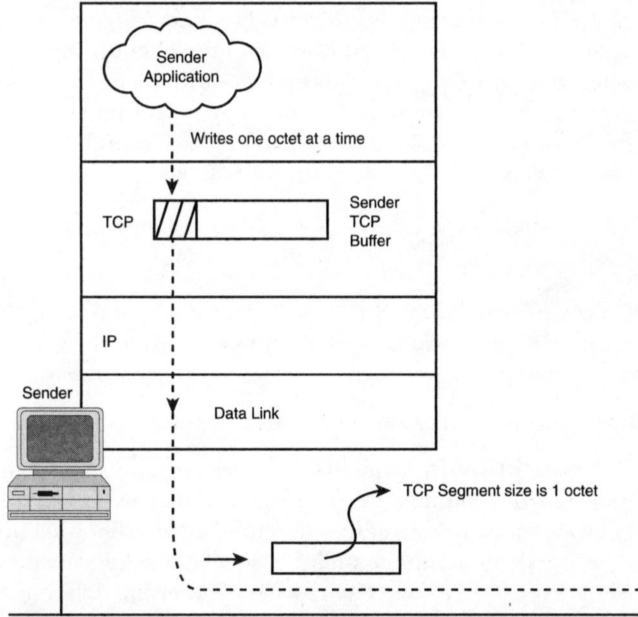

In figure 11.24, because the receiver sends a window size of 1 octet, the sender responds by sending only one octet of data. As soon as this octet is received, the receiver application reads just one octet of data, and the receiver TCP again advertises a window size of 1. And the cycle continues.

In figure 11.25, the sender application sends only one octet of data. The sender TCP does not wait to see whether other data is accumulated but sends this one octet immediately. As the sender application continues to generate data one octet at a time, each octet is sent immediately.

In both situations, the overhead of sending the data is enormous because of the following reasons:

- A large number of small packets is generated.
- Each packet is processed separately by each of the Data Link-, IP-, and TCP layers at the sender and the receiver. Intervening routers must process the packets at the Data Link- and IP layers.
- There is a large computational overhead in each of the protocol layers because each packet must be individually routed, checksummed, and encapsulated/decapsulated. Each packet must also have its sequence- and acknowledgment numbers computed, and must be handled by send/receive buffers.
- The ratio of the protocol headers to actual payload (data delivered) is high; that is, protocol efficiency is low. As a result, data throughput is low.
- As each octet segment is individually acknowledged, the delays for each octet accumulate to a significant value, and the data throughput is low. For 1,000 octets sent in 1,000 packets over a link with 50 ms delay, total delay is 1,000 × 50 ms = 5 seconds. Assuming that the time to transmit the packet to the link is small compared to the delay of the link, the overall throughput is only 1,000 octets × 8 bits/octet ÷ 5 seconds = 1,600 bps.

To avoid the SWS on the receiver side, TCP implementations use the following heuristics:

- **Delay advertising.** If the receive window size is smaller than a given size, the receiver delays advertising the window size until the receiver window size is at least equal to the following:

  min (0.5×Receiver buffer size, Maximum Segment Size)

- **Delay acknowledgments.** Acknowledgments that contain the receiver window size computed in the previous bullet are delayed. This delay reduces network traffic by decreasing the number of acknowledgments. Recall that TCP acknowledgments are cumulative, so a later acknowledgment can acknowledge all data received so far. The risk here is that the delaying of acknowledgments can cause the sender to time out and retransmit segments. To prevent this occurrence, ACKs are delayed to a maximum of 500 milliseconds after which they must be sent. Many implementations delay acknowledgments by no more than 200 milliseconds. Additionally, the receiver should acknowledge every other data segment to ensure that the sender has a sufficient number of round-trip time estimates to implement its adaptive time-out algorithm.

Rather than delaying the acknowledgment, you can use another approach. In this approach, the acknowledgment is not delayed, but it is sent immediately without advertising an increase in window size until the prespecified limit has been reached. This approach is not recommended by the TCP standards, however.

To avoid the SWS on the sender side, TCP implementations use the Nagle avoidance algorithm. The basic ideas behind Nagle's SWS avoidance algorithm include the following:

- The sender sends the first data segment. After the first data segment, the sender does not immediately send short size segments even if the sender application sets the PSH flag.
- Data is sent only if the following is true:
    1. There is sufficient data to send to fill a maximum-size segment.
    2. An acknowledgment arrives while waiting for data to send.
    3. A preset time-out occurs.

If an application rapidly generates data, it will rapidly fill up the sender TCP buffer to the maximum segment size. TCP will send the maximum segment size without delay. Also, when an acknowledgment is received, the segment data in the buffer is sent without delay even if it is smaller than the maximum segment size.

If the application slowly generates data, segments will be sent when successive acknowledgments are received. Meanwhile, the sender TCP buffer will accumulate data.

The Nagle avoidance algorithm can be disabled for real-time applications that require minimum delay and send large bursts of data at a time.

Dealing with Dead TCP Connections

When a remote computer crashes or the network links are down, the TCP connections will break. How does TCP detect a connection that is dead and release its resources? An ICMP message may arrive informing TCP that the destination is unreachable. TCP retries a few times by retransmitting segments before reporting the condition to the application. What if TCP does not receive any ICMP messages because they are lost in transmission? TCP then retries for a first threshold number of retransmissions, after which TCP notifies IP to check whether a dead router or route is the problem. IP tries to recompute the route to the destination. Meanwhile, TCP retries for a second threshold number of transmissions, after which TCP declares that the connection is dead. On detecting a dead connection, TCP must release all resources such as TCB (transmission control buffers) associated with the connection.

When neither end point has sent data for a long time, the connection is maintained in the idle state. In the idle state, the connection consumes resources to maintain the connection even if the network or one of the other end points is down. Some TCP implementations send a keep-alive TCP message, which periodically checks to see whether the connection is alive. When a keep-alive TCP message is sent, an acknowledgment is expected from the receiver. The suggested default for the keep-alive timer is two hours. In some TCP implementations, the default is much smaller (for example, 10–15 minutes). The keep-alive timers should be set to what makes sense for the majority of applications running on a TCP host. Keeping this timer too short will generate excessive traffic, and keeping the timer value too long will not quickly alert TCP that the connection is dead.

TCP Finite State Machine

Figure 11.26 shows the behavior of the TCP as a finite state machine. A *finite state machine* is a logical model for the behavior of a system whose internal state changes with the occurrence of specified events. The boxes represent the state of the machine, and the arrows represent the transition from one state to another. The labels on the arrows represent the event that caused the transition between the states and the response of TCP to that event in the following format:

event

---

response

In figure 11.26, an *x* for the *response* indicates that no special response occurs.

Each end point of a TCP connection starts from the closed state. Arrows from this closed state are shown to indicate that a connection can occur by an active OPEN or a passive OPEN.

An active OPEN causes TCP to create a TCB and send a SYN flag segment and enter into the SYN SENT state. When a SYN flag and ACK flag is sent by the other end point, TCP sends an acknowledgment to complete the three-way handshake and enters the CONNECTION ESTABLISHED state.

When a passive OPEN is issued by an end point, it creates a TCB and enters into the LISTEN state. When TCP receives a SYN flag in this state (active OPEN request), it sends the flag's sequence number and the SYN and ACK flags in a TCP segment and enters the SYN RCVD state. When TCP receives an ACK or SYN flag from the other end point, the connection moves to the CONNECTION ESTABLISHED state.

Figure 11.26 TCP finite state machine.

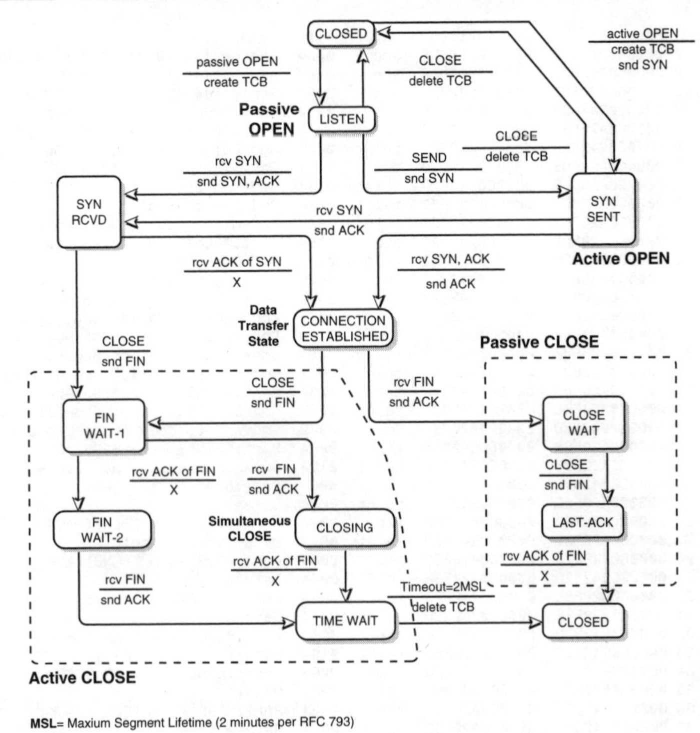

The TIME WAIT state is entered upon closing the connection to ensure that there is a delay of twice the MSL (maximum segment lifetime) time interval. This state is used to avoid duplicate segment numbers. See the earlier discussion in the section "The Flags Field" on avoiding duplicate sequence numbers.

The FIN WAIT-1 and FIN WAIT-2 states show the graceful close mechanism of TCP. Both sides have to agree on closing the connection before a connection is closed.

TCP Traces

The Telnet protocol uses TCP, and it is a good candidate for studying its protocol trace to examine the behavior of TCP. Figure 11.27 shows a complete Telnet trace of a user that performs the following activities:

1. Logging on to a Telnet server
2. Executing various commands at a Telnet server
3. Logging off from the Telnet server

Figure 11.27 Telnet trace.

No.	Source	Destination	Layer	Size	Summary
1	0000C024282D	FFFFFFFFFFFF	arp	0064	Req by 144.19.74.44 for 144.19.74
2	0000C024282D	FFFFFFFFFFFF	arp	0064	Req by 144.19.74.44 for 144.19.74
3	0000C0A20F8E	0000C024282D	arp	0064	Reply 144.19.74.201=0000C0A20F8E
4	0000C024282D	0000C0A20F8E	tcp	0064	Port:6295 ---> TELNET SYN
5	0000C0A20F8E	0000C024282D	tcp	0064	Port:TELNET ---> 6295 ACK SYN
6	0000C024282D	0000C0A20F8E	telnt	0069	Cmd=Do; Code=Echo; Cmd=Do; Code=S
7	0000C0A20F8E	0000C024282D	tcp	0064	Port:TELNET ---> 6295 ACK
8	0000C0A20F8E	0000C024282D	telnt	0064	Cmd=Do; Code=;
9	0000C024282D	0000C0A20F8E	telnt	0064	Cmd=Won't; Code=;
10	0000C0A20F8E	0000C024282D	telnt	0067	Cmd=Will; Code=Echo; Cmd=Will; Co
11	0000C0A20F8E	0000C024282D	tcp	0064	Port:TELNET ---> 6295 ACK
12	0000C024282D	0000C0A20F8E	telnt	0072	Cmd=Do; Code=Suppress Go Ahead; C
13	0000C0A20F8E	0000C024282D	telnt	0070	Cmd=Do; Code=Terminal Type; Cmd=D
14	0000C0A20F8E	0000C024282D	tcp	0064	Port:TELNET ---> 6295 ACK
15	0000C024282D	0000C0A20F8E	telnt	0072	Cmd=Will; Code=Terminal Type; Cmd
16	0000C0A20F8E	0000C024282D	tcp	0064	Port:TELNET ---> 6295 ACK
17	0000C0A20F8E	0000C024282D	telnt	0064	Cmd=Subnegotiation Begin; Code=Te
18	0000C024282D	0000C0A20F8E	telnt	0071	Cmd=Subnegotiation Begin; Code=Te
19	0000C0A20F8E	0000C024282D	tcp	0064	Port:TELNET ---> 6295 ACK
20	0000C0A20F8E	0000C024282D	telnt	0067	Cmd=Do; Code=Echo; Cmd=Will; Code
21	0000C024282D	0000C0A20F8E	telnt	0069	Cmd=Won't; Code=Echo; Cmd=Don't;
22	0000C0A20F8E	0000C024282D	tcp	0064	Port:TELNET ---> 6295 ACK
23	0000C0A20F8E	0000C024282D	telnt	0104	Data=..Linux 1.3.50 (ltreec1.ltre
24	0000C024282D	0000C0A20F8E	tcp	0064	Port:6295 ---> TELNET ACK
25	0000C0A20F8E	0000C024282D	telnt	0064	Data=..
26	0000C024282D	0000C0A20F8E	tcp	0064	Port:6295 ---> TELNET ACK
27	0000C0A20F8E	0000C024282D	telnt	0073	Data=ltreec1 login:
28	0000C024282D	0000C0A20F8E	tcp	0064	Port:6295 ---> TELNET ACK
29	0000C024282D	0000C0A20F8E	telnt	0064	Data=u
30	0000C0A20F8E	0000C024282D	tcp	0064	Port:TELNET ---> 6295 ACK
31	0000C0A20F8E	0000C024282D	telnt	0064	Data=u
32	0000C024282D	0000C0A20F8E	tcp	0064	Port:6295 ---> TELNET ACK
33	0000C024282D	0000C0A20F8E	telnt	0064	Data=s
34	0000C0A20F8E	0000C024282D	tcp	0064	Port:TELNET ---> 6295 ACK
35	0000C0A20F8E	0000C024282D	telnt	0064	Data=s
36	0000C024282D	0000C0A20F8E	tcp	0064	Port:6295 ---> TELNET ACK
37	0000C024282D	0000C0A20F8E	telnt	0064	Data=e
38	0000C0A20F8E	0000C024282D	tcp	0064	Port:TELNET ---> 6295 ACK
39	0000C0A20F8E	0000C024282D	telnt	0064	Data=e
40	0000C024282D	0000C0A20F8E	tcp	0064	Port:6295 ---> TELNET ACK
41	0000C024282D	0000C0A20F8E	telnt	0064	Data=r
42	0000C0A20F8E	0000C024282D	tcp	0064	Port:TELNET ---> 6295 ACK
43	0000C0A20F8E	0000C024282D	telnt	0064	Data=r
44	0000C024282D	0000C0A20F8E	tcp	0064	Port:6295 ---> TELNET ACK
45	0000C024282D	0000C0A20F8E	telnt	0064	Data=1
46	0000C0A20F8E	0000C024282D	tcp	0064	Port:TELNET ---> 6295 ACK
47	0000C0A20F8E	0000C024282D	telnt	0064	Data=1
48	0000C024282D	0000C0A20F8E	tcp	0064	Port:6295 ---> TELNET ACK
49	0000C024282D	0000C0A20F8E	telnt	0064	Data=..
50	0000C0A20F8E	0000C024282D	tcp	0064	Port:TELNET ---> 6295 ACK
51	0000C0A20F8E	0000C024282D	telnt	0064	Data=..
52	0000C024282D	0000C0A20F8E	tcp	0064	Port:6295 ---> TELNET ACK
53	0000C0A20F8E	0000C024282D	telnt	0068	Data=Password:
54	0000C024282D	0000C0A20F8E	tcp	0064	Port:6295 ---> TELNET ACK
55	0000C024282D	0000C0A20F8E	telnt	0064	Data=u
56	0000C0A20F8E	0000C024282D	tcp	0064	Port:TELNET ---> 6295 ACK
57	0000C024282D	0000C0A20F8E	telnt	0064	Data=s
58	0000C0A20F8E	0000C024282D	tcp	0064	Port:TELNET ---> 6295 ACK
59	0000C024282D	0000C0A20F8E	telnt	0064	Data=e
60	0000C0A20F8E	0000C024282D	tcp	0064	Port:TELNET ---> 6295 ACK
61	0000C024282D	0000C0A20F8E	telnt	0064	Data=r

```
 62 0000C0A20F8E  0000C024282D  tcp   0064  Port:TELNET ---> 6295 ACK
 63 0000C024282D  0000C0A20F8E  telnt 0064  Data=1
 64 0000C0A20F8E  0000C024282D  tcp   0064  Port:TELNET ---> 6295 ACK
 65 0000C024282D  0000C0A20F8E  telnt 0064  Data=p
 66 0000C0A20F8E  0000C024282D  tcp   0064  Port:TELNET ---> 6295 ACK
 67 0000C024282D  0000C0A20F8E  telnt 0064  Data=w
 68 0000C0A20F8E  0000C024282D  tcp   0064  Port:TELNET ---> 6295 ACK
 69 0000C024282D  0000C0A20F8E  telnt 0064  Data=..
 70 0000C0A20F8E  0000C024282D  tcp   0064  Port:TELNET ---> 6295 ACK
 71 0000C0A20F8E  0000C024282D  telnt 0064  Data=....
 72 0000C024282D  0000C0A20F8E  tcp   0064  Port:6295 ---> TELNET ACK
 73 0000C0A20F8E  0000C024282D  telnt 0113  Data=Last login: Wed May 28 18:33
 74 0000C024282D  0000C0A20F8E  tcp   0064  Port:6295 ---> TELNET ACK
 75 0000C0A20F8E  0000C024282D  telnt 0073  Data=Linux 1.3.50...
 76 0000C024282D  0000C0A20F8E  tcp   0064  Port:6295 ---> TELNET ACK
 77 0000C0A20F8E  0000C024282D  telnt 0064  Data=..
 78 0000C024282D  0000C0A20F8E  tcp   0064  Port:6295 ---> TELNET ACK
 79 0000C0A20F8E  0000C024282D  telnt 0069  Data=Power, n:..
 80 0000C024282D  0000C0A20F8E  tcp   0064  Port:6295 ---> TELNET ACK
 81 0000C0A20F8E  0000C024282D  telnt 0119  Data=.The only narcotic regulated
 82 0000C024282D  0000C0A20F8E  tcp   0064  Port:6295 ---> TELNET ACK
 83 0000C0A20F8E  0000C024282D  telnt 0064  Data=..
 84 0000C024282D  0000C0A20F8E  tcp   0064  Port:6295 ---> TELNET ACK
 85 0000C0A20F8E  0000C024282D  telnt 0069  Data=ltreec1:~$
 86 0000C024282D  0000C0A20F8E  tcp   0064  Port:6295 ---> TELNET ACK
 87 0000C024282D  0000C0A20F8E  telnt 0064  Data=l
 88 0000C0A20F8E  0000C024282D  tcp   0064  Port:TELNET ---> 6295 ACK
 89 0000C0A20F8E  0000C024282D  telnt 0064  Data=l
 90 0000C024282D  0000C0A20F8E  tcp   0064  Port:6295 ---> TELNET ACK
 91 0000C024282D  0000C0A20F8E  telnt 0064  Data=s
 92 0000C0A20F8E  0000C024282D  tcp   0064  Port:TELNET ---> 6295 ACK
 93 0000C0A20F8E  0000C024282D  telnt 0064  Data=s
 94 0000C024282D  0000C0A20F8E  tcp   0064  Port:6295 ---> TELNET ACK
 95 0000C024282D  0000C0A20F8E  telnt 0064  Data=
 96 0000C0A20F8E  0000C024282D  tcp   0064  Port:TELNET ---> 6295 ACK
 97 0000C0A20F8E  0000C024282D  telnt 0064  Data=
 98 0000C024282D  0000C0A20F8E  tcp   0064  Port:6295 ---> TELNET ACK
 99 0000C024282D  0000C0A20F8E  telnt 0064  Data=-
100 0000C0A20F8E  0000C024282D  tcp   0064  Port:TELNET ---> 6295 ACK
101 0000C0A20F8E  0000C024282D  telnt 0064  Data=-
102 0000C024282D  0000C0A20F8E  tcp   0064  Port:6295 ---> TELNET ACK
103 0000C024282D  0000C0A20F8E  telnt 0064  Data=a
104 0000C0A20F8E  0000C024282D  tcp   0064  Port:TELNET ---> 6295 ACK
105 0000C0A20F8E  0000C024282D  telnt 0064  Data=a
106 0000C024282D  0000C0A20F8E  tcp   0064  Port:6295 ---> TELNET ACK
107 0000C024282D  0000C0A20F8E  telnt 0064  Data=l
108 0000C0A20F8E  0000C024282D  tcp   0064  Port:TELNET ---> 6295 ACK
109 0000C0A20F8E  0000C024282D  telnt 0064  Data=l
110 0000C024282D  0000C0A20F8E  tcp   0064  Port:6295 ---> TELNET ACK
111 0000C024282D  0000C0A20F8E  telnt 0064  Data=..
112 0000C0A20F8E  0000C024282D  tcp   0064  Port:TELNET ---> 6295 ACK
113 0000C0A20F8E  0000C024282D  telnt 0064  Data=..
114 0000C024282D  0000C0A20F8E  tcp   0064  Port:6295 ---> TELNET ACK
115 0000C0A20F8E  0000C024282D  telnt 0067  Data=total 7..
116 0000C024282D  0000C0A20F8E  tcp   0064  Port:6295 ---> TELNET ACK
117 0000C0A20F8E  0000C024282D  telnt 0130  Data=drwxr-xr-x   3 user1     user
118 0000C024282D  0000C0A20F8E  tcp   0064  Port:6295 ---> TELNET ACK
119 0000C0A20F8E  0000C024282D  telnt 0131  Data=drwxr-xr-x  19 root      root
120 0000C024282D  0000C0A20F8E  tcp   0064  Port:6295 ---> TELNET ACK
121 0000C0A20F8E  0000C024282D  telnt 0138  Data=-rw-r--r--   1 user1     user
122 0000C024282D  0000C0A20F8E  tcp   0064  Port:6295 ---> TELNET ACK
123 0000C0A20F8E  0000C024282D  telnt 0132  Data=-rw-r--r--   1 user1     user
```

continues

```
124 0000C024282D   0000C0A20F8E   tcp    0064  Port:6295 ---> TELNET ACK
125 0000C0A20F8E   0000C024282D   telnt  0130  Data=-rw-r--r--    1 user1    user
126 0000C024282D   0000C0A20F8E   tcp    0064  Port:6295 ---> TELNET ACK
127 0000C0A20F8E   0000C024282D   telnt  0132  Data=-rw-r--r--    1 user1    user
128 0000C024282D   0000C0A20F8E   tcp    0064  Port:6295 ---> TELNET ACK
129 0000C0A20F8E   0000C024282D   telnt  0134  Data=drwxr-xr-x    2 user1    user
130 0000C024282D   0000C0A20F8E   tcp    0064  Port:6295 ---> TELNET ACK
131 0000C0A20F8E   0000C024282D   telnt  0064  Data=l
132 0000C024282D   0000C0A20F8E   tcp    0064  Port:6295 ---> TELNET ACK
133 0000C0A20F8E   0000C024282D   telnt  0068  Data=treec1:~$
134 0000C024282D   0000C0A20F8E   tcp    0064  Port:6295 ---> TELNET ACK
135 0000C024282D   0000C0A20F8E   telnt  0064  Data=p
136 0000C0A20F8E   0000C024282D   tcp    0064  Port:TELNET ---> 6295 ACK
137 0000C0A20F8E   0000C024282D   telnt  0064  Data=p
138 0000C024282D   0000C0A20F8E   tcp    0064  Port:6295 ---> TELNET ACK
139 0000C024282D   0000C0A20F8E   telnt  0064  Data=s
140 0000C0A20F8E   0000C024282D   tcp    0064  Port:TELNET ---> 6295 ACK
141 0000C0A20F8E   0000C024282D   telnt  0064  Data=s
142 0000C024282D   0000C0A20F8E   tcp    0064  Port:6295 ---> TELNET ACK
143 0000C024282D   0000C0A20F8E   telnt  0064  Data=
144 0000C0A20F8E   0000C024282D   tcp    0064  Port:TELNET ---> 6295 ACK
145 0000C0A20F8E   0000C024282D   telnt  0064  Data=
146 0000C024282D   0000C0A20F8E   tcp    0064  Port:6295 ---> TELNET ACK
147 0000C024282D   0000C0A20F8E   telnt  0064  Data=-
148 0000C0A20F8E   0000C024282D   tcp    0064  Port:TELNET ---> 6295 ACK
149 0000C0A20F8E   0000C024282D   telnt  0064  Data=-
150 0000C024282D   0000C0A20F8E   tcp    0064  Port:6295 ---> TELNET ACK
151 0000C024282D   0000C0A20F8E   telnt  0064  Data=a
152 0000C0A20F8E   0000C024282D   tcp    0064  Port:TELNET ---> 6295 ACK
153 0000C0A20F8E   0000C024282D   telnt  0064  Data=a
154 0000C024282D   0000C0A20F8E   tcp    0064  Port:6295 ---> TELNET ACK
155 0000C024282D   0000C0A20F8E   telnt  0064  Data=l
156 0000C0A20F8E   0000C024282D   tcp    0064  Port:TELNET ---> 6295 ACK
157 0000C0A20F8E   0000C024282D   telnt  0064  Data=l
158 0000C024282D   0000C0A20F8E   tcp    0064  Port:6295 ---> TELNET ACK
159 0000C024282D   0000C0A20F8E   telnt  0064  Data=x
160 0000C0A20F8E   0000C024282D   tcp    0064  Port:TELNET ---> 6295 ACK
161 0000C0A20F8E   0000C024282D   telnt  0064  Data=x
162 0000C024282D   0000C0A20F8E   tcp    0064  Port:6295 ---> TELNET ACK
163 0000C024282D   0000C0A20F8E   telnt  0064  Data=..
164 0000C0A20F8E   0000C024282D   tcp    0064  Port:TELNET ---> 6295 ACK
165 0000C0A20F8E   0000C024282D   telnt  0064  Data=..
166 0000C024282D   0000C0A20F8E   tcp    0064  Port:6295 ---> TELNET ACK
167 0000C0A20F8E   0000C024282D   telnt  0133  Data= F    UID   PID  PPID PRI NI
168 0000C024282D   0000C0A20F8E   tcp    0064  Port:6295 ---> TELNET ACK
169 0000C0A20F8E   0000C024282D   telnt  0140  Data=  0     0     1     0  30 15
170 0000C024282D   0000C0A20F8E   tcp    0064  Port:6295 ---> TELNET ACK
171 0000C0A20F8E   0000C024282D   telnt  0143  Data=  0     0     2     1  30 15
172 0000C024282D   0000C0A20F8E   tcp    0064  Port:6295 ---> TELNET ACK
173 0000C0A20F8E   0000C024282D   telnt  0140  Data=  0     0     8     1  30 15
174 0000C024282D   0000C0A20F8E   tcp    0064  Port:6295 ---> TELNET ACK
175 0000C0A20F8E   0000C024282D   telnt  0140  Data=  0     0    24     1  30 15
176 0000C024282D   0000C0A20F8E   tcp    0064  Port:6295 ---> TELNET ACK
177 0000C0A20F8E   0000C024282D   telnt  0140  Data=  0     0    38     1  30 15
178 0000C024282D   0000C0A20F8E   tcp    0064  Port:6295 ---> TELNET ACK
179 0000C0A20F8E   0000C024282D   telnt  0140  Data=  0     0    40     1  30 15
180 0000C024282D   0000C0A20F8E   tcp    0064  Port:6295 ---> TELNET ACK
181 0000C0A20F8E   0000C024282D   telnt  0140  Data=  0     1    42     1  30 15
182 0000C024282D   0000C0A20F8E   tcp    0064  Port:6295 ---> TELNET ACK
183 0000C0A20F8E   0000C024282D   telnt  0140  Data=  0     0    44     1  30 15
184 0000C024282D   0000C0A20F8E   tcp    0064  Port:6295 ---> TELNET ACK
185 0000C0A20F8E   0000C024282D   telnt  0139  Data=  0     0    46     1  30 15
```

```
186 0000C024282D  0000C0A20F8E  tcp    0064  Port:6295 ---> TELNET ACK
187 0000C0A20F8E  0000C024282D  telnt  0140  Data= 0     0    49     1   30 15
188 0000C024282D  0000C0A20F8E  tcp    0064  Port:6295 ---> TELNET ACK
189 0000C0A20F8E  0000C024282D  telnt  0140  Data= 0     0    51     1   30 15
190 0000C024282D  0000C0A20F8E  tcp    0064  Port:6295 ---> TELNET ACK
191 0000C0A20F8E  0000C024282D  telnt  0140  Data= 0     0    53     1   30 15
192 0000C024282D  0000C0A20F8E  tcp    0064  Port:6295 ---> TELNET ACK
193 0000C0A20F8E  0000C024282D  telnt  0140  Data= 0     0    57     1   30 15
194 0000C024282D  0000C0A20F8E  tcp    0064  Port:6295 ---> TELNET ACK
195 0000C0A20F8E  0000C024282D  telnt  0140  Data= 0     0    61     1   30 15
196 0000C024282D  0000C0A20F8E  tcp    0064  Port:6295 ---> TELNET ACK
197 0000C0A20F8E  0000C024282D  telnt  0140  Data= 0     0    62     1   30 15
198 0000C024282D  0000C0A20F8E  tcp    0064  Port:6295 ---> TELNET ACK
199 0000C0A20F8E  0000C024282D  telnt  0140  Data= 0     0    63     1   30 15
200 0000C024282D  0000C0A20F8E  tcp    0064  Port:6295 ---> TELNET ACK
201 0000C0A20F8E  0000C024282D  telnt  0140  Data= 0     0    64     1   30 15
202 0000C024282D  0000C0A20F8E  tcp    0064  Port:6295 ---> TELNET ACK
203 0000C0A20F8E  0000C024282D  telnt  0140  Data= 0     0    65     1   30 15
204 0000C024282D  0000C0A20F8E  tcp    0064  Port:6295 ---> TELNET ACK
205 0000C0A20F8E  0000C024282D  telnt  0131  Data= 0     0   145     1   30 15
206 0000C024282D  0000C0A20F8E  tcp    0064  Port:6295 ---> TELNET ACK
207 0000C024282D  0000C0A20F8E  telnt  0064  Data=.
208 0000C0A20F8E  0000C024282D  tcp    0064  Port:TELNET ---> 6295 ACK
209 0000C0A20F8E  0000C024282D  telnt  0136  Data= 0     0   258    44   29 15
210 0000C0A20F8E  0000C024282D  telnt  0064  Cmd=;
211 0000C024282D  0000C0A20F8E  telnt  0064  Data=.
212 0000C0A20F8E  0000C024282D  telnt  0064  Data=.
213 0000C0A20F8E  0000C024282D  tcp    0064  Port:TELNET ---> 6295 ACK
214 0000C024282D  0000C0A20F8E  tcp    0064  Port:6295 ---> TELNET ACK
215 0000C0A20F8E  0000C024282D  telnt  0071  Data=..ltreec1:~$
216 0000C024282D  0000C0A20F8E  tcp    0064  Port:6295 ---> TELNET ACK
217 0000C024282D  0000C0A20F8E  telnt  0064  Data=l
218 0000C0A20F8E  0000C024282D  tcp    0064  Port:TELNET ---> 6295 ACK
219 0000C0A20F8E  0000C024282D  telnt  0064  Data=l
220 0000C024282D  0000C0A20F8E  tcp    0064  Port:6295 ---> TELNET ACK
221 0000C024282D  0000C0A20F8E  telnt  0064  Data=o
222 0000C0A20F8E  0000C024282D  tcp    0064  Port:TELNET ---> 6295 ACK
223 0000C0A20F8E  0000C024282D  telnt  0064  Data=o
224 0000C024282D  0000C0A20F8E  tcp    0064  Port:6295 ---> TELNET ACK
225 0000C024282D  0000C0A20F8E  telnt  0064  Data=g
226 0000C0A20F8E  0000C024282D  tcp    0064  Port:TELNET ---> 6295 ACK
227 0000C0A20F8E  0000C024282D  telnt  0064  Data=g
228 0000C024282D  0000C0A20F8E  tcp    0064  Port:6295 ---> TELNET ACK
229 0000C024282D  0000C0A20F8E  telnt  0064  Data=o
230 0000C0A20F8E  0000C024282D  tcp    0064  Port:TELNET ---> 6295 ACK
231 0000C0A20F8E  0000C024282D  telnt  0064  Data=o
232 0000C024282D  0000C0A20F8E  tcp    0064  Port:6295 ---> TELNET ACK
233 0000C024282D  0000C0A20F8E  telnt  0064  Data=u
234 0000C0A20F8E  0000C024282D  tcp    0064  Port:TELNET ---> 6295 ACK
235 0000C0A20F8E  0000C024282D  telnt  0064  Data=u
236 0000C024282D  0000C0A20F8E  tcp    0064  Port:6295 ---> TELNET ACK
237 0000C024282D  0000C0A20F8E  telnt  0064  Data=t
238 0000C0A20F8E  0000C024282D  tcp    0064  Port:TELNET ---> 6295 ACK
239 0000C0A20F8E  0000C024282D  telnt  0064  Data=t
240 0000C024282D  0000C0A20F8E  tcp    0064  Port:6295 ---> TELNET ACK
241 0000C024282D  0000C0A20F8E  telnt  0064  Data=..
242 0000C0A20F8E  0000C024282D  tcp    0064  Port:TELNET ---> 6295 ACK
243 0000C0A20F8E  0000C024282D  tcp    0064  Port:TELNET ---> 6295 ACK FIN
244 0000C024282D  0000C0A20F8E  tcp    0064  Port:6295 ---> TELNET ACK FIN
245 0000C0A20F8E  0000C024282D  tcp    0064  Port:TELNET ---> 6295 ACK
```

Packets 1 through 3 in figure 11.27 deal with ARP resolution. ARP resolution is discussed in Chapter 5, "Address Resolution Protocols." The actual Telnet trace begins from packet 4.

The following sections examine only the TCP aspect of the Telnet trace in figure 11.27 and not the Telnet application data. The packet numbers in the following traces correspond to the packet numbers in figure 11.27. For this reason, the entire trace of the Telnet session is reproduced in figure 11.27 for your reference, even though the trace itself is somewhat long.

TCP Open Connection Three-Way Handshake Trace

Figures 11.28 through 11.30 show the three TCP packets involved in the three-way handshake that is used to open a TCP connection.

Figure 11.28 OPEN TCP connection request: sending the initial sender sequence number (ISS).

```
Packet Number : 4            6:38:38 PM
Length : 64 bytes
ether: ==================== Ethernet Datalink Layer ====================
       Station: 00-00-C0-24-28-2D ----> 00-00-C0-A2-0F-8E
       Type: 0x0800 (IP)
   ip: ====================== Internet Protocol ======================
       Station:144.19.74.44 ---->144.19.74.201
       Protocol: TCP
       Version: 4
       Header Length (32 bit words): 5
       Precedence: Routine
              Normal Delay, Normal Throughput, Normal Reliability
       Total length: 44
       Identification:     1
       Fragmentation allowed, Last fragment
       Fragment Offset: 0
       Time to Live: 100 seconds
       Checksum: 0xA1AF(Valid)
  tcp: ================= Transmission Control Protocol =================
       Source Port: 6295
       Destination Port: TELNET
       Sequence Number: 25784320
       Acknowledgement Number: 0
       Data Offset (32-bit words): 6
       Window: 4096
       Control Bits: Synchronize Sequence Numbers (SYN)
       Checksum: 0x4A87(Valid)
       Urgent Pointer: 0
       Option:MAXIMUM SEGMENT SIZE
              Option Length: 4
              Maximum Segment Size : 1024
```

```
 0: 00 00 C0 A2 0F 8E 00 00 C0 24 28 2D 08 00 45 00 |.........$(-..E.
10: 00 2C 00 01 00 00 64 06 A1 AF 90 13 4A 2C 90 13 |.,....d.....J,..
20: 4A C9 18 97 00 17 01 89 70 00 00 00 00 00 60 02 |J.......p.....`.
30: 10 00 4A 87 00 00 02 04 04 00 00 00             |..J.........
```

The OPEN connection request TCP packet has the following flags and sequence number and represents Step 1 in the three-way handshake:

e number = 25784320 (ISS)

Acknowledgment Number = 0 (not valid because ACK = 0)

Another interesting thing to note about the OPEN connection option is that the Data Offset field is 6, which indicates the existence of a TCP option. This option is the MSS option (option-kind= 2) with the following hex codes:

02 04 04 00

These codes translate to the following TCP option values:

Option:	MAXIMUM SEGMENT SIZE
Option Length:	4
Maximum Segment Size :	1,024

The source port, destination port, and window size of this initial packet are as follows:

Source Port:	6295
Destination Port:	23 (standard Telnet server port)
Window:	4,096

The source port represents the port on which the Telnet client is listening to receive data from the Telnet server. The destination port is the port on the Telnet server that is being contacted for opening a connection. The window is the number of octets that the Telnet client can receive; that is, it is the size of the Telnet client computer's TCP receive buffer.

Figure 11.29 shows the acknowledgment of the OPEN connection request TCP packet by the receiver. This is Step 2 in the three-way handshake:

SYN = 1

ACK = 1

All other TCP flags set to 0

Sequence Number = 1508167651 (IRS)

Acknowledgment Number = 25784321 (ISS +1)

Figure 11.29 Acknowledgment of OPEN connection request: sending the initial receiver sequence number (IRS).

```
Packet Number : 5            6:38:38 PM
Length : 64 bytes
ether: ==================== Ethernet Datalink Layer ====================
       Station: 00-00-C0-A2-0F-8E ----> 00-00-C0-24-28-2D
       Type: 0x0800 (IP)
   ip: ====================== Internet Protocol ======================
       Station:144.19.74.201 ---->144.19.74.44
       Protocol: TCP
       Version: 4
       Header Length (32 bit words): 5
       Precedence: Routine
              Normal Delay, Normal Throughput, Normal Reliability
       Total length: 44
       Identification: 21410
       Fragmentation allowed, Last fragment
       Fragment Offset: 0
       Time to Live: 64  seconds
       Checksum: 0x720E(Valid)
  tcp: ================= Transmission Control Protocol =================
       Source Port: TELNET
       Destination Port: 6295
       Sequence Number: 1508167651
       Acknowledgement Number: 25784321
       Data Offset (32-bit words): 6
       Window: 30719
       Control Bits: Acknowledgement Field is Valid (ACK)
              Synchronize Sequence Numbers (SYN)
       Checksum: 0xB8AE(Valid)
       Urgent Pointer: 0
       Option:MAXIMUM SEGMENT SIZE
              Option Length: 4
              Maximum Segment Size : 1024
```

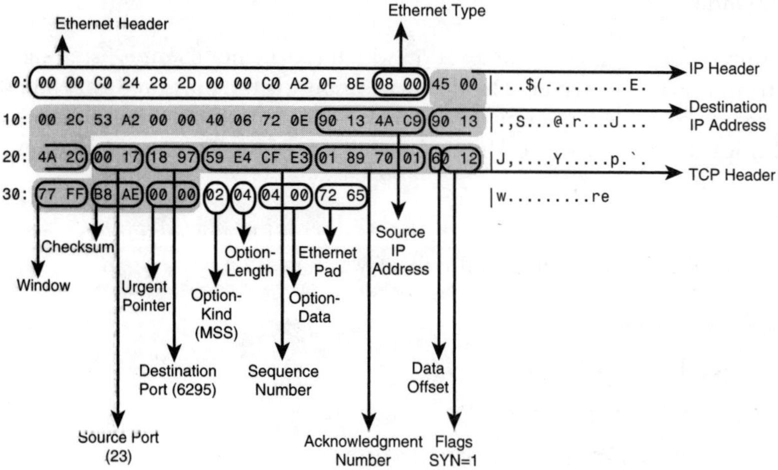

```
 0: 00 00 C0 24 28 2D 00 00 C0 A2 0F 8E 08 00 45 00 |...$(-........E.
10: 00 2C 53 A2 00 00 40 06 72 0E 90 13 4A C9 90 13 |.,S...@.r...J...
20: 4A 2C 00 17 18 97 59 E4 CF E3 01 89 70 01 60 12 |J,....Y.....p.`.
30: 77 FF B8 AE 00 00 02 04 04 00 72 65             |w.........re
```

The packet in figure 11.29 is sent by the Telnet server to synchronize its sequence number and contains the server's initial sequence number. Another interesting thing to note about the OPEN connection option is that the Data Offset field is 6, which indicates the existence of a TCP option. This option is the MSS option (option-kind = 2) with the following hex codes:

02 04 04 00

These codes translate to the following TCP option values:

Option: MAXIMUM SEGMENT SIZE

Option Length: 4

Maximum Segment Size : 1,024

In this example, both the Telnet client and server use the same MSS size, but this situation does not always have to exist. The source port, destination port, and window size of the OPEN connection acknowledgment packet are as follows:

Source Port: 23 (standard Telnet server port)

Destination Port: 6295

Window: 30,719

The source port represents the port on which the Telnet server is listening to receive data from the Telnet client. The destination port is the port on the Telnet client that made the request for opening a connection. The window is the number of octets that the Telnet server can receive; that is, it is the size of the Telnet server computer's TCP receive buffer. Note that this number is larger than that of the Telnet client.

Figure 11.30 shows the last step in the three-way handshake. In this step the Telnet server's sequence number received by the Telnet client is being acknowledged. This packet has the following flags and sequence numbers:

ACK = 1

PSH = 1

All other TCP flags set to 0

Sequence Number = 25784321 (ISS + 1)

Acknowledgment Number = 1508167652 (IRS + 1)

Figure 11.30 Acknowledgment of initial receiver sequence number (IRS).

```
Packet Number : 6          6:38:38 PM
Length : 69 bytes
ether: ==================== Ethernet Datalink Layer ====================
       Station: 00-00-C0-24-28-2D ----> 00-00-C0-A2-0F-8E
       Type: 0x0800 (IP)
   ip: ====================== Internet Protocol ======================
       Station:144.19.74.44 ---->144.19.74.201
       Protocol: TCP
       Version: 4
       Header Length (32 bit words): 5
       Precedence: Routine
              Normal Delay, Normal Throughput, Normal Reliability
       Total length: 49
       Identification:    2
       Fragmentation allowed, Last fragment
       Fragment Offset: 0
       Time to Live: 100 seconds
       Checksum: 0xA1A9(Valid)
  tcp: ================= Transmission Control Protocol =================
       Source Port: 6295
       Destination Port: TELNET
       Sequence Number: 25784321
       Acknowledgement Number: 1508167652
       Data Offset (32-bit words): 5
       Window: 4096
       Control Bits: Acknowledgement Field is Valid (ACK)
              Push Function Requested (PSH)
       Checksum: 0x18A9(Valid)
       Urgent Pointer: 0
telnt: ======================= Telnet Protocol =======================
       Command: Do
       Option Code: Echo
       Command: Do
       Option Code: Suppress Go Ahead
       Command: Will
       Option Code:
```

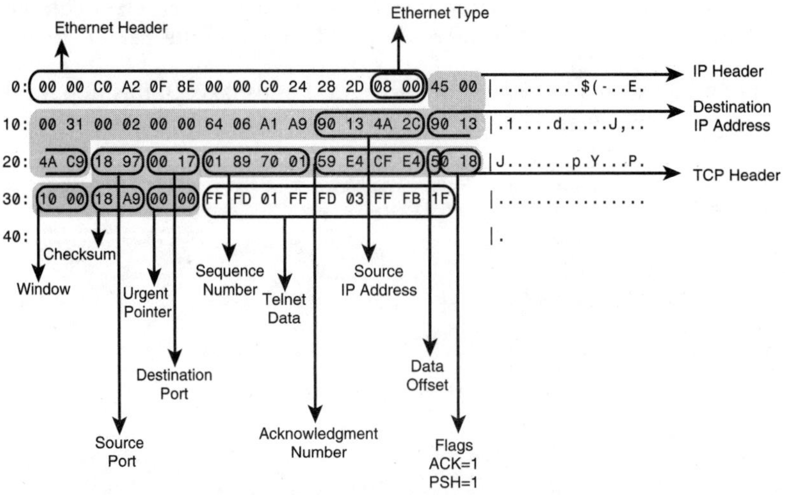

```
 0: 00 00 C0 A2 0F 8E 00 00 C0 24 28 2D 08 00 45 00 |........$(-..E.
10: 00 31 00 02 00 00 64 06 A1 A9 90 13 4A 2C 90 13 |.1....d.....J,..
20: 4A C9 18 97 00 17 01 89 70 01 59 E4 CF E4 50 18 |J.......p.Y...P.
30: 10 00 18 A9 00 00 FF FD 01 FF FD 03 FF FB 1F    |...............
40:                                                 |.
```

The PSH flag is set to suggest to TCP that it should send the data. Nagle's avoidance technique is used to prevent the Silly Window Syndrome (SWS). See the earlier section "Avoiding the Silly Window Syndrome" for details on Nagle's algorithm to avoid SWS.

Another interesting thing to note about the OPEN connection option is that the Data Offset field is 5 which indicates no TCP options.

The source port, destination port, and window size of this initial packet are as follows:

Source port:	6295
Destination port:	23 (standard Telnet server port)
Window:	4,096

The source port represents the end point of the TCP connection on the Telnet client. The destination port represents the end point of the TCP connection on the Telnet server. The window is the number of octets that the Telnet client can receive; that is, it is the size of the Telnet client computer's TCP receive buffer.

TCP Normal Data Mode Trace

In packet 6 (refer to fig. 11.30), which concludes the three-way handshake and acknowledges the TCP receiver's IRS, nine octets of Telnet data are sent:

FF FD 01 FF FD 03 FF FB 1F

How do you know that nine octets of Telnet data have been sent? Examine the IP header field to determine the size of the IP datagram (refer to fig. 11.30). The IP datagram is 49 octets. Of these 49 octets, 20 octets (Header Length = 5 words) are taken up by the IP header, and 20 octets (Data Offset = 5 words) are taken up by the TCP header. What remains is 49 – 20 – 20 = 9 octets for the Telnet data.

Packet 6 represents the start of data transmission mode in the TCP trace. Packet 7 (see fig. 11.31) contains an acknowledgment of this data from the Telnet server. The Telnet server at this point does not have any data to send and, therefore, sends only an acknowledgment.

Figure 11.31 Acknowledgment packet.

```
Packet Number : 7          6:38:38 PM
Length : 64 bytes
ether: ==================== Ethernet Datalink Layer ====================
       Station: 00-00-C0-A2-0F-8E ----> 00-00-C0-24-28-2D
       Type: 0x0800 (IP)
   ip: ====================== Internet Protocol ======================
       Station:144.19.74.201 ---->144.19.74.44
       Protocol: TCP
       Version: 4
       Header Length (32 bit words): 5
       Precedence: Routine
              Normal Delay, Normal Throughput, Normal Reliability
       Total length: 40
       Identification: 21411
       Fragmentation allowed, Last fragment
       Fragment Offset: 0
       Time to Live: 64  seconds
       Checksum: 0x7211(Valid)
  tcp: ================= Transmission Control Protocol =================
       Source Port: TELNET
       Destination Port: 6295
       Sequence Number: 1508167652
       Acknowledgement Number: 25784330
       Data Offset (32-bit words): 5
       Window: 30710
       Control Bits: Acknowledgement Field is Valid (ACK)
       Checksum: 0xCEB7(Valid)
       Urgent Pointer: 0
```

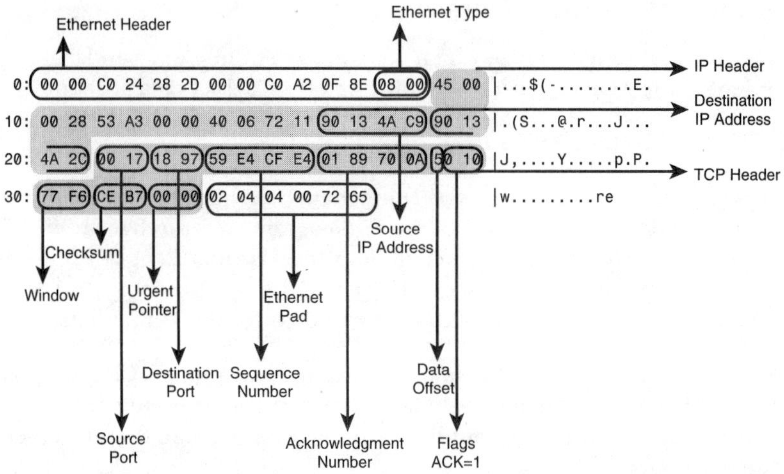

```
 0: 00 00 C0 24 28 2D 00 00 C0 A2 0F 8E 08 00 45 00 |...$(-........E.
10: 00 28 53 A3 00 00 40 06 72 11 90 13 4A C9 90 13 |.(S...@.r...J...
20: 4A 2C 00 17 18 97 59 E4 CF E4 01 89 70 0A 50 10 |J,....Y.....p.P.
30: 77 F6 CE B7 00 00 02 04 04 00 72 65             |w.........re
```

Ethernet Header
Ethernet Type
IP Header
Destination IP Address
TCP Header
Source IP Address
Checksum
Window
Urgent Pointer
Ethernet Pad
Destination Port
Sequence Number
Data Offset
Source Port
Acknowledgment Number
Flags ACK=1

Note that this packet has the following flags and sequence numbers:

ACK = 1

All other TCP flags set to 0

Sequence Number: 1508167652

Acknowledgment Number: 25784330

Note that the acknowledgment number that is sent back contains the acknowledgment for the nine octets of Telnet client data:

ISN from Telnet client = 25784321

Telnet data = 9

Acknowledgment Number data = ISN from Telnet client + Telnet
= 25784321 + 9
= 25784330

One second after the acknowledgment packet is sent, the Telnet server sends a response to the Telnet client data in packet 8 (see fig. 11.32). If the Telnet server had been ready to send this response right away, it could have done so in packet 7. TCP will delay sending acknowledgments to avoid sending small packets, but the maximum delay according to the TCP standard is 500 milliseconds (see the discussion in the previous section "Avoiding the Silly Window Syndrome"). You know that one second has transpired between packets 7 and 8 by examining the time stamps that are displayed on the first line in the protocol decodes. These time stamps indicate the time that a packet was captured by using a protocol analyzer.

The amount of application data that is sent in packet 8 is computed as before:

IP Total Length – IP Header Length – TCP Data Offset

= 43 – 20 – 20 = 3 octets

Figure 11.32 TCP data transmission.

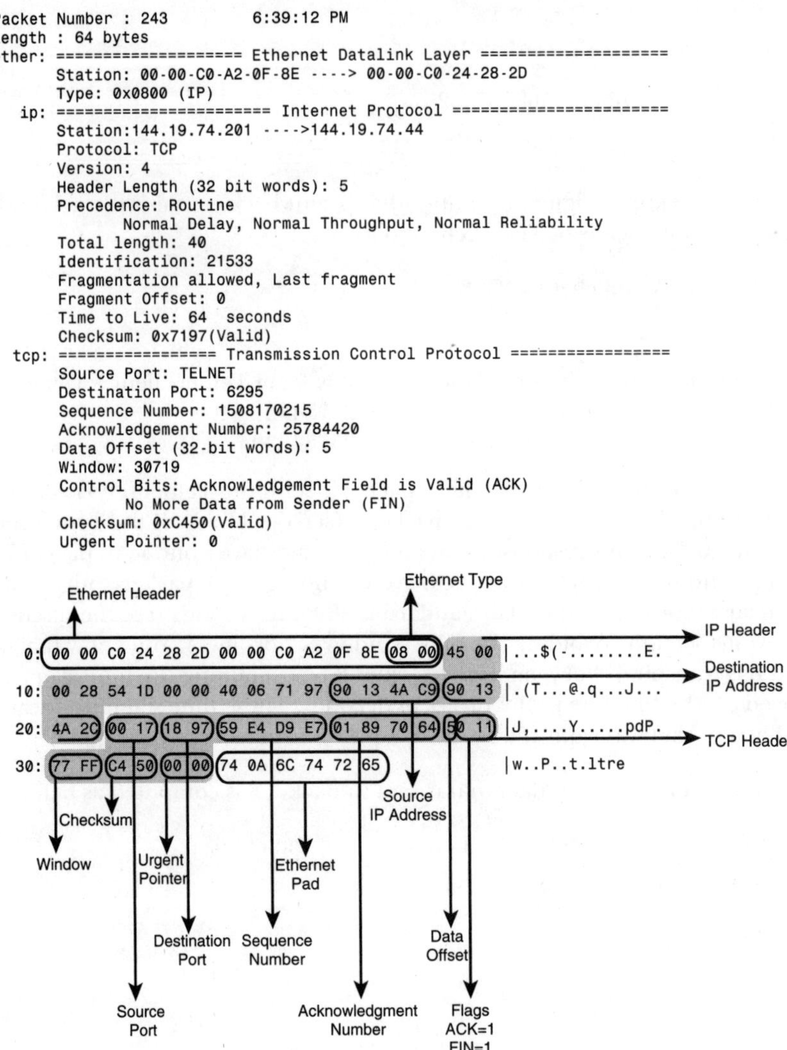

```
Packet Number : 243          6:39:12 PM
Length : 64 bytes
ether: ==================== Ethernet Datalink Layer ====================
          Station: 00-00-C0-A2-0F-8E ----> 00-00-C0-24-28-2D
          Type: 0x0800 (IP)
   ip: ====================== Internet Protocol ======================
          Station:144.19.74.201 ---->144.19.74.44
          Protocol: TCP
          Version: 4
          Header Length (32 bit words): 5
          Precedence: Routine
                 Normal Delay, Normal Throughput, Normal Reliability
          Total length: 40
          Identification: 21533
          Fragmentation allowed, Last fragment
          Fragment Offset: 0
          Time to Live: 64  seconds
          Checksum: 0x7197(Valid)
  tcp: ================ Transmission Control Protocol ================
          Source Port: TELNET
          Destination Port: 6295
          Sequence Number: 1508170215
          Acknowledgement Number: 25784420
          Data Offset (32-bit words): 5
          Window: 30719
          Control Bits: Acknowledgement Field is Valid (ACK)
                No More Data from Sender (FIN)
          Checksum: 0xC450(Valid)
          Urgent Pointer: 0
```


TCP Graceful Close Trace

Packets 217 through 242 (refer to fig. 11.27) show the Telnet client transmitting the logout command one character at a time to the Telnet server. Packets 243 through 245 illustrate the graceful close mechanism. In packet 243 (see fig. 11.33), the Telnet server that receives the logout command requests a close of the TCP connection by setting the FIN flag to 1. This flag indicates that the Telnet server has no more data to send.

Figure 11.33 Graceful close request issued by Telnet server.

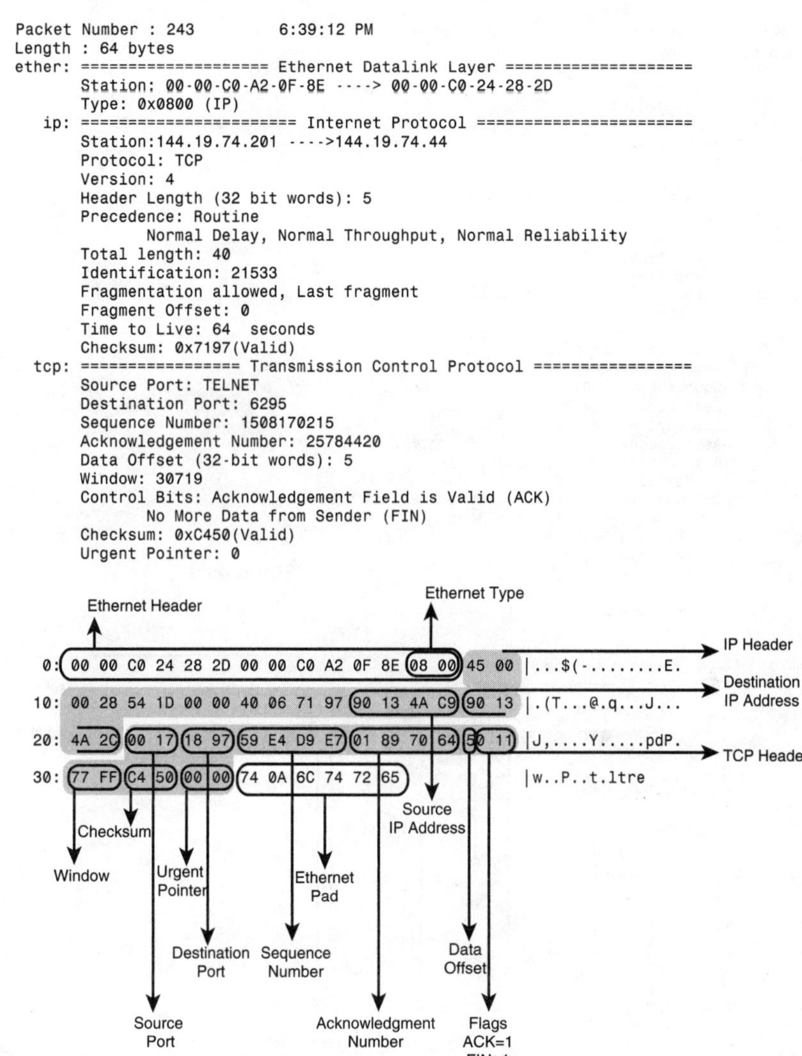

```
Packet Number : 243          6:39:12 PM
Length : 64 bytes
ether: ==================== Ethernet Datalink Layer ====================
       Station: 00-00-C0-A2-0F-8E ----> 00-00-C0-24-28-2D
       Type: 0x0800 (IP)
   ip: ====================== Internet Protocol ======================
       Station:144.19.74.201 ---->144.19.74.44
       Protocol: TCP
       Version: 4
       Header Length (32 bit words): 5
       Precedence: Routine
              Normal Delay, Normal Throughput, Normal Reliability
       Total length: 40
       Identification: 21533
       Fragmentation allowed, Last fragment
       Fragment Offset: 0
       Time to Live: 64  seconds
       Checksum: 0x7197(Valid)
  tcp: ================= Transmission Control Protocol =================
       Source Port: TELNET
       Destination Port: 6295
       Sequence Number: 1508170215
       Acknowledgement Number: 25784420
       Data Offset (32-bit words): 5
       Window: 30719
       Control Bits: Acknowledgement Field is Valid (ACK)
              No More Data from Sender (FIN)
       Checksum: 0xC450(Valid)
       Urgent Pointer: 0
```


In packet 244 (see fig. 11.34), the Telnet client responds by setting the FIN flag to 1, thereby indicating that the client is ready to close the connection and that it has no more data to send. Note that in this implementation, the window size is set to 0 to indicate that TCP at the Telnet client will not accept any more data.

Figure 11.34 Graceful close request agreed upon by Telnet client.

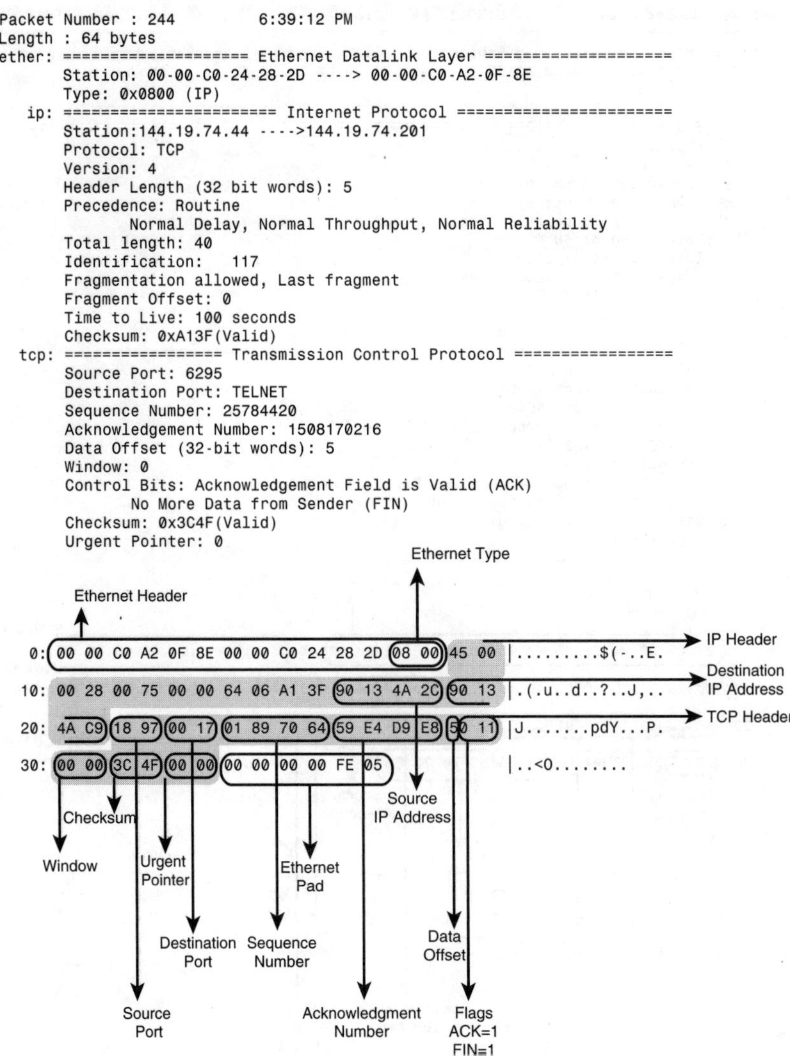

Packet Number : 244 6:39:12 PM
Length : 64 bytes
ether: ==================== Ethernet Datalink Layer ====================
Station: 00-00-C0-24-28-2D ----> 00-00-C0-A2-0F-8E
Type: 0x0800 (IP)
ip: ====================== Internet Protocol ======================
Station:144.19.74.44 ---->144.19.74.201
Protocol: TCP
Version: 4
Header Length (32 bit words): 5
Precedence: Routine
Normal Delay, Normal Throughput, Normal Reliability
Total length: 40
Identification: 117
Fragmentation allowed, Last fragment
Fragment Offset: 0
Time to Live: 100 seconds
Checksum: 0xA13F(Valid)
tcp: ================ Transmission Control Protocol ================
Source Port: 6295
Destination Port: TELNET
Sequence Number: 25784420
Acknowledgement Number: 1508170216
Data Offset (32-bit words): 5
Window: 0
Control Bits: Acknowledgement Field is Valid (ACK)
No More Data from Sender (FIN)
Checksum: 0x3C4F(Valid)
Urgent Pointer: 0
Ethernet Type
Ethernet Header
0: 00 00 C0 A2 0F 8E 00 00 C0 24 28 2D 08 00 45 00 |.........$(-..E.
10: 00 28 00 75 00 00 64 06 A1 3F 90 13 4A 2C 90 13 |.(.u..d..?..J,..
20: 4A C9 18 97 00 17 01 89 70 64 59 E4 D9 E8 50 11 |J.......pdY...P.
30: 00 00 3C 4F 00 00 00 00 00 00 FE 05 |..<0........
IP Header
Destination IP Address
TCP Header
Source IP Address
Checksum
Window
Urgent Pointer
Ethernet Pad
Destination Port
Sequence Number
Data Offset
Source Port
Acknowledgment Number
Flags ACK=1 FIN=1

In figure 11.35, the Telnet server acknowledges the reception of the FIN flag from the Telnet client. At this point, the TCP modules at the Telnet client and the server will release the resources associated with the TCP connection.

Figure 11.35 **Acknowledgment of graceful close request from Telnet client.**

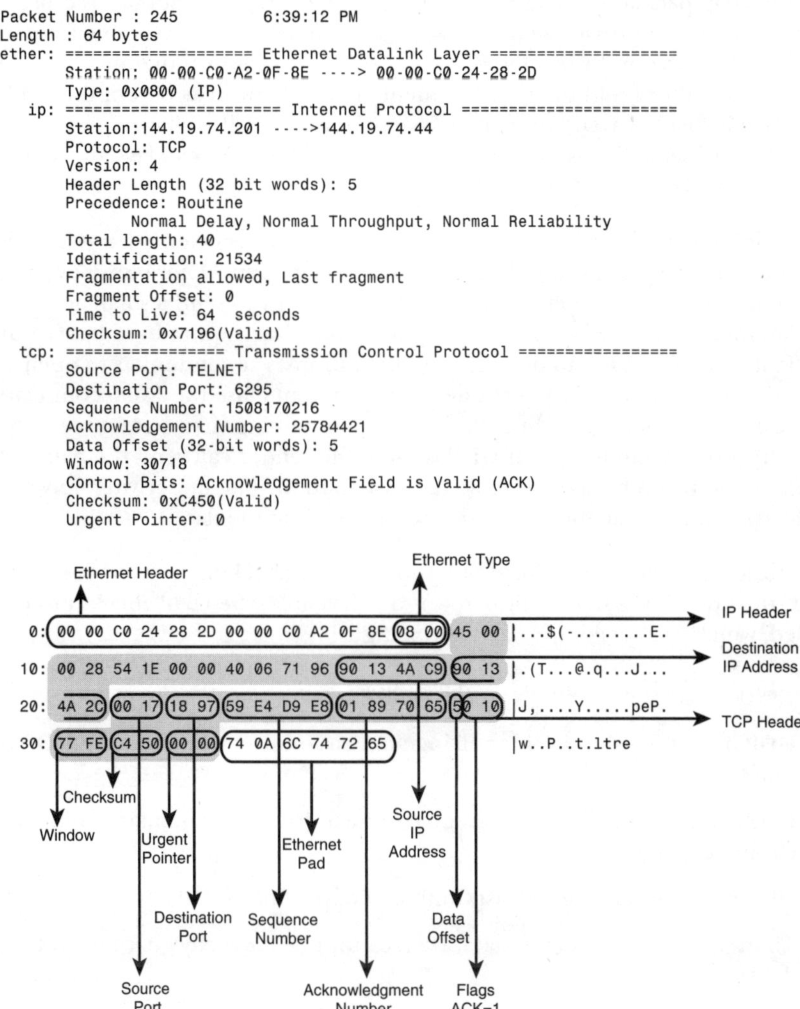

```
Packet Number : 245         6:39:12 PM
Length : 64 bytes
ether: ==================== Ethernet Datalink Layer ====================
       Station: 00-00-C0-A2-0F-8E ----> 00-00-C0-24-28-2D
       Type: 0x0800 (IP)
   ip: ======================= Internet Protocol =======================
       Station:144.19.74.201 ---->144.19.74.44
       Protocol: TCP
       Version: 4
       Header Length (32 bit words): 5
       Precedence: Routine
              Normal Delay, Normal Throughput, Normal Reliability
       Total length: 40
       Identification: 21534
       Fragmentation allowed, Last fragment
       Fragment Offset: 0
       Time to Live: 64  seconds
       Checksum: 0x7196(Valid)
  tcp: ================= Transmission Control Protocol =================
       Source Port: TELNET
       Destination Port: 6295
       Sequence Number: 1508170216
       Acknowledgement Number: 25784421
       Data Offset (32-bit words): 5
       Window: 30718
       Control Bits: Acknowledgement Field is Valid (ACK)
       Checksum: 0xC450(Valid)
       Urgent Pointer: 0
```


The User Datagram Protocol (UDP)

There are a number of applications for which the robustness of TCP is not required. Instead, what is needed is a transport protocol that can identify the applications on the computers and provide a rudimentary error check. The User Datagram Protocol (UDP) provides these capabilities.

Unlike TCP, which is connection oriented, UDP (as its name suggests) operates in the datagram mode. UDP makes no attempt to create a connection. Data is sent by encapsulating it in a UDP header and passing the data to the IP layer. The IP layer sends the UDP packet in a single IP datagram unless fragmentation is required. UDP does not attempt to provide sequencing of data; therefore, it is possible for data to arrive in a different order from which it was sent. Applications that need sequencing services must either build their own sequencing mechanism as part of the application or use TCP instead of UDP. In many LAN environments, the chance of data being received out of sequence is small because of small predictable delays and simple network topology.

UDP is useful in applications that are command/response oriented and in which the commands and responses can be sent in a single datagram. There is no overhead involved in opening and then closing a connection just to send a small amount of data. Another advantage of UDP is for applications that require broadcast/multicast. In TCP, if a broadcast has to be sent to 1,000 stations, the sender has to open 1,000 connections, send data on each connection, and then close the 1,000 connections. The overhead of opening these connections, maintaining them (resource utilization), and then closing them is high. If UDP is used, the sender can send the data to the IP module requesting a broadcast/multicast distribution. The underlying network's broadcast/multicast capability may be used in sending the data.

UDP provides a rudimentary form of optional error checking over the integrity of the data. If the underlying network is known to be reliable, the UDP checksums can be disabled, which will speed up UDP processing.

The features of UDP are summarized as follows:

- UDP has a provision for identifying application processes by using UDP port numbers.
- UDP is datagram oriented with no overhead for opening, maintaining, and closing a connection.
- UDP is efficient for broadcast/multicast applications.
- There is no sequencing of data. Data cannot be correctly guaranteed for delivery.
- UDP uses optional error checksum of data only.
- UDP is faster, simpler and more efficient than TCP; however, it is also less robust then TCP.

UDP provides unreliable, connectionless delivery services over TCP. UDP is regarded as a Transport layer protocol. As a Transport layer protocol, UDP is somewhat of a paradox because the function of a Transport layer is to provide end-to-end data integrity, which is something UDP does not do. Despite this drawback, a large number of practical applications are built around UDP. These applications include the following:

- TFTP (Trivial File Transfer Protocol)
- DNS (Domain Name System)
- NFS (Network File System) version 2
- SNMP (Simple Network Management Protocol)
- RIP (Routing Information Protocol)
- Many services that broadcast data, such as WHOD (Who daemon on Unix servers)

The upcoming sections explore UDP in greater detail.

UDP Header Format

The UDP header has a fixed length of eight octets. The format of the UDP header is shown in figure 11.36.

Figure 11.36 UDP header format.

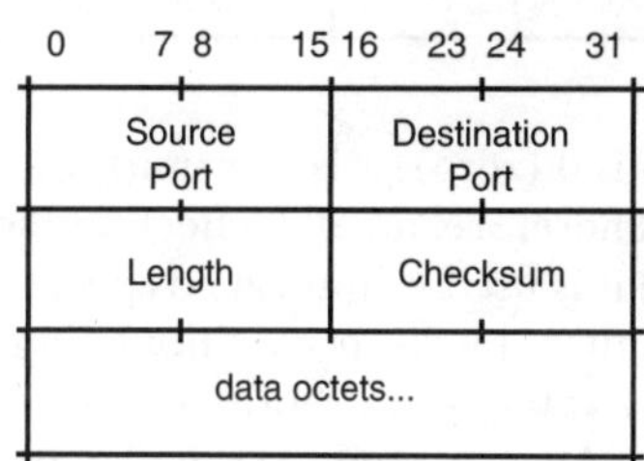

The Source Port is a 16-bit field. This field is optional. When meaningful, it indicates the following:

- The port number of the sending process.
- The source port number is the port to which a reply should be addressed in the absence of any other information.
- When set to 0, the field indicates that the source port number is not used.

The Destination Port field identifies the process at the destination IP address. This process is to receive the UDP data being sent. Like TCP, UDP performs demultiplexing of data to the destination process by using port number values. If UDP receives a datagram with a port number that is not in use (no UDP application associated with the port), UDP generates an ICMP port unreachable error message and rejects the datagram.

The Length field is the length of this UDP packet in octets. This length includes the UDP header and its data. The minimum value of the Length field is 8 and indicates a zero-size data field.

The checksum field is the 16-bit 1's complement of the 1's complement sum of a pseudoheader of information from the IP header, the UDP header, and the data, padded with zero octets at the end (if necessary) to make a multiple of two octets. The checksum procedure is the same as is used in TCP.

The pseudoheader, which is prefixed conceptually to the UDP header, contains the source address, the destination address, the protocol (UDP protocol number is 17), and the UDP length (see fig. 11.37). This information provides protection against misrouted datagrams. The pseudoheader has a fixed size of 12 octets. The information in the UDP pseudoheader completely specifies the half association of the destination, even though no connection is being set up.

Figure 11.37 UDP pseudoheader used in checksum calculations.

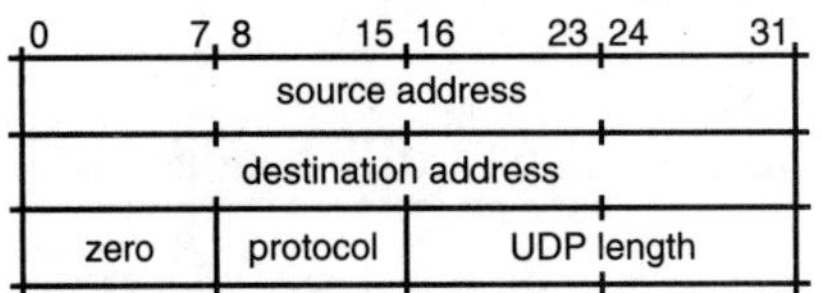

If the computed checksum is 0 (zero), it is transmitted as all 1s (the equivalent in 1's complement arithmetic). Therefore, an all 0 checksum will never be generated by the preceding calculation, and it is used to indicate a special condition: an all 0 transmitted checksum value means that checksums are not being used. Another way of looking at this situation is that 0 has two representations if you use 1's complement arithmetic: all 0s, and all 1s. All 1s is used for calculated checksum, and all 0s indicates that checksumming is disabled. An application running on a reliable IP network, such as a LAN, may want to disable the extra overhead of generating checksums on transmission and verifying them on receiving the UDP datagram.

The UDP protocol runs on top of IP. The IP checksum is done only over the header, whereas the UDP checksum is done over the UDP header and data. The UDP checksum is needed for guaranteeing the integrity of the data field.

UDP Layering and Encapsulation

UDP runs on top of IP, as you can see in figure 11.38. Applications that run on top of UDP are associated with a UDP port number. The UDP port number is in a different address space than the TCP port number address space. Thus it is possible to have a TCP port number of 1017 and a UDP port number of 1017 to refer to separate application processes. Table 2.5, in Chapter 2, shows both TCP and UDP port numbers.

Figure 11.38 UDP protocol layering.

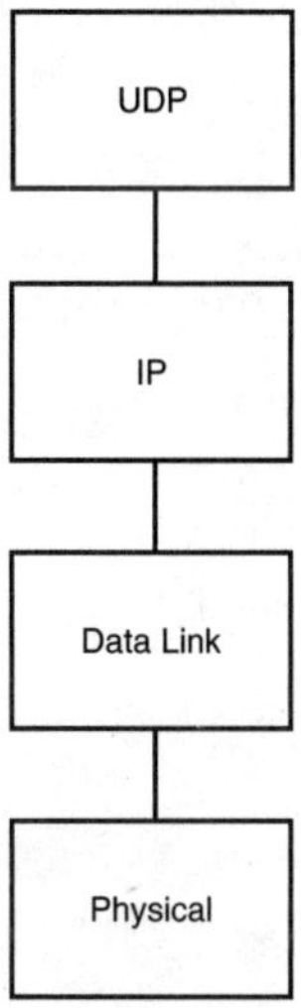

UDP

IP

Data Link

Physical

Figure 11.39 shows how UDP data is encapsulated in an IP header, which in turn is encapsulated by the Data Link layer. The protocol number assigned to UDP is 17.

Figure 11.39 UDP encapsulation.

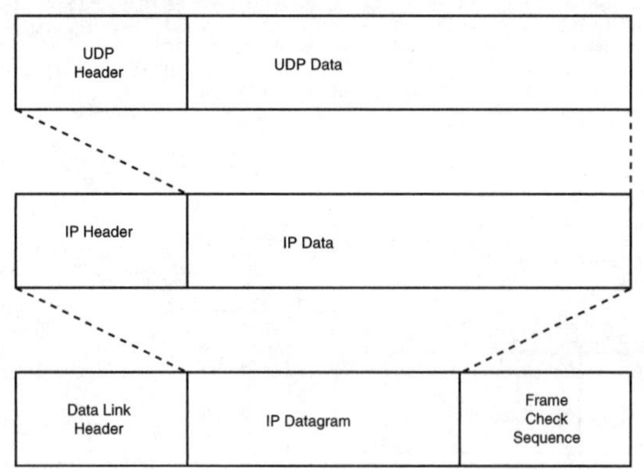

There is a strong degree of coupling between UDP and IP because of the necessity of the UDP layer to know the IP address for the pseudoheader. Recall that the pseudoheader is used as part of the UDP checksum. The implication here is that the UDP module must be able to determine the source and destination IP addresses and the Protocol field from the IP header. One possible UDP/IP interface would return the whole IP datagram, including all the IP header, in response to a RECEIVE operation issued by a UDP application. This interface then would enable UDP to pass a full IP datagram, complete with header, to the IP to send. The IP layer then would verify certain fields for consistency and would compute the IP header checksum.

UDP Trace

Figures 11.40 and 11.41 show two UDP packets: one generated by the Unix WHOD (Who daemon) and another generated by the RIP protocol.

Figure 11.40 UDP packet for the WHOD process.

```
Packet Number : 2            10:57:22 PM
Length : 130 bytes
ether: ==================== Ethernet Datalink Layer ====================
       Station: 00-00-C0-BB-E8-73 ----> FF-FF-FF-FF-FF-FF
       Type: 0x0800 (IP)
   ip: ====================== Internet Protocol ======================
       Station:199.245.180.15 ---->199.245.180.255
       Protocol: UDP
       Version: 4
       Header Length (32 bit words): 5
       Precedence: Routine
             Normal Delay, Normal Throughput, Normal Reliability
       Total length: 112
       Identification:   296
       Fragmentation allowed, Last fragment
       Fragment Offset: 0
       Time to Live: 64  seconds
       Checksum: 0x805B(Valid)
  udp: ==================== User Datagram Protocol ====================
       Source Port: WHO
       Destination Port: WHO
       Length = 92
       Checksum: 0x086A(Valid)
Data:
   0: 01 01 00 00 31 EE A4 F5 00 00 00 00 67 61 74 65 |....1.......gate
  10: 6B 65 65 70 65 72 00 00 00 00 00 00 00 00 00 00 |keeper..........
  20: 00 00 00 00 00 00 00 00 00 00 00 00 00 00 00 00 |................
  30: 00 00 00 00 00 00 00 00 31 EE 7F 85 63 6F 6E 73 |........1...cons
  40: 6F 6C 65 00 72 6F 6F 74 00 00 00 00 31 EE 80 10 |ole.root....1...
  50: 00 00 24 36                                     |..$6
```

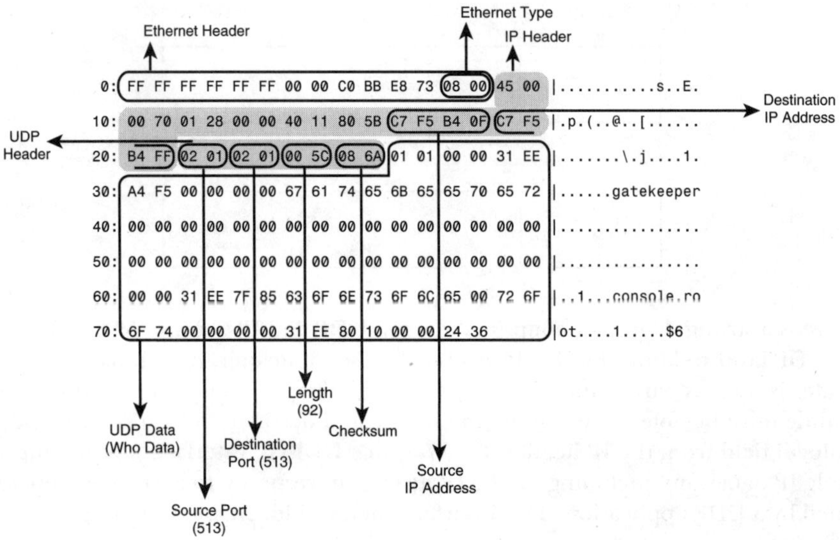

```
 0: FF FF FF FF FF FF 00 00 C0 BB E8 73 08 00 45 00 |...........s..E.
10: 00 70 01 28 00 00 40 11 80 5B C7 F5 B4 0F C7 F5 |.p.(..@..[......
20: B4 FF 02 01 02 01 00 5C 08 6A 01 01 00 00 31 EE |.......\.j....1.
30: A4 F5 00 00 00 00 67 61 74 65 6B 65 65 70 65 72 |......gatekeeper
40: 00 00 00 00 00 00 00 00 00 00 00 00 00 00 00 00 |................
50: 00 00 00 00 00 00 00 00 00 00 00 00 00 00 00 00 |................
60: 00 00 31 EE 7F 85 63 6F 6E 73 6F 6C 65 00 72 6F |..1...console.ro
70: 6F 74 00 00 00 00 31 EE 80 10 00 00 24 36       |ot....1.....$6
```

Ethernet Header
Ethernet Type
IP Header
Destination IP Address
UDP Header
UDP Data (Who Data)
Source Port (513)
Destination Port (513)
Length (92)
Checksum
Source IP Address

The WHOD UDP source and destination port numbers are 513. The RIP UDP source and destination port numbers are 520. Both UDP protocol decodes show a nonzero checksum, which means that checksums are in use.

Figure 11.41 UDP packet for the RIP process.

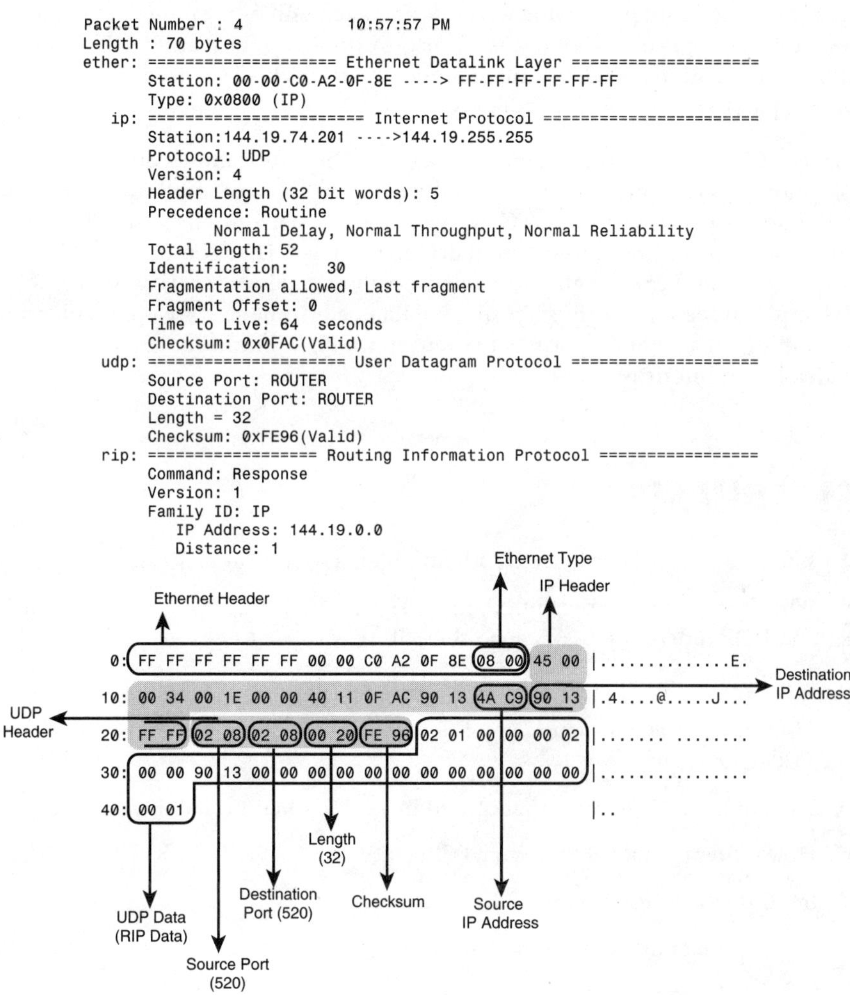

```
Packet Number : 4          10:57:57 PM
Length : 70 bytes
ether: ==================== Ethernet Datalink Layer ====================
       Station: 00-00-C0-A2-0F-8E ----> FF-FF-FF-FF-FF-FF
       Type: 0x0800 (IP)
   ip: ====================== Internet Protocol ======================
       Station:144.19.74.201 ---->144.19.255.255
       Protocol: UDP
       Version: 4
       Header Length (32 bit words): 5
       Precedence: Routine
              Normal Delay, Normal Throughput, Normal Reliability
       Total length: 52
       Identification:    30
       Fragmentation allowed, Last fragment
       Fragment Offset: 0
       Time to Live: 64  seconds
       Checksum: 0x0FAC(Valid)
  udp: ==================== User Datagram Protocol ====================
       Source Port: ROUTER
       Destination Port: ROUTER
       Length = 32
       Checksum: 0xFE96(Valid)
  rip: ================= Routing Information Protocol =================
       Command: Response
       Version: 1
       Family ID: IP
          IP Address: 144.19.0.0
          Distance: 1

 0: FF FF FF FF FF FF 00 00 C0 A2 0F 8E 08 00 45 00 |..............E.
10: 00 34 00 1E 00 00 40 11 0F AC 90 13 4A C9 90 13 |.4....@.....J...
20: FF FF 02 08 02 08 00 20 FE 96 02 01 00 00 00 02 |....... .......
30: 00 00 90 13 00 00 00 00 00 00 00 00 00 00 00 00 |................
40: 00 01                                           |..
```


Also, note that the IP Protocol field is set to 17 to indicate that UDP is being encapsulated.

Summary

TCP and UDP are standard Transport layer protocols that are implemented for IP networks. All nonrouter devices that implement the TCP/IP protocol suite are used to implement TCP. Pure router devices do not implement TCP or UDP. However, most commercial routers provide network management and remote logon capability. These services require the use of the Transport protocols TCP and UDP. In many TCP implementations, UDP is implemented as part of the TCP module, even though UDP is separate from TCP conceptually.

By using TCP and UDP, you can deliver data not just to a remote computer, but to an application process running on the remote computer. These application processes are identified by port numbers. TCP can ensure that data is delivered reliably to the destination by providing a connection-oriented service. UDP, on the other hand, is connectionless and cannot guarantee delivery of data. However, UDP is useful in many applications such as those in which data needs to be sent to a particular application running on a machine, or in situations in which application data needs to be broadcasted or multicasted.

Test Yourself

1. What feature in TCP and UDP identifies an application process?
2. What is the range of port numbers in TCP and UDP? Are port numbers in TCP and UDP independent of each other? If so, why?
3. List and briefly explain some of the TCP features.
4. List some of the consequences of using sequence numbers for every octet in a TCP data stream.
5. Explain the PAR scheme that is used in TCP to obtain reliability.
6. How is flow control achieved in TCP?
7. Suppose the following for a TCP data stream:

    Left edge of window = 1111

    Window size = 6,000 octets

    TCP segment sent but not acknowledged = 800 octets

    Answer the following questions:

    a) Has the data from octet numbers 900 to 1,110 been acknowledged?

b) Can data starting from octet number 7,111 be sent immediately?

c) Starting from sequence number 1911, list the sequence numbers of the data that can be sent immediately.

8. In question 7, suppose that an acknowledgment is received with the following parameters:

   ACK flag = 1

   Acknowledgment Number = 2111

   Window size = 3,000 octets

   What is the new window size and the left edge of the window at the sender? Draw a sketch of this window.

9. How is data multiplexing/demultiplexing achieved in TCP?

10. What is an end point in TCP? Given a TCP connection in which the sender and receiver have the following parameters, list the end points for this TCP connection:

    Sender IP = 200.13.44.2

    Sender TCP port number = 2012

    Destination IP = 132.44.45.66

    Destination TCP port number = 23

    Will the TCP connection have to cross a router boundary?

11. What is a half association in TCP? Given a TCP connection in which the sender and receiver have the following parameters, list the half associations for this TCP connection:

    Sender IP = 145.34.46.62

    Sender TCP port number = 3000

    Destination IP = 145.34.45.61

    Destination TCP port number = 21

    Does this TCP connection have to cross a router boundary? Under what conditions does this TCP connection have to cross a router boundary?

12. What is a full association in TCP? Given a TCP connection in which the sender and receiver have the following parameters, list the full association for this TCP connection:

    Sender IP = 33.23.24.12

    Sender TCP port number = 4234

Destination IP = 33.24.24.12

Destination TCP port number = 80

Does this TCP connection have to cross a router boundary? Under what conditions does this TCP connection have to cross a router boundary?

13. What is a TCB?
14. Describe the two types of TCP OPEN calls.
15. What is the difference between well-known port numbers and reserved port numbers?
16. How is a port number associated with an application process?
17. What is the purpose of the Sequence Number and Acknowledgment Number fields in TCP? How can you tell whether these fields carry valid information?
18. When is the Acknowledgment Number field not valid in TCP?
19. Does receiving an acknowledgment verify that a remote application process has received data? Explain your answer.
20. What is the purpose of the Data Offset field in the TCP header? What is a typical value for the Data Offset field?
21. A TCP header has a Data Offset field value of 6. What can you conclude from this value? Can you make any determination on the type of additional TCP information carried in the TCP header?
22. Describe the purpose of the TCP PSH flag.
23. Describe the purpose of the TCP RST flag.
24. Describe the purpose of the TCP URG flag. What other TCP header field is related to the URG flag?
25. Describe the use of the SYN and ACK flags to indicate different types of TCP messages.
26. What is a three-way handshake in TCP? Explain the three stages in the three-way handshake.
27. A TCP with an ISS value of 345435 opens a connection with another TCP with an IRS value of 675111. Assuming no data is transferred, describe the SYN, ACK, Sequence Number, and Acknowledgment Number field values in the TCP messages of the three-way handshake.
28. A TCP with an ISS value of 67200 opens a connection with another TCP with an IRS value of 893001. Assuming that the active OPEN connection sends 17 octets of data, describe the SYN, ACK, Sequence Number, and Acknowledgment Number field values in the TCP messages of the three-way handshake.

29. A TCP with an ISN value of 345001 opens a connection with another TCP with an ISN value of 234010. Assuming that the active OPEN connection sends 17 octets of data, the passive OPEN message sends 20 octets of data, and the acknowledgment of the IRS contains 12 octets of data, describe the SYN, ACK, Sequence Number, and Acknowledgment Number field values in the TCP messages of the three-way handshake.

30. What is MSL in TCP?

31. If a TCP implementation can retain memory of sequence numbers in use, does it have to wait for the MSL duration before it can start using sequence numbers larger than those recently used? Explain your answer.

32. If a TCP generates message octets at the rate of 1.44 Mbps, how long will it take before sequence numbers are reused?

33. How is the ISN value selected for TCP?

34. On startup, what would happen if a TCP always starts with an ISN value of 0? Will your answer be any different if an ISN value of 1 is used instead of 0?

35. Suppose that a TCP implementation uses the time of day to determine the ISN value for a connection. Will this solve the duplicate sequence number problem?

    (*Hint: Consider what happens in case of a crash.*)

36. What is the purpose of the FIN flag? Describe the graceful close mechanism in TCP.

37. How is the TCP checksum computed? Does the checksum apply to the message data? What is the purpose of including the pseudoheader in computing the checksum?

38. What is the purpose of the MSS option in TCP? When can the MSS option be sent?

39. What are the advantages and disadvantages of the fact that TCP acknowledgments are cumulative?

40. Why are adaptive time-outs necessary in TCP?

41. Describe the formulas used for adaptive retransmission time-out for TCP. Assuming that ALPHA = 0.8, BETA = 2, LBOUND = 1 ms, and UBOUND = 1 sec, compute the successive retransmission time-out values, assuming the following RTT values:

    RTT = 0.21

    RTT = 0.18

    RTT = 0.34

    RTT = 0.52

    RTT = 0.81

42. How can Karn's algorithm be used to improve the effectiveness of retransmission time-outs?
43. Describe Van Jacobson's congestion control algorithm.
44. What is the Silly Window Syndrome?
45. How can SWS be avoided on the sender side?
46. How can SWS be avoided on the receiver side?
47. Discuss how the Nagle avoidance technique works well for a sender sending small amounts of data as well as large amounts of data.
48. How does TCP deal with dead connections?
49. List the main features of UDP.
50. When will you use UDP in preference to using TCP?
51. When will you use TCP in preference to using UDP?
52. What does it mean when a UDP application uses a sender port number of 0?
53. Decode the transport protocol in the following hexadecimal dump. Assume Ethernet at the Data Link layer.

```
 0: 00 00 C0 24 28 2D 00 00 C0 A2 0F 8E 08 00 45 00 ¦...$(-........E.
10: 00 29 54 0C 40 00 40 06 31 A7 90 13 4A C9 90 13 ¦.)T.@.@.1...J...
20: 4A 2C 00 17 18 97 59 E4 D9 D2 01 89 70 5B 50 38 ¦J,....Y.....p[P8
30: 77 FF C5 44 00 01 FF 20 30 20 20 20             ¦w..D... 0
```

54. Decode the transport protocol in the following hexadecimal dump. Assume Ethernet at the Data Link layer.

```
 0: FF FF FF FF FF FF 00 00 C0 BB E8 73 08 00 45 00 ¦...........s..E.
10: 00 70 01 2A 00 00 40 11 80 59 C7 F5 B4 0F C7 F5 ¦.p.*..@..Y......
20: B4 FF 02 01 02 01 00 5C 07 02 01 01 00 00 31 EE ¦.......\......1.
30: A5 A9 00 00 00 00 67 61 74 65 6B 65 65 70 65 72 ¦......gatekeeper
40: 00 00 00 00 00 00 00 00 00 00 00 00 00 00 00 00 ¦................
50: 00 00 00 00 00 00 00 00 00 00 00 00 00 00 00 00 ¦................
60: 00 00 31 EE 7F 85 63 6F 6E 73 6F 6C 65 00 72 6F ¦..1...console.ro
70: 6F 74 00 00 00 00 31 EE 80 10 00 00 24 EA       ¦ot....1.....$.
```

Part III

TCP/IP Application Services

CHAPTER 12

Automatic Configuration

Configuring TCP/IP parameters for each workstation on a large network can be a difficult and time-consuming task, particularly when the TCP/IP parameters—such as IP addresses and subnet masks—need to be changed. The changes can occur because of a major restructuring of the network or because the network has a large number of mobile users with portable computers that can be connected to any of the network segments. The network connections can be direct physical connections or wireless connections. Because the TCP/IP parameters for computers depend on the network segment they connect to, appropriate values must be set up whenever a computer is connected to a different network segment.

Understanding the consequences of TCP/IP parameter changes requires knowledgeable network administrators. Several auto-configuration protocols, such as Boot Protocol (BOOTP) and Dynamic Host Configuration Protocol (DHCP), have been developed by the Internet Engineering Task Force (IETF) for TCP/IP internetworks.

Dynamic Configuration Using BOOTP

BOOTP is designed to use User Datagram Protocol (UDP) and Internet Protocol (IP) to carry configuration information for computers wanting to configure themselves. Computers making the request are called *BOOTP clients,* and computers that respond to the BOOTP client requests are called *BOOTP servers* (see fig. 12.1).

Figure 12.1 **BOOTP clients and servers.**

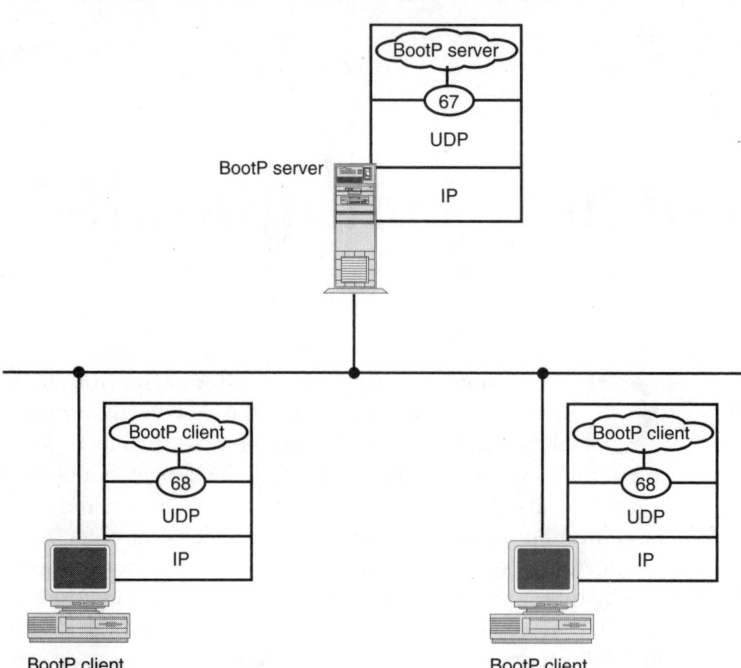

The purpose of the BOOTP client request is to discover the IP parameter settings for the computer running the BOOTP client.

BOOTP is discussed in RFC 951 on the "Bootstrap Protocol" and is updated by RFC 2132, RFC1532, RFC 1542, and RFC1395. The following sections describe the operation of BOOTP.

BOOTP Request/Reply IP Addresses

The BOOTP messages are encapsulated in a UDP header that identifies the port number used by the BOOTP processes. The UDP datagram is encapsulated in an IP header. What source and destination IP address values are used in the IP header? This is an interesting question because when the BOOTP client makes its request, it must use a source and destination IP address. Typically, the BOOTP client does not know its IP address; it uses a source IP address value of 0.0.0.0. If the BOOTP client knows its IP address, it uses this address in the BOOTP client request.

Does the BOOTP client know the IP address of the BOOTP server? Typically no. This is especially true in situations where the BOOTP client is a diskless workstation and has no way of knowing the BOOTP server address. In situations where the workstation can be configured with the BOOTP server address, the BOOTP client can use the BOOTP server address.

When the BOOTP client does not recognize the BOOTP server's IP address, it uses a limited IP broadcast. Recall from Chapter 4, "IP Addressing," that the IP limited broadcast has the following value:

255.255.255.255

The limited broadcast address is received by all IP nodes, including BOOTP servers, on the local network.

What if the BOOTP server is on a different IP subnet, beyond a router boundary? Recall from the discussion in Chapter 4 that a limited broadcast cannot cross a router boundary. In this case, the router must be configured with a BOOTP relay agent that checks to see if the UDP destination port number of 67 is being used in the limited broadcast datagram. (UDP port 67 is reserved for BOOTP/DHCP.) If this is the case, the limited broadcast is forwarded to the router's network interfaces (see fig. 12.2).

Figure 12.2 Forwarding of BOOTP messages across a router boundary.

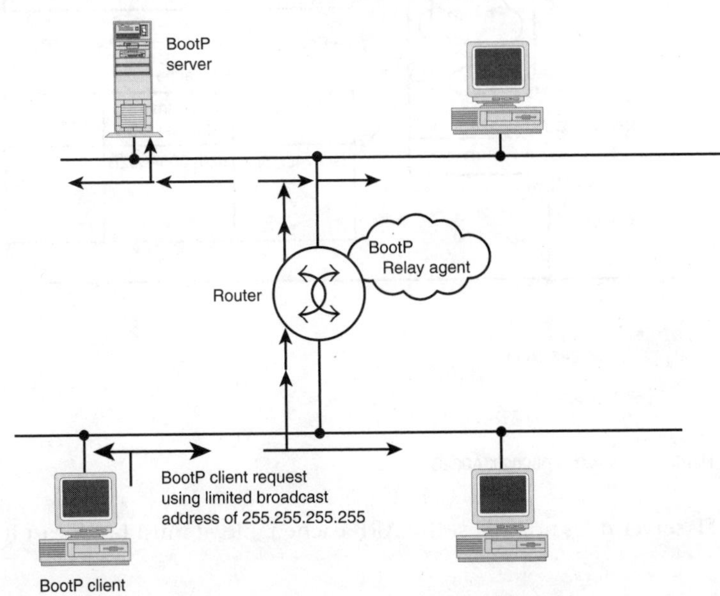

When the BOOTP server is on the local network, it can respond to the BOOTP client request message. Does the BOOTP reply message from the BOOTP server use the IP address of the client? In other words, can the BOOTP server send a directed reply? The answer depends on the BOOTP server implementation.

A problem is associated with sending a directed BOOTP reply to the BOOTP client. The BOOTP server knows the BOOTP client's IP address by looking it up in its BOOTP configuration database. Why can't the BOOTP server use this IP address to send a directed reply to the BOOTP client? The answer to this question lies in the fact that when the BOOTP server sends an ARP request message to discover the hardware address of the BOOTP client, the BOOTP client is unable to respond. Why? Because the BOOTP client does not know its IP address, as yet. The BOOTP server knows the hardware address of the BOOTP client from the Data Link layer header in the BOOTP client message. A BOOTP server implementation may add an entry in the ARP cache table for the BOOTP client (see fig. 12.3). If it does, the BOOTP server can use a directed reply. The BSD Unix BOOTP implementation uses the ARP modification technique.

Figure 12.3 Adjusting of the ARP cache table by a BOOTP server.

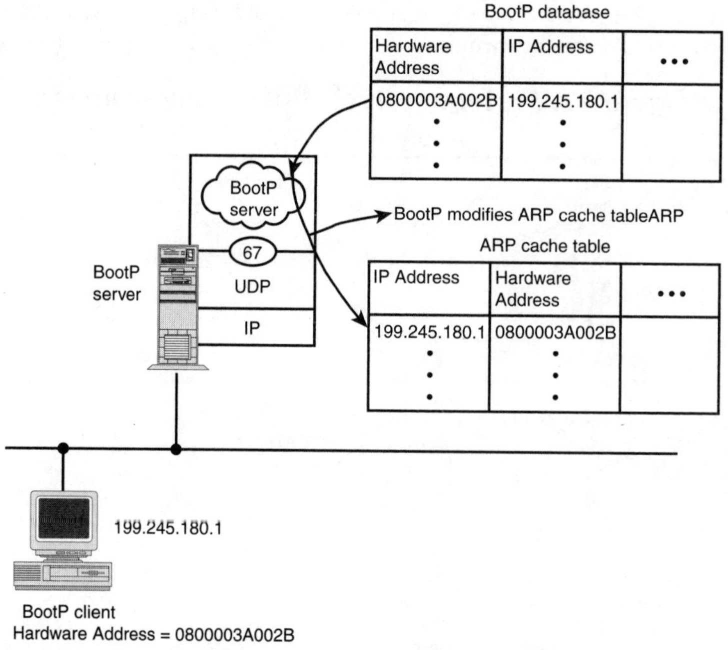

If a BOOTP server does not adjust the ARP cache table, it must broadcast its reply.

Handling Loss of BOOTP Messages

BOOTP uses UDP and IP protocols. These protocols cannot guarantee delivery of BOOTP messages. As a result BOOTP messages can become lost, delayed, duplicated, or delivered out of sequence. Because IP provides only a checksum to guard against errors in the IP header and not the data field, a BOOTP implementation may require that the UDP checksum be enabled. The UDP checksum can guard against error in the entire BOOTP message.

A BOOTP client sends requests using the IP Don't Fragment (DF) flag set to 1 to simplify the processing of BOOTP replies, and in case it does not have enough memory to reassemble fragmented datagrams.

BOOTP uses a time out and retransmission policy to handle message loss. When a BOOTP client sends its request, it also starts a timer. A BOOTP reply within the time out interval cancels the timer, but if the timer expires before a BOOTP reply is received, the BOOTP retransmits its request.

When BOOTP clients start at the same time, they can flood the network with BOOTP broadcast requests. To prevent this from occurring, the BOOTP specification recommends using a random delay starting with a random time out interval from zero to four seconds. Successive retransmissions cause the doubling of the random time out interval until a large value, such as 60 seconds, is reached. When this upper limit is reached, the random time out interval is not doubled, but random time delays within this interval are still used. Randomization is used to avoid simultaneous BOOTP client requests that could overload the server and cause packet collisions in an ethernet network. Doubling the random time out interval avoids overloading the network with too many BOOTP client broadcast requests.

BOOTP Message Format

Figure 12.4 shows the BOOTP message format, and table 12.1 discusses the meanings of the fields in the BOOT message.

Figure 12.4 BOOTP message format.

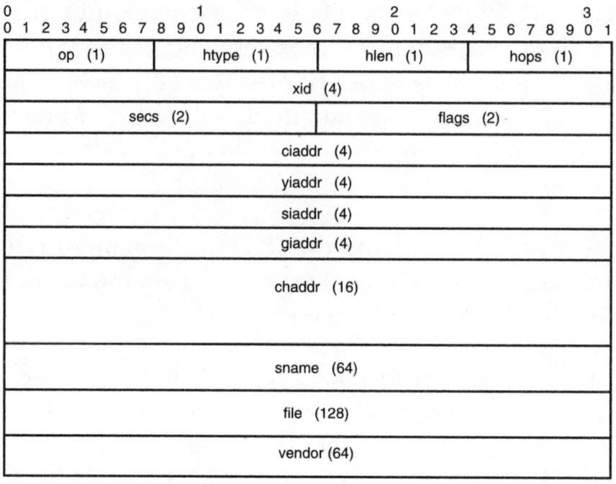

0–7	8–15	16–23	24–31
op (1)	htype (1)	hlen (1)	hops (1)
xid (4)			
secs (2)		flags (2)	
ciaddr (4)			
yiaddr (4)			
siaddr (4)			
giaddr (4)			
chaddr (16)			
sname (64)			
file (128)			
vendor (64)			

Numbers in parenthesis ( ) represent octets

TABLE 12.1
DHCP Fields

Field	Octets	Description
op	1	Message op code (message type). A value of 1 means it is a BOOTREQUEST message, and a value of 2 means it is a BOOTREPLY message.
htype	1	Hardware address type. The values are the same as those used for the ARP packet format. For example, a value of 1 is used for 10 Mbps ethernet.
hlen	1	Hardware address length in octets. Ethernet and token-ring hardware address length is 6 bytes.
hops	1	Set to zero by the BOOTP client. This is optionally used by relay agents running on routers when they forward BOOTP messages.
xid	4	Transaction ID. A randomly generated number chosen by the BOOTP client when it generates a BOOTP message. The BOOTP server uses the same Transaction ID in its BOOTP messages to the client. The Transaction ID enables the BOOTP clients and servers to associate BOOTP messages with the corresponding responses.

Field	Octets	Description
secs	2	Filled by the BOOTP client. It is the seconds elapsed since client started trying to boot.
unused	2	Not used.
ciaddr	4	The BOOTP client's IP address. It is filled by the BOOTP client in a BOOTPREQUEST message to verify the use of previously allocated configuration parameters. If the client does not recognize its IP address, this field is set to 0.
yiaddr	4	The BOOTP client's "your IP address." Returned by the BOOTP server.
siaddr	4	The server's IP address. Inserted by the BOOTP client if the client wants to contact a BOOTP server. The BOOTP server's IP address may have been initialized as part of the TCP/IP configuration database at the BOOTP client. The value returned by the BOOTP server may be the address of the next server to contact as part of the boot process. For example, this may be the address of a server that holds the operating system boot image.
giaddr	4	The IP address of the router that runs the BOOTP relay agent.
chaddr	16	The BOOTP client's hardware address. A value of 16 octets is used to enable different network hardware types. Ethernet and token-ring hardware use only 6 octets.
sname	64	An optional server host name if recognized by the BOOTP client. It is a null terminated string.
file	128	The boot file name. It is a null terminated string. If the BOOTP client wants to boot with an image of the operating system downloaded from a network device, it can specify a generic name, such as "unix," for booting a Unix image. The BOOTP server can hold more specific

continues

Table 12.1, Continued
DHCP Fields

Field	Octets	Description
		information about the exact operating system image needed for that workstation. This reply from the BOOTP server contains the fully qualified directory path name.
vendor	64	An optional vendor-specific area. This could be hardware type/serial on request, or "capability"/remote file system handle on reply. This information may be set aside for use by a third phase bootstrap or kernel.

Phases of the BOOTP Procedure

Contrary to what might be suggested by its name, BOOTP is not used for actually transferring the operating system image to the BOOTP client. The transfer of the operating system image is handled by a separate protocol called Trivial File Transfer Protocol (TFTP), which runs on the UDP transport. Diskless workstations need to download of the operating system image. Other workstations that are only using BOOTP to assign IP addresses from a central location don't download the operating system image.

Figure 12.5 shows the phases of the complete bootstrap procedure required to download an operating system image. In step 1, the BOOTP client makes a request to obtain the IP configuration image. In step 2, the BOOTP server returns the IP configuration information and the name of the operating system image file to download. In step 3, the BOOTP client passes a request to obtain the operating system image to the TFTP client. In step 4, the TFTP client issues a request to the TFTP server to obtain the operating system image. In step 5, the TFTP server returns a series of data packets containing the operating system image. After obtaining the operating system image, the BOOTP loads the operating system image in memory and initializes itself.

Figure 12.5 Typical bootstrap procedure.

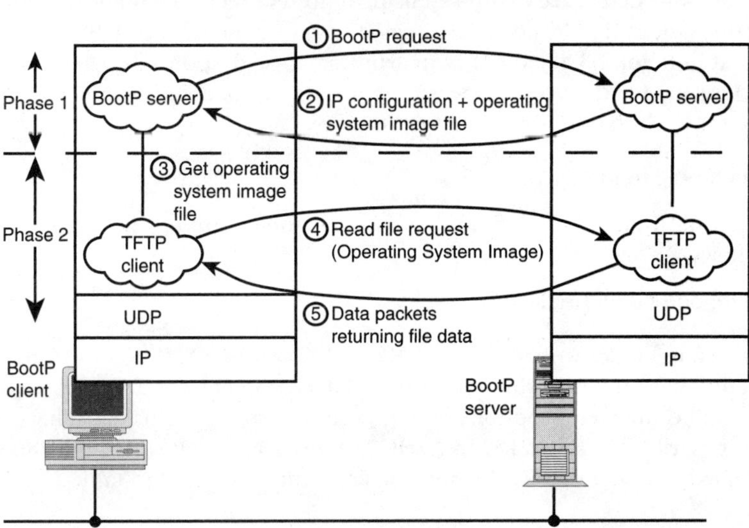

Keeping the BOOTP phase separate from the transfer of the operating system image has the advantage that the BOOTP server need not run on the same machine that stores the operating system images (TFTP server). Additionally, it enables BOOTP to be used in situations where only the configuration image is needed from the BOOTP server and there is no need to transfer the operating system image.

There may be situations in which an administrator may want to set up a workstation to boot up with a different operating system type depending on the user. In this case, the BOOTP request message can contain a generic label in the file name field, such as "unix," to download a Unix operating system image or "default" to download some other default operating system image. On seeing the generic name of the operating system image that has been requested, the BOOTP server can consult its configuration database and map the generic name to its fully qualified file name and return this name in the BOOTP reply. The BOOTP client can pass this fully qualified name to its local TFTP client for downloading the operating system image.

Vendor Specific Area

The BOOTP message format describes several common IP parameters. Many vendors need to describe additional parameters for their devices. The *Vendor Specific Area* field in BOOTP messages is used for these additional parameters.

The Vendor Specific Area field in the BOOTP message contains vendor-specific data for the BOOTP client. This field is optional, and its usage depends on the type of additional configuration information needed by the BOOTP client. The first four octets contain a "magic cookie" value that defines the format of the rest of the vendor field. These four octets are expressed using a dotted decimal notation—they should not be confused as IP addresses. The magic cookie value of 99.130.83.99 (hexadecimal dotted notation 63.82.53.63) is an arbitrary agreed-upon value that specifies a standard format for the vendor-specific area. The magic cookie value is followed by a list of items. Each item is identified by the following:

- 1-octet tag field or type field
- Optional 1-octet length field that specifies the length of the data field that follows
- Multi-octet data field

The BOOTP item tags were defined in RFC 1497 on "BOOTP Vendor Information Extensions." With the introduction of the DHCP protocol, the BOOTP vendor extensions and the DHCP options field now have a common format. This common format is described in RFC 2132 in "DHCP Options and BOOTP Vendor Extensions." Common examples of the vendor-specific tag values are listed in table 12.2.

Table 12.2
Common Vendor Specific Tags for BOOTP

Tag	Length	Meaning (octets)
0	-	Used only for padding. The pad option can be used to cause subsequent fields to align on word boundaries.
1	4	Subnet Mask field.
2	4	Time Offset field. Specifies time offset of the client's subnet in seconds from Coordinated Universal Time (UTC). The offset is expressed as a signed 32-bit integer.
3	N	Router option. Specifies a list of IP addresses for routers on the client's subnet. Routers should be listed in order of preference. The minimum length for the router option is 4 octets, and the length must always be a multiple of 4.
4	N	Time Server option. Specifies a list of RFC 868 time servers available to the client. Servers should be listed in order of preference. The minimum length for the router option is 4 octets, and the length must always be a multiple of 4.

Tag	Length	Meaning (octets)
5	N	Name Server option. Specifies a list of Internet Engineering Note (IEN) 116 name servers available to the client. Servers should be listed in order of preference. The minimum length for the router option is 4 octets, and the length must always be a multiple of 4.
6	N	Domain Name Server option. Specifies a list of Domain Name System (STD 13, RFC 1035) name servers available to the client. Servers should be listed in order of preference. The minimum length for the router option is 4 octets, and the length must always be a multiple of 4.
7	N	Log Server option. Specifies a list of MIT-LCS UDP log servers available to the client. Servers should be listed in order of preference. The minimum length for the router option is 4 octets, and the length must always be a multiple of 4.
8	N	Cookie Server option. Specifies a list of RFC 865 cookie servers available to the client. Servers should be listed in order of preference. The minimum length for the router option is 4 octets, and the length must always be a multiple of 4.
9	N	LPR Server option. Specifies a list of RFC 1179 line printer servers available to the client. Servers should be listed in order of preference. The minimum length for the router option is 4 octets, and the length must always be a multiple of 4.
10	N	Impress Server option. Specifies a list of Imagen Impress servers available to the client. Servers should be listed in order of preference. The minimum length for the router option is 4 octets, and the length must always be a multiple of 4.
11	N	Resource Location Server option. Specifies a list of RFC 887 Resource Location servers available to the client. Servers should be listed in order of preference. The minimum length for the router option is 4 octets, and the length must always be a multiple of 4.

continues

Table 12.2, Continued
Common Vendor Specific Tags for BOOTP

Tag	Length	Meaning (octets)
12	N	Host Name option. Specifies the name of the client. The name may or may not be qualified with the local domain name. See RFC 1035 for character set restrictions. Minimum length of the data field is 1 octet.
13	2	Boot File Size option. Specifies the length in 512-octet blocks of the default boot image for the client. The file length is specified as an unsigned 16-bit integer.
128-254	Undefined	Reserved for site-specific options. Interpretation depends on implementation.
255	-	End option. Marks the end of valid information in the vendor field. Subsequent octets should be filled with the pad option.

Dynamic Configuration Using DHCP

Dynamic Host Configuration Protocol (DHCP) is an extension of the BOOTP protocol that provides greater flexibility in IP address management. DHCP can be used for the dynamic configuration of essential TCP/IP parameters for hosts (workstations and servers) on a network. The DHCP protocol consists of two elements:

- A mechanism for allocating IP addresses and other TCP/IP parameters
- A protocol for negotiating and transmitting host-specific information

The TCP/IP host requesting the TCP/IP configuration information is called the *DHCP client*, and the TCP/IP host that supplies this information is called a *DHCP server*.

The DHCP protocol is described in RFC 2131 on "Dynamic Host Configuration Protocol." The following sections discuss the operation of DHCP.

Understanding IP Address Management with DHCP

DHCP uses the following three methods for IP address allocation:

- manual allocation
- automatic allocation
- dynamic allocation

In the manual allocation method, the DHCP client's IP address is set manually by the network administrator at the DHCP server, and DHCP is used to convey to the DHCP client the value of the manually configured IP address.

In the automatic allocation method, no manual assignments of IP addresses need to be made. The DHCP client is assigned an IP address when it first contacts the DHCP server. The IP address assigned using this method is permanently assigned to the DHCP client and is not reused by another DHCP client.

In the dynamic allocation method, DHCP assigns an IP address to a DHCP client on a temporary basis. The IP address is on loan or "leased" to the DHCP client for a specified duration. On the expiry of this lease, the IP address is revoked, and the DHCP client is required to surrender the IP address. If the DHCP client still needs an IP address to perform its functions, it can request another IP address.

The dynamic allocation method is the only one of the three methods that affords automatic reuse of an IP address. An IP address need not be surrendered by the DHCP client on the expiry of the lease. If the DHCP client no longer needs an IP address, such as when the computer is being gracefully shutdown, it can release the IP address to the DHCP server. The DHCP server then can reissue the same IP address to another DHCP client making a request for an IP address.

The dynamic allocation method is particularly useful for DHCP clients that need an IP address for temporary connection to a network. For example, consider a situation where 300 users have portable computers on a network and a class C address has been assigned to a network. This enables the network to have 253 nodes on the network (255–2 special addresses = 253). Because computers connecting to a network using TCP/IP are required to have unique IP addresses, all of the 300 computers cannot be simultaneously connected to the network. However, if there are at most only 200 physical connections on the network, it should be possible to use a class C address by reusing IP addresses that are not in use. Using DHCP's dynamic IP address allocation, IP address reuse is possible.

Dynamic IP address allocation is also a good choice for assigning IP addresses to new hosts that are being permanently connected and where IP addresses are scarce. As old hosts are retired, their IP addresses can be immediately reused.

Regardless of which of the three methods of IP address allocation is used, you can still configure IP parameters at a central DHCP server once, instead of repeating the TCP/IP configuration for each computer.

The DHCP IP Address Acquisition Process

Upon contacting a DHCP server, a DHCP client goes through several internal states during which it negotiates the use of an IP address and the duration of use. How a DHCP client acquires the IP address can best be explained in terms of a state transition diagram (also called a finite state machine). Figure 12.6 shows the state transition diagram that explains the interaction between the DHCP client and DHCP server.

Figure 12.6 DHCP state transition diagram showing DHCP client/server interaction.

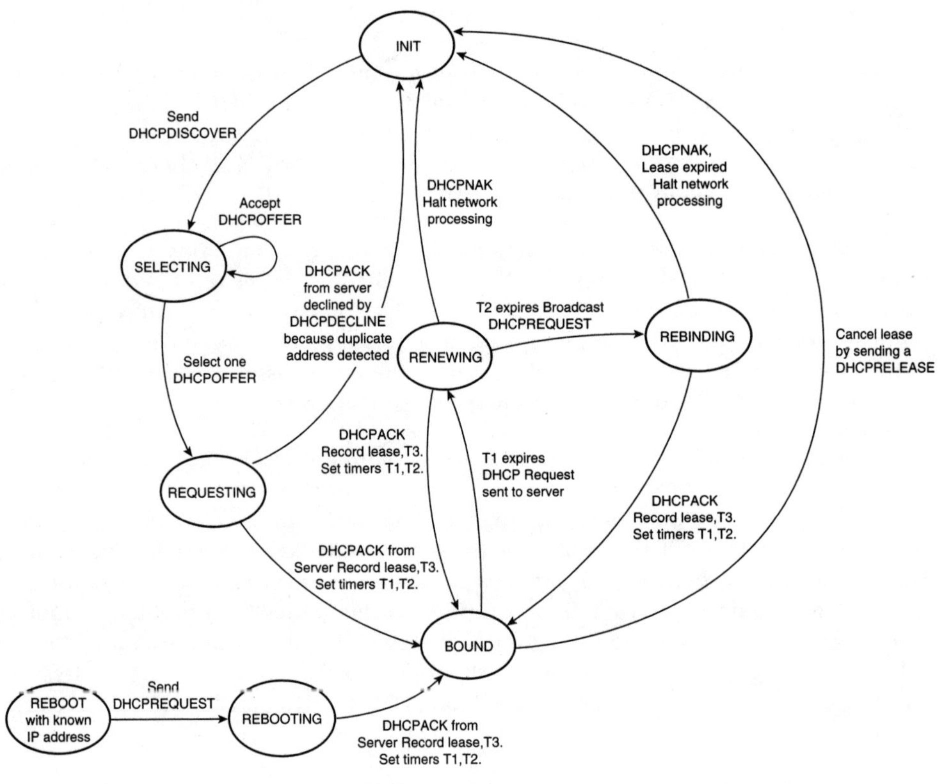

When the DHCP client is first started, it begins in the INIT (initialize) state. At this point the DHCP client does not recognize its IP parameters, and so sends a DHCPDISCOVER broadcast. The DHCPDISCOVER is encapsulated in a UDP/IP packet. The destination UDP port number is set to 67 (decimal), the same as that for a BOOTP server, because the DHCP protocol is an extension of the BOOTP protocol. A local IP broadcast address of 255.255.255.255 is used in the DHCPDISCOVER packet. If DHCP servers are not on the local network, the IP router must have DHCP-relay agent support to forward the DHCPDISCOVER request to other subnetworks. DHCP-relay agent support is discussed in RFC 1542.

Before sending the DHCPDISCOVER broadcast packet, the DHCP client waits for a random time interval between 1 to 10 seconds. This is to prevent DHCP clients from starting at the same time if they are powered up at the same time (as sometimes happens after a power failure).

After sending the DHCPDISCOVER broadcast, the DHCP client enters the SELECTING state. In this state, the DHCP client receives DHCPOFFER messages from the DHCP servers that have been configured to respond to the DHCP client. The time period over which the DHCP client waits to receive DHCPOFFER messages is implementation dependent. The DHCP client must select one DHCPOFFER response if it receives multiple DHCPOFFER responses. After selecting a DHCPOFFER message from a server, the DHCP client sends a DHCPREQUEST message to the selected DHCP server. The DHCP server responds with a DHCPACK.

The DHCP client may optionally perform a check on the IP address sent in the DHCPACK to verify if the address is not in use. On a broadcast network, the DHCP client can send an ARP request for the suggested IP address to see if there is an ARP response. An ARP response would imply that the suggested IP address is already in use, in which case the DHCPACK from the sever is ignored, a DHCPDECLINE is sent, and the DHCP client enters the INIT state and retries to get a valid unused IP address. When the ARP request is broadcast on the local network, the client uses its own hardware address in the sender hardware address field of the ARP packet, but sets a value of 0 in the sender IP address field. A sender IP address of 0 is used rather than the suggested IP address, so as not to confuse ARP caches on other TCP/IP hosts (in case the suggested IP address is already in use).

When the DHCPACK from the DHCP server is accepted, three timer values are set, and the DHCP client moves into the BOUND state. The first timer, T1, is the lease renewal timer; the second timer, T2, is the rebinding timer; and the third timer, T3, is the lease duration. The DHCPACK always returns the value of T3, which is the duration of the lease. The values of timers T1 and T2 can be configured at the DHCP server, but if they are not set, default values are used based on the duration of the lease. The following list shows the default values used for T1 and T2:

T1 = renewal timer

T2 = rebinding timer

T3 = duration of lease

$$T1 = 0.5 \times T3$$

$$T2 = 0.875 \times T3$$

The actual time at which the timer values expire is computed by adding to the timer value, the time at which the DHCPREQUEST that generated the DHCPACK response was sent. If the time at which the DHCP request was sent was T0, then the expiration values are computed as follows:

$$\text{Expiration of } T1 = T0 + T1$$

$$\text{Expiration of } T2 = T0 + T2$$

$$\text{Expiration of } T3 = T0 + T3$$

RFC 2131 recommends that a "fuzz" factor be added to the timers T1 and T2 to prevent several DHCP clients from expiring their timers at the same time.

At the expiration of timer T1, the DHCP client moves from the BOUND state to the RENEWING state. In the RENEWING state a new lease for the allocated IP address must be negotiated by the DHCP client from the DHCP server that originally allocated the IP address. If the original DHCP server does not renew the release, it sends a DHCPNAK message, and the DHCP client moves into the INIT state and tries to obtain a new IP address. If the original DHCP server sends a DHCPACK message, this message contains the new lease duration. The DHCP client sets its timer values and moves to the BOUND state.

If the timer T2 expires while DHCP client is waiting in the RENEWING state for a DHCPACK or DHCPNAK message from the original DHCP server, the DHCP client moves from the RENEWING state to the REBINDING state. The original DHCP server may not respond because it's down or a network link is down. Note from the previous equations that T2 > T1, so the DHCP client waits for the original DHCP server to renew the release for a duration of T2-T1.

At the expiration of a timer T2, a broadcast DHCPREQUEST is sent on the network to contact any DHCP server to extend the lease, and the DHCP client is in the REBINDING state. A broadcast DHCPREQUEST is sent because the DHCP client assumes, after spending T2-T1 seconds in the RENEWING state, that the original DHCP server is not available, and the DHCP client tries to contact any configured DHCP server to respond to it. If a DHCP server responds with a DHCPACK message, the DHCP client renews its lease (T3), sets the timers T1 and T2, and moves back to the BOUND state. If no DHCP server is able to renew the release after the expiration of timer T3, the lease expires and the DHCP client moves to the INIT state. Note that by this time, the DHCP client has tried to renew the lease, first with the original DHCP server and then with any DHCP server on the network.

When the lease expires (timer T3 expires), the DHCP client must surrender the use of its IP address and halt network processing with that IP address.

The DHCP client does not always have to wait for the expiration of the lease (timer T3) to surrender the use of an IP address. It could voluntarily relinquish control of an IP address by canceling its lease. For example, a user with a portable computer may connect to the network to perform a network activity. The DHCP server on the network may set the duration of the lease for one hour. Assume that the user finishes the network tasks in 30 minutes, and now wants to disconnect from the network. When the user gracefully shuts down his computer, the DHCP client sends a DHCPRELEASE message to the DHCP server to cancel its lease. The surrendered IP address is now available for use by another DHCP client.

If DHCP clients are run on computers that have a disk, the allocated IP address allocated can be stored on the disk, and when the computer reboots, it can make a request for the same IP address. This is shown in figure 12.6 in the state labeled "REBOOT with known IP address."

DHCP Packet Format

The DHCP packet format is shown in figure 12.7. The DHCP messages use a fixed format for all the fields, except the options field that has a minimum size of 312 octets. Readers who are familiar with the BOOTP protocol recognize that with the exception of the flags field and the options field, the message formats for DHCP and BOOTP are identical. In fact the DHCP server can be configured to answer BOOTP requests. The configuration details are operating system-specific.

Figure 12.7 DHCP packet format.

0 0 1 2 3 4 5 6 7	1 8 9 0 1 2 3 4 5	2 6 7 8 9 0 1 2 3	3 4 5 6 7 8 9 0 1
op (1)	htype (1)	hlen (1)	hops (1)
xid (4)			
secs (2)		flags (2)	
ciaddr (4)			
yiaddr (4)			
siaddr (4)			
giaddr (4)			
chaddr (16)			
sname (64)			
file (128)			
options (312)			

Numbers in parentheses ( ) represent octets

Table 12.3 provides an explanation of the fields used in the DHCP protocol. Only the leftmost bit of the DHCP options field is used (see fig. 12.8). The other bits in the options field must be set to 0.

TABLE 12.3
DHCP Fields

Field	Octets	Description
op	1	Message op code (message type). A value of 1 means it is a BOOTREQUEST message, and a value of 2 means it is a BOOTREPLY message.
htype	1	The hardware address type. The values are the same as that used for the ARP packet format. For example, a value of 1 is used for 10 Mbps ethernet.
hlen	1	The hardware address length in octets. Ethernet and token-ring hardware adders length is 6 bytes.
hops	1	Set to 0 by the DHCP client. This is optionally used by relay agents running on routers when they forward DHCP messages.
xid	4	A Transaction ID. A randomly generated number chosen by the DHCP client when it generates a DHCP message. The DHCP server uses the same Transaction ID in its DHCP messages to the client. The Transaction ID enables the DHCP clients and servers to associate DHCP messages with the corresponding responses.
secs	2	Filled by the DHCP client. It is the seconds elapsed since client started trying to boot.
flags	2	Used to indicate whether this is a broadcast message. If so, the leftmost bit has a value of 1. All other bits must remain zero.
ciaddr	4	The DHCP client's IP address. It is filled by the DHCP client in a DHCPREQUEST message to verify the use of previously allocated configuration parameters. If the client does not know its IP address, this field is set to 0.

Field	Octets	Description
yiaddr	4	The DHCP client's "your IP address" returned by the DHCP server.
siaddr	4	The server's IP address. If the DHCP client wants to contact a specific DHCP server, it inserts the server's IP address in this field. The DHCP server's IP address may have been discovered in prior DHCPOFFER and DHCPACK messages returned by the server. The value returned by the DHCP server may be the address of the next server to contact as part of the boot process. For example, this may be the address of a server that holds the operating system boot image.
giaddr	4	The IP address of the router that runs the relay agent
chaddr	16	The DHCP client's hardware address. A value of 16 octets is used to enable different network hardware types. Ethernet and token-ring hardware use only 6 octets.
sname	64	An optional server host name if known by the DHCP client. It is a null terminated string.
file	128	The boot file name. It is a null terminated string. If the DHCP client wants to boot with an image of the operating system downloaded from a network device, it can specify a generic name, such as "unix," for booting a Unix image in a DHCPDISCOVER. The DHCP server can hold more specific information about the exact operating system image needed for that workstation. This image name can be returned as a fully qualified directory path name in the DHCPOFFER message from the DHCP server.
options	312	An optional parameters field.

Most of the DHCP messages sent by the DHCP server to the DHCP client are unicast messages (messages sent to a single IP address). This is because the DHCP server learns about the DHCP client's hardware address in messages sent by the DHCP client to the server. The DHCP client may request that the DHCP server respond with a broadcast address by setting the leftmost bit in the options field to 1. The DHCP client will do this if it does not know its IP address yet. The IP protocol module in DHCP client rejects a received datagram if the destination IP address in the datagram does not match the IP address of the DHCP client's network interface. If the IP address of the network interface is not known, the datagram still is rejected. However, the IP protocol module accepts any IP broadcast datagram. Therefore, to ensure that the IP protocol module accepts the DHCP server reply when the IP address is not yet configured, the DHCP client requests that the DHCP server reply use broadcast messages instead of unicast messages.

Figure 12.8 DHCP options field.

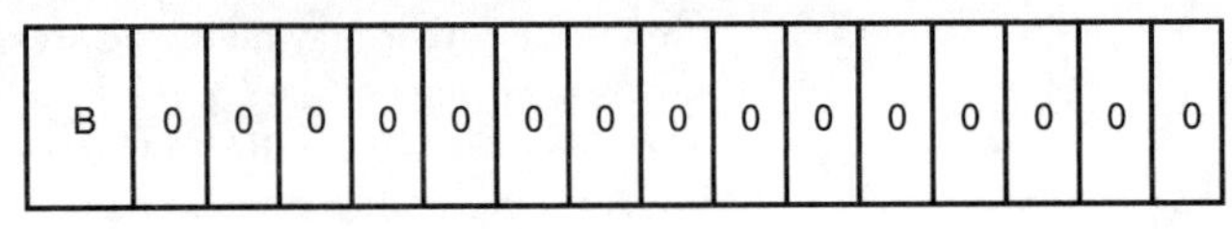

The options field is variable in length, with the minimum size extended to 312 octets, so that the total minimum size of a DHCP message is 576 octets, which is the minimum IP datagram size a host must be prepared to accept. If a DHCP client needs to use larger size messages it can negotiate this using the Maximum DHCP message size option. Because the sname and file fields are quite large and may not always be used, DHCP options may be further extended into these fields by specifying the Option Overload option. If present, the usual meanings of the sname and file fields are ignored, and these fields are examined for options. Options are expressed using the Type, Length, Value (T-L-V) format.

Figure 12.9 shows that in DHCP, the option consists of a 1-octet Type field, followed by a 1-octet Length field. The value of the Length field contains the size of the Value field. The different DHCP messages themselves are expressed using a special Type value of 53. The option values that describe the DHCP messages are shown in figure 12.10.

Figure 12.9 Option format for DHCP messages.

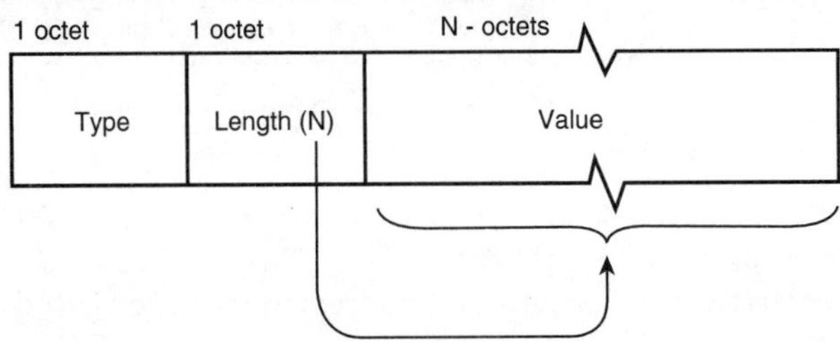

Figure 12.10 Option values for the DHCP messages.

	1 octet	1 octet	1 octet
DHCPDISCOVER	53 Type	1 length	1 value
DHCPOFFER	53 Type	1 length	2 value
DHCPREQUEST	53 Type	1 length	3 value
DHCPDECLINE	53 Type	1 length	4 value
DHCKACK	53 Type	1 length	5 value
DHCPNAK	53 Type	1 length	6 value
DHCPRELEASE	53 Type	1 length	7 value

DHCP Protocol Trace

This section describes the DHCP message format for packets captured on a real-life network. Because the DHCP protocol and its packet format are a superset of BOOTP, only DHCP traces are discussed in this chapter. In fact, the DHCP client and servers use the same port number assignments for the BOOTP client and BOOTP servers. That is, DHCP client uses UDP port number 68, and DHCP server uses UDP port number 67. Most protocol analyzers will attempt to decode DHCP and BOOTP messages in the same format.

DHCP Trace with Directed Reply from DHCP Server

Figures 12.11 and 12.12 show a DHCP client broadcast request and a DHCP server reply. The DHCP server reply is a directed reply. A directed reply was possible because this implementation of the DHCP server made a direct entry in the ARP cache table at the server to add an entry for the DHCP client.

Figure 12.11 DHCP broadcast request.

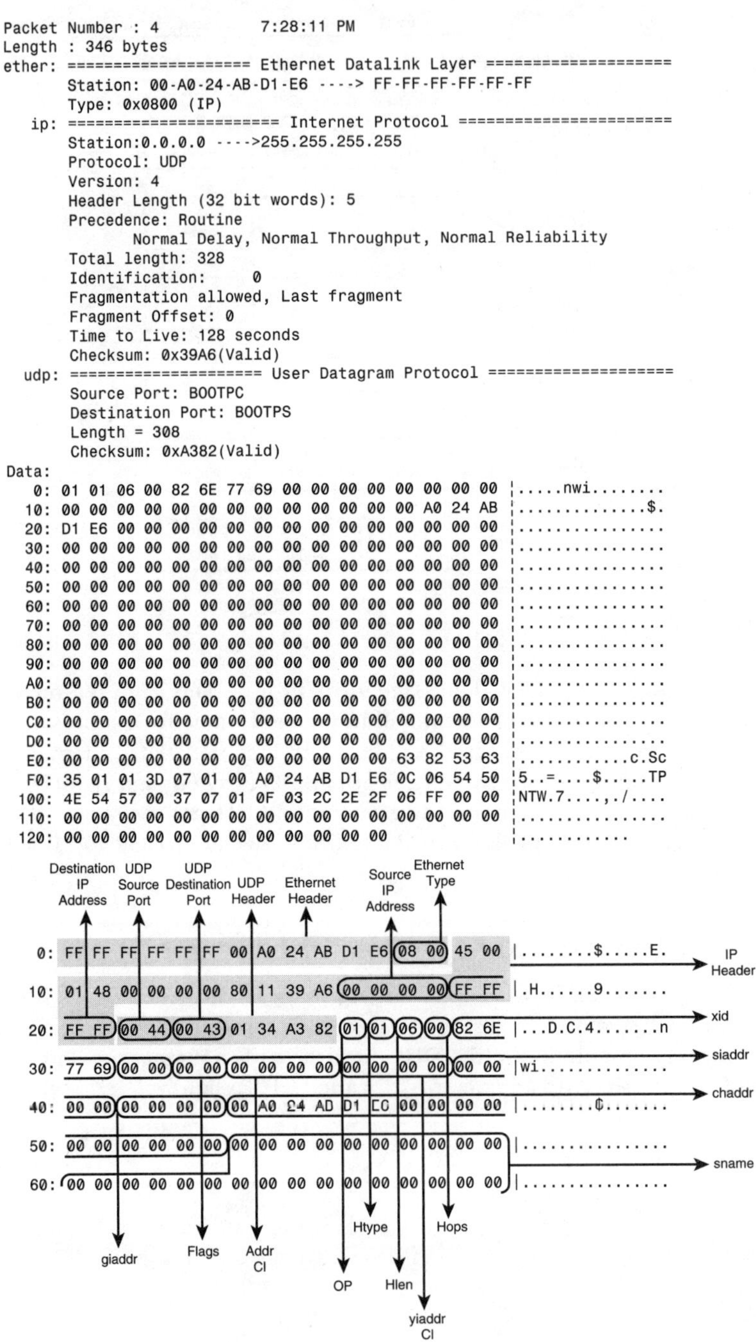

```
Packet Number : 4            7:28:11 PM
Length : 346 bytes
ether: ==================== Ethernet Datalink Layer ====================
       Station: 00-A0-24-AB-D1-E6 ----> FF-FF-FF-FF-FF-FF
       Type: 0x0800 (IP)
   ip: ======================= Internet Protocol =======================
       Station:0.0.0.0 ---->255.255.255.255
       Protocol: UDP
       Version: 4
       Header Length (32 bit words): 5
       Precedence: Routine
             Normal Delay, Normal Throughput, Normal Reliability
       Total length: 328
       Identification:     0
       Fragmentation allowed, Last fragment
       Fragment Offset: 0
       Time to Live: 128 seconds
       Checksum: 0x39A6(Valid)
  udp: ===================== User Datagram Protocol ====================
       Source Port: BOOTPC
       Destination Port: BOOTPS
       Length = 308
       Checksum: 0xA382(Valid)
Data:
   0: 01 01 06 00 82 6E 77 69 00 00 00 00 00 00 00 00 |.....nwi........
  10: 00 00 00 00 00 00 00 00 00 00 00 00 A0 24 AB |.............$.
  20: D1 E6 00 00 00 00 00 00 00 00 00 00 00 00 00 00 |................
  30: 00 00 00 00 00 00 00 00 00 00 00 00 00 00 00 00 |................
  40: 00 00 00 00 00 00 00 00 00 00 00 00 00 00 00 00 |................
  50: 00 00 00 00 00 00 00 00 00 00 00 00 00 00 00 00 |................
  60: 00 00 00 00 00 00 00 00 00 00 00 00 00 00 00 00 |................
  70: 00 00 00 00 00 00 00 00 00 00 00 00 00 00 00 00 |................
  80: 00 00 00 00 00 00 00 00 00 00 00 00 00 00 00 00 |................
  90: 00 00 00 00 00 00 00 00 00 00 00 00 00 00 00 00 |................
  A0: 00 00 00 00 00 00 00 00 00 00 00 00 00 00 00 00 |................
  B0: 00 00 00 00 00 00 00 00 00 00 00 00 00 00 00 00 |................
  C0: 00 00 00 00 00 00 00 00 00 00 00 00 00 00 00 00 |................
  D0: 00 00 00 00 00 00 00 00 00 00 00 00 00 00 00 00 |................
  E0: 00 00 00 00 00 00 00 00 00 00 00 00 63 82 53 63 |............c.Sc
  F0: 35 01 01 3D 07 01 00 A0 24 AB D1 E6 0C 06 54 50 |5..=....$.....TP
 100: 4E 54 57 00 37 07 01 0F 03 2C 2E 2F 06 FF 00 00 |NTW.7....,./....
 110: 00 00 00 00 00 00 00 00 00 00 00 00 00 00 00 00 |................
 120: 00 00 00 00 00 00 00 00 00 00 00 00             |............
```

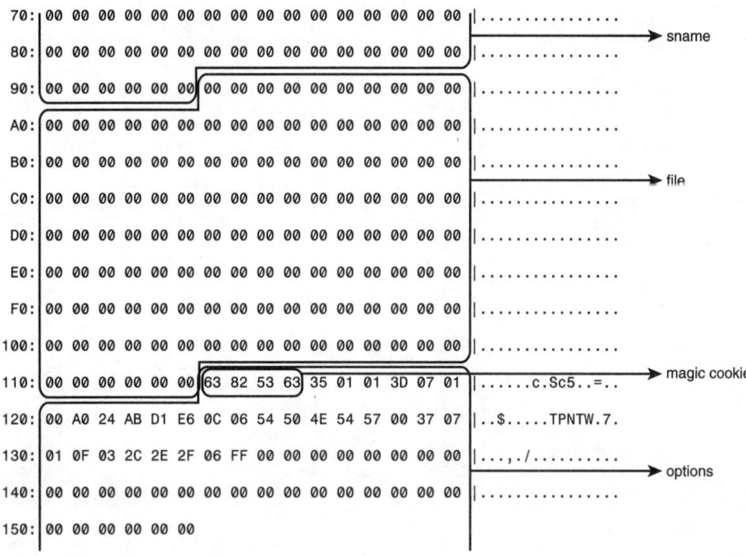
70: 00 00 00 00 00 00 00 00 00 00 00 00 00 00 00 00 |................
80: 00 00 00 00 00 00 00 00 00 00 00 00 00 00 00 00 |................
90: 00 00 00 00 00 00 00 00 00 00 00 00 00 00 00 00 |................
A0: 00 00 00 00 00 00 00 00 00 00 00 00 00 00 00 00 |................
B0: 00 00 00 00 00 00 00 00 00 00 00 00 00 00 00 00 |................
C0: 00 00 00 00 00 00 00 00 00 00 00 00 00 00 00 00 |................
D0: 00 00 00 00 00 00 00 00 00 00 00 00 00 00 00 00 |................
E0: 00 00 00 00 00 00 00 00 00 00 00 00 00 00 00 00 |................
F0: 00 00 00 00 00 00 00 00 00 00 00 00 00 00 00 00 |................
100: 00 00 00 00 00 00 00 00 00 00 00 00 00 00 00 00 |................
110: 00 00 00 00 00 00 63 82 53 63 35 01 01 3D 07 01 |......c.Sc5..=..
120: 00 A0 24 AB D1 E6 0C 06 54 50 4E 54 57 00 37 07 |..$.....TPNTW.7.
130: 01 0F 03 2C 2E 2F 06 FF 00 00 00 00 00 00 00 00 |...,./..........
140: 00 00 00 00 00 00 00 00 00 00 00 00 00 00 00 00 |................
150: 00 00 00 00 00 00
sname
file
magic cookie
options

The DHCP broadcast request has the following parameters:

op = 1

htype = 1

hlen = 6

hops = 0

xid = 826E7769 (hex)

secs = 0

flags = 0

ciaddr = 0.0.0.0

yiaddr = 0.0.0.0

siaddr = 0.0.0.0

giaddr = 0.0.0.0

chaddr = 00A024ABD1E6 00000000000000000000

sname = 0 (64 octets)

file = 0 (128 octets)

options = 0 (312 octets)

Figure 12.12 DHCP directed reply.

```
Packet Number : 5            7:28:11 PM
Length : 594 bytes
ether: ==================== Ethernet Datalink Layer ====================
       Station: 00-00-C0-DD-14-5C ----> 00-A0-24-AB-D1-E6
       Type: 0x0800 (IP)
   ip: ====================== Internet Protocol =======================
       Station:199.245.180.10 ---->199.245.180.41
       Protocol: UDP
       Version: 4
       Header Length (32 bit words): 5
       Precedence: Routine
              Normal Delay, Normal Throughput, Normal Reliability
       Total length: 576
       Identification: 47444
       Fragmentation allowed, Last fragment
       Fragment Offset: 0
       Time to Live: 128 seconds
       Checksum: 0x8739(Valid)
  udp: ==================== User Datagram Protocol ====================
       Source Port: BOOTPS
       Destination Port: BOOTPC
       Length = 556
       Checksum: 0x0000(checksum not used)
Data:
    0: 02 01 06 00 82 6E 77 69 00 00 00 00 00 00 00 00 |.....nwi........
   10: C7 F5 B4 29 C7 F5 B4 0A 00 00 00 00 00 A0 24 AB |...)..........$.
   20: D1 E6 00 00 00 00 00 00 00 00 00 00 00 00 00 00 |................
   30: 00 00 00 00 00 00 00 00 00 00 00 00 00 00 00 00 |................
   40: 00 00 00 00 00 00 00 00 00 00 00 00 00 00 00 00 |................
   50: 00 00 00 00 00 00 00 00 00 00 00 00 00 00 00 00 |................
   60: 00 00 00 00 00 00 00 00 00 00 00 00 00 00 00 00 |................
   70: 00 00 00 00 00 00 00 00 00 00 00 00 00 00 00 00 |................
   80: 00 00 00 00 00 00 00 00 00 00 00 00 00 00 00 00 |................
   90: 00 00 00 00 00 00 00 00 00 00 00 00 00 00 00 00 |................
   A0: 00 00 00 00 00 00 00 00 00 00 00 00 00 00 00 00 |................
   B0: 00 00 00 00 00 00 00 00 00 00 00 00 00 00 00 00 |................
   C0: 00 00 00 00 00 00 00 00 00 00 00 00 00 00 00 00 |................
   D0: 00 00 00 00 00 00 00 00 00 00 00 00 00 00 00 00 |................
   E0: 00 00 00 00 00 00 00 00 00 00 00 00 63 82 53 63 |............c.Sc
   F0: 35 01 02 36 04 C7 F5 B4 0A 33 04 00 00 0E 10 3A |5..6.....3.....:
  100: 04 00 00 07 08 3B 04 00 00 0C 3C 01 04 FF FF FF |.....;....<.....
  110: 00 06 04 C7 F5 B4 0A 0F 0C 6B 69 6E 65 74 69 63 |.........kinetic
  120: 73 2E 63 6F 6D FF 00 00 00 00 00 00 00 00 00 00 |s.com...........
  130: 00 00 00 00 00 00 00 00 00 00 00 00 00 00 00 00 |................
  140: 00 00 00 00 00 00 00 00 00 00 00 00 00 00 00 00 |................
  150: 00 00 00 00 00 00 00 00 00 00 00 00 00 00 00 00 |................
  160: 00 00 00 00 00 00 00 00 00 00 00 00 00 00 00 00 |................
  170: 00 00 00 00 00 00 00 00 00 00 00 00 00 00 00 00 |................
  180: 00 00 00 00 00 00 00 00 00 00 00 00 00 00 00 00 |................
  190: 00 00 00 00 00 00 00 00 00 00 00 00 00 00 00 00 |................
  1A0: 00 00 00 00 00 00 00 00 00 00 00 00 00 00 00 00 |................
  1B0: 00 00 00 00 00 00 00 00 00 00 00 00 00 00 00 00 |................
  1C0: 00 00 00 00 00 00 00 00 00 00 00 00 00 00 00 00 |................
  1D0: 00 00 00 00 00 00 00 00 00 00 00 00 00 00 00 00 |................
  1E0: 00 00 00 00 00 00 00 00 00 00 00 00 00 00 00 00 |................
  1F0: 00 00 00 00 00 00 00 00 00 00 00 00 00 00 00 00 |................
  200: 00 00 00 00 00 00 00 00 00 00 00 00 00 00 00 00 |................
  210: 00 00 00 00 00 00 00 00 00 00 00 00 00 00 00 00 |................
  220: 00 00 00 00
```

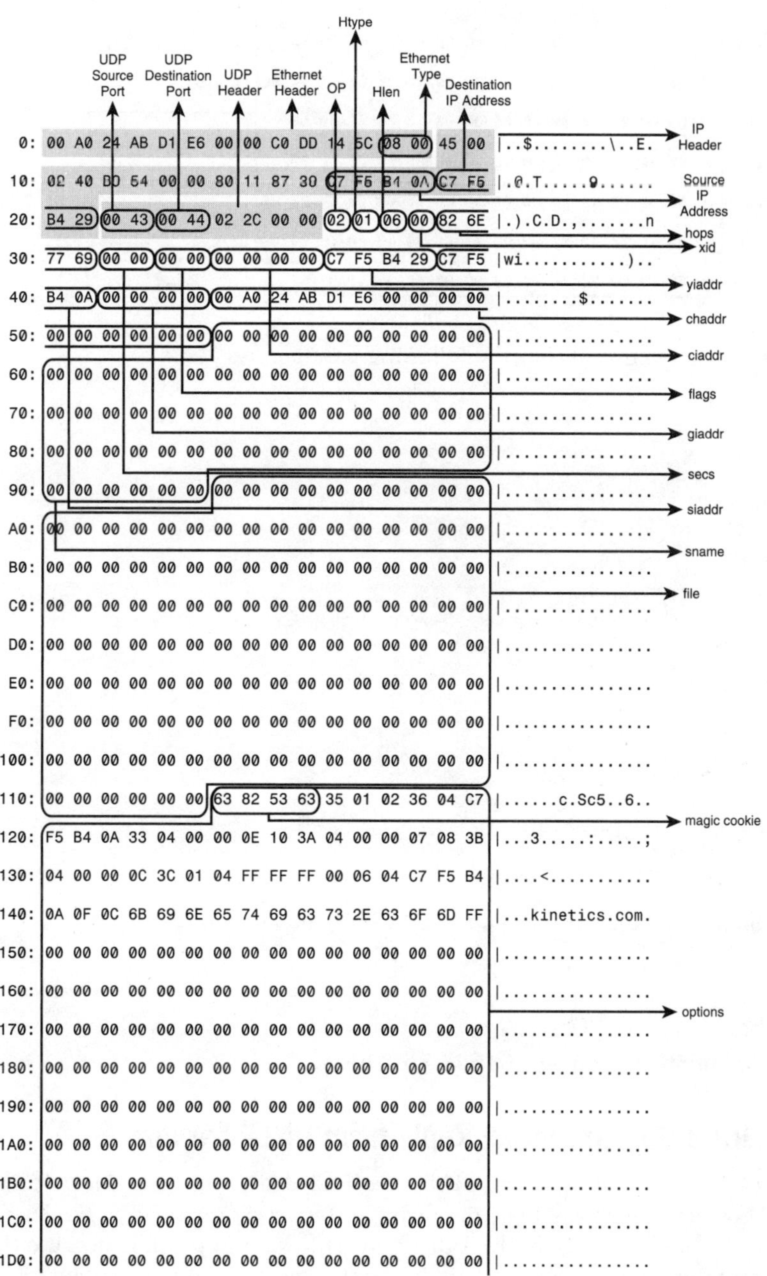
Htype
UDP Source Port
UDP Destination Port
UDP Header
Ethernet Header
OP
Hlen
Ethernet Type
Destination IP Address
IP Header
Source IP Address
hops
xid
yiaddr
chaddr
ciaddr
flags
giaddr
secs
siaddr
sname
file
magic cookie
options
|...kinetics.com.

continues

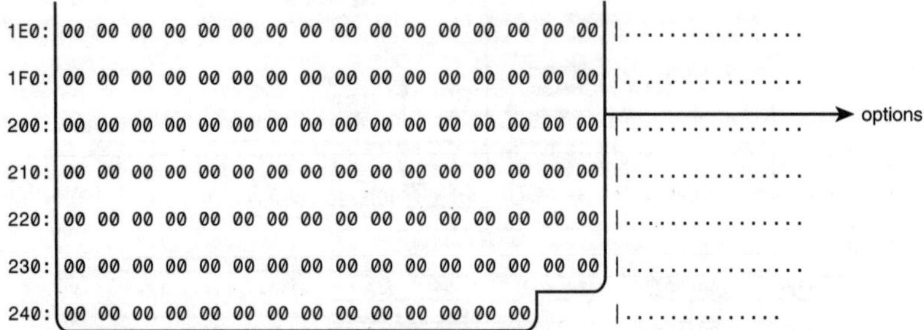
1E0: 00 00 00 00 00 00 00 00 00 00 00 00 00 00 00 00 |................
1F0: 00 00 00 00 00 00 00 00 00 00 00 00 00 00 00 00 |................
200: 00 00 00 00 00 00 00 00 00 00 00 00 00 00 00 00 |................
210: 00 00 00 00 00 00 00 00 00 00 00 00 00 00 00 00 |................
220: 00 00 00 00 00 00 00 00 00 00 00 00 00 00 00 00 |................
230: 00 00 00 00 00 00 00 00 00 00 00 00 00 00 00 00 |................
240: 00 00 00 00 00 00 00 00 00 00 00 00 00 00 |..............
options

The DHCP directed reply has the following parameters:

op = 2

htype = 1

hlen = 6

hops = 0

xid = 826E7769 (hex)

secs = 0

flags = 0

ciaddr = 0.0.0.0

yiaddr = 199.245.180.41

siaddr = 199.245.180.10

giaddr = 0.0.0.0

chaddr = 00A024ABD1E6 00000000000000000000

sname = 0 (64 octets)

file = 0 (128 octets)

options: magic cookie = 63 82 53 63 (hex)

DHCP Trace with Broadcast Reply from DHCP Server

Figures 12.13 and 12.14 show a DHCP client broadcast request and a DHCP server reply. However, unlike the trace discussed in the preceding section, the DHCP server reply is sent as a broadcast reply. A directed reply was not possible because this implementation of the DHCP server does not make a direct entry in the ARP cache table.

Figure 12.13 DHCP broadcast request.

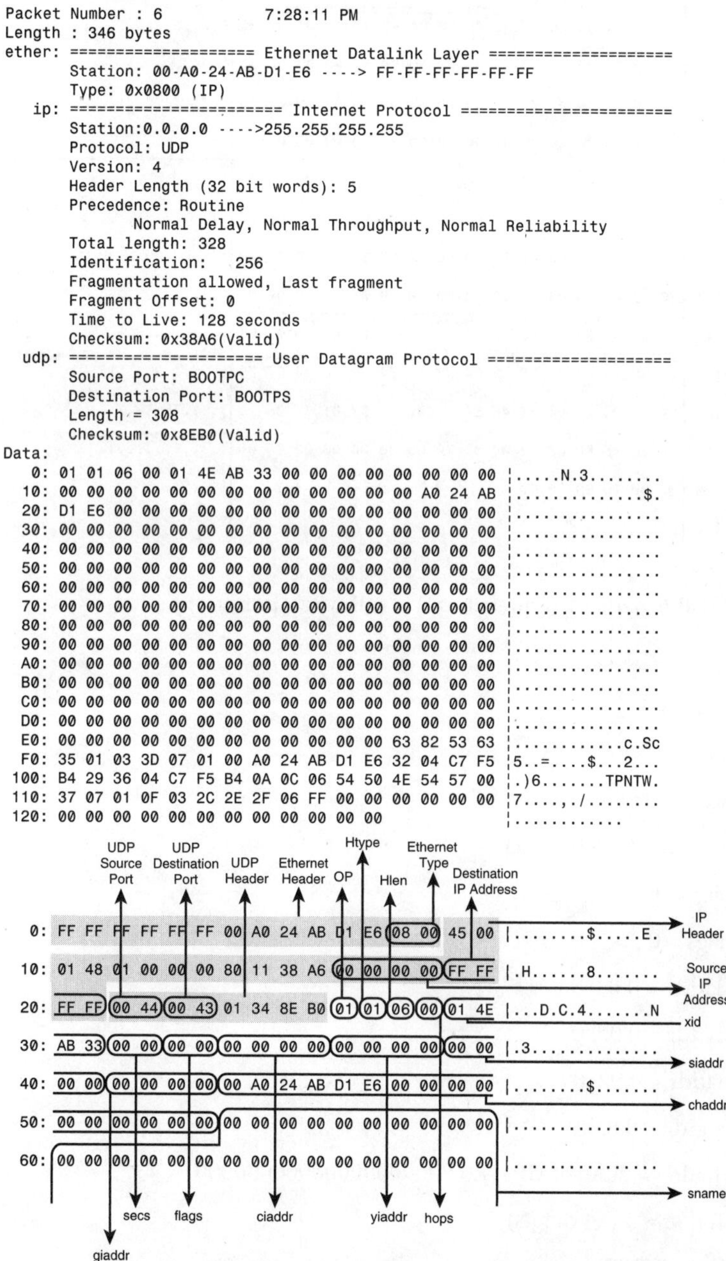

```
Packet Number : 6          7:28:11 PM
Length : 346 bytes
ether: ==================== Ethernet Datalink Layer ====================
       Station: 00-A0-24-AB-D1-E6 ----> FF-FF-FF-FF-FF-FF
       Type: 0x0800 (IP)
   ip: ====================== Internet Protocol ======================
       Station:0.0.0.0 ---->255.255.255.255
       Protocol: UDP
       Version: 4
       Header Length (32 bit words): 5
       Precedence: Routine
              Normal Delay, Normal Throughput, Normal Reliability
       Total length: 328
       Identification:   256
       Fragmentation allowed, Last fragment
       Fragment Offset: 0
       Time to Live: 128 seconds
       Checksum: 0x38A6(Valid)
  udp: ==================== User Datagram Protocol ====================
       Source Port: BOOTPC
       Destination Port: BOOTPS
       Length = 308
       Checksum: 0x8EB0(Valid)
Data:
    0: 01 01 06 00 01 4E AB 33 00 00 00 00 00 00 00 00 |.....N.3........
   10: 00 00 00 00 00 00 00 00 00 00 00 00 00 A0 24 AB |..............$.
   20: D1 E6 00 00 00 00 00 00 00 00 00 00 00 00 00 00 |................
   30: 00 00 00 00 00 00 00 00 00 00 00 00 00 00 00 00 |................
   40: 00 00 00 00 00 00 00 00 00 00 00 00 00 00 00 00 |................
   50: 00 00 00 00 00 00 00 00 00 00 00 00 00 00 00 00 |................
   60: 00 00 00 00 00 00 00 00 00 00 00 00 00 00 00 00 |................
   70: 00 00 00 00 00 00 00 00 00 00 00 00 00 00 00 00 |................
   80: 00 00 00 00 00 00 00 00 00 00 00 00 00 00 00 00 |................
   90: 00 00 00 00 00 00 00 00 00 00 00 00 00 00 00 00 |................
   A0: 00 00 00 00 00 00 00 00 00 00 00 00 00 00 00 00 |................
   B0: 00 00 00 00 00 00 00 00 00 00 00 00 00 00 00 00 |................
   C0: 00 00 00 00 00 00 00 00 00 00 00 00 00 00 00 00 |................
   D0: 00 00 00 00 00 00 00 00 00 00 00 00 00 00 00 00 |................
   E0: 00 00 00 00 00 00 00 00 00 00 00 00 63 82 53 63 |............c.Sc
   F0: 35 01 03 3D 07 01 00 A0 24 AB D1 E6 32 04 C7 F5 |5..=....$...2...
  100: B4 29 36 04 C7 F5 B4 0A 0C 06 54 50 4E 54 57 00 |.)6.......TPNTW.
  110: 37 07 01 0F 03 2C 2E 2F 06 FF 00 00 00 00 00 00 |7....,./........
  120: 00 00 00 00 00 00 00 00 00 00 00 00             |............
```


continues

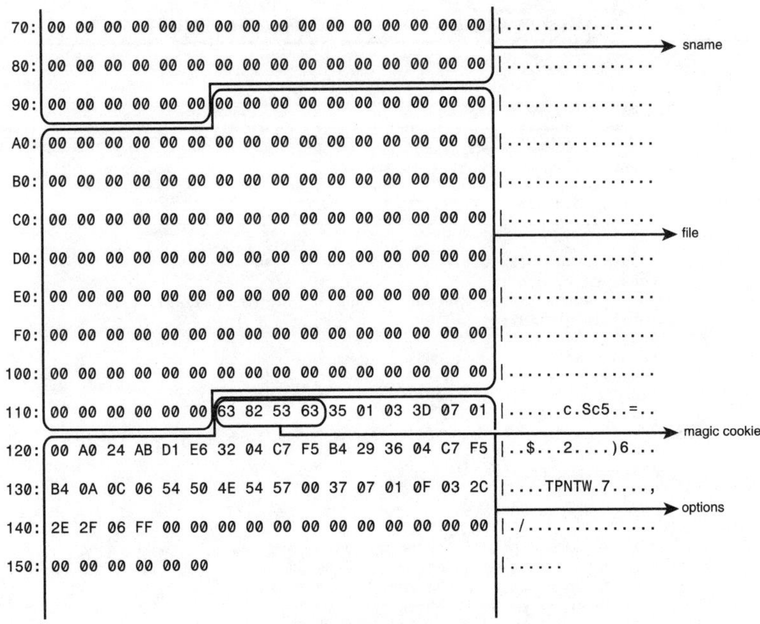
70: 00 00 00 00 00 00 00 00 00 00 00 00 00 00 00 00 |................
80: 00 00 00 00 00 00 00 00 00 00 00 00 00 00 00 00 |................
90: 00 00 00 00 00 00 00 00 00 00 00 00 00 00 00 00 |................
A0: 00 00 00 00 00 00 00 00 00 00 00 00 00 00 00 00 |................
B0: 00 00 00 00 00 00 00 00 00 00 00 00 00 00 00 00 |................
C0: 00 00 00 00 00 00 00 00 00 00 00 00 00 00 00 00 |................
D0: 00 00 00 00 00 00 00 00 00 00 00 00 00 00 00 00 |................
E0: 00 00 00 00 00 00 00 00 00 00 00 00 00 00 00 00 |................
F0: 00 00 00 00 00 00 00 00 00 00 00 00 00 00 00 00 |................
100: 00 00 00 00 00 00 00 00 00 00 00 00 00 00 00 00 |................
110: 00 00 00 00 00 00 63 82 53 63 35 01 03 3D 07 01 |......c.Sc5..=..
120: 00 A0 24 AB D1 E6 32 04 C7 F5 B4 29 36 04 C7 F5 |..$...2....)6...
130: B4 0A 0C 06 54 50 4E 54 57 00 37 07 01 0F 03 2C |....TPNTW.7....,
140: 2E 2F 06 FF 00 00 00 00 00 00 00 00 00 00 00 00 |./..............
150: 00 00 00 00 00 00 |......
sname
file
magic cookie
options

The DHCP broadcast request has the following parameters:

op = 1

htype = 1

hlen = 6

hops = 0

xid = 826E7769 (hex)

secs = 0

flags = 0

ciaddr = 0.0.0.0

yiaddr = 0.0.0.0

siaddr = 0.0.0.0

giaddr = 0.0.0.0

chaddr = 00A024ABD1E6 00000000000000000000

sname = 0 (64 octets)

file = 0 (128 octets)

options = 0 (312 octets)

Figure 12.14 DHCP broadcast reply.

```
Packet Number : 7           7:28:11 PM
Length : 594 bytes
ether: ==================== Ethernet Datalink Layer ====================
       Station: 00-00-C0-DD-14-5C ----> FF-FF-FF-FF-FF-FF
       Type: 0x0800 (IP)
   ip: ======================= Internet Protocol =======================
       Station:199.245.180.10 ---->255.255.255.255
       Protocol: UDP
       Version: 4
       Header Length (32 bit words): 5
       Precedence: Routine
              Normal Delay, Normal Throughput, Normal Reliability
       Total length: 576
       Identification: 47445
       Fragmentation allowed, Last fragment
       Fragment Offset: 0
       Time to Live: 128 seconds
       Checksum: 0x0358(Valid)
  udp: ===================== User Datagram Protocol ====================
       Source Port: BOOTPS
       Destination Port: BOOTPC
       Length = 556
       Checksum: 0x0000(checksum not used)
Data:
    0: 02 01 06 00 01 4E AB 33 00 00 00 00 00 00 00 00 |.....N.3........
   10: 00 00 00 00 C7 F5 B4 0A 00 00 00 00 00 A0 24 AB |..............$.
   20: D1 E6 00 00 00 00 00 00 00 00 00 00 00 00 00 00 |................
   30: 00 00 00 00 00 00 00 00 00 00 00 00 00 00 00 00 |................
   40: 00 00 00 00 00 00 00 00 00 00 00 00 00 00 00 00 |................
   50: 00 00 00 00 00 00 00 00 00 00 00 00 00 00 00 00 |................
   60: 00 00 00 00 00 00 00 00 00 00 00 00 00 00 00 00 |................
   70: 00 00 00 00 00 00 00 00 00 00 00 00 00 00 00 00 |................
   80: 00 00 00 00 00 00 00 00 00 00 00 00 00 00 00 00 |................
   90: 00 00 00 00 00 00 00 00 00 00 00 00 00 00 00 00 |................
   A0: 00 00 00 00 00 00 00 00 00 00 00 00 00 00 00 00 |................
   B0: 00 00 00 00 00 00 00 00 00 00 00 00 00 00 00 00 |................
   C0: 00 00 00 00 00 00 00 00 00 00 00 00 00 00 00 00 |................
   D0: 00 00 00 00 00 00 00 00 00 00 00 00 00 00 00 00 |................
   E0: 00 00 00 00 00 00 00 00 00 00 00 00 63 82 53 63 |............c.Sc
   F0: 35 01 06 FF 00 00 00 00 00 00 00 00 00 00 00 00 |5...............
  100: 00 00 00 00 00 00 00 00 00 00 00 00 00 00 00 00 |................
  110: 00 00 00 00 00 00 00 00 00 00 00 00 00 00 00 00 |................
  120: 00 00 00 00 00 00 00 00 00 00 00 00 00 00 00 00 |................
  130: 00 00 00 00 00 00 00 00 00 00 00 00 00 00 00 00 |................
  140: 00 00 00 00 00 00 00 00 00 00 00 00 00 00 00 00 |................
  150: 00 00 00 00 00 00 00 00 00 00 00 00 00 00 00 00 |................
  160: 00 00 00 00 00 00 00 00 00 00 00 00 00 00 00 00 |................
  170: 00 00 00 00 00 00 00 00 00 00 00 00 00 00 00 00 |................
  180: 00 00 00 00 00 00 00 00 00 00 00 00 00 00 00 00 |................
  190: 00 00 00 00 00 00 00 00 00 00 00 00 00 00 00 00 |................
  1A0: 00 00 00 00 00 00 00 00 00 00 00 00 00 00 00 00 |................
  1B0: 00 00 00 00 00 00 00 00 00 00 00 00 00 00 00 00 |................
  1C0: 00 00 00 00 00 00 00 00 00 00 00 00 00 00 00 00 |................
  1D0: 00 00 00 00 00 00 00 00 00 00 00 00 00 00 00 00 |................
  1E0: 00 00 00 00 00 00 00 00 00 00 00 00 00 00 00 00 |................
  1F0: 00 00 00 00 00 00 00 00 00 00 00 00 00 00 00 00 |................
  200: 00 00 00 00 00 00 00 00 00 00 00 00 00 00 00 00 |................
  210: 00 00 00 00 00 00 00 00 00 00 00 00 00 00 00 00 |................
  220: 00 00 00 00                                     |....
```

continues

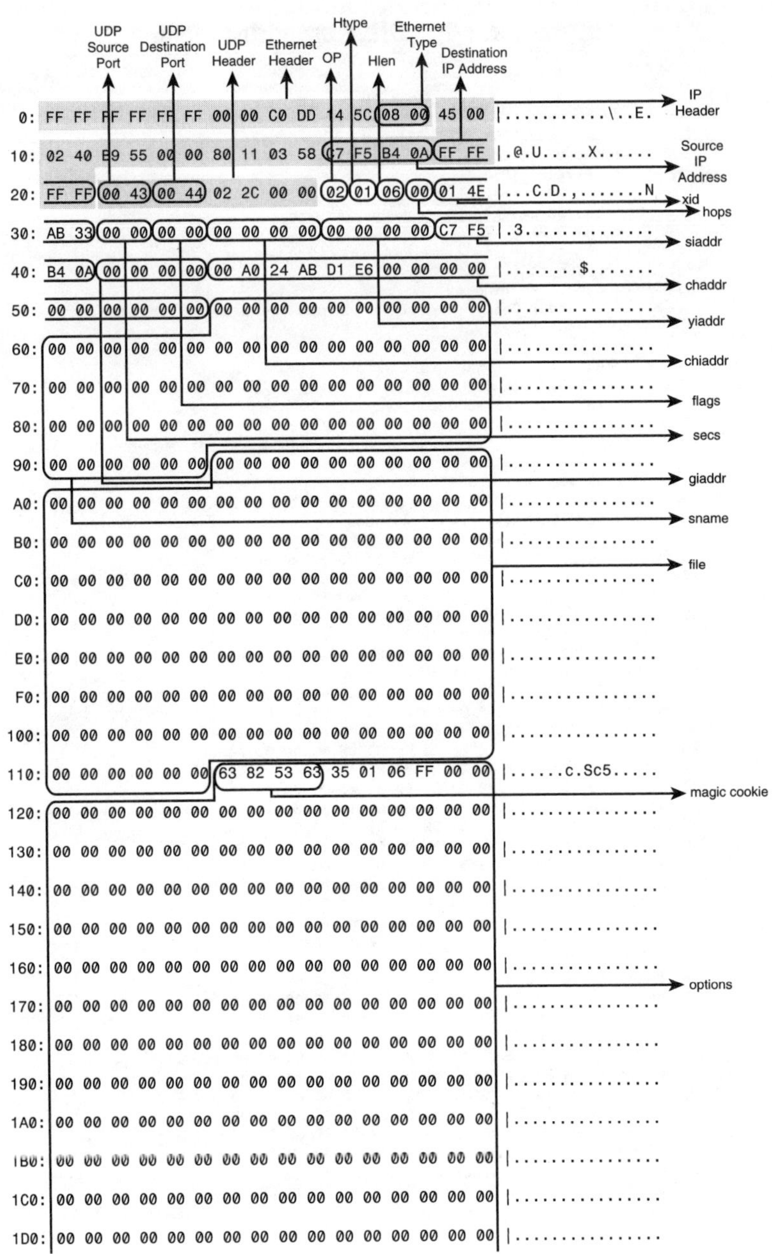
UDP Source Port
UDP Destination Port
UDP Header
Ethernet Header
OP
Htype
Hlen
Ethernet Type
Destination IP Address
IP Header
Source IP Address
xid
hops
siaddr
chaddr
yiaddr
chiaddr
flags
secs
giaddr
sname
file
magic cookie
options
0: FF FF FF FF FF FF 00 00 C0 DD 14 5C 08 00 45 00 |...........\..E.
10: 02 40 B9 55 00 00 80 11 03 58 C7 F5 B4 0A FF FF |.@.U.....X......
20: FF FF 00 43 00 44 02 2C 00 00 02 01 06 00 01 4E |...C.D.,.......N
30: AB 33 00 00 00 00 00 00 00 00 00 00 00 00 C7 F5 |.3..............
40: B4 0A 00 00 00 00 00 A0 24 AB D1 E6 00 00 00 00 |........$.......
50: 00 00 00 00 00 00 00 00 00 00 00 00 00 00 00 00 |................
60: 00 00 00 00 00 00 00 00 00 00 00 00 00 00 00 00 |................
70: 00 00 00 00 00 00 00 00 00 00 00 00 00 00 00 00 |................
80: 00 00 00 00 00 00 00 00 00 00 00 00 00 00 00 00 |................
90: 00 00 00 00 00 00 00 00 00 00 00 00 00 00 00 00 |................
A0: 00 00 00 00 00 00 00 00 00 00 00 00 00 00 00 00 |................
B0: 00 00 00 00 00 00 00 00 00 00 00 00 00 00 00 00 |................
C0: 00 00 00 00 00 00 00 00 00 00 00 00 00 00 00 00 |................
D0: 00 00 00 00 00 00 00 00 00 00 00 00 00 00 00 00 |................
E0: 00 00 00 00 00 00 00 00 00 00 00 00 00 00 00 00 |................
F0: 00 00 00 00 00 00 00 00 00 00 00 00 00 00 00 00 |................
100: 00 00 00 00 00 00 00 00 00 00 00 00 00 00 00 00 |................
110: 00 00 00 00 00 00 63 82 53 63 35 01 06 FF 00 00 |......c.Sc5.....
120: 00 00 00 00 00 00 00 00 00 00 00 00 00 00 00 00 |................
130: 00 00 00 00 00 00 00 00 00 00 00 00 00 00 00 00 |................
140: 00 00 00 00 00 00 00 00 00 00 00 00 00 00 00 00 |................
150: 00 00 00 00 00 00 00 00 00 00 00 00 00 00 00 00 |................
160: 00 00 00 00 00 00 00 00 00 00 00 00 00 00 00 00 |................
170: 00 00 00 00 00 00 00 00 00 00 00 00 00 00 00 00 |................
180: 00 00 00 00 00 00 00 00 00 00 00 00 00 00 00 00 |................
190: 00 00 00 00 00 00 00 00 00 00 00 00 00 00 00 00 |................
1A0: 00 00 00 00 00 00 00 00 00 00 00 00 00 00 00 00 |................
1B0: 00 00 00 00 00 00 00 00 00 00 00 00 00 00 00 00 |................
1C0: 00 00 00 00 00 00 00 00 00 00 00 00 00 00 00 00 |................
1D0: 00 00 00 00 00 00 00 00 00 00 00 00 00 00 00 00 |................

```
1E0: 00 00 00 00 00 00 00 00 00 00 00 00 00 00 00 00 |................
1F0: 00 00 00 00 00 00 00 00 00 00 00 00 00 00 00 00 |................
200: 00 00 00 00 00 00 00 00 00 00 00 00 00 00 00 00 |................  --> options
210: 00 00 00 00 00 00 00 00 00 00 00 00 00 00 00 00 |................
220: 00 00 00 00 00 00 00 00 00 00 00 00 00 00 00 00 |................
230: 00 00 00 00 00 00 00 00 00 00 00 00 00 00 00 00 |................
240: 00 00 00 00 00 00 00 00 00 00 00 00 00 00       |..............
```

The DHCP broadcast reply has the following parameters:

op = 2

htype = 1

hlen = 6

hops = 0

xid = 826E7769 (hex)

secs = 0

flags = 0

ciaddr = 0.0.0.0

yiaddr = 199.245.180.41

siaddr = 199.245.180.10

giaddr = 0.0.0.0

chaddr = 00A024ABD1E6 00000000000000000000

sname = 0 (64 octets)

file = 0 (128 octets)

options: magic cookie = 63 82 53 63 (hex)

Summary

Both BOOTP and DHCP solve the important problem of automatic configuration of IP parameters, such as IP addresses and subnet masks, for individual devices on the network. Both protocols are client-/server-based and use the same UDP port numbers. The DHCP protocol is designed to replace the older BOOTP protocol and is a superset of the BOOTP message format.

A major advantage of DHCP is that IP addresses can be leased on a time basis. This enables a more flexible reuse of IP addresses where IP addresses do not have to be permanently allocated to a station based on their hardware addresses. The BOOTP IP address allocation is less flexible than that of DHCP because IP addresses are associated with the hardware address of a network interface.

Test Yourself

1. Why is the BOOTP request typically broadcast? What destination IP broadcast address is used by BOOTP?
2. The source IP address for the BOOTP request set to what value? Why is it set to this value?
3. If the BOOTP server is on another IP subnet, how is the BOOTP request that uses the limited broadcast address forwarded to this subnet?
4. Why don't most BOOTP servers send a directed reply to the BOOTP client?
5. What would a BOOTP server be required to do in order to send a directed reply to the BOOTP client?
6. If a BOOTP server cannot send a directed reply to a BOOTP client, how is it able to send the reply to the client?
7. How does BOOTP guard against loss of messages?
8. Discuss what would happen if BOOTP clients started at the same time.
9. What mechanism does BOOTP use to prevent BOOTP server and network overload caused by BOOTP clients starting at the same time?
10. Draw a diagram of the BOOTP message format and briefly explain the purpose of the fields in the BOOTP message.
11. Is BOOTP to be used to download the operating system image?
12. Why is the bootstrap procedure for a station that uses BOOTP split into distinct phases? Describe these phases.
13. Why is TFTP used instead of FTP in conjunction with BOOTP?
14. How can BOOTP be configured to enable different operating system images to be downloaded for a given workstation.
15. What is the purpose of the vendor-specific area in BOOTP? What is this field called in DHCP? Does DHCP use the same format for this field?
16. What is the value of the magic cookie used in the option/vendor field in DHCP/BOOTP? If this magic cookie value is used, what is the format of the items in this field?

17. What is the purpose of the option/vendor items with tag values 0 and 255 in BOOTP/DHCP?
18. What BOOTP/DHCP tag values are reserved for site-specific options?
19. What are the two primary elements of the DHCP protocol?
20. Name the three methods for IP address allocation in DHCP and describe them.
21. How is an IP address allocated to a DHCP client given back to the DHCP server for reuse?
22. A network has 400 temporary connections, but at any time it has no more than 250 connections in use. How many class C addresses need to be used if IP address allocation is done using BOOTP? Justify your answer.
23. A network has 400 temporary connections, but at any time has no more than 250 connections in use. How many class C addresses need to be used if IP address allocation is done using DHCP? Justify your answer.
24. If a host provides services to users outside the network, what would be the consequence of assigning IP addresses dynamically using DHCP for this host?
25. Should routers initialize their network interfaces dynamically using DHCP?
26. In DHCP, what is the purpose of the DHCPDISCOVER broadcast?
27. What mechanism is used to prevent DHCP clients sending DHCPDISCOVER broadcasts at the same time?
28. In DHCP, what is the purpose of the DHCPOFFER message?
29. In DHCP, what is the purpose of the DHCPACK message?
30. What precaution can a DHCP client use to ensure that an address leased to it is not already in use?
31. When would a DHCP client decline an IP address leased by a DHCP server? What DHCP message is used for this purpose? How would the DHCP client proceed after the occurrence of this event?
32. Explain the purpose of the three timer values, T1, T2 and T3, used in DHCP. What is the relationship between these timer values?
33. Why does RFC 2131 suggest adding a fuzz factor to the timer values?
34. What happens in DHCP when the timer T1 expires?
35. What happens in DHCP when the timer T2 expires?
36. What happens in DHCP when the timer T3 expires?
37. Draw a diagram of the DHCP message format and briefly explain the purpose of the fields in the BOOTP message.
38. How does the DHCP message format differ from the BOOTP message format?

39. The DHCP client can request that the DHCP server unicast or broadcast its reply. Why and how does the DHCP client indicate this to the server?
40. What methods does DHCP use to provide a larger options field?
41. Decode the following DHCP message and label the fields and its values:

```
  0: FF FF FF FF FF FF 00 A0 24 AB D1 E6 08 00 45 00 ¦........$.....E.
 10: 01 48 00 00 00 00 80 11 39 A6 00 00 00 00 FF FF ¦.H......9.......
 20: FF FF 00 44 00 43 01 34 A3 82 01 01 06 00 82 6E ¦...D.C.4.......n
 30: 77 69 00 00 00 00 00 00 00 00 00 00 00 00 00 00 ¦wi..............
 40: 00 00 00 00 00 00 00 A0 24 AB D1 E6 00 00 00 00 ¦........$.......
 50: 00 00 00 00 00 00 00 00 00 00 00 00 00 00 00 00 ¦................
 60: 00 00 00 00 00 00 00 00 00 00 00 00 00 00 00 00 ¦................
 70: 00 00 00 00 00 00 00 00 00 00 00 00 00 00 00 00 ¦................
 80: 00 00 00 00 00 00 00 00 00 00 00 00 00 00 00 00 ¦................
 90: 00 00 00 00 00 00 00 00 00 00 00 00 00 00 00 00 ¦................
 A0: 00 00 00 00 00 00 00 00 00 00 00 00 00 00 00 00 ¦................
 B0: 00 00 00 00 00 00 00 00 00 00 00 00 00 00 00 00 ¦................
 C0: 00 00 00 00 00 00 00 00 00 00 00 00 00 00 00 00 ¦................
 D0: 00 00 00 00 00 00 00 00 00 00 00 00 00 00 00 00 ¦................
 E0: 00 00 00 00 00 00 00 00 00 00 00 00 00 00 00 00 ¦................
 F0: 00 00 00 00 00 00 00 00 00 00 00 00 00 00 00 00 ¦................
100: 00 00 00 00 00 00 00 00 00 00 00 00 00 00 00 00 ¦................
110: 00 00 00 00 00 00 63 82 53 63 35 01 01 3D 07 01 ¦......c.Sc5..=..
120: 00 A0 24 AB D1 E6 0C 06 54 50 4E 54 57 00 37 07 ¦..$.....TPNTW.7.
130: 01 0F 03 2C 2E 2F 06 FF 00 00 00 00 00 00 00 00 ¦...,./..........
140: 00 00 00 00 00 00 00 00 00 00 00 00 00 00 00 00 ¦................
150: 00 00 00 00 00 00                               ¦......
```

42. Decode the following DHCP message and label the fields and its values:

```
  0: 00 A0 24 AB D1 E6 00 00 C0 DD 14 5C 08 00 45 00 ¦..$........\..E.
 10: 02 40 B9 54 00 00 80 11 87 39 C7 F5 B4 0A C7 F5 ¦.@.T.....9......
 20: B4 29 00 43 00 44 02 2C 00 00 02 01 06 00 82 6E ¦.).C.D.,.......n
 30: 77 69 00 00 00 00 00 00 00 00 C7 F5 B4 29 C7 F5 ¦wi...........)..
 40: B4 0A 00 00 00 00 00 A0 24 AB D1 E6 00 00 00 00 ¦........$.......
 50: 00 00 00 00 00 00 00 00 00 00 00 00 00 00 00 00 ¦................
 60: 00 00 00 00 00 00 00 00 00 00 00 00 00 00 00 00 ¦................
 70: 00 00 00 00 00 00 00 00 00 00 00 00 00 00 00 00 ¦................
 80: 00 00 00 00 00 00 00 00 00 00 00 00 00 00 00 00 ¦................
 90: 00 00 00 00 00 00 00 00 00 00 00 00 00 00 00 00 ¦................
 A0: 00 00 00 00 00 00 00 00 00 00 00 00 00 00 00 00 ¦................
 B0: 00 00 00 00 00 00 00 00 00 00 00 00 00 00 00 00 ¦................
 C0: 00 00 00 00 00 00 00 00 00 00 00 00 00 00 00 00 ¦................
 D0: 00 00 00 00 00 00 00 00 00 00 00 00 00 00 00 00 ¦................
```

```
 E0: 00 00 00 00 00 00 00 00 00 00 00 00 00 00 00 00 ¦................
 F0: 00 00 00 00 00 00 00 00 00 00 00 00 00 00 00 00 ¦................
100: 00 00 00 00 00 00 00 00 00 00 00 00 00 00 00 00 ¦................
110: 00 00 00 00 00 00 63 82 53 63 35 01 02 36 04 C7 ¦......c.Sc5..6..
120: F5 B4 0A 33 04 00 00 0E 10 3A 04 00 00 07 08 3B ¦...3......:.....;
130: 04 00 00 0C 3C 01 04 FF FF FF 00 06 04 C7 F5 B4 ¦....<...........
140: 0A 0F 0C 6B 69 6E 65 74 69 63 73 2E 63 6F 6D FF ¦...kinetics.com.
150: 00 00 00 00 00 00 00 00 00 00 00 00 00 00 00 00 ¦................
160: 00 00 00 00 00 00 00 00 00 00 00 00 00 00 00 00 ¦................
170: 00 00 00 00 00 00 00 00 00 00 00 00 00 00 00 00 ¦................
180: 00 00 00 00 00 00 00 00 00 00 00 00 00 00 00 00 ¦................
190: 00 00 00 00 00 00 00 00 00 00 00 00 00 00 00 00 ¦................
1A0: 00 00 00 00 00 00 00 00 00 00 00 00 00 00 00 00 ¦................
1B0: 00 00 00 00 00 00 00 00 00 00 00 00 00 00 00 00 ¦................
1C0: 00 00 00 00 00 00 00 00 00 00 00 00 00 00 00 00 ¦................
1D0: 00 00 00 00 00 00 00 00 00 00 00 00 00 00 00 00 ¦................
1E0: 00 00 00 00 00 00 00 00 00 00 00 00 00 00 00 00 ¦................
1F0: 00 00 00 00 00 00 00 00 00 00 00 00 00 00 00 00 ¦................
200: 00 00 00 00 00 00 00 00 00 00 00 00 00 00 00 00 ¦................
210: 00 00 00 00 00 00 00 00 00 00 00 00 00 00 00 00 ¦................
220: 00 00 00 00 00 00 00 00 00 00 00 00 00 00 00 00 ¦................
230: 00 00 00 00 00 00 00 00 00 00 00 00 00 00 00 00 ¦................
240: 00 00 00 00 00 00 00 00 00 00 00 00 00 00       ¦..............
```

43. The DHCP/BOOTP client uses a well-known UDP port number of 68. Why does the DHCP/BOOTP client not pick a random port number for the UDP source port field?

44. Draw diagrams showing the protocol layering and encapsulation for BOOTP and DHCP.

CHAPTER 13

Application Services

In TCP/IP, the application services implement the functionality of layers 5, 6, and 7 of the OSI model. Not all TCP/IP applications need the services of layers 5 and 6. The application services deal with the formatting, sending, and receiving of application level data. They do not deal with the interaction with the user which is provided by end-user applications.

This chapter discusses the following major application services that use the TCP/IP protocol infrastructure described in previous chapters:

- Domain Name System (DNS)
- Mail protocols: SMTP, POP3, IMAP4
- Remote access protocols: Telnet, Berkeley r*
- File transfer protocols: FTP, TFTP
- File access protocols: NFS, Web NFS
- Web access protocols: HTTP/HTML, Gopher

Domain Name System

In the modern Internet, hosts are named by using the Domain Name System (DNS) mechanism. DNS provides a symbolic name for referring to hosts. DNS is employed indirectly by almost all application services because users typically submit references to host names as DNS names. For example, a user who wants to start a Telnet session with a host can issue the following command:

```
% telnet archie.ans.net
Trying 147.225.1.2...
Connected to nis.ans.net.
Escape character is '^]'.
AIX telnet (nis.ans.net)
IBM AIX Version 3 for RISC System/6000
(c) Copyrights by IBM and by Others 1982, 1990
login:
```

The immediate response from the Telnet session is the following message:

```
Trying 147.225.1.2...
```

The TCP/IP software translated the host name *archie.ans.net* to the 32-bit IP address 147.225.1.2. This translation was performed by DNS (see fig. 13.1).

TCP/IP application software can be configured to make use of DNS to resolve names. When a TCP/IP application encounters a host name, the application sends a query to a *name resolver* to translate the name to an IP address. On many systems, the name resolver can be on the same workstation where the query was issued. The name resolver is typically implemented as a set of library routines on the system.

If the name resolver cannot find the answer, it sends the query to a *name server* that it knows about. Typically, the name server exists on the workstation's network. If the name server cannot find the answer, the query can be sent to another name on the TCP/IP network.

Figure 13.1 DNS name resolution example.

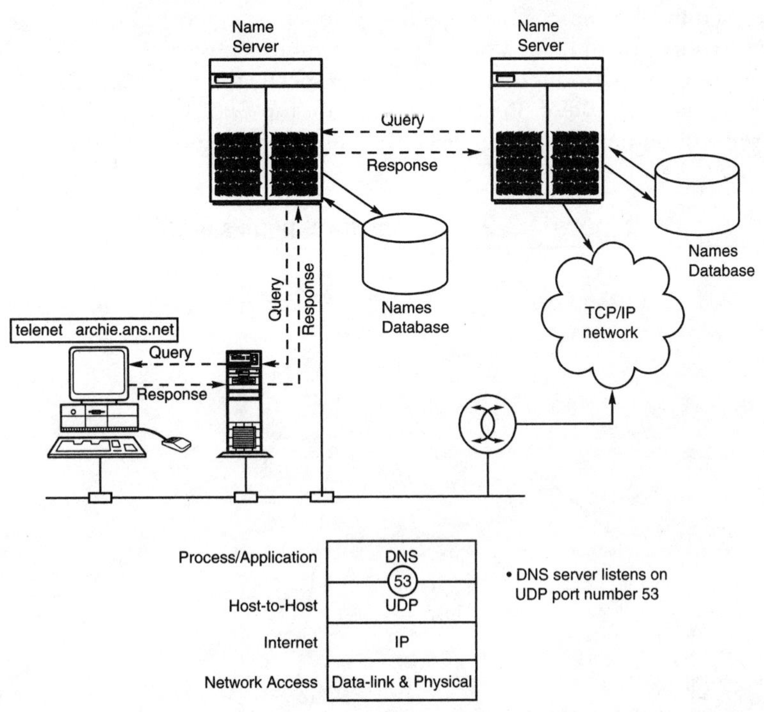

The DNS system relies on a query/response-type behavior and uses the UDP protocol as a transport protocol. The UDP protocol is more suited for applications that are query/response based because there is no overhead of maintaining a connection for transmitting data. The TCP protocol can also be used for query/response-based applications, but it requires an initial opening of a connection and a breakdown of the connection when the query/response is finished. If only a single query/response or an occasional query/response transaction is expected, the overhead of establishing and breaking a connection can be excessive.

In the Telnet example described in this section, DNS is used by the application service to resolve the DNS name to its equivalent IP address. In fact, this name resolution is the primary purpose of DNS, which provides a mapping between DNS symbolic names and IP addresses. DNS has another important use in connection with mail services: DNS is used to specify the mail server that is used for handling e-mail addresses.

The most widely used implementation of DNS is the Berkeley Internet Domain Name (BIND) server, which was originally available on BSD Unix. It is now available on most Unix platforms. On Unix systems, BIND is often called the *named* (name daemon) program.

Earlier in this section, the host names example was shown with periods in it. This type of name uses a hierarchical naming convention. In the hierarchical name scheme used in DNS, names are organized into a hierarchical tree. At the top of the tree is the root domain named by the period symbol (.). Because all names have this common root, the period is omitted when you specify the hierarchical name in most TCP/IP applications. Below the root domain are top-level domains (see fig. 13.2). These reflect how names are organized. Examples of top-level domains are shown in table 13.1.

Figure 13.2 Hierarchical names in DNS.

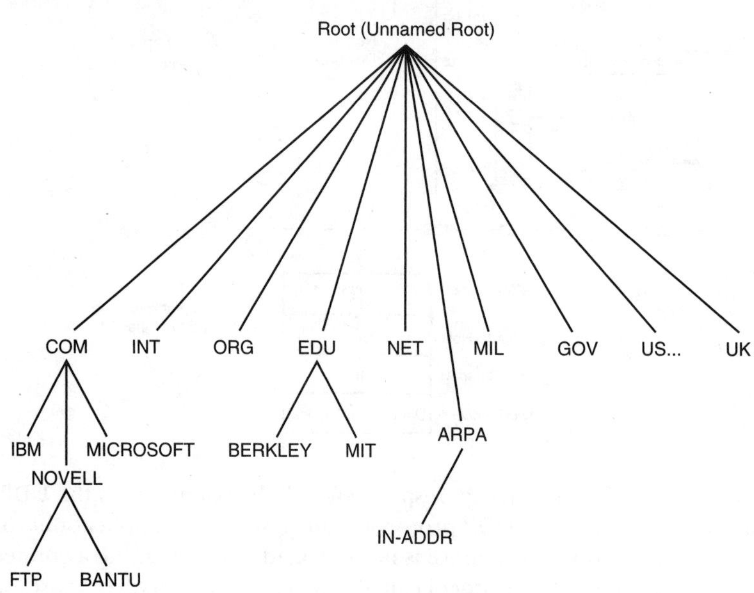

TABLE 13.1
Examples of Some Top-Level Domains

Top-Level Domain	Description
COM	Commercial organization
EDU	Education institution: universities, schools, and so on
MIL	Military
GOV	U.S. government
NET	Network provider

Top-Level Domain	Description
ORG	Organization
ARPA	ARPANET: historical, still used for inverse address mapping
INT	International organization
US	Country: United States
CA	Country: Canada
UK	Country: United Kingdom
DE	Country: Germany
SE	Country: Sweden
FR	Country: France
IN	Country: India
CN	Country: China
JA	Country: Japan

The two-letter designations are assigned to a country per the CCITT standards (now called International Telecommunications Union, or ITU, standards) and the ISO-3166 standard (except for Great Britain, which uses UK rather than GB as its designation). These are the same country designations that are used for specifying country objects in NetWare Directory Services. Below the top-level domains are middle-level domains. There can be a number of middle-level names. Each name is separated from another by use of the period (which can never occur as part of the name of a domain). Domain names are case insensitive. The length of a complete domain name cannot exceed 255 characters, as in the following example:

archie.ans.net

In archie.ans.net, the name of the host is archie, which is in the ans.net domain.

If another host has the name of sparky, and this host is also in the ans.net domain, then the fully qualified name (FQN) of the host would be the following:

sparky.ans.net

Many of the middle-level names refer to names of organizations. An organization is free to define subdomains within the organization, but if it does so, then the organization should implement appropriate domain name services to resolve names in these subdomains. For instance, consider the organization SCS that has been given the following domain name:

SCS.COM

If this organization has separate networks for its corporate, marketing and research arms, it can define three separate subdomains named CORP, MKTG, and RESCH, and it can provide a DNS server or a number of DNS servers to resolve names on its networks. The domains in this case would be as follows:

CORP.SCS.COM

MKTG.SCS.COM

RESCH.SCS.COM

Although a DNS server is not required for each domain, it is common to have one or more for each domain being served. In figure 13.2, there would be several DNS servers for the root domain. These servers would know about names of the top-level domains such as COM, EDU, MIL, ORG, NET, and so on.

There are a number of name servers that manage the domain names at the root domain. Table 13.2 lists some of the root domain servers.

TABLE 13.2
Example Root Domain Servers

Hostname	Net Addresses	Server Program
NS.INTERNIC.NET	198.41.0.4	BIND (Unix)
NS.NIC.DDN.MIL	192.112.36.4	BIND (Unix)
NS1.ISI.EDU	128.9.0.107	BIND (Unix)
AOS.ARL.ARMY.MIL	128.63.4.82	BIND (Unix)
	192.5.25.82	
C.NYSER.NET	192.33.4.12	BIND (Unix)
TERP.UMD.EDU	128.8.10.90	BIND (Unix)
NS.NASA.GOV	192.52.195.10	BIND (Unix)
	128.102.16.10	
NIC.NORDU.NET	192.36.148.17	BIND (Unix)

Several DNS servers can be used for a domain to perform load balancing and to avoid unnecessary network traffic, and for reliability in case the primary DNS server is not available. The COM domain can have one or more DNS servers that know the names of all commercial organizations in the COM domain. Within the COM domain, a subdomain such as IBM.COM will have its own DNS servers for that domain. Hosts within a domain will query the local DNS server for the domain to resolve names. For example, the host WORLD.STD.COM would query the DNS server for the domain STD.COM to find out the IP address of the host FTP.NOVELL.COM or the IP address of ATHENA.SCS.ORG. After this query is resolved, the results are usually cached locally for a configurable period of time.

The DNS servers for a domain need to resolve names of hosts in their domains. A secondary DNS server in a domain must know the IP address of the primary server in the domain that the secondary server can contact for resolving a name query. A DNS server must also know the IP address of the parent DNS server.

DNS uses UDP as a transport protocol to send DNS queries and receive responses from DNS servers. The DNS server listens on UDP port number 53.

DNS is described in RFCs 1034 (STD 13) on "Domain Names: Concepts and Facilities" and is updated by RFCs 1982, 1876, and 1101.

RFC 2137 on "Domain Name System Dynamic Update" and RFC 2136 on "Dynamic Updates in the Domain Name System (DNS UPDATE)" describe recent modifications to DNS.

Mail Protocols

Mail service is perhaps the most widely used application on the Internet. Several protocols for mail service are available, but the most widely used is the Simple Mail Transfer Protocol (SMTP). Because of a large number of mobile and workstation users on the Internet, other support protocols, such as POP3 (Post Office version 3) and IMAP4 (Internet Message Access Protocol version 4), have also been developed.

Simple Mail Transfer Protocol (SMTP)

SMTP enables ASCII text messages to be sent to mailboxes on TCP/IP hosts that have been configured with mail services. Figure 13.3 shows a mail session that uses SMTP. A user wanting to send mail interacts with the local mail system through the user agent (UA) component of the mail system. The mail is deposited in a local mail outgoing mailbox. A sender-SMTP process periodically polls the outgoing box, and when the process finds a mail message in the box, it establishes a TCP connection with the destination host to which mail is to be sent. The receiver-SMTP process at the destination host accepts the connection, and the mail message is sent on that connection. The receiver-SMTP process deposits the mail message in the destination mailbox on the destination host. If there is no mailbox with the specified name on the destination host, a mail message is sent to the originator. This message indicates that the mailbox does not exist. The sender-SMTP and receiver-SMTP processes that are responsible for the transfer of mail are called message transfer agents (MTAs).

Figure 13.3 SMTP user session.

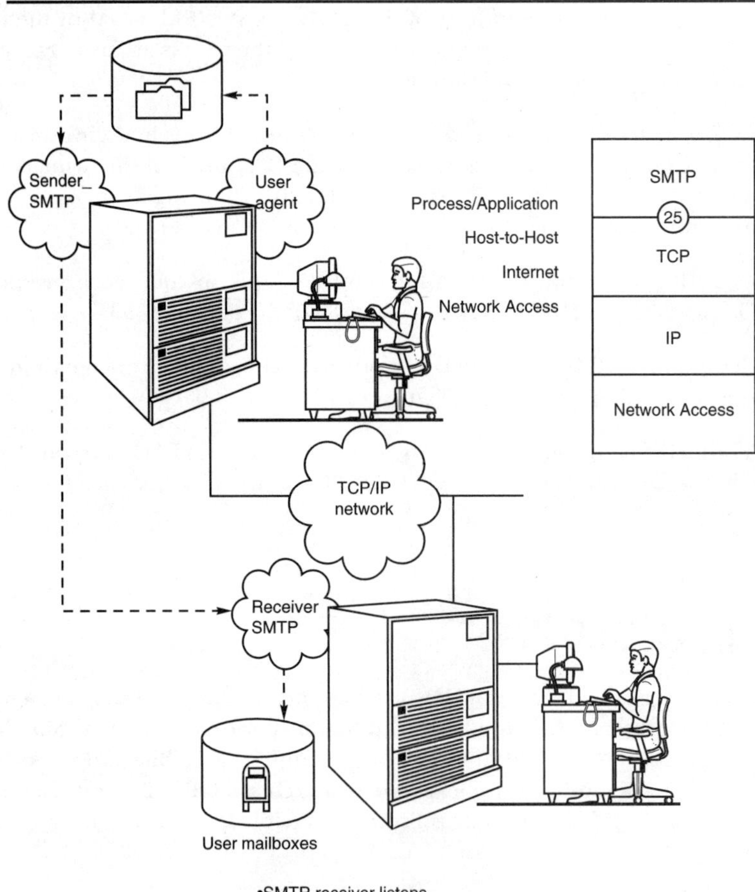

Mail addresses that are used in SMTP follow the RFC 882 standard. The mail headers are often referred to as *882 headers*. An example of an 882 address is the following:

KSS@SHIVA.COM

The text string before the @ symbol specifies the mailbox name, and the text string after the symbol specifies the host name. If the mailbox name contains special characters, such as %, the mailbox name contains a special encoding that is used by mail gateways. In the mail address of KSS@SHIVA.COM, the text string KSS is the name of the mailbox on host SHIVA.COM.

If you want to send nontext messages, such as binary files, audio, or images, by using SMTP, you can encode the message as a text message by using the UUENCODE utility that is available on many systems. The receiver will have to decode the encoded message by using a utility called UUDECODE. Another way of sending nontext messages is to use the MIME protocol. MIME (Multipurpose Internet Mail Extensions) is described in RFCs 1896 RFC2045, RFC2046, and RFC2049. MIME is used to encode different content types, such as plain text, richly formatted text, image, audio, video, HTML documents, and so on (see fig. 13.4).

Figure 13.4 MIME message. (Courtesy Learning Tree)

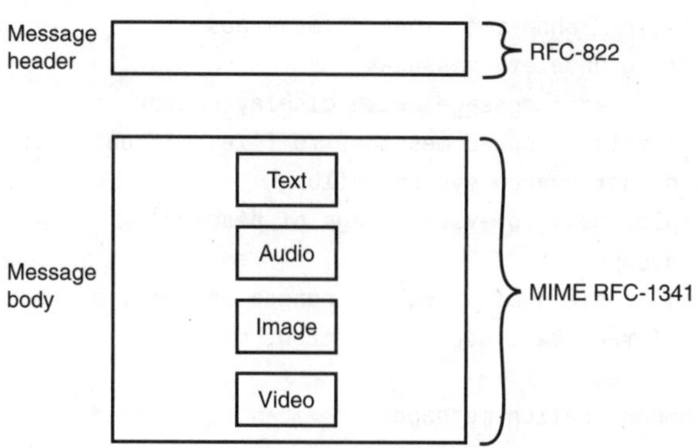

MIME message bodies can have nested contents, and MIME user agents can select among alternative representations of contents. For example, if a "dumb" terminal—which does not have the capability to display an audio/video message—is used, the terminal can display the text portion of this message. Another useful feature of MIME is that it can use a pointer to reference data that is stored elsewhere. For example, the pointer can refer to a document on an FTP site. This process prevents the necessity of including the document in every mail message that is sent out on a mail distribution list. Only users that are interested in the document on the FTP site have to retrieve this document.

A sample mail session that uses the Unix *mail* program follows to illustrate how the user can interact with the user agent (UA).

```
% mail
Mail version SMI 4.0 Thu Jul 23 13:52:20 PDT 1992 Type ? for help.
"/usr/spool/mail/karanjit": 1 message
> 1 kss@RAMA.COM Mon Apr 25 19:32 5148/153370
& ?
cd [directory]     chdir to directory or home if none given
```

```
d [message list]    delete messages
e [message list]    edit messages
f [message list]    show from lines of messages
h        print out active message headers
m [user list]     mail to specific users
n        goto and type next message
p [message list]    print messages
pre [message list]    make messages go back to system mailbox
q        quit, saving unresolved messages in mbox
r [message list]    reply to sender (only) of messages
R [message list]    reply to sender and all recipients of messages
s [message list] file   append messages to file
t [message list]    type messages (same as print)
top [message list]    show top lines of messages
u [message list]    undelete messages
v [message list]    edit messages with display editor
w [message list] file   append messages to file, without from line
x        quit, do not change system mailbox
z [-]       display next [previous] page of headers
!        shell escape
A [message list] consists of integers, ranges of same, or user names separated
by spaces. If omitted, Mail uses the current message.
& m karanjit@kscs.com
Subject: Mail demonstration message
This is a demonstration on using the
simple mail program interface.
When done you must type period (.)
:-)
.
EOT
& h
(Print out active message headers)
> 1 kss@RAMA.COM Mon Apr 25 19:32 5148/153370
& p
(Print message. Message now follows)
Message 1:
From kss@RAMA.COM Mon Apr 25 19:32:35 1994
Return-Path: <kss@RAMA.COM>
Received: by world.std.com (5.65c/Spike-2.0)
  id AA01519; Mon, 25 Apr 1994 19:31:33 -0400
Received: from sita.RAMA.COM by relay1.UU.NET with SMTP
  (5.61/UUNET-internet-primary) id AAwnfh17101; Mon, 25 Apr 94 19:21:26 -0
400
```

```
Received: by sita.RAMA.COM (5.67/PERFORMIX-0.9/08-16-92)
  id AA03921; Mon, 25 Apr 94 16:21:21 -0700
Date: Mon, 25 Apr 94 16:21:21 -0700
From: kss@RAMA.COM (K S)
Message-Id: <9404252321.AA03921@learn1.Lrntree.COM>
To: karanjit@world.std.com
Status: RO
X-Status: D
#! /bin/sh
# This is a shell archive. Remove anything before this line, then unpack
# it by saving it into a file and typing "sh file". To overwrite existing
# files, type "sh file -c". You can also feed this as standard input via
# unshar, or by typing "sh <file", e.g.. If this archive is complete, you
# will see the following message at the end:
#     "End of shell archive."
# Contents: INSTALL Makefile Prospero RCS README acalloc.c archie.c
# archie.man atalloc.c dirsend.c get_pauth.c get_vdir.c p_err_text.c
# pauthent.h pcompat.h perrno.h pfs.h pmachine.h pprot.h ptalloc.c
# regex.c stcopy.c support.c uw-copyright.h vl_comp.c vlalloc.c
# Wrapped by darwin@king.csri on Wed Jan 5 20:28:52 1994
PATH=/bin:/usr/bin:/usr/ucb ; export PATH
if test -f 'INSTALL' -a "${1}" != "-c" ; then
 echo shar: Will not clobber existing file \"'INSTALL'\"
else
echo shar: Extracting \"'INSTALL'\" \(1725 characters\)
sed "s/^X//" >'INSTALL' <<'END_OF_FILE'
X[Last changed: 07/31/91]
(Rest of message....)
& x
(Quit and do not change system mailbox)
%
```

The mail messages are sent by using the SMTP commands that are listed in tables 13.3 and 13.4. These tables contain the SMTP sender and receiver commands for a minimum implementation. All SMTP commands are four letters long. The SMTP receiver is typically a mail server and responds to SMTP commands with three-digit status codes that have the following syntax:

DDD Text message

DDD is the three-digit status code.

Table 13.3
SMTP Sender (Client) Commands for a Minimal Implementation

Command	Meaning
`HELO` *sender*	This command is a connection request from a sender-SMTP.
`MAIL FROM:` *fromaddr*	This command is used to initiate a mail transaction in which the mail data is delivered to one or more mailboxes.
`RCPT TO:` *sendto*	This command is used to identify an individual recipient of the mail data. Multiple recipients are specified by multiple use of this command.
`DATA`	The receiver treats the lines following the command as mail data from the sender. The mail data is terminated by a line containing only a period, as in the character sequence <CRLF>.<CRLF>.
`QUIT`	This command specifies that the receiver must send an OK reply and then close the connection.
`RESET`	This command specifies that the current mail transaction is to be aborted.
`NOOP`	This is a no operation command. It specifies no other action than that the receiver send an OK reply. This command can be used as a diagnostic aid to check whether the receiver responds with an OK reply.

Table 13.4
Example SMTP Receiver (Mail Server) Commands

Command	Meaning
`250`	Requested mail action OK, completed.
`251`	User not local; will forward to <forward-path>.
`450`	Requested mail action not taken: mailbox unavailable. For example, mailbox is busy.
`550`	Requested action not taken: mailbox unavailable.

Command	Meaning
451	Requested action aborted: error in processing.
551	User not local; please try <forward-path>.
452	Requested action not taken: insufficient system storage.
552	Requested mail action aborted: exceeded storage allocation.
553	Requested action not taken: mailbox name not allowed. For example, mailbox syntax may be incorrect.
354	Start mail input; end with <CRLF>.<CRLF>.
554	Transaction failed.

Figure 13.5 shows an SMTP session that uses some of these commands. Notice that in this example, mail is being sent from the user kss@scs.psi.com identified by the MAIL command.

Figure 13.5 Example SMTP session showing SMTP commands. (Courtesy Learning Tree)

Example SMTP Session

S: HELO machine
R: HELO machine, Pleased to meet you

S: MAIL FROM: kss@scs.psi.com
R: 250 OK

S: RCPT To: jones@scs.psi.com
R: 250 OK

S: RCPT To: bob@ltree.psi.com
R: 550 No such user here
} User bob does not have a mailbox at ltree.psi.com

S: RCPT To: john@ltree.psi.com
R: 250 OK

S: DATA
R: 354 Strart mail input; end with <CRLF>.<CRLF>
S: message text
S: message text
S: message text_etc.
S: <CRLF>.<CRLF>
R: 250 OK

R = SMTP receiver
S = SMTP sender

The mail is being sent to jones@scsi.psi.com and bob@ltree.psi.com. Note that the mailbox bob@ltree.psi.com does not exist, so an error message (550 status code) is returned to indicate that there is no such user. The mail server responds to all other commands with a status code of 250.

SMTP-related standards documents are described in table 13.5

Table 13.5
SMTP-Related Standard RFCs

Protocol	Name	Status	RFC#	STD#
SMTP	Simple Mail Transfer Protocol	Rec	821	10
SMTP-SIZE	SMTP Service Ext for Message Size	Rec	1870	10
SMTP-EXT	SMTP Service Extensions	Rec	1869	10
MAIL	Format of Electronic Mail Messages	Rec	822	11

Post Office Protocol Version 3 (POP3)

SMTP expects the destination host—the mail server receiving the mail—to be online; otherwise, a TCP connection cannot be established with the destination host. For this reason, it is not practical to establish an SMTP session with a desktop for receiving mail because desktop workstations are often turned off at the end of the day.

In many network environments, SMTP mail is received by a SMTP host that is always active on the network (see fig. 13.6). This SMTP host provides a mail-drop service. Workstations interact with the SMTP host and retrieve messages by using a client/server mail protocol, such as POP3 (Post Office Protocol version 3) described in RFC 1939. POP3 uses the TCP transport protocol, and the POP3 server listens on its well-known TCP port number 110.

Although POP3 is used to download messages from the server, SMTP is still used to forward messages from the workstation user to its SMTP mail server.

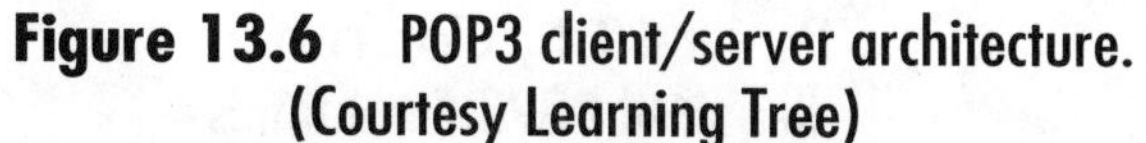

Figure 13.6 POP3 client/server architecture. (Courtesy Learning Tree)

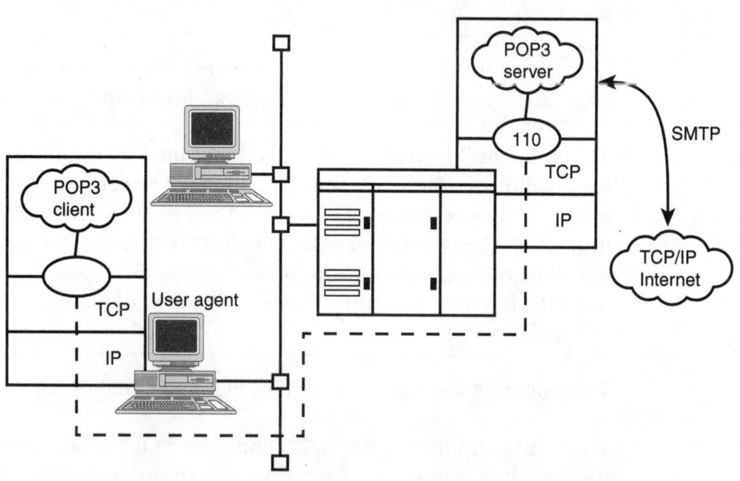

- **Message Transfer Agent (MTA) is run on a computer with more resources than that available to the workstation**
  - Offers a "maildrop" service to smaller nodes, such as workstations
- **POP3 provides dynamic access to maildrop server**

Tables 13.6 through 13.8 list the POP3 commands based on the RFC 1939 specification. Although the USER and PASS commands (see table 13.7) are listed as optional commands in RFC 1939, most POP3 implementations support these commands. The reason why USER/PASS can be regarded as optional is because they can be replaced by the MD5 (Message Digest version 5) authentication method used in the APOP command.

Table 13.6
Required POP3 Commands

Command	Meaning
`STAT`	This command is used to specify a positive response consisting of +OK followed by a single space, the number of messages in the mail drop, a single space, and the size of the mail drop in octets. Example response: +OK *msgid size.*
`LIST` *`[msg]`*	When a message number is specified, the POP3 server returns the scan listing for the message, such as its message number and size. When no message number is specified, a positive response is

continues

Table 13.6, Continued
Required POP3 Commands

Command	Meaning
	returned; and then the response goes multiline, where each line contains a scan listing of all messages waiting at the mailbox.
`RETR` *`msg`*	This command is used to retrieve a list of messages waiting for the user mailbox at the POP3 server. The POP3 server issues an initial positive response of +OK, and then the response given is multiline. After the initial +OK, the POP3 server sends the multiline message corresponding to the specified message number. If a message cannot be found, the +ERR response is returned.
`DELE` *`msg`*	This command marks the specified message as deleted.
`NOOP`	This command means No Operation. The POP3 server does nothing; it merely replies with a positive response of +OK. This command can be used as a diagnostic to check whether the POP3 connection is OK.
`RSET`	This command unmarks any messages that have been marked as deleted by the POP3 server. The POP3 server then replies with a positive response of +OK. Example response: +OK mail drop has 3 messages (430 octets)
`QUIT`	The POP3 server removes all messages marked as deleted from the mail drop and issues the following replies to the status of this operation: +OK or -ERR. The POP3 server releases any exclusive-access lock on the mail drop and closes the TCP connection.

Table 13.7
Optional POP3 Commands

Command	Meaning
`USER` *`name`*	This command is used to specify the name string to identify a mailbox.
`PASS` *`string`*	This command specifies a server/mailbox-specific password for the user name.
`TOP` *`msg n`*	The POP3 server sends an +OK response followed by the headers of the specified message, *msg*; then a blank line followed by *n* lines in the indicated message body. If the

Command	Meaning
	number of lines requested by the POP3 client is greater than the number of lines in the message body, the POP3 server sends the entire message.
`UIDL [msg]`	This command is used to return a unique identifier listing (UIDL) for the message. The POP3 server sends an +OK response with a line containing information for that message. This line is called a unique ID listing for that message. If no argument is given, the POP3 server issues a +OK positive response and then the response goes multiline. After the initial +OK for each message in the mail drop, the POP3 server responds with a line containing information for that message. A UIDL consists of the message number of the message followed by a single space and then the unique ID of the message.
`APOP name digest`	The *name* is a string that identifies the mailbox, and *digest* is the MD5 (Message Digest version 5) digest string. This command is used to provide an alternative authentication method to the normal USER/PASS exchange, which is sent as clear text. The APOP authentication method provides for both origin authentication and replay protection. More importantly, with APOP, the password is not sent in the clear over the network.

TABLE 13.8
POP3 Server Replies

Command	Meaning
`+OK`	Command was executed correctly
`-ERR`	Command execution resulted in error

Figure 13.7 shows a sample interaction between a POP3 client and a POP server. The interaction uses some of the commands listed in tables 13.6 though 13.8.

Figure 13.7 POP3 sample session. (Courtesy Learning Tree)

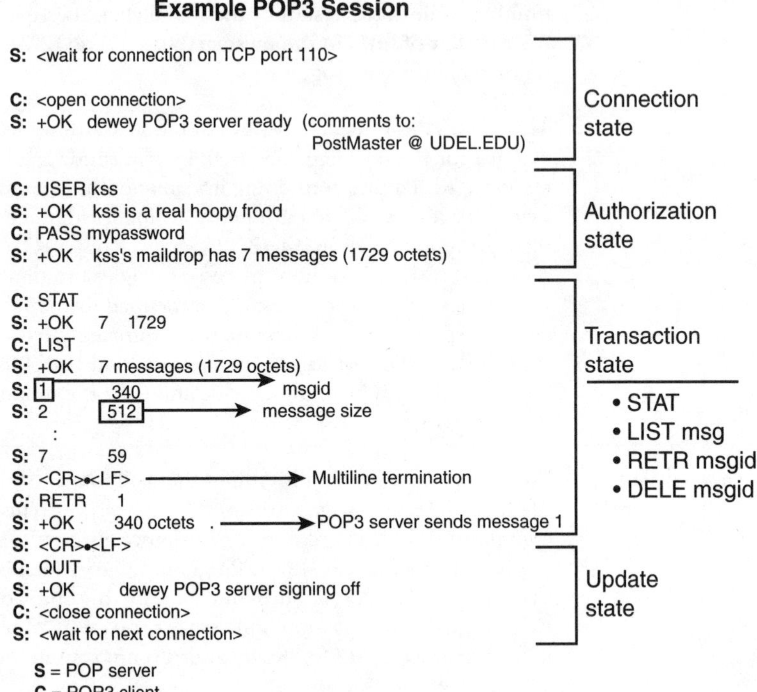

Example POP3 Session
S: <wait for connection on TCP port 110>
C: <open connection>
S: +OK dewey POP3 server ready (comments to: PostMaster @ UDEL.EDU)
Connection state
C: USER kss
S: +OK kss is a real hoopy frood
C: PASS mypassword
S: +OK kss's maildrop has 7 messages (1729 octets)
Authorization state
C: STAT
S: +OK 7 1729
C: LIST
S: +OK 7 messages (1729 octets)
S: 1 340
msgid
S: 2 512
message size
:
S: 7 59
S: <CR>•<LF>
Multiline termination
C: RETR 1
S: +OK 340 octets .
POP3 server sends message 1
S: <CR>•<LF>
Transaction state
• STAT
• LIST msg
• RETR msgid
• DELE msgid
C: QUIT
S: +OK dewey POP3 server signing off
C: <close connection>
S: <wait for next connection>
Update state
S = POP server
C = POP3 client

This sample POP3 session shows that the POP3 session initially enters into a *connection state.* In the connection state, the TCP connection with the POP3 server is established. Next, the POP3 session enters into the *authorization state.* In this state, the user must provide a user name and password to be authenticated by the POP3 server. In earlier POP3 implementations, the user name and password authentication information is sent as clear text and is susceptible to compromise, which means that someone examining the POP3 packet trace can discover the user name and password combination. In POP3 as specified in RFC 1939, an alternative, more secure authentication method based on MD5 can be used.

After the user has been authorized, the POP3 session enters the *transaction state.* In the transaction state, a number of commands—such as STAT, LIST, RETR, DELE, RSET, and so on—can be issued. In figure 13.7, the POP3 client issues a STAT command, and the server returns the number of messages with a total size (1,729 octets) of these messages. The POP3 client then uses the LIST command to ask for a list of all the messages. The POP3 server returns the message numbers for each message and its corresponding size. The client then issues the RETR commands and specifies each message identifier that is to be downloaded. Depending on the setting at the POP3 client, the POP3 client may issue a DELE command to delete a message that has been retrieved.

After the messages have been downloaded, the POP3 session enters the *update state.* In the update state, the POP3 client issues a QUIT command to close the connection. Both POP3 client and POP3 server may then update their internal states to reflect the new count of messages in their respective mailboxes. The TCP connection is then closed.

Internet Message Access Protocol Rev 4 (IMAP4)

While POP3 has served well as a client/server protocol for workstations to download their e-mail messages, it has a number of weaknesses. For example, mail must be downloaded to the workstation before it can be manipulated, and POP3 does not permit the direct manipulation of mail messages at the server. For these reasons, IMAP4 has been proposed as a replacement to POP3.

IMAP4 enables a client/server protocol to access and manipulate electronic mail messages on a server. This protocol permits manipulation of remote message folders, called *mailboxes,* in a way that is functionally equivalent to local mailboxes. IMAP4 also provides the capability for an offline client to resynchronize its mailboxes with the server.

IMAP4 client features include the following:

- Access and manipulate portions of e-mail messages on a server without downloading them
- Review messages and attachments without downloading them
- Download all messages for offline operation
- Resynchronize local mailboxes with those at the server

IMAP4 provides operations, such as the following:

- Creating, deleting, and renaming mailboxes
- Checking for new messages
- Permanently removing messages from mailboxes
- Setting and clearing flags that indicate the status of messages
- Recognizing RFC-822 headers and parsing of MIME encoded messages.
- Searching and selective fetching of message attributes, texts, and portions thereof.

Messages in IMAP4 are accessed by the use of numbers. These numbers are either message sequence numbers or unique identifiers. IMAP4 supports a single server. A mechanism for accessing configuration information to support multiple IMAP4 servers is also being considered by the IETF.

Like POP3, IMAP4 does not specify a means of posting mail. This function is handled by a mail transfer protocol such as SMTP. Figure 13.8 shows the client/server interaction for IMAP4.

Figure 13.8 IMAP4 client/server architecture. (Courtesy Learning Tree)

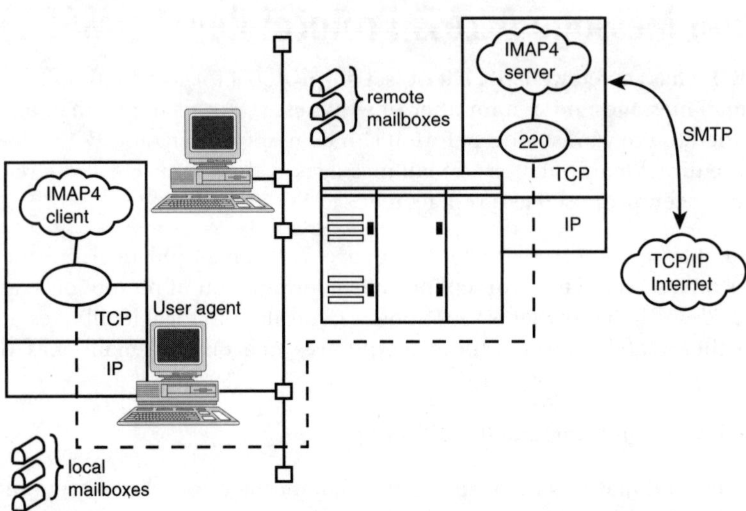

- **Message Transfer Agent (MTA) is run on a computer with more resources than that available to the workstation**
  - Offers a "maildrop" service to smaller nodes, such as workstations
- **POP3 provides dynamic access to maildrop server**

The behavior of IMAP4 can be described in terms of a state diagram (see fig. 13.9).

Figure 13.9 IMAP4 state diagram.

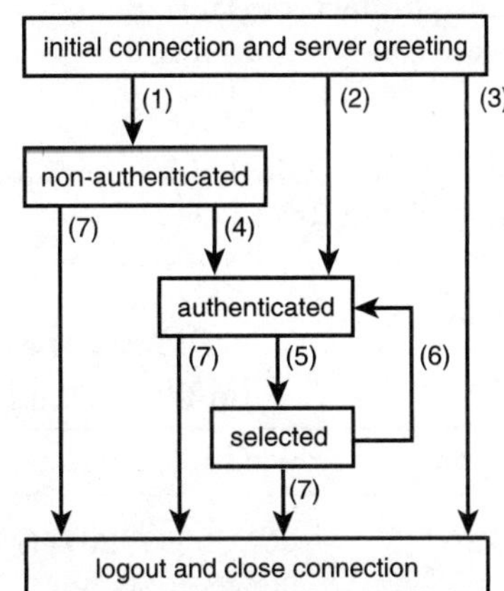

(1) connection without pre-authentication (OK greeting)
(2) pre-authenticated connection (PREAUTH greeting)
(3) rejected connection (BYE greeting)
(4) successful LOGIN or AUTHENTICATE command
(5) successful SELECT or EXAMINE command
(6) CLOSE command, or failed SELECT or EXAMINE command
(7) LOGOUT command, server shutdown, or connection closed

As figure 13.9 illustrates, IMAP4 can be in one of four states. Most IMAP4 commands are valid only in a particular state. A protocol error is generated if an IMAP4 client attempts a command in an inappropriate state. The following IMAP4 states are defined in this section:

- Nonauthenticated state
- Authenticated state
- Selected state
- Logout state

In the *nonauthenticated state*, the IMAP4 client supplies authentication credentials. Most commands are not permitted unless the client has been authenticated. This state is entered when a connection starts, unless the connection has been preauthenticated.

In the *authenticated state*, the client is authenticated and must select a mailbox before commands that affect messages are permitted. This state is entered when a preauthenticated connection starts or when acceptable authentication credentials have been provided. If an error is made in selecting a mailbox, this state is re-entered so that another mailbox can be selected.

The *selected state* is entered after a valid mailbox has been successfully selected.

In the *logout state*, the connection is terminated, and the IMAP4 server closes the connection. This state can be entered as a result of a client request or by a server decision.

IMAP4 is the subject of a great deal of interest among messaging vendors. Table 13.9 describes the IMAP4-related RFCs.

Table 13.9 IMAP4-Related RFCs

RFC#	Status	RFC Title
2095	PS	IMAP/POP AUTHorize Extension for Simple Challenge/Response
2088	PS	IMAP4 nonsynchronizing literals
2087	PS	IMAP4 QUOTA extension
2086	PS	IMAP4 ACL extension
2061	I	IMAP4 COMPATIBILITY WITH IMAP2BIS
2060	PS	INTERNET MESSAGE ACCESS PROTOCOL VERSION 4rev1
1733	I	DISTRIBUTED ELECTRONIC MAIL MODELS IN IMAP4
1732	I	IMAP4 COMPATIBILITY WITH IMAP2 AND IMAP2BIS
1731	PS	IMAP4 authentication mechanisms

PS = Proposed Standard

I = Information

Remote Access Protocols

The typical interaction with many minicomputer, mainframe-based host systems is that a user interacts with the host by logging on from a terminal. The terminal characteristics depend on the hardware of the terminal and the terminal model defined by the host operating system. After a connection between the terminal and the host is established (see fig. 13.10), the user types in keystrokes representing the user commands. The terminal driver at the host receives the keystrokes and buffers them to form the user command. The user command is submitted to the host; the host then performs the actions requested by the user command and sends its response back.

Figure 13.10 Terminal/host architecture.

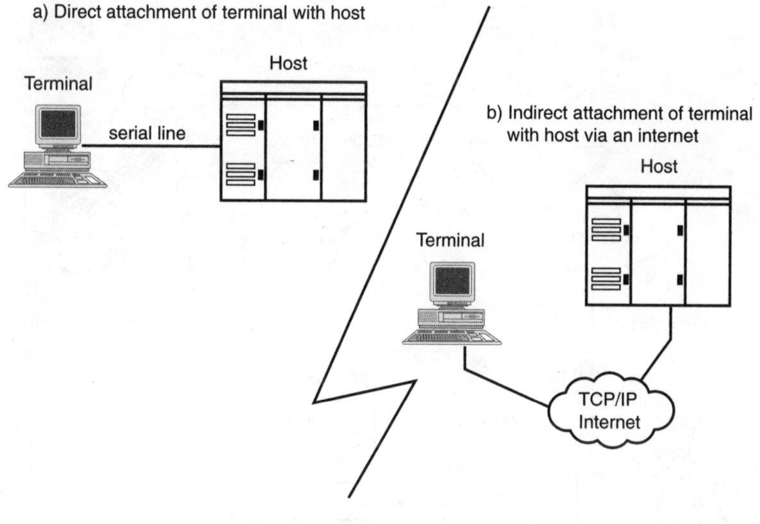

When the terminal and host are separated by a network a remote access protocol is needed to provide the same capabilities as when the terminal and host are directly attached (refer to fig. 13.10). The primary remote access protocols in the TCP/IP protocol suite are the following:

- Telnet
- Berkeley r* utilities

Telnet

The Telnet protocol is used for emulating a terminal connection to a remote host. Telnet makes use of TCP as a transport protocol to transmit the information between a user's keyboard to the remote host, and to display information from the remote host to the user workstation's display.

Figure 13.11 shows a Telnet session. In order to support a Telnet session, you must have a Telnet client component running at the user's workstation and a Telnet server running at the remote host. A TCP/IP session is set up between the Telnet client and the Telnet server. The Telnet server listens on TCP port number 23, which is dedicated for this purpose. On Unix systems, the Telnet server is called *telnetd* (Telnet daemon, pronounced *telnet-dee*) after the name of the program that implements the Telnet server.

Figure 13.11 Example Telnet session.

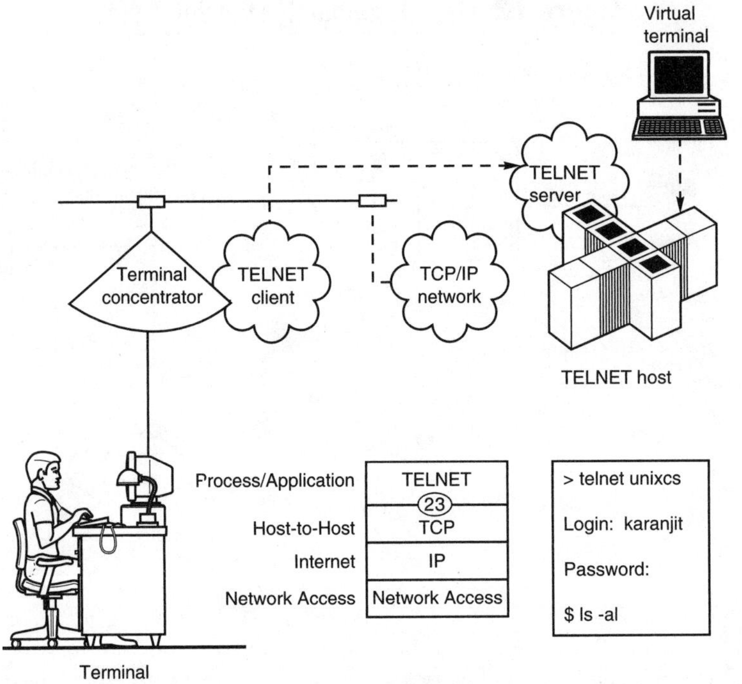

As the user types in the keyboard commands, the characters are received by the Telnet server component and sent to the operating system that the Telnet server runs on, as if the characters were typed in by a locally attached terminal. The results of the commands are sent by the Telnet server to the Telnet client. The Telnet client displays the results received from the Telnet server on the user workstation's display unit. To the user using the Telnet client, the response seems to be from a machine that is attached locally to the workstation. After you are logged in, you can type in any command that you are permitted on the remote operating system. To log in to a remote host, you must have an account on that machine.

The following is an example of a Telnet session to a Unix host:

```
% telnet world.std.com
Trying 192.74.137.5 ...
Connected to world.std.com.
Escape character is '^]'.
* To create an account on The World login as new, no password.
SunOS Unix (world)
login: karanjit
Password:password
Last login: Tue May 10 17:52:29 from karanjit-slip.cs
OS/MP 4.1C Export(STD/arlie)#15: Fri Mar 18 17:25:40 1994

           Welcome to the World! A 6 CPU Solbourne 6E/900.
       Public Access Unix — Home of the Online Book Initiative

          Type 'help' for help! — Stuck? Try 'help HINTS'.

       When you see MORE, hit the space bar for the next page.
              Use 'exit' or 'logout' to leave the system.
                  Still Stuck? Send mail to 'staff'.

You have mail.
Over disk quota on /home/ie, time limit has expired, remove 120K
TERM = (vt100)
Erase is Backspace
No new messages.
An authority is a person who can tell you more about something than you
really care to know.
from: postel@isi.edu [no subject]

% ls -alr
total 1011

-rw------- 1 karanjit  21852 Apr 13 21:56 veronica
drwx------ 2 karanjit    512 Dec 28 1992 temp
-rw------- 1 karanjit   4780 Jun 4 1993 snapip.dmp
-rw------- 1 karanjit   1319 Jul 9 1993 Index
-rw------- 1 karanjit      8 Apr 13 20:43 .sh_history
-rw------- 1 karanjit   7035 May 10 17:53 .pinerc
drwx------ 2 karanjit    512 Apr 13 20:01 .nn
-rw------- 1 karanjit 138402 Apr 13 20:01 .newsrc.bak
-rw-r--r-- 1 karanjit 138102 Apr 13 20:01 .newsrc
-rw-r--r-- 1 karanjit      4 Apr 7 12:55 .msgsrc
```

```
-rw------- 1 karanjit     11 Dec 28 1992 .mh_profile
-rw-r--r-- 1 karanjit    386 Dec 19 1992 .login
-rw------- 1 karanjit      0 Apr 7 17:35 .gopherrc
-rw-r--r-- 1 karanjit    538 Dec 19 1992 .emacs
drwx------ 2 karanjit    512 Jan 22 1993 .elm
-rw-rw-r-- 1 karanjit    799 Feb 1 1993 .cshrc
-rw------- 1 karanjit      0 Dec 19 1992 .addressbook
drwxrwxr-x1911 root    61952 May 24 12:55 ..
drwx------ 7 karanjit   1024 May 10 17:56 .

% ping novell.com
novell.com is alive

% logout
```

After you are logged in with Telnet, the commands that you type are those that are specific to the operating system that you are logged in to.

The next sections discuss Telnet in greater detail.

Telnet Architecture

Figure 13.12 shows the Telnet client/server model. When a user starts a Telnet application and specifies a destination host name, a TCP connection is established with port 23 on the destination host. The data between the Telnet client and Telnet host (also called Telnet server) is sent over this TCP connection. Normally, the TCP connection is closed when the user issues a logout command to terminate the Telnet session.

Figure 13.12 Telnet client/server model. (Courtesy Learning Tree)

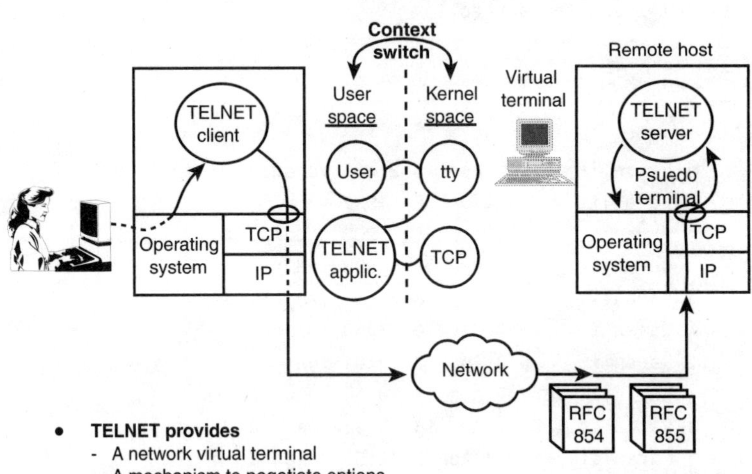

After a TCP connection has been established, the Telnet client and Telnet server negotiate parameters that determine the type of terminal device being used. The parameters also establish the mode in which the Telnet session will operate. For example, the Telnet client can be configured to negotiate a line mode of operation in which each line entered by a user is sent in one TCP segment. The default is to send each character typed in by the user in its own message segment.

As the user types in keystrokes, they are accepted by the terminal driver and transmitted to the Telnet client. The Telnet client typically sends each character data in its own TCP segment. There is a very high protocol overhead in this mode of operation; but for a fast network with sufficient bandwidth, this overhead is not a serious concern if there are only a few Telnet users. The Telnet server sends its response as TCP message segments. The server response contains several characters of data and has a better protocol efficiency than the Telnet client data.

In many implementations, the Telnet server is started by an Internet daemon (super daemon) server that listens for connections on a list of ports defined in its configuration database. When a connection is received for TCP port 23—the well-known port for the Telnet server—the Telnet server process starts to listen on TCP port 23. There may be several instances of the Telnet server program running simultaneously to handle a large number of Telnet clients. Alternatively, a single Telnet server instance that uses multiple threads to handle different Telnet sessions can be used.

In figure 13.12, the Telnet client and server are shown to be running in the user mode. Modern operating systems provide two modes of operation for running a program: *user mode* and *kernel mode.* Most applications run in user mode, where they have restricted access to the computer hardware. This restricted access prevents an error-prone application from crashing the system. Access to operating system services and access to protocols and devices are handled through system calls via the operating system interface. The operating system services and the protocol and device handlers typically run in the kernel mode. In the kernel mode, programs have unrestricted access to the computer's hardware.

If the Telnet client and server run in the user mode and need access to system services such as the TCP/IP protocol, the machine must perform a *context switch* to switch to the kernel mode in which the TCP/IP protocol is running. An operating system context switch involves the execution of several computer cycles and takes up the CPU resources of the computer.

When a character from the terminal is delivered, a context switch takes place from the user mode to the kernel mode to access the operating systems teletype (tty) driver, which runs in the kernel mode. The tty driver passes this character to the Telnet client, which runs in the user mode. Therefore, a context switch has to take place from the kernel mode back to the user mode. When the Telnet client sends the character data to the TCP/IP stack, another context switch takes place because the TCP/IP stack runs in the kernel mode. In this example, three context switches take place for every character sent by the Telnet client machine.

On the server side, a context switch takes place as the received character data is sent up the TCP/IP stack to the Telnet server program. The Telnet server sends character data to the operating system via a pseudoteletype (ptty) interface that involves one or more context switches. With a large number of characters being received by the Telnet server machine, there will be many context switches that add to the processing load on the machine and cause it to slow down. If other applications are running on the Telnet host, they are affected by the Telnet load, also.

The Telnet standard, called STD 8, is defined in the following RFCs:

- RFC 854 on "Telnet Protocol Specification"
- RFC 855 on "Telnet Option Specification"

The NVT Terminal and Format

To accommodate a large variety of terminal hardware and Telnet server capabilities, the Telnet protocol provides for negotiation of parameters. The parameters that are negotiated define a network virtual terminal (NVT) device, as shown in figure 13.13.

Figure 13.13 **Network virtual terminal. (Courtesy Learning Tree)**

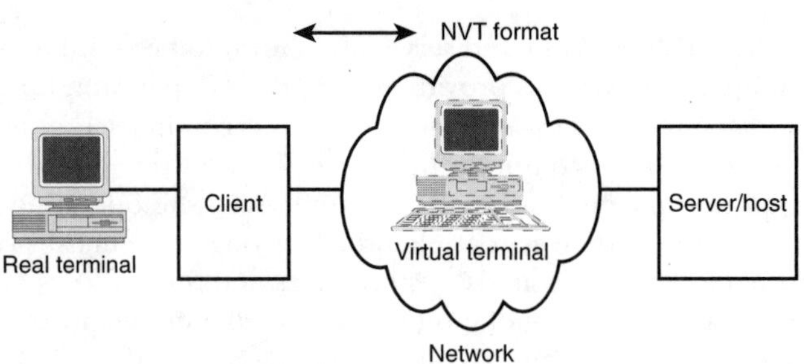

- **Goal: remote login capability**
- **Network Virtual Terminal (NVT) protocol**
  - Defines common language for transferring control and data information
- **Client translates between NVT format and client machine's format**
- **Server translates between NVT format and server machine's format**

The NVT device is associated with a NVT protocol that defines the method for transferring control and data information. Differences in terminal hardware, control, and data information is handled by the NVT device model and the NVT protocol.

The Telnet client translates user keystrokes into a stream of characters in the NVT format. The NVT format handles the encoding of user data and control data. *User data* consists of the letter/digit codes for the keystrokes that are pressed. *Control data* consists of characters to halt a running process (CTRL+C in many systems), erase characters (backspace), erase lines, and so on. The Telnet server accepts the NVT data format and translates it to the local character format for the operating system used at the server. The response sent by the server machine is converted to an NVT data stream by the Telnet server. On receiving the response, the Telnet client converts the NVT data stream to the local character format on the client machine. To summarize,

- The Telnet client translates between the NVT format and the client machine format.
- The Telnet server translates between the NVT format and the server machine format.

The NVT format uses seven-bit US ASCII code for character data and reserves the most significant bit in the character for command sequences. The U.S. ASCII character set includes 95 printable characters, such as letters, digits, punctuation marks, and 33 control codes. Printable characters have the same meaning as in the U.S. ASCII character set. Table 13.10 shows the definitions for some standard control characters.

TABLE 13.10
NVT Control Characters

Name	Code	Meaning
NUL	0	No operation
BEL	7	Produce audible/visible signal
BS	8	Move one position to the left
HT	9	Move right to next horizontal tab
LF	10	Move down (vertically) to the next line
V	T11	Move down to the next vertical tab
FF	12	Move to top of next page
CR	13	Move to beginning of current line

Figure 13.14 shows an NVT format example. The user must type in the following character sequence for a command:

```
cp inpo<bs>ut.doc x
```

Figure 13.14 NVT format example. (Courtesy Learning Tree)

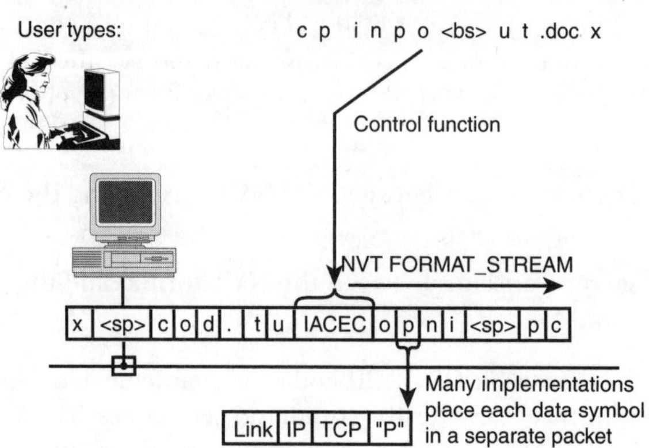
User types:
c p i n p o <bs> u t .doc x
Control function
NVT FORMAT_STREAM
x <sp> c o d . t u IACEC o p n i <sp> p c
Many implementations place each data symbol in a separate packet
Link IP TCP "P"
• Control functions are passed as part of data stream
- Escape sequence is the IAC character followed by command code
IAC = interpret as command ASCII code 255

The *<bs>* represents the backspace character that will erase the last character *o* that was typed incorrectly. The NVT characters that are sent by the Telnet client use the US ASCII representation of these characters and send each character in a separate TCP segment. Notice what happens when the *<bs>* is encountered. It is translated into the following command sequence:

```
IAC EC
```

The IAC means the interpret-as-command character, which has a code value of 255. The EC character is the erase character, which has a code value of 247. Notice that each of these control codes has its most significant bit set to 1.

Telnet Option Negotiation

After a TCP connection is established for the Telnet session, the two sides—Telnet client and server—negotiate the options that will be used for the Telnet session. During Telnet option negotiation, information—such as the terminal type, half- or full-duplex mode, line mode, character mode, and other parameters—is agreed upon by both sides.

The Telnet client sends option requests by using special Telnet codes such as DO, WILL, DON'T, or WON'T. The Telnet server responds with WON'T, DON'T, WILL, or DO. These codes are sent as character codes that begin with the special code of 255, which tells the server to interpret as command (IAC) the character that follows. Special character codes with their most significant bit set to 1 are reserved for the

Telnet option command requests and responses. For example, the code 253 is reserved for a DO command, and the code 253 is reserved for a WON'T command. Therefore, the following character codes have the indicated meanings:

255 253 = IAC DO = DO option indicator

255 252 = IAC DON'T = DON'T option indicator

Figure 13.15 shows the Telnet commands reference list, and table 13.11 shows the code values for some of the Telnet options.

Figure 13.15 Example Telnet command codes. (Courtesy Learning Tree)

TELNET Commands Reference List

IAC (255)		Interpret next octet as command
IAC (255)	DON'T (254)	Sender wants receiver to disable option
IAC (255)	DO (253)	Sender wants receiver to enable option
IAC (255)	WON'T (252)	Sender wants to disable option
IAC (255)	WILL (251)	Sender wants to enable option
IAC (255)	GA (249)	"Go Ahead" signal
IAC (255)	EL (248)	"Erase Line" signal
IAC (255)	EC (247)	"Erase Character" signal
IAC (255)	AYT (246)	"Are You There?" signal
IAC (255)	AO (245)	"Abort Output" signal
IAC (255)	IP (244)	"Interrupt Process" signal
IAC (255)	BRK (243)	"Break Signal"
IAC (255)	DMARK (242)	The datastream portion of the SYNC signal, accompanied by TCP Urgent Notification, causes the data path to be cleared until DMARK character
IAC (255)	NOP (241)	"No Operation" signal
IAC (255)	SB (250)	Start of subnegotiation of indicated option
IAC (255)	SE (240)	End of subnegotiation parameters

TABLE 13.11
Telnet Code Values

Name	Code	RFC#	Meaning
Echo	1	857	Allow receiver to echo data
SGA	3	858	Suppress sending of "Go Ahead" signal at data end
Status	5	859	Request for status of TESNET option from remote side
Timing Mark	6	860	Request that timing mark be inserted in return stream for synchronization
Terminal Type	24	884	Exchange information about terminal type
NAWS	31	1073	Negotiate about window size
Tspeed	32	1079	Send terminal speed information
TFC	33	1080	Terminal (Remote) Flow Control
Linemode	34	1116	Send complete lines instead of individual characters
Xdisploc	35	1096	X Display Location

Berkeley r* Utilities

BSD Unix, as part of its distribution, made available a number of commands called the r commands—or r* utilities. On remote computers, these commands perform such tasks as remote login and remote execution. These commands are designed to provide transparent access to remote computers in a network where the users can be trusted. This situation is particularly true on a university campus, such as the University of California, Berkeley, where students and faculty have accounts on several computers and need transparent access to these accounts. Many other platforms—such as other Unix implementations, VMS, MVS, DOS, NT, and so on—have ported the r* utilities to their operating systems, so these utilities are now widely available.

Table 13.12 shows some of the common "r" commands.

Table 13.12
Berkeley r* Utilities

Command	Meaning
`rlogin`	Similar to Telnet. It allows users to log on to remote computers.
`rexec`	Enables a command to be executed on a remote computer.
`rsh`	Enables the start of a shell (command processor) on a remote computer to execute the specified command.
`rcp`	Permits the copying of files between remote systems or between a remote and a local system.
`rwho`	Displays a list of users who are logged on to the network.
`rwall`	Writes a message to all users on the specified machines.
`ruptime`	Displays computers on the network, their load, number of users, and the up time of each machine.

The upcoming sections provide details of the more common Berkeley r* commands.

The rlogin Command

The rlogin command does not have the same level of negotiation utilities as Telnet and, therefore, the remote host must either know or be configured to accept the terminal type of the user requesting the logon. Some rlogin implementations export the local user environment to the remote machine as part of the login session.

The transparent access of the r* utilities is implemented on the notion of trust. For a user to have transparent access to a host, the user computer's IP address must be placed on either of the following files on the remote computer:

- **hosts.equiv file.** On Unix systems, this file is kept in the /etc directory. This file enables hosts listed in it to be *trusted*, which means that these hosts have transparent access to the remote host.
- **.rhosts file.** A user can use this file to enable users on other computers to use the user's login name.

Along with the host name or IP address in the hosts.equiv and .rhosts files, the list of users that have transparent access on the machine can also be specified. If users are not explicitly listed, all users on the listed machine are given transparent access. Details of the use of these files and their contents may differ from system to system, so you should consult the host's documentation on using these commands.

On Unix systems, the /etc/passwd file that contains a list of valid user accounts is also used to verify that the user has an account on the system.

Typically, a user will issue a command, such as rlogin, by specifying the name of the remote host, as follows:

```
rlogin hostname
```

There is no need to supply the user name and password because the user is authenticated by the rlogin server (called *rlogind* and pronounced as *rlogin-dee* on Unix systems). The rlogin server runs on the remote system that checks the hosts.equiv, .rhosts, and /etc/passwd (for Unix system) files (see fig. 13.16).

Figure 13.16 Example of rlogin usage.

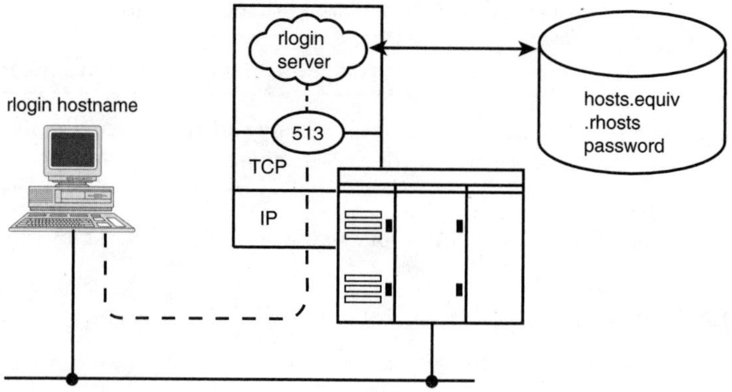

The rsh Utility

The rsh command can be used to run a command on the remote computer and return the results back. For example, the following rsh command runs the specified command *ps -a* on the remote computer rama.kinetics.com and sends the results back to the local computer:

```
rsh rama.kinetics.com ps -a
```

The r* utilities understand the environments on both machines, and they understand the file system notions of *standard input, standard output,* and *standard error* that are supported on many operating systems other than Unix. Thus, it is possible to save the output of the preceding rsh command in a local file by using the following command:

```
rsh rama.kinetics.com ps -a > local_file
```

The rcp Utility

The rcp utility can be used to copy files between two remote systems or between a remote and a local system. Remote files are referenced by using the following syntax:

```
hostname:pathname
```

The *hostname* specifies the name of the host (or its IP address) that contains the file with the *pathname.*

The following command copies a file from the remote system rama.kinetics.com to a local file:

```
rcp rama.kinetics.com:/etc/passwd passwd.loc
```

The following command copies a file from the remote system rama.kinetics.com to the remote system kama.kinetics.com:

```
rcp rama.kinetics.com:/etc/ftpusers kama.kinetics.com:/ftpusers
```

Security Concerns with Berkeley r* Utilities

The problem with transparent access is that if an intruder gains access to the critical files that contain the host names of the trusted machines, a user can gain access to the system by modifying these files.

Some r* implementations do not work with IP addresses but only with domain names. This extra security ensures that the computers are at least registered in DNS. Intruders attempting to gain access to the system must at least register themselves as part of the DNS, which increases their exposure to detection.

Many non-Unix r* implementations prompt the user for a local password before running the r command. However, the valid passwords are stored in a local file. If this file can be stolen by the intruder, the file can be used to gain access to the remote system.

File Access Protocols

Data on most systems is represented in units called *files.* A file on a system has the following attributes: the file name; the time stamp on which it was created, last modified, and last accessed; the size of the file; and other details that are operating-system dependent.

Data transfer between systems usually involves transfer of a file or a portion of a file.

The TCP/IP application services provide the following two standard protocols for transferring the complete contents of files between systems: the File Transfer Protocol (FTP) and the Trivial File Transfer Protocol (TFTP).

For direct access to files, where a remote file system appears as a part of the local file system, another standard protocol called NFS (Network File System) can be used.

These protocols are discussed in the following sections.

File Transfer Protocol (FTP)

FTP uses TCP to transfer files between two systems across an IP network. There are two components in an FTP implementation: FTP client and FTP server. Figure 13.17 shows the FTP operation model.

Figure 13.17 FTP operation model. (Courtesy Learning Tree)

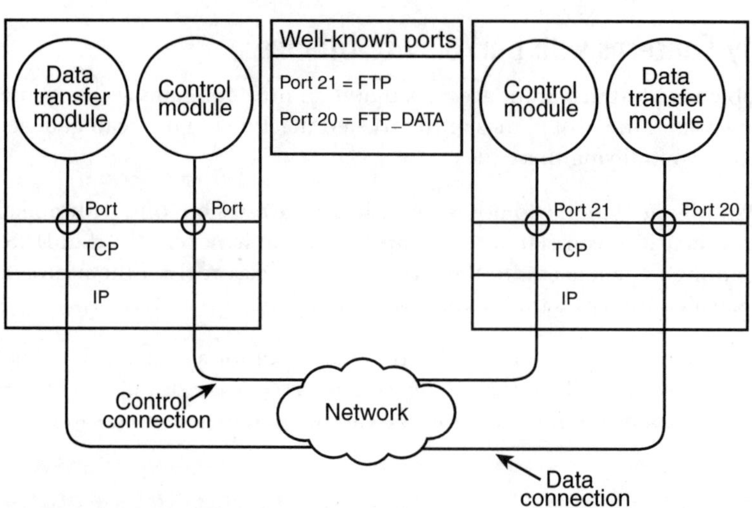

- **Control connection**
  - Created when connection to FTP server is established
  - Used for FTP commands/replies only
- **Data transfer connection**
  - Created on demand for each data transfer
  - Destroyed on end of each data transfer

The FTP client runs on the user's machine and initiates connections to the FTP server. The FTP server listens on the well-known TCP port 21 and waits for connection requests. When a connection request is received, a three-way handshake ensues to establish a TCP connection. This TCP connection is called the *control connection,* and it is used for sending FTP commands and responses. When the FTP client issues a command to start a data transfer, the client starts a data transfer process on the client side on a local TCP port number. This local TCP port number is sent to the FTP server through the control connection. When the FTP server receives the port number of the data process on the FTP client, the server starts a data process on the well-known TCP port 20 that issues a TCP connection request to connect with the data process port number on the FTP client. This connection is called the *data connection*, and it is used only for transferring data from the requested files. FTP permits both download and upload of files to the FTP server. These files are sent through the data connection. In summary, the following two FTP connections are created in an FTP session:

- Control connection: (TCP, FTP_CLIENT_IP, CLIENT_PORT1, FTP_SERVER_IP, 21)
- Data Connection: (TCP, FTP_CLIENT_IP, CLIENT_PORT2, FTP_SERVER_IP, 20)

The data connection exists only for the duration of the file transfer and is closed after the data transfer is completed. A new data connection is opened every time a file is transferred. The FTP connection remains open until the user or FTP server closes the connection. Typically, the FTP session is closed by the FTP user, but an FTP server may also close a connection in situations of overload at the FTP server or some other problem with the FTP server.

In the FTP operation model, the data process is shown to be created as a separate process. This separate process may not be the case in situations where FTP is run on a limited operating system that does not provide the facility for creating multiple processes or when FTP is run in an embedded system without operating system support. In this case, a single monolithic program or process is used to implement each FTP component. Regardless of how the FTP client and FTP server executing environments are managed, the FTP protocol requires that two TCP connections be used: one for the control connection and the other for the data connection.

The FTP standard is described in RFC 959 (STD 9) on "File Transfer Protocol." The upcoming sections describe the structure of the FTP command and give examples of its usage.

FTP Commands

The control commands sent on the FTP connection use the data format used in a Telnet session. Recall that Telnet uses the NVT format for sending data. The FTP control connection does not use all the capabilities of the NVT format; it uses only a subset of these capabilities. Specifically, FTP does not use the NVT commands for option negotiation.

The FTP control commands are sent as a four-letter character string followed by optional arguments. These commands and their meanings are outlined in table 13.13.

TABLE 13.13
FTP Control Commands

Control Command	Meaning
USER **uname**	Specifies the user name of the user starting the FTP session.
PASS **password**	Specifies the password for the user name specified by the USER command.
ACCT **account**	Specifies additional accounting information after a successful PASS command. This command is optional.
CWD **directory**	Specifies that the current working directory at the server be changed to the one specified in the command.
CDUP	Specifies that the current working directory at the server be changed to the parent directory.
SMNT **path**	Specifies that a different file system data structure be mounted without altering the login or password information.
REIN	Reinitializes the user session information. Session information is set to the default. A USER command is expected to follow.
QUIT	Terminates the FTP session.
PORT h1, h2, h3, h4, p1, p2	Specifies the TCP end point information. Used to identify the data process port number for the FTP client to the FTP server. h1, h2, h3, and h4 are the numbers in the dotted-decimal notation for the client's IP address. p1 and p2 are the numbers in the dotted-decimal notation for the data process port number.
PASV	Specifies that the FTP server listen for the data connection to be issued by the FTP client. Response to this command is the TCP end point on which the server is listening.

Control Command	Meaning
TYPE **code**	Specifies the data representation type.
STRU **code**	Specifies the file structure. Example: file, record, page.
MODE **code**	Specifies the transfer mode. Example: stream, block, compressed.
RETR **path**	Used to retrieve the specified file.
STO **path**	Used to store the specified file at the FTP server.
STOU **path**	Similar to STO except that the resultant file to be created must have a name unique to that directory.
APPE **path**	Similar to STO except that if the file name exists, the data must be appended to the file.
ALLO **arguments**	Used to allocate storage space for the file at the server.
REST **argument**	Used to specify the server marker at which the file transfer is to be restarted. Used to position to the specified data point.
RNFR **path**	Specifies the old pathname that is to be renamed. Must be followed by the RNTO command.
RNTO **path**	Specifies the pathname of the new file. Must be preceded by the RNTO command.
ABOR	Specifies that the FTP server should abort the preceding command.
DELE **path**	The specified file is to be deleted.
RMD **directory**	The specified directory should be deleted.
MKD **directory**	The specified directory should be created.
PWD	Print Working Directory. Returns the name of the current working directory at the FTP server.
LIST **[directory]**	Causes the list of files and their attributes for the specified directory to be returned. If the directory argument is not specified, the current directory is assumed.

continues

Table 13.13, Continued
FTP Control Commands

Control Command	Meaning
`NLST [directory]`	Name List. Causes only the list of file names for the specified directory to be returned. Other file attributes are not returned. If the directory argument is not specified, the current directory is assumed. Used in the implementation of the FTP user command MGET.
`SITE parameters`	Used to specify site specific commands to the FTP server.
`SYST`	Used to find out the type of operating system at the FTP server.
`STAT [path]`	Used to return status information on files or the FTP transfer.
`HELP [command]`	Used to obtain help for a command; when no argument is specified, a list of commands is implemented at the server.
`NOOP`	No Operation. Causes the FTP server to send a reply.

In response to the FTP commands, the FTP server returns a three-digit reply code followed by a space and optional text message, as follows:

```
ddd Text Message
```

ddd represents the three-digit response code.

As an example, the FTP server may reply with the following code:

```
200 Command okay.
```

Table 13.14 lists some command response codes and their meanings that are returned by the FTP server.

Table 13.14
FTP Server Response Codes and Their Meanings

200 Command okay.
500 Syntax error, command unrecognized.
501 Syntax error in parameters or arguments.

202 Command not implemented, superfluous at this site.
502 Command not implemented.
503 Bad sequence of commands.
504 Command not implemented for that parameter.
110 Restart marker reply.
211 System status, or system help reply.
212 Directory status.
213 File status.
214 Help message.
215 *NAME* system type.
120 Service ready in nnn minutes.
220 Service ready for new user.
221 Service closing control connection.
421 Service not available, closing control connection.
125 Data connection already open; transfer starting.
225 Data connection open; no transfer in progress.
425 Can't open data connection.
226 Closing data connection.
426 Connection closed; transfer aborted.
227 Entering Passive Mode (h1,h2,h3,h4,p1,p2).
230 User logged in, proceed.
530 Not logged in.
331 User name okay, need password.
332 Need account for login.

continues

Table 13.14, Continued
FTP Server Response Codes and Their Meanings

532 Need account for storing files.
110 Restart marker reply.
120 Service ready in nnn minutes.
125 Data connection already open; transfer starting.
150 File status okay; about to open data connection.
200 Command okay.
202 Command not implemented, superfluous at this site.
250 Requested file action okay, completed.
257 "PATHNAME" created.
350 Requested file action pending further information.
450 Requested file action not taken.
451 Requested action aborted: local error in processing.
452 Requested action not taken.
550 Requested action not taken.
551 Requested action aborted: page type unknown.
552 Requested file action aborted.
553 Requested action not taken.

FTP from a User Perspective

FTP enables the user to interactively access files and directories on remote hosts and to perform directory operations such as the following:

- Listing of files in a remote or local directory
- Renaming and deleting of files (if you have permission)
- Transferring files from remote host to local host (downloading)
- Transferring files from local host to remote host (uploading)

In general, to use FTP or any other TCP/IP application service, you must have a client version of these applications. These client TCP/IP applications are available on a large variety of platforms. Some platforms have a graphical user interface (GUI), while others are command-line driven. From an educational viewpoint, it is better to discuss the command-line interface because you can more readily see the correspondence between the FTP user command and the FTP internal commands listed in table 13.13.

To start an FTP session, you can use the following command:

```
ftp [hostname]
```

The *hostname* is the symbolic name or IP address of the host that you are logging on to. If the *hostname* is left out, you can issue a number of FTP commands. If you type the help command or a question mark (?), you can obtain help on the FTP commands. The following listing outlines some of the FTP commands available while you are logged on to a host named INTERNIC.NET:

```
ftp> ?
Commands may be abbreviated. Commands are:

!          cr          macdef     proxy       send
$          delete      mdelete    sendport    status
account    debug       mdir       put         struct
append     dir         mget       pwd         sunique
ascii      disconnect  mkdir      quit        tenex
bell       form        mls        quote       trace
binary     get         mode       recv        type
bye        glob        mput       remotehelp  user
case       hash        nmap       rename      verbose
cd         help        ntrans     reset       ?
cdup       lcd         open       rmdir
close      ls          prompt     runique
```

If you want to perform an FTP session to the host INTERNIC.NET, you would use the following command:

```
ftp INTERNIC.NET
```

If you know the IP address of the host—for example, the FTP server for Novell—you can use the following command:

```
ftp 137.65.4.1
```

It is important to realize that you must specify a user name and a password to log into an FTP host. The FTP server uses the FTP host's underlying authentication mechanism to verify the privileges an FTP user should have. Therefore, if you have a user account with the name of Bob on the computer acting as the FTP host, you can log in as user Bob and use the same password that you would normally use to log on to that computer's native operating system.

Many FTP hosts provide *anonymous* logins. Then if you were to specify the user name as *anonymous* and the password as *guest* (some computers expect an e-mail address containing the @ character), you can log in to the FTP host with a limited set of privileges determined by the system administrator of the FTP host.

The following example is a short guided tour of an FTP session to an FTP server.

1. Enter the FTP command and supply the name of the host.

   ```
   % ftp internic.net
   ```

   The % in the preceding command is the default Unix prompt.

2. If the host is reachable, you will see a message similar to the following. Details of the sign-on messages may differ.

   ```
   Connected to internic.net.
   220-*****Welcome to the InterNIC Registration Host *****
   *****Login with username "anonymous" and password "guest"
   *****You may change directories to the following:
   policy    - Registration Policies
   templates    - Registration Templates
   netinfo    - NIC Information Files
   domain    - Root Domain Zone Files
   220 And more!
   Name (internic.net:karanjit):
   ```

   As the message indicates, you can log in as the user *anonymous* with password *guest*.

3. Supply the user name and password.

   ```
   Name (internic.net:karanjit): anonymous
   331 Guest login ok, send "guest" as password.
   Password:guest
   230 Guest login ok, access restrictions apply.ftp>
   ```

4. After you are logged in, you can use the ? or help command:

   ```
   ftp>?
   ```

   Commands may be abbreviated. Commands are listed earlier in this section.

5. The command to see your current directory on the FTP host is *pwd.*

```
ftp> pwd
257 "/" is current directory.
```

The status of each FTP command is returned as a numeric code, such as 257, and a text message accompanying it.

6. To see a listing of files in the current directory, use the *ls* or *DIR* command.

```
ftp> ls
200 PORT command successful.
150 Opening ASCII mode data connection for file list.
bin
usr
dev
etc
pub
policy
templates
home
netinfo
domain
ls-ltR
netprog
archives
rfc
226 Transfer complete.
99 bytes received in 0.04 seconds (2.4 Kbytes/s)
```

The preceding list just lists the files and does not give information about the size of a file or whether it is a directory. To see this information, it is preferable to use the *DIR* command as follows:

```
ftp> dir
200 PORT command successful.
150 Opening ASCII mode data connection for /bin/ls.
total 22
drwxr-xr-x 2 root  1    512 Mar 22 21:40 archives
dr-xr-xr-x 2 root  1    512 Feb 25 1993 bin
drwxr-xr-x 2 root  1    512 Mar 9 1993 dev
drwxr-xr-x 2 root  1    512 Apr 1 1993 domain
dr-xr-xr-x 2 root  1    512 Feb 25 1993 etc
drwxr-xr-x 2 root  1    512 Mar 9 1993 home
-rw-r--r-- 1 root  1   9035 May 4 19:12 ls-ltR
drwxr-xr-x 2 root  1   1024 Apr 14 14:57 netinfo
```

```
drwxr-xr-x 2 root  1    512 Apr  1 1993 netprog
drwxr-xr-x 2 root  1   1024 May  4 19:11 policy
drwxr-xr-x 4 root  1    512 Apr 20 15:01 pub
lrwxrwxrwx 1 root  1    6 Aug 9 1993 rfc -> policy
drwxr-xr-x 2 root  1    512 May  3 19:54 templates
drwxr-xr-x 3 root  1    512 Feb 25 1993 usr
226 Transfer complete.
875 bytes received in 0.25 seconds (3.4 Kbytes/s)
```

The information is reported in the Unix-style listing format because you are logged on to a Unix system.

7. If you know that you are logged on to a Unix system acting as an FTP server, you can use the following useful trick.

   If you use the *ls* command, the Unix *ls* command is executed. You can supply to the *ls* command any of the Unix options, such as the *-lR* option, that give a recursive long-form listing of files in subdirectories. You should realize that the *-lR* option is not a part of the standard FTP commands and will work only for Unix FTP servers or those FTP servers that emulate this behavior. The following example shows the output of *the ls -lR* command. You can use this command to get a quick overview of the files that are available on the FTP host:

```
ftp> ls -lR
200 PORT command successful.
150 Opening ASCII mode data connection for /bin/ls.
total 22
drwxr-xr-x 2 root   512 Mar 22 21:40 archives
dr-xr-xr-x 2 root   512 Feb 25 1993 bin
drwxr-xr-x 2 root   512 Mar 9 1993 dev
drwxr-xr-x 2 root   512 Apr 1 1993 domain
dr-xr-xr-x 2 root   512 Feb 25 1993 etc
drwxr-xr-x 2 root   512 Mar 9 1993 home
-rw-r--r-- 1 root   9035 May 4 19:12 ls-ltR
drwxr-xr-x 2 root   1024 Apr 14 14:57 netinfo
drwxr-xr-x 2 root   512 Apr 1 1993 netprog
drwxr-xr-x 2 root   1024 May 4 19:11 policy
drwxr-xr-x 4 root   512 Apr 20 15:01 pub
lrwxrwxrwx 1 root   6 Aug 9 1993 rfc -> policy
drwxr-xr-x 2 root   512 May 3 19:54 templates
drwxr-xr-x 3 root   512 Feb 25 1993 usr
     :
  (and more output)
       :
usr/lib:
```

```
total 576
-r-xr-xr-x 1 root  40960 Feb 25 1993 ld.so
-rwxr-xr-x 1 root  516096 Feb 25 1993 libc.so.1.8
-rwxr-xr-x 1 root  24576 Feb 25 1993 libdl.so.1.0
226 Transfer complete.
remote: -lR
9228 bytes received in 1.2 seconds (7.5 Kbytes/s)
```

8. To change your directory to a particular directory, such as *rfc,* use the *CD* command:

```
ftp> cd rfc
250 CWD command successful.
```

9. To see a listing of the files in the */rfc* directory, use *ls* or *DIR,* as follows:

```
ftp> ls
200 PORT command successful.
150 Opening ASCII mode data connection for file list.
asn.index
domain.index
index
master.index
network.index
rfc1009.txt
rfc1011.txt
rfc1031.txt
        :
 (and more output)
        :
226 Transfer complete.
496 bytes received in 0.045 seconds (11 Kbytes/s)
```

10. If you try to get a file that does not exist, such as the file rfc1365.txt, FTP will indicate this as follows:

```
ftp> get rfc1365.txt
200 PORT command successful.
550 rfc1365.txt: No such file or directory.
```

11. To copy a file from the FTP server to the local host, the FTP command is the following:

```
get remotefile [localfile]
```

In this command, *remotefile* is the name of the file on the remote host and *localfile* is the name of the file on the local machine. If *localfile* is not specified, the local file is given the same name as the remote file.

For text files, FTP performs the proper carriage-return-to-carriage-return/linefeed conversions between different operating systems if the transfer mode is ascii. To use the transfer mode of ascii, use the FTP *ascii* command. To transfer binary files, use the *image* or *binary* command to disable carriage-return/linefeed conversions.

The following shows the FTP *GET* command:

```
ftp> get rfc1400.txt
200 PORT command successful.
150 Opening ASCII mode data connection for rfc1400.txt (13009 bytes).
226 Transfer complete.
local: rfc1400.txt remote: rfc1400.txt
13404 bytes received in 0.78 seconds (17 Kbytes/s)
```

12. To close the current FTP connection, use the *close* command:

```
ftp> close
221 Goodbye.
ftp>
```

13. To exit out of FTP completely, use the *BYE* command. This command will also close existing FTP connections before exiting FTP:

```
ftp> bye
%
```

Trivial File Transfer Protocol (TFTP)

TFTP uses the UDP protocol as its transport protocol. Because UDP does not guarantee data delivery, TFTP must perform its own error connection. TFTP uses a simple PAR (Positive Acknowledgment Retransmission) scheme for error correction. TFTP defines acknowledgment messages that are used to acknowledge receipt of data. If an acknowledgment message is not received in a specified time-out period, the data packet is retransmitted.

TFTP was designed for its simplicity and for the small code size required for its implementation. TFTP's small code size permits the protocol to be implemented in the bootstrap ROMs of many workstations. TFTP is often used in connection with BOOTP. BOOTP is used to obtain configuration information from a BOOTP server, and TFTP is used to download an operating system image.

The TFTP standard is described in RFC 1350 on "The TFTP Protocol (Revision 2)" and updated by RFCs 1782, 1783, 1784, and 1785.

The following two sections discuss TFTP in greater detail by first exploring its message format and then its operation.

TFTP Message Format

TFTP defines five types of messages. These message types are listed in table 13.15.

Table 13.15
TFTP Message Types

Operation Code	Description
1	Read request (RRQ)
2	Write request (WRQ)
3	Data (DATA)
4	Acknowledgment (ACK)
5	Error (ERROR)

The TFTP client sends an initial read (RRQ) or write (WRQ) request message (see fig. 13.18) to UDP port 69 on a TFTP server. The TFTP server listens for read/write requests on this port.

Figure 13.18 TFTP client/server interaction. (Courtesy Learning Tree)

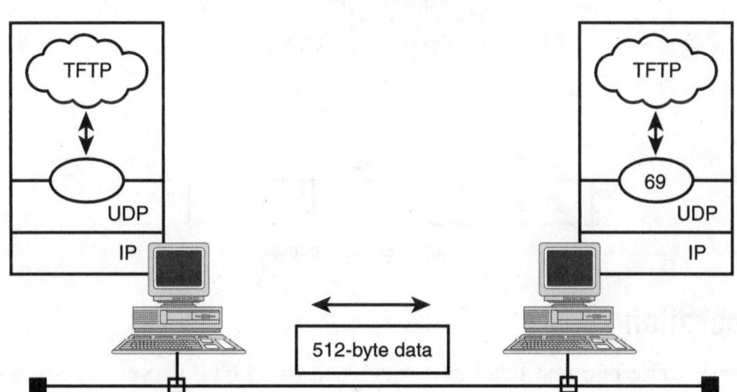

- **Trivial File Transfer Protocol (TFTP)**
  - Runs on top of UDP and is simpler than FTP
    - TFTP provides its own error management
  - Does not provide authentication
  - Easily implemented in Read-Only Memory (ROM)
    - Ideal for diskless workstations

The format of read and write requests is shown in figure 13.19. All TFTP messages have an Opcode field whose values and meanings are listed in table 13.15. The read and write request messages have filename and mode of operation fields. The filename field is a string of characters terminated by null (zero value) octets. The mode field is used to specify the different types of files that can be transferred. Its values can be NETASCII, BINARY or MAIL and are terminated by null (zero value) octets. Because both filename and mode fields are terminated by null octets, they can be variable in size because the null octets mark the end of these fields.

Figure 13.19 TFTP message formats.

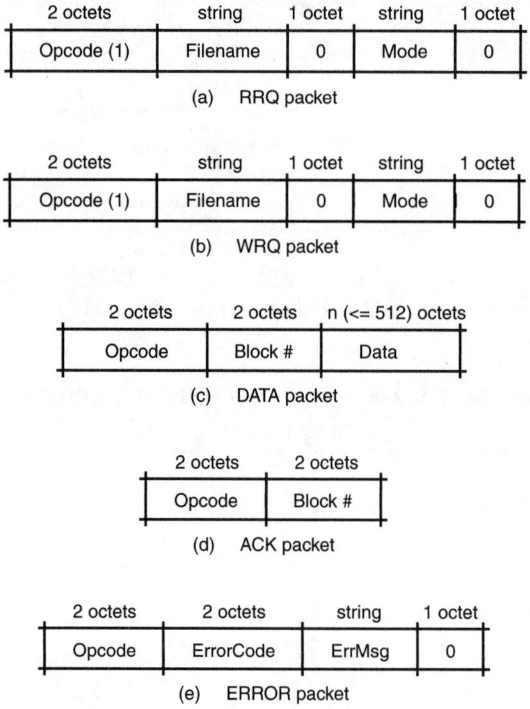

2 octets	string	1 octet	string	1 octet
Opcode (1)	Filename	0	Mode	0

(a) RRQ packet

2 octets	string	1 octet	string	1 octet
Opcode (1)	Filename	0	Mode	0

(b) WRQ packet

2 octets	2 octets	n (<= 512) octets
Opcode	Block #	Data

(c) DATA packet

2 octets	2 octets
Opcode	Block #

(d) ACK packet

2 octets	2 octets	string	1 octet
Opcode	ErrorCode	ErrMsg	0

(e) ERROR packet

TFTP Operation

After a read/write request has been received, the TFTP server registers the IP address and port number of the client. In subsequent responses sent to the TFTP client, the TFTP server uses the client IP address and port number. The read/write request message is acknowledged and followed by data messages and their acknowledgments. TFTP sends messages in 512 octet-size blocks. A data block of a size less than 512 octets signals the end of data transmission. If the file size is an exact multiple of 512 octets, an extra data message with zero size is sent. Data blocks are numbered sequentially. Data and Acknowledgment messages include a field that contains the block number of the data being transmitted. Figure 13.20 shows a TFTP transmission where a write message has been issued by a TFTP client.

Figure 13.20 Example TFTP transaction. (Courtesy Learning Tree)

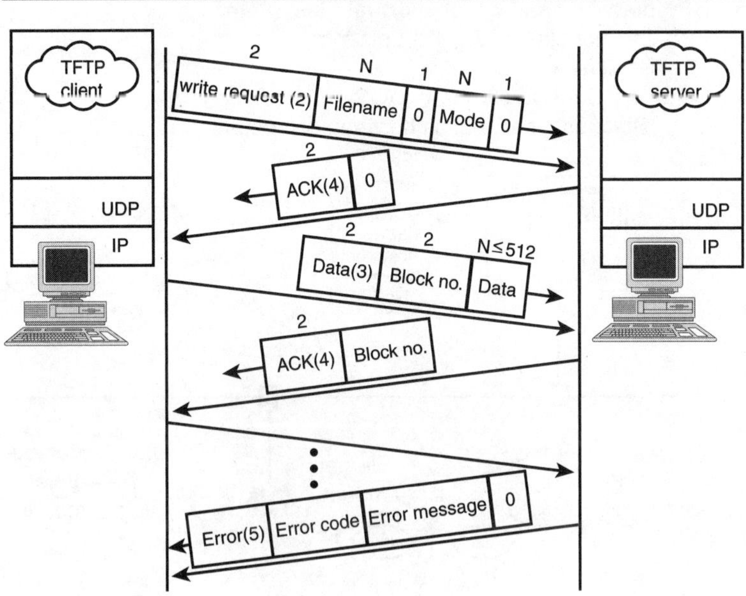

- **Only five TFTP message types are defined**
- **Data block of size < 512 signals end of data**

TFTP can be used to transfer files between hosts without requiring user authentication. Files can be transferred by just specifying the file name. Because a user account and a password are not required for transferring files in TFTP, many system administrators disable TFTP on their systems or restrict the types of files that can be transferred. Implementations can also deny access to a file unless every user on the host can access the file.

Network File System Protocol

Network File System (NFS) is a file-service protocol originally developed by SUN Microsystems and licensed to a large number of vendors. NFS enables a computer on which the NFS server software is running to *export* its file systems to other clients. *Exporting* a file system means that it is made available to clients on a variety of different operating system platforms as long as they are running the NFS client software.

Figure 13.21 shows that the NFS server is exporting the /users directory. This exported directory can be accessed simultaneously by clients running different operating systems.

Figure 13.21 Using NFS. (Courtesy Learning Tree)

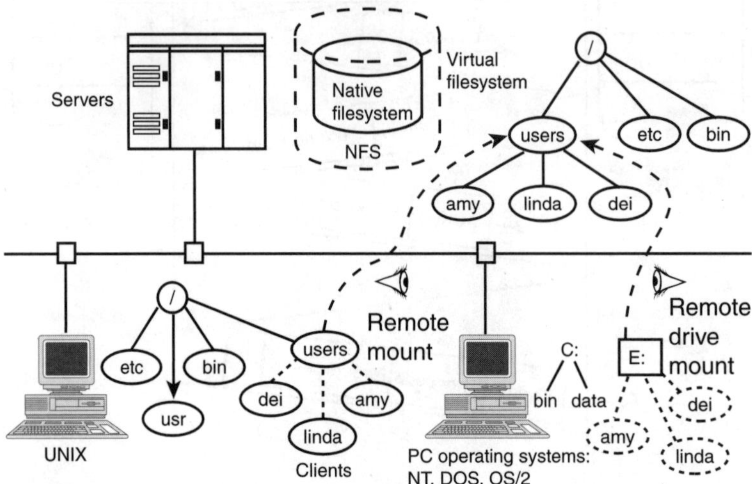

Each NFS client views the file system exported by the NFS server in the environment of the client's native file system. For example, a PC DOS NFS client will access the exported file system through a network-drive letter assignment, and a Unix NFS client will see the exported file system as being linked to its local file system.

The following sections discuss the different NFS versions and the NFS protocols.

NFS Versions

NFS consists of a number of protocols that act together to implement a transparent file system. NFS was developed by SUN Microsystems in the early 1980s and has been licensed to over 200 vendors. The NFS protocol is documented in RFC 1094 on "NFS: Network File System Protocol Specification."

The original NFS protocol as documented in RFC 1094 was designed to use UDP as the transport protocol. The UDP transport protocol was used in NFS versions 1 and 2. The use of UDP is optimized for LANs but has some disadvantages when used on WANs. NFS version 2 supported TCP, but there was an overhead associated with using TCP because its use was not optimized.

More recent advances in NFS version 3 permit NFS to run on top of TCP. NFS version 3 is designed to run on TCP and is better suited for WAN usage, which is more error prone and has a wide variation in time delays. NFS version 3 removed the arbitrary 8 KB size transfer limit of NFS version 2.

NFS version 3 is required by Web NFS, a new protocol that enables Web browsers to access NFS servers. NFS version 3 is documented in RFC 1813 on "NFS Version 3 Protocol Specification."

NFS Protocols

The NFS application service is implemented by a set of upper-layer NFS protocols. Figure 13.22 shows the different NFS protocols. At the Data Link and Physical layers of the OSI, NFS supports the wide variety of technologies that are available. At the Network layer, NFS uses IP. At the Transport layer, NFS uses UDP or TCP. When NFS is used over UDP, it is highly recommended that the optional UDP checksum be used.

Figure 13.22 The NFS protocols. (Courtesy Learning Tree)

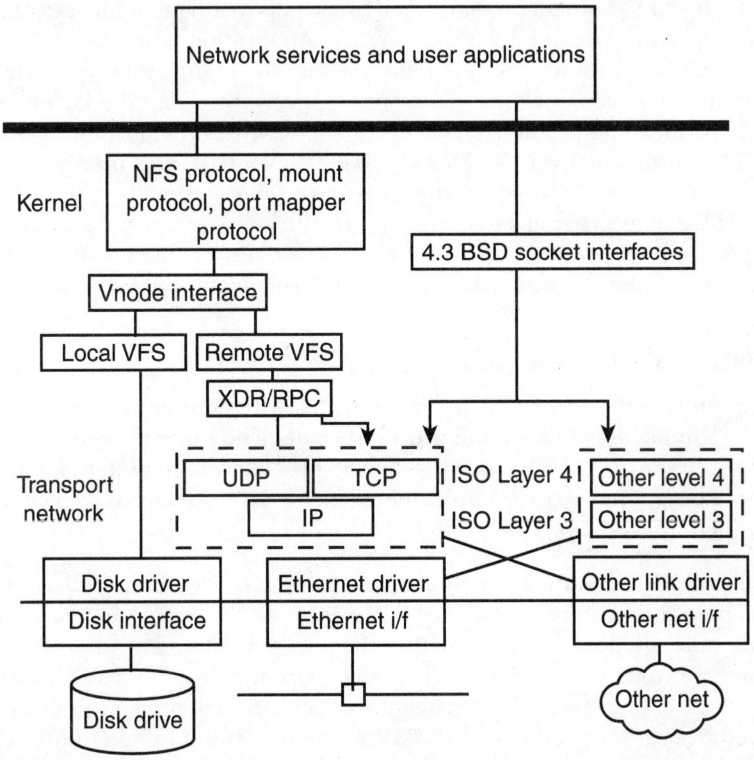

At the Session layer of the OSI model, NFS uses the Remote Procedure Call (RPC) protocol. Several RPC protocols that are quite different from each other exist, yet they are all called RPC. NFS's RPC is often called Sun-RPC to distinguish it from other RPC protocols. RPC enables NFS services at the server to be accessed by using the procedure call paradigm, which is familiar to programmers. RPC provides a high-level access to NFS services without getting involved with details of communications protocols. Programmers that use RPC do not have to be communications experts to use the networking services that can be accessed by using RPC. The Sun-RPC protocol is documented in RFC 1057 on "RPC: Remote Procedure Call Protocol Specification version 2."

At the Presentation layer of the OSI model, NFS uses the External Data Representation (XDR) protocol. The XDR provides a uniform way of representing data. For example, number data is represented by using 2's complement notation. If a system uses a different number representation, conversion is done by XDR. The XDR protocol is documented in RFC 1832 on "XDR: External Data Representation Standard."

At the Application layer of the OSI model, NFS uses the Network File System (NFS) protocol. The NFS protocol provides such services as writing to a file, creating a file, reading a file, and so on at the NFS server. The Application layer also consists of a number of support protocols for NFS, such as the *Mount* and *Portmapper* protocol. The Mount protocol implements the NFS mounting procedure, and the Portmapper protocol provides clients that need access to a service with the port number for the service. The Portmapper protocol uses the well-known UDP port number 111. An NFS client that wants to access a particular service sends a request to the UDP port number 111. Server programs that want to provide a service register with the Portmapper. On receiving a request for a registered service, the Portmapper responds with the port number of the service to which the requests should be sent.

NFS Remote Procedure Calls

NFS communication between client and server uses the Remote Procedure Call model. NFS implements 18 remote procedure calls. The software code for these 18 procedures resides at the NFS server. The NFS procedures are used by NFS clients to access the network file services implemented by the NFS server. An NFS client accesses these procedures through the RPC mechanism.

The RPC protocol contains a program number and a procedure number. The program number identifies the service being accessed. For example, the NFS service has a program number of 100003. Within the program, there are 18 procedures that are numbered from 0 to 17. For instance, the procedure number 6 deals with the reading of a file. An NFS client that needs to read a file will send an RPC request that contains the program number of 100003 and the procedure number of 6 (see fig. 13.23). Other parameters for the read operation will also have to be supplied in the NFS client's RPC request packet.

Figure 13.23 Example RPC call.

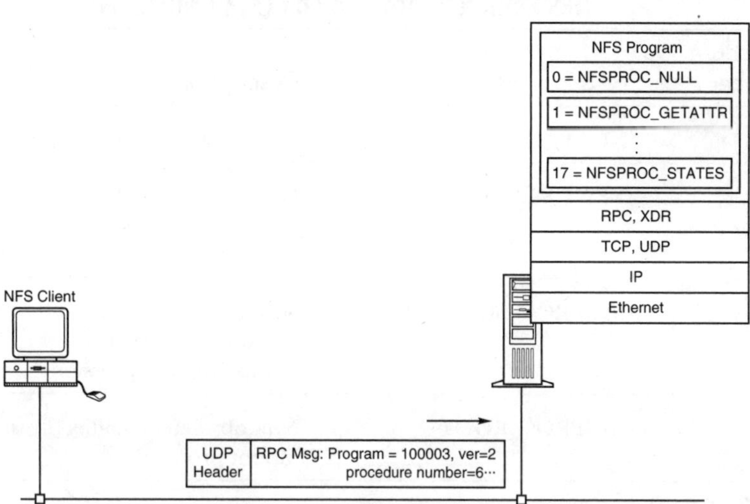

The RPC request also specifies the version number of the program that should provide the service. All programs that advertise their services have a version number. The version number allows a graceful way of enabling old and new versions of a program service to coexist. This coexistence enables existing NFS clients that use the older service to be supported, while newer NFS clients can access the newer (and hopefully better) version of the program.

Table 13.16 lists the different procedure numbers for the NFS program and a brief description of their meanings. The NFS_PROC, procedure 0, is described as a *do-nothing procedure.* In all programs, procedure number 0 does nothing. In actual fact, it does more than nothing. If an RPC request is sent to procedure number 0, the procedure number simply returns the request back to the sender. In other words, procedure number 0 acts as a simple echo service. Many NFS clients use this echo feature as the basis for providing a diagnostic utility called *nfsping,* which does what the name suggests. When the host name or IP address is supplied as a parameter to the nfsping utility, it sends an echo request to procedure number 0 for the NFS program and awaits a reply. The following is the syntax for using nfsping:

nfsping *hostname*

If the NFS service is active at the host, a reply will be received; otherwise, you can conclude that the service is not available or that the host is unreachable.

TABLE 13.16
NFS Remote Procedure Call (RPC) Numbers

Procedure Number	NFS Procedure	Description
0	NFS_PROC	Does nothing; diagnostic check
1	NFS_GETATTR	Gets attributes of file/directory, such as owner and group owner permissions
2	NFSPROC_SETATTR	Sets the attribute of a file/directory, such as owner and group owner permissions
3	NFSPROC_ROOT	Now obsolete; Handled by the Mount protocol
4	NFSPROC_LOOKUP	Obtains a file handle to a file in a specific directory
5	NFSPROC_READLINK	Reads contents of a symbolic link
6	NFSPROC_READ	Reads from a file
7	NFSPROC_WRITECACHE	Used in NFS version 3 to write to cache
8	NFSPPROC_WRITE	Writes to a file
9	NFSPROC_CREATE	Creates a file
10	NFSPROC_REMOVE	Removes a directory entry from a directory
11	NFSPROC_RENAME	Renames a file
12	NFSPROC_LINK	Creates a hard link to a file
13	NFSPROC_SYMLINK	Creates a symbolic link to a file
14	NFSPROC_MKDIR	Creates a directory
15	NFSPROC_RMDIR	Removes a directory

Procedure Number	NFS Procedure	Description
16	NFSPROC_READDIR	Reads a directory
17	NFSPROC_STATFS	Gets the file system attributes

Web NFS

The Web NFS protocol is designed to enable web browsers to access NFS servers across the Internet. The Web NFS protocol requires the use of NFS version 3, which supports TCP connections and uses public handles.

In NFS, a *handle* is an internal data structure that is created by the NFS server when a Mount request is made by using the Mount NFS protocol. The Mount NFS protocol relies on RPC for communication between the NFS client and server. The handle is returned when the Mount daemon (a Unix term for an independent process) that runs at the NFS server mounts the requested file system. The mounting process involves verifying whether the Mount request is permitted for the user and initializing data structures with information about accessing the requested file system. The returned handle is then used in all subsequent operations for accessing the file system.

A public handle is a specially reserved file system handle that is used as an initial file-system handle by web browsers. The use of a public handle makes it possible for a web browser to access a file system at a NFS server without having to issue a NFS Mount command.

Figure 13.24 shows the use of Web NFS. The Web NFS server listens on TCP port 2049 for requests from web clients.

Figure 13.24 Web NFS. (Courtesy Learning Tree)

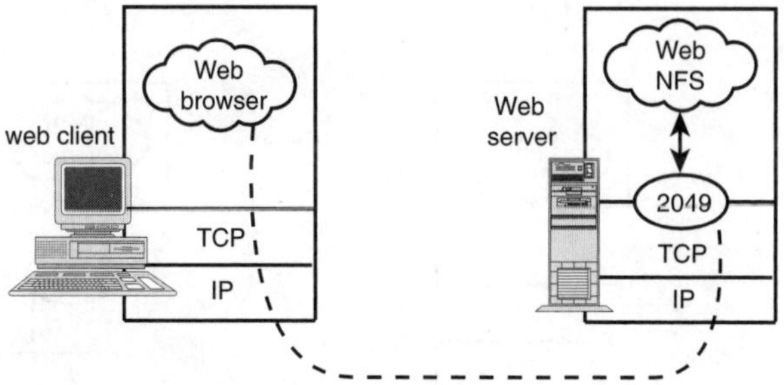

The Web NFS protocols are documented in RFC 2054 on "Web NFS Client Specification" and RFC 2055 on "Web NFS Server Specification."

Internet Access Protocols

A number of protocols have evolved to provide access to documents on the Internet. The two most prominent ones are the HTTP (HyperText Transfer Protocol) and Gopher. Of these protocols, the most widely used is HTTP, otherwise known by the more popular name of the World Wide Web (WWW) protocol.

World Wide Web (WWW)

Figure 13.25 illustrates the use of the World Wide Web. The World Wide Web is often called simply the web. The web is comprised of many web servers. The web servers store documents that contain such information as text, graphics, sound, and video that are organized in *web pages*. Each web page contains instructions called hyperlinks that link the web documents. The hyperlinks can point to documents on the same server or a different server on the Internet. The resulting set of hyperlinked documents appear as a maze of web pages that can span countries and continents—hence, the name World Wide Web.

Figure 13.25 The World Wide Web. (Courtesy Learning Tree)

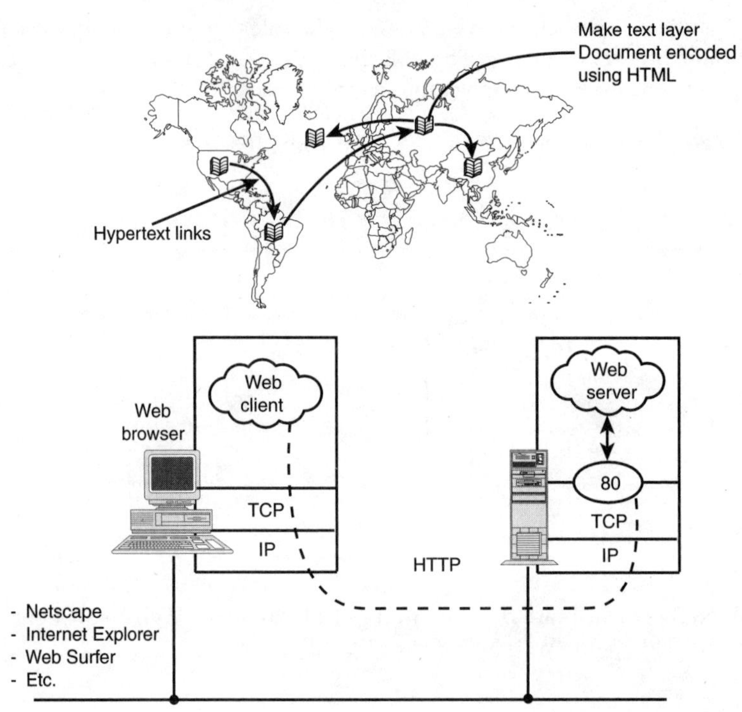

The web documents are accessed by web clients called web browsers, who run on user machines. The document is encoded by using a special markup language called HTML (HyperText Markup Language). After a web browser downloads an HTML document, the browser renders the document graphically on the display. The HTML contains the description of the different components of the web page, and the web browser uses this description to graphically draw the page. Hyperlinks appear as underlined text. When you access this text, it causes the web browser to download the corresponding linked document.

The upcoming sections discuss HTML encoding and the HTTP protocol.

HyperText Markup Language (HTML)

HTML is an implementation of the Standard Generalized Markup Language (SGML). The SGML standard, also designated as ISO-8879 by the International Organization of Standards (ISO), provides a generalized method of specifying how to represent documents that have hyperlinks. A *hyperlink* is a phrase or sentence in a document that is highlighted in a special way so that when it is selected, another document is displayed or a specified action is performed. Actions that can be performed when a hyperlink is selected include the following: displaying an image, sending mail, soliciting information from the user by using a form, initiating a remote logon or file transfer session, querying a database, executing a program, and so on. The documents containing hyperlinks are also called hyperdocuments.

All HTML documents contain tags that have the following structure:

```
<tag>
</tag>
```

The *tag* is a reference to special keywords that are used to describe the components of an HTML document. The end tag specifier </*tag*> ends the scope of the corresponding <*tag*>. Almost every HTML tag has a corresponding end tag specifier. For example, HTML documents begin and end with the following specifiers:

```
<HTML>
The different elements of the HTML document
go between these tags.
</HTML>
```

Between the <HTML> and </HTML> tags, you specify the head and body of the HTML document. The head is specified by using the <HEAD> and </HEAD> tags. The body of the HTML is specified by the <BODY> and </BODY> tags:

```
<HTML>
<HEAD> The Head goes over here </HEAD>
<BODY> The Body goes here </BODY>
</HTML>
```

Blank lines and new lines placed between tags are not significant. For example, the preceding HTML syntax can be written as follows:

```
<HTML><HEAD> The Head goes over here </HEAD><BODY> The Body goes here </BODY>
</HTML>
```

Blank lines and new lines are generally added to improve readability of the HTML document. Also, tags are case insensitive. If you want to break a paragraph of text or add a blank line that will appear in the rendering of the HTML document by the web browser, you need to add special HTML tags. Within the head section, you define the title of the HTML document. The title is defined by the tags <TITLE> and </TITLE>. The text in the title tags is displayed at the title area of the browser, as follows:

```
<HTML>
<HEAD>
    <TITLE>
        My first simple HTML page!
</TITLE>
</HEAD>
<BODY> The Body goes here </BODY>
</HTML>
```

To create a hyperlink, you use the following anchor tag:

```
<A HREF= URLaddress otherparameters> hyperlink text </A>
```

The anchor tag can have a number of parameters indicated by *otherparameters,* which modifies the behavior of the anchor tag. Typically, you have the HREF parameter that is set to an URL address. An URL address is a standard way of specifying a resource or location on the Internet. The URL has the following general syntax:

protocol://hostname/pathname

The *protocol* can be any of the protocols used on the Internet, such as HTTP, FTP, Telnet, Gopher, File, and so on, which are used to access the resource. If you are specifying an HTML document on another host computer, the protocol that you will specify will be HTTP (HyperText Transfer Protocol), which is used to fetch an HTML document. If you want to access a document by using file transfer, you will specify the FTP protocol, and so on. If you are accessing a local file on the same computer that you are using to run the web browser, you can specify the protocol to be File.

The *hostname* is the IP address or DNS (Domain Name System) of the host on which the resource is located. The *pathname* is the directory and the file name of the document/file that is being accessed. The *pathname* may be case sensitive if the web server runs on a Unix host. The *pathname* is optional. If not specified for an HTML document, the default name of index.html or index.htm is assumed. Here are some examples of URL addresses:

http://www.novell.com

http://www.hp.com/peripherals

http://www.tsl.org

ftp://ftp.novell.com

telnet://usa.net

file:///F|/PUBS/NWEB/simple.html

Consider the following HTML document, which uses an anchor tag to point to different resources. Note that comments can be embedded in an HTML document by using <!-- *comment*>.

```
<HTML>
<HEAD><TITLE>Anchor tags</TITLE></HEAD>
<BODY>
<!-- This is a comment for HTML documents. Notice its syntax.>
<!
<H1>Demonstration of the use of anchor tags</H1>
<p>Anchor tags can be used to create hyperlinks. Notice how we began this
paragraph with a paragraph tag. Paragraph tags automatically format a paragraph
of text for display. When you end with a hard new line, a line break is gener-
ated to separate the paragraph from any text that may follow.
<br> <!-- The tag to the left creates a line break. You go to a new line>
Actually, anchor tags have many different parameters, but we will consider only
the simple ones here.
<hr><!-- This creates a horizontal line>
<p> Here are the anchor tags:
<p><A HREF=http://www.novell.com>Novell's web server</A>
<p><A HREF=ftp://www.novell.com>Novell's FTP server</A>
<p><A HREF=telnet://usa.net>Logon to USA.NET</A>
<p><A HREF=mailto:tslinfo@tsl.org>Mail us</A>
</BODY>
</HTML>
```

By studying the HTML code and its actual appearance in a web browser, you can better understand the different elements of HTML.

In the preceding HTML document, the paragraph tag <p> was used to put the different anchors on separate lines. HTML provides an ordered or unordered list to represent items on separate lines. The ordered list numbers each list item, and the unordered list places a bullet before each list item. The syntax of using these lists is shown next:

```
<!-- Ordered list>
<OL>
       <LI> List item1
       <LI> List item2
                        :
       <LI> List itemN
</OL>
<!-- Unordered list>
<UL>
       <LI> List item1
       <LI> List item2
                        :
       <LI> List itemN
</UL>
```

The following shows the HTML code for putting the anchor tags as a numbered list. Notice that two additional anchor tags are defined. The HREF parameter contains the string preceded with the # character. This location refers to a position defined by an anchor tag in the same document. This location to jump to has an anchor tag that has the NAME parameter whose value is the same as the HREF value without the # character:

```
<HTML>
<HEAD><TITLE>Anchor tags</TITLE></HEAD>
<BODY>
<!-- This is a comment for HTML documents. Notice its syntax.>
<!
<H1>Demonstration of the use of anchor tags</H1>
<p>Anchor tags can be used to create hyperlinks. Notice how we began this
paragraph with a
paragraph tag. Paragraph tags automatically format a paragraph of text for
display. When you end
with a hard new line, a line break is generated to separate the paragraph from
any text that might
follow.
<br> <!-- The tag to the left creates a line break. You go to a new line>
Actually, anchor tags have many different parameters, but we will consider only
the simple ones
here.
<hr><!-- This creates a horizontal line>
<p> Here are the anchor tags:
<B><!-- Make things bold until /B>
```

```
<OL><! -- Begin Ordered List>
<LI><A HREF=http://www.ibm.com>IBM's web server</A>
<LI><A HREF=ftp://ftp.cisco.org>Cisco's FTP server</A>
<LI><A HREF=telnet://usa.net>Logon to USA.NET</A>
<!-- Next two Anchors cause jump to named location in current document>
<LI><A HREF="#Heading1">Heading 1</A>
<LI><A HREF="#Heading2">Heading 2</A>
</OL><!-- End Ordered List>
</B><!-- End bold>
<hr>
<!-- Heading levels can be from H1 to H6>
<A NAME="Heading1"><H2>Heading1 topic</H2></A>
<A NAME="Heading2"><H2>Heading2 topic</H2></A>
</BODY>
</HTML>
```

Figure 13.26 shows the rendering of the preceding HTML code in a web browser. You may also notice the use of the <B> and </B> tags to display text in bold. Similarly, the <I> and </I> tags exist for displaying text in italics. You can also use up to six levels of headings <H1> to <H6> to display headings in different sizes.

Figure 13.26 Rendering of HTML document in a web browser.

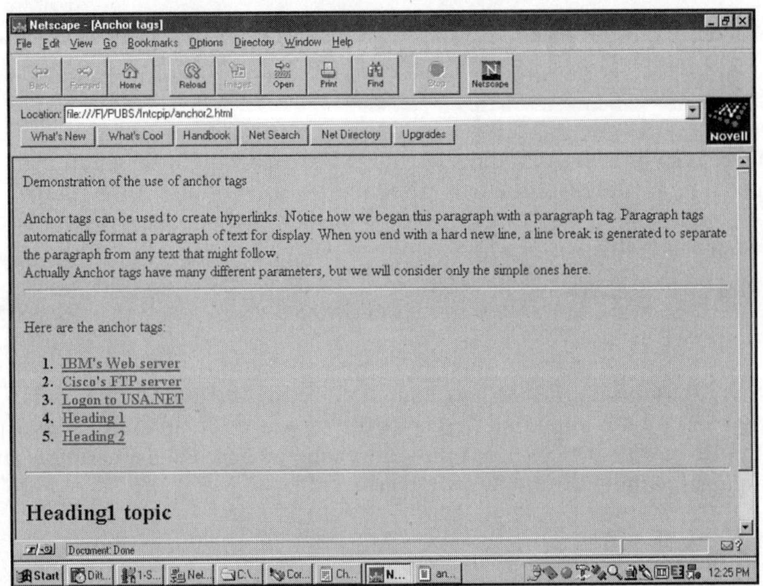

HyperText Transfer Protocol (HTTP)

The web client commands and the HTML documents that are sent in response to the web client commands are transmitted by using a special protocol called the HyperText Transfer Protocol (HTTP). The web server is also called an HTTP server (or HTTP daemon on Unix systems) because it responds to HTTP requests.

When a web browser requests an HTML document, a connection is established between the web browser and the web server. A TCP connection is established on TCP port number 80 on the server by default. You can specify other ports, such as TCP port number 8080, but the default port of 80 is reserved for HTTP.

If a nonstandard value is being used by the web browser, the TCP port number must be specified as part of the URL address. The following is an example of an URL address that requests service from port 8080 of the web server:

http://www.someorg.com:8080

After the connection is established, the web browser sends a request for the document by using the HTTP protocol. The request includes the method to be used to fetch the document, the object's name, and the HTTP protocol version in use at the web browser. The HTTP protocol uses text strings so that human beings can more readily understand the protocol. For example, the following HTTP request may be sent by the web browser to the web server requesting a document:

```
GET /web/docs/index.html HTTP/1.0
```

In this request, the GET HTTP request is used to obtain the document /web/docs/index.html. The version number of HTTP to be used for transferring the document is 1.0.

The server responds to the request for the HTML document by sending an HTTP response. The HTTP response from the server is composed of three parts:

- Response status
- Response header
- Response data

The response status is a line of text that contains the version number of HTTP used by the server, a status code that describes the server result, and a text description that sheds a little more light into what the status code means. The following is an example of a response status returned by a web server:

```
HTTP/1.0 200 OK
```

After the response code comes the response header. The response header contains information on the server type, the MIME version number used to describe the content type, the content type that describes the contents to follow in the response data, and a blank line. The blank line is mandatory because it separates the response header from the response data. Here is an example of a response header:

```
Date: Tuesday, 05-Nov-96 23:42:34 GMT
Server: Novell-HTTP-Server/2.5
MIME-version: 1.0
Content-type:text/plain
Body follows after the mandatory blank line
```

MIME is a method of encoding data that was originally used in Internet mail for transmitting documents containing a mix of text, image, audio, and video data. HTTP uses MIME to describe the different data types that it must deal with. The Content-type is a MIME description of the data. The text/html says that the major category of the data that is to be sent is text, and the subcategory is HTML. On seeing the text type, the browser interprets the response data that follows as HTML code. Another content type that is understood by all web browsers is text/plain, which means that the response data is to be treated as plain text.

If the document that was requested was an HTML document, the response data will contain the text in the HTML document. An example of the response data is shown next:

```
<HTML>
<HEAD><TITLE>Simple HTML doc</TITLE></HEAD>
<BODY>
<P> This is a simple HTML document...
</BODY>
</HTML>
```

Putting together all the different pieces of the web server's response, the following is seen by the web browser:

```
HTTP/1.0 200 OK
Date: Tuesday, 05-Nov-96 23:42:34 GMT
Server: Novell-HTTP-Server/2.5
MIME-version: 1.0
Content-type:text/plain
<HTML>
<HEAD><TITLE>Simple HTML doc</TITLE></HEAD>
<BODY>
<P> This is a simple HTML document...
</BODY>
</HTML>
```

After the HTTP request/response is complete, the underlying TCP/IP connection is terminated. A TCP/IP connection is made for each HTTP request/response.

Figure 13.27 shows a typical HTTP interaction. Note that the first step is to open a TCP connection to port 80 on the web server. Next, the GET/HTTP 1.0 command is sent by the web client. The document transfer takes place. At the end of the HTML document transfer, the connection is closed by the HTTP server. As other documents are fetched, a separate TCP connection is opened.

Figure 13.27 Typical HTTP interaction. (Courtesy Learning Tree)

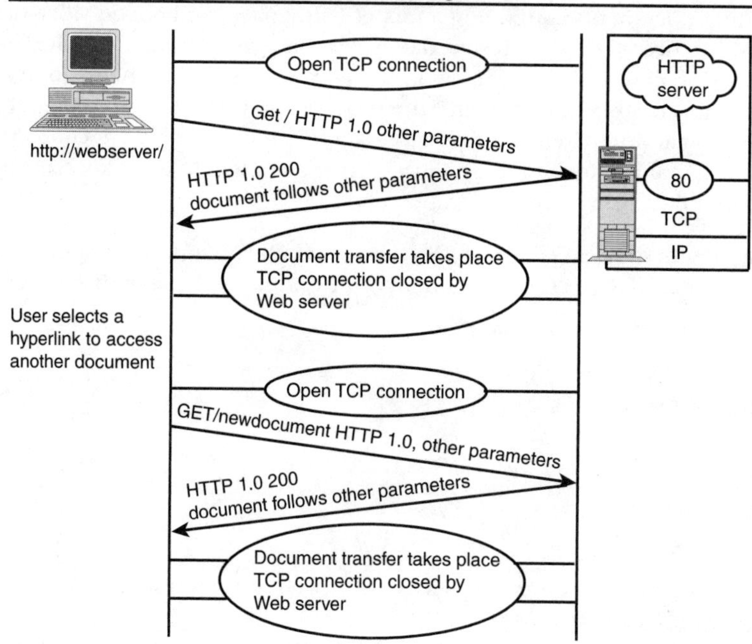

- **HTTP parameters are MIME encoded**

To understand how the HTTP protocol works, you can try an experiment to connect to the web server at port number 80. If you have access to a Telnet client application, you can try the experiment by using the following command:

```
telnet webhost        80
```

You must replace *webhost* with the IP address or host name of the NetWare web server. The number 80 tells the Telnet client to connect at TCP port 80 on the web server. Without an explicit port number, Telnet will try to connect to its default port number of 23. You can use Telnet from any Unix host or a MS Windows-based application. If you are using a GUI-enabled application, you will have to set the port number to 80 in the appropriate dialog box.

After you make the connection, you will see messages similar to the following from the web server:

```
Trying 199.245.180.11...
Connected to 199.245.180.11
Escape character is '^['.
```

The preceding response assumes that the IP address of the web server is 199.245.180.11. Your web server's IP address will undoubtedly be different.

Now you are going to simulate a web browser client that is making an HTTP GET request. Enter the following command to fetch the index.htm file:

```
GET /index.html HTTP/1.0
```

After you press the enter key, you will notice that nothing happens because the HTTP request must be followed by two <CR><LF> characters. Press the Enter key one more time. You will see the HTTP response from the web server scroll by quickly. The following is a response from an experimental web server in the author's network laboratory:

```
HTTP/1.0 200 OK
Date: Sat, 02 Aug 1997 04:17:19 GMT
Server: Novell-HTTP-Server/2.5
Content-type: text/html
Last-modified: Thu, 29 Feb 1996 14:26:58 GMT
Content-length: 2761
<HTML><TITLE>NetWare Web Server CGI SDK Home Page</TITLE>
<BODY TEXT="#000000" LINK="#FF0000">
<BODY BACKGROUND=images/blue_pap.gif>
<IMG SRC="/images/novlogo.gif" align="right" hspace=10> <P>
<H2>Novell NetWare Web Server</H2>
This NetWare Web Server product contains the CGI SDK that allows
programmers to extend the functionality of the NetWare Web Server.
<P>
This is the sample home page installed on your Early Access
Web Server. You can edit this file or replace it with any other
HTML document. This file can be found in your document root
as <I>index.htm</I>.
<HR>
<H2>About this web server...</H2>
This web page is served from a NetWare File server running HTTP.NLM.
The CGI implementation is beta software, and is provided to allow
for developers to begin development of extensions to the
NetWare Web Server.
<p>
```

```
<B>Please send e-mail to the address at the bottom of this page to let
us know that you're developing applications to the NetWare Web Server,
and for any technical support issues you might have.</B>
<hr>
Try out these three examples of applications that are written to the
NetWare CGI. The SDK provides the source code for the <I>cgiparse</I>
and <I>cginph</I> applications that you can use as development templates.
<P>
1. LoadableModule    /nds/    sys:web/nds-bin/
<DD>http://localhost<A HREF="/nds/ndsobj">/nds/ndsobj</A>
<P>
2. LoadableModule /cgi/ sys:web/cgi-bin
<DD>http://localhost<A HREF="/cgi/cgiparse">/cgi/cgiparse</A>
<DD><I>Use as a template for parsed-header extensions.</I><P>
3. LoadableModule /cgi/ sys:web/cgi-bin
<DD>http://localhost<A HREF="/cgi/cginph">/cgi/cginph</A>
<DD><I>Use as a template for non-parsed header extensions.</I><P>
<hr>
The following is an implementation of an image map processor
written to the NetWare CGI. The NetWare Web Server implements
image maps natively, but this demonstrates that you can implement your
own processing if you wish.
<p>
Try clicking on the pillar, a fish's eye, the plant, etc.
<p>
<br>
<A href="/cgi-bin/imagemap.nlm/ncsafish.imp"><IMG src="/images/ncsafish.gif"
ISMAP></A>
<HR>
<H2>Known problems</H2>
Sometimes there may be some problems when you UNLOAD the HTTP.NLM.
The System Console may hang for a bit before unloading.
Also, sometimes unloading HTTP.NLM does not successfully unload your CGI
extensions. If this happens, manually unload the extensions before
trying to unload HTTP.NLM again.
<P>
More examples and code will be provided with later updates. Be sure
to send us email to the address below to get on our update list!
<HR>
<ADDRESS>Novell, Inc., San Jose, CA<br>
<A HREF="mailto:nwwebdev@novell.com"><i>nwwebdev@novell.com</i></A>
</ADDRESS>
</BODY>
</HTML>
```

Notice that the HTTP response contains some header information, a blank line, and then the contents of the actual document that was requested. The HTML document that is requested may be different on your web server because the contents of the index.html file may be different. At the end of the HTML document transfer, the Telnet connection is closed automatically. If you need to get another document with HTTP/1.0, you will have to open another connection. The process of opening and closing a connection each time an HTML document is transferred is somewhat inefficient especially when several files need to be downloaded to the web browser. Newer improvements to the HTTP protocol are expected to have options to overcome these limitations.

In the preceding experiment, you were fetching a document that already existed. What if you tried to fetch a document that did not exist? Try the following experiment by using HTTP where you attempt to fetch a document you know does not exist. As before, make a Telnet connection to the HTTP server and enter the following command:

```
GET /xyzzy.htm HTTP/1.0
```

Press the Enter key twice. You should see an output similar to the following:

```
HTTP/1.0 404 Not Found
Date: Sat, 02 Aug 1997 04:18:29 GMT
Server: Novell-HTTP-Server/2.5
Content-type: text/html
<HEAD><TITLE>404 Not Found</TITLE></HEAD>
<BODY><H1>404 Not Found</H1>
The requested URL /xyzzy.htm was not found on this server.<P>
</BODY>
```

Notice that the HTTP response contains a HTML document that announces that the requested resource was not found. The error code that is returned is 404, which indicates that the resource was not found. The HTML document that was returned by the web server is a *virtual document.* It does not exist in the HTML documents directory on the server, but it was created dynamically by the web server to indicate the nature of the error.

You may want to try some other experiments, such as sending an invalid request to see what kind of response is returned by the server, as follows:

```
GETX this is an invalid request
```

The web server response indicates an error code of 400, which means that this is a bad HTTP request:

```
HTTP/1.0 400 Bad Request
Date: Sat, 02 Aug 1997 04:20:09 GMT
```

```
Server: Novell-HTTP-Server/2.5
Content-type: text/html
<HEAD><TITLE>400 Bad Request</TITLE></HEAD>
<BODY><H1>400 Bad Request</H1>
Your client sent a query that this server could not
understand.<P>
Reason: Invalid or unsupported method.<P>
</BODY>
```

HTTP is undergoing major modifications to support persistent TCP connections, where a TCP connection can be held open for longer than the document transfer period to avoid the overhead of opening a TCP connection every time a document is accessed. HTTP version 1.1 is described in RFC 2068 on "Hypertext Transfer Protocol—HTTP/1.1."

Web Indexing and CGI Gateways

To find specific topics on the web, you can use a number of search engines that are available. These search engines index web documents, follow all links in a web document, and index all documents obtained by following links. Some of these search engines are run by separate organizations. Many web browsers contain methods of accessing these search engines directly. Examples of search engines may be found at www.yahoo.com, www.excite.com, and www.lycos.com.

Many of the search engines employ a Common Gateway Interface (CGI), which permits the running of other application services (see fig. 13.28). The CGI is used to transfer a request to another application that is running on the same server or on a different server. The execution results from the application service are sent to the HTTP server via CGI, and then they sent back to the web client.

Figure 13.28 Common Gateway Interface (CGI). (Courtesy Learning Tree)

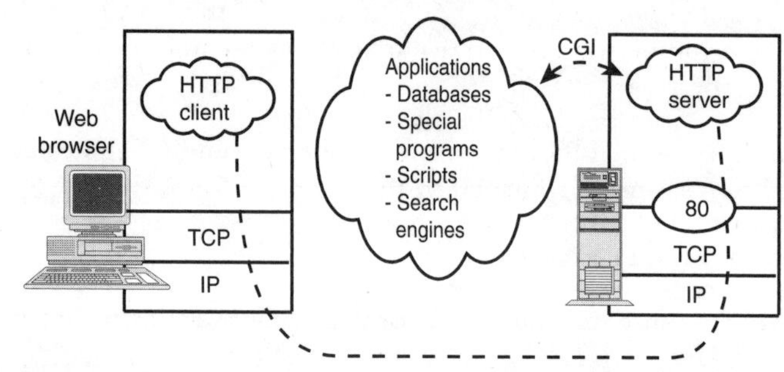

Gopher

Although most new information for public use is placed on web servers on the Internet, there is useful older information that is accessible only by using older tools such as FTP and Gopher. Gopher has lost its popularity because of the more common use of the World Wide Web.

The Gopher protocol and tool was developed at the University of Minnesota and provides a system of menus that you can navigate for topics of interest. In Gopher, the hyperlinks are the menu titles. After you select a menu title, you can access other menus or documents that may be on the same server or on a different server. The set of menus that are linked together is called *gopher space.*

Figure 13.29 shows the interaction between a Gopher client and a Gopher server. The Gopher server listens on TCP port 70 and waits for text retrieval strings that are sent by the Gopher client. The Gopher server returns menu items based on the text retrieval string.

Figure 13.29 Gopher client/server. (Courtesy Learning Tree)

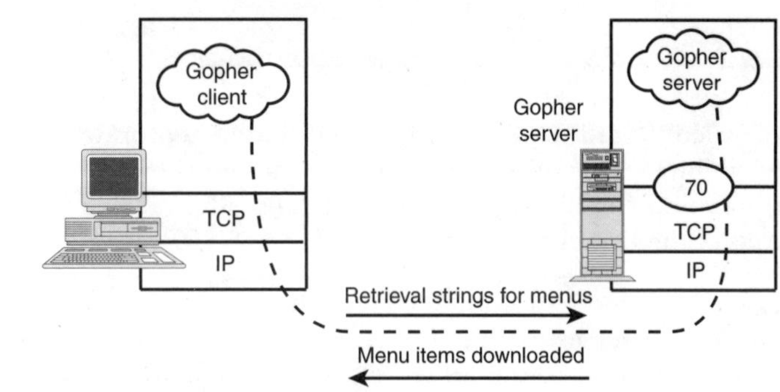

Figure 13.30 shows a sample screen of menus that is reported by a Gopher client.

Figure 13.30 Gopher menu example. (Courtesy Learning Tree)

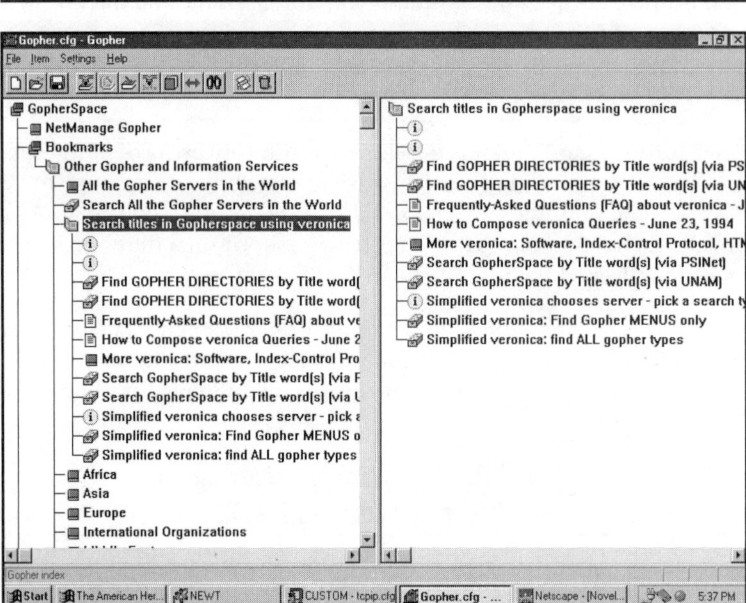

A special tool called Veronica (very easy rodent-oriented networkwide index to computerized archives) is associated with Gopher and is primarily used for searching topics in the menus of Gopher servers. Veronica is usually available as a menu choice at the top levels of the Gopher menu system.

A Gopher session is started by a Gopher client that sends a TCP connection request to port 70 on the Gopher server (see fig. 13.31). The Gopher server accepts the connection, and a TCP connection is established. The Gopher client then sends an empty string ("") that is terminated by the carriage-return and line-feed characters. The Gopher server responds to this string by sending menu items in its top-level menu directory. The menu items are sent by using the format shown in figure 13.32.

Figure 13.31 Gopher operation. (Courtesy Learning Tree)

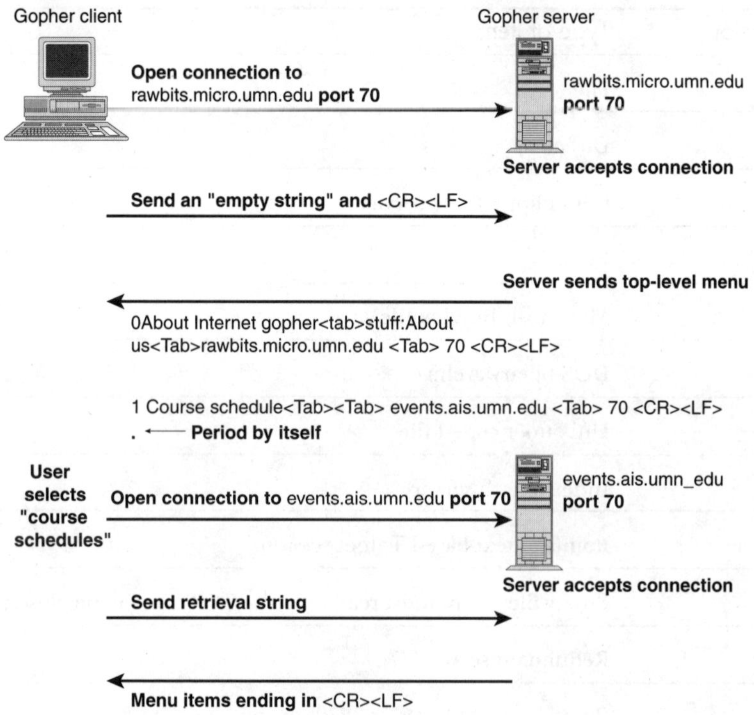

Gopher client

Gopher server

Open connection to
rawbits.micro.umn.edu **port 70**

rawbits.micro.umn.edu
port 70

Server accepts connection

Send an "empty string" and <CR><LF>

Server sends top-level menu

0About Internet gopher<tab>stuff:About us<Tab>rawbits.micro.umn.edu <Tab> 70 <CR><LF>

1 Course schedule<Tab><Tab> events.ais.umn.edu <Tab> 70 <CR><LF>

. ← **Period by itself**

User selects "course schedules"

Open connection to events.ais.umn.edu **port 70**

events.ais.umn_edu
port 70

Server accepts connection

Send retrieval string

Menu items ending in <CR><LF>

Figure 13.32 Gopher menu item format.

Selector	<Tab>	Display string	<Tab>	File reference	<Tab>	Host name	<Tab>	Host port number

<Tab> = ASCII tab character

The selector field (see fig. 13.32) has the values defined in table 13.17. The display string field is the menu item string to be displayed by the Gopher client. The file reference field is a special string that must be sent to the Gopher server to retrieve the items associated with the current selection. The host name and host port number fields define the Gopher server TCP end point where the specified file reference can be found.

TABLE 13.17
Selector Field Values

Selector	Type of Item
0	File
1	Directory
2	CSO Phone Book service
3	Error
4	Macintosh BinHex file
5	DOS binary archive
6	Unix uuencoded file
7	Index-search server
8	Points to text-based Telnet session
9	Binary file; client must read until the TCP connection closes; beware
+	Redundant server
T	Points to a text-based tn3270 session
g	GIF format graphics file
I	Image file; client decides how to display

The Gopher protocol is described in RFC 1436 on "The Internet Gopher Protocol (a distributed document search and retrieval protocol)."

Summary

This chapter discusses the following services that use the TCP/IP protocol infrastructure: Domain Name System (DNS); mail protocols: SMTP, POP3, and IMAP4; remote access protocols: Telnet and Berkeley r*; file transfer protocols: FTP and TFTP; file access protocols: NFS, Web NFS; web access protocols: HTTP/HTML, Gopher.

The application services implement the functionality of layers 5, 6, and 7 of the OSI model. These application services deal with the formatting, sending, and receiving of application-level data. They do not deal with interaction with the user, which is provided by end-user applications.

Test Yourself

1. What is the purpose of DNS?
2. What is a name resolver in DNS?
3. Why does DNS use UDP instead of TCP?
4. Draw a diagram showing the client/server nature of DNS, the DNS service running on the DNS server, and the port numbers used for DNS.
5. What is the most widely used implementation of DNS?
6. Typically, what do the two-letter designations for the top-level domain name in DNS signify?
7. Are domain names in DNS case sensitive? Are there any limitations to the length of the domain names?
8. List some of the top-level domains in DNS.
9. What is the purpose of assigning more than one DNS server for a top-level domain?
10. The organization SITA, Inc. has a host with a domain name of *ramu.eng.sita.com.* Assuming that the organization has DNS servers for the *eng.sita.com* and *sita.com* domains, discuss the order of querying the DNS servers. Your answer should mention what would happen if the organization's DNS servers are unable to resolve the query.
11. Is SMTP designed to send binary data? How can binary data be sent by using SMTP?
12. Describe the format of an 822 mail address.
13. How does MIME accommodate a display of multimedia messages on dumb terminals?
14. If a document is sent to a number of e-mail addresses on a mailing list, how can the amount of data sent in the e-mail be minimized by using MIME?
15. Describe the differences between a mail UA and a mail MTA.
16. A user with an e-mail address of kss@hoopy.frood.com sends a three-line text message to a user at veena@scs.sing.org. Describe the sequence of SMTP commands and responses needed to transfer such a message.
17. A user with an e-mail address of kss@hoopy.frood.com sends a three-line text message to multiple destinations at veena@scs.sing.org, anita@scs.sing.org, and linda@scs.sing.org. Describe the sequence of SMTP commands and responses needed to transfer such a message.

18. Why is SMTP not suitable for receiving e-mail at workstations? What mail protocols are better suited for this task?
19. Draw a diagram showing the client/server nature of POP3 and the port numbers used by POP3.
20. If POP3 is used at a workstation, is it used for both sending and receiving e-mail messages? What other protocols, if any, are needed?
21. A user uses POP3 to download three e-mail messages from a mail server that have the following message sizes:

Message ID	Size
1	121
2	300
3	290

The mail messages are *not* deleted after downloading. Describe the sequence of POP3 client commands and server responses that you can expect to see when this operation is performed.

Assume that the user's name is *belinda* and her password is *magic*.

22. A user uses POP3 to download four e-mail messages from a mail server that have the following message sizes:

Message ID	Size
1	345
2	443
3	4425
4	7450

The mail messages are deleted after downloading. Describe the sequence of POP3 client commands and server responses that you can expect to see when this operation is performed.

Assume that the user's name is *linda* and her password is *saralfont*.

23. Describe the four states that are involved in a typical POP3 session.
24. What is a major weakness in POP3 that IMAP4 overcomes?
25. Draw a diagram showing the client/server nature of IMAP4 and the port numbers used by IMAP4.
26. Describe some of the features of IMAP4 clients.
27. List some of the operations that IMAP4 can perform.

28. If IMAP4 is used at a workstation, is it used for both sending and receiving e-mail messages? What other protocols, if any, are needed?

29. Describe the behavior of IMAP4 in terms of a state diagram.

30. Draw a diagram showing the client/server nature of Telnet and the port numbers used by Telnet.

31. A user types the following command by using Telnet:

    mv file.1 file.2 *cr lf*

    cr and *lf* are the carriage return line-feed characters that mark the end of the command.

    How many data packets are sent by the Telnet client to send this command when the Telnet line mode option is being used? How does your answer change if the line mode option is not being used?

32. What is the NVT format? Why is it used?

33. How is a Telnet command sent by using NVT?

34. If each character typed by a user in a Telnet session is sent as a separate TCP segment, what is the typical protocol overhead of sending this character? Take into account protocols from the Data Link layer and above. Assume that the Data Link protocol is Ethernet.

35. If each character typed by a user in a Telnet session is sent as a separate TCP segment, what is the typical protocol overhead of sending this character? Take into account protocols from the Physical layer and above. Assume that the Physical layer and Data Link layer protocols are Ethernet.

36. If a user makes a mistake in a Telnet session and uses the backspace key to erase her mistake, what NVT command is sent?

37. What is the purpose of Telnet option negotiation? How is it done?

38. List some of the common Berkeley r* commands and describe them briefly.

39. In order to provide transparent access in using the Berkeley r* commands, what files are used?

40. Draw a diagram showing the protocol stack and port numbers used by rlogin.

41. The following command is to be run at the machine at 142.44.45.44 and the results sent to a local file called local.cpy:

    cat /etc/passwd

    Write the rsh command to perform this task.

What does the rsh command do?

(HINT: In Unix, the cat command on a single file name prints the contents of the file to the standard output.)

42. How can the command in question 41 be performed by using the Berkeley rcp command?
43. List some of the security concerns in using the Berkeley r* commands.
44. List the TCP connections used in an FTP session and describe their purpose. Are these connections kept open for the entire duration of the FTP session?
45. Draw a diagram that shows the protocol stack and port numbers used in an FTP session.
46. How does an FTP server know which port to connect to at the FTP client for the data connection?
47. List the message types used for TFTP.
48. Draw a diagram that shows the protocol stack and port numbers used in a TFTP session.
49. How many data packets are sent in a TFTP session to send a file of 10,000 bytes?
50. How many data packets are sent in a TFTP session to send a file of 8,192 bytes?
51. What is the relationship between NFS version numbers and the transport protocol that is used?
52. What Session and Presentation layer protocols are used in NFS? Describe them briefly.
53. What Application layer protocols are used in NFS? Describe them briefly.
54. How can the NFS_PROC, procedure 0, be used in troubleshooting NFS?
55. What is Web NFS?
56. What is a handle in NFS? Why is a public handle used in Web NFS?
57. What is HTTP and HTML?
58. Draw a diagram that shows the client/server interaction between a web client and a web server. Label any port numbers that are used.
59. What is a tag in HTML? What is an anchor tag? Give an example of an anchor tag.
60. What is an URL? Describe its syntax and give an example of how it can be used to specify that the /usr/public.doc file should be downloaded from the host krishna.vaikunth.heaven.org.

61. What is the purpose of CGI on a web server?
62. Draw a diagram that shows a typical HTTP interaction between a web browser and a web server.
63. What is Gopher and Veronica?
64. Draw a diagram that shows the client/server interaction between a Gopher client and a Gopher server. Label any port numbers that are used.
65. Describe the interaction between a Gopher client and a Gopher server in terms of the types of messages exchanged.

CHAPTER 14

TCP/IP Network Management

TCP/IP networks use a standard management protocol called Simple Network Management Protocol (SNMP). The SNMP protocol is widely used in the industry. While SNMP was developed as a solution for network management on TCP/IP networks, it is not limited to TCP/IP networks. The SNMP protocol can be run on other transport protocols, such as IPX, AppleTalk, and OSI.

Introduction to TCP/IP Network Management

In this section the fundamental concepts of SNMP will be presented. These concepts apply to SNMP implementations on any platform. A model for network management is discussed before discussing SNMP. This model describes the goal of network management and is applicable for most modern network management protocols, including SNMP.

A Model for Network Management

Figure 14.1 shows a model for network management. In this model, the network consists of several devices with a *management agent* running in them. The management agent has knowledge of the device parameters it runs on. Some of the device parameters are specific to the managed device. For instance, router devices have parameters describing the routing table. All devices can be expected to have some common parameters, such as the name of device, how long the device has been active (*up time*), and so on.

Figure 14.1 Model for network management. (Courtesy Learning Tree)

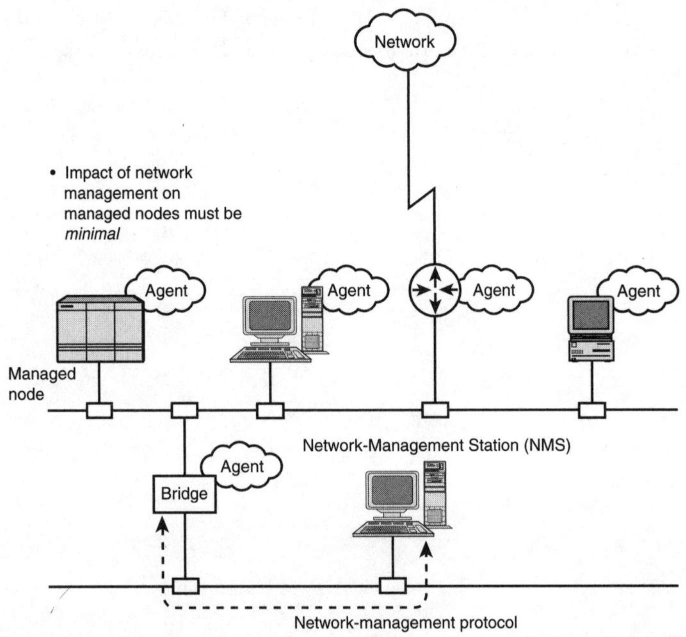

Figure 14.1 shows that the agents can be managed by a special device called the Network Management Station (NMS). The Network Management Station can issue specific requests to a device for information on its network parameters. The agent for the device receives these requests and sends back the requested information. Upon receiving the reply, the Network Management Station knows the value of the requested parameters. It can use this information to deduce information on the state of the device and whether the device requires attention.

It would also be important to prevent an unauthorized Network Management Station from obtaining information on the devices on the network. This requires the implementation of some authentication scheme that will prevent unauthorized access.

Figure 14.2 shows the goal of network management. The network is shown as a "cloud" that has both *input* and *output*. The network input is the shared data and the activity generated by users of the network. The network output is the increased efficiency resulting from information sharing. The network is subject to disturbances in the form of computers, devices, and network links becoming inoperational. The goal of network management is to monitor the status of the network, and use control mechanisms to achieve the desired output (increased efficiency) despite the network disturbances.

Figure 14.2 Goal of network management.

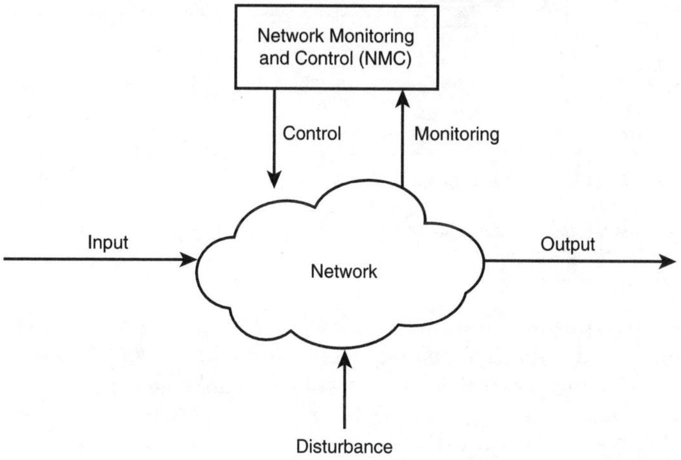

The mechanisms used for monitoring and controlling the network should have a minimal impact on the network. In other words the protocols used to collect information should not impact the performance of the network and the devices that are managed. If the network management mechanism uses up most of the network bandwidth, very little is available for the network users. In this case the network traffic will be disrupted. Similarly, the network agents running on the devices should not consume a great deal of processing power on their devices; otherwise, the devices may not be able to perform their normal functions within the desired time.

The Managed Node and SNMP

The device being managed by the Network Management Station is called the *managed node.* The managed node (see fig. 14.3) has parameters that the Network Management Station can *query* and obtain values for. A *management protocol* is used as the means to establish communications between the Network Management Station and the managed node and send queries and receive responses. An example of this management protocol is SNMP.

Figure 14.3 The Managed node. (Courtesy Learning Tree)

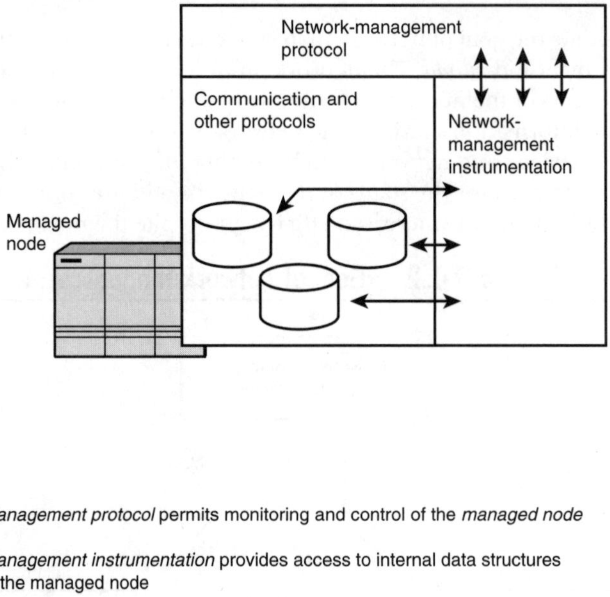

- *Management protocol* permits monitoring and control of the *managed node*
- *Management instrumentation* provides access to internal data structures of the managed node

The management protocol interfaces with the *network management instrumentation* within the managed node. The management instrumentation has internal knowledge of the parameters and memory locations within the managed node. When a query is received through the management protocol, such as SNMP, the network management instrumentation receives the request and accesses the managed node's parameters. The results are reported back to the Network Management Station by the management instrumentation using the network management protocol.

In the discussion on SNMP, the managed node is often called the *managed device.* These terms are used interchangeably in this chapter.

There has been considerable activity in the development of SNMP and MIBs for various devices (see next section, "Management Information Base (MIB)"). The following are some of the more recent and relevant RFCs as they pertain to SNMP:

- RFC 2128 PS G. Roeck, "Dial Control Management Information Base using SMIv2," 03/31/1997. (Pages = 34) (Format = .txt)
- RFC 2127 PS G. Roeck, "ISDN Management Information Base," 03/31/1997. (Pages = 49) (Format = .txt)
- RFC 2096 PS F. Baker, "IP Forwarding Table MIB," 01/30/1997. (Pages = 21) (Format = .txt) (Obsoletes RFC1354)
- RFC 2037 PS K. McCloghrie, A. Bierman, "Entity MIB," 10/30/1996. (Pages = 35) (Format = .txt)
- RFC 2021 PS S. Waldbusser, "Remote Network Monitoring Management Information Base Version 2 using SMIv2," 01/16/1997. (Pages = 130) (Format = .txt)
- RFC 2020 PS J. Flick, "Definitions of Managed Objects for IEEE 802.12 Interfaces," 10/17/1996. (Pages = 31) (Format = .txt)
- RFC 2013 PS K. McCloghrie, "SNMPv2 Management Information Base for the User Datagram Protocol using SMIv2," 11/12/1996. (Pages = 6) (Format = .txt) (Updates RFC1213)
- RFC 2012 PS K. McCloghrie, "SNMPv2 Management Information Base for the Transmission Control Protocol," 11/12/1996. (Pages = 10) (Format = .txt) (Updates RFC1213)
- RFC 2011 PS K. McCloghrie, "SNMPv2 Management Information Base for the Internet Protocol using SMIv2," 11/12/1996. (Pages = 18) (Format = .txt) (Updates RFC1213)
- RFC 1910 E G. Waters, "User-based Security Model for SNMPv2," 02/28/1996. (Pages = 44) (Format = .txt)
- RFC 1909 E K. McCloghrie, "An Administrative Infrastructure for SNMPv2," 02/28/1996. (Pages = 19) (Format = .txt)
- RFC 1908 DS J. Case, K. McCloghrie, M. Rose, S. Waldbusser, "Coexistence between Version 1 and Version 2 of the Internet-standard Network Management Framework," 01/22/1996. (Pages = 10) (Format = .txt) (Obsoletes RFC1452)
- RFC 1907 DS J. Case, K. McCloghrie, M. Rose, S. Waldbusser, "Management Information Base for Version 2 of the Simple Network Management Protocol (SNMPv2)," 01/22/1996. (Pages = 20) (Format = .txt) (Obsoletes RFC1450) .
- RFC 1906 DS J. Case, K. McCloghrie, M. Rose, S. Waldbusser, "Transport Mappings for Version 2 of the Simple Network Management Protocol (SNMPv2)," 01/22/1996. (Pages = 13) (Format = .txt) (Obsoletes RFC1449)
- RFC 1904 DS J. Case, K. McCloghrie, M. Rose, S. Waldbusser, "Conformance Statements for Version 2 of the Simple Network Management Protocol (SNMPv2)," 01/22/1996. (Pages = 24) (Format = .txt) (Obsoletes RFC1444).

- RFC 1903 DS J. Case, K. McCloghrie, M. Rose, S. Waldbusser, "Textual Conventions for Version 2 of the Simple Network Management Protocol (SNMPv2)," 01/22/1996. (Pages = 23) (Format = .txt) (Obsoletes RFC1443).
- RFC 1902 DS J. Case, K. McCloghrie, M. Rose, S. Waldbusser, "Structure of Management Information for Version 2 of the Simple Network Management Protocol (SNMPv2)," 01/22/1996. (Pages = 40) (Format = .txt) (Obsoletes RFC1442).
- RFC 1901 E J. Case, K. McCloghrie, M. Rose, S. Waldbusser, "Introduction to Community-based SNMPv2," 01/22/1996. (Pages = 8) (Format = .txt)
- RFC 1759 PS R. Smith, F. Wright, T. Hastings, S. Zilles, J. Gyllenskog, "Printer MIB," 03/28/1995. (Pages = 113) (Format = .txt)
- RFC 1757 DS S. Waldbusser, "Remote Network Monitoring Management Information Base," 02/10/1995. (Pages = 91) (Format = .txt) (Obsoletes RFC1271)
- RFC 1749 PS K. McCloghrie, F. Baker, E. Decker, "IEEE 802.5 Station Source Routing MIB using SMIv2," 12/29/1994. (Pages = 10) (Format = .txt) (Updates RFC1748)
- RFC 1748 DS K. McCloghrie, E. Decker, "IEEE 802.5 MIB using SMIv2," 12/29/1994. (Pages = 25) (Format = .txt) (Updated by RFC1749)
- RFC 1724 DS G. Malkin, F. Baker, "RIP Version 2 MIB Extension," 11/15/1994. (Pages = 18) (Format = .txt) (Obsoletes RFC1389)
- RFC 1697 PS D. Brower, R. Purvy, A. Daniel, M. Sinykin, J. Smith, "Relational Database Management System (RDBMS) Management Information Base (MIB) using SMIv2," 08/23/1994. (Pages=38) (Format=.txt)
- RFC 1696 PS J. Barnes, L. Brown, R. Royston, S. Waldbusser, "Modem Management Information Base (MIB) using SMIv2," 08/25/1994. (Pages = 31) (Format = .txt)
- RFC 1695 PS M. Ahmed, K. Tesink, "Definitions of Managed Objects for ATM Management Version 8.0 using SMIv2," 08/25/1994. (Pages = 73) (Format = .txt)
- RFC 1694 DS T. Brown, K. Tesink, "Definitions of Managed Objects for SMDS Interfaces using SMIv2," 08/23/1994. (Pages = 35) (Format = .txt) (Obsoletes RFC1304)
- RFC 1666 PS Z. Kielczewski, D. Kostick, K. Shih, "Definitions of Managed Objects for SNA NAUs using SMIv2," 08/11/1994. (Pages = 68) (Format = .txt)
- RFC 1660 DS B. Stewart, "Definitions of Managed Objects for Parallel-printer-like Hardware Devices using SMIv2," 07/20/1994. (Pages = 10) (Format = .txt) (Obsoletes RFC1318)

- RFC 1659 DS B. Stewart, "Definitions of Managed Objects for RS-232-like Hardware Devices using SMIv2," 07/20/1994. (Pages = 21) (Format = .txt) (Obsoletes RFC1317)
- RFC 1658 DS B. Stewart, "Definitions of Managed Objects for Character Stream Devices using SMIv2," 07/20/1994. (Pages = 18) (Format = .txt) (Obsoletes RFC1316)
- RFC 1657 PS S. Willis, J. Burruss, J. Chu, "Definitions of Managed Objects for the Fourth Version of the Border Gateway Protocol (BGP-4) using SMIv2," 07/21/1994. (Pages = 21) (Format = .txt)
- RFC 1650 PS F. Kastenholz, "Definitions of Managed Objects for the Ethernet-like Interface Types using SMIv2," 08/23/1994. (Pages = 20) (Format = .txt)
- RFC 1643 S F. Kastenholz, "Definitions of Managed Objects for the Ethernet-like Interface Types," 07/13/1994. (Pages = 19) (Format = .txt) (Obsoletes RFC1623) (STD 50)
- RFC 1905 DS J. Case, K. McCloghrie, M. Rose, S. Waldbusser, "Protocol Operations for Version 2 of the Simple Network Management Protocol (SNMPv2)," 01/22/1996. (Pages = 24) (Format = .txt) (Obsoletes RFC1448)
- RFC 1628 PS J. Case, "UPS Management Information Base," 05/19/1994. (Pages = 45) (Format = .txt)
- RFC 1612 PS R. Austein, J. Saperia, "DNS Resolver MIB Extensions," 05/17/1994. (Pages = 36) (Format = .txt)
- RFC 1611 PS R. Austein, J. Saperia, "DNS Server MIB Extensions," 05/17/1994. (Pages = 32) (Format = .txt)
- RFC 1604 PS T. Brown, "Definitions of Managed Objects for Frame Relay Service," 03/25/1994. (Pages = 46) (Format = .txt) (Obsoletes RFC1596)
- RFC 1595 PS T. Brown, K. Tesink, "Definitions of Managed Objects for the SONET/SDH Interface Type," 03/11/1994. (Pages = 59) (Format = .txt)
- RFC 1567 PS G. Mansfield, S. Kille, "X.500 Directory Monitoring MIB," 01/11/1994. (Pages = 19) (Format = .txt)
- RFC 1566 PS N. Freed, S. Kille, "Mail Monitoring MIB," 01/11/1994. (Pages = 21) (Format = .txt)
- RFC 1565 PS N. Freed, S. Kille, "Network Services Monitoring MIB", 01/11/1994. (Pages=18) (Format=.txt)
- RFC 1525 PS E. Decker, K. McCloghrie, P. Langille, A. Rijsinghani, "Definitions of Managed Objects for Source Routing Bridges," 09/30/1993. (Pages = 18) (Format = .txt) (Obsoletes RFC1286)
- RFC 1503 I K. McCloghrie, M. Rose, "Algorithms for Automating Administration in SNMPv2 Managers," 08/26/1993. (Pages = 19) (Format = .txt)

- RFC 1461 PS D. Throop, "SNMP MIB extension for MultiProtocol Interconnect over X.25," 05/27/1993. (Pages = 30) (Format = .txt)
- RFC 1451 PS J. Case, K. McCloghrie, M. Rose, S. Waldbusser, "Manager to Manager Management Information Base," 05/03/1993. (Pages = 36) (Format = .txt)
- RFC 1447 PS K. McCloghrie, J. Galvin, "Party MIB for version 2 of the Simple Network Management Protocol (SNMPv2)," 05/03/1993. (Pages = 50) (Format = .txt)
- RFC 1446 PS J. Galvin, K. McCloghrie, "Security Protocols for version 2 of the Simple Network Management Protocol (SNMPv2)," 05/03/1993. (Pages = 51) (Format = .txt)
- RFC 1445 PS J. Davin, K. McCloghie, "Administrative Model for version 2 of the Simple Network Management Protocol (SNMPv2)," 05/03/1993. (Pages = 47) (Format = .txt)
- RFC 1441 PS J. Case, K. McCloghrie, M. Rose, S. Waldbusser, "Introduction to version 2 of the Internet-standard Network Management Framework," 05/03/1993. (Pages = 13) (Format = .txt)
- RFC 1420 PS S. Bostock, "SNMP over IPX," 03/03/1993. (Pages = 4) (Format = .txt) (Obsoletes RFC1298)
- RFC 1419 PS G. Minshall, M. Ritter, "SNMP over AppleTalk," 03/03/1993. (Pages = 7) (Format = .txt)
- RFC 1418 PS M. Rose, "SNMP over OSI," 03/03/1993. (Pages = 4) (Format = .txt) (Obsoletes RFC1283)

Management Information Base (MIB)

The parameters in the managed node are called *management objects.* The set of parameters in a managed node is called the *Management Information Base* (MIB). The MIB can be regarded conceptually as a database. The objects in the MIB, called *variables,* have a number associated with them that is used to uniquely identify the object. This number is called the *object id.* The *object id* is based on a hierarchical numbering scheme and enables the variable in the MIB to be *ordered.* The ordering of the variables means that given an object id for a variable, you can determine the "next" variable that follows. The ordering of the MIB variables is conceptually similar to the indexing that orders records in a database. SNMP messages typically request and return the values of MIB variables.

An MIB variable also includes a status flag indicating if the variable is read-only or has read-write access.

A certain set of standard MIB variables exists for the different protocol elements of TCP/IP. These MIB variables deal with parameter values for IP, ICMP, TCP, SNMP, Exterior Gateway Protocol (EGP), and Address Translation tables.

Data-link interfaces, such as Ethernet, Token Ring, SMDS, and ATM have their own set of MIB variables. It is even possible for a special device vendor to have MIB variables specific to that device. MIB variables that are specific to a vendor's device are called *proprietary MIBs.* There are interface mechanisms that enable an SNMP manager to take a description of a proprietary MIB and *compile* it so that it becomes one of the MIB variables recognized by the SNMP Manager.

The Management Paradigm in SNMP

The Network Management Station for SNMP is called the *SNMP Manager.* The SNMP Manager uses a management paradigm called the *remote debugging* paradigm (see fig. 14.4). In this paradigm, the SNMP Manager is like a programmer at a workstation debugging programs from a remote location. Such a hypothetical programmer would be interested in reading the values of variables in the program and changing the values of certain critical variables. Likewise, the SNMP Manager should be able to read and update the values of MIB variables on the managed devices. The SNMP Manager should be able to perform the following actions:

- Read or Read-Write MIB variables
- Perform trap-directed polls
- Perform simple traversal of variables in the managed node

Figure 14.4 The SNMP management paradigm. (Courtesy Learning Tree)

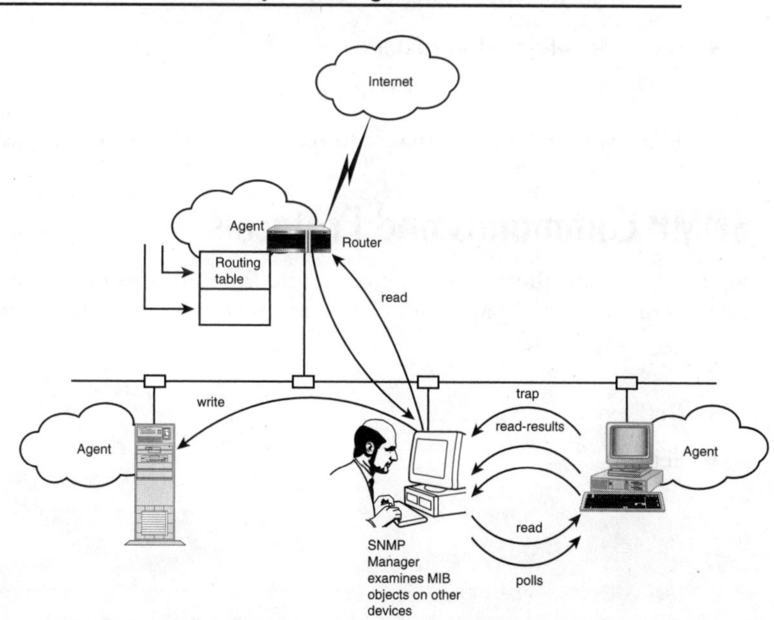

When an exceptional condition occurs at a managed device, such as a link failure or a critical change in the status of a device, the managed device sends a *Trap SNMP* message to the SNMP Manager. The Trap SNMP message contains an indication of the event that caused the generation of the message. It is up to the SNMP Manager to respond to the Trap SNMP message. The SNMP Manager can simply log the message in a trap log file or take more extensive action. The SNMP Manager can, for instance, request additional information from the device that generated the trap message. The additional information can be obtained through read requests for specific MIB variables. If the SNMP Manager is programmed for control of the device, it can issue a write request to modify the value of an MIB variable.

All control actions within SNMP occur as a "side effect" of modifying an MIB variable. For example, if a device is to be powered off remotely from an SNMP Manager, the SNMP Manager could send a write request to modify an MIB variable called the *ifPowerOff* variable. The managed device can be programmed so that the *ifPowerOn* variable causes the following side effect: the value of the variable is normally 1; if the value is 0, the device will be powered off. Upon sensing a value of 0 in its *ifPowerOn* variable, the managed device can initiate a device shutdown.

Because the MIB variables are ordered according to their object identifiers, the SNMP manager can traverse all the variables in the device using an SNMP command called *GetNext*. This is a simple traversal of the MIB.

Because SNMP uses side effects to initiate control actions, the SNMP commands consist only of the following:

- Get (Read an MIB variable)
- Set (Write of an MIB variable)
- GetNext (Return the next MIB variable)
- Trap (Sent to SNMP manager to report exceptional conditions)

SNMP Commands and Protocols

Figure 14.5 shows the SNMP commands and the transport protocols that SNMP depend on. The SNMP Manager can issue any of the following commands:

- Get
- GetNext
- Set

Figure 14.5 The SNMP architecture. (Courtesy Learning Tree)

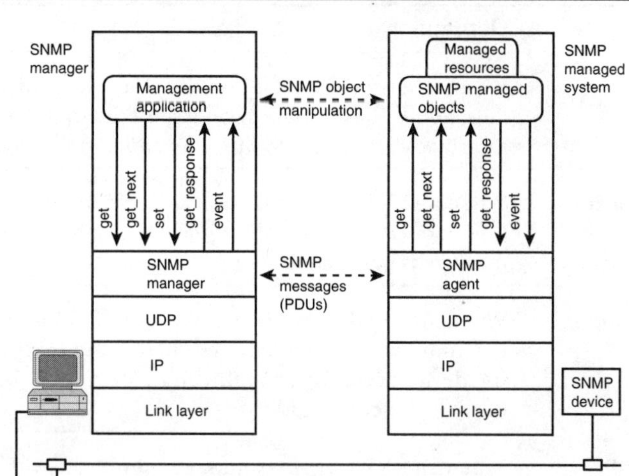

These commands are sent to the SNMP agent using the UDP/IP protocols. The SNMP agent can send a GetNext_Response SNMP command in reply to the SNMP Get request or GetNext request from the SNMP Manager. The SNMP Set command from the SNMP Manager is not explicitly acknowledged. In other words, there is no such command as a Set_Response command sent from the SNMP agent to the SNMP Manager. The Trap events are sent from the SNMP agent to the SNMP Manager when exceptional conditions occur in the managed device.

SNMP Traps

When an unusual condition occurs in the SNMP device, the SNMP agent alerts the SNMP Manager through SNMP traps. Figure 14.6 shows a sample network showing some of the Trap messages that can be generated by SNMP agents. The Trap messages can be *link up or down,* which occurs if the network interface comes up or goes down; *cold or warm start,* which occurs when a device boots and the SNMP agent initializes itself; *authentication failure,* which occurs if an incorrect COMMUNITY name is specified with the request; *loss of EGP neighbor,* which occurs if an agent cannot communicate with its EGP neighbor. On a NetWare network, except for the *loss of EGP neighbor* trap, any of the previous Trap messages can occur.

At one time the EGP protocol was widely used on the Internet. Its inclusion as a Trap SNMP message is to support those sites that may still be using it. The SNMP agent must be configured to send Trap messages to an SNMP Manager station.

Table 14.1 summarizes the different SNMP Trap messages that can occur.

Table 14.1
SNMP Trap Messages

Parameter	Description
Link up or down	When a network interface on the managed device fails, a *link down* trap message is generated; if the network interface comes back to life, a *link up* trap message is generated.
Cold or warm start	When an SNMP agent starts, a *cold start* trap message is generated. If the SNMP initializes its table, a *warm start* trap message is generated.
Authentication failure	When an SNMP agent receives an SNMP request with a community name that does not match the community name the device is configured with, an *authentication failure* trap message is generated.
Loss of EGP neighbor	When an SNMP agent cannot communicate with its EGP neighbor, a *loss of EGP neighbor* trap message is generated.

Figure 14.6 SNMP Traps.

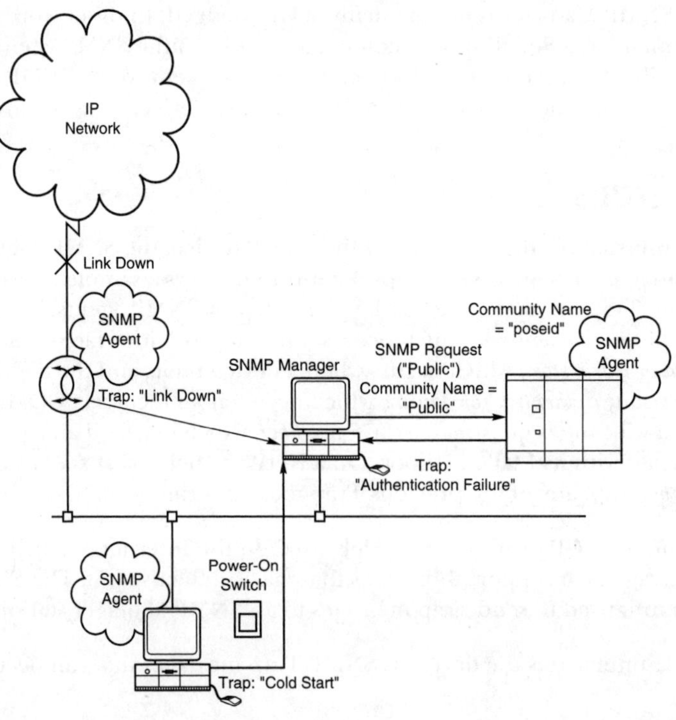

SNMP Object Identifiers and Messages

The following sections discuss the structure of SNMP messages. In this treatment only the widely used SNMP version 1 message structure is discussed. Currently SNMP version 2 is not widely used.

Many SNMP messages and replies contain the name of the MIB object whose value is being sought. Before discussing the SNMP message structure, the names used to describe MIB objects are discussed.

MIB Object Identifiers

In SNMP MIB objects are given a unique object identifier consisting of a sequence of numbers separated by ".". This sequence of numbers is read from left to right and corresponds to nodes of the object name tree. Figure 14.7 show a partial object name tree that shows the object identifiers for the MIB objects sysDescr and sysLocation. The topmost nodes in the tree represent different committees and high-level organizations responsible for the composition of the name underneath their tree branch. The following topmost nodes are defined:

- **ccitt(0).** The nodes under the ccitt(0) branch are administered by the International Telegraph and Telephone Consultative Committee.
- **iso(1).** The nodes under the iso(1) branch are administered by the International Organization for Standardization and the International Electrotechnical Committee (ISO/IEC).
- **joint-iso-ccitt(2).** The nodes under the joint-iso-ccitt(1) branch are jointly administered by the International Telegraph and Telephone Consultative Committee, the International Organization for Standardization, and the International Electrotechnical Committee.

Network management is defined under the iso(1) tree branch. Under this tree branch are a number of subordinate organization definitions. Network Management falls under the org(3) node shown in figure 14.7.

Under the org(3) node are a number of subordinate organizations. Network Management falls under the dod(6) node for the Department of Defense (DoD), shown in figure 14.7.

Under the dod(6) node are a number of subordinate networks. Network Management falls under the internet(1) node for the Internet, shown in figure 14.7.

Under the internet(1) node are a number of subordinate nodes representing different services and standardization efforts. Standardized Network Management objects fall under the mgmt(2) node, shown in figure 14.7.

Figure 14.7 An object name tree. (Courtesy Learning Tree)

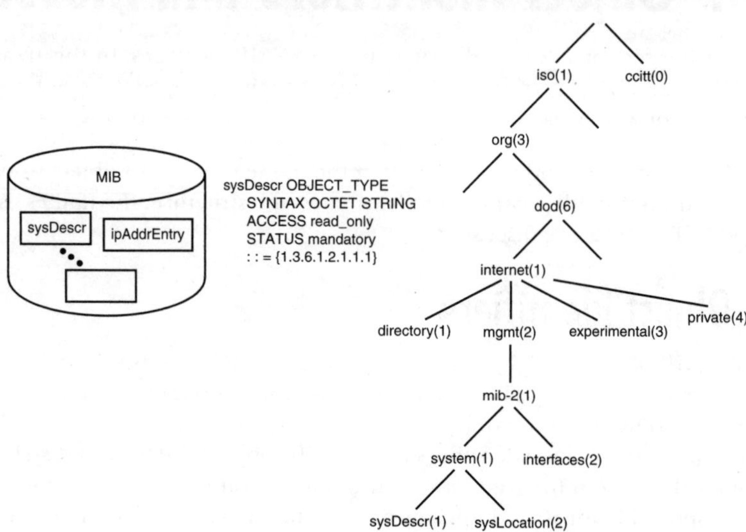

Under the mgmt(2) node are a number of subordinate nodes representing different standardization efforts. Standardized Network Management objects fall under the mib-2(1) node, shown in figure 14.7.

Under the mib-2(1) node are a number of subordinate nodes representing groupings of MIB variables. Figure 14.7 shows the system(1) and interfaces(2) MIB variable groupings.

Under the system(1) node are shown the two MIB variables, sysDescr(1) and sysLocation(2). The object identifiers for these variables are defined by enumerating the node numbers starting from the top of the object name tree to the MIB variable object. These numbers are written from left to right and are separated by periods. Therefore, the object identifiers for these MIB variables have the following names:

- sysDescr: 1.3.6.1.2.1.1.1
- sysLocation: 1.3.6.1.2.1.1.2

Notice that there is a natural ordering of the MIB variables. The "next" variable after sysDescr is sysLocation because the last number in the object identifier representation changes from 1 to 2.

SNMP Messages

SNMP message formats vary in length and are complex. A subset of the Abstract Syntax Notation, version 1 (ASN.1) language is used to describe the SNMP message structure. ASN.1 is a fairly intuitive language, although its rigorous definition is beyond the scope of this book. As an example of the intuitive nature of this language, consider the following, which describes the structure of an ethernet frame using ASN.1:

```
Ethernet-Frame ::= SEQUENCE {
               destAddr  OCTET STRING (SIZE(6)),
               srcAddr   OCTET STRING (SIZE(6)),
               etherType INTEGER (1501..65535),
               data      ANY(SIZE(46-1500)),
               crc       OCTET STRING(SIZE(4))
               }
```

Note that the "::=" defines on its right-hand side, the variable defined on the left-hand side (Ethernet-Frame). The SEQUENCE {} represents an ordered list of items inside the {}. This ordered list is the fields of the ethernet frame such as the destination address, source address, ethernet type, data, and CRC.

The type of each field is named immediately after the name of the field variable. For example, destAddr and srcAddr are each defined as the type OCTET STRING, which defines a data type taking 0 or more octets as its value. Each octet in the octet string can vary in value from 0 to 255. The size of the octet string is placed after the OCTET STRING type.

EtherType is defined to be an INTEGER that is an integer value of arbitrary size and precision. The "(1501..65535)" placed immediately after the INTEGER defines its size.

The data field is of type ANY, which is between 46 to 1,500 octets long.

The crc field is a 4-octet length OCTET STRING.

Using the ASN.1 notation, all SNMP messages can be considered to have the following format:

```
SNMP-message ::= SEQUENCE {
              version INTEGER {version-1(1)},
              community OCTET STRING,
              data ANY}
```

This message format is shown in figure 14.8, which explains the meanings of the fields.

Figure 14.8 The SNMP message format. (Courtesy Learning Tree)

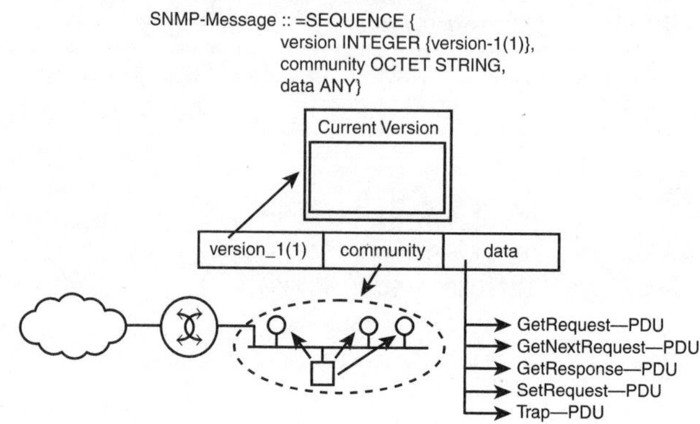

The version number is the version number of the message format. *Community* is a string value that is sent in every SNMP message. An agent receiving an SNMP message checks the community name against its configured community name value. If there is a match, the operation requested in the SNMP message is performed. If there is no match, the SNMP agent sends an SNMP trap message indicating an authentication failure. This is a very simple authentication scheme because the community name is like a password. The problem with this authentication scheme is that the password is not encrypted and sent in the clear.

The data field represents the details of the different SNMP messages, such as the GetRequest, GetNextRequest, GetResponse, SetRequest, and Trap. The format of these message types is described in figures 14.9 and 14.10.

Summary

TCP/IP networks use a standard network management protocol called Simple Management Protocol (SNMP). The SNMP protocol is widely used in the industry. SNMP was originally developed as a solution for network management on TCP/IP networks. SNMP is no longer limited to TCP/IP networks. The SNMP protocol can be run on other transport protocols, such as IPX and OSI.

This chapter discussed the basics of SNMP. The discussion on SNMP message format was confined to SNMP version 1. The sequel to this book, "TCP/IP: The Professional Reference," by the same author and publisher discusses SNMP version 2, MIB-2, and authentication issues in SNMP.

Figure 14.9 The SNMP PDU format. (Courtesy Learning Tree)

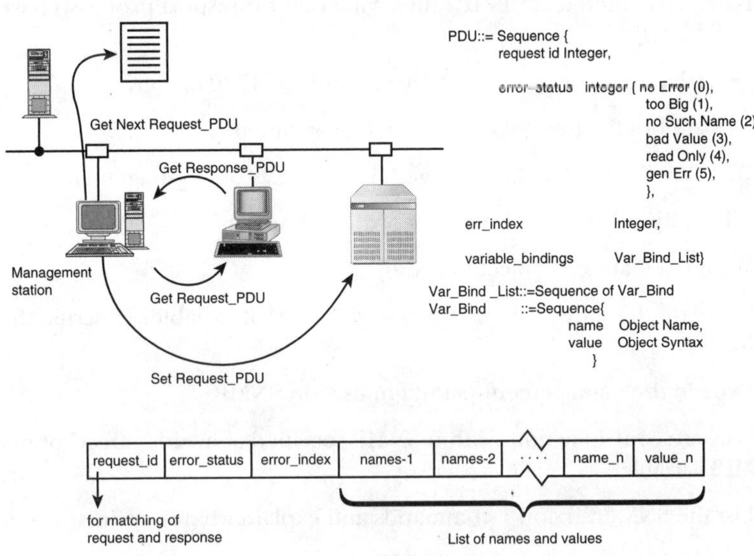

Figure 14.10 The Trap PDU format. (Courtesy Learning Tree)

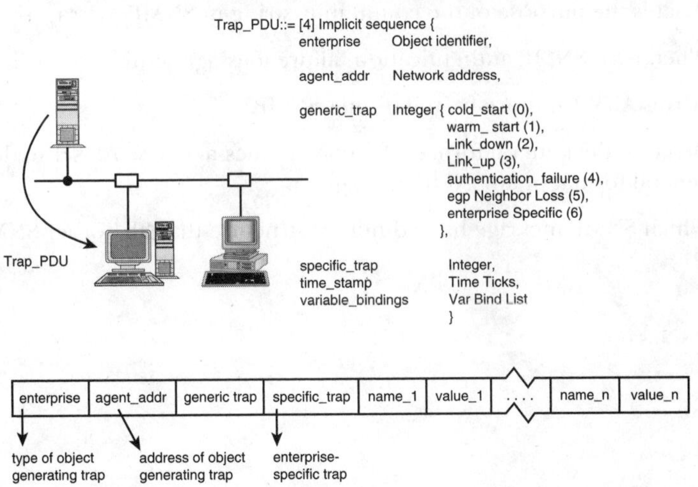

Test Yourself

1. Is SNMP limited to TCP/IP only? What other transport protocols have been used with SNMP?
2. Describe the roles of an SNMP agent and SNMP manager.
3. Explain briefly the goal of network management.
4. Describe the model of a managed node in network management.
5. Which RFC deals with DNS server MIB extensions?
6. What is a managed object in SNMP?
7. What are the status flags associated with an MIB variable? Describe their meaning.
8. Explain the management paradigm used in SNMP.
9. Why are control actions within SNMP specified as a "side effect" of modifying a MIB variable?
10. List the SNMP version 1 commands and explain what they do.
11. Draw a diagram showing the SNMP architecture and the SNMP messages between an SNMP agent and an SNMP manager.
12. What is an SNMP trap? Give examples of SNMP trap messages.
13. What is the purpose of the community string in SNMP messages?
14. When is an SNMP authentication failure message sent?
15. Why is ASN.1 important in defining SNMP?
16. Describe the general format of an SNMP message. Use ASN.1 to describe the general format of an SNMP message.
17. Which SNMP message has a different structure than the other SNMP messages?

Part IV

Future Directions

CHAPTER 15

IP Next Generation and ATM

This chapter discusses two exciting technologies that can do much to shape the future of the new generation of intranets and internets. These technologies are IP Next Generation (IPv6) and ATM. This chapter should serve as an overview of what is on the horizon, and is not intended as a detailed exposition of these topics.

Some IP Next Generation issues are discussed in earlier chapters. In Cchapter 4, "IP Addressing," you learned that the long-term solution to the problem of depletion of IPv4 addresses is IPv6, or IP Next Generation. This chapter will explore IPv6 in greater depth and will address the important issues surrounding the protocol. Besides IPv6, another promising technology that is seeing a great deal of deployment is ATM. ATM is important because it provides a technology that can be used for both LANs and WANs and for carrying different types of data, including voice and video, on the same network. This chapter will introduce you to the issues of running the TCP/IP protocol stack over the ATM hardware fabric.

IPv6

The primary motivation for IPv6 was to increase the address size to meet the growing demands of modern networks that have large numbers of devices connected to a network. Rather than simply increasing the address size, however, the designers of IPv6 made other improvements based on their experience of over 15 years of running Ipv4.

A number of competing proposals were made to solve the problems of Ipv4 addressing and to improve the protocol. Ipv6 is the culmination of the best ideas in the competing proposals. The following sections describe the structure of the Ipv6 header format in detail.

The IPv6 Header Format

The IPv6 header consists of a basic fixed-size 40-octet header that contains 16 octets each for the source and destination IPv6 addresses. The basic IPv6 header can be followed optionally by special IPv6 extension headers that include the following:

- Routing header
- Fragment header
- Destination Options header
- No Next header
- Hop-by-Hop Options header
- Authentication header
- Encrypted Security Payload header

The Ipv6 headers permit additional information to be supplied with the basic Ipv6 header.

The *extension headers* provide additional information to handle IPv6 processing. Extension headers follow the Ipv6 basic header and describe subprotocol layers within the Ipv6 layer. Using extension headers, Ipv6 defines additional facilities and even enables the definition of new facilities.

An IPv6 datagram can contain zero or several extension headers. Typically, destination devices examine these headers so that intermediate devices, such as routers, do not have to waste time processing extension headers although the intermediate devices are required to transmit them. An exception to this rule includes those extension headers—such as the Hop-by-Hop Options header and the Routing extension header—that are designed to be processed by routers.

Figure 15.1 shows the basic IPv6 header.

Figure 15.1 IPv6 basic header.

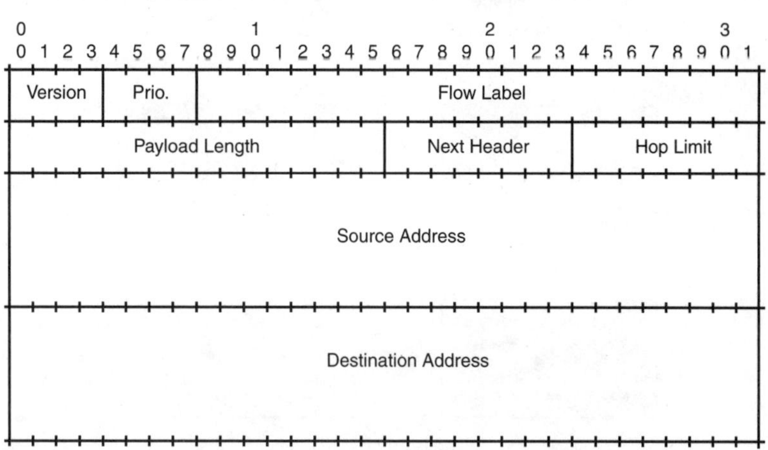

Note that the first field is the four-bit Version field. This field is the same as the IPv4 field except that its value is 6 instead of 4 for the IPv4 header. The value of 6 for the Version field indicates that the fields that follow use the IPv6 header format. Originally, it was intended that the IPv4 and IPv6 protocols would run on the same physical network, using the same Data Link layer drivers. Demultiplexing of the two formats would be done by examining the Version field. For reasons of efficiency, it is intended that the demultiplexing of IPv4 and IPv6 be performed wherever possible at the Data Link layer. For this reason, a Ethernet Type value of 86DD (hex) has been assigned for IPv6. Figure 15.2 shows how demultiplexing of IPv4 and IPv6 headers can be done by using the Ethernet Type field.

The Priority field is four-bits long and can have 16 possible values. This field enables the sender to assign a level of importance to datagrams that are originated by the sender. This field plays a similar role to the Precedence field in IPv4. The Priority values are divided into two ranges:

- **Values 0–7.** These values are used to specify the priority of traffic for which the source is providing congestion control. This traffic, such as TCP traffic, "backs off" in response to congestion.
- **Values 8–15.** These values are used to specify the priority of traffic that does not back off in response to congestion, such as real-time packets that are sent at a constant rate.

Figure 15.2 Demultiplexing of IPv4 and IPv6 headers.

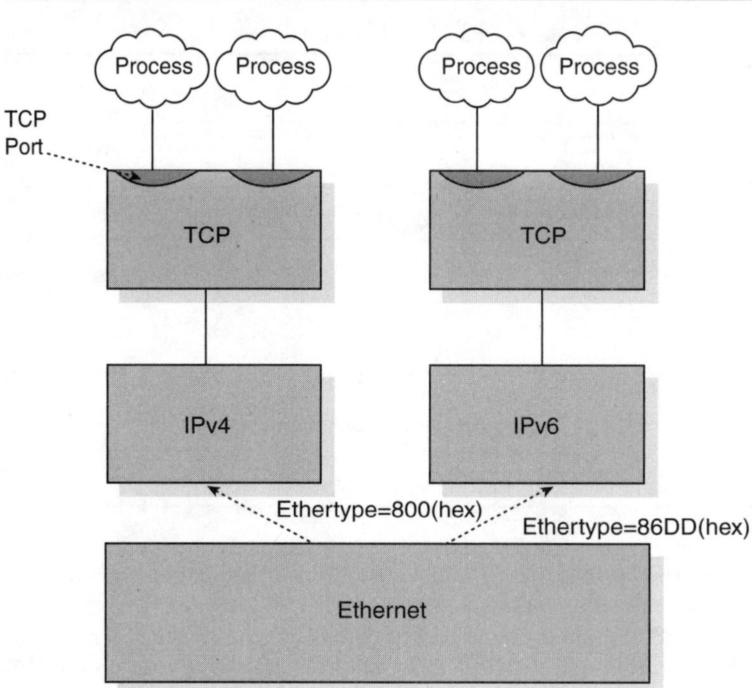

Table 15.1 defines priority values for congestion-controlled traffic.

TABLE 15.1
IPv6 Priority Field Values

Priority Value	Meaning
0	Uncharacterized traffic
1	"Filler" traffic (for example, netnews)
2	Unattended data transfer (for example, e-mail)

Priority Value	Meaning
3	(Reserved)
4	Attended bulk transfer (for example, FTP, NFS)
5	(Reserved)
6	Interactive traffic (for example, Telnet, X)
7	Internet control traffic (for example, routing protocols, SNMP)

For noncongestion-controlled traffic, such as in real-time applications, the lowest Priority value, which is 8, should be used for those packets that the sender is most willing to have discarded under conditions of congestion. The highest value, which is 15, should be used for those packets that the sender is least willing to have discarded. The actual priority levels to be used will be decided by the applications or configuration options within the applications that run on the Ipv6 network.

The Flow Label is a 24-bit field that is used to identify datagrams that are transmitted between a source and destination and need a similar treatment. Datagrams that have the same label value between the specified source and destination are considered to part of the same "flow." For example, datagrams carrying video or audio data from a server to a multimedia station may have different flow label values. This enables traffic with the same flow label values to be treated in the same manner throughout the network.

Payload Length is a 16-bit field that contains an unsigned value that represents the size of the data carried after the header. This length does not include the IPv6 basic header. The Payload Length field is similar to the Total Length field in the IPv4 header. The difference is that in IPv4, the Total Length field includes the IP header; in IPv6, the Payload Length field does not include the IP header. The size of the payload length is limited to 64 KB. IPv6 uses a jumbogram option to transport larger-size datagrams.

The Next Header is an eight-bit field that identifies the type of header immediately following the IPv6 basic header. The header that immediately follows can be the protocol type value that identifies a transport protocol such as TCP (6) or UDP (17); or the header can be a value that identifies an IPv6 extension header. IPv6 extension headers are used to specify IPv6 options and other information. Figure 15.3 shows the use of the Next Header field to specify a TCP message that follows immediately. A Next Header value of 59 indicates no next header; in other words, there is no encapsulation of any other protocol or data. Table 15.2 shows some of the Next Header values.

Figure 15.3 Use of Next Header field.

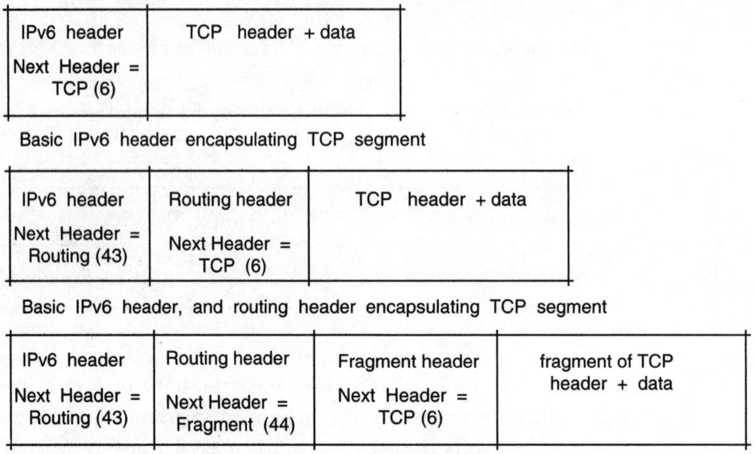

Basic IPv6 header, routing header, and fragmentation header encapsulating TCP segment

TABLE 15.2
Common Protocol Types and Next Header Values

Decimal	Abbreviation	Description
0		Reserved (Ipv4)
0	HBH	Hop-by-hop option (IPv6)
1	ICMP	Internet Control Message Protocol (IPv4)
2	IGMP	Internet Group Management Protocol (IPv4)
2	ICMP	Internet Control Message Protocol (IPv4)
3	GGP	Gateway-to-Gateway Protocol
4	IP	IP in IP (IPv4 encapsulation)
5	ST	Stream

Decimal	Abbreviation	Description
6	TCP	Transmission Control Protocol
17	UDP	User Datagram Protocol
29	ISO-TP4	ISO Transport Protocol Class 4
37	DDP	Datagram Delivery Protocol
43	RH	Routing header (IPv6)
44	FH	Fragment header (IPv6)
45	IDRP	Inter-Domain Routing Protocol
51	AH	Authentication header (IPv6)
52	ESP	Encrypted Security Payload (IPv6)
59	Null	No Next header (IPv6)
80	ISO-IP	ISO Internet Connectionless Protocol (CLNP)
88	IGRP	IGRP
89	OSPF	Open Shortest Path First
255		Reserved

The Hop Limit is an eight-bit field that contains an unsigned integer value. This field is decreased by 1 every time a router forwards the IPv6 datagram. When the value reaches 0, the device that is handling the datagram discards the datagram. This field prevents old datagrams from endlessly circulating around the network, a problem that can easily occur if a routing loop is created. The initial value of Hop Limit is set by the sender. The Hop Limit is similar to the TTL field in the IPv4 header. The difference is that in IPv4, the TTL field is measured in seconds; and in IPv6, the Hop Limit is measured in hops. Actually, even in IPv4, the TTL—for all practical considerations—has the property of a hop count because routers decrease the TTL value by 1 instead of the time it takes to process the datagram. In reality, protocols such as TCP use large Sequence Number fields (see Chapter 11, "Transfer Protocols") to guard against the resurgence of old packets.

The Source Address and Destination Address fields are 16 octets long and represent the new IPv6 addresses. These addresses are discussed in Chapter 4, "IP Addressing."

The upcoming sections discuss the different Ipv6 extension headers.

Routing Header

The IPv6 Routing Extension header (see fig. 15.4) is used to specify one or more intermediate routers that an IPv6 datagram must visit on its way to the destination. This header is used to implement the idea of the source routing option that is also used in IPv4. The IPv6 Routing extension header is identified by the Next Header value of 43 in the IPv6 basic header.

Figure 15.4 IPv6 Routing extension header.

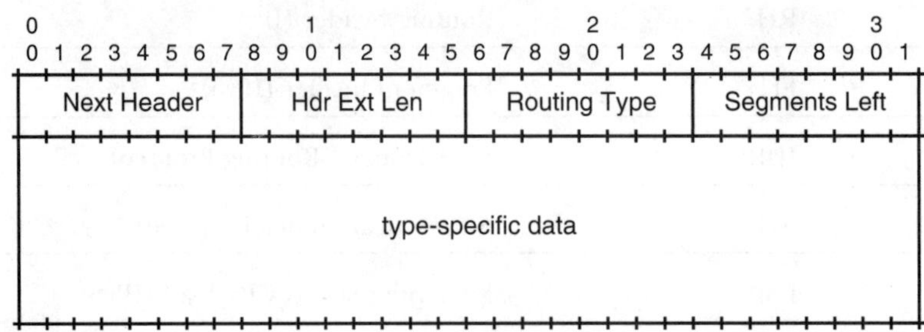

The fields in the IPv6 Routing extension header have the following meaning:

- **Next Header.** This is an eight-bit selector that identifies the type of header that immediately follows the Routing header. It can be another IPv6 extension header as part of a chain of IPv6 extension headers, or it can be an upper-layer transport protocol.
- **Hdr Ext Len.** This is an eight-bit unsigned integer that indicates the length of the Routing header in eight-octet units, excluding the first eight octets.
- **Routing Type.** This field is an eight-bit identifier of a particular Routing header variant. Currently, a Routing Type of 0 is defined in the IPv6 specification (RFC 1883). Other values can be used to identify alternative Routing header formats.
- **Segments Left.** This field is an eight-bit unsigned integer and specifies the number of route segments remaining. The number of remaining route segments is the number of explicitly listed intermediate nodes that still need to be visited before reaching the final destination.
- **Type-Specific Data.** This is a variable-length field whose format is determined by the Routing Type field. The length of the field is such that the complete Routing header length is an integer multiple of eight octets.

If a node encounters a Routing header with an unrecognized Routing Type value, it processes the packet based on the value of the Segments Left field. If Segments Left is zero, the node ignores the Routing header and proceeds to process the next header in the packet. The next header is identified by the Next Header field in the Routing header.

If Segments Left is nonzero, the node must discard the packet and send an ICMP Parameter Problem, Code 0, message to the packet's destination, which is indicated by the Source Address field and points to the unrecognized Routing Type value.

Figure 15.5 shows a Routing header for Routing Type 0. Note that the first 32 bits of this header are the same as shown in figure 15.4. The Type-specific data field contains a list of router addresses that enable the source to override the route that may have been otherwise followed by the IPv6 datagram as determined by the routing protocol running at the router.

Figure 15.5 Routing type 0, IPv6 Routing header.

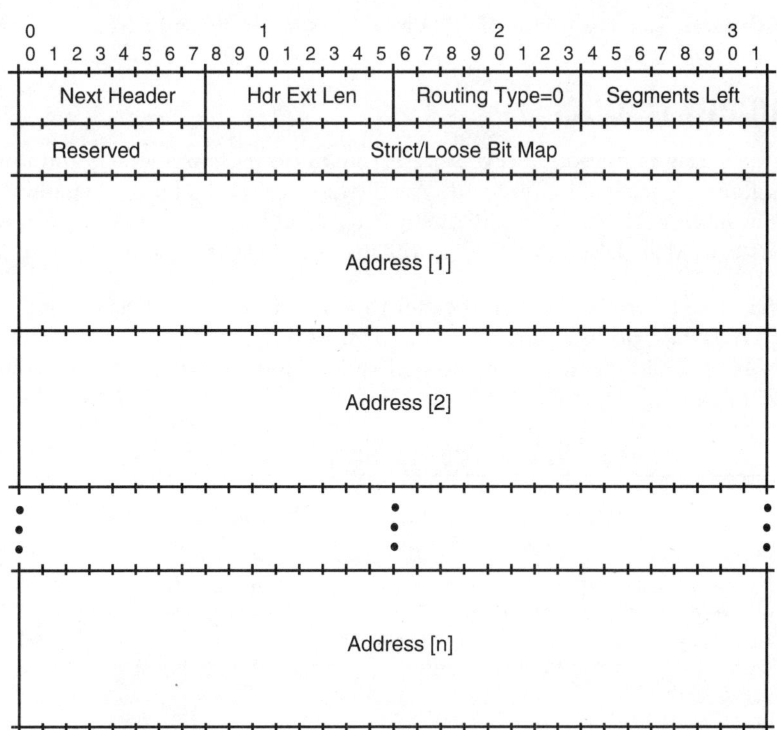

The fields in the IPv6 type 0 Routing extension header have the following meaning:

- **Next Header.** An eight-bit selector that identifies the type of header immediately following the Routing header.
- **Hdr Ext Len.** An eight-bit unsigned integer. This field is the length of the Routing header in eight-octet units, excluding the first eight octets. For the Type 0 Routing header, the Hdr Ext Len is equal to two times the number of addresses in the header and must be an even number less than or equal to 46.

- **Segments Left.** An eight-bit unsigned integer. This field is the number of route segments remaining, and its maximum legal value is 23 for route type 0.
- **Reserved.** An eight-bit reserved field that is initialized to zero for transmission and ignored on reception.
- **Strict/Loose Bit Map.** A 24-bit bitmap, numbered 0 to 23, left to right. Each bit corresponds to a segment of the route and indicates whether the next destination address must be a neighbor of the preceding address. A bit value of 1 means a strict-source routing; that is, the next destination address must be a neighbor. A bit value of 0 means loose-source routing; that is, the next destination address does not have to be a neighbor.
- **Address[1..n].** A vector of 128-bit addresses, numbered 1 to *n*.

Fragment Header

Unlike IPv4, fragmentation in IPv6 is performed only by source nodes and not by routers along a packet's delivery path. An IPv6 source node knows the path MTU size to the destination. IPv6 nodes implement Path MTU Discovery as defined in RFC 1191 on "Path MTU Discovery" to discover the path MTU to the destination.

An IPv6 source inserts a Fragment header to send packets larger than would fit in the path MTU to their destinations. The Fragment header is identified by a Next Header value of 44 in the immediately preceding header. Figure 15.6 shows the format of the Fragment header.

Figure 15.6 IPv6 Fragment extension header.

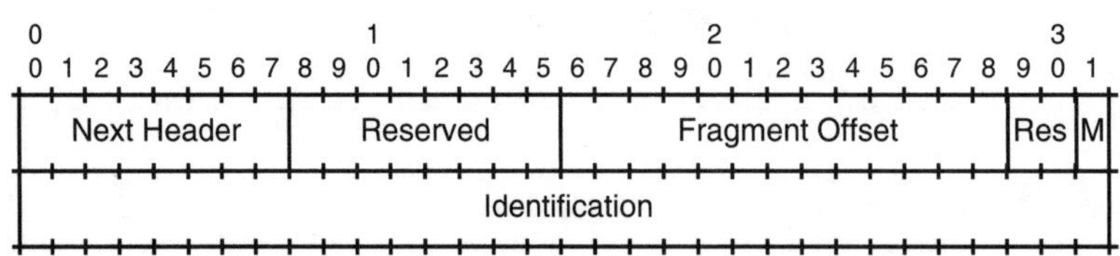

The fields in the Fragment header have the following meanings:

- **Next Header.** An eight-bit selector that identifies the type of header that immediately follows the Routing header. This header can be another IPv6 extension header as part of a chain of IPv6 extension headers, or it can be an upper-layer transport protocol.
- **Reserved.** An eight-bit reserved field that is initialized to zero for transmission and ignored on reception.

- **Fragment Offset.** A 13-bit unsigned integer that indicates the offset, in 8-octet units, of the data following this header. Offsets are measured relative to the start of the fragmentable part of the original packet.
- **Res.** A two-bit reserved field that is initialized to zero for transmission and ignored on reception.
- **M flag.** This field is set to 1 for more fragments, and 0 for the last fragment.
- **Identification.** A 32-bit field. For every packet that is to be fragmented, the source node generates an Identification value. The Identification value must be different from that of any other fragmented packet sent recently with the same Source Address and Destination Address fields.

Destination Options Header

The Destination Options header is used to carry optional information that needs to be examined only by a packet's destination nodes. The Destination Options header is identified by a Next Header value of 60 in the immediately preceding header (see fig. 15.7).

Figure 15.7 IPv6 Destination Options extension header.

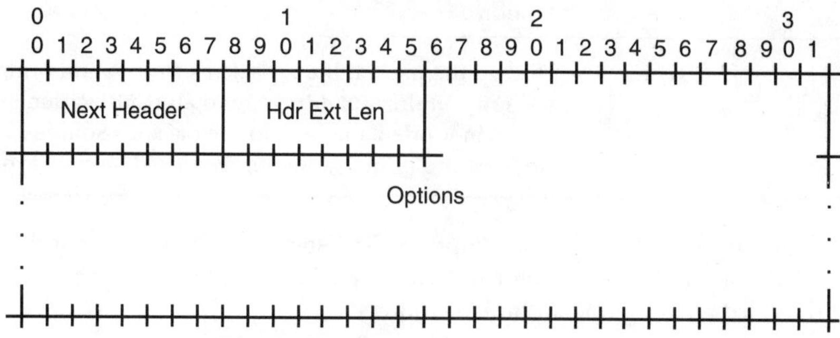

The fields in the Destination Options header have the following meaning:

- **Next Header.** An eight-bit selector that identifies the type of header immediately following the Routing header.
- **Hdr Ext Len.** An eight-bit unsigned integer. This field is the length of the Routing header in eight-octet units, excluding the first eight octets.
- **Options.** A variable-length field. The complete Destination Options header length is an integer multiple of eight octets.

Option values are used by the Hop-by-Hop and the Destination Options header. The option values are encodes that use the Type-Length-Value (TLV) format. The option type is one octet, and the option length is one octet and has the size of the option data that immediately follows. The Option Type identifiers are encoded so that their most significant two bits specify the action that must be taken if the processing IPv6 node does not recognize the Option Type. Table 15.3 shows this encoding.

TABLE 15.3
Most Significant Two Bits in Option Type for IPv6

Bits	Meaning
00	Skip over this option and continue processing the header.
01	Discard the packet.
10	Discard the packet. Regardless of whether the packet's Destination Address was a multicast address, send an ICMP Parameter Problem, Code 2 message to the packet's Source Address that points to the unrecognized Option Type.
11	Discard the packet. If the packet's Destination Address was not a multicast address, send an ICMP Parameter Problem, Code 2 message to the packet's Source Address and point to the unrecognized Option Type.

The third most significant bit of the Option Type specifies whether or not the option data of that option can change en route to the packet's final destination. The meaning of the third most significant bit is as follows:

- **0** Option Data does not change en route.
- **1** Option Data may change en route.

Two *padding options*—Pad1 and PadN (see fig. 15.8)—are used when necessary to align subsequent options and to pad out the containing header to a multiple of eight octets in length.

The Pad1 option is used to insert one octet of padding into the Options area of a header. If more than one octet of padding is required, the PadN option is used.

Figure 15.8 Padding options.

Pad1 option (alignment requirement: none)

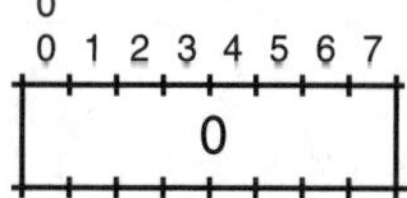

Note: the format of the Pad1 option is a special case – it does not have lengths and value fields.

PadN option (alignment requirement: none)

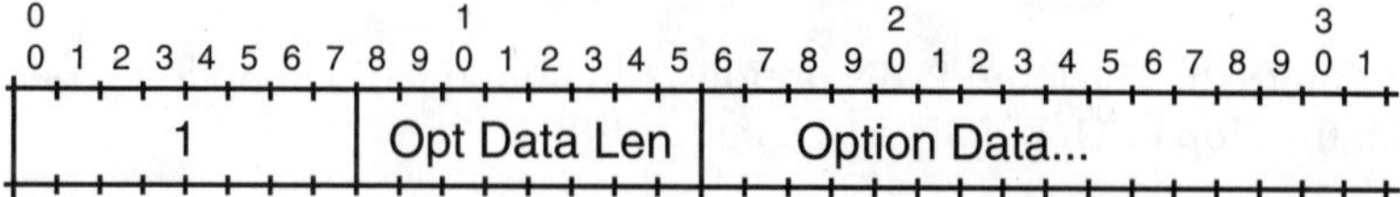

No Next Header

If a value of 59 is used in the Next Header field of an IPv6 header or any extension header, it indicates that nothing is following that header. If the Payload Length field of the IPv6 header indicates the presence of octets past the end of a header whose Next Header field contains 59, those octets must be ignored and passed on unchanged if the packet is forwarded.

Hop-By-Hop Options Header

The Hop-by-Hop Options header is used to carry optional information that is required by all intermediary nodes along a packet's delivery path. The Hop-by-Hop Options header is identified by a Next Header value of 0 in the IPv6 header and has the format shown in figure 15.9.

The fields in the Hop-by-Hop Options header have the following meaning:

- **Next Header.** An eight-bit selector that identifies the type of header immediately following the Routing header.
- **Hdr Ext Len.** An eight-bit unsigned integer. This is the length of the Routing header in eight-octet units, excluding the first eight octets.

- **Options.** A variable-length field, on which the complete Destination Options header length is an integer multiple of eight octets. The option values are encodes that use the Type-Length-Value (TLV) format.

Figure 15.9 IPv6 hop-by-Hop Options header.

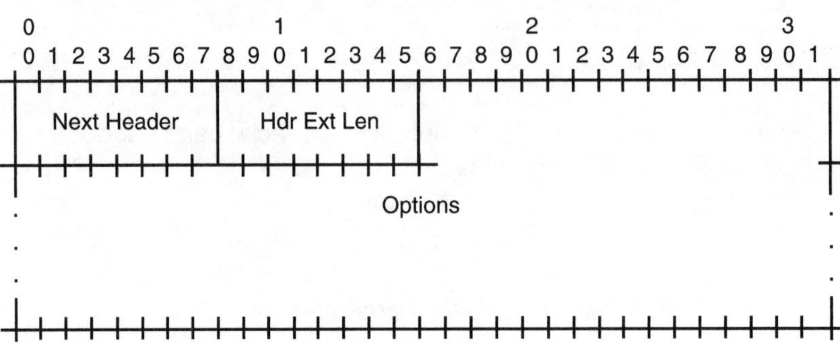

In addition to the Pad1 and PadN options, the Jumbo Payload option is defined for use with the Hop-by-Hop option (see fig. 15.10).

Figure 15.10 IPv6 Jumbo Payload option.

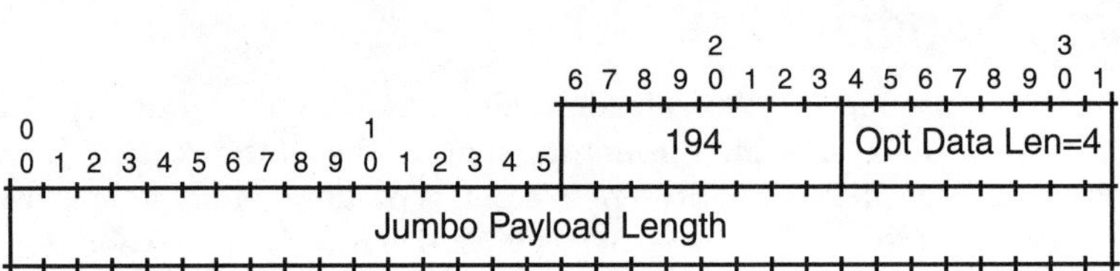

The alignment requirement for the Jumbo Payload option is *4n + 2*. This alignment means that the start of the option must be a multiple of four octets plus two from the start of the header.

The Jumbo Payload option is used to send IPv6 packets with payloads longer than 65,535 octets. The Jumbo Payload Length field is 32 bits wide and represents the length of the packet in octets, excluding the IPv6 header but including the Hop-by-Hop Options header. The Jumbo Payload length must be greater than 65,535. If a packet is received with a Jumbo Payload option containing a Jumbo Payload Length less than or equal to 65,535, an ICMP Parameter Problem message, Code 0, is sent to the packet's source. The message points to the high-order octet of the invalid Jumbo Payload Length field.

In addition, the Payload Length field in the IPv6 header must be set to zero in every packet that carries the Jumbo Payload option. If a packet is received with a valid Jumbo Payload option present and a nonzero IPv6 Payload Length field, an ICMP

Parameter Problem message, Code 0, is sent to the packet's source. This message points to the Option Type field of the Jumbo Payload option.

Authentication Header

The Authentication header (see fig. 15.11) is used to provide strong integrity and authentication for IP datagrams. The IPv6 Authentication header provides security by adding authentication information to an IP datagram. This authentication information is calculated by using all the fields that do not change in transit in the IPv6 datagram. Fields or options that need to change in transit—such as hop count, time to live, and so on—are considered to be zero for the calculation of the authentication data. The IPv6 header immediately preceding the Authentication header contains the value of 51 in its Next Header field. The Authentication header is used to detect whether the packet has been altered. It has no facilities for encrypting the packet. Packet encryption is handled by the IPv6 Encrypted Security Payload header (see the next section).

Figure 15.11 IPv6 Authentication header.

Bits 0–7	Bits 8–15	Bits 16–31
Next Header	Length	Reserved
Security Parameters Index		
Authentication Data (variable number of 32-bit words)		

The fields of the Authentication header have the following meaning:

- **Next Header.** This field is an eight-bit selector that identifies the type of header immediately following the Routing header.
- **Length.** This field is eight bits wide and specifies the length of the Authentication Data field in 32-bit words. Its minimum value is 0 words, which is used only in the special case when no authentication algorithm is used.
- **Reserved.** This field is 16 bits wide and is reserved for future use. It must be set to all zeros by the sender. The value is included in the Authentication Data calculation, but it is otherwise ignored by the recipient.
- **Security Parameters Index (SPI).** This is a 32-bit pseudorandom value that identifies the security association for this datagram. The Security Parameters Index value of 0 is reserved to indicate that no security association exists. The

set of Security Parameters Index values in the range 1 through 255 is reserved to the Internet Assigned Numbers Authority (IANA) for future use. A reserved SPI value will not normally be assigned by IANA unless the use of that particular assigned SPI value is openly specified in an RFC.

- **Authentication Data.** This is a variable-length field, but it is always an integral number of 32-bit words and contains the calculated authentication data for this packet.

Encrypted Security Payload Header

The IPv6 Encrypted Security Payload (ESP) is used for providing integrity and confidentiality of IP datagrams. Nonrepudiation and protection from traffic analysis are not provided by ESP. The IPv6 Authentication header can provide nonrepudiation if it is used with certain authentication algorithms.

The IP Authentication header can be used in conjunction with ESP to provide authentication. An application requiring integrity and authentication without confidentiality should use the Authentication header rather than ESP because the IP Authentication header is designed for authentication, and the ESP header is designed for confidentiality.

ESP encrypts data to be protected and places the encrypted data in the data portion of the Encapsulating Security Payload. This mechanism can be used to encrypt either a Transport layer segment or an entire IP datagram.

ESP has the following two modes of operation:

- Tunnel-mode ESP
- Transport-mode ESP

In Tunnel-mode ESP, the original IP datagram is placed in the encrypted portion of the Encapsulating Security Payload, and that entire ESP frame is placed within a datagram having unencrypted IP headers. The information in the unencrypted IP headers is used to route the secure datagram from origin to destination. An unencrypted IP Routing header may be included between the IP header and the Encapsulating Security Payload.

In Transport-mode ESP, the ESP header is inserted into the IP datagram immediately prior to the Transport Layer Protocol header. In this mode, bandwidth is conserved because there are no encrypted IP headers or IP options.

ESP can appear anywhere after the IP header and before the final Transport Layer Protocol header. The header immediately preceding an ESP header must contain the value of 50 in its Next Header field. ESP consists of an unencrypted header followed by encrypted data. The encrypted data includes both the protected ESP header fields and the protected user data, which is either an entire IP datagram or a Transport layer protocol. A high-level diagram of a secure IP datagram is shown in figure 15.12.

Figure 15.12 IPv6 Encrypted Security Payload header.

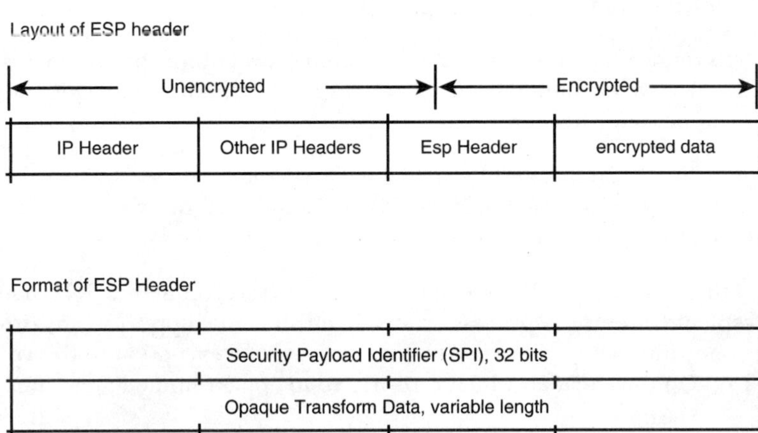

Encryption and authentication algorithms, and the precise format of the Opaque Transform Data associated with them, are known as *transforms.* The ESP format is designed to support new transforms in the future to support new or additional cryptographic algorithms.

The SPI field (see fig. 15.12) is a 32-bit pseudorandom value identifying the security association for this datagram. If no security association has been established, the value of the SPI field is set to 0. An SPI is similar to the Security Association Identifier (SAID) used in other security protocols. SPI values from 0 through 255 are reserved by the Internet Assigned Numbers Authority (IANA) for future use. The SPI is the only mandatory transform-independent field.

IPv6 Extension Header Order

When more than one extension header is used in the same packet, the RFCs recommend that headers should appear in the following order:

1. IPv6 header
2. Hop-by-Hop Options header
3. Destination Options header
4. Routing header
5. Fragment header

6. Authentication header
7. Encapsulating Security Payload header
8. Destination Options header
9. Upper-layer header

Each extension header should occur once, at most, except for the Destination Options header, which should occur twice: once before a Routing header and once before the upper-layer header.

If the upper-layer header is another IPv6 header—as in the case where IPv6 is being tunneled over or encapsulated in IPv6—it may be followed by extensions headers, which are separately subject to the same ordering recommendations.

Although the preceding order of extension headers is recommended, IPv6 nodes must accept and attempt to process extension headers that appear in any order and that occur any number of times in the same packet. The exception to this rule is the Hop-by-Hop Options header, which is restricted to appear immediately after an IPv6 header.

IP on ATM

Asynchronous Transfer Mode (ATM) is a technology that uses cell-level switching to provide large data rates and bandwidth. The fundamental component in an ATM network is a switch (see fig. 15.13). Typically, fiber-optic cables are used as the media for an ATM network. A pair of fiber-optic cables is used to carry data to and from a switch. The ATM switch uses small packet sizes of 53 octets. Of the 53 octets in an ATM cell, 5 octets are used as an ATM header, and the remaining 48 octets are used for data. The actual protocol efficiency of an ATM cell (taking into account on the ATM overhead) is quite good: it is 90.6 percent.

Original data is broken down into small cells and sent rapidly across the network. Figure 15.14 shows a network built by using a number of ATM switches. The interface between ATM switches is called Network to Network Interface (NNI), and the interface between a computer and an ATM switch is called User to Network Interface (UNI). The set of ATM switches in a network is also called an *ATM fabric*.

Before discussing the actual transport of IP datagrams in ATM networks, you must have additional background information on ATM, such as ATM circuits and the ATM adaptation layer. These concepts are covered in the upcoming sections.

Figure 15.13 An ATM switch.

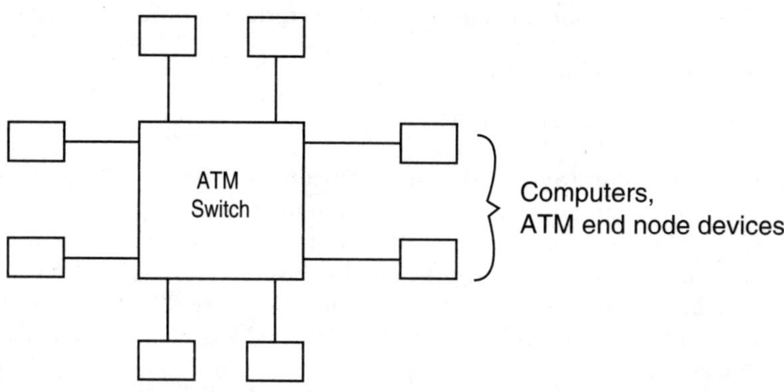

Figure 15.14 ATM network and interfaces.

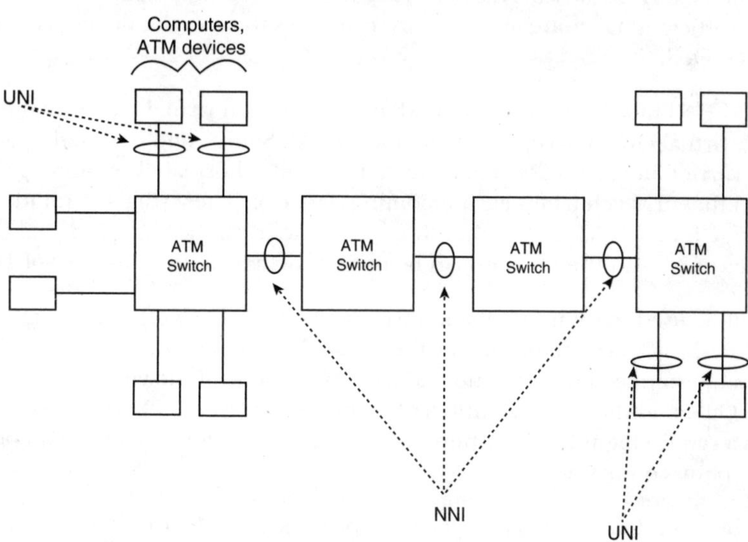

ATM Circuits

ATM provides two types of connection-oriented interfaces between two IP nodes:

- Switched virtual circuits (SVCs)
- Permanent virtual circuits (PVCs)

A switched virtual circuit (SVC) call is similar to a telephone call. The SVC goes through a call-establishment phase, a connection-maintenance phase where data is transferred, and finally a connection-termination phase that closes the connection. The computer makes the request for the call establishment to its local ATM switch and specifies the complete address of the remote computer. The computer then waits for the local ATM switch to complete the call. The ATM signaling mechanism is used to establish a circuit from the originating computer to the destination computer through a series of ATM switches. During the call-establishment phase, each ATM switch on the path examines the *quality of service* (QoS) requested for the virtual circuit. If an ATM switch can meet the demands of the requested QoS, it forwards the call to the next ATM switch. After an ATM switch agrees to accept the call, it must commit sufficient hardware and software resources to meet the demands of the requested QoS.

The ATM UNI interface uses a 24-bit identifier for each virtual circuit that is assigned for each virtual circuit accepted by the local ATM. Source and destination addresses are not carried in each ATM cell. Instead, the sender host labels each outgoing data cell, and the ATM cell labels each incoming data cell. The virtual circuit identifiers are unique for each ATM hop; therefore, the sender can be using a virtual circuit identifier of 33, and the receiver can be using a virtual circuit identifier of 108.

ATM can be used to set up permanent virtual circuits (PVCs) that act as telephone leased lines. PVCs are established by the network administrator, who manually specifies the source and destination address end points of the virtual circuit, the desired QoS, and the 24-bit identifiers for the virtual circuit. PVCs are useful when there is a requirement for a continuous (or near continuous) data stream between two end points on the network.

The 24-bit circuit identifier consists of two parts (see fig. 15.15):

- An 8-bit virtual path identifier (VPI)
- A 16-bit virtual circuit identifier (VCI)

The 24-bit circuit identifier is often called the VPI/VCI pair. The VPI value is the same for the set of virtual circuits that follow the same path value. The VPI field can be used to route data traffic more efficiently by using the VPI field to identify the route of the circuit. It is also possible for commercial carriers to charge for connections based on the path identified by the VPI value. The customers then have the flexibility of how they will multiplex virtual circuits along this path.

The VPI/VCI pair constitutes an important part of the information in each ATM cell header (see fig. 15.16). The ATM cell header is only five octets long.

Figure 15.16 An ATM cell header.

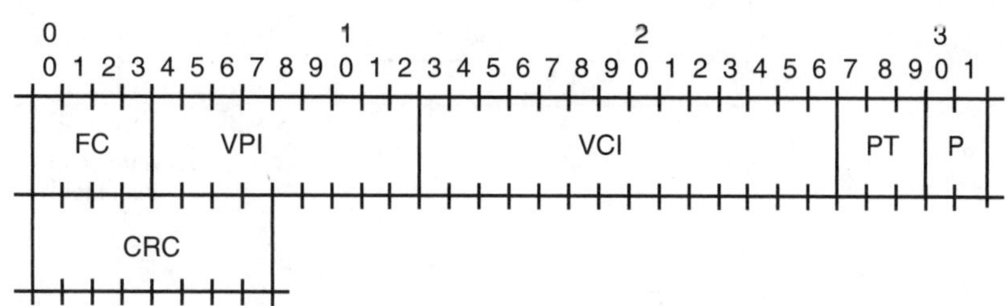

FC=Flow Control
VPI=Virtual Path Identifier
VCI=Virtual Circuit Identifier
PT=Payload Type
P=Priority
CRC=Cyclic Redundancy Checksum

ATM Adaptation Layer

ATM uses 53 octet cells at its lowest level. It is not efficient for IP running on ATM to break datagrams into such small sizes. Instead, the IP layer continues to treat datagrams normally and passes the datagrams to an ATM Adaptation layer (AAL). The AAL functions are located in the firmware on the ATM network-interface board. Software drivers running on the host computer interact with the AAL (see fig. 15.17).

You can use several choices of the Adaptation layer protocols: ATM Adaptation layer 1 (AAL1), ATM Adaptation layer 2 (AAL2), ATM Adaptation layer 3 (AAL3), ATM Adaptation layer 4 (AAL4), and ATM Adaptation layer 5 (AAL5). Most of the attention today is focused on AAL1, which is used for fixed-rate data streams, such as audio and video data; and AAL5, which is used for conventional computer communications. such as TCP/IP.

AAL5 provides an interface to IP with an MTU size of 65,535 octets. The AAL5 format is shown in figure 15.18. Rather than a header, AAL5 uses an eight-octet trailer.

The UU (User-to-User indication) field is used to transparently transfer user-to-user information. The field has no function for AAL5 and can be set to any value. The CPI (Common Part Identifier) field is used to align the AAL5 trailer to 64 bits. Because only the 64-bit alignment function is used, this field is set to 0.

Figure 15.17 An ATM interface.

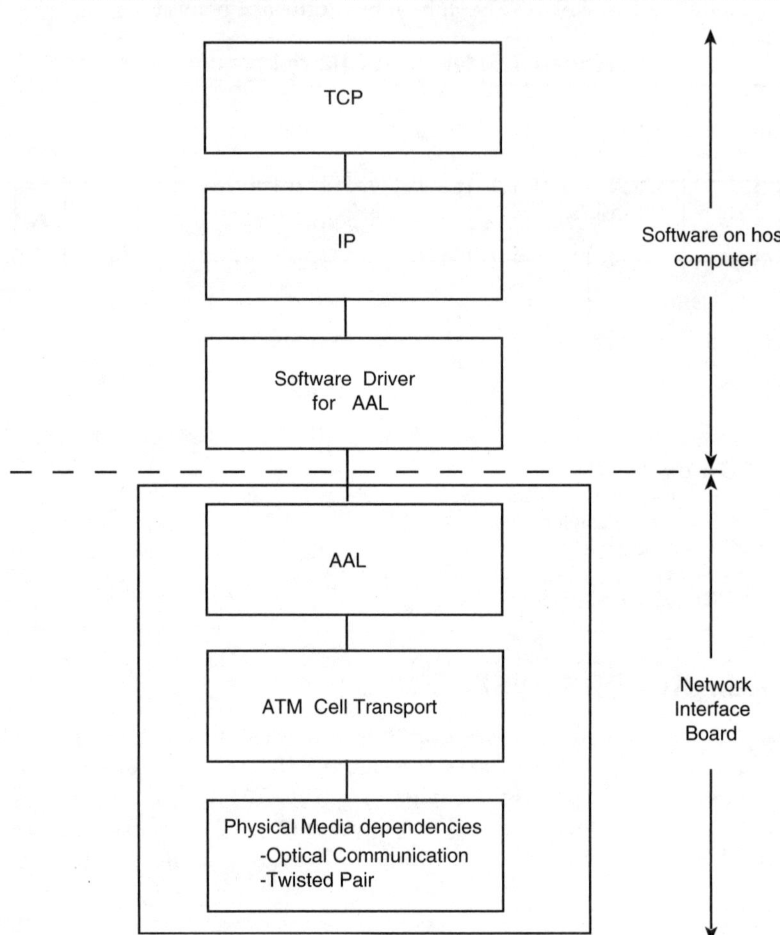

The Length field is 16 bits long and contains the length of the AAL5 packet. The Length field can be used to describe a packet that is 65,535 octets long.

The CRC field is the 32-bit Cyclic Redundancy Checksum used for error detection. The receiving AAL5 uses the CRC field to detect errors in the AAL5 packet.

Figure 15.18 The AAL5 format.

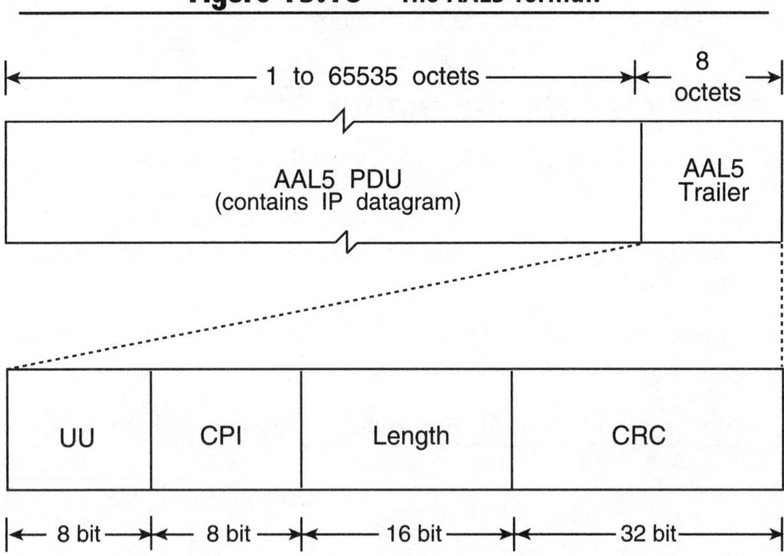

The IP datagram received by AAL5 is appended with the 8-octet AAL5 trailer and then divided into 48-octet units. This process is called segmentation and is performed by the ATM network-interface board inside the computer. Because segmentation is done in hardware, it is very rapid. Each 48-octet data unit is sent with a 5-octet ATM cell header to form a 53-octet ATM cell. The receiver AAL5 strips off the ATM cell headers and recombines the 48-octet data units to form the original IP datagram. The CRC is computed and checked against the original CRC for detecting errors in transmission. The process of recombining the 48-octet data units to form the original datagrams is called *reassembly* and is performed by the ATM network interface board at the receiver.

If the IP datagram size plus the 8-octet trailer is an exact multiple of 48 octets, the cell division will produce full cells. If the IP datagram size plus the 8-octet trailer is *not* an exact multiple of 48 octets, the last cell will not be full. AAL5 allows the last cell to be 0 to 40 octets long, followed by zero padding and then the 8-octet AAL5 trailer. AAL5 always places the AAL5 header in the last eight octets of the last ATM cell. This positioning enables the receiver AAL5 to quickly extract the AAL5 trailer without knowing the overall length of the packet.

How does the receiving AAL5 recognize the last cell in the series of AAL5 cells that constitute the AAL5 packet? AAL5 sets the low-order bit of the payload type field in the ATM cell header to indicate the last cell. The AAL5 receiver looks for this bit in the incoming cells that mark the end of the AAL5 packet. The process of recognizing the last cell of the AAL5 packet is called *convergence.*

Encoding Type Information for ATM

The AAL5 trailer format does not include a Type field for the data to be transmitted. If an ATM circuit is used for carrying data of only one protocol type such as IP, then the Type field is not necessary because both sender and receiver will have an agreement as to the type of protocol traffic being carried. However, in a multiprotocol environment, a Type field is needed.

To carry multiprotocol traffic, AAL5 uses SNAP (subnetwork attachment point) encapsulation. Figure 15.19 shows SNAP encapsulation for running IP on ATM.

Figure 15.19 SNAP encapsulation for running IP on ATM.

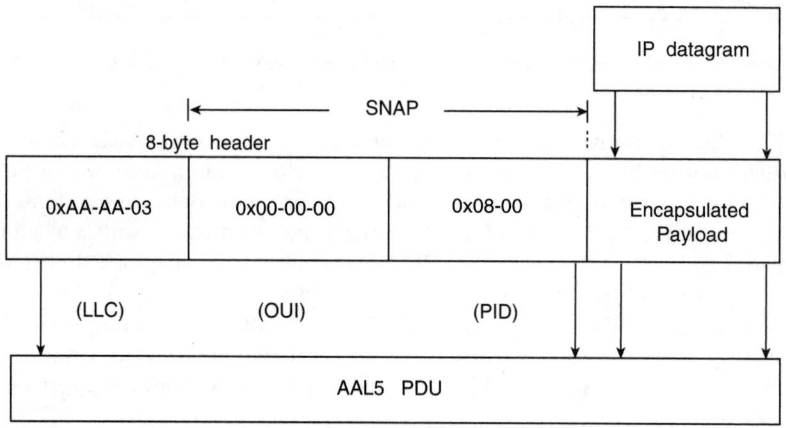

SNAP encapsulation is based on the IEEE 802.2 standard. It consists of the IEEE 802.2 header followed by the SNAP header.

The IEEE 802.2 header consists of the following consecutive fields:

- **DSAP field.** This field is one octet long and is the Destination Service Access Point field. Its value is set to AA (hex) to indicate SNAP encapsulation.
- **SSAP field.** This field is one octet long and is the Source Service Access Point field. Its value is set to AA (hex) to indicate SNAP encapsulation.

- **Control field.** This field is one octet long and, in IEEE 802.2, indicates the type of communication mode. Its value is set to 03 (hex) for SNAP encapsulation. A Control field value of 03 (hex) is for unnumbered information (UI), which means that no sequence numbers are used at the AAL5 level for numbering packets.

The SNAP header consists of the following consecutive fields that immediately follow the IEEE 802.2 header:

- **Organizational Unit Identifier (OUI).** This field is three octets long. Its value is a code for the organization or authority responsible for the further structuring of the fields that follow. An OUI value of 0 is used for the SNAP header format.
- **Type.** This is a two-octet field. Its value is the Ethernet Type field for the protocol type that is being encapsulated. For IPv4 datagrams, a value of 800 (hex) is used. For IPv6 datagrams, a value of 86DD (hex) is used. Other Ethernet Type values for other protocols are defined in RFC 1700 on "Assigned Numbers."

Summary

This chapter introduces two exciting technologies that have the potential to shape the future of the new generation of intranets and internets. These technologies are IP Next Generation and ATM.

In this chapter, you learned about the IPv6 protocol header format and the meanings of these fields. IPv6 not only extends the address range of IPv4 from 4 octets to 16 octets, but it also provides new facilities through extension headers. Extension headers follow the IPv6 basic header and describe subprotocol layers within the IPv6 layer. The IPv6 protocol is itself extensible through mechanisms such as the Destination Options header, which leaves the encoding of the Data field in this extension header up to the sender and the receiver.

Another topic discussed in this chapter is ATM. The ATM fabric provides a seamless interface between LANs and WANs. Traditionally, different hardware technologies have been used for building LANs and WANs. ATM can be used for both LANs and WANs and for a mix of a wide variety of data streams, such as audio, video, and data streams. The basics of the ATM technology as they apply to IP networks were discussed in this chapter.

A lot more can be said about IPv6 and ATM than is discussed in this chapter. But, alas, you have come to the end of the book and reached a ceiling—the page constraint and scope of this book—that does not permit a more detailed treatment of these exciting technologies. This treatment of these topics must then await another time when the sequel to this book, "TCP/IP: The Professional Reference," will be written.

Test Yourself

1. What is the purpose of dividing the IPv6 header into a basic header and extension headers?
2. What kind of information is kept in the IPv6 basic header? Draw a diagram of the IPv6 basic header format; label and briefly explain the fields.
3. How is protocol demultiplexing between IPv4 and IPv6 datagrams done?
4. Why is the IP Version field not used to perform protocol demultiplexing between IPv4 and IPv6?
5. What is the Priority field used for in the IPv6 basic header? Describe the values used for the priority field.
6. What is the purpose of the Next Header field in the IPv6 basic header and extension header?
7. List the different extension headers defined in IPv6. What mechanism is used in IPv6 that identifies an extension header as a particular type?
8. An IPv6 basic header encapsulates a TCP segment. What value of Next Header is used for this purpose? Draw a diagram that shows this encapsulation.
9. An IPv6 basic header encapsulates a UDP segment. What value of Next Header is used for this purpose? Draw a diagram that shows this encapsulation.
10. An IPv6 basic header and the routing header encapsulate a TCP segment. What values of the Next Header fields are used for this purpose? Draw a diagram that shows this encapsulation.
11. An IPv6 basic header, a Fragment header, and a Routing header encapsulate a TCP segment. What values of the Next Header fields are used for this purpose? Draw a diagram that shows this encapsulation.
12. What is the recommended order for IPv6 extension headers? What happens when an IPv6 does not use this recommended order?
13. Why does the IPv6 header use hops in the Hop field instead of using the TTL value?
14. Compare the IPv4 header with the IPv6 basic header. What are the similarities and dissimilarities between them?

15. What is the purpose of the IPv6 Routing extension header?
16. Draw a diagram of the IPv6 Routing extension header and explain the meaning of its fields.
17. What happens when an IPv6 node encounters a Routing extension header with an unrecognized Routing Type value?
18. Draw a diagram of a Routing extension header for Routing type 0. How is it different from the format of the general routing header?
19. How is IPv6 fragmentation different from IPv4 fragmentation?
20. What is the purpose of the IPv6 Fragment extension header?
21. Draw a diagram of the IPv6 Fragment extension header and explain the meaning of its fields.
22. What is the purpose of the IPv6 Destination Options extension header?
23. Draw a diagram of the IPv6 Destination Options extension header and explain the meaning of its fields.
24. How can the IPv6 Destination Options extension header be used to extend the functionality of IPv6?
25. When is the No Next header used?
26. What is the purpose of the IPv6 Hop-by-Hop Options extension header?
27. Draw a diagram of the IPv6 Hop-by-Hop Options extension header and explain the meaning of its fields.
28. What is the purpose of the Jumbo Payload option in the IPv6 Hop-by-Hop Options extension header? Describe the Jumbo Payload option format.
29. What is the purpose of the IPv6 Authentication extension header?
30. Draw a diagram of the IPv6 Authentication extension header and explain the meaning of its fields.
31. What is the purpose of the IPv6 Encrypted Security Payload header?
32. Draw a diagram of the IPv6 Encrypted Security Payload header and explain the meaning of its fields.
33. Describe the two modes of IPv6 Encrypted Security Payload operation.
34. What is the IPv6 extension headers order?
35. Describe the basic format of the ATM cell.
36. What is the difference between a UNI and a NNI in ATM?
37. Describe the two types of ATM circuits.

38. How is an ATM circuit identified? What are the two components of this identification?
39. Draw a diagram that identifies the components of an ATM interface inside a computer running TCP/IP.
40. Draw a diagram showing the AAL5 PDU format. Explain the meaning of the fields.
41. What mechanism is used for a receiver ATM station to efficiently identify the AAL5 trailer?
42. How is the last cell in an AAL5 PDU identified? What is this mechanism called?
43. For transmitting IP and other protocols over ATM, what mechanism is used? Describe this mechanism for sending IPv4 and IPv6 datagrams over an ATM interface.

Appendix A

Standard Protocols

This appendix lists the Standard, Draft, and Proposed protocols as defined in RFC 2200. These protocols are listed in tables to provide a ready reference to help you track the statuses of these protocols.

Table A.1 offers a list of standard protocols as described in RFC 2200.

Table A.1
Standard Protocols

Protocol	Name	Status	RFC	STD
	Internet Official Protocol Standards	Req	2200	1
	Assigned Numbers	Req	1700	2
	Host Requirements—Communications	Req	1122	3
	Host Requirements—Applications	Req	1123	3
IP	Internet Protocol as amended by:	Req	791	5
	IP Subnet Extension	Req	950	5
	IP Broadcast Datagrams	Req	919	5
	IP Broadcast Datagrams with Subnets	Req	922	5
ICMP	Internet Control Message Protocol	Req	792	5
IGMP	Internet Group Multicast Protocol	Rec	1112	5
UDP	User Datagram Protocol	Rec	768	6
TCP	Transmission Control Protocol	Rec	793	7
TELNET	Telnet Protocol	Rec	854,855	8
FTP	File Transfer Protocol	Rec	959	9
SMTP	Simple Mail Transfer Protocol	Rec	821	10
SMTP-SIZE	SMTP Service Ext for Message Size	Rec	1870	10
SMTP-EXT	SMTP Service Extensions	Rec	1869	10

Protocol	Name	Status	RFC	STD
MAIL	Format of Electronic Mail Messages	Rec	822	11
CONTENT	Content Type Header Field	Rec	1049	11
NTPV2	Network Time Protocol (Version 2)	Rec	1119	12
DOMAIN	Domain Name System	Rec	1034,1035	13
DNS-MX	Mail Routing and the Domain System	Rec	974	14
SNMP	Simple Network Management Protocol	Rec	1157	15
SMI	Structure of Management Information	Rec	1155	16
Concise-MIB	Concise MIB Definitions	Rec	1212	16
MIB-II	Management Information Base-II	Rec	1213	17
NETBIOS	NetBIOS Service Protocols	Ele	1001,1002	19
ECHO	Echo Protocol	Rec	862	20
DISCARD	Discard Protocol	Ele	863	21
CHARGEN	Character Generator Protocol	Ele	864	22
QUOTE	Quote of the Day Protocol	Ele	865	23
USERS	Active Users Protocol	Ele	866	24
DAYTIME	Daytime Protocol	Ele	867	25
TIME	Time Server Protocol	Ele	868	26

continues

Table A.1, Continued
Standard Protocols

Protocol	Name	Status	RFC	STD
TFTP	Trivial File Transfer Protocol	Ele	1350	33
TP-TCP	ISO Transport Service on top of the TCP	Ele	1006	35
ETHER-MIB	Ethernet MIB	Ele	1643	50
PPP	Point-to-Point Protocol (PPP)	Ele	1661	51
PPP-HDLC	PPP in HDLC Framing	Ele	1662	51
IP-SMDS	IP Datagrams over the SMDS Service	Ele	1209	52
POP3	Post Office Protocol (Version 3)	Ele	1939	53

Applicability Statements: RFC 2200 makes the following notes about some the protocols listed in table A.1. These notes are called Applicability Statements.

- **IGMP.** The Internet Architecture Board intends to move toward general adoption of IP multicasting as a more efficient solution than broadcasting for many applications. The host interface has been standardized in RFC-1112; however, multicast-routing gateways are in the experimental stage and are not widely available. An Internet host should support all of RFC-1112, except for the IGMP protocol itself, which is optional; see RFC-1122 for more details. Even without IGMP, implementation of RFC-1112 will provide an important advance: IP-layer access to local network multicast addressing. It is expected that IGMP will become recommended for all hosts and gateways at some future date.
- **SMI, MIB-II SNMP.** The Internet Architecture Board recommends that all IP and TCP implementations be network manageable. At the current time, this implies implementation of the Internet MIB-II (RFC-1213), and at least the recommended management protocol SNMP (RFC-1157).
- **RIP.** The Routing Information Protocol (RIP) is widely implemented and used in the Internet. However, both implementors and users should be aware that RIP has some serious technical limitations as a routing protocol. The IETF is currently devpeloping several candidates for a new standard "open" routing

protocol with better properties than RIP. The IAB urges the Internet community to track these developments, and to implement the new protocol when it is standardized; improved Internet service will result for many users.

- **TP-TCP.** As OSI protocols become more widely implemented and used, there will be an increasing need to support interoperation with the TCP/IP protocols. The Internet Engineering Task Force is formulating strategies for interoperation. RFC-1006 provides one interoperation mode, in which TCP/IP is used to emulate TP0 in order to support OSI applications. Hosts that wish to run OSI connection-oriented applications in this mode should use the procedure described in RFC-1006. In the future, the IAB expects that a major portion of the Internet will support both TCP/IP and OSI (inter-)network protocols in parallel, and it will then be possible to run OSI applications across the Internet using full OSI protocol "stacks."

Table A.2 lists Network-Specific Standard Protocols. All Network-Specific Standards have Elective status.

Table A.2
Network-Specific Standard Protocols

Protocol	Name	Status	RFC	STD
IP-ATM	Classical IP and ARP over ATM	Prop	1577	
IP-FR	Multiprotocol over Frame Relay	Draft	1490	
ATM-ENCAP	Multiprotocol Encapsulation over ATM	Prop	1483	
IP-TR-MC	IP Multicast over Token-Ring LANs	Prop	1469	
IP-FDDI	Transmission of IP and ARP over FDDI Net	Std	1390	36
IP-X.25	X.25 and ISDN in the Packet Mode	Draft	1356	
ARP	Address Resolution Protocol	Std	826	37
RARP	A Reverse Address Resolution Protocol	Std	903	38

continues

Table A.2, Continued
Network-Specific Standard Protocols

Protocol	Name	Status	RFC	STD
IP-ARPA	Internet Protocol on ARPANET	Std	BBN1822	39
IP-WB	Internet Protocol on Wideband Network	Std	907	40
IP-E	Internet Protocol on Ethernet Networks	Std	894	41
IP-EE	Internet Protocol on Exp. Ethernet Nets	Std	895	42
IP-IEEE	Internet Protocol on IEEE 802	Std	1042	43
IP-DC	Internet Protocol on DC Networks	Std	891	44
IP-HC	Internet Protocol on Hyperchannel	Std	1044	45
IP-ARC	Transmitting IP Traffic over ARCNET Nets	Std	1201	46
IP-SLIP	Transmission of IP over Serial Lines	Std	1055	47
IP-NETBIOS	Transmission of IP over NETBIOS	Std	1088	48
IP-IPX	Transmission of 802.2 over IPX Networks	Std	1132	49
IP-HIPPI	IP over HIPPI	Draft	2067	

Applicability Statements: RFC 2200 makes the following notes about some of the protocols listed in table A.2.

It is expected that a real-life network will support one or more physical networks, and for each physical network supported, the appropriate protocols from the preceding list must be supported. That is, it is elective to support any particular type of physical network, but it is required that the supported physical networks be supported exactly according to the protocols in the preceding list. See also the Host and Gateway Requirements RFCs (1122 and 1123) for more specific information on network-specific ("link layer") protocols.

Table A.3 lists the Draft Standard Protocols.

TABLE A.3
Draft Standard Protocols

Protocol	Name	Status	RFC
BOOTP	DHCP Options and BOOTP Extensions	Recommended	2132
DHCP	Dynamic Host Configuration Protocol	Elective	2131
	Clarifications and Extensions BOOTP	Elective	1542
DHCP-BOOTP	Interoperation Between DHCP and BOOTP	Elective	1534
MIME-CONF	MIME Conformance Criteria	Elective	2049
MIME-MSG	MIME Msg Header Ext for Non-ASCII	Elective	2047
MIME-MEDIA	MIME Media Types	Elective	2046
MIME	Multipurpose Internet Mail Extensions	Elective	2045
PPP-CHAP	PPP Challenge Handshake Authentication	Elective	1994
PPP-MP	PPP Multilink Protocol	Elective	1990
PPP-LINK	PPP Link Quality Monitoring	Elective	1989
COEX-MIB	Coexistence between SNMPV1 & SNMPV2	Elective	1908
SNMPv2-MIB	MIB for SNMPv2	Elective	1907
TRANS-MIB	Transport Mappings for SNMPv2	Elective	1906

continues

Table A.3, Continued
Draft Standard Protocols

Protocol	Name	Status	RFC
OPS-MIB	Protocol Operations for SNMPv2	Elective	1905
CONF-MIB	Conformance Statements for SNMPv2	Elective	1904
CONV-MIB	Textual Conventions for SNMPv2	Elective	1903
SMIV2	SMI for SNMPv2	Elective	1902
CON-MD5	Content-MD5 Header Field	Elective	1864
OSPF-MIB	OSPF Version 2 MIB	Elective	1850
STR-REP	String Representation ...	Elective	1779
X.500syn	X.500 String Representation ...	Elective	1778
X.500lite	X.500 Lightweight ...	Elective	1777
BGP-4-APP	Application of BGP-4	Elective	1772
BGP-4	Border Gateway Protocol 4	Elective	1771
PPP-DNCP	PPP DECnet Phase IV Control Protocol	Elective	1762
RMON-MIB	Remote Network Monitoring MIB	Elective	1757
802.5-MIB	IEEE 802.5 Token Ring MIB	Elective	1748
BGP-4-MIB	BGP-4 MIB	Elective	1657
RIP2-MIB	RIP Version 2 MIB Extension	Elective	1724
RIP2	RIP Version 2-Carrying Additional Info.	Elective	1723
RIP2-APP	RIP Version 2 Protocol App. Statement	Elective	1722
SIP-MIB	SIP Interface Type MIB	Elective	1694
	Def Man Objs Parallel-printer-like	Elective	1660

Protocol	Name	Status	RFC
	Def Man Objs RS-232-like	Elective	1659
	Def Man Objs Character Stream	Elective	1658
SMTP-8BIT	SMTP Service Ext or 8-bit MIME transport	Elective	1652
OSI-NSAP	Guidelines for OSI NSAP Allocation	Elective	1629
OSPF2	Open Shortest Path First Routing V2	Elective	1583
ISO-TS-ECHO	Echo for ISO-8473	Elective	1575
DECNET-MIB	DECNET MIB	Elective	1559
BRIDGE-MIB	BRIDGE-MIB	Elective	1493
NTPV3	Network Time Protocol (Version 3)	Elective	1305
IP-MTU	Path MTU Discovery	Elective	1191
FINGER	Finger Protocol	Elective	1288
NICNAME	WhoIs Protocol	Elective	954

Applicability Statements: RFC 2200 makes the following notes about some of the protocols listed in table A.3.

Point-to-Point Protocol (PPP) is a method of sending IP over serial lines, which are a type of physical network. It is anticipated that PPP will be advanced to the network-specifics standard protocol state in the future.

Table A.4 lists the Proposed Standard Protocols.

Table A.4
Proposed Standard Protocols

Protocol	Name	Status	RFC
IPv6-Jumbo	TCP and UDP over IPv6 Jumbograms	Elective	2147
MAIL-SERV	Mailbox Names for Common Services	Elective	2142
URN-SYNTAX	URN Syntax	Elective	2141
RADIUS	Remote Authentication Dial In Service	Elective	2138
SDNSDU	Secure Domain Name System Dynamic Update	Elective	2137
DNS-UPDATE	Dynamic Updates in the DNS	Elective	2136
DC-MIB	Dial Control MIB using SMIv2	Elective	2128
ISDN-MIB	ISDN MIB using SMIv2	Elective	2127
ITOT	ISO Transport Service on top of TCP	Elective	2126
BAP-BACP	PPP-BAP, PPP-BACP	Elective	2125
VEMMI-URL	VEMMI URL Specification	Elective	2122
ROUT-ALERT	IP Router Alert Option	Elective	2113
MIME-RELAT	MIME Multipart/Related Content-type	Elective	2112
CIDMID-URL	Content-ID and Message-ID URLs	Elective	2111
MHTML	MIME E-mail Encapsulation	Elective	2110
HTTP-STATE	HTTP State Management Mechanism	Elective	2109
802.3-MIB	802.3 Repeater MIB using SMIv2	Elective	2108

Protocol	Name	Status	RFC
PPP-NBFCP	PPP NetBIOS Frames Control Protocol	Elective	2097
TABLE-MIB	IP Forwarding Table MIB	Elective	2096
IMAPPOPAU	IMAP/POP AUTHorize Extension	Elective	2095
RIP-TRIG	Trigger RIP	Elective	2091
IMAP4-LIT	IMAP4 non-synchronizing literals	Elective	2088
IMAP4-QUO	IMAP4 QUOTA extension	Elective	2087
IMAP4-ACL	IMAP4 ACL Extension	Elective	2086
HMAC-MD5	HMAC-MD5 IP Auth. with Replay Prevention	Elective	2085
RIP2-MD5	RIP-2 MD5 Authentication	Elective	2082
RIPNG-IPV6	RIPng for Ipv6	Elective	2080
URI-ATT	URI Attribute Type and Object Class	Elective	2079
GSSAP	Generic Security Service Application	Elective	2078
MIME-MODEL	Model Primary MIME Types	Elective	2077
RMON-MIB	Remote Network Monitoring MIB	Elective	2074
IPV6-UNI	IPv6 Provider-Based Unicast Address	Elective	2073
HTML-INT	HTML Internationalization	Elective	2070
DAA	Digest Access Authentication	Elective	2069
HTTP-1.1	Hypertext Transfer Protocol—HTTP/1.1	Elective	2068
DNS-SEC	Domain Name System Security Extensions	Elective	2065

continues

Table A.4, Continued
Proposed Standard Protocols

Protocol	Name	Status	RFC
IMAPV4	Internet Message Access Protocol v4rev1	Elective	2060
URLZ39.50	Uniform Resource Locators for Z39.50	Elective	2056
SNANAU-APP	SNANAU APPC MIB using SMIv2	Elective	2051
PPP-SNACP	PPP SNA Control Protocol	Elective	2043
RTP-MPEG	RTP Payload Format for MPEG1/MPEG2	Elective	2038
ENTITY-MIB	Entity MIB using SMIv2	Elective	2037
RTP-JPEG	RTP Payload Format for JPEG-compressed	Elective	2035
SMTP-ENH	SMTP Enhanced Error Codes	Elective	2034
RTP-H.261	RTP Payload Format for H.261	Elective	2032
RTP-CELLB	RTP Payload Format of Sun's CellB	Elective	2029
SPKM	Simple Public-Key GSS-API Mechanism	Elective	2025
DLSW-MIB	DLSw MIB using SMIv2	Elective	2024
IPV6-PPP	IP Version 6 over PPP	Elective	2023
MULTI-UNI	Multicast over UNI 3.0/3.1 based ATM	Elective	2022
RMON-MIB	RMON MIB using SMIv2	Elective	2021
802.12-MIB	IEEE 802.12 Interface MIB	Elective	2020
IPV6-FDDI	Transmission of IPv6 Packets Over FDDI	Elective	2019
TCP-ACK	TCP Selective Acknowledgement Options	Elective	2018

Protocol	Name	Status	RFC
URL-ACC	URL Access-Type	Elective	2017
MIME-PGP	MIME Security with PGP	Elective	2015
MIB-UDP	SNMPv2 MIB for UDP	Elective	2013
MIB-TCP	SNMPv2 MIB for TCP	Elective	2012
MIB-IP	SNMPv2 MIB for IP	Elective	2011
MOBILEIPMIB	Mobile IP MIB Definition using SMIv2	Elective	2006
MOBILEIPAPP	Applicability Statement for IP Mobility	Elective	2005
MINI-IP	Minimal Encapsulation within IP	Elective	2004
IPENCAPIP	IP Encapsulation within IP	Elective	2003
MOBILEIPSUP	IP Mobility Support	Elective	2002
TCPSLOWSRT	TCP Slow Start, Congestion Avoidance ...	Elective	2001
BGP-COMM	BGP Communities Attribute	Elective	1997
DNS-NOTIFY	Mech. for Notification of Zone Changes	Elective	1996
DNS-IZT	Incremental Zone Transfer in DNS	Elective	1995
SMTP-ETRN	SMTP Service Extension ETRN	Elective	1985
SNA	Serial Number Arithmetic	Elective	1982
MTU-IPV6	Path MTU Discovery for IP version 6	Elective	1981
PPP-FRAME	PPP in Frame Relay	Elective	1973
IPV6-ETHER	Transmission IPv6 Packets Over Ethernet	Elective	1972

continues

Table A.4, Continued
Proposed Standard Protocols

Protocol	Name	Status	RFC
IPV6-AUTO	IPv6 Stateless Address Autoconfiguation	Elective	1971
IPV6-ND	Neighbor Discovery for IP Version 6	Elective	1970
PPP-ECP	PPP Encryption Control Protocol	Elective	1968
GSSAPI-KER	Kerberos Version 5 GSS-API Mechanism	Elective	1964
PPP-CCP	PPP Compression Control Protocol	Elective	1962
GSSAPI-SOC	GSS-API Auth for SOCKS Version 5	Elective	1961
LDAP-STR	String Rep. of LDAP Search Filters	Elective	1960
LDAP-URL	LDAP URL Format	Elective	1959
ONE-PASS	One-Time Password System	Elective	1938
TRANS-IPV6	Transition Mechanisms IPv6 Hosts/Routers	Elective	1933
AUTH-SOCKS	Username Authentication for SOCKS V5	Elective	1929
SOCKSV5	SOCKS Protocol Version 5	Elective	1928
WHOIS++M	How to Interact with a Whois++ Mesh	Elective	1914
WHOIS++A	Architecture of Whois++ Index Service	Elective	1913
DSN	Delivery Status Notifications	Elective	1894
EMS-CODE	Enhanced Mail System Status Codes	Elective	1893

Protocol	Name	Status	RFC
MIME-RPT	Multipart/Report	Elective	1892
SMTP-DSN	SMTP Delivery Status Notifications	Elective	1891
RTP-AV	RTP Audio/Video Profile	Elective	1890
RTP	Transport Protocol for Real-Time Apps	Elective	1889
DNS-IPV6	DNS Extensions to support Ipv6	Elective	1886
ICMPv6	ICMPv6 for Ipv6	Elective	1885
IPV6-Addr	IPv6 Addressing Architecture	Elective	1884
IPV6	IPv6 Specification	Elective	1883
HTML	Hypertext Markup Language—2.0	Elective	1866
SMTP-Pipe	SMTP Serv. Ext. for Command Pipelining	Elective	1854
MIME-Sec	MIME: Object Security Services	Elective	1848
MIME-Encyp	MIME: Signed and Encrypted	Elective	1847
WHOIS++	Architecture of the WHOIS++ service	Elective	1835
	Binding Protocols for ONC RPC Version 2	Elective	1833
XDR	External Data Representation Standard	Elective	1832
RPC	Remote Procedure Call Protocol V. 2	Elective	1831
	ESP DES-CBC Transform	Ele/Req	1829
	IP Authentication using Keyed MD5	Ele/Req	1828

continues

Table A.4, Continued
Proposed Standard Protocols

Protocol	Name	Status	RFC
ESP	IP Encapsulating Security Payload	Ele/Req	1827
IPV6-AH	IP Authentication Header	Ele/Req	1826
	Security Architecture for IP	Ele/Req	1825
RREQ	Requirements for IP Version 4 Routers	Elective	1812
URL	Relative Uniform Resource Locators	Elective	1808
CLDAP	Connection-less LDAP	Elective	1798
OSPF-DC	Ext. OSPF to Support Demand Circuits	Elective	1793
TMUX	Transport Multiplexing Protocol	Elective	1692
TFTP-Opt	TFTP Options	Elective	1784
TFTP-Blk	TFTP Blocksize Option	Elective	1783
TFTP-Ext	TFTP Option Extension	Elective	1782
OSI-Dir	OSI User Friendly Naming ...	Elective	1781
MIME-EDI	MIME Encapsulation of EDI Objects	Elective	1767
Lang-Tag	Tags for Identification of Languages	Elective	1766
XNSCP	PPP XNS IDP Control Protocol	Elective	1764
BVCP	PPP Banyan Vines Control Protocol	Elective	1763
Print-MIB	Printer MIB	Elective	1759
ATM-SIG	ATM Signaling Support for IP over ATM	Elective	1755

Protocol	Name	Status	RFC
IPNG	Recommendation for IP Next Generation	Elective	1752
802.5 SSR	802.5 SSR MIB using SMIv2	Elective	1749
SDLCSMIv2	SNADLC SDLC MIB using SMIv2	Elective	1747
BGP4/IDRP	BGP4/IDRP for IP/OSPF Interaction	Elective	1745
AT-MIB	Appletalk MIB	Elective	1742
MacMIME	MIME Encapsulation of Macintosh files	Elective	1740
URL	Uniform Resource Locators	Elective	1738
POP3-AUTH	POP3 AUTHentication command	Elective	1734
IMAP4-AUTH	IMAP4 Authentication Mechanisms	Elective	1731
RDBMS-MIB	RDMS MIB—using SMIv2	Elective	1697
MODEM-MIB	Modem MIB—using SMIv2	Elective	1696
ATM-MIB	ATM Management Version 8.0 using SMIv2	Elective	1695
SNANAU-MIB	SNA NAUs MIB using SMIv2	Elective	1666
PPP-TRANS	PPP Reliable Transmission	Elective	1663
	Postmaster Convention X.400 Operations	Elective	1648
TN3270-En	TN3270 Enhancements	Elective	1647
PPP-BCP	PPP Bridging Control Protocol	Elective	1638
UPS-MIB	UPS Management Information Base	Elective	1628
AAL5-MTU	Default IP MTU for use over ATM AAL5	Elective	1626

continues

Table A.4, Continued
Proposed Standard Protocols

Protocol	Name	Status	RFC
PPP-SONET	PPP over SONET/SDH	Elective	1619
PPP-ISDN	PPP over ISDN	Elective	1618
DNS-R-MIB	DNS Resolver MIB Extensions	Elective	1612
DNS-S-MIB	DNS Server MIB Extensions	Elective	1611
FR-MIB	Frame Relay Service MIB	Elective	1604
PPP-X25	PPP in X.25	Elective	1598
OSPF-NSSA	The OSPF NSSA Option	Elective	1587
OSPF-Multi	Multicast Extensions to OSPF	Elective	1584
SONET-MIB	MIB SONET/SDH Interface Type	Elective	1595
RIP-DC	Extensions to RIP to Support Demand Cir.	Elective	1582
	Evolution of the Interfaces Group of MIB-II	Elective	1573
PPP-LCP	PPP LCP Extensions	Elective	1570
X500-MIB	X.500 Directory Monitoring MIB	Elective	1567
MAIL-MIB	Mail Monitoring MIB	Elective	1566
NSM-MIB	Network Services Monitoring MIB	Elective	1565
CIPX	Compressing IPX Headers Over WAM Media	Elective	1553
IPXCP	PPP Internetworking Packet Exchange Control	Elective	1552
SRB-MIB	Source Routing Bridge MIB	Elective	1525
CIDR-STRA	CIDR Address Assignment ...	Elective	1519

Protocol	Name	Status	RFC
CIDR-ARCH	CIDR Architecture ...	Elective	1518
CIDR-APP	CIDR Applicability Statement	Elective	1517
	802.3 MAU MIB	Elective	1515
HOST-MIB	Host Resources MIB	Elective	1514
	Token Ring Extensions to RMON MIB	Elective	1513
FDDI-MIB	FDDI Management Information Base	Elective	1512
KERBEROS	Kerberos Network Authentication Ser (V5)	Elective	1510
GSSAPI	Generic Security Service API: C-bindings	Elective	1509
DASS	Distributed Authentication Security ...	Elective	1507
	X.400 Use of Extended Character Sets	Elective	1502
HARPOON	Rules for Downgrading Messages ...	Elective	1496
Mapping	MHS/RFC-822 Message Body Mapping	Elective	1495
Equiv	X.400/MIME Body Equivalences	Elective	1494
IDPR	Inter-Domain Policy Routing Protocol	Elective	1479
IDPR-ARCH	Architecture for IDPR	Elective	1478
PPP/Bridge	MIB Bridge PPP MIB	Elective	1474
PPP/IP MIB	IP Network Control Protocol of PPP MIB	Elective	1473
PPP/SEC MIB	Security Protocols of PPP MIB	Elective	1472

continues

Table A.4, Continued
Proposed Standard Protocols

Protocol	Name	Status	RFC
PPP/LCP MIB	Link Control Protocol of PPP MIB	Elective	1471
X25-MIB	Multiprotocol Interconnect on X.25 MIB	Elective	1461
SNMPv2	Introduction to SNMPv2	Elective	1441
PEM-KEY	PEM—Key Certification	Elective	1424
PEM-ALG	PEM—Algorithms, Modes, and Identifiers	Elective	1423
PEM-CKM	PEM—Certificate-Based Key Management	Elective	1422
PEM-ENC	PEM—Message Encryption and Auth	Elective	1421
SNMP-IPX	SNMP over IPX	Elective	1420
SNMP-AT	SNMP over AppleTalk	Elective	1419
SNMP-OSI	SNMP over OSI	Elective	1418
FTP-FTAM	FTP-FTAM Gateway Specification	Elective	1415
IDENT-MIB	Identification MIB	Elective	1414
IDENT	Identification Protocol	Elective	1413
DS3/E3-MIB	DS3/E3 Interface Type	Elective	1407
DS1/E1-MIB	DS1/E1 Interface Type	Elective	1406
BGP-OSPF	BGP OSPF Interaction	Elective	1403
	Route Advertisement In BGP2 and BGP3	Elective	1397
SNMP-X.25	SNMP MIB Extension for X.25 Packet Layer	Elective	1382

Protocol	Name	Status	RFC
SNMP-LAPB	SNMP MIB Extension for X.25 LAPB	Elective	1381
PPP-ATCP	PPP AppleTalk Control Protocol	Elective	1378
PPP-OSINLCP	PPP OSI Network Layer Control Protocol	Elective	1377
SNMP-PARTY-MIB	Administration of SNMP	Elective	1353
SNMP-SEC	SNMP Security Protocols	Elective	1352
SNMP-ADMIN	SNMP Administrative Model	Elective	1351
TOS	Type of Service in the Internet	Elective	1349
PPP-IPCP	PPP Control Protocol	Elective	1332
	X.400 1988 to 1984 downgrading	Elective	1328
	Mapping between X.400 (1988)	Elective	1327
TCP-EXT	TCP Extensions for High Performance	Elective	1323
FRAME-MIB	Management Information Base for Frame	Elective	1315
NETFAX	File Format for the Exchange of Images	Elective	1314
IARP	Inverse Address Resolution Protocol	Elective	1293
FDDI-MIB	FDDI-MIB	Elective	1285
	Encoding Network Addresses	Elective	1277
	Replication and Distributed Operations	Elective	1276

continues

Table A.4, Continued
Proposed Standard Protocols

Protocol	Name	Status	RFC
	COSINE and Internet X.500 Schema	Elective	1274
BGP-MIB	Border Gateway Protocol MIB (Version 3)	Elective	1269
ICMP-ROUT	ICMP Router Discovery Messages	Elective	1256
OSI-UDP	OSI TS on UDP	Elective	1240
STD-MIBs	Reassignment of Exp MIBs to Std MIBs	Elective	1239
IPX-IP	Tunneling IPX Traffic through IP Nets	Elective	1234
IS-IS	OSI IS-IS for TCP/IP Dual Environments	Elective	1195
IP-CMPRS	Compressing TCP/IP Headers	Elective	1144
NNTP	Network News Transfer Protocol	Elective	977

For your convenience, all the Telnet options are shown with their states and statuses in table A.5.

Table A.5
Telnet Options

Protocol	Name	#	State	Status	RFC	STD
TOPT-BIN	Binary Transmission	0	Std	Rec	856	27
TOPT-ECHO	Echo	1	Std	Rec	857	28
TOPT-RECN	Reconnection	2	Prop	Ele		
TOPT-SUPP	Suppress Go Ahead	3	Std	Rec	858	29
TOPT-APRX	Approx Message Size Negotiation	4	Prop	Ele		

Protocol	Name	#	State	Status	RFC	STD
TOPT-STAT	Status	5	Std	Rec	859	30
TOPT-TIM	Timing Mark	6	Std	Rec	860	31
TOPT-REM	Remote Controlled Trans and Echo	7	Prop	Ele	726	
TOPT-OLW	Output Line Width	8	Prop	Ele		
TOPT-OPS	Output Page Size	9	Prop	Ele		
TOPT-OCRD	Output Carriage-Return Disposition	10	Prop	Ele	652	
TOPT-OHT	Output Horizontal Tabstops	11	Prop	Ele	653	
TOPT-OHTD	Output Horizontal Tab Disposition	12	Prop	Ele	654	
TOPT-OFD	Output Formfeed Disposition	13	Prop	Ele	655	
TOPT-OVT	Output Vertical Tabstops	14	Prop	Ele	656	
TOPT-OVTD	Output Vertical Tab Disposition	15	Prop	Ele	657	
TOPT-OLD	Output Linefeed Disposition	16	Prop	Ele	658	
TOPT-EXT	Extended ASCII	17	Prop	Ele	698	
TOPT-LOGO	Logout	18	Prop	Ele	727	
TOPT-BYTE	Byte Macro	19	Prop	Ele	735	
TOPT-DATA	Data Entry Terminal	20	Prop	Ele	1043	
TOPT-SUP	SUPDUP	21	Prop	Ele	736	
TOPT-SUPO	SUPDUP Output	22	Prop	Ele	749	
TOPT-SNDL	Send Location	23	Prop	Ele	779	
TOPT-TERM	Terminal Type	24	Prop	Ele	1091	

continues

TABLE A.5, CONTINUED
Telnet Options

Protocol	Name	#	State	Status	RFC	STD
TOPT-EOR	End of Record	25	Prop	Ele	885	
TOPT-TACACS	TACACS User Identification	26	Prop	Ele	927	
TOPT-OM	Output Marking	27	Prop	Ele	933	
TOPT-TLN	Terminal Location Number	28	Prop	Ele	946	
TOPT-3270	Telnet 3270 Regime	29	Prop	Ele	1041	
TOPT-X.3	X.3 PAD	30	Prop	Ele	1053	
TOPT-NAWS	Negotiate About Window Size	31	Prop	Ele	1073	
TOPT-TS	Terminal Speed	32	Prop	Ele	1079	
TOPT-RFC	Remote Flow Control	33	Prop	Ele	1372	
TOPT-LINE	Linemode	34	Draft	Ele	1184	
TOPT-XDL	X Display Location	35	Prop	Ele	1096	
TOPT-ENVIR	Telnet Environment Option	36	Hist	Not	1408	
TOPT-AUTH	Telnet Authentication Option	37	Exp	Ele	1416	
TOPT-ENVIR	Telnet Environment Option	39	Prop	Ele	1572	
TOPT-TN3270E	TN3270 Enhancements	40	Prop	Ele	1647	
TOPT-AUTH	Telnet XAUTH	41	Exp			
TOPT-CHARSET	Telnet CHARSET	42	Exp		2066	
TOPT-EXTOP	Extended-Options-List	255	Std	Rec	861	32

INDEX

Symbols

A

B

C

D

F

G

H

I-J-K

L

N

O

P-Q

R

S

T

U

V

PLUG YOURSELF INTO...

THE MACMILLAN INFORMATION SUPERLIBRARY™

Free information and vast computer resources from the world's leading computer book publisher—online!

FIND THE BOOKS THAT ARE RIGHT FOR YOU!

A complete online catalog, plus sample chapters and tables of contents!

- STAY INFORMED with the latest computer industry news through our online newsletter, press releases, and customized Information SuperLibrary Reports.
- GET FAST ANSWERS to your questions about Macmillan Computer Publishing books.
- VISIT our online bookstore for the latest information and editions!
- COMMUNICATE with our expert authors through e-mail and conferences.
- DOWNLOAD SOFTWARE from the immense Macmillan Computer Publishing library:
  - Source code, shareware, freeware, and demos
- DISCOVER HOT SPOTS on other parts of the Internet.
- WIN BOOKS in ongoing contests and giveaways!

TO PLUG INTO MCP:

WORLD WIDE WEB: **http://www.mcp.com**

FTP: ftp.mcp.com

REGISTRATION CARD

Inside TCP/IP Third Edition

Name ______________________________ Title ______________________

Company ___________________________ Type of business ______________

Address ____

City/State/ZIP ____

Have you used these types of books before? ☐ yes ☐ no

If yes, which ones? ____

____

How many computer books do you purchase each year? ☐ 1–5 ☐ 6 or more

How did you learn about this book? ___________________________

Where did you purchase this book? ___________________________

Which applications do you currently use? ______________________

____

Which computer magazines do you subscribe to? _________________

____

What trade shows do you attend? _____________________________

____

Comments: ____

____

____

Would you like to be placed on our preferred mailing list? ☐ yes ☐ no

☐ **I would like to see my name in print!** You may use my name and quote me in future New Riders products and promotions. My daytime phone number is: ______________________

New Riders Publishing 201 West 103rd Street ◆ Indianapolis, Indiana 46290 USA

Fax to **317-817-7448**

Fold Here

NO POSTAGE
NECESSARY
IF MAILED
IN THE
UNITED STATES

BUSINESS REPLY MAIL

FIRST-CLASS MAIL PERMIT NO. 9918 INDIANAPOLIS IN

POSTAGE WILL BE PAID BY THE ADDRESSEE

NEW RIDERS PUBLISHING
201 W 103RD ST
INDIANAPOLIS IN 46290-9058

Support:

If you need assistance with the information in this book or with a CD/Disk accompanying the book, please access the Knowledge Base on our Web site at **http://www.superlibrary.com/general/support**. Our most Frequently Asked Questions are answered there. If you do not find the answer to your questions on our Web site, you may contact Macmillan Technical Support **(317) 581-3833** or e-mail us at **support@mcp.com**.